MW00781635

"'R.C. Sproul,' someone said to me in the 1970s, 'is the finest communicator in the Reformed world.' Now, four decades later, his skills honed by long practice, his understanding deepened by years of prayer, meditation, and testing (as Martin Luther counseled), R.C. shares the fruit of what became perhaps his greatest love: feeding and nourishing his own congregation at St. Andrew's from the Word of God and building them up in faith and fellowship and in Christian living and serving. Dr. Sproul's expositional commentaries have all R.C.'s hallmarks: clarity and liveliness, humor and pathos, always expressed in application to the mind, will, and affections. R.C.'s ability to focus on 'the big picture,' his genius of never saying too much, leaving his hearers satisfied yet wanting more, never making the Word dull, are all present in these expositions. They are his gift to the wider church. May they nourish God's people well and serve as models of the kind of ministry for which we continue to hunger."

—Dr. Sinclair B. Ferguson
Teaching Fellow
Ligonier Ministries

"Dr. R.C. Sproul, well known as a master theologian and extraordinary communicator, showed that he was a powerful, insightful, helpful expository preacher. This collection of sermons is of great value for churches and Christians everywhere."

—Dr. W. Robert Godfrey
President emeritus and professor of church history emeritus
Westminster Seminary California, Escondido, California

"I tell my students again and again, 'You need to buy good commentaries and do so with some discernment.' Among them there must be preacher's commentaries, for not all commentaries are the same. Some may tell you what the text means but provide little help in answering the question, 'How do I preach this text?' Dr. R.C. Sproul was a legend in our time. His preaching held us in awe for half a century, and these pages represent the fruit of his exposition at the very peak of his abilities and insights. Dr. Sproul's expositional commentary series represents Reformed theology on fire, delivered from a pastor's heart in a vibrant congregation. Essential reading."

—Dr. Derek W.H. Thomas
Senior minister
First Presbyterian Church, Columbia, South Carolina

"Dr. R.C. Sproul was the premier theologian of our day, an extraordinary instrument in the hand of the Lord. Possessed with penetrating insight into the text of Scripture, Dr. Sproul was a gifted expositor and world-class teacher, endowed with a strategic grasp and command of the inspired Word. When he stepped into the pulpit of St. Andrew's and committed himself to the weekly discipline of biblical exposition, this noted preacher demonstrated a rare ability to explicate and apply God's Word. I wholeheartedly recommend Dr. Sproul's expositional commentaries to all who long to know the truth better and experience it more deeply in a life-changing fashion. Here is an indispensable tool for digging deeper into God's Word. This is a must-read for every Christian."

—Dr. Steven J. Lawson
Founder and president
OnePassion Ministries, Dallas

"How exciting! Thousands of us have long been indebted to Dr. R.C. Sproul the teacher, and now, through Dr. Sproul's expositional commentaries, we are indebted to Sproul the preacher, whose sermons are thoroughly biblical, soundly doctrinal, warmly practical, and wonderfully readable. Sproul masterfully presents us with the 'big picture' of each pericope in a dignified yet conversational style that accentuates the glory of God and meets the real needs of sinful people like us. This series of volumes is an absolute must for every Reformed preacher and church member who yearns to grow in the grace and knowledge of Christ Jesus. I predict that Sproul's pulpit ministry in written form will do for Christians in the twenty-first century what Martyn Lloyd-Jones' sermonic commentaries did for us last century. *Tolle lege*, and buy these volumes for your friends."

—Dr. Joel R. Beeke
President and professor of systematic theology and homiletics
Puritan Reformed Theological Seminary, Grand Rapids, Michigan

LUKE

AN EXPOSITIONAL COMMENTARY

LUKE

AN EXPOSITIONAL COMMENTARY

R.C. SPROUL

Reformation Trust A DIVISION OF LIGONIER MINISTRIES, ORLANDO, FL

Luke: An Expositional Commentary

Published by Reformation Trust Publishing
a division of Ligonier Ministries
421 Ligonier Court, Sanford, FL 32771
Ligonier.org ReformationTrust.com

Printed in China
RR Donnelley
0000820
First edition

ISBN 978-1-64289-281-9 (Hardcover)
ISBN 978-1-64289-282-6 (ePub)
ISBN 978-1-64289-283-3 (Kindle)

Cover design: Ligonier Creative
Interior typeset: Katherine Lloyd, The DESK

Library of Congress Cataloging-in-Publication Data

Names: Sproul, R. C. (Robert Charles), 1939-2017, author.
Title: Luke : an expositional commentary / R.C. Sproul.
Description: First edition. | Orlando, FL : Reformation Trust Publishing, a division of Ligonier Ministries, 2020. | Includes index.
Identifiers: LCCN 2020008038 (print) | LCCN 2020008039 (ebook) | ISBN 9781642892819 (hardback) | ISBN 9781642892826 (epub) | ISBN 9781642892833 (kindle edition)
Subjects: LCSH: Bible. Luke--Commentaries.
Classification: LCC BS2595.53 .S77 2021 (print) | LCC BS2595.53 (ebook) | DDC 226.4/07--dc23
LC record available at https://lccn.loc.gov/2020008038
LC ebook record available at https://lccn.loc.gov/2020008039

CONTENTS

SERIES PREFACE

When God called me into full-time Christian ministry, He called me to the academy. I was trained and ordained to a ministry of teaching, and the majority of my adult life has been devoted to preparing young men for the Christian ministry and to trying to bridge the gap between seminary and Sunday school through various means under the aegis of Ligonier Ministries.

Then, in 1997, God did something I never anticipated: He placed me in the position of preaching weekly as a leader of a congregation of His people—St. Andrew's in Sanford, Florida. Over the past twelve years, as I have opened the Word of God on a weekly basis for these dear saints, I have come to love the task of the local minister. Though my role as a teacher continues, I am eternally grateful to God that He saw fit to place me in this new ministry, the ministry of a preacher.

Very early in my tenure with St. Andrew's, I determined that I should adopt the ancient Christian practice of *lectio continua*, "continuous expositions," in my preaching. This method of preaching verse-by-verse through books of the Bible (rather than choosing a new topic each week) has been attested throughout church history as the one approach that ensures believers hear the full counsel of God. Therefore, I began preaching lengthy series of messages at St. Andrew's, eventually working my way through several biblical books in a practice that continues to the present day.

Previously, I had taught through books of the Bible in various settings, including Sunday school classes, Bible studies, and audio and video teaching series for Ligonier Ministries. But now I found myself appealing not so much to the minds of my hearers but to both their minds and their hearts. I knew that I was responsible as a preacher to clearly explain God's Word *and* to show how we ought to live in light of it. I sought to fulfill both tasks as I ascended the St. Andrew's pulpit each week.

What you hold in your hand, then, is a written record of my preaching labors amidst my beloved Sanford congregation. The dear saints who sit under my preaching encouraged me to give my sermons a broader hearing. To that end, the chapters that follow were adapted from a sermon series I preached at St. Andrew's.

Please be aware that this book is part of a broader series of books containing adaptations of my St. Andrew's sermons. This book, like all the others in the series, will *not* give you the fullest possible insight into each and every verse in this biblical book. Though I sought to at least touch on each verse, I focused on the key themes and ideas that comprised the "big picture" of each passage I covered. Therefore, I urge you to use this book as an overview and introduction.

I pray that you will be as blessed in reading this material as I was in preaching it.

—R.C. Sproul
Lake Mary, Florida
April 2009

1

AN ORDERLY ACCOUNT

Luke 1:1–4

Inasmuch as many have undertaken to compile a narrative of the things that have been accomplished among us, just as those who from the beginning were eyewitnesses and ministers of the word have delivered them to us, it seemed good to me also, having followed all things closely for some time past, to write an orderly account for you, most excellent Theophilus, that you may have certainty concerning the things you have been taught.

Luke is mentioned in several places in the New Testament, not the least of which is in his own book of Acts where he served as a companion to the Apostle Paul in his missionary journeys. Luke was not only a doctor but also a missionary, a medical missionary who was a close companion and friend of the Apostle to the Gentiles, Saul of Tarsus. Luke was born and raised in Antioch, was of Gentile descent, and died in his eighties in a peaceful manner, unlike most of the other writers of the biblical narratives and epistles.

When I was last in Rome, we made a special visit to the Mamertine Prison where the Apostle Paul endured his second and final Roman imprisonment before his execution under that emperor, Nero, whose nickname was "the Beast." The holding cell was situated across the street from the Roman forum. It was not a large prison but simply a large cistern that had been cut out of the rock and originally had been used to keep a supply of water for the Romans. But, as history would have it, it was emptied of water and turned into a cell for those who were about to be executed. It was a moving experience to go down the stairs into that cistern, that dank, dark, cold, wet place where the great Apostle was held, and presumably there wrote his final letter to Timothy, whom he had left behind in Ephesus. In that epistle, Paul writes these final words:

> For I am already being poured out as a drink offering, and the time of my departure has come. I have fought the good fight, I have finished the race, I have kept the faith. Henceforth there is laid up for me the crown of righteousness, which the Lord, the righteous judge, will award to me on that day, and not only to me but also to all who have loved his appearing.
>
> Do your best to come to me soon. For Demas, in love with this present world, has deserted me and gone to Thessalonica. Crescens has gone to Galatia, Titus to Dalmatia. Luke alone is with me. Get Mark and bring him with you, for he is very useful to me for ministry. Tychicus I have sent to Ephesus. When you come, bring the cloak that I left with Carpus at Troas, also the books, and above all the parchments. (4:6–13)

He goes on to say in verses 17–18:

> But the Lord stood by me and strengthened me, so that through me the message might be fully proclaimed and all the Gentiles might hear it. So I was rescued from the lion's mouth. The Lord will rescue me from every evil deed and bring me safely into his heavenly kingdom. To him be the glory forever and ever. Amen.

The last admonition to Timothy, in the New King James Version, is "Do your utmost to come before winter" (2 Tim. 4:21). In 2 Timothy 4, Paul essentially tells Timothy, "Come before winter, bring the parchments, bring my coat, and bring Mark because I am alone except for the Lord and for the beloved physician Luke."

Luke the Historian

The last statement of the Apostle Paul speaks volumes about his companion who went with him on his missionary journeys and stood next to Paul in all the trials and tribulations that are recorded in the book of Acts. Most significantly, Luke stood side by side with Paul in that dreadful, dank prison cell. All the rest had departed or fled. Luke, we know, was a physician and a missionary. But most importantly, Luke has emerged as one of the most important, if not the most important, historians of the ancient world.

As we look back at how he begins his Gospel, he acknowledges at the outset that others had taken time to give a narrative account of the things they knew of the person and work of Jesus. We have, survived to this day, the inspired writings of Matthew, Mark, and John. But, presumably besides those Gospel writers, there were others in the first century who tried their hand at writing a summary of the history of Jesus.

Luke acknowledges that at the beginning and makes it clear that he is aware that others have gone before him in this venture of providing a history. And so he says, **Inasmuch as many have undertaken to compile a narrative of the things that have been accomplished among us, just as those who from the beginning were eyewitnesses and ministers of the word have delivered them to us** (vv. 1–2). Of course, Matthew and John were disciples. Mark was not one of the Twelve, but he was considered to be the amanuensis, or the secretary, of the Apostle Peter. Also, Luke was not a disciple, but he had been converted by the Apostles and had come under the tutelage of the great Apostle Paul.

So much of what Luke knows he gains from his association with Paul as well as with the others who were among the first disciples. This is those who, from the beginning, were eyewitnesses and ministers of the Word. Luke is saying, "I am not an eyewitness, but I am a historian, and as a historian, I check the sources." Luke gives us more information about the birth of Jesus than anybody else, and it's with almost total certainty that we know Luke had the privilege of interviewing Mary, the mother of Christ. Luke said, "After we have received these from the eyewitnesses, it seemed good to me also, having had a complete understanding of all the things from the very first, to write to you an orderly account, most excellent Theophilus."

There is a lot of conjecture about the one who is addressed here and also in the book of Acts. The name Theophilus means "friend or lover of God." Some argue that the person who is mentioned here represents, in a certain way, "Christian everyman," that there was no actual Theophilus. It seems, however, that Luke is addressing and dedicating this volume, as was commonplace in the ancient world, to a person of noble position. He is devoting or dedicating this to a man by the name of Theophilus because he calls him **most excellent Theophilus** (v. 3), which was a title given not to symbolic characters but rather to real historical persons.

Luke goes on to say the reason he's writing is **that you may have certainty concerning the things you have been taught** (v. 4). That was his burden, and that was his passion: "I am writing these things down that you can be sure that the things that you have heard, the things that have been preached, and the things that have been declared to you by eyewitnesses are available in an orderly, historical, and carefully documented account. I do this to strengthen your faith, to give you certitude, and so that you can have the full assurance of the truth of the gospel." That was Luke's task as a historian.

The ancient world had many notable historians, both Roman and Greek, and Jewish as well. You have the historians Thucydides, Xenophon, Herodotus, Suetonius, Tacitus, Pliny, and the Jewish historian Josephus, all of whose works are still read. I have a collection in my house of all the works of the great Greek historians, and there were many. And they were excellent in the work they did. But no historian of the ancient world has been subjected to as much academic and archaeological scrutiny as Luke, the writer of this Gospel.

Historians have sometimes been skeptical about the biblical writers, and in the early part of the twentieth century, a British atheist historian, William Mitchell Ramsay, set out to debunk the truth claims of the Gospels. He decided to follow the alleged footsteps of the Apostle Paul throughout his missionary journeys, going to all those places that the archaeologists have examined. Dr. Ramsay was converted to Christianity along the way, because he discovered that every time a spade of dirt was turned over in those days, some historical aspect of the Gospels was verified and authenticated. Ramsay and other secular historians have said that Luke, apart from inspiration, apart from the divine assistance that he enjoyed, was the most accurate historian of the entire ancient world.

2

THE ANGEL AND ZECHARIAH, PART 1

Luke 1:5–12

In the days of Herod, king of Judea, there was a priest named Zechariah, of the division of Abijah. And he had a wife from the daughters of Aaron, and her name was Elizabeth. And they were both righteous before God, walking blamelessly in all the commandments and statutes of the Lord. But they had no child, because Elizabeth was barren, and both were advanced in years.

Now while he was serving as priest before God when his division was on duty, according to the custom of the priesthood, he was chosen by lot to enter the temple of the Lord and burn incense. And the whole multitude of the people were praying outside at the hour of incense. And there appeared to him an angel of the Lord standing on the right side of the altar of incense. And Zechariah was troubled when he saw him, and fear fell upon him.

Luke promised to give an orderly account of all the things that came to pass with respect to the person and work of Christ. When giving an orderly account of things that have taken place, one has to decide where to begin. Luke begins not with the birth of Jesus, nor with the appearance of John the Baptist and his public ministry, but with the appearance of the angel Gabriel to Zechariah, the father of John the Baptist. Of all the Gospel writers, Luke is the only one who starts at this point and gives us information regarding the pending birth of John the Baptist.

John the Baptist may be the most underrated person in the whole New Testament. That is, he is underrated by us, but certainly not by the biblical writers, and above all, not by the Lord Jesus Christ. Jesus said of John that none greater has ever appeared than John the Baptist and that the Law and the Prophets ruled until John (Matt. 11:11–13).

But a new era, a new epoch, breaks through with the birth of John the Baptist. It had been four hundred years since the last prophecy had been uttered in Israel. After many prophets had spoken God's word to Israel in the Old Testament, suddenly, after Malachi, God became silent. Not for a year, not for ten years, but for four hundred years. Think of all the history that has transpired in the last four centuries before our time. That's a long time for God to be silent.

And now, Luke tells us, that silence is broken with the coming of a new prophet whose birth is announced here in this episode. Luke tells us it takes place **in the days of Herod, king of Judea** (v. 5). That's not an incidental historical point that we should overlook, because these were days of trial and days of darkness for the people of Israel. Herod was not a Jew; he was a puppet king of the oppressing Roman Empire, and he ruled for thirty-six years, from 40 BC to 4 BC. During that time, he had some magnificent accomplishments, such as the rebuilding of the temple in all its grandeur. Not only did he rebuild the Jewish temple, but he also built pagan temples and initiated pagan religious rites among the people.

For all that he accomplished, he never was secure in his standing. He was so paranoid about his power and authority that he killed everyone who seemed to him to be a threat, including many members of his own family. He was to the Jews what Nero was to the Romans, and so these were dark days indeed when this episode that Luke records takes place.

Zechariah

In the days of Herod, king of Judea, there was a priest named Zechariah, of the division of Abijah. And he had a wife from the daughters of Aaron, and her name was Elizabeth (v. 5). It is interesting to look at the meaning of some of the names of people in Scripture. The name Zechariah means "God has remembered again." David, in the Psalms, says, "Bless the Lord, O my soul, and forget not all his benefits" (Ps. 103:2). It is our habit to forget the things that God has done for us. We tend to live from one blessing to the next, and as soon as our memory of our last blessing from the hand of the Lord fades, we begin to be dull in our ardor and love for the Lord until He blesses us again. So, David reminds us that our soul should bless the Lord and not be given to forgetfulness, because God is a God who never forgets.

After four hundred years, the people were beginning to think that the Lord

God, omnipotent in His omniscience, had laid that attribute aside and had suddenly become forgetful. Maybe He's forgotten the promises that He made to Abraham. Where is the Messiah He promised us centuries ago? Did He forget the promises that He made to the people of antiquity? Now Israel has a priest whose name means "God has remembered again." This is the pattern of God throughout redemptive history, that He remembers every promise He's ever made. We have to live by that. It's one thing to believe in God; it's another thing to believe Him, to believe what He says, to believe His promises, and to live not by the allure of this world but by the promises of God, knowing that the Lord does not forget.

Now, after four hundred years of silence, Zechariah appears on the scene. He is called a priest in **the division of Abijah** (v. 5) and his wife was also from a priestly line, and her name was Elizabeth. Zechariah and Elizabeth are described here as **righteous before God, walking blamelessly in all the commandments and statutes of the Lord** (v. 6). This of course does not negate what the Scriptures tell us elsewhere that there are none righteous, no not one, that no one is perfect in their obedience before God (Rom. 3:10–11), but the Bible does speak about those who manifest exemplary godliness, such as Job, Noah, and other characters of the Old Testament who were singularly godly. We find in this couple two people who manifest unusual, extraordinary godliness, so that in God's sight they are righteous, not simply through the righteousness of Christ but also in contrast to other people. They keep the law; they love the law; they are devoted to the things of God, and God is pleased with them.

But there is one great problem: they have no children. Elizabeth was barren, just as Sarah had been barren, Hannah had been barren, and the mother of Samson had been barren. In those days, people considered barren women with a sense of reproach. The assumption they made is that there had to be some dark sin that lurked in the souls of a childless couple. Many would have thought that God had shut up the womb of Elizabeth as an expression of His divine displeasure. But Scripture says otherwise. There was no hidden sin. They were godly, blameless. Nevertheless, they were old and they were childless.

Now while he was serving as priest before God when his division was on duty, according to the custom of the priesthood, he was chosen by lot to enter the temple of the Lord and burn incense (vv. 8–9). Israel had eighteen thousand priests, divided among the different groups. Fourteen priests of those eighteen thousand were given the privilege of offering the incense on the altar during the course of a single year. Only once could a priest have the opportunity to offer the prayers of intercession for the people by means of the offering of the incense, which was to represent the prayers of God's people, a sweet aroma to God.

That means that the vast majority of priests never in their lifetime had the opportunity to offer this sacred task in the Holy Place of the temple. How did a priest get the opportunity for this sacred task? He wasn't elected by his fellow priests to do it, nor was there a contest to determine who was the most righteous of the priests. No, the only one who could choose a priest for this sacred service was God Himself, and He did it through the casting of lots. When Zechariah got the word, he must have been overwhelmed to receive such a spiritual blessing that would be the high point of his entire priesthood.

The Angel Appears

And the whole multitude of the people were praying outside at the hour of incense (v. 10). Prayers were offered for the nation on these occasions, both in the morning and the evening, but the vast multitude of people came in the late afternoon, at dusk, for the offering of these prayers. They gathered outside the temple to pray and watch the smoke that came out of the temple, because when the incense burned, the smoke spiraled up through the roof of the temple, and that was the signal for the people to fall on their faces in the courtyard, in thanksgiving that the prayers of intercession on their behalf had been offered.

They were accustomed, after they saw the smoke, to seeing the priest soon come out of the temple, and they would all rejoice together. But on this day, nothing happened. Something had gone wrong, it seemed to the watching multitude. **And there appeared to him an angel of the Lord standing on the right side of the altar of incense. And Zechariah was troubled when he saw him, and fear fell upon him** (vv. 11–12). Zechariah, in his service, was dramatically interrupted by the appearance of an angel.

Luke tells us at the beginning of his Gospel that he is going to give us the facts, and in this case he speaks of an angel. In our modern era, this seems to smack of the mythological. It's one of the supernatural elements of Scripture that the skeptics and the cynics repudiate.

Scripture testifies unashamedly about the existence of angels. In the New Testament, the word for *angel* occurs more often than the word for *love*, more often than the word for *sin*. So, in a numeric sense at least, the New Testament speaks more about angels than it does about love, more about angels than it does about sin. Angels are an integral part of Scripture. But Zechariah was just like we are. When an angel appeared to him, he was on his face in terror. The angel came and gave an astonishing message, a message that would change the course of Zechariah's life, of Elizabeth's life, of Israel's life, and of our lives.

3

THE ANGEL AND ZECHARIAH, PART 2

Luke 1:13–25

But the angel said to him, "Do not be afraid, Zechariah, for your prayer has been heard, and your wife Elizabeth will bear you a son, and you shall call his name John. And you will have joy and gladness, and many will rejoice at his birth, for he will be great before the Lord. And he must not drink wine or strong drink, and he will be filled with the Holy Spirit, even from his mother's womb. And he will turn many of the children of Israel to the Lord their God, and he will go before him in the spirit and power of Elijah, to turn the hearts of the fathers to the children, and the disobedient to the wisdom of the just, to make ready for the Lord a people prepared."

And Zechariah said to the angel, "How shall I know this? For I am an old man, and my wife is advanced in years." And the angel answered him, "I am Gabriel. I stand in the presence of God, and I was sent to speak to you and to bring you this good news. And behold, you will be silent and unable to speak until the day that these things take place, because you did not believe my words, which will be fulfilled in their time." And the people were waiting for Zechariah, and they were wondering at his delay in the temple. And when he came out, he was unable to speak to them, and they realized that he had seen a vision in the temple. And he kept making signs to them and remained mute. And when his time of service was ended, he went to his home.

After these days his wife Elizabeth conceived, and for five months she kept herself hidden, saying, "Thus the Lord has done for me in the days when he looked on me, to take away my reproach among people."

In Luke's orderly account, he began with the visitation of the angel to the priest Zechariah. I mentioned that the word *angel* (Greek *angelos*) occurs more often in the New Testament than the word for *sin* and more often than the word for *love*. This is not simply a peripheral matter in the biblical accounts, for angels play a significant role throughout the New Testament, not only here with the annunciation to Zechariah but also shortly thereafter as the same angel appeared to Mary the mother of Jesus.

The heavenly host attended and announced the birth of our Lord Jesus Christ on that Christmas night outside Bethlehem. We see the angels appearing at the end of Jesus' time of temptation in the wilderness when they came to minister to Him. We see the angels appear again at the time of His resurrection, as they announced to the women that He was not there but that He had risen. We see angels escorting Jesus to heaven on the shekinah cloud of glory at the time of His ascension, and we are promised that we will see Him again descending from heaven on clouds of glory, escorted once more by these heavenly agents.

Angels appear in the New Testament, but their occurrences and manifestations were exceedingly rare. Before this moment, Zechariah—this godly, righteous, obedient priest—had never in his life had the privilege of seeing a real live angel. When the angel Gabriel came into the Holy Place by the altar of incense, Zechariah's response was the same as yours and mine would have been: he was overcome with terror. The first thing the angel had to say to him was **"Do not be afraid, Zechariah, for your prayer has been heard, and your wife Elizabeth will bear you a son, and you shall call his name John"** (v. 13). This message suggests that when Zechariah was chosen out of eighteen thousand priests to have this privilege of going into the Holy Place to offer the incense on the altar of incense, which symbolized the prayers of the people, he took that opportunity in his old age to pray: "Oh dear Lord, please, please let me have a son. Let Elizabeth have offspring through Your power."

Clearly, for many years Zechariah and Elizabeth had prayed fervently for a child. God's answer was no. Most likely, as they grew older and realized Elizabeth was past the age of childbearing, their prayer changed to "Lord, give us the grace to accept our childlessness." When Zechariah came into the temple and prayed, he wasn't praying for a child, but for Israel, for his people who were oppressed under the heavy hand of Rome and the heavy hand of Herod the Tetrarch. So the answer was stunning when the angel said, "Your prayer is heard. You've been praying for your people, for the nation; and the Lord has heard your prayer. He's going to give you a son who is sent by God for the well-being of the people of Israel."

The Birth of John the Baptist Foretold

Gabriel goes on to say, **"Your wife Elizabeth will bear you a son, and you shall call his name John"** (v. 13). In biblical terms, it was always the privilege of the parents, particularly the father, to name their children. All the way back to creation, the giving of the name indicated an expression of authority. When God set Adam and Eve over the whole creation and gave them dominion, He tasked Adam with naming the animals. This was not just an exercise in zoology or taxonomy but an expression of mankind's authority over the animals.

So, throughout biblical history, it was the custom and the tradition for the parents to name the child because it indicated their authority over the child. But there were those rare occasions, when a special child was born, that God would take from the parents the authority to name the child. "His name shall be Isaac." "His name shall be Samuel." "His name shall be John." "His name shall be Jesus." When God named a child, the child was set apart for a specific purpose. "This child will be sanctified and consecrated for a special task that I have called him to perform." And so, the angel told Zechariah not only that he was going to have a son but also what his son's name was to be. This will become important when the child is born, as we will read later in Luke's narrative. The Lord was naming this child because he was on a mission and he belonged to God.

For he will be great before the Lord (v. 15). Gabriel said John would drink neither wine nor strong drink, not because he was going to be a Nazirite but because he was to have a special role as a prophet, an ascetic prophet, one who would come out of the desert just like Elijah.

The angel goes on to say that John **will be filled with the Holy Spirit, even from his mother's womb** (v. 15). Those who think the womb can be disturbed because that which is in it is only so much undifferentiated protoplasm and not a human being should take heed. Before John the Baptist was even born, while he was still in his mother's womb, he was filled by the Holy Ghost. **And he will turn many of the children of Israel to the Lord their God** (v. 16). The prophecy went on to say that John would be an evangelist, as it were, an instrument of God to confront many of the people whose hearts had been hardened—people of Israel who were the heirs of the covenant of grace but who had come to despise it.

John was going to be the instrument of God to change these things: **"he will turn many of the children of Israel to the Lord their God, and he will go before him in the spirit and power of Elijah"** (vv. 16–17). He was not going to be Elijah; he was going to be Elijah reborn in the sense that he was going to fulfill the Old Testament prophecy of the return of Elijah, not because God was going to bring Elijah back from heaven, but because He was going to anoint this child with the same power and the same spirit that he had given to the great prophet Elijah. Why? **"To turn the hearts of the fathers to the children, and the disobedient to the wisdom of the just, to make ready for the Lord a people prepared"** (v. 17).

What does he mean, **to turn the hearts of the fathers to the children**? Some commentators say that Israel was finally going to have a generation of godly people who would make the patriarchs in heaven happy to see them. I don't think it means that. Rather, it's probably simply that the hostility, the breakdown of family relationships that sin engenders in nations when they depart from the Lord God, was going to change. A new era was coming. A new epoch was about to break through in history, and there would be a dramatic change in families, in houses, and in relationships between the parents and their children. And not only that, but the disobedient who scoffed at the truth of God would finally see the wisdom of the just.

Throughout world history and biblical history, those who embrace the truth of God appear to be fools in the eyes of the world. But the real fool is the one who says in his heart, "There is no God" (Ps. 14:1). "But your son," the angel tells Zechariah, "is going to turn many of the people around, and they will see the wisdom of righteousness, the wisdom of the just who embrace it. And then he is going to make ready a people prepared for the Lord. In fact, that will be his chief task. His number one responsibility will be to make straight the way of the Lord, to be the herald of the coming Messiah, to be the one who goes before Him whom the Lord is sending to redeem His people. Your son is going to do that."

The Sin of Unbelief

This is overwhelming for this old priest. **And Zechariah said to the angel, "How shall I know this? For I am an old man, and my wife is advanced in years"** (v. 18). Filled with doubt, Zechariah says: "This can't be. It can't happen. We can't do it." Zechariah needed to read *The Little Engine That Could*. He needed to study his theology of the Lord God omnipotent. When Zechariah says, "I can't," he means, "God can't." The angel then reminds him of some important truths: "My normal habitation is in the immediate presence of God, and it's the Lord God Himself who sent me here with all the power of His might and all the might of His truth. Don't tell me you're too old. I was sent to speak to you, to bring you this gospel, these glad tidings. But you don't want to hear them, and you will pay a price for that, Zechariah."

Early on in the first chapter, beginning in verse 6, Zechariah and his wife, Elizabeth, are described as righteous before God, walking in all the commandments and ordinances of the Lord, blameless. Until this surprise announcement from Gabriel, God had been pleased with the singular posture of obedience and righteousness displayed by Zechariah. In fact, Scripture describes him as having been blameless. That's a little bit of hyperbole. If we look at it carefully, we'll certainly find something that was blameworthy. But in general, his character was one that was blameless. However we measure it, that streak of blamelessness comes to an abrupt halt here, in the Holy Place, when the angel announces that he and his wife are going to have this child who will be the forerunner of the Messiah. Zechariah says to the angel, **"I am an old man"** (v. 18).

Consider the response of God's ambassador, God's authorized messenger, to Zechariah's doubt: **"I am Gabriel. I stand in the presence of God, and I was sent to speak to you and to bring you this good news. And behold, you will be silent and unable to speak until the day that these things take place, because you did not believe my words, which will be fulfilled in their time"** (vv. 19–20). There are consequences to unbelief. "Though you were known as righteous and devout and blameless, now I'm going to take away your ability to speak because of your unbelief." Gabriel administers a judgment of God on this righteous man for his unbelief.

I don't think we take seriously enough the sinfulness of unbelief. We have a tendency in our culture, and even in the church, to think that belief in Christ or unbelief in Christ, believing and trusting in the things of God or not trusting in the things of God, are optional. They don't carry any dire consequences if we dismiss them. But we need to understand that unbelief in the Word of God is sin. And not only is it sin, but it's an egregious sin. And not only is it an egregious sin, but it's a sin that has eternal consequences.

Many dimensions of theology are related to the problem we face here with Zechariah. Why does God punish Zechariah for his struggle when he didn't punish Abraham, for example, in the Old Testament? He said, "Fear not, Abram, I am your shield; your reward shall be very great" (Gen. 15:1). And Abram said, "O Lord God, what will you give me, for I continue childless, and the heir of my house is Eliezer of Damascus?" (v. 2). And God said, "This man shall not be your heir; your very own son shall be your heir" (v. 4). And what happened? In verse 6, we read, "And he believed the Lord, and he counted it to him as righteousness." This is the first clear example of a man being justified by faith alone, the cardinal issue of the sixteenth-century Protestant Reformation.

Paul labors the point that before Abraham offered up Isaac on the altar in Genesis 22 and that already in chapter 15, he was counted righteous before God. As soon as faith was born in his soul, he was justified. He didn't have to have faith plus works in order to be justified, but faith alone was all that was necessary for Abraham to have righteousness imputed to him. The only righteousness that could have been imputed to him was the righteousness of Christ, who was not even born yet.

Even after this marvelous profession of faith by which Abraham was justified, he staggered for a moment and asked, "O Lord GOD, how am I to know that I shall possess it?" (Gen. 15:8). You see, even with the saving faith that Abraham had—he had enough faith to have the righteousness of Christ imputed to him, to have his salvation guaranteed—there was still that element of doubt in his heart. And God went to elaborate measures to convince Abraham that His word could be trusted, and there wasn't the slightest hint of judgment given to Abraham for wanting to have the word of God confirmed, as was the case with Hezekiah (Isa. 38) and as was the case with Gideon and his fleece (Judg. 6). Throughout Scripture, we see people hearing the word of God and staggering in unbelief and God being patient with them, forbearing, tender, and kind.

Now, all of a sudden, here's Zechariah, who had been told something equally astonishing and was struggling with believing it. Instead of having a covenant ratified with him as God did for Abraham, or an answer through a fleece as He did for Gideon, He said, **"And behold, you will be silent and unable to speak until the day that these things take place, because you did not believe my words, which will be fulfilled in their time"** (v. 20).

Abraham got mercy. Zechariah got justice. Once again, we see that God will have mercy on whom He will have mercy and be gracious to whom He will be gracious (Rom. 9:15). Because He gives grace to one and then again to another and to another for the same thing does not mean that we can then assume He will be ever so gracious to everyone else who commits the same sin. Sometimes God says: "No! Stop right here. That's enough."

Limited Atonement

In the Bible, people die in one of two ways. They either die in faith or they die in their sin. If you die in your sin, it is too late. The judgment of God will be upon you, not simply for a few months as it was for Zechariah, but forever.

Remember the doctrines of grace, that famous acrostic TULIP, which stands for total depravity, unconditional election, limited atonement, irresistible grace, and perseverance of the saints. Many of our evangelical brothers and sisters embrace TULIP. Many more, however, will affirm the T, the U, the I, and the P, but they knock the L out of TULIP.

How can we say that the atonement of Jesus Christ is limited? The Bible says that He died for the whole world. Are we saying that Jesus' atoning death was not sufficient to save everybody in the world? The same people who ask these questions, however, say that not everybody in the world is saved. Well, why isn't everybody in the world saved? Because a necessary condition to be saved by the atoning death of Jesus Christ is to have faith in Him. If someone has no faith in Jesus Christ, the atoning death of Christ only exacerbates his guilt before God and will do nothing to alleviate it because he has rejected the perfect sacrifice that was offered once for all.

If Jesus, on the cross, died for every sin of every person who ever lived, and made atonement for every sin of every person who ever lived, how can we therefore resist the conclusion of universalism? If Jesus died for every sin of every person, nothing is left for God to punish. Everybody would be saved because every sin has already been atoned for. Obviously, the atonement of Christ is made only for those who believe, and so in that sense the efficacy of that atonement is limited—it is limited to believers. Jesus didn't die for everybody; He died for believers. You can take it to the next step. He died for the elect. And everyone for whom He died, everyone for whom He made an atonement, has their sins forgiven forever. This was not an afterthought in the economy of God's plan of salvation, but from all eternity God had planned to send His Son into the world to atone for the sins of His people.

I mention limited atonement to help us see how important unbelief is. It is a sin. We have the tendency to think that if someone doesn't believe, if he is not convinced, he may be wrong but at worst it's an error in judgment. No. What made it so serious that Zechariah didn't believe this message? When somebody speaks, the credibility of what is said is directly related to the character and integrity of the person who's making the statement. That's why we want, in a court of law, to have witnesses who are credible. It's one thing for me not to believe everything I'm told, because I have had numerous experiences in my lifetime when people have lied to me. But God has never lied to me or to you. When I don't believe what God says, I am assaulting the very integrity of the Almighty. My unbelief is an accusation against God Himself, saying, "God, I can't trust what You say." That's why the issue of the source of the announcement to Zechariah is so central to this passage. **"How shall**

I know this? For I am an old man, and my wife is advanced in years" (v. 18), followed by, **"I am Gabriel. I stand in the presence of God"** (v. 19). "It was God who sent me to announce these things to you. I am not speaking on my own authority, Zechariah. I'm speaking the word of God." To not believe the word of God is to sin.

To not just believe *in* God but to believe God is the very essence of what it means to be a Christian. Back in the Old Testament, the prophet Habakkuk made the comment, "The righteous shall live by his faith" (Hab. 2:4). We can translate it, "The righteous shall live by trust." It's not by accident that this statement by Habakkuk is repeated three times in the New Testament, not the least of which is in Paul's thematic statement of the doctrine of justification in the first chapter of Romans. It's not a coincidence that, in the sixteenth century, this was the core issue between Rome, and Luther and the Reformers. To be justified is to live by faith. To be righteous is to be righteous by faith. It's why the Reformers called faith the sole instrument of our justification. It's not faith plus something else. By trusting the Word of God and trusting in God alone for salvation—that's the only way anybody can ever be saved.

Augustine belabored the difference between faith and credulity. Credulity involves an undue readiness to believe anything with uncertain evidence, for no reason at all. But authentic biblical faith is grounded in the trustworthiness of God. Nothing could be more unreasonable or more irrational than to doubt a word that comes from God.

Zechariah said he and his wife were too old. Gabriel responded that he stands in the presence of God who told him to tell Zechariah that he was going to have a son. Having heard God say that, was Gabriel supposed to discount the truthfulness of the word of the One who sent him? This wasn't an intellectual problem; it was a moral problem. The reason for Zechariah's doubt was his abiding sin. The reason we doubt the Word of God is not because His Word is unbelievable or not credible but because we project onto God the untrustworthiness that describes our own condition. Let every man be a liar, but God's Word is true.

The just shall live by faith. Jesus said, "Man shall not live by bread alone, but by every word that comes from the mouth of God" (Matt. 4:4). There is no justification for denying the Word of God. Not your age, not your culture, not your profession. Nothing. If God says it, it's settled.

In that instant, Zechariah's lips were closed. In the outer court, the people were waiting for Zechariah to appear, wondering what was taking him so long. He came out and they wanted an explanation. He tried to tell them but could not speak. Zechariah gestured, trying to communicate what he saw. The people thought he had seen a vision. So he went home—the story goes—and Elizabeth became pregnant and went into seclusion until her days were fulfilled in the birth of her son.

How do you respond to the Word of God? Justly or unjustly? Those are the only two options.

4

THE ANNUNCIATION

Luke 1:26–38

In the sixth month the angel Gabriel was sent from God to a city of Galilee named Nazareth, to a virgin betrothed to a man whose name was Joseph, of the house of David. And the virgin's name was Mary. And he came to her and said, "Greetings, O favored one, the Lord is with you!" But she was greatly troubled at the saying, and tried to discern what sort of greeting this might be. And the angel said to her, "Do not be afraid, Mary, for you have found favor with God. And behold, you will conceive in your womb and bear a son, and you shall call his name Jesus. He will be great and will be called the Son of the Most High. And the Lord God will give to him the throne of his father David, and he will reign over the house of Jacob forever, and of his kingdom there will be no end."

And Mary said to the angel, "How will this be, since I am a virgin?"

And the angel answered her, "The Holy Spirit will come upon you, and the power of the Most High will overshadow you; therefore the child to be born will be called holy—the Son of God. And behold, your relative Elizabeth in her old age has also conceived a son, and this is the sixth month with her who was called barren. For nothing will be impossible with God." And Mary said, "Behold, I am the servant of the Lord; let it be to me according to your word." And the angel departed from her.

The archangel Gabriel was dispatched from the presence of God on a mission to give an announcement of extraordinary importance. He had been selected by God to give a similar announcement to Zechariah, one that caused Zechariah to stagger before its content. If Gabriel had his hands full with Zechariah, the announcement he was to give to Mary was even more extraordinary.

In the pages of the Old Testament were historical precedents of women who were barren and past the age of childbearing whose wombs God had quickened, granting them sons. But never in the history of the world had any woman had a child while she remained a virgin. This would be the first and last time in history that such an event would take place.

Gabriel Appears to Mary

We are told in the text that during the sixth month of Elizabeth's pregnancy, **Gabriel was sent from God to a city of Galilee named Nazareth** (v. 26), a tiny village that was situated almost halfway between the Mediterranean Sea, which was twenty-two miles to its west, and the Sea of Galilee, which was fifteen miles to its east and slightly north. This little village, of no grand significance historically, was visited by the heavenly messenger who came to a virgin who was betrothed to a man.

When the angel came to Mary, he greeted her with these somewhat strange words: **"Greetings, O favored one, the Lord is with you!"** (v. 28). Those who are of Roman Catholic background may notice immediately the familiarity of these words, as they are part of the Rosary. The words are uttered, "Hail Mary, full of grace, blessed are thou among women, and blessed is the fruit of your womb, Jesus." The translation here has the angel saying, **"Greetings, O favored one."** In the Latin Vulgate, translated by the church father Jerome, the words are *gratia plena*, which literally mean "full of grace."

The angel recognized that Mary had received such an abundance of grace that no woman before this moment in history had experienced. Her favor with the Lord was without equal, and so, with this greeting, Mary was stunned and bewildered. She must have thought, What can this possibly mean? Who is this angel? What does he say? That I am filled with grace, that I am highly favored, and that I am supposedly supremely blessed and that the Lord is with me?

The angel says: **"Do not be afraid, Mary, for you have found favor with God. And behold, you will conceive in your womb and bear a son, and you shall call his name Jesus"** (vv. 30–31). Just as the angel instructed Zechariah about the name of his son, so the angel instructed Mary what her Son would be named. **"He will be great and will be called the Son of the Most High. And the Lord God will give to him the throne of his father David"** (v. 32). He would be known as the Son of the Most High God and as the Son of David, the One whom God promised would be David's Son and David's Lord. **"He will reign over the house of Jacob forever, and of his kingdom there will be no end"** (v. 33).

This young girl was a godly woman. Surely, she knew the pages of the Old

Testament Scriptures. Surely, she understood that David's Son, whose kingdom would last forever, would be the Messiah of Israel. One would think she would first say, "Why?" but instead she asked, "How?": **"How will this be, since I am a virgin?"** (v. 34).

The Providence of God

Mary responded as any child of nature would respond. Even in her day, people assumed there were such things as natural laws, laws of nature that act independently of the sovereign providence of God. This is the view we have of nature today. We somehow think that the laws—what we call the laws of nature, such as the law of gravity and the law of inertia—are laws that are inherent in the created universe and that operate independently from the power of God, from the providence of God, and from the sovereignty of God. That's the reason why, historically, theologians have defined miracles as actions of God that are *contra naturam*, or "against nature."

But we need to stop for a minute and realize what we call natural laws are simply the ordinary way God governs His creation. God does this according to a pattern that He establishes, and that pattern includes, for example, the regularity of things falling when you drop them because of gravity. But even gravity has no power whatsoever apart from the sustaining power of God. We believe in the Lord God Almighty who reigns over everything, who sets the planets in their courses, who sends the birds south in the winter. But from Mary's perspective, from the perspective of the natural, there was no way this announcement could come true. It was against the laws of nature.

But the angel has the answer to her question, and he takes the time to explain it to her. **"The Holy Spirit will come upon you, and the power of the Most High will overshadow you"** (v. 35). The Holy Spirit, in biblical terms, is often referred to as the *dynamis*, the power of God. We get the English word *dynamite* from it. That is, the Spirit of God has supernatural sovereign power.

It is by the Holy Spirit's brooding over the waters that the original creation came into existence. If we go back to Genesis 1, we see "In the beginning, God created the heavens and the earth. The earth was without form and void, and darkness was over the face of the deep. And the Spirit of God was hovering over the face of the waters" (vv. 1–2). There in that uncreated state, the universe is described as formless, amorphous, empty, and enveloped in total darkness. The Spirit of God hovered over the waters and brooded, and hovered over the unformed creation as a hen broods over her eggs, and God spoke: "Let there be light" (v. 3). And the lights came on. Soon after, the earth was formed and shaped and structured by the omnipotent Creator.

When I taught classes in seminary, I would often be asked about a seeming conundrum regarding the power of God: "Professor, do you believe that God is omnipotent?" Yes. "That God can do all things?" Yes. "Nothing is impossible for God?" Yes. "Well, can God build a rock so big that He can't move it?" If I say, "Yes, He can build a rock so big that He can't move it," then there's something that's not possible for Him to do. So He's not really omnipotent. And if I say, "No, He can't build a rock so big that He can't move it," then again I'm on the horns of this dilemma, and I'm again saying that God is not omnipotent, that there are certain things that He can't do.

There is a right answer to that question and it's very simple. Can God build a rock so big that He can't move it? Of course not. Because He's omnipotent. Why not? To be omnipotent does not mean that God can do anything. God can't die. God can't lie. God can't be God and not be God at the same time and in the same relationship. He can't stop being God, and as long as He is God, whatever He makes, whatever He creates, He controls and He has power over. He can do anything that He purposes to do, anything that accords with His character as God. That's the theological lesson that the angel is reiterating here to Mary: "With God, nothing is impossible; all things are possible. That is, He has power over everything in His creation, including your empty womb."

The Place of Mary

And Mary said, "Behold, I am the servant of the Lord; let it be to me according to your word." And the angel departed from her (v. 38). In the sixteenth century, the greatest schism in the history of Christendom took place with the Protestant Reformation. At the time of the Reformation, the dispute became so bitter and the hostilities so escalated that we saw the formation of the Spanish Inquisition, where people were tortured on the rack and burned at the stake. Christendom was at war with itself.

Today, we see the attitudes that prevailed in the sixteenth century greatly nullified, and we think of the rack and burning at the stake as aberrations of the past and not something commonplace in the theological disputes of our time. In fact, so much has the division between Rome and Protestantism been ameliorated that there have been initiatives in recent decades to announce to the world a certain accord, an agreement, between Rome and Protestantism.

In 1870, at the Council of Trent, Protestants were described as schismatics and heretics. Fast-forward to the 1960s, to the Second Vatican Council, and there Protestants were referred to as separated brethren. Note the stark contrast in the language between the two councils, how the hostilities have settled down. I'll hear frequently that the things that divide Rome from Protestantism are not that great anymore. The truth is the differences between evangelical Protestantism and Roman Catholicism are as great today as they were in the sixteenth century. The issue of the gospel is still very much at stake.

The Roman Catholic Catechism of 1994 reaffirmed the Council of Trent and its teaching on the doctrine of justification, its understanding of salvation, and the treasury of merits, indulgences, and purgatory. These are major points of difference between Rome and evangelical Protestantism. There is also the doctrine of papal infallibility, which, though many in the Roman church believed it, was not formally defined by the church until 1870, at the First Vatican Council. But in addition to the issue of the authority of the church and the doctrine of justification, we have the whole phenomenon of Rome's Mariology, the uniquely Roman devotion to Jesus' mother. Since this devotion is so strongly associated with the Roman Catholic Church, we might expect that Rome's doctrines concerning Mary have been around for centuries. But the truth is that most of these decrees have come since the mid-1800s.

Three important papal decrees bear on Mary. The first is *Ineffabilis Deus*, issued by Pope Pius IX in 1854. It defined the doctrine of the Immaculate Conception, meaning that Mary was born sinless; that is, she did not inherit the effects of original sin. The idea was that she had to be sinless in order not to pass on original sin to her Son. The second decree is *Munificentissimus Deus*, issued by Pope Pius XII in 1950. It defined the bodily assumption of Mary, meaning that Mary did not die but went bodily into heaven. The third decree is *Ad Caeli Reginam*, issued by Pope Pius XII in 1954. It defined the coronation of Mary as the queen of heaven, meaning that God chose her to be the mother of Christ because He willed her to have a unique and exceptional role in salvation as the second Eve associated with the second Adam. These changes inform the actual daily practice of devout Roman Catholics, who frequently have shrines to Mary in their yards. As recently as the catechism of 1994, Mary is referred to as the mother of the Christian church, the queen of heaven, the exemplar of true Christianity, and as mediatrix between the church and God.

Theology can hardly sink lower than to obscure the uniqueness of our Lord's saving work as the Mediator between man and God, and as the Apostle Paul wrote in his Pastoral Epistles, "There is one mediator between God and men, the man Christ Jesus" (1 Tim. 2:5).

These changes didn't happen overnight. It was already an issue in the sixteenth century, and the Protestant leaders even then were concerned that the veneration of Mary transgressed the biblical laws against idolatry, the veneration of creatures. The church responded by making a distinction between two Latin terms: *latria* and *dulia*. *Latria* means "worship," while *dulia* means "service, honor, or veneration." Church officials said that Roman Catholics were not committing idolatry when it came to Mary and other idols because they were offering *dulia* rather than *latria*. Mary, however, as early as the sixteenth century, was said to be accorded *hyperdulia*, a kind of veneration that stops short of *latria* but goes beyond *dulia*.

Calvin responded that this distinction between *dulia* and *latria* was a distinction without a difference. When you kneel down before the likeness of a mortal person, pray to this likeness, and invoke the power of that person to improve your life and to mediate your prayers to God, how does that differ in any way from worship? When you observe the contemporary pilgrimages and religious behavior of multitudes of people in the Roman Catholic Church in their special festivals devoted to Mary, it's hard to say that they are not worshiping Mary.

This issue came to the fore in the Second Vatican Council. Many people think that at Vatican II, all kinds of doctrinal changes took place in the Roman system. They are mistaken. Pope John XXIII, when he called this unexpected council, said, "Let fresh winds blow through the church." He was looking for church renewal; he was very much concerned about the church's pastoral role with the people. He ruled out major theological disputes from discussion. They didn't discuss providence or election or justification or Christology. The focus of Vatican II was on ecclesiology, on matters of the church.

The one great doctrinal issue that emerged at Vatican II had to do with the role of Mary in the church, but again it was subsumed under the study of the church and where Mary fits into the church. There was a significant debate between two factions at the council: the Latin wing of the church and the Western wing of the church. These two groups, with respect to Mary, were called minimalists and maximalists, respectively. The great issue that divided them was whether Mary should be regarded not only as mediatrix (which was already accepted doctrine) but as co-redemptrix, a redeemer alongside Jesus. Now, happily, the church did not embrace the maximalist position in its fullness, but there remains a strong current in favor of maximalism in the Roman Catholic communion to this day.

Mary's Fiat

Where does this all come from? One of the pivotal passages was Luke 1:38, which records Mary's response to the announcement of the angel Gabriel that she was going to conceive and have a child by the power of the Holy Ghost. The virgin birth was announced to Mary by Gabriel, and her initial response was one of stunned amazement: **"How will this be, since I am a virgin?"** (v. 34). We noted it was going to take place through the power of the Holy Ghost, the same power that brought the world into being and creation. He was going to overshadow her so that the child in her womb would be called the Son of God. He would be Most Holy, and He would be the Son of the Most High.

What did Mary say after the angel explained all these things? **"Behold, I am the servant of the Lord; let it be to me according to your word"** (v. 38). In the Roman Catholic Church, this is referred to as the Fiat of Mary. The term *fiat* is the present imperative form of the verb "to be" in Latin, meaning "let it be."

At the time of creation, the first fiat in all of history occurred, the divine imperative by which the whole universe was created, when the fiat came from the mouth of God: "'Let there be light,' and there was light" (Gen. 1:3). Let the oceans teem with fish and the fields with verdant growth, and all the work of creation was accomplished through the command, the imperative, of God, what we call the Divine Fiat. At the grave of Lazarus, Jesus didn't invite the dead man to come back to life; He spoke to him with the imperative, "Lazarus, come out" (John 11:43). There was nothing that Lazarus could do but come out under the weight and the authority of the imperative command of Jesus.

So the idea of the fiat has a rich history throughout redemptive history, and when the Roman Catholic theologians come to this text, they say, "Here it is, out of the lips of Mary—let it be!" The maximalists use this text to say the incarnation took place because of the will of God and also because of the will of Mary. Mary exercised her authority, without which there would be no virgin birth, without which there would be no redeeming Jesus, without which there would be no salvation. So salvation depended, according to the maximalists, on Mary's imperative response to the angel's announcement.

If ever a statement had been rudely torn and ripped of context, it is Mary's Fiat. Yes, the imperative form, at least in the Latin Vulgate, is used here, but notice the context. The first thing Mary says is **"Behold, I am the servant of the Lord."** If there is any "Let it be," there is first "Who am I?" The attitude being expressed by this girl to the announcement of the angel is "Gabriel, I am a handmaiden. I am not the owner of the house. I don't have any authority in this matter, but I am your servant, and if the Lord wants me to have this baby, so be it." There is much difference between "Let it be" and "If the Lord wants me to have this baby, whatever the Lord wants I will do because I am His servant."

How do maximalists handle this? They make another parallel. They say there's a parallel between Adam and Jesus. In the New Testament, Jesus is called the new Adam or the second Adam. Through the first Adam's disobedience, death came into the world. Through the second Adam's obedience, life comes into the world (see Rom. 5:12–21). Destruction, disaster, and damnation came through the first Adam; salvation and deliverance come through the second

Adam, Jesus. They say the same parallel exists between Eve and Mary, as through one woman's disobedience death came into the world, so through the other woman's obedience life came into the world.

That's why they are jealous to elevate Mary to the level of co-redemptrix. In their view, she participates virtually as an equal with her Son in effecting our redemption. Her Son is the second Adam, she is the second Eve, and together, mother and Son, they bring about salvation. The truth is that Mary, who is in heaven right now, would be offended by anyone suggesting there is a real parallel between Eve and herself. Mary is not the queen of the universe. The church is the queen of the universe. The church is the bride of Christ, and Christ is the King, and His only queen is His bride, not His mother.

But again, we need to understand what a singularly blessed woman Mary was. The early creeds call Mary *theotokos*, "God-bearer" or "mother of God." This was not understood in the sense that Jesus derived His divine nature from Mary but in the sense that she was mother to the One who is God incarnate.

Mary is due honor for her example of obedience, but she is not a co-redemptrix. She was merely human. She will participate in the bodily resurrection when Christ's kingdom comes in its fullness. But she died. She went to heaven. She doesn't have the eschatological glorification of her body as Rome claims. There was no bodily ascension to heaven. We don't pray to Mary. I've had my Catholic friends say: "Why not pray to Mary? If she asks her Son for something, He's not going to refuse her." Scripture doesn't instruct us to pray to Mary. We're told to pray to the One who is the Mediator. We have our Great High Priest. We don't have a great high priestess. We have our Great High Priest who intercedes for us. Is that not enough? Should we pray to His grandmother or grandfather? Who else? No. Mary is not divine; she is a sinner saved by grace, just as we are. But what a gracious sinner she was.

I read in this text a willingness to do the will of the Lord. That is what we can learn from Mary: how to be in subjection to God, as she was.

5

MARY'S VISIT TO ELIZABETH

Luke 1:39–45

In those days Mary arose and went with haste into the hill country, to a town in Judah, and she entered the house of Zechariah and greeted Elizabeth. And when Elizabeth heard the greeting of Mary, the baby leaped in her womb. And Elizabeth was filled with the Holy Spirit, and she exclaimed with a loud cry, "Blessed are you among women, and blessed is the fruit of your womb! And why is this granted to me that the mother of my Lord should come to me? For behold, when the sound of your greeting came to my ears, the baby in my womb leaped for joy. And blessed is she who believed that there would be a fulfillment of what was spoken to her from the Lord."

I once made a trip to the cradle of Christianity, where I visited the Holy Land, Ephesus, Rome, and other important places of Christian history. Several people asked me what I thought was the highlight. Was it preaching on the site of the tomb of the Apostle John in Ephesus? Certainly, that was one of the highlights. Seeing the sights in Jerusalem, speaking on the Sea of Galilee, and going to Capernaum and the other places were all meaningful to me, but the moment I enjoyed the most was riding in the bus, going up to Jerusalem.

When the Bible speaks of going up to Jerusalem, it speaks of going to a city of higher elevation, just as in America people would go up to Denver from the lower portions of the Midwest. So in Palestine, when one wanted to go to the capital city, he had to go up through the hill country. So much of the history in 1 and 2 Samuel took place in the hill country, and it was like I was seeing ghosts out the window everywhere I went. The hill country of Judea has a beautiful terrain. As I consider this text, I'm right back there in the hills of Judea where Mary is making haste, hurrying as fast as she can to go and see her cousin Elizabeth.

The Worth of the Unborn

I can't just pass over the reality of what's taking place here. We have a response to Mary's presence not only from Elizabeth but also from Elizabeth's unborn child, whose first testimony to Jesus—his first heralding of the King—takes place before he's even born. At this time, six months into the pregnancy, the child that Elizabeth carried in her womb was alive, was human, and was a person. Now those three things are extremely important as we consider what I believe is the greatest ethical crisis that has ever visited the United States of America, far exceeding the moral travesty of slavery: the wanton destruction of more than half a million unborn babies every year in this nation, with hardly a peep out of the church.

We hear the rhetoric. I hear people say, "A woman has a right to her own body." There are two things I want to observe just quickly in passing. In the first instance, an unborn child in the womb of a mother is not part of the woman's body. It may be in the woman's body, but it is not the woman's body. The clearest evidence that we have to distinguish individual human beings in our society today is DNA. The DNA code of an unborn baby is different from every DNA cell in the woman's body. The fetus is in the woman's womb, in her body, but it is not part of her body.

Second, one person's rights end where another's begin. A mother may currently have the legal right in the United States of America to destroy her unborn child, but where did she get the moral right to do it? Where does the Lord God, who is the author, protector, and sustainer of life, grant to any woman or any man the right to destroy another person? How far we have come. If you look at the history of theology in the last two thousand years, you will see innumerable issues of debate between conservatives and liberals, theologians of every different stripe. Until the feminist movement of the twentieth century, however, if there was a consensus on any doctrine or on any moral issue in the history of Christianity, it was on abortion, which the *Didache* in the early church unabashedly called murder.

But if we can argue that what is growing in the womb is not a person, is not alive, is not an individual entity of its own, then we can use phrases such as this: "It's just a blob of undifferentiated protoplasm." Or this: "The unborn child is just so much domestic sewage." We can't become more pagan than that. The reason government exists at all, the raison d'être for government historically, under God, is primarily to protect, to sustain, and to maintain human life. And when a government willfully fails to do that, it has not only become pagan, it has become demonic.

Now, that's my opinion. Yes, I am a trained theologian. That's my vocation, that's my education. I've spent my entire adult life studying the things of God, and I am by no means infallible. But if I know anything at all about God, I know beyond a shadow of a doubt that He hates abortion. If you've had one, it's a grave and heinous sin but not unforgivable. If you've had one and you're a Christian, you know it's a grave sin and it haunts you every hour. If you've assisted in it or encouraged it as a man, you are in profound need of the forgiving grace of God, which is available. Don't try to excuse it. Don't try to rationalize it. Get it forgiven and stop this practice.

Elizabeth Blesses Mary

And when Elizabeth heard the greeting of Mary, the baby leaped in her womb. And Elizabeth was filled with the Holy Spirit (v. 41). After she was filled with the Holy Spirit, what did she do? **And she exclaimed with a loud cry, "Blessed are you among women, and blessed is the fruit of your womb!"** (v. 42).

Elizabeth was not praying a prayer but singing a song in praise of Mary's faith. This is the first of five songs in Luke's account of the infancy narrative of Jesus. It's the first, and it sets the stage for perhaps the greatest one, which will be the focal point of our further study. The five songs are these: this song of Elizabeth; the *Magnificat*, the song of Mary; the *Benedictus*, the song of Zechariah; the *Gloria in Excelsis Deo*, the song of the angels on Christmas Eve; and the *Nunc Dimittis*, the song of Simeon when the baby Jesus is presented at the temple. We should take note of the content of these songs. These songs are glorious. They are majestic, and their content is so enriching that as we meditate on them, it can change our lives.

Throughout sacred Scripture, music is often referenced. Songs communicate much, in some cases bad and arrogant ideas, and yet some music can be used of God to elevate the soul to the highest levels humanly possible. Even Plato understood in ancient Greece that one had to pay attention to the music that the youth were listening to, because Plato observed the powerful effect music had on the young people. Listen to the music today, and you'll learn something about the behavior of our age. We need to have music that praises, that blesses, that thanks God, and that responds to God.

Exodus 15 contains one of the lengthier songs of the Old Testament. After the people of Israel were released from bondage and rescued from the chariots of Pharaoh, Moses and the children of Israel were caught between Migdol and the Red Sea. The sea was in front of them, and the pursuing chariots of Pharaoh behind them. They were completely helpless, like lambs ready to be slaughtered. Moses raised his arms and called on God to deliver His people, and God caused a great wind to blow. The Red Sea parted, and the children of Israel walked across on dry ground while the sea was held back by the wind that God in His providence had ordained. As soon as the Israelites reached the other side, Pharaoh and his armies, spewing out death, went into the vacant portion of the sea with their chariots, and as they were in the middle of the Red Sea, the wall of water that the wind had been holding back suddenly collapsed and drowned them.

This was the biggest moment of salvation in the Old Testament, and it was celebrated in song. Moses sang:

> "I will sing to the Lord, for he has triumphed gloriously;
> the horse and his rider he has thrown into the sea.
> The Lord is my strength and my song,
>   and he has become my salvation;
> this is my God, and I will praise him,
>   my father's God, and I will exalt him.
> The Lord is a man of war;
>   the Lord is his name.
>
> "Pharaoh's chariots and his host he cast into the sea,
>   and his chosen officers were sunk in the Red Sea.
> The floods covered them;
>   they went down into the depths like a stone." (Ex. 15:1–5)

This was a great hymn. Miriam echoes the same sentiment (v. 21). During the period of the judges, Deborah sang, "From heaven the stars fought, from their courses they fought against Sisera" (Judg. 5:20). David lamented at the news of the death of Jonathan and Saul, "Tell it not in Gath, publish it not in the streets of Ashkelon" (2 Sam. 1:20). The song of Hannah concerned the promised birth of Samuel (1 Sam. 2:1–10). The book of Revelation tells us that when the kingdom of Christ is consummated, He will give to His people a new song (Rev. 14:3).

We have five songs at the advent of Jesus, with His birth announced by a chorale from heaven and celebrated by the human agents under the inspiration of the Holy Spirit, beginning with this simple couplet in metrical style: **"Blessed are you among women, and blessed is the fruit of your womb!"** (v. 42) She goes on to say, **"And why is this granted to me that the mother of my Lord should come to me?"** (v. 43) "Who am I?" Elizabeth says. "I can't believe it. I can't believe you're visiting me." She's the elder cousin and yet she's saying, "Who are you? What are you doing here? I can't believe you're gracing my house, that the mother of my Lord should come to me." As the Spirit moved Elizabeth to say those things, the same Spirit came upon Mary.

6

THE MAGNIFICAT

Luke 1:46–56

And Mary said,

> "My soul magnifies the Lord,
>   and my spirit rejoices in God my Savior,
> for he has looked on the humble estate of his servant.
>   For behold, from now on all generations will call me blessed;
> for he who is mighty has done great things for me,
>   and holy is his name.
> And his mercy is for those who fear him
>   from generation to generation.
> He has shown strength with his arm;
>   he has scattered the proud in the thoughts of their hearts;
> he has brought down the mighty from their thrones
>   and exalted those of humble estate;
> he has filled the hungry with good things,
>   and the rich he has sent away empty.
> He has helped his servant Israel,
>   in remembrance of his mercy,
> as he spoke to our fathers,
>   to Abraham and to his offspring forever."

And Mary remained with her about three months and returned to her home.

One of the things that's clear from this text is that Mary, as a young Jewish girl, did something that most Jewish girls did in her day: she memorized Scripture. We see strains of similarity between this song and the song of praise and thanksgiving sung by Hannah in the Old Testament when she was told of the impending birth of her son Samuel (1 Sam. 2:1–10). This song also has several references to elements found in the Psalms. The more we ingest Scripture and hide it in our hearts, memorize it, and become familiar with it, the more we will find that in our prayers we will turn to the language of the Word of God itself. This is modeled for us in this marvelous hymn by Mary.

Mary sings this hymn under the inspiration of the Holy Spirit, and its content reveals much about Mary and also much about the character of God. She begins, **"My soul magnifies the Lord, and my spirit rejoices in God my Savior"** (vv. 46–47). One of the things Scripture warns us of more than once is the danger of rendering to God mere lip service, going through the motions, offering rote worship where we say the words and confess with our mouths while our hearts remain far from Him.

What is noteworthy about Mary's hymn is that she is not giving lip service to God. This song of praise and adoration is welling up out of the depths of her being. She says, **"My soul magnifies the Lord."** Mary is not saying that God could become any greater than He already is, but her meaning is this: "My soul has been saturated by a sense of the divine and by His presence and by His mercy. And so, from the deepest part of my being, I want to exalt Him." That's what it means to magnify, to lift God up in exaltation.

Mary is not making a distinction between her soul and her spirit like some people would like to believe, but what we have here is a common Hebrew form of poetry, which is parallelism and in this case, synonymous parallelism, where the first line and the second line mean essentially the same thing. She says it once—**"My soul magnifies the Lord"**—and she says it again—**"my spirit rejoices in God my Savior."**

The Savior of Mary

Theologians have paid particular attention to the last two words of the second line, the words **my Savior.** What does Mary mean by that? Thomas Aquinas believed that Mary could not have been sinless because here she confesses her need of a Savior. That insight of Thomas may be correct, but it's not a necessary inference from the text. The words translated "to save" and "salvation" in the Bible can mean something other than the ultimate salvation we have from the consequences of our sins, but anytime God rescues His people and spares them from any calamity, it is expressed as a kind of salvation. The salvation that Mary has in view here may be the rescue from the calamity of being humiliated—being a forgotten, insignificant person—as she specifies in the next line the sense in which God has been merciful to her.

"For he has looked on the humble estate of his servant" (v. 48). She speaks initially of her being overwhelmed by the tenderness of God. In former Christmas seasons, I've preached on the *Magnificat* and I've pointed out that in that line we have contained the original Cinderella story. This Cinderella story was not a fairy tale, not a myth, but was sober reality and truth because God Himself looked at this young woman in her low estate.

"For behold, from now on all generations will call me blessed" (v. 48). Just as the child who was conceived in her womb would be called David's greater Son and not only David's Son but also David's Lord, so the babe would be not only Mary's Son but also her Savior. No woman in the history of the world could sing that song because only Mary was given the unspeakable privilege of being the mother of our Savior.

The Mighty, Holy, Merciful God

In the *Magnificat*, Mary specifically mentions three attributes of God: **"For he who is mighty has done great things for me, and holy is his name. And his mercy is for those who fear him from generation to generation"** (vv. 49–50). We see here that God is mighty, He is holy, and He is merciful. The One who has recognized her is the Almighty One, the One who possesses all power on heaven and earth, the One who can create a universe by the sound of His voice, by the power of His command. It is this power that the angel Gabriel mentioned to Mary when she was confounded by his announcement. "How will this be, since I am a virgin?" (v. 34). "The Holy Spirit will come upon you, and the power of the Most High will overshadow you" (v. 35).

Often, when people in our culture speak of God, they do so in meaningless terms. People will speak about a power, a higher power, a force greater than oneself. There's hardly any difference between that kind of language and the language of an animist who bows down and worships an idol made of wood. Why do they talk about God that way? Because as long as we can depersonalize God—make Him an impersonal force of vague, amorphous power—we have nothing to worry about. Because impersonal forces will never hold us accountable for our behavior. We will never have to face judgment. But the God who is, is the God who has a name. He is not simply a power, though He has all power. He is the mighty God who **"has done great things for me"** (v. 49).

"Holy is his name" (v. 49). How beautiful is this description of the character of God. God, Mary is saying, is so holy, so transcendentally majestic, that His very name is holy. That's who He is. That's His identity. He is the Holy One of Israel, not just mighty—not just raw force or brute power, but it's a holy power, a holy might, a holy strength—and **"his mercy is for those who fear him"** (v. 50). Don't miss the impact of those words. The One from whom we receive mercy is the Almighty One, the Holy One. How else could we exist in the presence of the Holy One, except by mercy?

The Strength of God

It is interesting that Mary mentions this in the middle of a hymn that is filled with reverence and adoration. **"He has shown strength with his arm"** (v. 51). Here we have an image of God in human form, in which His arm is a symbol of His strength. I think the funniest chapter in the Bible is Numbers 11. That's the occasion where Moses is distraught because the multitude of people that he has led in the exodus are now complaining day after day. They want to go back to Egypt because now they miss their leeks and garlic and onions, and all they have to eat every day is the manna that God supernaturally provides for them from heaven. They had manna for breakfast, manna for lunch, manna for dinner, and if they wanted to have a midnight snack, they had manna for that too. They had roast manna, fried manna, sautéed manna, boiled manna—everything they could possibly do to alter the taste of it.

They said: "Let's go back to Egypt. Give us Pharaoh. At least under Pharaoh, even while we were slaves, we had onions, garlic, and leeks." Moses wants to die and says: "Did I conceive all this people? Did I give them birth, that you should say to me, 'Carry them in your bosom, as a nurse carries a nursing child,' to the land that you swore to give their fathers? Where am I to get meat to give to all this people? For they weep before me and say, 'Give us meat, that we may eat.' I am not able to carry all this people alone; the burden is too heavy for me. If you will treat me like this, kill me at once, if I find favor in your sight, that I may not see my wretchedness" (Num. 11:12–15).

And God says: "The Lord will give you meat, and you shall eat. You shall not eat just one day, or two days, or five days, or ten days, or twenty days, but a whole month, until it comes out at your nostrils and becomes loathsome to you, because you have rejected the Lord who is among you and have wept before him, saying, 'Why did we come out of Egypt?'" (vv. 18–20). Now Moses is deeply upset and says, "The people among whom I am number six hundred thousand on foot, and you have said, 'I will give them meat, that they may eat a whole month!' Shall flocks and herds be slaughtered for them, and be enough for them? Or shall all the fish of the sea be gathered together for them, and be enough for them?" (vv. 21–22).

God answers Moses' question with another question: "Is the LORD's hand shortened? Now you shall see whether my word will come true for you or not" (v. 23). What a great, great image. That's the image that finds its way now into this song: **"He has shown strength with his arm."**

In the *Magnificat*, Mary focuses attention on the power of God. Mary's song celebrates the providence of God, a concept that has all but disappeared from the thinking and speaking of Christian people today.

When we look to the providence of God, we look to that sense in which God sovereignly sustains and governs His entire creation. It's not as though God created the universe and then stepped out of the picture and put inherent laws into nature; that's deism. God didn't wind up the universe like a clock and let the clock run down on its own. What God creates, He sustains. Not just over the long haul, but moment by moment, second by second. Every moment of history unfolds under His omnipotent, divine government.

Mary's song is replete with allusions and references to the Old Testament. You can see the influence of the Psalms throughout this particular song. If there was any central theme that defined the entire faith of Old Testament Israel, it was this fundamental assertion: the Lord God omnipotent reigns. God is the Lord, and there is none other. In His omnipotence, He is the King of all things. The doctrine of the government of God in His providence means simply this: He raises kingdoms up; He brings kingdoms down. No one exercises power in this world apart from the sovereign government of God. At Christmas, we celebrate the One who comes, whose government is on His shoulders, and to whom the Father gives the authority to reign with a government that will have no end. We fuss and fret and stew and worry every day about the problems we face from the earthly governments of this world, even in our own nation. Sometimes we forget who is actually running things. It is the Lord God omnipotent who reigns.

Mary goes on to say, **"He has brought down the mighty from their thrones and exalted those of humble estate"** (v. 52). Thrones are the symbols of authority and power for earthly kings. The Lord God omnipotent topples the thrones of monarchs and drags the mighty down from their positions of exaltation. In contrast, He raises up and exalts those of low estate. Mary is thinking that she is a lowly handmaiden of the Lord. Her estate is low in her culture, and yet God raised her up.

The Care of God

"He has filled the hungry with good things, and the rich he has sent away empty" (v. 53). This verse features antithetical parallelism, which marks a stark contrast. In the first case, God in His mercy and providence has provided for the poor. This presupposes the sermon that Mary's Son will preach one day in years to come: "Blessed are you who are poor, for yours is the kingdom of God. Blessed are you who are hungry now, for you shall be satisfied" (6:20–21).

There is not throughout Scripture an absolute negation or condemnation of the rich, but there is a universal condemnation of God against the rich who are the self-satisfied rich, for those who see no sense of dependence on their redeeming God. The people with a bootstrap mentality think that everything they have they have earned; they have acquired it without any assistance from the mercy and grace of God. People who think they are self-sufficient run a severe risk of opposition from God. "God opposes the proud but gives grace to the humble" (James 4:6).

When the judgment of God comes upon the rich in Scripture, in most cases that judgment is not directed against the merchant class of Israel. The rich who are in view are the rulers who use their seats of authority, like King Ahab, to exploit the people and sell the poor for a pair of shoes. **"He has filled the hungry with good things,"** Mary says. And in contrast to that, He looks to the self-sufficient, arrogant rich and sends them away empty. For self-sufficient, wealthy people, there is no worse consequence they can imagine than to go away empty. It's God who gives grace to the poor, and it's God who will take away from the self-sufficient rich, because it is the Lord who gives, and it's the Lord who takes away. Blessed be the name of the Lord (see Job 1:21).

We read in Isaiah 45, "For the sake of my servant Jacob, and Israel my chosen, I call you by your name, I name you, though you do not know me" (v. 4). The refrain throughout this and following chapters is "I am the Lord, and there is no other, besides me there is no God; I equip you, though you do not know me, that people may know, from the rising of the sun and from the west, that there is none besides me; I am the Lord, and there is no other. I form light and create darkness; I make well-being and create calamity; I am the Lord, who does all these things" (vv. 5–7). This is the sovereignty of God. This is His providence.

We sometimes have a naive view of God, looking at the things of God through rose-colored glasses. We affirm that all good things come from the hands of God, but any problems, suffering, or afflictions are far removed from Him. No. He brings peace; He brings calamity. He fills; He empties. He heals; He hurts. People tell me that they experience unanswered prayers. There's no such thing as an unanswered prayer from God. God's no is as much an answer as His yes. The same God who says yes to our prayers also sometimes says no when we plead our case with Him. Whether His response is yes or no, He is the same God who is holy and merciful and who does all things well. Mary may not have understood all the depths of theology or fathomed the consequences of what she was told by Gabriel, but when she asked, "How will this be?" (v. 34), the answer was "Nothing will be impossible with God" (v. 37).

The Faithfulness of God

Mary finishes her song in a magnificent style: **"He has helped his servant Israel, in remembrance of his mercy, as he spoke to our fathers, to Abraham and to his offspring forever"** (vv. 54–55). Remember David's cry, "Bless the Lord, O my soul, and forget not all his benefits" (Ps. 103:2). Our tendency as Christians is to be as strong in our faith as the recollection of our latest blessing. But we forget all the benefits that God has poured out on us in our lives. That's our nature, to forget.

This is one of the ways we differ so profoundly from God. He does not know how to forget. Once God makes a promise, it is sure. His promise can never be broken or forgotten. The national faith of Israel and the spiritual vitality of the people were weak at the time of Jesus' coming. People such as Elizabeth, Zechariah, Joseph, and Mary, who kept the faith handed down through the ages, felt all alone. They wondered, Where's God? And then in the *Magnificat*, Mary said: "Oh, yes! He remembers. He remembers the covenant He made with Abraham and with our fathers forever." That's the God we come to worship every Sunday morning. The God of providence, the God of promises, the God who doesn't know how to forget His promises to Abraham and to his seed forever.

7

THE BIRTH OF JOHN

Luke 1:57–66

Now the time came for Elizabeth to give birth, and she bore a son. And her neighbors and relatives heard that the Lord had shown great mercy to her, and they rejoiced with her. And on the eighth day they came to circumcise the child. And they would have called him Zechariah after his father, but his mother answered, "No; he shall be called John." And they said to her, "None of your relatives is called by this name." And they made signs to his father, inquiring what he wanted him to be called. And he asked for a writing tablet and wrote, "His name is John." And they all wondered. And immediately his mouth was opened and his tongue loosed, and he spoke, blessing God. And fear came on all their neighbors. And all these things were talked about through all the hill country of Judea, and all who heard them laid them up in their hearts, saying, "What then will this child be?" For the hand of the Lord was with him.

Luke tells us that Elizabeth's days were fulfilled, that it was time for her to deliver her child, and so she brought forth a son. Then we have this simple note from Luke: **And her neighbors and relatives heard that the Lord had shown great mercy to her, and they rejoiced with her** (v. 58). We know that when Elizabeth first received the news that in her old-age barrenness she would conceive and bear a child, she withdrew to her residence and kept herself hidden.

Luke tells us this: **her neighbors and relatives heard that the Lord had**

shown great mercy to her, and they rejoiced with her. This is the communion of saints. This is the community of people who believe and put their trust in God. The Word of God tells us in Romans 12 that we are to weep with those who weep and to rejoice with those who rejoice, so that we are united in our joys and sorrows, empathizing with each other. That's how it is to be with the people of God.

Luke goes on to say that **on the eighth day they came to circumcise the child** (v. 59). This was in accordance with Jewish law. **And they would have called him Zechariah after his father, but his mother answered, "No; he shall be called John"** (vv. 59–60).

The people gathered weren't satisfied with the response from Elizabeth. **And they said to her, "None of your relatives is called by this name." And they made signs to his father, inquiring what he wanted him to be called** (vv. 61–62).

And he asked for a writing tablet and wrote, "His name is John" (v. 63). The deed was done. The discussion was over. He already had his name. His name was John, and at that point Zechariah showed he was controlled not by custom but by the word of God, and **they all wondered** (v. 63).

And immediately his mouth was opened and his tongue loosed, and he spoke, blessing God (v. 64). Zechariah's tongue that had been bound, shut up tight, was loosed, and he spoke, praising God. The first words from this man's mouth after he had suffered through nine months of silence were praise and adoration for his God.

When that happened, we are told, **fear came on all their neighbors. And all these things were talked about through all the hill country of Judea** (v. 65). Every village in the hill country of Judea was abuzz with the news of these extraordinary events, **and all who heard them laid them up in their hearts, saying, "What then will this child be?"** (v. 66). They couldn't wait to see what this little baby would grow up to be like.

For the hand of the Lord was with him (v. 66). The hand of the Lord was with John the day he was born. It was with him before he was born, when he leaped in his mother's womb. It was with him when he came to the Jordan River to baptize and to call Israel to repentance. It was with him when he was in prison, and it was with him when he was martyred.

8

THE BENEDICTUS

Luke 1:67–80

And his father Zechariah was filled with the Holy Spirit and prophesied, saying,

"Blessed be the Lord God of Israel,
 for he has visited and redeemed his people
and has raised up a horn of salvation for us
 in the house of his servant David,
as he spoke by the mouth of his holy prophets from of old,
that we should be saved from our enemies
 and from the hand of all who hate us;
to show the mercy promised to our fathers
 and to remember his holy covenant,
the oath that he swore to our father Abraham, to grant us
 that we, being delivered from the hand of our enemies,
might serve him without fear,
 in holiness and righteousness before him all our days.
And you, child, will be called the prophet of the Most High;
 for you will go before the Lord to prepare his ways,
to give knowledge of salvation to his people
 in the forgiveness of their sins,
because of the tender mercy of our God,
 whereby the sunrise shall visit us from on high

to give light to those who sit in darkness and in the shadow of death,
to guide our feet into the way of peace."

And the child grew and became strong in spirit, and he was in the wilderness until the day of his public appearance to Israel.

We've already considered two of the other songs of the infancy of Jesus, Elizabeth's song and the *Magnificat* of Mary. Later on, we will look at the *Gloria in Excelsis Deo* of the heavenly chorus outside Bethlehem and the *Nunc Dimittis*, the song of Simeon. But the other great hymn in Luke's Gospel is this one sung by Zechariah, the father of John the Baptist. In this song is both celebration and prophecy of what is to come. But the central theme—I think the most important theme—is expressed at the very beginning of this song, and it has to do with God's visiting His people.

The song begins, **"Blessed be the Lord God of Israel"** (v. 68). Why is Zechariah attributing a beatific view of God at the beginning of the hymn? He answers that for us clearly. The reason he is blessing God is because **"he has visited and redeemed his people and has raised up a horn of salvation for us in the house of his servant David"** (vv. 68–69).

God Visits His People

What's somewhat unusual that we don't see when we read the English translation of the text is the language that is used for such divine visitation. The Greek verb that is translated "visited" here is the verb form of an extremely important noun in biblical categories. The noun is *episkopos*. That word sounds at least somewhat familiar to us, because we think of the Episcopalian Church, which is called *episcopalian* because of its form of government. It is a church that is ruled by bishops. When we talk of that which is episcopal, we're talking about that which has to do with bishops.

Indeed, one of the ways that *episkopos* is translated into English is "bishop." *Episkopos* is made up of two parts, a prefix and a root. The root is the word *skopos*. That comes right over into English. It's the word that we translate into "scope." Long-range rifles have scopes mounted on them. We have microscopes. We have telescopes. The scope is something that we look through.

But the idea here is "vision," or looking, and as we look at this word, think of the relationship between the word *vision* and the word *visit*. They are closely related. When people come to your house to visit you, it's because they want to see you, and therein is the connection going back to the Latin *videre*. Both *vision* and *visit* come from that Latin root. The root of the word translated "bishop" is *skopos* with a prefix *epi* attached to it. That prefix *epi* intensifies the root. In Latin, the corresponding term is *supervidere*, meaning "super-looking."

In our culture, on the job we have people who do their work and while they are doing their work, somebody is watching them; that person is called the supervisor. A supervisor is not just a visor. He's not just a looker; he's a super-looker. He's watching closely. The supervisor or the bishop is not a casual observer. The supervisor is one who looks at things deeply and carefully and fully so that he sees every single detail of what is going on.

I labor this point because this title of *episkopos* is in the New Testament given to Jesus. Jesus, we are told in the book of Hebrews, is the "Bishop of your souls" (1 Peter 2:25, KJV). That title is given to Jesus merely as a transfer of the understanding of the nature of God to His Son. Ultimately, the supreme bishop is God, who observes everything in the world totally and comprehensively. Jesus tells us there's not a single bird that lands on the ground that our heavenly Father doesn't see. He tells us that the very hairs on our head are numbered (Matt. 10:29–30). David exclaimed: "Where shall I go from your Spirit? Or where shall I flee from your presence? If I ascend to heaven, you are there! If I make my bed in Sheol, you are there!" (Ps. 139:7–8).

God Provides for His People

Related to this is another word we have in our theological vocabulary that's critically important for the Christian to understand, and that's the concept of divine providence. With *providence* we have a root and a prefix. The root is *videre*, which has to do with vision. *Pro-videre* means to see things beforehand. But it's more than that. It's not just that the providence of God refers to His knowledge of things before they happen, but more importantly, it has to do with His sovereign plan of things that will come to pass. It is His provision for His people.

The first time we find the concept of divine providence in the Bible is in Genesis 22. There, God said to Abram, "Take your son, your only son Isaac, whom you love, and go to the land of Moriah, and offer him there as a burnt offering on one of the mountains of which I shall tell you" (v. 2). If God came to Abraham and said, "Take your son to that mountain and sacrifice him to Me," and that was all the information God gave to Abraham, Abraham might have taken Ishmael, his son by Hagar, his wife's servant, and sacrificed him. But God was very specific. He named Isaac.

Abraham got up early in the morning. He chopped wood for the sacrifice and loaded his beast of burden and took Isaac. As they saw Mount Moriah in the distance, Isaac asked, "Behold, the fire and the wood, but where is the lamb for a burnt offering?" (v. 7). I think this is one of the most poignant moments in the history of redemption. What was going on in Abraham's heart? Abraham said to his son, "God will provide for himself the lamb for a burnt offering, my son" (v. 8). Jehovah-Jireh—the Lord will provide. Abraham said he was going to trust in the provision—the providence of God.

When they got to the top of the mountain, Abraham took his son and bound him with the ropes and placed him on the altar and raised the knife above his head. At the last second, as Abraham was about to plunge the knife into the heart of his son, God spoke and said: "Abraham, Abraham! . . . Do not lay your hand on the boy or do anything to him, for now I know that you fear God, seeing you have not withheld your son, your only son, from me" (vv. 11–12). And behind Abraham was a ram caught in a thicket by his horns. That ram was used as a substitute for the sacrifice. God had provided. Jehovah-Jireh had provided the lamb to be slain as a substitute.

Two thousand years later, near that same mountain, God took His Son, His only Son, the Son whom He loved, Jesus, and put Him on the altar of sacrifice. Only this time no one shouted "Stop!" The ultimate provision was made. All that is incorporated in this concept of divine visitation.

Divine Visitation

The idea of the bishop was similar to that of Greek generals, who from time to time came to inspect the troops to see if they were battle ready or if they were negligent and had grown rusty, lazy, and incompetent during his absence. If he found the troops battle ready, he pronounced his benediction on them, but if he found them ill-prepared, the general brought judgment on the troops. The troops never knew when the general would pay them a visit.

In the Old Testament, there is the idea of the supreme, providential Lord who will visit His people. These visits could be either wonderful and redemptive or tragic as they brought His judgment. The people of God in the Old Testament looked forward to the promised day of the Lord. In the beginning, the day of the Lord was this future day when God would come and redeem His people, bringing peace and justice to them and redeeming them from their enemies and fulfilling all His covenant promises. But as the people of Israel grew cold in their hearts and stiff-necked, they were warned that the day of the Lord might not be as they had anticipated.

The prophet Amos said to them, "Is not the day of the Lord darkness, and not light, and gloom with no brightness in it?" (Amos 5:20). There is a two-edged sword in the Old Testament. On the one hand, they looked forward to the bright dawn of the day of God's visitation, and on the other hand, they feared that this day might be one of judgment. The ultimate visit from on high was the entrance of Christ into the world. For those who receive Him, to them He gives authority to be called the children of God (John 1:12). It is the day of the Lord's redemption. But for those who reject Him, it is the day of darkness, with no light in it.

How many times have the great saints and we, the lesser saints, felt the absence of God? We wonder where He is. We don't sense His nearness. I think of Martin Luther at Worms, the night before his trial, praying and crying out: "God, where are You? Send help. I need You. This isn't my cause; this is Your cause. The cause is Yours, and I am Yours." Luther prayed that the next day God would visit him and give him strength. In the morning the Lord God omnipotent indeed visited His servant and upheld him.

God visited Zechariah and Elizabeth, and He was about to visit the whole nation with the birth of His Son. That made Zechariah sing, "**Blessed be the Lord God of Israel, for he has visited and redeemed his people**" (v. 68).

A Horn of Salvation

When Zechariah praised God, he went on to say that God **"has raised up a horn of salvation for us"** (v. 69). It would be almost impossible to count all the titles used to describe the Messiah in sacred Scripture. But here is one we could easily miss if we pass over the text too quickly. This visitation and redemption involves the coming of the Messiah, who is here referenced as a horn of salvation in the house of His servant David.

The image of the horn refers to those beasts of the earth that use their horns in battle. It is a symbol of great strength. In Jewish imagery, one such animal that is referenced again and again is the ox. In our own language, we have the expression "as strong as an ox."

In the early church, the four Gospel writers were associated with various symbols. One of these symbols was the ox, and it was associated with Luke, the author of the Gospel we're considering. He records the description of the Messiah as having the horn of salvation, as One who comes in His messianic office with enormous strength, a strength that cannot be overcome. And He comes **"in the house of his servant David"** (v. 69).

In this part of the hymn, Zechariah is not celebrating the role that God is giving to his son, who has been named John. That prophetic utterance comes at the end of the hymn. In this section of the hymn, he is extolling the greatness of God's Messiah, whom God is raising up in the house of David. His own son

John would be from the house of Levi and not from the tribe of Judah, which is the tribe from which the Messiah was to come.

He mentions that the realization of the visitation of the horn of salvation is not something that has come without any word of preparation, but rather it happens **"as he spoke by the mouth of his holy prophets from of old"** (v. 70). The prophecy of the coming Messiah begins with Adam and Eve and the curse on the serpent, whose seed would be crushed by the Seed of the woman. Throughout the pages of the Old Testament, the prophets again and again reiterate the gospel promise of the coming Messiah who would bring redemption with Him.

God Keeps His Promises

"That we should be saved from our enemies and from the hand of all who hate us" (v. 71). This reference in biblical terminology is not simply a promise that God is going to rescue the Jews from the Romans, the Philistines, the Amorites, or any of those other nations that constantly besieged Israel. Rather, the ultimate enemy that will be crushed by the horn of salvation is the devil, the prince of darkness, and all his minions who are part of the curse—death, darkness, disease, and everything else that puts a shadow over the joy of human life. All these enemies will be conquered by the Messiah, who will rise from the house of David **"to show the mercy promised to our fathers and to remember his holy covenant"** (v. 72). Notice that this is the same theme that Mary focused on in the *Magnificat* when she said that God has remembered the promise that He has made to our father Abraham.

In the mid-1960s in Boston, when I was a college professor, one of our administrative members became sick unto death. I visited him several times a week during his dying days. He was called Deacon, because he was a deacon in his church. He was such a wonderful man and a dear friend. When I visited him, the thing Deacon loved the most was when I read the Word of God to him. The last text that I read was from Hebrews 6:13–20, where we read these words: "For when God made a promise to Abraham, since he had no one greater by whom to swear, he swore by himself, saying, 'Surely I will bless you and multiply you.' And thus Abraham, having patiently waited, obtained the promise. For people swear by something greater than themselves, and in all their disputes an oath is final for confirmation. So when God desired to show more convincingly to the heirs of the promise the unchangeable character of his purpose, he guaranteed it with an oath" (vv. 13–17).

God was determined to make it absolutely clear, so that there would be no doubt about not only the promise but the immutability, the impossibility of its being changed or weakened. Because He was so determined to do this, "he guaranteed it with an oath, so that by two unchangeable things, in which it is impossible for God to lie, we who have fled for refuge might have strong encouragement to hold fast to the hope set before us" (vv. 17–18). What are those two immutable things that make it impossible for God to lie? The first thing is a promise that comes from God. When God makes a promise, it is there forever and cannot be broken. And the second thing is the oath by which He confirms that promise. By these two things we see that it is impossible for God to lie.

I told Deacon, "We have this as a sure and steadfast anchor of the soul, a hope that enters into the inner place behind the curtain, where Jesus has gone as a forerunner on our behalf, having become a high priest forever after the order of Melchizedek" (vv. 19–20).

That's what drives the Christian life, that we are children of Abraham, that he is the father of the faithful, and that to Abraham God made a promise and confirmed it by an oath, a promise that was not only to him as an individual but was to Abraham and his seed. Paul emphasizes in his letter to the Romans that as many who put their faith in Christ are indeed the children of Abraham (Rom. 4:1–12).

Let's just take a moment to rehearse that promise and that oath, going back to Genesis 12, where we read these words: "Now the Lord said to Abram, 'Go from your country and your kindred and your father's house to the land that I will show you'" (v. 1). Abram's land and family were given to idolatry. God said: "And I will make of you a great nation, and I will bless you and make your name great, so that you will be a blessing. I will bless those who bless you, and him who dishonors you I will curse, and in you all the families of the earth shall be blessed" (vv. 2–3). So Abram departed as the Lord had commanded him. That's where it starts.

A few chapters later, we find the confirmation of this promise. When people ask me what my life verse is, I tell them Genesis 15:17. They often come back and ask if I said the wrong verse. I reply, "No, this is the verse that if I'm ever in prison, in solitary confinement, and I could have only one verse of the Bible, this is the one I'd want." Genesis 15:17 reads, "When the sun had gone down and it was dark, behold, a smoking fire pot and a flaming torch passed between these pieces."

The story starts in the beginning of chapter 15 where we read, "The word of the Lord came to Abram in a vision: 'Fear not, Abram, I am your shield; your reward shall be very great.' But Abram said, 'O Lord God, what will you give me, for I continue childless, and the heir of my house is Eliezer of Damascus?'" (vv. 1–2). Abram must have thought, What do you mean You're going to be my exceedingly great reward? I'm one of the wealthiest men in the world. What can You give me that would be a great reward that would make up for the fact that I have no son? "And Abram said, 'Behold, you have given me no offspring, and a member of my household will be my heir.' And behold, the word of the Lord came to him: 'This man shall not be your heir; your very own son shall be your heir.' And he brought him outside and said, 'Look toward heaven, and number the stars, if you are able to number them.' Then he said to him, 'So shall your offspring be'" (vv. 3–5).

We read these pregnant words in verse 6: "And he believed the Lord, and he counted it to him as righteousness." The Apostle Paul uses this verse in Romans 4:3 to illustrate the doctrine of justification by faith alone through the imputation of a righteousness from God to those who have no righteousness. "But he said, 'O Lord God, how am I to know that I shall possess it?'" (Gen. 15:8). And now Abram stumbles. He's like all of us. We believe; help our unbelief. After Abram's remarkable profession of faith, he wavers. "I believe You, but how can I know for sure that this promise that You've made will come true?"

"He said to him, 'Bring me a heifer three years old, a female goat three years old, a ram three years old, a turtledove, and a young pigeon.' And he brought him all these, cut them in half, and laid each half over against the other. But he did not cut the birds in half" (vv. 9–10). God has Abraham form a gauntlet of sorts by putting one half of the animal and the other half of the animal on each side of the aisle. "And when birds of prey came down on the carcasses, Abram drove them away" (v. 11).

> As the sun was going down, a deep sleep fell on Abram. And behold, dreadful and great darkness fell upon him. Then the Lord said to Abram, "Know for certain that your offspring will be sojourners in a land that is not theirs and will be servants there, and they will be afflicted for four hundred years. But I will bring judgment on the nation that they serve, and afterward they shall come out with great possessions. As for you, you shall go to your fathers in peace; you shall be buried in a good old age. And they shall come back here in the fourth generation, for the iniquity of the Amorites is not yet complete."
>
> When the sun had gone down and it was dark, behold, a smoking fire pot and a flaming torch passed between these pieces. (vv. 12–17)

This is a theophany. The smoking fire pot and the flaming torch are visible manifestations of the invisible God. This is God Himself going between these pieces of these carcasses that have been set there in that aisle.

What God is acting out dramatically and demonstratively to Abram is this:

"I'm cutting a covenant with you, Abram, and what I'm saying is if I don't keep My word, if I fail to keep My promise, may I be torn asunder just as you've cut in half this heifer, this ram, and this goat. May the immutable God suffer a permanent mutation. May the infinite surrender to finitude, the immortal to mortality. Abram, there's nothing higher upon which I can swear an oath than on My own self-existent, infinite, eternal being." When God made this covenant with Abram and his seed, He swore an oath by Himself, by His own divine being. God put His deity on the line to confirm the promise that God made to Abraham and to his seed.

Is it any wonder that when these promises are fulfilled, the servant of God, Zechariah, sings under the inspiration of the Holy Spirit? For God has kept His promise to Abraham and to his seed. That's why many in the church baptize their babies. Because in that original covenant with Abram, he was to be circumcised as a sign of that covenant, and he was commanded by God to circumcise his son, who had not yet come to faith, as a sign of the promise of God (17:1–14). That covenantal sign was not a sign of Abraham's faith, and it was not a sign of Isaac's faith; it was the sign of God's promise to all who believe. Baptism fulfills circumcision just as the Lord's Supper fulfills Passover. That principle of family solidarity is never abolished, even in the New Testament.

In the book of Acts, when people come to faith as adults and receive the covenant sign, not only do they receive it, but their household does also. The principle that had been the view for centuries is that the children of believers are not saved automatically because their parents are saved. They don't have faith automatically because their parents have faith. But they do have the promise of God given to Abraham and renewed again and again throughout the history of the old covenant and into the new covenant.

We are the people of the covenant. The covenant that is extolled by Zechariah, that God has remembered His holy covenant, **"the oath that he swore to our father Abraham, to grant us that we, being delivered from the hand of our enemies, might serve him without fear, in holiness and righteousness before him all our days"** (vv. 73–75). Martin Luther coined the Latin phrase *coram Deo*. Central to the Reformation, it means "in the presence of God." Every Christian is to live their life always aware that we're living before the face of God, in His presence, under His authority, to His glory, **"in holiness and righteousness before him all our days"** (v. 75).

A New Prophet

In the final section of the *Benedictus*, Zechariah prophesies about his son and his son's ministry for the Son of God. We read in verse 76, **"And you, child,**

will be called the prophet of the Most High; for you will go before the Lord to prepare his ways." We noted already that the work of prophecy had ceased after the words of Malachi, the last of the minor prophets of the Old Testament.

In Malachi 4:4–6, the last prophecy in the Old Testament, we read these words: "Remember the law of my servant Moses, the statutes and rules that I commanded him at Horeb for all Israel. Behold, I will send you Elijah the prophet before the great and awesome day of the LORD comes. And he will turn the hearts of fathers to their children and the hearts of children to their fathers, lest I come and strike the land with a decree of utter destruction." The last prophecy of the Old Testament was that the day of the Lord was coming, but before it comes, God will send His prophet Elijah. Remember that Elijah did not die but was carried up bodily into heaven in the chariots of fire (2 Kings 2). Because of this prophecy in Malachi, the ancient Jews looked forward to the return of Elijah. Every time the Jews celebrate the Passover even to this day, there is a chair at the table that sits there empty. The empty chair is for Elijah because God promised that he would come back.

As we will see later in the unfolding of the New Testament record and from the teaching of our Lord, Jesus said of John the Baptist, "He is Elijah who is to come" (Matt. 11:14). John is the one who comes in the spirit and the power of Elijah, and in this prophetic hymn, Zechariah says, **"And you, child, will be called the prophet of the Most High; for you will go before the Lord to prepare his ways"** (v. 76). It is also part of Isaiah's prophecy that before the Messiah comes, the forerunner, anointed by God to restore the voice of prophecy, would appear and cry to the people, "In the wilderness prepare the way of the LORD; make straight in the desert a highway for our God" (Isa. 40:3). Be ready when He comes. Under the inspiration of the Holy Ghost, Zechariah now prophesies that his son will fulfill that Old Testament prophecy, that John will be the forerunner of the Messiah. And together with the Messiah, he will **"give knowledge of salvation to his people in the forgiveness of their sins, because of the tender mercy of our God, whereby the sunrise shall visit us from on high"** (vv. 77–78).

The Gospel of Salvation

We sometimes think that Jesus' purpose in coming was to do miracles, and He certainly did that. Or that His purpose in coming was to give us salvation through His atonement, and that's certainly true. But His earthly ministry, just as John's began with preaching, was proclamation—the announcement of the gospel. Early on, it wasn't called the gospel of Jesus Christ; it was called the gospel of the kingdom of God. He called His hearers to learn, to gain knowledge. John and Jesus both taught the knowledge of salvation.

Some years ago, I spoke at the Christian bookseller's convention. There were six or seven thousand booksellers, and I had been asked to give the plenary address. I gave a message titled "Saved from What?" speaking of what salvation means, and I feared I was running the risk of insulting their intelligence, as they were all engaged in Christian publishing. If anybody should have a knowledge of salvation, it was these people.

Christians talk about being saved, but an important question to ask is, Saved from what? We might think we are saved from sin or the devil, and in some sense that is true, as in Christ we are freed from slavery to sin and bondage to the devil. But truly, what we are saved from is God Himself. This can be a shocking idea to grasp. Many Christians know they are saved, but they don't realize that it is God's wrath from which they are saved.

If God were a higher being or a cosmic force, people would have nothing to fear. A "higher being" has no authority over people and makes no demands of them. But when we talk about the personal God of the Bible who holds each of us accountable and who tells us that we will experience everlasting damnation if we don't repent, we become exposed to the reality of our fear. In our culture, we're expected to remain vague and speak about God "in general," but let a football player announce to the public that he's a disciple of Jesus Christ and watch the hostility explode. We can talk about God generally, but when we come to Jesus, we're down to the ultimate issue. If we are not in Christ, we are not reconciled; we are still at war.

The *Benedictus* goes on to give us more of the content of salvation, the knowledge of salvation to His people by the remission of their sins. For cancer patients, there's usually no better news than when the doctor tells them, "Your disease is in remission." That means it's gone away. It doesn't always stay away. We know the crushing disappointment some experience when it comes back. But with the remission of sins, it never comes back. When God forgives a sinner, He forgives him forever.

I knew no theology the night I became a Christian. I listened to a friend talk about Jesus as if He were real, as if my friend had a personal relationship with Him. I'd never heard anything like that in my life, but as I listened, I knew. I got my first knowledge of salvation, and then I went to my college dormitory room, walked in, turned off the light, and got on my knees before the bed. The only thing I could say was, "God, forgive me of my sins." In that moment, I experienced the unspeakable joy of having my soul flooded with the absolute assurance that every sin I had ever committed and ever would commit was forgiven. In that moment, I experienced salvation, which was the most decisive and defining moment of my life. Nobody can have their sins remitted and remain the same.

God's Tender Mercy

Zechariah's song says we have forgiveness of sins **"because of the tender mercy of our God"** (v. 78). The forgiveness of sins is not something we merit. It's not something we strive to achieve. It's not that we can make up for our sins by works of righteousness. That is the worst myth ever perpetrated in the church. If you want to go on a fool's errand, chase the hope of redeeming yourself by your own achievements. If any activity is doomed to failure, it would be this.

The only way a person can know salvation and have remission of his sins is through the mercy of God. It's not through the justice of God but through God's mercy. Notice here, under the influence of the Holy Spirit, how the mercy of God is described. It is **"because of the tender mercy of our God."**

Women want a husband who is strong but also tender—not overbearing but also not a weakling. We find that combination of strength and tenderness in the husband of the church, the strong and mighty Jesus, whose mercy is tender. When God forgives us of our sins, the mercy that He pours out on our souls is sweet and gentle and tender. That's how the mercy of God functions.

After Zechariah's song comes what seems almost like a footnote: **And the child grew and became strong in spirit, and he was in the wilderness until the day of his public appearance to Israel** (v. 80). The desert was the traditional meeting place between man and God. It was to the desert that Elijah fled for refuge, where he was fed by the ravens, and where he lived in a cave. John the Baptist lived in the desert, and there he ate wild locusts and honey (Matt. 3:4). John grows stronger and stronger until the summons comes, saying, "Prepare the way of the LORD" (Isa. 40:3).

9

THE BIRTH OF JESUS

Luke 2:1–20

In those days a decree went out from Caesar Augustus that all the world should be registered. This was the first registration when Quirinius was governor of Syria. And all went to be registered, each to his own town. And Joseph also went up from Galilee, from the town of Nazareth, to Judea, to the city of David, which is called Bethlehem, because he was of the house and lineage of David, to be registered with Mary, his betrothed, who was with child. And while they were there, the time came for her to give birth. And she gave birth to her firstborn son and wrapped him in swaddling cloths and laid him in a manger, because there was no place for them in the inn.

And in the same region there were shepherds out in the field, keeping watch over their flock by night. And an angel of the Lord appeared to them, and the glory of the Lord shone around them, and they were filled with great fear. And the angel said to them, "Fear not, for behold, I bring you good news of great joy that will be for all the people. For unto you is born this day in the city of David a Savior, who is Christ the Lord. And this will be a sign for you: you will find a baby wrapped in swaddling cloths and lying in a manger." And suddenly there was with the angel a multitude of the heavenly host praising God and saying,

> "Glory to God in the highest,
> and on earth peace among those with whom he is pleased!"

When the angels went away from them into heaven, the shepherds said to one another, "Let us go over to Bethlehem and see this thing that has happened, which the

Lord has made known to us." And they went with haste and found Mary and Joseph, and the baby lying in a manger. And when they saw it, they made known the saying that had been told them concerning this child. And all who heard it wondered at what the shepherds told them. But Mary treasured up all these things, pondering them in her heart. And the shepherds returned, glorifying and praising God for all they had heard and seen, as it had been told them.

The first thing we see about Luke's narrative of Christ's birth is found in the opening words. He begins his account by saying, **In those days** (v. 1). Luke speaks of the activity of the emperor of the Roman Empire and of **Quirinius**, the **governor of Syria** (v. 2), real people in real places in real history. This story does not begin with the words "Once upon a time," because this is no fairy tale. This is sober history, announcing the entrance into this world of our Savior. Luke sets his narrative squarely in the context of real history. **In those days a decree went out from Caesar Augustus that all the world should be registered** (v. 1).

This story is about three kings. One of those kings sits on the throne as the ruler and emperor of the greatest power on the face of the earth at that time, Rome. The second King does not sit on a throne but lies in a manger wrapped in swaddling cloths. This little King is the King of kings. He rules over the king in Rome. And it's about the eternal King, the Lord God omnipotent, who reigns from the moment of His work of creation to the moment of His work of the fulfillment of His cosmos. He is the great King who reigns over all things.

The story proximately speaks of an earthly decree, issued and executed by the emperor in Rome, that all people return to their cities of birth to be registered for the census in order to be taxed by the empire. This decree is done in obedience to a decree that took place much earlier, even in eternity, when God decreed that His Son would come into this world to do His work of redemption for His people and that He would be born at a specific time, in the fullness of time; at a specific place, in the village of Bethlehem; and for a specific mission, to save His people from their sins.

Caesar Augustus, born Gaius Octavius, was the first and probably the most celebrated of all the Roman emperors. He succeeded his great-uncle and adoptive father, Julius Caesar, as the leader of Rome after Julius was assassinated in 44 BC. Julius named Octavius his heir, and the senate of Rome named him emperor and gave him the title Caesar Augustus. *Augustus* means "the supreme, sublime, majestic one." The Jews shrank in horror from that title because they believed that only God was worthy of such a title. The true August One was in the manger because there was no room for Him in the inn. Caesar Augustus celebrated the memory of his great-uncle by building a temple in his honor, acknowledging the deity of Julius Caesar.

A Humble, Glorious Birth

In obedience to the decree of Caesar Augustus, **Joseph also went up from Galilee, from the town of Nazareth, to Judea, to the city of David, which is called Bethlehem** (v. 4). He did this **because he was of the house and lineage of David** (v. 4), and he brought **Mary, his betrothed**, with him (v. 5). Roman law did not require that a man bring his wife to register for the census, but we can speculate as to why Joseph subjected his betrothed to such an arduous journey. The proximate reason seems clear. She **was with child** (v. 5). He knew the time had come for her to deliver, and he did not want her to have to be without him, so he brought her with him. But the ultimate reason is that it had been decreed from all eternity that the babe would be born in Bethlehem. The prophet Micah had announced centuries before: "But you, O Bethlehem Ephrathah, who are too little to be among the clans of Judah, from you shall come forth for me one who is to be ruler in Israel, whose coming forth is from of old, from ancient days" (Mic. 5:2).

And while they were there, the time came for her to give birth. And she gave birth to her firstborn son and wrapped him in swaddling cloths and laid him in a manger, because there was no place for them in the inn (vv. 6–7). The entrance of Jesus into this world is against the backdrop of humiliation. A cloak of shame and reproach is spread across the infant who is wrapped in rough, bandage-like strips of cloth and placed either in a niche of rock used as a feeding trough for animals or in a crude cradle. Humiliation began in His entrance into the world and ended in His exit from the world.

However, at the very moment the babe is wrapped in the cloth of humiliation, God is not satisfied that the circumstances of the Son's birth be only humiliation. God desired that shame be balanced with glory and exaltation. On the outskirts of the village, out in the fields, were the most lowly valued people of the land: **shepherds out in the field, keeping watch over their flock by night** (v. 8). Shepherds watched these flocks through the night, taking turns sleeping and keeping vigil, lest the sheep be attacked by wild animals or taken by thieves. It truly was a silent night.

And an angel of the Lord appeared to them, and the glory of the Lord shone around them, and they were filled with great fear (v. 9). Almost every time the Bible records a theophany, an outward visible manifestation of the invisible God, it is accompanied by the presence of the shekinah. The shekinah was the blazing, refulgent, blinding glory of God. We read that when that glory was visible, people hid their eyes from it; they were overwhelmed by it, driven to their knees, because there was nothing in nature that could compare to the shekinah glory of God.

Luke gives us the notation that when the shekinah glory appeared, the shepherds **were filled with great fear**. I like the old King James: "They were sore afraid." When you are sore afraid, you are afraid like you've never been afraid in your life. Who wouldn't be trembling in fear at the manifestation of the glory of God at that moment?

The angel speaks and gives the most frequently uttered negative prohibition in the New Testament: **"Fear not"** (v. 10). It seems that in the New Testament record of the life of Jesus, every time He came into the presence of His disciples, instead of saying, "Peace be with you," or "Hello," He would say, "Don't be afraid." Nothing is more common for fallen creatures than to be terrified in the presence of God.

Every time I hear the prohibition "Don't be afraid," I think of my days teaching nineteenth-century philosophy and teaching the writings of Friedrich Nietzsche, the existential nihilist. Nietzsche said that there is no meaning to life, that everything is an exercise in futility. All there is at the end of the day is nothingness. At the same time, Nietzsche called for the superman, the *Übermensch*, to demonstrate what he called "dialectical courage." He said: "The superman is the man who builds his house on the slope of Vesuvius. He sends his ship into uncharted seas." He's afraid of nothing. He's defiant. He challenges this meaningless world in which he lives, and he lives his life with a spirit of courage.

What is dialectical courage? What Nietzsche meant is contradictory courage, irrational courage. He called on people to be courageous, even though their courage is equally meaningless. That is, he could give no sound reason for calling anyone to be courageous or to be fearless. In the New Testament, Jesus says to His followers, "Take heart," and He gives a reason for that command. "Take heart," Jesus says. "I have overcome the world" (John 16:33). Years before, the angel said, **"Fear not, for behold, I bring you good news of great joy that will be for all the people. For unto you is born this day in the city of David a Savior, who is Christ the Lord"** (vv. 10–11).

The shepherds likely understood that the word *Christ* was the Greek translation of the Hebrew word *Messiah*, or "anointed one," and this was an announcement that the long-awaited Savior had come into the world. **"And this will be a sign for you: you will find a baby wrapped in swaddling cloths and lying in a manger." And suddenly there was with the angel a multitude of the heavenly host praising God** (vv. 12–13). No sooner had the angel announced this than suddenly he was surrounded by a **multitude of the heavenly host**, that army of angels that inhabits heaven and surrounds the presence of our eternal God. Now, it's not Zechariah or Mary who is singing. It's the angels who bring a chorus from heaven saying, **"Glory to God in the highest, and on earth peace among those with whom he is pleased!"** (v. 14). This is the next song recorded in Luke's infancy narrative, *Gloria in Excelsis Deo*. Do you love the hymn "Angels We Have Heard on High," with its majestic refrain, "Gloria in excelsis Deo"? This is the first singing of that refrain.

The Shepherds Tell Everyone

When the angels went away from them into heaven, the shepherds said to one another, "Let us go over to Bethlehem and see this thing that has happened, which the Lord has made known to us." And they went with haste and found Mary and Joseph, and the baby lying in a manger (vv. 15–16). They weren't coming to see Mary or pay homage to Joseph. They were coming to see the babe who was lying in the manger. **And when they saw it, they made known the saying that had been told them concerning this child** (v. 17). They told everyone they knew. They did evangelism by opening their mouths. They told everyone what they had heard and seen, and **all who heard it wondered at what the shepherds told them** (v. 18).

I wonder how long they marveled and how long the excitement lasted. What was the duration of their zeal and happiness from this experience, which had to be a converting experience? Maybe every Christmas they made mention of it. Not Mary. **But Mary treasured up all these things, pondering them in her heart** (v. 19). Eight days later, when she took the child to the temple for circumcision, she pondered these things. When the boy was twelve and confounded the doctors in the temple, she pondered them. Every night as she tucked her son into bed, she pondered them, to the day she stood at the foot of a cross and watched Him die. She pondered until that Sunday morning came and He arose, not in humility, not in shame, not in disgrace, but in glory, in triumph, in exaltation.

And the shepherds returned, glorifying and praising God for all they had heard and seen, as it had been told them (v. 20). That's the destiny of the Christian, to give glory and honor, dominion and power and praise. We join the angels, saying, "Worthy is the Lamb who was slain, to receive power and wealth and wisdom and might and honor and glory and blessing!" (Rev. 5:12). That's Christmas.

10

THE SONG OF SIMEON

Luke 2:21–38

And at the end of eight days, when he was circumcised, he was called Jesus, the name given by the angel before he was conceived in the womb.

And when the time came for their purification according to the Law of Moses, they brought him up to Jerusalem to present him to the Lord (as it is written in the Law of the Lord, "Every male who first opens the womb shall be called holy to the Lord") and to offer a sacrifice according to what is said in the Law of the Lord, "a pair of turtledoves, or two young pigeons." Now there was a man in Jerusalem, whose name was Simeon, and this man was righteous and devout, waiting for the consolation of Israel, and the Holy Spirit was upon him. And it had been revealed to him by the Holy Spirit that he would not see death before he had seen the Lord's Christ. And he came in the Spirit into the temple, and when the parents brought in the child Jesus, to do for him according to the custom of the Law, he took him up in his arms and blessed God and said,

"Lord, now you are letting your servant depart in peace,
 according to your word;
for my eyes have seen your salvation
 that you have prepared in the presence of all peoples,
a light for revelation to the Gentiles,
 and for glory to your people Israel."

And his father and his mother marveled at what was said about him. And Simeon blessed them and said to Mary his mother, "Behold, this child is appointed for the fall and rising of many in Israel, and for a sign that is opposed (and a sword will pierce through your own soul also), so that thoughts from many hearts may be revealed."

And there was a prophetess, Anna, the daughter of Phanuel, of the tribe of Asher. She was advanced in years, having lived with her husband seven years from when she was a virgin, and then as a widow until she was eighty-four. She did not depart from the temple, worshiping with fasting and prayer night and day. And coming up at that very hour she began to give thanks to God and to speak of him to all who were waiting for the redemption of Jerusalem.

The Bible doesn't tell us much about **Simeon**, only that he was **righteous and devout** (v. 25) and that God had given him a special revelation. He was **waiting for the consolation of Israel, and the Holy Spirit was upon him. And it had been revealed to him by the Holy Spirit that he would not see death before he had seen the Lord's Christ** (vv. 25–26). God the Holy Spirit was pleased to tell this presumably elderly man that he would not die until first he laid eyes on the promised Messiah.

If you'll give me license to use my imagination a little, I don't know how often Simeon came to the temple looking for the Messiah, but I assume that he came almost every day, looking for **the consolation of Israel**. Notice that this is another title that is given to Jesus in the early chapters of Luke. Jesus was called the Messiah who would bring God's consolation to a suffering people (see Isa. 40).

I don't know for sure, but I'm convinced that Simeon was an object of derision and scorn as he waited day by day in the temple. But finally, one day the Spirit of God came upon Simeon, and he arrived at the temple as Mary and Joseph brought their infant child for His presentation, at the end of the forty days of purification for Mary after childbirth.

Jesus Is Circumcised

But before we look at what happened that day, we need to know why Joseph and Mary took Jesus to the temple in the first place. We look here at the beginning of this section: **And at the end of eight days, when he was circumcised, he was called Jesus, the name given by the angel before he was conceived in the womb** (v. 21). That one sentence tells us, first of all, that **eight days** after the birth of Jesus, **he was circumcised**. People wonder why the Lord Jesus Christ would have to submit to the Old Testament ritual of circumcision, which was given to Abraham and his seed as a sign of God's covenant promise.

The Apostle Paul tells us in the fourth chapter of Romans that the sign of circumcision included, among other things, the sign of that righteousness that was by faith. It had a twofold significance. On the one hand, those who were circumcised symbolically were cut off from the rest of the world—the world of paganism, the world of idolatry—and set apart and consecrated to be a part of the covenant people of God. But also, the sign of circumcision was a sign of a person's having his sin removed from himself, just as the foreskin of his flesh had been removed ceremonially.

Why, then, should Jesus be circumcised? He wasn't born with original sin. Jesus was perfectly sinless from the moment of His conception to the moment of His death. The Scriptures tell us, however, that the Lord Jesus was born under the law, and everything that the law required of Israel was required of Israel's Redeemer and Israel's Champion. It was therefore necessary as devout parents that Joseph and Mary would see to it that their firstborn son would be circumcised.

Circumcision, in the old covenant, was, among other things, a sign of salvation that came only through faith; it did not automatically confer salvation. Paul labors that point in his letter to the Romans. Many Jews believed that because they were circumcised, they were automatically saved. The doctrine of justification by faith, Paul tells us, was not an innovation in the New Testament. It was the same way Abraham was saved in the Old Testament. The covenant promise came to adults in the Old Testament only after they made a true profession of faith.

God mandated that the same sign be given to their children before the children were capable of professing faith, because the sign was not a sign of the children's faith. It was a sign of God's promise of salvation to all who believe. That's why for two thousand years the children of Old Testament believers were included in receiving the sign of the covenant, and that didn't change in the New Testament. God gave a new covenant and a new sign, the sign of baptism, and required that only those who made profession of faith as adults could receive that sign, but their children were to receive it, as we see in the book of Acts (see Acts 16:15, 33–34). With household baptism, the principle of family solidarity remained intact and was never abrogated or repealed. That's why we think it's important, not just optional, that the children of believers receive the sign of the new covenant, which is the sign of the promise of salvation to all who believe. Baptism does not convey salvation, just as in the Old Testament circumcision did not convey salvation. It's a sign of the promise of God, and our own Lord, as an infant, received the sign of the covenant, circumcision, in His time.

Circumcision of baby boys on the eighth day was established in Old Testament law. There was also a ritual that involved the presentation of the firstborn son in the temple, which was accompanied by the giving of sacrifices. This presentation was a sign of the redeeming of the people. Symbolically, before He redeemed His people from sins, the baby Jesus experienced the sign of that redemption Himself. The Redeemer, because He had to follow the law, had to be "redeemed" before He could ever save anyone. Those were the requirements of the law that brought Joseph and Mary with the baby Jesus to the temple. They arrived there at the same moment Simeon came.

The *Nunc Dimittis*

And he came in the Spirit into the temple, and when the parents brought in the child Jesus, to do for him according to the custom of the Law, he took him up in his arms and blessed God (vv. 27–28). Under the influence of the Holy Spirit, Simeon began to sing a new song, the *Nunc Dimittis*, one of the greatest of the New Testament hymns celebrating God's salvation. The name of the song is taken from the first words of the song in Latin. This old man Simeon, holding the baby, says, **"Lord, now you are letting your servant depart in peace, according to your word; for my eyes have seen your salvation that you have prepared in the presence of all peoples, a light for revelation to the Gentiles, and for glory to your people Israel"** (vv. 29–32). Simeon is saying, in effect: "I've looked into the face of my Savior. I don't have to watch Him grow up or see Him in His public ministry or listen to His public teaching or watch the miracles He will perform. I don't need to see the transfiguration or be an eyewitness of the atoning death on the cross or of His resurrection from the dead. I see the light of salvation that God has promised His people, that consolation that we've been waiting for. I've seen the salvation that You've promised. Now let me go home."

My grandfather died in 1945, and my grandmother lived as a widow for more than twenty years after that, dying when she was eighty-nine years old. She was a devout Christian, and in the latter years of her life, she would say to me when I was a young boy: "I just don't understand why the Lord won't take me home. I want to go." Think of that motif in the Old Testament. Moses begged God: "God, if You have any love for me at all, slay me. The burden that You've put on my back of leading these people who complain and grumble all the time is too much. If you love me at all, take me away." Job cursed the day he was born.

It was a common thing for the saints of antiquity, after enduring so much suffering, to long and look for a better country. That was Simeon's hope. "Now, Lord, let me go. Now allow Your servant to depart in peace that I can enter into the heavenly kingdom."

And his father and his mother marveled at what was said about him (v. 33). Then Simeon turned his attention to them, and he uttered a blessing on the parents of Jesus. He said specifically to Mary, **"Behold, this child is appointed for the fall and rising of many in Israel, and for a sign that is opposed"** (v. 34). In other words, "Yes, He will raise many people up, but He will be a rock of offense, and people will stumble because of Him and they will fall into greater and greater wickedness. Every time they reject this One, the sin that they carry will be greatly magnified. There will be no neutrality toward Him."

All of this was not only foreseen but decreed from the foundation of the world in the covenant of redemption in the Godhead. Jesus' coming into the world was not an afterthought, not plan B in God's providence. But notice the words of the prophet: "**Behold, this child is appointed for the fall and rising of many in Israel**." In essence, "He is only a baby now, but He has a destiny, a destiny that began in eternity and a destiny that will surely come to pass because that destiny has been set before Him by His heavenly Father." You may not like the doctrine of predestination, but if you're going to be biblical, you cannot avoid it, for here we see it with respect to the ministry of our Lord Himself.

Further, Simeon told Mary, a time is coming that **"a sword will pierce through your own soul also"** (v. 35). We saw earlier that Mary pondered these things in her heart (v. 19). I wonder how many times she remembered what Simeon had said. What did he mean? Did she think of that moment when her child grew up and before her eyes was hanging on the cross, and at His death the soldier took his spear and pierced Jesus' side? Do you think Mary felt that not just in her side but in her soul? She must have known then that that prophecy had come to pass.

Finally, there is this mention of the **prophetess, Anna** (v. 36), who was also there in the temple. She had been there every day for decades. Anna came each day with prayers, and she joined Simeon, Mary, Joseph, and Jesus in that very moment, giving thanks to God and speaking of Him to all who looked for redemption in Jerusalem. That very day, Jerusalem's redemption was in the temple with her.

11

JESUS IN THE TEMPLE

Luke 2:39–52

And when they had performed everything according to the Law of the Lord, they returned into Galilee, to their own town of Nazareth. And the child grew and became strong, filled with wisdom. And the favor of God was upon him.

Now his parents went to Jerusalem every year at the Feast of the Passover. And when he was twelve years old, they went up according to custom. And when the feast was ended, as they were returning, the boy Jesus stayed behind in Jerusalem. His parents did not know it, but supposing him to be in the group they went a day's journey, but then they began to search for him among their relatives and acquaintances, and when they did not find him, they returned to Jerusalem, searching for him. After three days they found him in the temple, sitting among the teachers, listening to them and asking them questions. And all who heard him were amazed at his understanding and his answers. And when his parents saw him, they were astonished. And his mother said to him, "Son, why have you treated us so? Behold, your father and I have been searching for you in great distress." And he said to them, "Why were you looking for me? Did you not know that I must be in my Father's house?" And they did not understand the saying that he spoke to them. And he went down with them and came to Nazareth and was submissive to them. And his mother treasured up all these things in her heart.

And Jesus increased in wisdom and in stature and in favor with God and man.

Luke gives us more information about Jesus' birth and infancy than any other Gospel writer. We looked at Jesus' presentation in the temple when He was about six weeks old. But then there's a gap that goes from six weeks old to twelve years old. After that, we have another gap that goes from age twelve to about age thirty, when Jesus appears to begin His public ministry.

I've often wondered why it is that the Gospel writers don't fill us in with the details of Jesus' childhood. Attempts were made to do that by the fraudulent writings of the second-century Gnostics in the so-called apocryphal gospels, where fanciful stories are told of the child Jesus. They tell of His being lonely as He played in the dirt and His shaping birds from the mud, then turning these dirt birds into live birds so that He could have pets to play with. These fanciful stories really did not add truth or honor to our understanding of Jesus.

All we're told is that between the time Jesus was presented in the temple until the time He appeared again at age twelve that **the child grew and became strong, filled with wisdom. And the favor of God was upon him** (v. 40). At age thirteen, a Jewish young man becomes responsible for his own actions; he becomes a *bar mitzvah*, or son of the commandment, and he undergoes a ceremony to mark the occasion. According to the custom of the Jews at that time, when the boy was twelve, a year before bar mitzvah, the parents would take him to Jerusalem. He would be shown the temple and the different sites all around the Holy City so that he could be prepared for the following year's ceremony. In all probability, that's why, on this occasion when Jesus' parents came to Jerusalem for the feast of the Passover, they brought Him with them.

Luke tells us that when the time was finished for the celebration of the Passover, the people who had traveled many miles as pilgrims returned to their homes. The custom in the day was to travel by caravan. The caravan would include the family—aunts and uncles and cousins—and neighbors from the village and nearby villages. In this case, it would most likely have included all the family and friends from Nazareth and probably also from Cana and perhaps also from Capernaum and the other cities nearby.

In these caravans, women and children walked at the front, and in the back would be the men and the older boys. Jesus was on the threshold between child and young man, so it's safe for us to assume that on this occasion, Mary, with the children at the front of the caravan, assumed that Jesus was at the back of the caravan with Joseph, because she realized He certainly wasn't with her. And in like manner, in all probability, Joseph, being at the rear of the caravan with other men and young men, noticed that Jesus wasn't with him, and so he assumed Jesus must be with His mother at the front of the caravan. Finally, they realized He wasn't with them. As they searched for Him among their family and friends, their anxiety must have grown intense. Alone, Mary and Joseph began their journey back to Jerusalem.

They got back to Jerusalem, and Jesus wasn't waiting for them at the gates of the city. They scoured the city looking for Him, looking at the bazaar, looking at all the shops that dotted the streets even in those days. They couldn't find Him.

The Two Natures of Christ

After three days they found him in the temple, sitting among the teachers, listening to them and asking them questions (v. 46). At that time, after the celebration of the Passover, the visiting rabbis, scholars, theologians of the day remained in the city to discuss matters of theology. They were all in a room talking back and forth, discussing their theological theories. To Mary and Joseph's astonishment, they find Jesus sitting in the midst of these doctors, participating in the theological dialogue. **And all who heard him were amazed at his understanding and his answers** (v. 47).Though Mary and Joseph were astonished to find their Son involved in these discussions, the teachers were even more amazed by Jesus and His knowledge.

How did He know so much? How is it possible for this twelve-year-old boy Jesus to confound the experts in the law and the Scriptures? There is a quick and simple answer that people often give. They look at this event and say: "Well, why wouldn't He know all this? Jesus is God incarnate, and God is omniscient. He doesn't have to be taught by the scholars. He knows everything, and if Jesus is God incarnate, doesn't that mean that He knew everything?"

Well, yes and no. Now we bump right up against one of the greatest mysteries and one of the most important doctrines of the Christian faith, and that is the mystery of the incarnation of Christ, whom we confess to be the God-man, whom we profess to be the very incarnation of God. During the fifth century AD, the church faced one of the most critical crises it had endured up till that time. There was a rise of two distinct and separate heresies at the same time, both of which seriously threatened the well-being of the church.

The first heresy was called the Monophysite heresy, and it had been advanced by a man named Eutyches. The Monophysite heresy taught this: if Jesus was one person, clearly He must have had only one nature, like every other person we've ever met. If He only had one nature, however, was it divine or human? If you were to ask a Monophysite, "Was Jesus' single nature divine or was it human?" he would say that the one nature was a blend of deity and humanity. They called it a single *theanthropic* nature. *Theos* means God and *anthrōpos* means man, so they say one theanthropic nature means Jesus had one nature, a divinely human nature or a humanly divine nature.

The Council of Chalcedon in 451 condemned this view. The council pointed out that in conceiving of Jesus as having one theanthropic nature, the Monophysites had said that He is neither human nor divine but something else. If His human nature has been deified, then it's no longer human. And if His divine nature has been humanized, then it's no longer divine. So the Monophysite view was condemned.

The other heresy was Nestorianism, which is named after the theologian Nestorius. The view taught that if Christ has two natures, a human nature and a divine nature, then He must also be two persons, human and divine. This view was condemned at the Council of Ephesus in 431 and again at the Council at Chalcedon. In condemning this view, Chalcedon first made a positive affirmation. It said that Jesus, in the mystery of the incarnation, is *vera homo, vera Deus*, "truly man and truly God." We must affirm both the true humanity of Jesus in the incarnation and affirm His true deity. Then, the council gave the famous four negatives of Chalcedon. The council wisely didn't try to totally explain the mystery of the incarnation. It didn't answer all the questions. Instead, it set the borders. It defined the incarnation in terms of what it was not with these four negatives. They said Jesus is truly human, truly divine, having two natures, perfectly united, but without mixture or confusion, separation or division.

A pox on both houses was pronounced at Chalcedon. The council said that however we understand the incarnation, we can't understand it in terms of a mixture or blend of deity and humanity, nor can we understand it in terms of a separation or division between the two natures. If we cross these boundaries, we must choose our heresy.

Then the council went on to say that each nature retains its own attributes. That simple theological affirmation has been trampled on and brutally violated throughout church history and even today. If we could remember those four negatives as well as that each nature retains its own attributes, we would spare ourselves much grief in trying to understand the God-man.

So, how did Jesus know all that He knew? Those who say He knew it because of His divine nature are saying that because the divine nature is omniscient, then the human nature must be omniscient too. But that is to confuse the two natures and to fail to recognize that each nature retains its own attributes.

When looking at Jesus' two natures, we should see that we can't divide them, but we must distinguish them. For example, when Jesus walked down the street, He had physical legs, arms, fingers, and toes. Now we have to ask this: Were His legs and arms and fingers and toes a manifestation of His deity? Of course not. God is not physical. The divine nature doesn't have legs. It doesn't have arms, fingers, or toes. When Jesus was hungry or thirsty, did that show His deity or His humanity? It showed His humanity, of course. This is what it is to distinguish but not separate. We recognize that the one person of Christ acted according to one or the other nature at various times. When the one person of Christ was thirsty, it was according to His human nature, but that does not mean that He was thirsty according to His divine nature. God never gets thirsty, but humans get thirsty. That's easy enough to understand when we're talking about flesh and blood and getting thirsty and getting hungry.

But what about when it comes to knowledge? One of the things that drove the great theologian Thomas Aquinas to distraction was the problem in Mark's Gospel where near the end of His life, the disciples ask Jesus when He is coming back. Jesus gave them some general answers to the question and then said this: "But concerning that day or that hour, no one knows, not even the angels in heaven, nor the Son, but only the Father" (Mark 13:32). Thomas said: "That can't be. Jesus had to know the day and the hour. He was God incarnate." What Thomas thought was that Jesus' divine nature knew, and if the two natures were perfectly united, then the human nature had to know too. Thomas wasn't thinking correctly here. Jesus' human knowledge was as limited as anybody else's human knowledge unless the divine nature communicated information to the human nature.

In the Old Testament, prophets like Isaiah, Jeremiah, Ezekiel, and Daniel had supernatural knowledge of the future. Did they gain that knowledge from their own insight? No, they gained that knowledge because God revealed it to them. Just as Jesus said, touching His humanity, "The words that I say to you I do not speak on my own authority, but the Father who dwells in me does his works" (John 14:10). There surely were times when Jesus displayed supernatural knowledge, such as when He knew Nathaniel before He met him (1:43–51) and when He knew about the woman at the well (ch. 4). But that didn't rise up out of Jesus' reservoir of human knowledge; rather, the Father or the divine nature revealed it to Him on that occasion.

It's possible that in the temple, on the occasion of Jesus' discussion with the teachers, that the divine nature somehow transferred knowledge to His human nature and gave Him answers for all the questions by the rabbis. But I don't think so. I don't think it's necessary for us to speculate that the way Jesus showed such prodigious knowledge at age twelve was because the divine nature was giving Him this insight.

The Communication of Attributes

There's another concept in the doctrine of Christ called the *communicatio idiomatum*, or communication of attributes, which is understood in different ways by different traditions. Roman Catholics and Lutherans believe that one nature of Christ can share attributes with the other. This is how, for instance, Christ can be physically present in the Lord's Supper in these traditions' conception: the divine nature communicates or shares the attribute of omnipresence with the human nature.

The Reformed tradition rejects this view, pointing out that it violates the Chalcedonian formula; it takes us right back to the Monophysites, who tried to blend and mix together the divine and human natures. We must say no to that. The Reformed tradition states that the *communicatio idiomatum* means that the two natures of Christ each communicate their attributes to the one person; so, the person of Christ is omnipresent according to His divine nature, not according to His human nature.

It is not that the divine nature shared knowledge with the human nature. So, how was Jesus able to amaze the Ph.D.s in the temple with His knowledge? I've studied theology seriously for more than fifty years, but I would have been confounded by the twelve-year-old Jesus had I been there. In His human nature, by the time He was twelve, He knew more about theology than I know today. How?

The Great Commandment is that we're to love the Lord our God with all of our hearts, souls, and minds. I have to confess I haven't loved God with all my mind for one minute in my life. The ravages of sin that fall on humanity from the fall affect not just the body and the will but also the mind. When we reject God, our foolish minds are darkened. We're still able to add two and two and come up with four. We're able to follow a logical argument sometimes, but we make errors in math and in logic even after much education, because our minds have been weakened, just as our bodies have been weakened by the influence of sin.

I will be embarrassed to stand before my Lord at the end of my days and have it revealed how much I don't know about the Bible and the things of God that I would have known if I had applied myself more seriously and ardently throughout my lifetime. Jesus didn't have the slightest influence of original sin in His life; His thinking was not for one second clouded by darkness, because for all of His twelve years Jesus had loved the Lord His God with His entire mind.

Jesus didn't need to rely on His divine nature to astound anyone. He was perfect in His humanity. Jesus knew His Father better than anyone ever has, even as a twelve-year-old. And He kept growing in wisdom, so that by the time

He was thirty, the people "were astonished at his teaching, for he taught them as one who had authority, and not as the scribes" (Mark 1:22).

Mary asked: **"Son, why have you treated us so? Behold, your father and I have been searching for you in great distress"** (v. 48). Jesus answered her question with a question. He said to them: **"Why were you looking for me? Did you not know that I must be in my Father's house?"** (v. 49).

Then Luke tells us: **And they did not understand the saying that he spoke to them. And he went down with them and came to Nazareth and was submissive to them. And his mother treasured up all these things in her heart. And Jesus increased in wisdom and in stature and in favor with God and man** (vv. 50–53). The next time we see Him is when He comes to be baptized by John.

12

JOHN THE BAPTIST

Luke 3:1–6

In the fifteenth year of the reign of Tiberius Caesar, Pontius Pilate being governor of Judea, and Herod being tetrarch of Galilee, and his brother Philip tetrarch of the region of Ituraea and Trachonitis, and Lysanias tetrarch of Abilene, during the high priesthood of Annas and Caiaphas, the word of God came to John the son of Zechariah in the wilderness. And he went into all the region around the Jordan, proclaiming a baptism of repentance for the forgiveness of sins. As it is written in the book of the words of Isaiah the prophet,

> "The voice of one crying in the wilderness:
> 'Prepare the way of the Lord,
>   make his paths straight.
> Every valley shall be filled,
>   and every mountain and hill shall be made low,
> and the crooked shall become straight,
>   and the rough places shall become level ways,
> and all flesh shall see the salvation of God.' "

Previously we looked at the experience of Jesus at age twelve when His parents brought Him to the temple and He astounded the doctors of the law with His knowledge. Then the Bible is silent for the next approximately eighteen years of Jesus' life. Luke now moves to the appearance of John the Baptist, and he is careful, indeed meticulous, in giving us the historical framework in which John the Baptist appeared. Notice what he says: **In the fifteenth year of the reign of Tiberius Caesar** (v. 1). Augustus Caesar was no longer emperor of Rome as he was at the time of the birth of Jesus. Now the emperor is Tiberius.

Luke goes on to say that at that time, **Pontius Pilate** was **governor of Judea**. Pilate was the fifth governor named by the Roman emperors to rule over conquered Palestine. We are then told that **Herod** was the **tetrarch of Galilee**. This is not Herod the Great. When Herod the Great was in his later years, he put together a will and testament that divided his kingdom among his sons. The Herod mentioned here is Herod Antipas, who replaced his brother Archelaus. Archelaus was first appointed tetrarch over Judea and Samaria, but he was deposed by the Roman emperor for cruelty. The Roman Empire was known for governmental cruelty, so the brutality of Archelaus must have been cruel indeed for him to have been thrown out of office by the Romans at that time.

Luke goes on to mention others: Herod's **brother Philip** was **tetrarch of the region of Ituraea and Trachonitis, and Lysanias tetrarch of Abilene**. Philip, who restored an ancient city and named it in honor of the Caesar and of himself, Caesarea Philippi, was one of the most noble of the rulers of the Jews at this time. Luke also mentions that it was **during the high priesthood of Annas and Caiaphas** (v. 2). Israel only had one high priest at any given time, and Annas had been the high priest, but he was removed from office by the Romans. The Jews, who had Caiaphas replace Annas, still gave tribute and honor to Annas and counted him as at the level of high priest. So, at this time there were effectively two high priests, Annas and Caiaphas. All this information is given by Luke to provide the time frame in which the ministry of John the Baptist began.

The Dangers of Syncretism

What is significant about this is the text shows that the ministry of John and the ministry of Jesus were both solidly rooted and grounded in real history. From antiquity, the people of God have always had to battle the threat of syncretism, where pagan elements are blended into pure worship. Syncretism borrows a little bit from the temple of Baal and a little bit from the Ashtaroth, and then mixes them together with the Jewish religion. Anytime syncretism takes place, something corrupt is added to the religion of God, and at the same time, something vitally important is removed from the truth of God.

The church has had to deal with that from the first century until today. It seems every time a popular philosophical movement arises, some theologian tries to create a synthesis between that movement and historical Christianity. The twentieth century, for example, saw two important syntheses come into being, and both did immeasurable damage to Christianity and to the church.

One was liberation theology, which was a conscious attempt to blend or synthesize biblical Christianity with the philosophy of Karl Marx. Christianity was then seen as having its purpose as not the personal salvation of the soul for eternal life but the establishment of what is called social justice. Liberation theology sought to translate the meaning of the gospel to the here and now, to social and political issues. In this view, the whole meaning of the gospel is about political revolution and freedom. One New Testament scholar wrote a book in which he claimed that whether Jesus lived is unimportant, because the meaning of Jesus is freedom. Wherever there is a struggle for freedom, that's where God is, and that's what Jesus means.

Even more widespread than liberation theology was the theology of Rudolf Bultmann, who became one of the most influential New Testament scholars of the twentieth century. What Bultmann tried to do, as others had attempted before him, was create a synthesis between New Testament Christianity and existential philosophy.

Bultmann said that a person can't live in this post-scientific era, in this time of enlightenment, using electricity, television, computers, and modern medicine, and still believe in a world inhabited by demons, a world where people die and are raised again from the dead. The New Testament content, in that regard, is to be understood as mythological. There is what Bultmann called "a kernel of truth" in the pages of the New Testament, buried underneath this mythology, and it's the task of the theologian to tear off the husk of all this mythology so that we can get to the kernel of truth that really matters. And that kernel of truth is this: that redemption is something that takes place vertically rather than horizontally.

For Bultmann, salvation takes place "immediately and directly from above," in an existential instant, in the here and now, with an existential experience of the sense of God. That's what Christianity is all about. Bultmann's theology rudely ripped Christianity out of any foundation in real history.

When I was in graduate school in the Netherlands, my professor, G.C. Berkouwer, observed about Bultmann that "theology can sink no lower." My professor was incorrect, however, because that was before the "death of God" theology that followed and radical feminist theology that started hosting conferences celebrating the goddess Sophia in reimagining God. That's lower than Bultmann's theology ever descended.

The Bible and History

There is an issue in theology with the relationship of Christianity to history. *Heilsgeschichte* is a word used to refer to salvation history. The claim is that the Bible is not real history; it's "redemptive" history or it's "salvation" history. Whether the Bible is accurate in the things that it reports is irrelevant; it's the message of how to have authentic human existence that matters.

Critics of this thinking came to the defense of orthodoxy, saying that it's true that the Bible is not an ordinary history book. It is redemptive history, but while it's redemptive history, it's also redemptive *history*. It's real history. The Apostle Paul understood these tendencies even when he wrote to the Corinthians, to those who were denying the historical reality of the resurrection of Jesus. He wrote, "If in Christ we have hope in this life only, we are of all people most to be pitied" (1 Cor. 15:19).

Since the Christian faith is tied to history, shouldn't we want to know if it's true? When we ask whether the truth claims of Christianity are trustworthy, we are asking, Did Jesus really die on the cross as an atoning death? Did Jesus actually rise from the dead? Did He truly ascend into heaven? If you remove those elements from Christianity, Christianity has been taken away and replaced with something else.

Why don't people have the honesty to say, "We've turned our churches into monuments of unbelief and we don't believe the Bible anymore," rather than try to reconstruct it or recast it in a way that will appeal to people? This happens with attempts to synthesize biblical Christianity with the prevailing notions of relativism and pluralism. You'll hear self-proclaimed evangelical preachers say: "Jesus isn't the only way. He's one way among many." That is bowing before the idol of secular pluralism, and it's a complete betrayal of the teaching of Jesus.

The Word Comes to John

Luke has been heralded as the greatest historian of antiquity, and he tells us things that happened, where they happened, when they happened, and why they happened as he now gives us the setting for the appearance of John the Baptist. **The word of God came to John the son of Zechariah in the wilderness** (v. 2). This happened in that desolate wilderness between the hill country of Judea and the Dead Sea, that piece of real estate where nothing grows except a few scrub bushes here and there, where the land is covered not with sand—not that kind of desert—but by pebbles and stones and rocks under which live scorpions and snakes.

John the Baptist lived in that austere environment, eating locusts and wild honey, because he was committed to the service of God. In the midst of that desolation, the word of the Lord came to John, telling him the time had come to leave the wilderness. John was to go to the River Jordan on a mission that had been prophesied of in the Old Testament. He was to prepare the way for the coming of the Messiah.

And he went into all the region around the Jordan, proclaiming a baptism of repentance for the forgiveness of sins (v. 3). A new rite was required of the Jews—they were to be baptized for the remission of their sins. The rite of baptism was a radical concept to the Jews, because before this time the only baptism that was of significance among them was proselyte baptism, a cleansing ritual that the Jews imposed on Gentiles who wanted to convert to Judaism. The reason proselyte baptism was inaugurated was because, from the Jewish perspective, Gentiles were unclean, too dirty to be involved in the sacred rites of Judaism. If they wanted to convert to Judaism, they had to profess faith in the content of Judaism, they had to be circumcised, and they had to take a bath (baptism) as a symbol of their cleansing. But that requirement was only for Gentiles.

After four hundred years of silence of the voice of prophecy, out of the wilderness comes John, who acts like the prophet Elijah in the Old Testament. He tells the Jewish people to come to the river and be baptized for the remission of sins. This is not New Testament baptism. This is not the baptism that is the covenant sign that Jesus instituted. This is a preparatory baptism. We find many points of similarity between the baptism of John and the baptism of Jesus, but they're not identical. This baptism is given to the Jews because God is telling them through John that everything has changed. The kingdom of God is at hand. The Messiah is about to appear. Salvation has come close, and the Jews are not ready. The Jews need to repent and be baptized, indicating the remission of their sins.

John Prepares the Way

In explaining this, Luke writes, **As it is written in the book of the words of Isaiah the prophet, "The voice of one crying in the wilderness: 'Prepare the way of the Lord, make his paths straight'"** (v. 4; see Isa. 40:3). This is the voice of John the Baptist. Initially, however, the reference was to the return of the Jews from captivity under Cyrus. In the ancient world, when a visiting king, monarch, or dignitary came to a country, it was the custom to "prepare the way," to adorn the streets, to roll out the red carpet, and to announce the imminent arrival of the distinguished monarch with the blowing of the trumpet.

That was the primary fulfillment of the prophecy that took place at the return from exile, but the ultimate fulfillment takes place here, as John the Baptist is that voice in the wilderness saying, **"Prepare the way of the Lord."**

It's interesting that in the New Testament, before followers of Christ were called Christians, which was kind of an insulting term, they were first called "the people of the Way" (see Acts 19:9, 23; 22:4; 24:14, 22), the narrow way, Christ's way, the One who is the way and the truth and the life. John calls the Jews to prepare the way.

Make his paths straight does not describe actual topographical changes that were to take place on the roads of Palestine. This is the prophetic word delivered in poetic imagery speaking about what has to happen to people as God comes to them. The proud—the arrogant who have exalted themselves and appear as high mountains—have to be brought low. Those who have been abased, those who have been oppressed, have to be lifted up. And all the thorns and rocks and stones and obstacles that fill our sinful hearts—our hearts of stone—have to be changed. The crooked places must be made straight, the rough places made smooth, because He is here and people are not ready. All flesh will see the manifestation of the salvation of God. This is the message: Prepare for the presence of Jesus.

13

JOHN PREACHES

Luke 3:7–20

He said therefore to the crowds that came out to be baptized by him, "You brood of vipers! Who warned you to flee from the wrath to come? Bear fruits in keeping with repentance. And do not begin to say to yourselves, 'We have Abraham as our father.' For I tell you, God is able from these stones to raise up children for Abraham. Even now the axe is laid to the root of the trees. Every tree therefore that does not bear good fruit is cut down and thrown into the fire."

And the crowds asked him, "What then shall we do?" And he answered them, "Whoever has two tunics is to share with him who has none, and whoever has food is to do likewise." Tax collectors also came to be baptized and said to him, "Teacher, what shall we do?" And he said to them, "Collect no more than you are authorized to do." Soldiers also asked him, "And we, what shall we do?" And he said to them, "Do not extort money from anyone by threats or by false accusation, and be content with your wages."

As the people were in expectation, and all were questioning in their hearts concerning John, whether he might be the Christ, John answered them all, saying, "I baptize you with water, but he who is mightier than I is coming, the strap of whose sandals I am not worthy to untie. He will baptize you with the Holy Spirit and fire. His winnowing fork is in his hand, to clear his threshing floor and to gather the wheat into his barn, but the chaff he will burn with unquenchable fire."

So with many other exhortations he preached good news to the people. But Herod the tetrarch, who had been reproved by him for Herodias, his brother's wife, and for all the evil things that Herod had done, added this to them all, that he locked up John in prison.

Try to imagine thousands of people gathered at the Jordan River seeking to undergo baptism at the hands of this new prophet who has come to them out of the desert. Multitudes flocked to the Jordan, from every walk of life, the common people and tax collectors. Even Roman soldiers gathered.

In this milling throng, pushing up against John the Baptist, he doesn't choose friendly or encouraging words to begin his address. Instead, he says: **"You brood of vipers! Who warned you to flee from the wrath to come?"** (v. 7). Vipers in Israel usually didn't grow to be more than two feet long, but they were deadly with their venom. They would often stretch themselves straight out on the ground and be mistaken for sticks, which people would pick up, as the book of Acts tells us (Acts 28:1–6).

John the Baptist violated every principle of political correctness and Dale Carnegie's book *How to Win Friends and Influence People*. He said, **"Who warned you to flee from the wrath to come?"** "Is that why you're here? Are you coming to be cleansed because you know that wrath is coming, and someone warned you and suggested that you flee from this wrath?" John, of course, was not denying that wrath was at the gates and that it would be a good thing to flee from it.

It's amazing to me that so many people at this time considered it a matter of urgency to flee from the wrath of God. We live in a time when it seems that no one has great fear of the wrath of God. Even in the church, there is a calloused sense that God gives love unconditionally and we have nothing to fear from His wrath.

The Fruit of Repentance

How do you know if you're a candidate for that wrath? How do you know if you're converted and safe from that wrath? We can learn something from John the Baptist here: **"Bear fruits in keeping with repentance"** (v. 8). There were people who came to be baptized by John who understood what he was saying to them: "Repent and be baptized. You're not clean." The symbolic significance of John's baptism was to point to a cleansing from sin and forgiveness to those who would repent.

It is appropriate to distinguish between different kinds of repentance. There is a repentance of *contrition*, which was manifested by David in his prayer of contrition in Psalm 51. There he poured out his heart before God, and his sorrow for his sin was genuine and deep. But there's also *attrition*, the kind of repentance that children show when they are caught with their hands in the cookie jar and say: "Please don't spank me. I'm sorry." They are repenting to get out of punishment. Their repentance is not genuine; it doesn't come from the heart.

Many of the people who came to the Jordan came to get the latest theological and ecclesiastical provision to cover their sins, but they went into the water with no real sense of repentance, and they came out unconverted. So, John said: "If you're converted, show me. Bring forth the fruit worthy of repentance." He wasn't saying the fruit will convert you or the fruit will save you or the works will justify you; he's saying if your faith is real, if your conversion is genuine, then you can't help but have fruit.

Do you have the fruit of repentance in your life? Do you have evidence in your life of your conversion? That's a question that each one of us has to ask ourselves pointedly and honestly, because true conversion always, inevitably, necessarily brings forth the fruit of repentance.

John warns the crowd, **"And do not begin to say to yourselves, 'We have Abraham as our father'"** (v. 8), as if that would save them from the wrath to come. That's like our saying: "I'm a church member. My parents were Christians. I was raised Christian. I don't have to bring forth fruits of repentance." John warns them, **"For I tell you, God is able from these stones to raise up children for Abraham"** (v. 8). If God made Adam out of the dirt, He can make children of Abraham out of the stones.

John goes on to say: **"Even now the axe is laid to the root of the trees. Every tree therefore that does not bear good fruit is cut down and thrown into the fire"** (v. 9). Again, it's not that the woodsman has gone to the barn and picked up his ax and started honing it to a sharp edge, or that he is chipping away at the outer bark of the tree. He's already penetrated to the very pith, to the very core of that tree. One more swing of the ax and the tree will come crashing down. "That's how near and urgent the crisis is," John is saying. "The ax is at the root of the tree. The crisis is right now. Don't wait till tomorrow. You may not have a tomorrow. The ax is at the root of the tree, and every tree that doesn't bring forth fruit is worthy only to be cut down and thrown in the fire."

What do you do with a dead fruit tree in your yard? Do you just let it stand there for decoration for twenty years? Of course not. If it's not bearing fruit, you cut it down. Break up the branches and throw it in the fire or let the garbage collector take it away. You need to get rid of it because it's worthless. So is everyone who brings forth no fruit from their conversion.

Practical Changes

In response, the people ask him, **"What then shall we do?"** (v. 10). He answers, **"Whoever has two tunics is to share with him who has none, and whoever has food is to do likewise"** (v. 11). John the Baptist did not ask Herod to institute a redistribution program or a welfare state, whereby the granting of relief from poverty would be forced on the people. The message of the gospel is voluntary compassion, voluntary giving to those in need, and if the church would do what the church is called to do, we wouldn't have the government's involvement in this matter as we have now. John says one of the fruits of conversion is compassion. If you're a converted person, you can't see somebody naked and not give them something to clothe them. If you see somebody hungry, you give them food.

The fruit of conversion is a heart that loves people—our neighbors—whether they're believers or unbelievers. If someone has AIDS, we don't ask him how he got it. If he's in the gutter, we don't ask how he got there. We get him out of there. That's what converted people do. They show compassion.

Then the tax collectors ask their question: **"Teacher, what shall we do?"** And John says to them, **"Collect no more than you are authorized to do"** (vv. 12–13). The tax collectors were not popular. A tax collector could collect oppressive taxes and then add to the oppression by taking extra for himself and lining his own pockets. John tells them to stop stealing. Paul tells us in his epistles, "Let the thief no longer steal" (Eph. 4:28). So one of the fruits of conversion is you don't steal.

When I was in ninth grade and played basketball at our junior high school, we had practice every afternoon. We had combination locks on our lockers, or at least most of the guys did. One poor soul didn't, and one day after practice, he discovered that his watch and wallet had been stolen. I remember thinking, not as a Christian but as a pagan, How can anybody be that selfish, that self-centered? How can they look in the mirror and know that they've actually reached into somebody else's locker and taken for themselves that which belongs to somebody else? How immoral that is.

Then the soldiers ask their question: **"And we, what shall we do?"** John said, **"Do not extort money from anyone by threats or by false accusation, and be content with your wages"** (v. 14). Another fruit of conversion is to be content with your wages. People aren't always content with their wages, and when we're not content, we have a tendency to shake our fists at God, saying: "God, You in Your providence have not been kind enough to us. If You were really a good God, You would make us more prosperous than we are."

Church and State

As the people were in expectation, and all were questioning in their hearts concerning John, whether he might be the Christ (v. 15). The people wonder whether John is the Messiah, but we're told almost as a footnote that Herod **locked up John in prison** (v. 20). Why? Why did Herod shut him in prison and subsequently cut off his head (see Matt. 14:1–12)? Because John, following a long line of prophets of God, was engaged with what we call in theology "prophetic criticism." He publicly criticized the tetrarch, the ruler of that territory, Herod, for his illicit marriage to his sister-in-law. John the Baptist called him out publicly (Luke 3:19–20).

A man once asked me, "R.C., are you going to tell the folks at St. Andrew's Chapel who to vote for in the next presidential election?" I said, "No, I don't do that." He said: "Why not? You're their shepherd. Don't you care about how your parishioners express their Christian faith in government elections?" Of course I do. And I try to teach principles that can help them in their decisions. But I know the government tells us that we're not supposed to endorse candidates, that there is to be this wall of separation between church and state. That wall, however, seems to have only one side. The government doesn't like it if we criticize it openly, but it doesn't hesitate to tell the church what it's not allowed to preach about. The state doesn't hesitate to enforce its views regarding abortion on Christian institutions.

Suppose one of the people running for the presidency in the next election adopted a platform to reinstitute slavery. Would you vote for him? I hope not. Do you realize that when unethical and immoral laws and customs become entrenched in a culture, it's almost impossible to excise them? William Wilberforce's efforts to abolish slavery in England were defeated time after time in Parliament until finally enough consciences were aroused that England did what was right and abolished slavery. Think what it cost the United States to get rid of slavery: eight hundred thousand American lives. Abortion on demand is far more wicked than slavery, and many in Washington, D.C., are totally committed to continuing the process of abortion on demand and even partial-birth abortion.

The government of the United States may claim a legal right to tell the church that it cannot discuss political issues from the pulpit, but it doesn't have the moral right. The office of the preacher and the office of prophetic criticism go through the whole of sacred Scripture, beginning with Moses, who told Pharaoh, "God told me to tell you to let His people go, because He has seen the oppression of His people and it is wrong." Moses was God's prophetic voice to Pharaoh, and Elijah was to Ahab and Jezebel, who tried to impose paganism on Israel. Isaiah went before kings and called them to repentance. Nathan confronted David in his sin, which was a sin not just against Uriah but against the nation he ruled. Ezekiel challenged the kings of Babylon for their evil.

Throughout the history of the church, it has been the function of the church not to be the state but to be the conscience of the state. God establishes government for the purpose of sustaining, protecting, and maintaining the sanctity of human life. When a government fails to do that, it has been demonized, and it is the responsibility of the church to stand up to that government and say: "Stop. God won't tolerate you people who have no regard for human life or ethics."

It is not the duty of the church to be the state, but it is the duty of the state to be the state. When we speak to the state about abortion, we're not asking the state to be the church; we're asking the state to be the state, to do what it is tasked by God to do: protect human life. This isn't China or Russia. This isn't the Third Reich. This is the United States of America that kills and sanctions the killing of more than half a million babies every year. Where is the church? Intimidated, terrified, cringing.

14

THE BAPTISM OF JESUS

Luke 3:21–22

Now when all the people were baptized, and when Jesus also had been baptized and was praying, the heavens were opened, and the Holy Spirit descended on him in bodily form, like a dove; and a voice came from heaven, "You are my beloved Son; with you I am well pleased."

In 1929, the Presbyterian Church in the United States of America, known as the Northern Presbyterian church, reached a critical stage. Theological liberalism, which is foundationally a theology of unbelief, had spread through Europe in the nineteenth century, had infected the mainline denominations in our country, and sadly had even reached the seminary in Princeton, N.J., which historically had been the greatest seminary in America. Several of the faculty members of that school left to start a new seminary in Philadelphia that would be committed to orthodox Christianity. The brain trust that came to establish Westminster Theological Seminary included such stalwart theologians as Oswald T. Allis, Robert Dick Wilson, Cornelius Van Til, John Murray, Paul Woolley, and a host of others. They were led by J. Gresham Machen.

In December 1936, Machen fell ill while in North Dakota to give a series of lectures. He was hospitalized after Christmas with pleurisy, and as he lay dying, he sent a telegram to his friend and colleague John Murray. It was a brief telegram but pregnant in its meaning. He said: "I'm so thankful for the active obedience of Christ. No hope without it."

Many Christians have never heard of the active obedience of Christ, and yet it's an extremely important doctrine in Christian theology. The distinction is between the active obedience of Jesus and His passive obedience. Christ's passive obedience refers to His willingly coming to earth and paying the penalty for sin, both throughout His earthly life and especially in His sacrificial death. Jesus willingly endured the miseries of this life. He did not resist His executioners. He was passive in His reception of the penalty for sin as our sin bearer.

In contrast to Christ's passive obedience, we have His active obedience, which refers to His whole life of living under the law in total subjection to the Father, actively and willingly obeying everything that the Lord God commanded Him to do. It was said of Him that His meat and His drink was to do the will of the Father, and zeal for His Father's house consumed Him.

The Meaning of Jesus' Baptism

This is directly related to the text we are considering about the baptism of Jesus. Many people are perplexed and question, Why was Jesus baptized at all? Wasn't the baptism of John the Baptist a baptism for repentance of sin? Wasn't the ritual a cleansing rite, in which John the Baptist commanded people to be cleansed and to repent of their sins? Jesus had no sins to repent of. He was the Lamb without blemish. He lived a life of perfect active obedience without sin. Though we're perplexed by why Jesus submitted to baptism, no one was more perplexed about it than John the Baptist. The people asked about John: "Is he the Christ? Is he the Messiah that is to come?" John put those rumors to rest. He said: "I baptize you with water, but he who is mightier than I is coming, the strap of whose sandals I am not worthy to untie. He will baptize you with the Holy Spirit and fire" (Luke 3:16).

John pointed people toward Jesus. We are told in the Gospel of Matthew that when Jesus went to John to be baptized, John tried to prevent it, but Jesus said, "Let it be so now, for thus it is fitting for us to fulfill all righteousness" (Matt. 3:15).

Let me speculate as to what Jesus could have said to John at that moment: "John, this is a covenant ritual that we're doing here. Baptize Me, and I'll explain it later." Or He could have said, "John, you need to do this because this is a matter of life and death."

We have no record that Jesus said either of these things to John. But the concept that I've given in my speculation is completely sound, because Jesus' baptism was a matter of life and death. Why? To understand that, we have to understand something about Jesus' role in His earthly ministry as the new Adam or, as Paul sometimes calls Him, the second Adam, the One who comes after the father of the human race. Adam, we are told, was a type of the One who was to come, the greater Adam who would come to bring salvation to the human race. Paul writes to the Romans:

> Therefore, just as sin came into the world through one man, and death through sin, and so death spread to all men because all sinned—for sin indeed was in the world before the law was given, but sin is not counted where there is no law. Yet death reigned from Adam to Moses, even over those whose sinning was not like the transgression of Adam, who was a type of the one who was to come.
>
> But the free gift is not like the trespass. For if many died through one man's trespass, much more have the grace of God and the free gift by the grace of that one man Jesus Christ abounded for many. And the free gift is not like the result of that one man's sin. For the judgment following one trespass brought condemnation, but the free gift following many trespasses brought justification. For if, because of one man's trespass, death reigned through that one man, much more will those who receive the abundance of grace and the free gift of righteousness reign in life through the one man Jesus Christ.
>
> Therefore, as one trespass led to condemnation for all men, so one act of righteousness leads to justification and life for all men. For as by the one man's disobedience the many were made sinners, so by the one man's obedience the many will be made righteous. Now the law came in to increase the trespass, but where sin increased, grace abounded all the more, so that, as sin reigned in death, grace also might reign through righteousness leading to eternal life through Jesus Christ our Lord. (Rom. 5:12–21)

It was a matter of life and death. Through Adam's original transgression, the whole world was plunged into ruin, and death came upon the entire human race. In contrast, by one man's obedience comes life. Without the obedience of Jesus, without His perfect active obedience, He would not have done for us what Adam failed so miserably to accomplish.

The Covenant of Works

To understand this, we have to go back to the Old Testament and look at it in the context of covenant. There are covenants all through the Bible. We have God's covenant with Noah, His covenant with Abraham, His covenant with

Moses, and the new covenant in the New Testament. But the first covenant made with human beings was made with Adam in the garden of Eden, and we call it the covenant of works (see Gen. 2:15–17). The name *Adam* means "man." He represented the entire human race, so when God entered into a covenant with Adam, He was entering into a covenant with every human being who would ever live. He promised the benefit and the blessing of this covenant of creation, of eternal life, if Adam obeyed the provisions and the stipulations of that covenant. However, the negative sanction was this: "If you disobey the terms of this covenant, you will die. And not only will you die sometime in the future, but the day in which you disobey, you will surely die."

The serpent came to Eve with a subtle and crafty question: "Did God actually say, 'You shall not eat of any tree in the garden'?" (Gen. 3:1). Of course God didn't say that, and Satan knew that God didn't say that. Satan was implying, "He might as well have said that, because if He put any restriction on you, you aren't really free." Initially, Eve says, "We may eat of the fruit of the trees in the garden, but God said, 'You shall not eat of the fruit of the tree that is in the midst of the garden, neither shall you touch it, lest you die'" (vv. 2–3). Now the direct assault comes from the serpent, who says: "You will not surely die. For God knows that when you eat of it your eyes will be opened, and you will be like God, knowing good and evil" (vv. 4–5). And seeing that the fruit appeared beautiful, Eve ate the fruit from the tree and then encouraged her husband to join her in this rebellion (v. 6).

We would expect that at the moment they put that fruit in their mouth and tasted it, they would have died instantly. They did die spiritually, but not physically. Their physical death was postponed in an act of mercy as God tempered His judgment with grace. The first experience that Adam and Eve had when they ate of the forbidden fruit was that they suddenly became aware of their nakedness. They were ashamed and hid themselves from God (v. 7). When the Lord God came in the cool of the evening, He asked, "Adam, where are you? Why are you hiding?" "We're naked and ashamed," they responded. God said: "I made you naked; you weren't ashamed. You didn't have any guilt. Why, all of a sudden, do you feel exposed? Why do you want to hide from Me?" (see vv. 8–11).

In His first act of redemption, God condescended to fashion clothes for Adam and Eve, to cover their nakedness and their shame (v. 21). He made a promise to them, that the Seed of the woman would crush the head of the serpent (v. 15). In that promise, God said there will come another Adam, a second Adam who will do what the first Adam failed to do, who will bring life rather than death.

In recent years, there's been a movement among professing evangelical Christians to reject the doctrine of the perfect, active obedience of Jesus. They want to do that because they reject the idea of this first covenant, the covenant of works. We distinguish between the covenant that God made with Adam (the covenant of works) and every covenant after that, which are sub-covenants of the one covenant of grace. Some object to the term *covenant of works* because they believe that any covenant that God gives to human beings is an act of grace because mankind doesn't deserve to be in a covenant relationship with God. Nobody argues that point. When we distinguish between the covenant of works and the covenant of grace, we know that God was not required to make a covenant with us at all. We won't argue that point, but those covenants that He did make differ as to how the benefits are received.

In the garden of Eden, Adam and Eve were on trial. They were in a period of probation. If they obeyed, they would get life. If they disobeyed, they would get death. In other words, if their works were righteous, they would live. If their works were evil, they would perish. I have long labored in behalf of the Reformed doctrine of justification by faith alone. However, as much as I believe in the doctrine of justification by faith alone, I encourage people to remember that there's only one way to be justified in the sight of God, and that's by works.

You may ask, How can you say that justification is by faith alone and then say justification is by works? Because the covenant of works that God gave to Adam and Eve is still in effect. The only way to satisfy the demands of God is through good works. Nothing less will do. The reason the covenant of grace is called the covenant of grace is because now God is saying, "It's not by your good works that you'll be saved but by somebody else's good works." We perish because of the first Adam's bad works. We will be saved by the perfect righteousness of the new Adam, whose works are without blemish, and whose works are given to us, if we put our trust in Him.

There are people even in the church who believe their good deeds and their trying to live a good life will get them into heaven. But they have no chance. Only one person has ever satisfied the law of God, and that's Jesus. That's why His submission to the baptism of John the Baptist was a matter of life and death. God required it of everyone, and as the new Adam entering into corporate solidarity with His people, Jesus submitted to that requirement of the law so that His acts of righteousness would be perfect. We are justified by works—not our own works, but the works of Jesus. He is our righteousness.

The Spirit Empowers Jesus

Jesus went into the water and was baptized by John, and this marked the beginning of His earthly public ministry. At that time, **the heavens were opened, and the Holy Spirit descended on him in bodily form, like a dove; and**

a voice came from heaven, "You are my beloved Son; with you I am well pleased" (vv. 21–22). The Holy Spirit came upon Jesus to empower Him for His redemptive mission. And this One, who had known and would know only a perfect active obedience, heard the voice from heaven, saying, **"You are my beloved Son; with you I am well pleased."** It is because of the Father's pleasure that we escape from the consequences of the sin of Adam, who plunged us into ruin. The new Adam, the second Adam, is the only One who can help us. There's no other name under heaven through which men may be saved but the name of Jesus (Acts 4:12).

Now I hope we understand what J. Gresham Machen was saying to his colleagues with his telegram: "I'm so thankful for the active obedience of Christ." Without it, we perish.

15

THE GENEALOGY OF JESUS

Luke 3:23–38

Jesus, when he began his ministry, was about thirty years of age, being the son (as was supposed) of Joseph, the son of Heli, the son of Matthat, the son of Levi, the son of Melchi, the son of Jannai, the son of Joseph, the son of Mattathias, the son of Amos, the son of Nahum, the son of Esli, the son of Naggai, the son of Maath, the son of Mattathias, the son of Semein, the son of Josech, the son of Joda, the son of Joanan, the son of Rhesa, the son of Zerubbabel, the son of Shealtiel, the son of Neri, the son of Melchi, the son of Addi, the son of Cosam, the son of Elmadam, the son of Er, the son of Joshua, the son of Eliezer, the son of Jorim, the son of Matthat, the son of Levi, the son of Simeon, the son of Judah, the son of Joseph, the son of Jonam, the son of Eliakim, the son of Melea, the son of Menna, the son of Mattatha, the son of Nathan, the son of David, the son of Jesse, the son of Obed, the son of Boaz, the son of Sala, the son of Nahshon, the son of Amminadab, the son of Admin, the son of Arni, the son of Hezron, the son of Perez, the son of Judah, the son of Jacob, the son of Isaac, the son of Abraham, the son of Terah, the son of Nahor, the son of Serug, the son of Reu, the son of Peleg, the son of Eber, the son of Shelah, the son of Cainan, the son of Arphaxad, the son of Shem, the son of Noah, the son of Lamech, the son of Methuselah, the son of Enoch, the son of Jared, the son of Mahalaleel, the son of Cainan, the son of Enos, the son of Seth, the son of Adam, the son of God.

What do you do with a genealogy? How do you preach from a genealogy, particularly this genealogy in Luke's Gospel, which presents some problems for us? When we compare Luke's genealogy with Matthew's genealogy (Matt. 1), we see that there are clear and glaring differences in their accounts. First, Luke begins with Jesus and works backward to Adam, while Matthew begins with Abraham and works forward to Jesus. While that's not too much of a difficulty to deal with, we see also that the total number of names differs. For example, between Abraham and Jesus, Luke provides fifty-seven names, while Matthew gives us only forty-one. Obviously, at least one of these genealogies is not comprehensive. In all probability, in keeping with the ancient custom of the Jewish genealogies, neither one was comprehensive, in that they would skip over individuals from time to time.

Some of the names that occur in Matthew's genealogy also occur in Luke's. But then, when you least expect it, the names differ. In Matthew's genealogy, Jesus is traced through Solomon, the son of David. In Luke's genealogy, Jesus is traced through Nathan, the son of David. Now, which was it, Nathan or Solomon? Those who are critical of the trustworthiness of sacred Scripture jump on these variations in the genealogies and argue that here is proof that the Bible is not inspired; it's not the Word of God because there are these discrepancies and disagreements between the two Gospel writers.

Others in the field of New Testament studies have labored to find a way to harmonize these two accounts. One of the most popular ways is to argue that Matthew gives us the legal genealogy of Jesus, one that follows the lineage of Joseph even though Joseph is not the biological father of Jesus because of the virgin birth. In Jewish legal terms, in the Jewish court system, Joseph would be considered the father; the lineage of Joseph would be of particular importance to the Jewish community. Some argue that Matthew's genealogy follows the history of the family of Joseph and that, therefore, Luke's follows the family of Mary.

I wish I could say that the problem could be resolved that easily. However, the debate has been fierce between those who argue that both genealogies trace the lineage of Joseph and those who say that one is for Joseph and the other is for Mary. I don't know how to resolve the question, and I leave it in the hands of the experts who deal with such questions as they uncover the patterns and processes that were used by the priests in the ancient world in keeping track of genealogical tables.

What I am concerned about most significantly is where these genealogies go. I said from Matthew, we see that the genealogy of Jesus is traced to Abraham.

It's clear that Matthew is trying to communicate to those who read his Gospel that Jesus is the Son of Abraham, which would be of extreme importance for any Jewish audience. Luke is not satisfied to trace the genealogy of Jesus simply to Abraham, but he goes before Abraham, back to Adam and beyond. Luke shows that Jesus is a descendent of Adam and that Adam was the son of God, having been created by God. Luke traces Jesus' lineage to Adam and to God. At this point, we have to ask, Why?

Understanding the Text

Let me suggest that there are some important considerations in these genealogies. First, anytime we are trying to interpret a book of the Bible, we have to be careful of what we infer from the pages of Scripture. In the difficult task of getting an accurate understanding of Scripture, certain things help us. Obviously, the words that are written are important. If we're going to interpret the Bible accurately, we want to know what the words that were used in the original text actually meant. If you're a New Testament student and you're interested in the meaning of the Greek words of the text, you look at a simple Greek-English dictionary and you look up the Greek word, and it might give you two or three English words by which that Greek word is properly rendered.

In the twentieth century, New Testament scholarship received one of the greatest tools that we've ever known. It's called Gerhard Kittel's *Theological Dictionary of the New Testament*, known simply as Kittel. It is amazing. Kittel might take a word, for example *pisteuō*, for which a normal Greek-English dictionary might give two or three definitions, such as "to believe," "to trust," or "to have faith." Kittel might instead give thirty-five pages defining the meaning of the Greek word *pisteuō*. How does it do that? The editors examine every time that a certain word occurs in the Gospels, every time it occurs in the Epistles, every time it occurs in the early church or in the church fathers, and every time it occurs in the Septuagint (the Greek translation of the Old Testament). Beyond that, they search for every time the word occurs in classical Greek literature such as in Greek poetry of Euripides. At the end of all that, there are thirty-five pages of explanation of the meaning of that Greek word, and there is a solid understanding of what it means.

One of the important things we study to get a more accurate understanding of the Bible is the original setting of the book in question. That includes questions like this: Who wrote it? To whom was it written? What prompted its writing? Those factors will go a long way in helping us glean the exact meaning of the text.

The Writing of the Gospels

What does that have to do with the genealogy? One of the things New Testament scholars seek to do is reconstruct as reasonably as possible the order and the manner in which the Gospels were written. When we look into this question, we see that there is an easily drawn distinction between the Synoptic Gospels—Matthew, Mark, and Luke—and the Gospel of John. The Synoptic Gospels contain more accounts about the life and ministry of Jesus, often offering different perspectives on the same events, whereas John's Gospel contains fewer accounts of events and more extended stretches of teaching. The focus of John's Gospel is more theological than it is biographical.

Trying to reconstruct the way in which the Gospels were written is an important matter, and there's debate as to which one was first. The vast majority say that Mark was written first and John's Gospel was written last. Almost everything that is found in Mark is also found in Matthew and Luke. Scholars say that in all probability, when Matthew and Luke wrote their Gospels, they used Mark's Gospel as a source in composing their own Gospels. We can also see that there is material common to Matthew and Luke that is not found in Mark. The speculation is that Matthew and Luke probably had another resource that Mark didn't use, maybe another set of sayings or a document or an oral tradition. This hypothetical source is called *Q*, from the German *Quelle*, which means "source" or "fountain."

If we set aside all the material in Matthew and Luke that is also in Mark and that may come from Q, what's left is the material in Matthew that's only in Matthew and the material in Luke that's only in Luke. When we look at those portions of Luke's Gospel and Matthew's Gospel, something jumps out. Almost all the material that is unique to Matthew deals with the application of Old Testament prophecy to Jesus' claims of being the Messiah. It becomes clear that Matthew was writing for a Jewish audience. When you pick up his book, you have to realize that it was written for Jews.

Luke, on the other hand, was writing to Gentiles and for Gentiles, because his great stress here is on the universality of the lordship of Jesus Christ. He wanted his audience to know that Jesus is not simply the Savior of the Jews but that he is the Savior of the Gentiles and that the kingdom of God is not limited to the geographical borders of the Holy Land but is for every tongue and tribe and nation.

Christ the Second Adam

Why does Luke not stop his genealogy with Abraham? Why does he go to Adam, who is the representative of the whole human race? Luke, before he begins the account of Jesus' public ministry, introduces Jesus as Savior of the world and as Savior of Jew and Gentile alike.

Why does Luke take his genealogy back to Adam? In part, it is again to show that the message of salvation through Christ is not just for the Jews but is for Gentiles as well. But I suggest there is another reason, one that would get me in a lot of debate in the theological world, because nowhere in his Gospel does Luke ever mention the role of Jesus as the new Adam or second Adam, which is so important to the teaching of the Apostle Paul. But here, Luke mentions Jesus' descent from the first Adam. Luke accompanied Paul on his missionary journeys, and it's inconceivable to me that Paul wouldn't have discussed with Luke the significance of Jesus as the new Adam to redeem us from the failure of the first Adam.

In looking at his genealogy, we get a hint, a little glimpse, of Luke's concern. Though I like to think that Luke's version is from Mary's side of the family, I can't prove that beyond a shadow of a doubt.

One of the features that's unique to Luke's Gospel is that he has more references to Jesus dealing with women than any of the other Gospels, so that Jesus is the Savior not just of the Jews or of the Gentiles or of men but of women as well. All this may be implied, but not explained, in the genealogy of our Lord Jesus Christ.

Finally, the one thing about which Luke is so concerned is the historical reality of the person and work of Christ. The presence of this extended genealogy underscores Luke's concern that the account that he provides is not of a mythological figure but of One who came in space and in time, indeed in the fullness of time, to be our Savior.

16

THE TEMPTATION OF JESUS

Luke 4:1–13

And Jesus, full of the Holy Spirit, returned from the Jordan and was led by the Spirit in the wilderness for forty days, being tempted by the devil. And he ate nothing during those days. And when they were ended, he was hungry. The devil said to him, "If you are the Son of God, command this stone to become bread." And Jesus answered him, "It is written, 'Man shall not live by bread alone.' " And the devil took him up and showed him all the kingdoms of the world in a moment of time, and said to him, "To you I will give all this authority and their glory, for it has been delivered to me, and I give it to whom I will. If you, then, will worship me, it will all be yours." And Jesus answered him, "It is written,

" 'You shall worship the Lord your God,
and him only shall you serve.' "

And he took him to Jerusalem and set him on the pinnacle of the temple and said to him, "If you are the Son of God, throw yourself down from here, for it is written,

" 'He will command his angels concerning you,
to guard you,'

and

> " 'On their hands they will bear you up,
> lest you strike your foot against a stone.' "
>
> And Jesus answered him, "It is said, 'You shall not put the Lord your God to the test.' " And when the devil had ended every temptation, he departed from him until an opportune time.

Jesus' disciples came to our Lord, asking Him, "Lord, teach us how to pray." In response, Jesus gave them a model prayer that has since been called the Lord's Prayer. He gave them those matters of priority for which they should entreat the Almighty in their prayers. Among those petitions is one that is sometimes confusing to us, for Jesus said to them, "When you pray say, 'Lord, lead us not into temptation, but deliver us from evil' " (see Matt. 6:9–13; Luke 11:1–4).

In the first place, nothing is more repugnant to the Christian mind than the idea that the holy and perfect and righteous God would ever lead anybody to be tempted to sin. God never entices us to disobey Him. As James tells us: "Let no one say when he is tempted, 'I am being tempted by God.' . . . But each person is tempted when he is lured and enticed by his own desire" (James 1:13–14).

The second part of the petition "Lead us not into temptation" is translated "but deliver us from evil" (Matt. 6:13). Evil in an abstract or general sense would be signified by the Greek word *ponēron*, which is in the neuter gender. But in this case, it is the Greek word *ponēros*, which is the masculine gender, with the definite article *the*. This refers not to evil in general but to *the evil one*. The word *ponēros* is a title ascribed by sacred Scriptures to the prince of lies, Satan. Jesus is saying, "Pray that you not be put to the test, that you may be protected from the hands of Satan."

Testing by God

Throughout biblical history, we see occasions where people are put to the test. We think of the time the patriarch Abraham was called of God to go to Mount Moriah and to offer his son, the son whom he loved, Isaac, as a sacrifice. That was a test of Abraham's faith, and he passed with flying colors (see Gen. 22). In the book of Job, Satan came to God and said: "You've put a hedge around Job. I can't touch him. But let me at him. Tear down that wall, and You'll see how quickly Job will curse You." And in the abject misery that followed, Job passed the test (see Job 1).

We see in various times and sundry places where God puts people to the test, but nowhere in Scripture do we see tests as significant as that which was given to our earthly parents, Adam and Eve, in the garden of Eden, and the test here at the beginning of our Lord's ministry when He is driven into the wilderness to be tempted by Satan. We've already seen in Luke's Gospel the link between the first Adam and now this new Adam. We read in sacred Scripture that **Jesus, full of the Holy Spirit, returned from the Jordan and was led by the Spirit in the wilderness** (v. 1). This was the same Spirit that descended upon Him like a dove at the Jordan River. It was the Holy Spirit sent by the Father to lead the Son into this place of testing in the Judean wilderness.

During the Reformation in the sixteenth century, Martin Luther was besieged by the assaults and the attacks of Satan. Luther felt the presence of Satan so keenly that on one occasion, he picked up an inkwell from his desk and threw it at Satan. He lamented that he suffered what he called the *Anfechtung* of the devil, the unbridled assault of Satan. But the *Anfechtung* that besieged Martin Luther was not worthy to be compared to the assault that was waged against Jesus. The devil tormented Martin Luther, assaulted him and attacked him, but now in the Judean wilderness it's all-out war. It is the blitzkrieg of hell coming against our Savior.

There are some strong contrasts between the temptation of Adam and Eve and the temptation of Jesus. Consider the setting. The setting for the test of Adam and Eve was a glorious garden of paradise. A gourmet feast was available for our first parents. Of all the trees of the garden, they could eat freely in this beautiful place that showed no evidence of the fall of nature. There were no briars, no thorns, no pain, no death. Adam was subjected to his temptation while he was in the presence of his helpmate, where he had companionship and was not exposed to the wiles of the serpent while he was alone. By contrast, Jesus was driven into the Judean wilderness, one of the most desolate pieces of real estate on the face of this earth, inhabited only by scorpions, snakes, and a few species of birds.

Adam was tempted on a full stomach. Jesus was subjected to a fast that lasted forty days. People tend to skate lightly over this and say: "Well, this is the Son of God. This is God incarnate. A forty-day fast isn't going to hurt Him." Jesus may not have gotten hungry according to His divine nature, because God doesn't need food, but according to His human nature, He could certainly be hungry. The text confirms that for us, as in a masterful example of understatement, it tells us **he ate nothing during those days. And when they were ended, he was hungry** (v. 2).

The Trustworthiness of God's Word

We see the radical differences between the circumstances of the tests that came to the first Adam and now the test that comes to the second Adam. But we must not miss the similarities of the test. The point of the attacks of Satan on Adam and Eve and on Jesus was at the same place. When Satan came into the garden with his craftiness and his guile, he approached the woman with a question: "Did God really say? Did God say that you can't eat of any of the trees of the garden?" Of course, God didn't say that and Satan knew it, but the suggestion was implicit that when God put one restriction on them, He may as well have put them all on them.

As Jean-Paul Sartre said, if you're not autonomous, you're not really free. Eve's first response was to fight for the integrity of her Creator and say: "He didn't say that. He said that of all the trees of the garden we may freely eat, but He did give one restriction. He said if we touch that tree over there, we will surely die."

Now the subtle implication becomes an explicit contradiction. Satan says: "No, no! You will not die." God speaks the truth; Satan utters the lie, the lie that contradicts boldly and clearly the veracity of what God said. You see what's at issue in the original temptation. "Eve, whom will you believe? Whom do you trust? Who speaks the word of truth? Is it God or is it Satan?" Eve weighed the options. She looked at the serpent. She heard what he said. She recalled what her Creator had said, and then she looked at the tree and thought: "The fruit looks so appetizing. Maybe the serpent is right. What harm will there be in one little taste of disobedience? After all, he said that if I taste it, I won't die. I'll be like God and have knowledge like God." She tasted it and gave it to her husband, who tasted it, and together they plunged the world into ruin, as God's word stood firm.

As the Son of God in the wilderness of Judea hears the words of the devil, it's the same point of attack Satan comes with when he says, **"If you are the Son of God, command this stone to become bread"** (v. 3). "If You are the Son of God, You shouldn't have to put up with this humiliation and self-denial. If You are the Son of God, You should be able to change these stones into bread and break Your fast. If, that is, You really are the Son of God."

What were the last words that Jesus heard at His baptism before the Spirit drove Him into the wilderness? The heavens opened and the voice of God was heard audibly: "You are my beloved Son; with you I am well pleased" (3:22). God's Word came to Jesus at His baptism, at His anointing to be the Messiah. And then, Satan came with the suggestion that God's word is not true, that God's word cannot be trusted.

The Power of God's Word

Satan unleashed that temptation in a time of suffering, a time of want, when Jesus was hungry. Jesus' reply was **"It is written"** (v. 4). These words among the Jews were the same as "The Bible says." It wasn't written in the Midrash, in the Talmud. It was written in sacred Scripture. Satan's temptation was countered by Jesus' quoting the Bible. **And Jesus answered him, "It is written, 'Man shall not live by bread alone'"** (v. 4). "Though bread would taste good, I live not only by bread but by every word that comes from the mouth of My Father, so I won't turn those stones to bread to satisfy My physical hunger."

And the devil took him up and showed him all the kingdoms of the world in a moment of time, and said to him, "To you I will give all this authority and their glory, for it has been delivered to me, and I give it to whom I will. If you, then, will worship me, it will all be yours" (vv. 5–7). Satan, undaunted, said to Jesus: "All the authority that goes with the monarchies of every kingdom I will give to You because it's mine to give. I am the prince of this world, and I can give authority to kings, to politicians, to whomever I please. I'll give You all authority over every nation, Jesus, if You will worship me. Nobody is looking. If You worship me, You won't have to go to a cross. You won't have to suffer and die in order to be king."

And Jesus answered him, "It is written, 'You shall worship the Lord your God, and him only shall you serve'" (v. 8). Jesus couldn't do what Satan tempted Him to do because the only One we may serve and worship is God.

Satan, seeing Jesus' unwavering commitment to Scripture, decided to quote some verses of his own. Satan knows the Bible better than you and I. The first rule of hermeneutics is that Scripture interprets Scripture, which means we are not to set one portion of Scripture against another. Satan ignored that. **And he took him to Jerusalem and set him on the pinnacle of the temple and said to him, "If you are the Son of God, throw yourself down from here, for it is written, 'He will command his angels concerning you, to guard you,' and 'On their hands they will bear you up, lest you strike your foot against a stone'"** (vv. 9–11). It's as if he was saying: "Let's see if You can really trust the Word of God. You keep quoting to me, 'The Bible says it.' If it's really true that the angels have been given charge over You, jump off the temple pinnacle here. You have nothing to worry about."

And Jesus answered him, "It is said, 'You shall not put the Lord your God to the test'" (v. 12). Jesus may have commended Satan and said to him: "Your quotation of Scripture is accurate, but your interpretation of it conflicts with everything the Word of God says. If I jump from this pinnacle, I would be putting God to the test, and it is not allowable for Me to test God. He's testing Me. I don't have to jump off this temple to know that the angels will guard Me. My Father said it, and His word is truth" (see John 17:17).

And when the devil had ended every temptation, he departed from him until an opportune time (v. 13). Satan, in his frustration, left the Savior, but his departure was not permanent but only temporary. Throughout Jesus' earthly ministry, Satan lurked in the shadows, speaking even through the lips of His own disciple. Jesus recognized Satan's influence in Peter's protest against our Lord's going to Jerusalem to be delivered: Peter said, "Never." Jesus said, "Get behind me, Satan!" (Matt. 16:21–23).

Amazingly, in Matthew and Mark, we are told that as soon as Satan departed, the heavenly host who had been there all along manifested themselves to Jesus and ministered to Him (Matt. 4:11; Mark 1:13). He received the angelic support, the angelic chorale of triumph that would have been given to the first Adam had he not succumbed to the temptations of the devil.

Before He began His earthly ministry, as soon as He was anointed for it, the Messiah had to pass this test, and He passed it at every point. Not only in those forty days, but up until He drew His last breath in which He said, "Father, into your hands I commit my spirit!" (Luke 23:46). The whole world attacks the Word of God, but we, as Christian people, are to live by every word that comes from God's mouth.

17

JESUS IN THE SYNAGOGUE

Luke 4:14–30

And Jesus returned in the power of the Spirit to Galilee, and a report about him went out through all the surrounding country. And he taught in their synagogues, being glorified by all.

And he came to Nazareth, where he had been brought up. And as was his custom, he went to the synagogue on the Sabbath day, and he stood up to read. And the scroll of the prophet Isaiah was given to him. He unrolled the scroll and found the place where it was written,

> "The Spirit of the Lord is upon me,
> because he has anointed me
> to proclaim good news to the poor.
> He has sent me to proclaim liberty to the captives
> and recovering of sight to the blind,
> to set at liberty those who are oppressed,
> to proclaim the year of the Lord's favor."

And he rolled up the scroll and gave it back to the attendant and sat down. And the eyes of all in the synagogue were fixed on him. And he began to say to them, "Today this Scripture has been fulfilled in your hearing." And all spoke well of him and marveled at the gracious words that were coming from his mouth. And they said, "Is not this Joseph's son?" And he said to them, "Doubtless you will quote to me this proverb, ' "Physician, heal yourself." What we have heard you did at Capernaum, do here in your hometown as well.' " And he said, "Truly, I say to you, no prophet is acceptable in his hometown. But in truth, I tell you, there were many widows in Israel in the days of Elijah, when the heavens were shut up three years and six months, and a great famine came over all the land, and Elijah was sent to none of them but only to Zarephath, in the land of Sidon, to a woman who was a widow. And there were many lepers in Israel in the time of the prophet Elisha, and none of them was cleansed, but only Naaman the Syrian." When they heard these things, all in the synagogue were filled with wrath. And they rose up and drove him out of the town and brought him to the brow of the hill on which their town was built, so that they could throw him down the cliff. But passing through their midst, he went away.

After Jesus' temptation in the wilderness, Luke tells us He **returned in the power of the Spirit to Galilee, and a report about him went out through all the surrounding country. And he taught in their synagogues, being glorified by all** (vv. 14–15). This brief statement is a transitional statement that goes between the conclusion of the temptation and the beginning of the event that took place in the synagogue at Nazareth. We don't know how much time took place between the temptation and His appearance at Nazareth. We don't know where His travels took Him, but looking at the rest of the Gospels, it is clear that a considerable period of time passed between His temptation and His appearance at Nazareth, perhaps as much as a full year.

In Luke's telling of the story, it is clear he wants to focus our attention on this event in Nazareth because in this incident, the mission of Jesus is clearly revealed. We see it in the light of the Old Testament teaching of the coming Messiah. Obviously, the mission of Jesus was the mission of the Messiah, and conversely the mission of the Messiah was the mission of Jesus because Jesus was the promised Messiah of Israel.

And he came to Nazareth, where he had been brought up. And as was his custom, he went to the synagogue on the Sabbath day, and he stood up to read (v. 16). He appeared here as a guest, as a visiting rabbi, and it was the custom in the synagogue to allow a visiting rabbi to give the meditation or the exposition of the Word of God by way of the sermon. First Jesus stood up in order to read the text of the day. Every week at the synagogue, the custom was to read a portion of the Torah or Law and then another reading from the Prophets. On this day, the prophet that was to be read was the prophet Isaiah.

Jesus stood up and read from Isaiah 61. Of the more than two thousand prophecies in the Old Testament that point to the coming Redeemer and the

Messiah, there is perhaps none more important than this prophecy from Isaiah. It is included in Isaiah's book in which he describes the mission of the Servant of God that culminates, or at least had been explained earlier, in chapter 53 of the mission of the Servant of the Lord to be the sin bearer of the people, to be the Savior of the people. But this Servant is not only to be the Savior of the people by bearing their sins; He is supposed to be their Lord and their conqueror who will bring two things ultimately: salvation and judgment, the redemption of God and His wrath.

Jesus reads this critical passage from Isaiah to those who are assembled in the synagogue, and it begins with these words: **"The Spirit of the Lord is upon me, because he has anointed me to proclaim good news to the poor"** (v. 18). We find other men in the Bible who performed miracles besides Jesus, such as Moses, Elijah, Elisha, and the Apostles of the New Testament. None of these men had a divine nature. So, by what power did these men perform their miracles? The Bible makes it clear that they did it by the power of the Holy Ghost, the third person of the Trinity, who, though He is distinguished from the Father and the Son, cannot be separated from Them, as They are all one in substance or essence. It's important that the ministry of Jesus on this earth takes place after He was anointed by the Holy Ghost. So, it's safe to assume that God incarnate was performing these works through the power of the third person of the Trinity, the Holy Ghost.

The Mission of the Messiah

The name *Christ* is the Greek translation of the Old Testament word for "Messiah," and it literally means "the anointed one." Jesus was anointed by the power of the sovereign God. Jesus came into the synagogue and read the text that promised a future Messiah who would come and minister in the power of the sovereign God, being anointed by God Himself. It was Jesus who was the subject of Isaiah's prophecy. To be anointed meant two different things. On the one hand, it referred to anointing by the Holy Spirit in the sense of being set apart, consecrated for a sacred vocation. Kings were anointed. Prophets were anointed, set apart, just as we ordain ministers and elders in the church. It's an act of consecration. But when Isaiah speaks about the anointing of the Messiah, he's not simply speaking about the Messiah as being set apart or consecrated, but rather he's saying that the Messiah is endowed with power from God. The first manifestation of that power is here in the text: **"The Spirit of the Lord is upon me, because he has anointed me."** To do what? **"To proclaim good news to the poor"** (v. 18). The Messiah, Jesus, was anointed by the Holy Ghost to preach.

The most powerful preacher who walked the face of the earth was Jesus of Nazareth. He had the full anointing promised to the Messiah. He was anointed **to proclaim good news to the poor**, not just to the physically poor as we see in His teaching on the Beatitudes (see 6:20–22), but to those who are poor in spirit, who are numbered among the brokenhearted, who are poverty stricken spiritually. You can be a person of great wealth and still be spiritually impoverished, desperately needing to hear the preaching of the gospel. When the Lord Jesus preached that gospel and the Holy Spirit quickened those words, people who heard Him knew of their poverty-stricken spiritual condition. When they were awakened by the power of the preaching of Jesus and the accompanying ministry of the Holy Ghost, they were converted.

He was anointed to heal the brokenhearted. Do you know a doctor who can heal a broken heart? Is there any more painful condition to suffer and endure than a broken heart? Remember, as an infant Jesus was brought to the temple, and the venerable Simeon saw the promised Messiah. God had promised that he would not die until he saw the Lord's anointed, and he patiently waited for the consolation of Israel (2:25–35). That was at the center of the task of the Messiah that was promised by God, that He would come to console the brokenhearted.

Jesus read the prophecy of Isaiah: **"He has anointed me to proclaim good news to the poor. He has sent me to proclaim liberty to the captives and recovering of sight to the blind, to set at liberty those who are oppressed"** (v. 18). The message of Jesus was really the greatest Emancipation Proclamation in the history of the world, because Jesus came to proclaim liberty to not only those who were enslaved and in chains but also those who were held captive by Satan, those who were in bondage to sin, slaves to the power of evil. Jesus came to set them free. He came to proclaim liberty to all of us who by nature are enslaved to the impulses of sin. He came to proclaim **"recovering of sight to the blind, to set at liberty those who are oppressed, to proclaim the year of the Lord's favor"** (vv. 18–19). **"The year of the Lord's favor"** is the Year of Jubilee, the time when all debts were canceled. That cyclical experience in the history of Israel was a foreshadowing of the ultimate work of the Messiah, who would cancel the debts of all His people permanently. The Messiah says, "I am anointed to do all these things."

The Prophecy Fulfilled

After Jesus read the summary Isaiah gives of the mission and agenda of the Lord's Messiah, **he rolled up the scroll and gave it back to the attendant and sat down** (v. 20). In the synagogue, after standing to read the Scripture, the rabbi sat down, and that was the signal for the beginning of the sermon. The rabbi sat on a chair or a bench, and the rest of the people sat on the floor at his feet. That is where we get the saying "sitting at the feet of a great teacher." Jesus sat down, and that was the signal now for Him to give His exposition, His explanation of the meaning of this text that He had just read.

It's easy to imagine the scene. **And the eyes of all in the synagogue were fixed on him** (v. 20). "What is He going to say? We know this man. We watched Him grow up here in Nazareth, and He has been gone for a while. He has been living in Capernaum, and we have heard all the stories of His incredible ministry, doing miracles and healings and speaking to multitudes all throughout the land and especially here in Galilee. But He hasn't come back home, but now here He is, and He is going to preach here for the first time." Every person in that crowd had their eyes fixed on Him, their ears listening intently. This is the shortest sermon recorded by anyone in all of sacred Scripture. Jesus sat down and looked out at this congregation who were peering at Him relentlessly, and He said to them, **"Today this Scripture has been fulfilled in your hearing"** (v. 21). Amen, end of the sermon.

Jesus read the mission of the Messiah set forth by the prophet Isaiah. The people of Israel had been reading that prophetic passage for centuries, as they waited generation after generation for the Lord's anointed, the Lord's deliverer, the Lord's conqueror to come. That day He was in their midst. They understood what Jesus was saying. After all these centuries, when the anointed one of God appeared on the scene, the people from His hometown were astounded.

There is no more important judgment you will ever make than answering the question, Who is Jesus? Sit there for a moment in your imagination on the floor in the synagogue. You've just heard the text, you've just heard the Word of God, and now you hear the Son of God saying, "I am He." What is your response? Do you leap for joy and say: "Thank You, God! We've waited so patiently"? Do you want to run up and hug His neck and say, "We're so glad, Jesus, to know that You are the Messiah"? That was not the response in Nazareth. People heard these words, looked at Him, shocked, and said, **"Is not this Joseph's son?"** (v. 22). Yes, it was Joseph's adopted son, but it was Yahweh's Son. It was the servant of the sovereign God, the anointed Son in whom the Father was well pleased, but they couldn't endure it. They choked on the words of Jesus.

Initially, Jesus was welcomed eagerly by the people of Nazareth as One who had already developed a reputation as a rabbi—that is, as a great teacher. Also, rumors had spread to Nazareth of the mighty works that He had done in the region of Galilee, particularly in and around Capernaum, which was the place where He was residing, presumably in the home of Peter (see v. 23). These rumors told of miraculous works that Jesus had accomplished. So, His reputation of greatness, which was unexpected by the people at Nazareth, certainly piqued the people's curiosity when Jesus spoke at their synagogue.

The people were astonished by what Jesus was saying. They understood that what He was saying was, "Right now, here in your presence, this text is fulfilled in Me. I am the promised Anointed One of Israel." Then we read, **And all spoke well of him and marveled at the gracious words that were coming from his mouth** (v. 22). They were stunned. They were amazed, and they marveled. Still, they were positive in their response, and they said, "Isn't this Joseph's son?"

A Prophet without Honor

Jesus understood what they were thinking. He knew they wanted a sign. They had heard the rumors of His miraculous works there in Galilee. They wanted Him to do miracles and show His power there. "If You are the Messiah, then give us a sign, here and now."

That's what He was reading in their responses, so He said: **"Doubtless you will quote to me this proverb, '"Physician, heal yourself." What we have heard you did at Capernaum, do here in your hometown as well'"** (v. 23). Jesus went on to say, **"Truly, I say to you, no prophet is acceptable in his hometown"** (v. 24). We've heard that proverbial statement that a prophet is not without honor except in his own country. That is, a person may achieve great fame, great respect, and be lauded throughout the land, except in his own hometown.

Jesus went on to give two historical examples to illustrate His point. Both were from the Old Testament, from the history of the office of the prophet. He first looked to Elijah and said, **"But in truth, I tell you, there were many widows in Israel in the days of Elijah, when the heavens were shut up three years and six months, and a great famine came over all the land, and Elijah was sent to none of them but only to Zarephath, in the land of Sidon, to a woman who was a widow"** (vv. 25–26). Jesus was telling the people that the miracle that Elijah performed was not for somebody from Elijah's home nation. There were many widows to whom he could have ministered in this miraculous fashion, but God in His providence sent him to Sidon, to the widow there who was to receive the blessing Elijah would bring to her.

In the second example, He said, **"And there were many lepers in Israel in the time of the prophet Elisha, and none of them was cleansed, but only Naaman the Syrian"** (v. 27). Jesus was telling them of the economy of God. "Why should I come to Nazareth and do miracles for you? You have not honored or received Me as the Messiah. The point is, in the Old Testament, Elijah didn't come to the widows in Israel. Elisha didn't come to the lepers in Israel. So, I'm not coming to the sinners in Nazareth."

When they heard these things, all in the synagogue were filled with wrath (v. 28). A paroxysm of anger and fury erupted in that very moment against Jesus. Instead of having their curiosity piqued regarding what this hometown man was going to do in Nazareth, they were now **filled with wrath**. They didn't just get angry and walk out. **And they rose up and drove him out of the town and brought him to the brow of the hill on which their town was built, so that they could throw him down the cliff. But passing through their midst, he went away** (vv. 29–30).

The Messiah Rejected

At the early stage of Jesus' ministry, the response of the people of Nazareth to one of their own was unqualified rejection. Isaiah spoke of the future One who would come as the sin bearer and the suffering servant of Israel: "He was despised, and we esteemed him not" (Isa. 53:3).

The Apostle John writes: "He was in the world, and the world was made through him, yet the world did not know him. He came to his own, and his own people did not receive him" (John 1:10–11). Let me change the language here, by way of illustrative license, and have it read like this: "He was in Nazareth, and Nazareth was made through Him. But Nazareth did not know Him. He came to His own Nazarenes, and His own Nazarenes did not receive Him." That merely is an application of the universal to the particular, because this happened throughout Israel. He came to Israel; He made Israel. Israel was His own, but they received Him not. Or, let's go beyond the scope of Nazareth, beyond the scope of Israel, to the whole world. He came to the world, as John says, and the world was made by Him, but the world didn't know Him. That is as true today as it was true that day in Nazareth.

The Scriptures make it abundantly clear that with Jesus, there is no neutrality. Those who are not with Him are against Him. If you are not His disciple, you are His enemy. And your natural state, the state in which you were born, the Scriptures tell us, is a state of enmity. By nature, God is your enemy, and by nature, God's Son is your enemy. Only a supernatural work of grace can change the disposition of your heart from one of antagonism to one of devoted love and religious affection. Unless God the Holy Spirit regenerates your soul and changes the disposition of your heart, you will be recalcitrant in your disavowal of the Lord's Anointed.

People sometimes say, "I accepted Jesus." But in the final analysis, it is not whether we accept Jesus; it's whether He accepts us. Perhaps a better term is *receive*. To receive Jesus is not exactly the same as accepting Him. To accept somebody, in our modern language, is to tolerate them. To receive Him, in biblical categories, is to embrace Him.

The language of the New Testament is not one of acceptance; it's of embracing. In fact, when the Bible speaks of believing in Christ, it means welcoming Him, receiving Him, trusting Him, embracing Him with all of one's heart.

We read in the prologue of John: "He came to his own, and his own people did not receive him. But to all who did receive him, who believed in his name, he gave the right to become children of God, who were born, not of blood nor of the will of the flesh nor of the will of man, but of God" (John 1:11–13). The word translated "right" is the Greek word *exousia*, which can also be translated as "power" or "authority." Sometimes it is used to describe the transcendent force and power of God, and other times it refers to the supernatural authority of God.

When you receive Christ, you put your faith in Him. Because you have faith, you are justified before God, and as a consequence of that justification, you are also immediately adopted into the family of God. Now you have the privilege and the authority to say, "Abba, Father." God is no longer your enemy. He is your heavenly Father. Because you received the Lord Jesus Christ and embraced Him, the Lord Jesus Christ covers you with His heavenly mantle. Christ becomes your older brother. Christ is God's only begotten Son, and every other child of God is His adopted child. We are not by nature the children of God; we are by nature children of wrath (Eph. 2:3). The only thing that changes our status ultimately from hell to heaven is receiving the Lord Jesus Christ, which the people of Nazareth were not willing to do.

Take a moment to think about how the culture in which we live responds to the law of almighty God. Are the people in our country willing to embrace sexual chastity and purity? Or do we revolt body and soul against God's prohibiting sexual sin? We live in a culture where many people constantly blaspheme the name of God or the name of Christ. Christ stands as the supreme obstacle to our sin. If you receive Him, you have to recognize your sin. You have to fall on your face in repentance. You have to beg for the forgiveness of God for the way that you have violated His law. But if you can reject Jesus and reject the One who sent Him, you are free from the law.

But the day comes for every man and woman where you will stand before the throne of almighty God. He has appointed the day on which He will judge the world through the One whom He has appointed judge, whom He has vindicated by the power of the resurrection. On that day, Jesus will either be your judge or He will be your defense attorney, because if you reject Him now, He will reject you then. Luke tells us this is how it started in Nazareth, and all of what happened in Nazareth was a foretaste of what was waiting for Jesus in Jerusalem. Are you with Him or are you against Him? Do you reject Him or do you receive Him?

18

JESUS MEETS A DEMON

Luke 4:31–37

And he went down to Capernaum, a city of Galilee. And he was teaching them on the Sabbath, and they were astonished at his teaching, for his word possessed authority. And in the synagogue there was a man who had the spirit of an unclean demon, and he cried out with a loud voice, "Ha! What have you to do with us, Jesus of Nazareth? Have you come to destroy us? I know who you are—the Holy One of God." But Jesus rebuked him, saying, "Be silent and come out of him!" And when the demon had thrown him down in their midst, he came out of him, having done him no harm. And they were all amazed and said to one another, "What is this word? For with authority and power he commands the unclean spirits, and they come out!" And reports about him went out into every place in the surrounding region.

Jesus went into the synagogue, as was His custom. We read that on more than one occasion, He served as the visiting rabbi interpreting the scroll of the week and giving His sermons. We are told that the people were utterly amazed and astonished at His teaching because He spoke with such authority. We've seen this before, and we will see it again. Jesus had a manner with which He spoke that the Scriptures describe as speaking with *exousia*, "power" or "authority." And we can call it a mixture of the two, an authoritative power or a powerful authority, so that when Jesus spoke, the people marveled at His words, at His truth, at the solemnity, the sobriety, the depth and seriousness of

His word. They didn't realize it at the time, but they were listening to sermons presented by the One who was the very incarnation of truth and who had in Himself the power of life that attended the proclamation of His word. When Jesus spoke, there was a moment of crisis for everyone in the room, as they felt the thunderous weight of His message.

The Reality of the Demonic Realm

On this occasion, as Jesus was preaching, He was rudely interrupted by the cry of a demon, who cried out, **"Ha!"** (v. 34). It was a brief word of mockery and sneering at the teaching of Jesus.

This text presents matters that seem bizarre to our ears. I remember as a graduate student in the Netherlands that our professor, G.C. Berkouwer, once commented in a lecture that there cannot be any theology without demonology. The New Testament so clearly propounds the idea of the reality of the demonic world and of the angelic world, populated by supernatural beings who are usually invisible to us but nevertheless are real and powerful. The New Testament speaks more often about angels than it does about love or even sin. Like it or not, the Christian faith contains an affirmation of an angelic realm where not all the angels are good and righteous but some are fallen and are of the minions of Satan.

When Luke and the other Gospel writers talk about demonic occurrences, they make a distinction between demonic possession and lunacy. Contemporary people sometimes say that first-century observers confused demonic possession with insanity. That is incorrect. The Bible distinguishes between those two and also distinguishes between demonic possession and what we would call forms of convulsions or epilepsy. There were separate categories distinguishing demonic possession from other maladies in the New Testament.

There has probably never been a period in human history when the demonic world was more actively at work and more furiously engaged against the kingdom of God than in the first century, because the Son of God was walking the earth and all the power of hell was unleashed against Him. Virtually every miracle that we see Jesus performing in the New Testament was also performed in the Old Testament by prophets such as Elijah, Elisha, or Moses. What was radically new about the supernatural ministry of Jesus was His ministry of exorcising demons. The New Testament writers were keen to let us know that Jesus' power over the demonic world is significant. It is a sign of His supernatural origin and supreme authority, that even the devils of this world tremble at His presence.

The accounts that we find in Scripture of encounters between Jesus and the demonic realm follow a similar pattern. There's always a protest where the demon complains: **"What have you to do with us, Jesus of Nazareth? Have you come to destroy us?"** (v. 34). Elsewhere, the question is, "Have you come here to torment us before the time?" (Matt. 8:29). The demons know that their days are numbered and that God in His providence has established a day when the demons will be wiped out and have their power completely removed. But that day had not yet come, and they were aware of it.

The demons have elements of a sound theology. They know who Jesus is. They know the truth. They know who God is, as James tells us: "You believe that God is one; you do well. Even the demons believe—and shudder!" (James 2:19). Their understanding of the identity of Jesus is, strangely enough, impeccable. Their problem is not that they don't know the truth; their problem is that they hate it. No one hates Jesus more than these demonic beings. When He appeared, they trembled, they feared, they protested, they resisted, and nothing could quench their fierce hatred of Him.

Christ Victorious

But the demon said, **"I know who you are—the Holy One of God"** (v. 34). You see, nothing recognizes the holy more clearly than the unholy. No one recognizes the intrusion of heaven more than those who inhabit hell. Here we find the testimony of the devil as to the identity of Jesus. **But Jesus rebuked him, saying, "Be silent and come out of him!" And when the demon had thrown him down in their midst, he came out of him, having done him no harm. And they were all amazed and said to one another, "What is this word? For with authority and power he commands the unclean spirits, and they come out!" And reports about him went out into every place in the surrounding region** (vv. 35–37).

In Ephesians 6:10–13, Paul writes:

> Finally, be strong in the Lord and in the strength of his might. Put on the whole armor of God, that you may be able to stand against the schemes of the devil. For we do not wrestle against flesh and blood, but against the rulers, against the authorities, against the cosmic powers over this present darkness, against the spiritual forces of evil in the heavenly places. Therefore take up the whole armor of God, that you may be able to withstand in the evil day, and having done all, to stand firm.

The Apostle Paul concludes this epistle the same way he began it, with the cosmic struggle in the heavens between the victor, the Son of God, who leads a host of captives, and these invisible but powerful forces from hell. Paul said,

"You need the whole armor of God because we're in a battle, and it's not with people." The battle that a Christian must endure is a spiritual battle, not just a struggle with their own sinful tendencies but also a war that is cosmic in scope. Paul said, "Do you realize as a Christian, you are engaged in a battle against powers, principalities, cosmic powers, and spiritual wickedness in high places?" The Bible tells us with respect to the world empires that God raises them up and God tears them down. There is this idea that entire empires, nations, and states can be demonized so that their political structure and their political actions are really actions that they are carrying on under the influence of the devil. We're fighting against supernatural forces, and we're fighting that battle with supernatural power, with the Holy Spirit and the armor of God.

A question I am often asked is, Can a Christian be demon possessed? I don't think so. You can be harassed, oppressed, frustrated by the enemy, but where the Spirit of God lives, there is liberty. Satan cannot inhabit the same space as the Holy Spirit. If you are indwelled by God the Holy Spirit, Satan can't get in you. He can come up against you and harass you, but he cannot possess you. "He who is in you is greater than he who is in the world" (1 John 4:4). That's good news for Christians, but it's bad news for those who want to find excuses for their sinful behavior by saying, "The devil made me do it." The devil may have made you do it, but if he did, you're not a believer. If you are a believer, Satan is an adversary to be warned of, but God says, "Resist the devil, and he will flee from you" (James 4:7).

The mission that we have as Christians is despised by Satan and by the forces of hell, and they will do everything they can to push us out of the battle and onto the sidelines, to paralyze us, to hold us captive, to put us into retreat. But we are called to pursue this battle until every tongue confesses Christ as Lord and Savior.

19

HEALING AND PREACHING

Luke 4:38–41

And he arose and left the synagogue and entered Simon's house. Now Simon's mother-in-law was ill with a high fever, and they appealed to him on her behalf. And he stood over her and rebuked the fever, and it left her, and immediately she rose and began to serve them.

Now when the sun was setting, all those who had any who were sick with various diseases brought them to him, and he laid his hands on every one of them and healed them. And demons also came out of many, crying, "You are the Son of God!" But he rebuked them and would not allow them to speak, because they knew that he was the Christ.

Luke has been giving us a chronicle of the activity of Jesus in the early years of His Galilean ministry. We saw what happened when He preached at His home synagogue of Nazareth, when the response of the people was "We know who You are. You're Joseph's son." Then He went to Capernaum and was confronted by a demon who said something different from what the people said at Nazareth. He said: "We know who You are. You're the Holy One, the Son of God." So, He is identified first simply as the son of Joseph and then not so simply as the Son of almighty God.

Luke continues his narrative by telling us what happened when Jesus returned to the house of Simon Peter, where presumably He was staying. When they arrived, **Simon's mother-in-law was ill**. Luke the physician tells us that she was ill because of **a high fever**. This was a serious matter for Peter and his wife. In those days, a high fever could indicate a fatal illness. They were profoundly concerned, and so **they appealed to him on her behalf** (v. 38). I'm interested in how Jesus responded to the beseeching of that family.

And he stood over her and rebuked the fever (v. 39). What? It's one thing for Jesus to rebuke a demon and have the demon leave the person that it had possessed, but we don't think of fevers as being capable of being admonished or rebuked. We might administer aspirin or put cold compresses on somebody's forehead or at least call the doctor, but usually if anybody in the family is running a fever, we don't stand there and admonish the fever. Whoever heard of such a thing?

Whatever was producing this fever in Peter's mother-in-law, the One who was there, who could calm the sea and still the storm by the word of rebuke, has the power and the authority to command rocks to speak or bacteria to leave a human body. The authority of Jesus over all power and every force of nature is manifest in this event when He healed Peter's mother-in-law by admonishing the fever. In an instant, not only did the fever break, but the fever left her so completely that with the departure of the fever also went all the consequences of that fever that had beset her. She was so completely, instantly healed that **immediately she rose and began to serve them** (v. 39).

The Purpose of Miracles

Luke goes on to say after this that **all those who had any who were sick with various diseases brought them to him, and he laid his hands on every one of them and healed them** (v. 40). As I've said before, during the earthly ministry of Jesus, His ministry was accompanied by a blaze of miracles. I'd like to consider the questions: Why all these miracles? What was the point?

The answer is not so simple. Certainly, one of the strongest motivations for Jesus' miraculous ministry was His compassion for people who were suffering. He demonstrated His concern and His care in His healings. He had the power to relieve the suffering, and so He did it out of compassion.

But there is a larger question about the function of miracles altogether in sacred Scripture. Here we find a lot of confusion even in the church today. For example, I hear people say frequently that the miracles of the Bible are there to prove the existence of God. I don't know of a place in sacred Scripture that says the function of miracles is to prove the existence of God. God doesn't need miracles to have His existence proven. The creation proves the existence of God. Paul tells us in Romans 1 that God's general revelation—that is, the revelation that He gives of Himself, both externally in nature and internally in the conscience of every human being—reveals Him clearly, plainly, manifestly, and utterly convincingly to every human being who walks on earth and to such a degree, the Apostle tells us, that every person knows that God exists (Rom. 1:18–20).

There are, of course, people who deny this. They say they don't believe in the existence of God, but the truth is that they can't avoid believing in His existence. They can bury that knowledge, repress it, deny it, and despise it, but they can't destroy the knowledge of God that He has planted in them and that He reveals to them through creation.

The function of a miracle, then, is not to prove the existence of God or even to give corroborative evidence of the existence of God. There is no actual word for *miracle* in the New Testament. You may find it in some English translations, but there is no Greek word that means "miracle." We have instead three words that are sometimes translated *miracle* or that refer to events that we might call miracles: *sēmeion*, meaning "sign"; *teras*, meaning "wonder"; and *dynamis*, meaning "power." We look at those three words—*signs*, *wonders*, and *powers*—and extrapolate from them the common essence of the three and then articulate our concept of the miraculous.

Take, for example, the word *sign* in John's Gospel. When Jesus changes the water into wine, John said, "This, the first of his signs, Jesus did at Cana in Galilee" (John 2:11). It's called a sign because it's significant. The point of the work that we call a miracle, that John calls a sign, is to do what a signpost ordinarily does, which is to point beyond itself to something else. That is, the miracles of Jesus and of the Apostles are signs that point beyond the immediate action to something else. What is this something else? What is it that the miracles point to?

The miracles point to the attestation of God to the person who is performing the miracle. That is, the miracles are God's certification of His agents who speak and proclaim His Word. Let's look for a moment back in the book of Exodus, where the first outbreak of plenteous miracles occurred. These miracles accompanied the ministry of Moses in preparation for and in connection with the exodus out of Egypt. God appeared to Moses in the burning bush in the Midianite wilderness. He gave Moses the task to go to the most powerful monarch in all the world, Pharaoh, and to say to him: "God says, 'You are to let My people go. I've heard the cries and the groanings of these people that you have enslaved. And I want you, Pharaoh, to set them free that they can come out and worship Me at My mountain'" (see Ex. 3).

God instructed Moses to tell the Israelites that they were going to be involved in the greatest act of deliverance in the history of the world. The Hebrews were to revolt against Pharaoh and leave Egypt. Now, this would be no small task, and Moses was puzzled. He said, "You want me to go to Pharaoh and say, 'Let My people go'"? Moses believed neither Pharaoh nor the Israelites would believe him. "How," Moses queried, "is anybody going to believe that You are sending me and I am speaking Your word?" Moses objected, "But behold, they will not believe me or listen to my voice, for they will say, 'The LORD did not appear to you'" (Ex. 4:1). The text tells us what happened next:

> The LORD said to him, "What is that in your hand?" He said, "A staff." And he said, "Throw it on the ground." So he threw it on the ground, and it became a serpent, and Moses ran from it. But the LORD said to Moses, "Put out your hand and catch it by the tail"—so he put out his hand and caught it, and it became a staff in his hand—"that they may believe that the LORD, the God of their fathers, the God of Abraham, the God of Isaac, and the God of Jacob, has appeared to you." Again, the LORD said to him, "Put your hand inside your cloak." And he put his hand inside his cloak, and when he took it out, behold, his hand was leprous like snow. Then God said, "Put your hand back inside your cloak." So he put his hand back inside his cloak, and when he took it out, behold, it was restored like the rest of his flesh. "If they will not believe you," God said, "or listen to the first sign, they may believe the latter sign." (vv. 2–8)

So, Moses did as the Lord commanded. He went to Pharaoh and made the demands that God had instructed him to make. Pharaoh brought out all his magicians, but their magic proved to be inferior to the miracles of God (8:18–19).

Let me fast-forward to the book of Hebrews, which says: "Therefore we must pay much closer attention to what we have heard, lest we drift away from it. For since the message declared by angels proved to be reliable, and every transgression or disobedience received a just retribution, how shall we escape if we neglect such a great salvation? It was declared at first by the Lord, and it was attested to us by those who heard, while God also bore witness by signs and wonders and various miracles and by gifts of the Holy Spirit distributed according to his will" (Heb. 2:1–4).

The author of Hebrews says the word was declared first by the Lord, and God confirmed that it was His word through miracles. The higher point of the miracles that we find in the New Testament was to authenticate the spokesmen for God, that they were sent from God. Nicodemus understood this when he came to Jesus by night, saying, "Rabbi, we know that you are a teacher come from God, for no one can do these signs that you do unless God is with him" (John 3:2).

Miracles for Today

I'm sometimes asked if I believe that miracles happen today. The simple answer is no. I've seen the sign that says "Expect a miracle." If you expect a miracle, if miracles are to be expected, there's nothing miraculous about them. If they're ordinary, they carry no certifiable weight. It's by their extraordinary character that they have sign power.

If I'm asked if I believe God is still working supernaturally in the world, the answer is, of course. Do I believe God answers prayers? Of course I do. Do I believe that God heals people in response to prayers? Of course I do. Theologians often make tight but real distinctions. When I say I don't believe in miracles today, I'm thinking of the narrow sense in which a miracle is defined as an extraordinary work that occurs in the external, perceivable world, against the laws of nature, by the immediate power of God. It is a work that only God can do, such as bringing life out of death, restoring a body part that has been cut off, walking on water, or turning water into wine.

Why do we labor so hard for this tight definition? For this reason: if a non-agent of revelation can perform a miracle, then a miracle cannot authenticate or certify a bona fide agent of revelation. That would mean that the New Testament's claim that miracles carry the authenticating authority of God Himself, as shown by Christ's and the Apostles' miracles, would be a false claim and a false argument.

What's at stake here is the authority, the authenticity, and the truthfulness of the Bible. That's why I have this tight definition and why I don't expect miracles, because I don't expect to find Apostles alive today. Miracles, in the narrow definition, stopped at the end of the Apostolic age. God is still alive, still working, and still answering prayers in an amazing way. I've seen marvelous answers to prayers, and I've seen people healed of so-called terminal illnesses. But I have never seen anybody raised out of a cemetery or an arm grow back or a preacher walk on water.

The Lord Jesus did miracles not only in the broad sense but in the narrow sense. It's these narrow-sense miracles of the New Testament that are so important to us, because they are God's attestation of Jesus and of the Apostles, to whose authority we submit.

20

THE GOSPEL OF THE KINGDOM

Luke 4:42–44

And when it was day, he departed and went into a desolate place. And the people sought him and came to him, and would have kept him from leaving them, but he said to them, "I must preach the good news of the kingdom of God to the other towns as well; for I was sent for this purpose." And he was preaching in the synagogues of Judea.

If someone asked you, "What is the kingdom of God?" how would you answer? If there is any theme that unites the Old Testament with the New Testament, any single thread that runs through the Bible from Genesis to Revelation, it is the concept of the kingdom of God.

What I find particularly significant about this text is this: there are a few occasions where Jesus tells people why He came to earth. He tells them what His mission is, the mission that has been given to Him by the Father, and He gives different concepts at different times, none of which are mutually exclusive. On one occasion He says, "I came that they may have life and have it abundantly" (John 10:10). He also said, "For even the Son of Man came not to be served but to serve, and to give his life as a ransom for many" (Mark 10:45). On another occasion He said, "For the Son of Man came to seek and to save the lost" (Luke 19:10). And when He was on trial before Pontius Pilate,

He said: "For this purpose I was born and for this purpose I have come into the world—to bear witness to the truth. Everyone who is of the truth listens to my voice" (John 18:37).

All these things have a connection with each other, but here Jesus explains His mission this way. When the crowds try to persuade Him to stay and not to depart from them, He said, **"I must preach the good news of the kingdom of God to the other towns as well; for I was sent for this purpose"** (v. 43). Jesus said the purpose of His coming was to preach and to proclaim the kingdom of God. Since this is the reason why Jesus came, it is imperative that we have some understanding of what He's talking about when He speaks of the kingdom of God.

To understand this, it is helpful to look at the word *gospel*. This word translates the Greek *euangelion*, meaning "good news," and there are three distinct ways that the word *gospel* is used in New Testament studies. The first way is to describe a particular genre of literature—namely, the four books that give us biographical information about the person and work of Jesus. We speak of the Gospel of Matthew, the Gospel of Mark, the Gospel of Luke, and the Gospel of John.

The second, and most frequent, way that the term *gospel* is used is in connection with the work of Christ. It is described as "the gospel of Jesus Christ" (Mark 1:1), "the gospel of the grace of God" (Acts 20:24), "the gospel of God" (Rom. 1:1), "the gospel of the glory of Christ" (2 Cor. 4:4), "the gospel of Christ" (Gal. 1:7), "the gospel of your salvation" (Eph. 1:13), "the gospel of peace" (Eph. 6:15), and "the gospel of our Lord Jesus" (2 Thess. 1:8). This sense of the word *gospel* has to do with a message, one that comes to us from God. It is God's possession, but the content of that message has to do with the person and work of Jesus. A related sense is how the benefits of Christ's work are appropriated. So normally when we talk about the gospel, we're talking about the gospel of Jesus Christ, the message concerning Jesus and what His person and work mean for us.

The third meaning is actually the earliest. It has to do with the kingdom of God, as we see when Jesus began His ministry. He said, "The time is fulfilled, and the kingdom of God is at hand; repent and believe in the gospel" (Mark 1:15). Matthew also refers to "the gospel of the kingdom" (Matt. 4:23; 9:35), as does Jesus in Matthew 24:14.

Initially, the gospel of Jesus Christ was known as the gospel of the kingdom of God. What is the **"good news of the kingdom of God"** (v. 43) that Jesus must preach to all these different cities? What does He mean when He says, "But if it is by the finger of God that I cast out demons, then the kingdom of God has come upon you" (11:20)? What does He mean when He says, "The kingdom of God is in the midst of you" (17:21)?

What is puzzling is that the Old Testament speaks of the kingdom of God and makes it clear that the Lord God omnipotent reigns and has reigned over His creation from the very moment that He made it. His sovereignty is from everlasting to everlasting, and so God has been King from the beginning. What is new about this kingdom that Jesus must preach?

The Revelation of the Kingdom of God

To understand this, let's look at that thread that goes from Genesis to Revelation. In Genesis 49, we have the record of the blessing of Jacob to his sons. We would expect the greatest blessing to go to his firstborn, Reuben, but it doesn't. Instead, we read these words:

> "Judah, your brothers shall praise you;
> your hand shall be on the neck of your enemies;
> your father's sons shall bow down before you.
> Judah is a lion's cub;
> from the prey, my son, you have gone up.
> He stooped down; he crouched as a lion
> and as a lioness; who dares rouse him?
> The scepter shall not depart from Judah,
> nor the ruler's staff from between his feet,
> until tribute comes to him;
> and to him shall be the obedience of the peoples.
> Binding his foal to the vine
> and his donkey's colt to the choice vine,
> he has washed his garments in wine
> and his vesture in the blood of grapes.
> His eyes are darker than wine,
> and his teeth whiter than milk." (vv. 8–12)

What is the scepter Jacob mentions in verse 10? The scepter is the rod of the king. It signifies his royal authority. Jacob was prophetically announcing to Judah that God's earthly king would come through the tribe of Judah, not through Zebulun, Reuben, Gad, Naphtali, Issachar, or anyone else. It was through Judah's line that God promised a king would come who would be known as "the Lion of Judah." There are references throughout the Old Testament to the coming of the kingdom of God; for example, Psalm 132 speaks of One who will manifest the kingdom of God on earth.

A kingdom is the realm that is ruled by a king, and it is usually understood in terms of geography—geographical boundaries and borders. It is the realm over which the king presides. In biblical terms, God's kingdom is not merely an area, a land, with geographical borders over which He reigns and rules. He reigns already over the entire world, over all things. But in biblical categories, the kingdom of God doesn't just describe that place where God rules; it also describes preeminently the place where God saves. The kingdom of God is the realm of the redeemed, the society of those who have experienced the salvation of the King. The promised Messiah will not only be a ruler, but He will be the King who is also a Priest. He is a King who will redeem His subjects through His priestly ministry.

Let's jump forward to the book of Revelation. When John received the visions that he recorded in this book, he was in exile on the island of Patmos. God drew back the curtain of heaven and let John peer into the heavenly court. John saw a spectacular scene, where the books of judgment had been prepared. "Then I saw in the right hand of him who was seated on the throne a scroll written within and on the back, sealed with seven seals" (Rev. 5:1). It was sealed so tightly that it seemed an impossible task for anybody to open the scroll and look into its contents.

John continues, "And I saw a mighty angel proclaiming with a loud voice, 'Who is worthy to open the scroll and break its seals?'" (v. 2). In John's vision of the heavenly court, the angels and the archangels were present, and one angel proclaimed with a loud voice, "Who is worthy to open the scroll?" As the psalmist asked in the Old Testament, "Who shall ascend the hill of the LORD?" (Ps. 24:3). The answer was, "He who has clean hands and a pure heart" (v. 4).

The requirement to open this book is not strength but worth. Who is worthy to open this book? And then we read these sad words from John: "I began to weep loudly because no one was found worthy to open the scroll or to look into it" (Rev. 5:4). John had been so excited when he heard the angel ask the question, and he was waiting to see somebody come forward to open up the scroll, but no one was found worthy. So, the Apostle was crushed with disappointment, and he writes, "And one of the elders said to me, 'Weep no more; behold, the Lion of the tribe of Judah, the Root of David, has conquered, so that he can open the scroll and its seven seals'" (v. 5).

The Lion of Judah was worthy and able to take these seals away and open this scroll to see every word that is contained in it. The Lion of Judah had prevailed. "And between the throne and the four living creatures and among the elders I saw a Lamb standing, as though it had been slain, with seven horns and with seven eyes, which are the seven spirits of God sent out into all the earth. And he went and took the scroll from the right hand of him who was seated on the throne" (vv. 6–7). When John looked for the lion, no lion was there. Just a lamb as if He had been slain. The Lion of Judah was also the Lamb of God, who takes away the sin of the world. The King is also our High Priest who offers Himself for our salvation. That's the good news. That's what Jacob could only dream of, what David could only hope for. Now it had come to pass. This One from the tribe of Judah has prevailed.

> And when he had taken the scroll, the four living creatures and the twenty-four elders fell down before the Lamb, each holding a harp, and golden bowls full of incense, which are the prayers of the saints. And they sang a new song, saying,
>
> "Worthy are you to take the scroll
> and to open its seals,
> for you were slain, and by your blood you ransomed people for God
> from every tribe and language and people and nation,
> and you have made them a kingdom and priests to our God,
> and they shall reign on the earth."
>
> Then I looked, and I heard around the throne and the living creatures and the elders the voice of many angels, numbering myriads of myriads and thousands of thousands, saying with a loud voice,
>
> "Worthy is the Lamb who was slain,
> to receive power and wealth and wisdom and might
> and honor and glory and blessing!"
>
> And I heard every creature in heaven and on earth and under the earth and in the sea, and all that is in them, saying,
>
> "To him who sits on the throne and to the Lamb
> be blessing and honor and glory and might forever and ever!"
> (vv. 8–13)

The King Has Come

Jesus was compelled to leave Capernaum that He might **"preach the good news of the kingdom of God to the other towns as well"** (v. 43). He taught His disciples in their prayers to say, "Your kingdom come, your will be done, on earth as it is in heaven" (Matt. 6:10). Sadly, many Christians today believe that the kingdom of God is something that's totally, completely, and utterly future. Others believe that it has been totally realized and consummated already. A pox on both of those houses. To think of the kingdom of God as totally and completely future is to miss one of the most important announcements of the New Testament, that our King has come, He has ascended into heaven, He has gone to His coronation, He has been crowned as the King of kings and the Lord of lords, and that our King reigns already, as invisible as it may seem. But He's not finished. The Lion of Judah will return, and when He returns, every knee will bow, either willingly or because He will break those knees until they bow in submission to Him (Ps. 2).

Every election year, we read daily the latest polls and discussion of the political candidates. We get worked up about it because it is important who is elected. In proximate terms, it's extremely important how the future of this country will work out. But ultimately, it's not who sits in the White House that matters; it's who sits over the White House.

We talk about the elements in the life of Jesus—His birth, His ministry, His life, His transfiguration, His atoning death, His resurrection from the dead. We talk about His ascension to heaven, and we also speak of His session. The session of Jesus is when He takes His seat at the right hand of God, and from that seat He rules over the kingdom that His Father has given to Him. All who put their faith in that King—all His loyal subjects—experience now and forever the fullness of the salvation that He has achieved for us, for behold, the Lion of Judah has prevailed, and the Lamb of God is worthy to receive glory, honor, dominion, and power now and forevermore.

21

THE CATCH OF FISH

Luke 5:1–11

On one occasion, while the crowd was pressing in on him to hear the word of God, he was standing by the lake of Gennesaret, and he saw two boats by the lake, but the fishermen had gone out of them and were washing their nets. Getting into one of the boats, which was Simon's, he asked him to put out a little from the land. And he sat down and taught the people from the boat. And when he had finished speaking, he said to Simon, "Put out into the deep and let down your nets for a catch." And Simon answered, "Master, we toiled all night and took nothing! But at your word I will let down the nets." And when they had done this, they enclosed a large number of fish, and their nets were breaking. They signaled to their partners in the other boat to come and help them. And they came and filled both the boats, so that they began to sink. But when Simon Peter saw it, he fell down at Jesus' knees, saying, "Depart from me, for I am a sinful man, O Lord." For he and all who were with him were astonished at the catch of fish that they had taken, and so also were James and John, sons of Zebedee, who were partners with Simon. And Jesus said to Simon, "Do not be afraid; from now on you will be catching men." And when they had brought their boats to land, they left everything and followed him.

Here the Bible records that the people continued to press around Jesus. On this occasion, however, they weren't insisting on healings and miracles; rather, the multitude was pressing about Jesus so that they might hear the Word of God.

Jesus **was standing by the lake of Gennesaret, and he saw two boats by the lake, but the fishermen had gone out of them and were washing their nets** (vv. 1–2). I can see that in my mind's eye. We used to live on the North Shore of Boston, and frequently we would drive to Gloucester to eat at the wharf there. We would watch as the fishing fleet would come in, and we would see the old, grizzled sailors on the sidewalks working with their nets, just as they did two thousand years ago. Meticulously, these men with gnarled fingers would work on the nets to make sure any weak portion was strengthened and anything that had ripped was repaired, so they could continue on their vocation of bringing fish to the land. So here, just as in Gloucester, these fishermen were sitting by the way, washing their nets.

Getting into one of the boats, which was Simon's, he asked him to put out a little from the land. And he sat down and taught the people from the boat. And when he had finished speaking, he said to Simon, "Put out into the deep and let down your nets for a catch" (vv. 3–4). We aren't told for sure why Jesus asked Peter to let down his nets, but we get a strong hint. Jesus, as prophets in the Old Testament were wont to do, would frequently accent His verbal proclamation with some kind of visible object lesson. After teaching the multitudes with His word, Jesus was going to teach Simon Peter something by way of an object lesson. He said: "Peter, I want you now to launch out into the deep. We're going to go fishing."

And Simon answered, "Master, we toiled all night and took nothing! But at your word I will let down the nets" (v. 5). You can sense the tension in Peter here, the frustration. You can guess what he was thinking. He was a professional fisherman. He knew how and where to fish. He had come up empty all night, and there was no reason to think his fortunes would change now. But he remained relatively polite.

Some people wonder why, if God is sovereign, we evangelize. Aren't people going to be saved whether we preach the gospel or not? The answer is, in part, because Jesus commands us to evangelize. If the Lord God omnipotent commands you to do something, you do it—not reluctantly, not smugly, as if you're ready to say when you fail, "I told you so." Peter responds appropriately here, as if to say: "OK, Lord. You're the Master. If You command it."

What was the result? **And when they had done this, they enclosed a large number of fish, and their nets were breaking** (v. 6). We need to understand how that happened. Jesus is the Maker, the Lord of those fish. He made the lake. When Jesus told His men to put the net in the water, the fish came to do the bidding of the Master. There was hesitancy on the part of Peter, but no hesitancy on the part of the fish. **They signaled to their partners in the other**

boat to come and help them. And they came and filled both the boats, so that they began to sink (v. 7). This was the greatest catch of fish these fishermen had ever experienced in all their years of fishing in this lake.

In the Presence of the Holy

I want us to note Peter's response. You would think that Peter would have said to Jesus: "Look, Jesus, 50 percent of the business is Yours. All You need to do is come down here once a week and tell us where to fish."

That wasn't Peter's response. His response is profound and profoundly important for us. Luke tells us Peter fell on his knees in front of Jesus, begging Him, not to go into business, but begging Him to leave, to go away. **But when Simon Peter saw it, he fell down at Jesus' knees, saying, "Depart from me, for I am a sinful man, O Lord"** (v. 8).

Do you know why our churches aren't filled right now? Because there are hundreds of thousands of people who want to stay as far away from Jesus as they possibly can. The reason they want to avoid the worship of Jesus and His presence is the same reason Peter gave to Jesus. Sinners don't want to come to church because they're sinners, and nothing makes a sinner more uncomfortable than to be in the presence of a holy God. In my book *The Holiness of God*, I have an entire chapter on the holiness of Christ. We've already seen the response of the demons to Jesus: "Jesus, please leave. Why are You tormenting us here before the time?" The demons couldn't stand to be in the presence of the holy, and neither can sinners.

About forty years ago or so, I was speaking at a college in western Pennsylvania in a town that was situated along one of the rivers in the Steel Valley. It was a bleak day at the end of winter. Snow had not yet completely melted from the sidewalks, and the snow was black from soot and dirt. It was a dreary day, overcast. Already on the bus, I looked at the people who were getting on. These were people who were depressed, who were oppressed, who were just trying to eke out some kind of a subsistence living. I could see them with their stooped shoulders and lines etched into their faces, and with the looks of the despair they wore.

I wondered, "Do these people have any hope whatsoever?" When I looked out the grimy windows on the bus, the first thing I noticed was that we were passing by a storefront church with a rudimentary cross in the front window. Suddenly my spirits were buoyed and I thought: "There it is. There's the sign of hope for these people—the cross." We went a little farther, and I saw another church. I was amazed to realize that I couldn't go a city block in this town without seeing a cross, the universal symbol of the Christian faith, the symbol of humanity's hope.

Without the cross, people are without hope in this world. But the cross is not just a sign of hope; it's also a sign of guilt, because when we see that cross, we know that it represents the work of Christ who saves His people who were in sin. Just as a vampire in the movies shrinks in horror at the sign of the cross, so a fallen human creature shrinks in horror at the sign of Christ, because Christ is holy and we are not. People who are unholy are always uncomfortable in the presence of the holy.

How many times have people accused you of being holier than thou? You often don't have to say a word. If people know you're a Christian, you'll make them feel uncomfortable, not because you're holy, but because you're associated with One who is. People are not comfortable in the presence of Jesus unless He's healing them or feeding them. Peter wanted Jesus to leave. This was not merely a wicked desire on Peter's part but a stupid one. It was foolish because of the reason he gave: **"Depart from me, for I am a sinful man, O Lord."** If Peter had any sense at all, he would have said: "Lord, don't go! Come here, because I'm a sinful man." What Peter needed more than anything was a Savior.

Hundreds of times people have said to me, "Religion may be good for you, and going to church and all that is fine if you get something out of it, but I don't feel the need for Jesus." I want to respond: "You don't feel the need for Jesus? Is your heart that hard? Don't you realize that there is nothing on this earth that you need more desperately than you need Jesus? What else can satisfy your need except Jesus?" Instead, I say to people: "What do you do with your sin? What do you do with your guilt?" I've yet to have somebody say, "I don't have any guilt" or "I don't have any sin." All impenitent sinners, even sociopaths, know that they have guilt, that they have sin. If you know you have sin, how can you be so foolish as to think you don't need Jesus? No one else can fix your problem.

Leaving Everything

And Jesus said to Simon, "Do not be afraid; from now on you will be catching men" (v. 10). In other words, "I don't need you to catch them. I can catch them without you. My Father can print His Word up in the clouds if He wants to, but He has chosen the foolishness of preaching as the means to save the world, and I'm choosing the foolishness of you disciples to bring My people into the fold."

And when they had brought their boats to land, they left everything and followed him (v. 11). Fame, glory, riches, power—all these things were forsaken because they realized that nothing could compare with this One who had just performed that miracle before their eyes. Nothing could compare with the One who was the Pearl of Great Price. They had nothing to trade for the greatness of the benefits from Jesus, and so they stopped running from Him. That's what happens at conversion. That's what happens when your life is turned around by God the Holy Spirit. You stop being a fugitive.

Once you hear the Holy One say to you, "Your sins are forgiven. Come, follow Me," then the Spirit of God changes that rock that's in your chest that you call a heart and causes it to beat anew under the Spirit's breath. Then all you want to do is get as close as you possibly can to Jesus and to follow Him the rest of your life. That's what it means to be a Christian.

22

HEALING OF THE LEPER

Luke 5:12–16

While he was in one of the cities, there came a man full of leprosy. And when he saw Jesus, he fell on his face and begged him, "Lord, if you will, you can make me clean." And Jesus stretched out his hand and touched him, saying, "I will; be clean." And immediately the leprosy left him. And he charged him to tell no one, but "go and show yourself to the priest, and make an offering for your cleansing, as Moses commanded, for a proof to them." But now even more the report about him went abroad, and great crowds gathered to hear him and to be healed of their infirmities. But he would withdraw to desolate places and pray.

Luke has told us repeatedly that multitudes of people were brought to Jesus and that He healed them of all kinds of calamitous diseases and afflictions. But on a few occasions, Luke isolates specific cases where Jesus manifested this ministry. In this case, He singled out the occurrence of the healing of a leper.

Leprosy in the New Testament was not as specifically defined as modern-day leprosy, or Hansen's disease, is now. A multitude of serious afflictions were subsumed under the general category of leprosy, so we don't know exactly the type of leprosy with which this man was afflicted.

In Leviticus, extensive instructions are given to people for diagnostic purposes to find out if the rash, scab, or lesion on a person's skin was a harmless problem or was one that was deemed to be leprosy. It was the priests' task in Israel to make the definitive diagnosis. Such texts seem foreign to us, and people grumble at sacred Scripture, losing their interest when reading the detailed matters involved. But if a Jew in that day awoke with a rash and he didn't know what it was, he knew from those instructions in Leviticus that his life was at stake. It was, in a sense, much worse for the Jew going through this process of diagnosis than it is for a modern person who is awaiting the results, from bloodwork or a biopsy, that might indicate a horrible disease.

For Jews, being diagnosed with leprosy was not only a sentence of a miserable illness, but it was also considered a kind of living death. One who was diagnosed with leprosy was not simply ill but was also considered unclean. Notice that in the other diseases that Jesus confronts, He heals them. But the leper who comes to Jesus doesn't ask to be healed; he asked to be made clean (v. 12). That is, he was asking to be healed, but more than to be healed, to be healed of a disease that made him an outcast from the covenant community of Israel, where the lepers had to live outside the camp, outside the community, and outside the town. Sometimes, they gathered together in colonies because the only people with whom they were allowed to have contact was other lepers. But in this story the man is by himself, and obviously somehow the word had gone around the countryside about the power of Jesus' ministry. This was the man's last hope to get rid of this walking death.

Luke tells us this man wasn't merely afflicted with the beginning touches of leprosy, but his case was severely advanced. As Luke the physician tells us, the man was **full of leprosy. And when he saw Jesus, he fell on his face and begged him, "Lord, if you will, you can make me clean"** (v. 12). The leper made a distinction between Jesus' power and His willingness to exercise that power on behalf of this poor wretch.

At this level, as badly mangled as this man's health was, his theology was sound. He was correct in his assessment that Jesus could make him clean, and in his whole life he had never met anyone who had the power to make him clean. In our lives, we will never meet anyone who can make us clean, save this One, Jesus, who met the poor leper on this day.

Faith Healing

A number of healing ministries are sprinkled across the Christian landscape in our day, and various types of these movements have come and gone in the past. But one of the most dangerous concepts we hear in these circumstances is the idea that faith healing means that in order to be healed, a necessary condition is to have the faith that you are going to be healed. If you don't have that faith, then the lack of that faith will be the fatal impediment against your becoming healed. I've heard this time and again. Such thinking goes along with the idea that if you ask for healing or for mercy from God and you preface your request by saying, "If it be Your will," that somehow you're manifesting a lack of faith and that in the very request, you are committing a sin.

Years ago, I met a delightful young man on our campus in western Pennsylvania, where Ligonier Ministries began. Each January, we had a one-month course of collegiate studies called a January term. A number of students would come from different colleges, and among them was our dear friend Harvey. Harvey was an exceptionally bright young man, alert and contagious with his loving spirit and attitude and deeply devoted as a Christian. He suffered from a severe form of cerebral palsy. In fact, he used to laugh at himself when he would try to navigate the pathways during snowstorms, because it was always a matter literally of touch and go for Harvey. He had a great spirit.

One day, he came to me deeply distressed. He said, "R.C., do you think that I'm demon possessed?" I said, "Harvey, what in the world ever gave you the idea that you might be demon possessed?" He went on to relate the story to me that he had some friends, zealous charismatics in his dorm at college, and they had decided to pray and lay hands on Harvey that he might be healed of his cerebral palsy. They, in the name of Jesus, demanded that Harvey be cured of cerebral palsy, but Harvey wasn't cured. So the next thing these students did was tell Harvey that the reason he wasn't cured was because he didn't have the faith. They explained that you have to believe that you are healed before you can actually be healed. It is like talking to a blind man and saying, "If you want to have your sight back, you have to believe that you can see before God will open your eyes." To believe that you can see when you can't see is not faith; it's credulity, and it's destructive to the soul. These students became more and more harsh with Harvey, chastising him for his lack of faith, which had to be the reason he hadn't been healed. When he persisted in not being healed, they accused Harvey of being demon possessed.

These young students began from a virtuous posture of concern and compassion for one of their fellow students to serious intercessory prayer for that student, and they ended up accusing this poor soul of being demon possessed and leaving him in a state far worse than he was in before they began their intercession. After Harvey told me of his experience, he asked me again if I thought he was demon possessed. I assured him he wasn't and then I prayed for him. I'm happy to report that Harvey, who is still burdened with cerebral palsy, has not let his condition become a real impediment to him. He has a very productive Christian life, is in the business world, and continues his devout faith and brilliant testimony to the Lord, because when he prays he says, "If it be Your will," and he is satisfied with however God responds.

God is good even when He does not answer our prayers the way we would like. I hear people talk about the difficulty of dealing with unanswered prayer. I'm not sure what that is. I've never had an unanswered prayer. Sometimes the answer is no, but that's an answer. If the answer comes from the Lord God omnipotent, who is more compassionate than any of us, then it's a good answer because He is saying, "That's not My will right now for you, at least in the immediate circumstances." His promises remain for the glory that awaits us in heaven, and He tells us that the afflictions we have to deal with in this world aren't worthy to be compared to the glory that He has laid up for us in heaven (Rom. 8:18). But in the meantime, we may experience great pain, suffering, and affliction, and it's according to the sovereign will of God.

And Jesus stretched out his hand and touched him, saying, "I will; be clean." And immediately the leprosy left him (v. 13). When Jesus healed the leper, the response was immediate and complete.

Cleansing Rites

And he charged him to tell no one, but "go and show yourself to the priest, and make an offering for your cleansing, as Moses commanded, for a proof to them" (v. 14). What was Jesus referring to here? The leper had been made clean by Jesus, but the priests, who were called to be health inspectors of sorts, needed to certify that he was clean. It was necessary so the man could be welcomed back into the fellowship of the village, the synagogue, and the temple. Before those things could happen, before the leper's exile from his family and community could be lifted, he had to follow the prescriptions of the law that God gave through Moses in the Old Testament. Only the priests could verify that he had been cleansed and was legally permitted to rejoin his family and community. He had to go through all of the ritual that's involved, including the offering of the sacrifice.

In Leviticus 14:1–7, we read:

> The LORD spoke to Moses, saying, "This shall be the law of the leprous person for the day of his cleansing. He shall be brought to the priest, and the priest shall go out of the camp, and the priest shall look. Then, if the case of leprous disease is healed in the leprous person, the priest shall command them to take for him who is to be cleansed two live clean birds and cedarwood and scarlet yarn and hyssop. And the priest shall command them to kill one of the birds in an earthenware vessel over fresh water. He shall take the live bird with the cedarwood and the scarlet yarn and the hyssop, and dip them and the live bird in the blood of the

> bird that was killed over the fresh water. And he shall sprinkle it seven times on him who is to be cleansed of the leprous disease. Then he shall pronounce him clean and shall let the living bird go into the open field."

There are some secondary ramifications of this seemingly obscure ritual in the Old Testament, and they have to do with baptism. Some people say that the only valid mode of baptism is immersion, and that, in fact, if someone is not baptized by immersion, he is not truly baptized. One line of argument for this view holds that the biblical word *baptizō* always means "to immerse." However, this is not the case. *Baptizō* does not always mean immerse. It may mean that, but it is used at other times to refer to an activity that is less than immersion.

One of the most important ancient documents we have is the Septuagint, the Greek translation of the Old Testament. It is so named because it was composed by seventy scholars, and it was aimed at Hellenistic Jews, for the Jews of the Diaspora who had lost their command of the Hebrew language and were now speaking Greek. The scholars translated with great care and meticulous concern the Old Testament Hebrew into the Greek. This translation was done about a century before Christ's birth.

Ironically, when they translated this portion of Leviticus 14, they used a form of *baptizō* to describe this process by which two small birds are taken. One is sacrificed and the blood is drained from that bird's death into a basin. When that is done, the second bird is then "baptized" in the blood of the first bird. The problem is that it's impossible to immerse the second bird in the blood of the first bird. There's not enough blood. That's why the English translation "to dip" (v. 6) is used for the second bird that is dipped into the blood of the first bird.

A very old piece of Christian art found in the catacombs depicts the baptism of Jesus in the Jordan. In it, Jesus is standing alongside John as John takes water and pours it over His head. Of course, that's not sacred Scripture, but it is a very early witness to the practice of baptism by pouring or sprinkling rather than by immersion.

Should we be baptizing infants? It's one small but significant point, that when Paul wrote to the Corinthians, he addressed a practical matter that the Corinthian believers encountered. It had to do with mixed marriages between Christians and non-Christians. Now, the Apostolic command is that a Christian is not allowed to marry a non-Christian. We still hold to that. But what happens when two pagans marry and one of them is converted and the other one isn't? There is now a mixed marriage, not by design but by consequence. What is the status, Paul is asked, of that person who is the unbeliever in this relationship? That's where Paul gives this seemingly strange advice: "For the unbelieving husband is sanctified by the wife, and the unbelieving wife is sanctified by the husband" (1 Cor. 7:14, NKJV). What does that mean? Does it mean that there is more than one way to be justified? Since sanctification follows justification, can we be justified by marriage as well as by faith? If we don't have faith, can we marry somebody who has that faith and be sanctified because of our spouse's status?

Here the term *sanctified* does not mean what we normally mean by that term, which is the process by which we are being conformed to the image of Christ after our conversion. Rather, Paul is speaking in Jewish covenantal language. When he says, "For the unbelieving husband is sanctified by the wife," he means the unbelieving husband is set apart, consecrated—not sent outside the camp, not considered unclean—but is now ritually clean and is allowed to be involved within the congregation of the faithful. Why would Paul allow an unbeliever to be consecrated or sanctified and to be within the broader confines of the covenant community? We don't have to guess. He gives the reason: "Otherwise your children [the word there is *infants*] would be unclean" (1 Cor. 7:14, NKJV). Your infants, your little children, would be unclean outside the covenant. But Paul says, "Now they are holy," not because they are righteous but because they are considered consecrated, sanctified inside the covenant community.

That's one reason why the vast majority of Christians for two thousand years have included their children in receiving the sign of the covenant, just as God commanded Israel for two thousand years in the Old Testament to receive the sign of the covenant. We recognize our children as members of the covenant community, and we give them the sign of the new covenant, which is baptism. It's not the only reason, but it's one reason. We need to understand the biblical language of being clean and of being unclean. As we've seen most dramatically, the most unclean, the leper, is now made clean through the power of Christ.

But now even more the report about him went abroad, and great crowds gathered to hear him and to be healed of their infirmities. But he would withdraw to desolate places and pray (vv. 15–16). When my car is running out of gas, I go to the gas station because I know it won't work once it's completely out of gas. Every time Jesus healed somebody, it drained Him. On some occasions, we read explicitly that the power went out of Him. The more the people came and the more they demanded from Him, the more important it became for Him to withdraw, to get alone with the Father, to have His strength recharged.

If it was necessary for the Lord Jesus to find that strengthening and intimate power from being alone with the Father, how much more important is it for us to be before the Father, gaining strength from His Spirit?

23

THE AUTHORITY TO FORGIVE

Luke 5:17–26

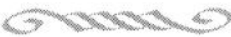

On one of those days, as he was teaching, Pharisees and teachers of the law were sitting there, who had come from every village of Galilee and Judea and from Jerusalem. And the power of the Lord was with him to heal. And behold, some men were bringing on a bed a man who was paralyzed, and they were seeking to bring him in and lay him before Jesus, but finding no way to bring him in, because of the crowd, they went up on the roof and let him down with his bed through the tiles into the midst before Jesus. And when he saw their faith, he said, "Man, your sins are forgiven you." And the scribes and the Pharisees began to question, saying, "Who is this who speaks blasphemies? Who can forgive sins but God alone?" When Jesus perceived their thoughts, he answered them, "Why do you question in your hearts? Which is easier, to say, 'Your sins are forgiven you,' or to say, 'Rise and walk'? But that you may know that the Son of Man has authority on earth to forgive sins"—he said to the man who was paralyzed—"I say to you, rise, pick up your bed and go home." And immediately he rose up before them and picked up what he had been lying on and went home, glorifying God. And amazement seized them all, and they glorified God and were filled with awe, saying, "We have seen extraordinary things today."

It was some thirty years ago that a small movie studio in Hollywood contacted me and asked me if I would write a screenplay from a book I had written. They wanted to produce a full-length Hollywood motion picture. I kind of chuckled at the invitation because, as I told them, I didn't know the first thing about writing a screenplay. They said: "That's all right. We'll help you and show you the basics that you have to do." So I agreed under duress to make the attempt. The screenplay was finished, but the movie was never produced for lack of interest in the story.

But in writing that screenplay, I learned I had to try to imagine the story through the lens of the camera. Every shot of the camera had a particular perspective, or what the Hollywood people call a POV, a point of view.

As I read the text of this incident involving the healing of the paralytic, I thought of all these different people involved in this incident in the life of Jesus. I want to look at this narrative from the various points of view of those who participated in it. Let me begin with the point of view of those who brought this paralyzed man to where Jesus was teaching the crowds. Obviously, they were men who not only had compassion for their paralyzed friend but also went out of their way to do something about it.

I had a little existential response to this because in my high school years, my father, who had been a very popular man in the community, was stricken with a terminal illness, and all he could do was sit in a chair for three years without being involved in any external activities. During that whole time, not a single one of his friends came to the house to visit him. I was disillusioned by that. I couldn't understand it, and I would say to my mother: "Where are Dad's friends? Why haven't they come?" She tried to comfort me and said, "You have to understand that it's difficult for them to see your father in this condition." I replied, "It may be difficult for Dad's friends, but it's far more difficult for him to be in this condition and to have no one come to see him."

The Love of the Paralytic's Friends

That stands in stark contrast to what we read here. **And behold, some men were bringing on a bed a man who was paralyzed, and they were seeking to bring him in and lay him before Jesus** (v. 18). This man who was paralyzed had friends who not only said their prayers and would send over meals or other such things, but they also went out of their way to do something to help him ultimately. They heard about Jesus. Perhaps some of them had even been eyewitnesses of the miraculous healings that He had performed in their region. These fellows decided to take their friend to Jesus.

They got a stretcher and placed the man on it. If you look at it from their perspective, you can imagine how their hearts sank when they saw that not only was the house in which Jesus was teaching filled to capacity, but there were large crowds outside so that there seemed no possible way to even get near Jesus. But they were not to be denied. The homes at that time for the most part were small. They had flat, tiled roofs, and much of the family activity took place on the roof, because the rooms were so small.

But finding no way to bring him in, because of the crowd, they went up on the roof and let him down with his bed through the tiles into the midst before Jesus (v. 19). Access to the roof would have been from an outside staircase attached to the wall. These men had the difficult task of carrying this man on the stretcher up the stairs to the roof. When they got there, they set the stretcher down and began to take the roof apart. They had to remove many tiles and make a hole big enough to slide the man down on the stretcher.

We can also look at this story from the perspective of the man who was paralyzed. His friends came to him one day and said: "There's a man in the land who is healing all kinds of diseases. The blind are seeing, the deaf are hearing, and we want to take you to Him because we believe that He can and He will heal you." I'm sure the man was afraid to believe, afraid to try one more possible remedy that might free him from his paralysis and give him the opportunity to walk and to be productive again. However weak or strong his faith was at the moment, his friends said: "Come on! We're going to take you on a stretcher, and whatever it takes, we're going to bring you to this man Jesus." Obviously, hope stirred in the breast of this paralytic, and he allowed himself to be lifted up and placed on the litter.

What was going through his mind as he was bumped along on the stretcher? When they came to the house where Jesus was, he could see that the place was a teeming multitude of people. It was so crowded that he must have thought: "This was a wasted trip. There is no way I'm going to be able to see this man called Jesus." What was going through his mind when his friends carried him up the stairs? They obviously would have a difficult time keeping the stretcher balanced so he wouldn't slide off the back or the front of it. Then, when they set him down on the roof in the midday sun, he was probably thinking: "What good is this? I still can't even see Jesus. He can't see me."

Then he saw his friends removing tiles from the roof. He saw them take ropes and attach them to the four corners of the litter. He had to take a deep breath and trust the strength of his friends as they began to lower him down through the roof in front of all the people. I doubt he had ever been more self-conscious than at that moment.

But what about the people who were there? They were trying to listen to

Jesus teach. They were hanging on every word, and all of a sudden they saw some dust falling down from the ceiling, and they looked up. Soon there was a little hole in the ceiling. They wondered what it was and tried to return their attention to Jesus. Then more debris started to fall down from the ceiling. They looked up, and the hole grew bigger and bigger. Everybody was looking up at the ceiling. Then they saw a stretcher being lowered right in their midst as they scrambled to get out of the way of this man who was being dropped down in front of Jesus.

Jesus Forgives the Paralytic

Of course, there's Jesus' perspective. We can't know exactly what He was thinking, but He may have thought: "I've seen people go to desperate measures to come into My presence. The kingdom is being taken by force by these people who are pressing into My kingdom, but I've never seen faith like this in all of Israel." His eyes were on this poor man as he was lowered down in front of Him.

Often, we're told in the New Testament writings that when Jesus looked upon people who were suffering, He had compassion for them. So it was when He saw this man. He knew that every eye in the room and those that peered through the windows were watching to see what He would do. He knew the scribes and the Pharisees gathered there were also watching carefully, not only to see what He would do but to hear what He would say.

And when he saw their faith, he said, "Man, your sins are forgiven you" (v. 20). Can you hear the ripple through the crowd? "What did He say?" "What did He say?" He said the man's sins were forgiven. What did that have to do with this whole event? This paralytic man didn't come to have his sins forgiven. He was coming to be healed. And Jesus said, **"Your sins are forgiven you."**

What about the point of view of the **scribes and the Pharisees** (v. 21)? They had come from Galilee, Judea, and Jerusalem to examine the work of Jesus, to catch Him in some unlawful act. They were skeptics and they were hostile toward Jesus. They saw the spectacle of the man being dropped down from the roof and probably thought it was an insult to proper decorum. Then they heard the words of Jesus. They said: **"Who is this who speaks blasphemies? Who can forgive sins but God alone?"** (v. 21). "What? What did He say? Did He tell that man that his sins were forgiven? Who does this Jesus think He is? We know that only God has the authority to forgive sins."

On this one point, their theology was sound. Only God has the authority to forgive sins. He may delegate that authority to His representatives to speak in His name, but the ultimate authority rests with God Himself. During the Reformation, Rome and the Protestant Reformers disputed over the sacrament of reconciliation. But the dispute was over the legitimacy of works of satisfaction, not the point when the priest gives absolution and says "*Te absolvo*" ("I absolve you") after somebody makes a confession of their sins.

The Reformers recognized that the Roman church had taught that the priest does not have the authority in himself to forgive sins, for only God can ultimately forgive sins, and the Reformers also recognized that Christ had said to His disciples, "If you forgive the sins of any, they are forgiven them" (John 20:23). Jesus delegated that authority to the church, and when the church gives the assurance of pardon or the assurance of forgiveness, it's not doing it on its own authority but only on the authority of Christ, to whom all authority in heaven and on earth was given by the Father (Matt. 28:18).

But the scribes and Pharisees said: **"Who is this who speaks blasphemies? Who can forgive sins but God alone?"** (v. 21). Jesus (back to His point of view) knew what they were thinking. **When Jesus perceived their thoughts, he answered them, "Why do you question in your hearts? Which is easier, to say, 'Your sins are forgiven you,' or to say, 'Rise and walk'?"** (vv. 22–23).

Jesus was responding to what they were saying and thinking. He didn't tell us what the answer is. If you read all the commentaries, they are divided about which is easier to say. In one sense, both are easy to say. Anybody can say, "Your sins are forgiven," and anybody can say, "Rise up and walk." But that doesn't make it happen. But on the one hand, it's easier to say, "Your sins are forgiven," than to say, "Rise up and walk." Why? It's easier to say it because there's no way that anyone can prove that what you've just said is true or that they can refute it. Forgiveness is something that takes place in the invisible realm. It's hidden from our view.

On the other hand, if a preacher says, "Rise up and walk," you're going to know very quickly whether what he says is true because the proof is readily observable. If Jesus would have said, "Rise up and walk," and the man was unable to rise up and walk, Jesus would be shown to be a fraud. So in one sense, it would be much easier to simply say, "Your sins are forgiven." However, for Jesus to say "Rise up and walk" was not a difficult thing. He had done much more difficult things in the past, but to say "Your sins are forgiven" in front of the Pharisees and scribes was to risk His life. Blasphemy was a capital offense.

The Power to Forgive

I think, given the circumstances, that Jesus took the more difficult tack here when He publicly announced that this man's sins were forgiven. Further, He said: **"But that you may know that the Son of Man has authority on earth to forgive sins"—he said to the man who was paralyzed—"I say to you, rise,**

pick up your bed and go home" (v. 24). With that, Jesus told the scribes and Pharisees that the Son of Man is also the Son of God, the One who descends from heaven, from the throne of judgment, who will judge the earth. He is the One who has the authority and the power to pardon the sinner.

And immediately he rose up before them and picked up what he had been lying on and went home, glorifying God. And amazement seized them all, and they glorified God and were filled with awe, saying, "We have seen extraordinary things today" (vv. 25–26). The second Jesus spoke the words, the paralyzed man's legs were filled with strength. He got up from that stretcher, and he didn't need his friends to carry him. He took the stretcher, walked on his own, free from the paralysis, free from sin.

I don't want to spiritualize this text. This man wasn't spiritually paralyzed; he was physically paralyzed. But each one of us who deals with unforgiven guilt suffers from an amazingly paralyzing force. If you suffer from that kind of paralysis, if there's a sin that has haunted you for years and years, that has spoiled your liberty as a Christian, this text tells you what to do about it, because there's only one cure for guilt, and that's forgiveness. And here is the One who has the power and the authority ultimately to say, "*Te absolvo*—I forgive you."

24

THE CALL OF LEVI

Luke 5:27–32

After this he went out and saw a tax collector named Levi, sitting at the tax booth. And he said to him, "Follow me." And leaving everything, he rose and followed him.

And Levi made him a great feast in his house, and there was a large company of tax collectors and others reclining at table with them. And the Pharisees and their scribes grumbled at his disciples, saying, "Why do you eat and drink with tax collectors and sinners?" And Jesus answered them, "Those who are well have no need of a physician, but those who are sick. I have not come to call the righteous but sinners to repentance."

It was 1964, and I was walking by myself down a street that was called the van der Helstlaan in the ancient, walled city of Naarden in the Netherlands. I was returning to the house where we had rented rooms during my graduate studies there. As I approached our house, I saw an elderly lady coming from the other direction. She was carrying a bag of groceries, and I smiled and greeted her. She stopped suddenly, and her face lit up and she spoke to me. It was like she wanted to hold me there, to not let me pass on. I spoke to her for five minutes and bade her goodbye, and she went on her way and I went into the house.

As I walked in the door, I was met by our landlady, who was livid. She screamed at me, asking me how I could speak to that terrible woman I had met on the street. I didn't understand what was behind all this intense anger.

The landlady finally explained that during World War II, which had ended only nineteen years before, this woman had been a Nazi collaborator. She was a traitor to her own people. She gave comfort and help to the occupying Nazis in the town.

Then our landlady went on to tell how the Germans were taking the sons, the young men, from the village and shipping them to Germany and putting them to work in slave labor camps to help in the military production effort. The woman in whose house we lived, together with her next-door neighbor, had conspired to dig a safe place under the landlady's living room floor, where they put a bed, water, food, and some flashlights, so if the Germans came near, they could hide her son and the next-door neighbor's son. She told how one day the Gestapo came into her house carrying machine guns and asked the woman, "Do you have any sons?" She said, "No." They ran to the bedroom and felt the bed and looked in the closet to see if there was any evidence of young men, and then to finish their examination, they came back to the living room. The leader pointed his gun at the floor, then started to shoot into the floor where the two young men were in hiding.

While they were shooting into the floor, they were watching the boy's mother to see what her reaction would be. When they finished and were satisfied that there were no young men there, the Germans left. This woman rushed over to the concealed trapdoor and went down into this cubbyhole and discovered to her relief that neither of the young men had been hit by the bullets. Can you imagine that? Can you imagine hiding your own son in your house and having somebody come in with a gun and start shooting at the floorboards? That's the kind of thing you see in movies, and it's hard to imagine that it actually happened. When I heard that story, I understood the intensity of her hatred toward her collaborator neighbor that had lasted for nineteen years.

I tell this story for a reason. The kind of hatred the woman had for the traitor, the collaborator, was how the Jewish people felt about tax collectors. In Israel, the terms **sinners** and **tax collectors** (v. 30) were virtually synonymous, because the people believed the worst sin was the sin of collaboration with the Romans who so severely oppressed the Jewish people. Perhaps the most miserable way in which the Romans oppressed the Jews was through taxation. The burden of the taxes that the Roman government imposed on captive Israel was incredible.

A Tax Collector Named Levi

After this he went out and saw a tax collector named Levi, sitting at the tax booth (v. 27). Here was a Jewish man who worked for the Romans, sitting outside at his tax booth, along the shore of the Sea of Galilee, on the trade route from Syria to Egypt, and he collected a toll tax or a tariff of some sort, keeping a percentage of what he collected for himself. The pious Jews, who prayed for their deliverance from the Romans every day, couldn't stand to look at this man named Levi. He was lining his own pockets by means of the oppressive, confiscatory taxes levied by the Roman government.

In God's structure of a nation, there was a distinction between priests and kings, between what we call the civil government and the religious establishment. God imposed a tax, as it were, upon His church in Israel. It was called a tithe, and every Jew was required to bring of his firstfruits, 10 percent of his yield. In addition to the tithes and the offerings, the people also supported the priests and the Levites, the religious life and the educational life of the people. God also imposed a head tax that was given to support the civil government.

The same principle is given implicitly to governments around the world, and we are told as Christians that we are to pay taxes to whom taxes are due (20:25). Yet at the same time, God holds governments responsible for requiring only the payment of taxes that are legitimate in His sight and chiefly through the imposition of a head tax where everybody pays the same amount of money. There is no progressive tax, no class warfare, no politicization of the economy in God's order of things. Government is established by God and is responsible to God to seek safety, peace, and justice.

Levi was a wealthy man, and most likely he wasn't tithing. Jesus came to him, a man who routinely stole from God and stole from his own people, and called him to be His disciple. Jesus called him to write the gospel, because Levi's other name was Matthew. He wrote the Gospel according to Matthew. Jesus said, **"Follow me." And leaving everything, he rose and followed him** (vv. 27–28). Levi packed up his ledger, threw away his account books, folded up his table, and said, "Yes, Lord, I'm going with You."

Calling Sinners to Repentance

And Levi made him a great feast in his house, and there was a large company of tax collectors and others reclining at table with them (v. 29). Not only did he follow Jesus, but he also threw a feast for Jesus. He opened his house. He invited all his tax-collector friends over for this party, and they reclined and enjoyed the feast. **And the Pharisees and their scribes grumbled at his disciples, saying, "Why do you eat and drink with tax collectors and sinners?"** (v. 30). Of course, it was known by the Pharisees. How could Jesus go to a party with tax collectors? They grumbled to Jesus' disciples over the company Jesus was keeping.

The Pharisees believed in salvation by segregation, by separating themselves from the *am haaretz*, the people of the land, by which they meant the people of the dirt, the dirty people, the outcasts, the sinners. To the Pharisees, salvation meant staying a safe distance from such people, because if you came close to them, you could become contaminated. When they saw Jesus going to this party with tax collectors, it was more than they could stand. They thought He was going too far with forgiving sins and eating and drinking with tax collectors. Jesus responded to them with very simple wisdom, saying: **"Those who are well have no need of a physician, but those who are sick. I have not come to call the righteous but sinners to repentance"** (vv. 31–32).

Jesus was making a simple point to the Pharisees: "You don't know who I am or why I'm here. I'm the Son of Man, and I've come to seek and to save the lost. I found one of those people who was lost at that table, sitting along the toll road, and I asked him to join My group, and he left everything to follow Me. I came for Matthew. I came for tax collectors, for prostitutes, for the people of the land, the dirty people. They are My people. I'm going to shed My blood for these people, for your enemies. I didn't come to save the righteous or to call the righteous to repentance, but to call sinners to repentance."

There was, the night of that banquet, no one who needed repentance more than the scribes and the Pharisees. Nobody needs a physician more than somebody who is fatally ill but doesn't know it. So it was with the Pharisees, and so it was with the scribes, and so it is with all of us who think that we don't need the ministrations of the Son of God to cover our sins, to forgive us, and to redeem us. This is our Savior who calls tax collectors to join Him; who calls tithe evaders to be His; and who wants His people to be made whole, to delight in the things that He delights in and to delight in the law of God.

25

NEW WINESKINS

Luke 5:33–39

And they said to him, "The disciples of John fast often and offer prayers, and so do the disciples of the Pharisees, but yours eat and drink." And Jesus said to them, "Can you make wedding guests fast while the bridegroom is with them? The days will come when the bridegroom is taken away from them, and then they will fast in those days." He also told them a parable: "No one tears a piece from a new garment and puts it on an old garment. If he does, he will tear the new, and the piece from the new will not match the old. And no one puts new wine into old wineskins. If he does, the new wine will burst the skins and it will be spilled, and the skins will be destroyed. But new wine must be put into fresh wineskins. And no one after drinking old wine desires new, for he says, 'The old is good.'"

Earlier we looked at Luke's description of the call of Matthew the tax collector and how he had a feast at his home for Jesus and invited all of his friends, the other tax collectors of the day. The Pharisees were put out by that because Jesus was now associating with known sinners. But that was not the end of their distress; they continued in their critical attitude toward Jesus. They raised a new issue in this passage. We're told that they came to Jesus and said, **"The disciples of John fast often and offer prayers, and so do the disciples of the Pharisees, but yours eat and drink"** (v. 33). They were upset about Jesus' apparent neglect of their tradition of fasting.

In the Old Testament, God commanded that the people of Israel fast on one occasion, on the Day of Atonement (Lev. 16:29), but for the rest of the year fasting was a matter of voluntary activity and practice. We see two particular times when fasting occurred in the Old Testament. The first was when people sought for a deeper and sharper focus on the things of God. They would withdraw from normal activities and devote themselves exclusively to contemplation and meditation on the things of God. The other prevalent reason for additional fasting was as an expression of mourning. When death came to a loved one, or great defeat came to the nation, or a time of repentance was at hand, the people expressed their grief and their mourning by rending their garments and entering into a fast.

But the Pharisees, who were the archconservatives of Israel, created new laws that God hadn't imposed upon the people. They created their own traditions, and their tradition sought to require the Jews to fast twice a week for at least a portion of the day. Not only that, but in their zeal for righteousness, they began to teach the idea that fasting was such a righteous enterprise that it would bring merit to the person who fasted. So this was just one more element of the Pharisees' attempt of self-justification.

On another occasion, Jesus rebuked them for substituting their traditions, the traditions of men, for the law of God (Matt. 23:1–36). This is the first rule of the legalist. The legalist legislates where God leaves people free. He takes "you may" and turns it into "you must," and that is absolutely fatal to a healthy Christian life. The Pharisees, who considered themselves the ultimate standard of righteousness, were the fathers of this kind of legalism. The second point of legalism is the idea that you can earn your way into heaven by doing good works or by obeying the law. Again, the Pharisees were at the forefront of those who taught this fatal error. They were, as I say, archconservatives. But what they were zealous to conserve was not the law of God. They were zealous to conserve their own traditions.

We must be careful here, because the New Testament speaks of another kind of tradition. Jesus was sharply critical of the traditionalism of the Pharisees, but during the Apostolic age, the Apostle Paul spoke warmly and approvingly about what he called in Greek the *paradosis*, which he received and which he instructed his readers to pass on. *Paradosis* is the Greek word for "tradition." So there is a godly tradition, the Apostolic tradition, which is to be maintained and guarded in every age of the church.

Some people believe something can't be good unless it's new. They, like the people and the philosophers who gathered together at the Areopagus in Athens (see Acts 17:16–34), think the old is always outmoded. As Luke tells us, they were always discussing "something new " (v. 21). We see this same tendency in the church, where we always are receiving new insights, new theologies that come down the pike to challenge classic Christian orthodoxy. It takes great discernment, great wisdom and knowledge of the things of God, to know when to be conservative and when to be open.

We always have to ask ourselves, "What is it that we're trying to conserve and why?" I don't care about preserving human traditions just because they're traditions, but I do care about preserving the biblical and Apostolic tradition.

A New Day

And Jesus said to them, "Can you make wedding guests fast while the bridegroom is with them? The days will come when the bridegroom is taken away from them, and then they will fast in those days" (vv. 34–35). We have a conflict now between Jesus and the Pharisees. How did Jesus respond to the question, "What about You and Your disciples?" What Jesus says in so many words is this: "What time is it?" Jesus wasn't asking them what time it was in the day. He was asking them what time it was in terms of redemptive history.

The Bible was written over literally thousands of years, and God's revelation of Himself and of His plan of redemption and of salvation was revealed gradually and progressively, beginning in Genesis and then expanding through the Prophets and the whole Old Testament where God was adding new information about the kingdom that was to come. He established feasts that were to be celebrated: the feast of the Passover, the Day of Atonement, and the Feast of Weeks. All of these things were not to be fulfilled in and of themselves. The New Testament tells us, "For it is impossible for the blood of bulls and goats to take away sins" (Heb. 10:4), and yet there was this elaborate procedure in the Old Testament of the slaying of the animals on the Day of Atonement (Lev. 16). These things were the shadows of what was to come. They were symbols that pointed beyond themselves to that which would come in the fullness of time when the final sacrifice would be made and the ultimate atonement offered. Then, these shadows would be discarded.

There are people today who want to take all of the Old Testament and bring it over into the new covenant, and there are those people who say the Old Testament is totally obsolete. They don't care a bit about it, and all they care about is the New Testament. No. There is an intimate relationship between Old Testament revelation and New Testament revelation. But at the same time, there are things that pass away, that are abrogated. The ceremonial law and the dietary laws of the Old Testament, for instance, have been set aside. The moral law of God has not been set aside.

Jesus understood that, but the Pharisees didn't get it. In talking about the coming of **"the bridegroom"** (v. 34), Jesus was speaking of Himself and His incarnation. Just as Israel was the bride of God in the Old Testament, so the New Testament church is the bride of Christ, and He's the Bridegroom who had been promised for centuries before, and now He was here. When the Bridegroom is here, you don't fast, you don't mourn, you don't rend your garments. You rejoice, you throw a party, but the Pharisees didn't know what time it was.

"The days will come when the bridegroom is taken away from them, and then they will fast in those days" (v. 35). Jesus was referring to His execution and His removal at the end of His incarnation. That's why in the early church, after the departure of Jesus, there was a great revival of voluntary fasting among Christian people. During times of persecution, when Christians were being thrown to the lions and suffering, their fellow believers would pray and fast for them.

New Wineskins

I don't know how closely the Pharisees listened to this illustration, but I'm sure they paid attention to the next one, because it touched upon something important to them, and that was their wine. Jesus gave this illustration: **"No one puts new wine into old wineskins. If he does, the new wine will burst the skins and it will be spilled, and the skins will be destroyed. But new wine must be put into fresh wineskins. And no one after drinking old wine desires new, for he says, 'The old is good'"** (vv. 37–39).

The old wineskins made out of goatskin or sheepskin had been stretched because the wine that was in them was continuing to ferment and stretching the leather to its limit. Jesus said: "If you put new wine in the old wineskins and that new wine starts to ferment, in the fermentation process the gases expand and stretch the old wineskins. The old wineskins have already been stretched, so if you put new wine in there and leave it in, you're going to lose the wineskin because it's going to break. What else are you going to lose? You'll lose the wine. You put the wine in the wineskin to preserve the wine so you can carry it about and enjoy the wine. In this case, you put new wine in the old wineskins, and you're going to lose both the wineskin and the wine."

What Jesus was saying is simple. You can't just take the kingdom of God and the arrival of Jesus and just put it on top of the Pharisees' traditions. It won't fit. Something new was happening. There was a new covenant. Yes, it built on the old, but it couldn't be absorbed totally by the old. You need to have a new aspect if you're going to fit into the new covenant, and by extension you can't have Christ and squeeze Him into your old life and expect that to work. A dreadful teaching has spread throughout evangelical Christianity, the teaching that someone can be a carnal Christian, that someone can become converted to Christ and never change. This is blasphemy. It is completely against the teaching of Christ and against the New Testament.

When you are born again by the Holy Ghost, you're a changed person. If you never experience change, your conversion experience is false. You can't be born of the Holy Spirit and not experience change. It is impossible. The sanctification that follows takes your whole lifetime and then into glory, but at conversion change begins immediately. One way you can check yourself, if you question whether you are converted, is by asking, "Has there been any change in my life, or am I still living the old way in the old wineskins?" If you are in Christ, you are a new creature. You need a new skin to carry the wine of the Holy Ghost.

26

JESUS AS LORD OF THE SABBATH

Luke 6:1–5

On a Sabbath, while he was going through the grainfields, his disciples plucked and ate some heads of grain, rubbing them in their hands. But some of the Pharisees said, "Why are you doing what is not lawful to do on the Sabbath?" And Jesus answered them, "Have you not read what David did when he was hungry, he and those who were with him: how he entered the house of God and took and ate the bread of the Presence, which is not lawful for any but the priests to eat, and also gave it to those with him?" And he said to them, "The Son of Man is lord of the Sabbath."

Once again, Luke tells us of a conflict that arises between Jesus and the Pharisees, and again it occurs **on a Sabbath** day. We read the somewhat innocuous report that Jesus **was going through the grainfields** and **his disciples plucked and ate some heads of grain, rubbing them in their hands** (v. 1). While this was happening, the Pharisees took notice and objected, as was their custom. They said, **"Why are you doing what is not lawful to do on the Sabbath?"** (v. 2). They began to nitpick this action of Jesus' disciples.

Keep this in mind that according to the Deuteronomic law of the Old Testament, it was permissible for passersby to go into a grainfield and help themselves to the basic necessities that were available there (Lev. 23:22). Of course, sojourners were not allowed to harvest all the crop and steal it from the farmer, but the disciples' action was part of the broader principles of gleaning that were set forth in the Old Testament. So by no means were Jesus and His disciples breaking the law of God.

The Pharisees were not content for the law of God to stand by itself. They added numerous regulations—more than a thousand—regarding what they thought was permitted and forbidden in terms of Sabbath keeping. According to their traditions, Jesus and His disciples had violated the Sabbath by engaging in unnecessary labor on the Sabbath day. For by picking an ear of grain, Jesus and His disciples were guilty of harvesting, and by rubbing the grain together, they were guilty of threshing. And so, the Pharisees were shaking their finger once again in the face of Jesus.

It's a wonder that Jesus, God incarnate, didn't at this point decide He had had enough and unleash the full power of His deity on the Pharisees. In any case, He patiently answered their objection and reminded them of Old Testament history by calling attention to the account of an event in the life of David and his comrades: **"Have you not read what David did when he was hungry, he and those who were with him: how he entered the house of God and took and ate the bread of the Presence, which is not lawful for any but the priests to eat, and also gave it to those with him?"** (vv. 3–4). When they were very hungry and had no food available to them, they went into the tabernacle and into the Holy Place (not into the Holy of Holies), where the showbread was on the altar as part of the ceremonies of Old Testament worship. David, realizing this was the only available food nearby for him and his comrades, took the bread from the altar and fed his soldiers and himself with it (1 Sam. 21:1–6).

Jesus showed His approval for David's actions regarding the bread; He enunciated the principle that no ceremony outweighs the fundamental needs of human life. David and his men were not involved in an act of vandalism, nor were they in a frivolous way helping themselves to food from the altar. They were eating because they had genuine hunger and needed the bread's sustenance. Jesus rebuked the Pharisees for their failure to understand what David had done in the Old Testament and for their failure to be concerned about the needs of Jesus and His disciples.

The Son of Man

However, this passage is about much more than what Jesus and His disciples did and how He answered the criticism of the Pharisees. In this narrative, Jesus makes a pronouncement that is overwhelming in its importance for us and for our understanding of Him: **And he said to them, "The Son of Man is lord of the Sabbath"** (v. 5).

We can divide this statement into two parts. The first is where Jesus calls Himself, once again, the **"Son of Man."** We've heard Him do this before. When He announced the forgiveness of sins for the paralytic, the Pharisees were angry, and Jesus said on that occasion, "But that you may know that the Son of Man has authority on earth to forgive sins" (5:24).

If we count the times Jesus is described in the New Testament by various titles and we look at their frequency, we see that far and away the number one title ascribed to Jesus in the New Testament is the title *Christ*, or *Christos*. It's used so often that we sometimes think that Christ is Jesus' last name. Jesus is His name; Christ is His title, which is the New Testament equivalent to the Old Testament word for *Messiah*. So when the New Testament talks about Jesus Christ, it means Jesus Messiah, Jesus the Anointed One.

The second most frequently given title to Jesus in the New Testament is *Lord*, which is significant because it is the Greek word *kyrios*. *Lord* corresponds to the Old Testament title *Adonai*, "Lord," which is used to denote God's supreme authority. When the Bible says, "O LORD, our Lord, how majestic is your name in all the earth!" (Ps. 8:9), what the Hebrew is saying is, "O Yahweh" (that's His name) "our Adonai" (that's His supreme title), "how majestic is your name."

Paul wrote to the Philippians: "Have this mind among yourselves, which is yours in Christ Jesus, who, though he was in the form of God, did not count equality with God a thing to be grasped, but emptied himself, by taking the form of a servant, being born in the likeness of men. And being found in human form, he humbled himself by becoming obedient to the point of death, even death on a cross. Therefore God has highly exalted him and bestowed on him the name that is above every name" (2:5–9). Then Paul says, "So that at the name of Jesus every knee should bow, in heaven and on earth and under the earth, and every tongue confess that Jesus Christ is Lord, to the glory of God the Father" (vv. 10–11). The name that is above every name is not the name Jesus. It's that title *Lord—Adonai, kyrios*.

In third place in terms of frequency is the title *Son of Man*. What is interesting about this is that this title occurs in the New Testament eighty-three times, but seventy-eight of them are from Jesus Himself. That means that *Son of Man* is the title that Jesus used most frequently for Himself.

We might think that *Son of Man* is a reference to Jesus' humanity. But, though the title includes a reference to His humanity, the dominant reference is to His deity. We can see this in a passage where this title appears in the Old Testament. In Daniel 7, the prophet writes regarding a vision of heaven:

> "As I looked, thrones were placed, and the Ancient of Days took his seat; his clothing was white as snow, and the hair of his head like pure wool; his throne was fiery flames; its wheels were burning fire. A stream of fire issued and came out from before him; a thousand thousands served him, and ten thousand times ten thousand stood before him; the court sat in judgment, and the books were opened. . . . I saw in the night visions, and behold, with the clouds of heaven there came one like a son of man, and he came to the Ancient of Days and was presented before him. And to him was given dominion and glory and a kingdom, that all peoples, nations, and languages should serve him; his dominion is an everlasting dominion, which shall not pass away, and his kingdom one that shall not be destroyed." (vv. 9–10, 13–14)

The "one like a son of man" in this passage is an exalted figure, one who is given power to rule and reign in the name of God, the "Ancient of Days." He is no mere human but one with divine authority. In using this title for Himself, Jesus is claiming deity. So, when Jesus uses the title "Son of Man" in Luke 6:5, He is claiming to be the One who comes from heaven, who carries the full measure of His deity with Him, and with that deity the full authority that is associated with Him.

Lord of the Sabbath

The second part of the statement, **"lord of the Sabbath"** (v. 5), would have been startling to the Pharisees. When was the Sabbath day established? Of course, it was one of the Ten Commandments that Moses brought down from Sinai. We may think that the sanctity of the Sabbath was established with the covenant God made with His people through Moses. No. Though the Sabbath is part of the Ten Commandments, it was instituted in creation.

The Sabbath is a creation ordinance established by God in His original work, where He worked for six days creating all that there was. On the seventh day He rested, and He hallowed it, He sanctified it. The Sabbath was sanctified in creation, and the only one who had authority to hallow the Sabbath day was God Himself—not the birds of the air or the fish of the sea or even the creatures that God made in His own image. Only the Creator can be Lord of the Sabbath day. And here, the Lord of the Sabbath day, the One who made all things, is now in His incarnation being challenged by the Pharisees for His behavior on the Sabbath day. He responds by asserting absolute authority over the Sabbath, asking in effect, "Who do you think made the Sabbath day?" We can understand why they couldn't wait to kill Him as a blasphemer. Jesus was claiming nothing less than absolute divine authority.

A controversy that has raged throughout Christian history is the question of which is the proper day for Christians to come together for worship. The original Sabbath in Israel was established on the seventh day of the week, and now Christians almost universally worship God on the first day of the week. The Sabbath cycle is still maintained, one in seven, because that's what the word *Sabbath* means. But now it's the first day rather than the seventh day. Why? Because the Lord of the Sabbath was resurrected on the first day of the week, and in His resurrection He proved the ultimate intent and purpose of the original Sabbath day by which God provides for His people a time of rest. It points forward to the future time when His people will enter into their rest by resurrection. The Lord of the Sabbath was raised on the first day of the week, and so the early church came together to worship, to celebrate the sacraments, and to hear the Word of God preached on the Lord's Day, on the Lord of the Sabbath's day, which is now the first day of the week.

These things and so much more are contained in the title *Son of Man* and the claim by our Lord that He as the Son of Man is the Lord of the Sabbath. This is a clear declaration of the deity of Christ that the One who went into the grainfield to feed Himself and His friends is the One who came down from heaven and would return there to take His seat at the right hand of the Father. It is this Son of Man whom we serve and worship on His day.

27

THE MAN WITH THE WITHERED HAND

Luke 6:6–11

On another Sabbath, he entered the synagogue and was teaching, and a man was there whose right hand was withered. And the scribes and the Pharisees watched him, to see whether he would heal on the Sabbath, so that they might find a reason to accuse him. But he knew their thoughts, and he said to the man with the withered hand, "Come and stand here." And he rose and stood there. And Jesus said to them, "I ask you, is it lawful on the Sabbath to do good or to do harm, to save life or to destroy it?" And after looking around at them all he said to him, "Stretch out your hand." And he did so, and his hand was restored. But they were filled with fury and discussed with one another what they might do to Jesus.

Christians often formulate all kinds of laws that have nothing whatsoever to do with the law of God. No drinking, no dancing, no going to movies or the theater—how do these rules and regulations come up to be tests of Christianity when they're nowhere in the Word of God? We, like the Pharisees, create rules that we can keep instead of obeying the ones that God gives us, which are much harder to keep. Anybody can refrain from seeing movies—but to not slander? That is difficult to obey.

On another Sabbath, he entered the synagogue and was teaching, and a man was there whose right hand was withered. And the scribes and the Pharisees watched him, to see whether he would heal on the Sabbath, so that they

might find a reason to accuse him (vv. 6–7). Jesus knew what to expect when He entered the synagogue that Sabbath day. He knew the Pharisees would be watching Him to see if they could find a reason to accuse Him of breaking the law.

But he knew their thoughts, and he said to the man with the withered hand, "Come and stand here." And he rose and stood there (v. 8). Jesus enlisted a man with a withered hand for His own purposes, and He told the man to step forward. In a sense, it seems that Jesus was putting this man at risk. The man didn't want to be used as exhibit A in a trial against Jesus. He didn't want to be the center of this controversy, and so, like most people, he probably wanted to shrink back into the shadows. But even more, the man wanted to get back the use of his hand. He stepped forward, and when Jesus said, **"Stretch out your hand,"** he did, and **his hand was restored** (v. 10).

Jesus had put the question to His enemies here, **"I ask you, is it lawful on the Sabbath to do good or to do harm, to save life or to destroy it?"** (v. 9). Jesus was not asking whether it was lawful to do on the Sabbath what the rabbis permitted. He was asking whether it was proper or just to do good. Healing a man's hand is a good thing, and good things like this may be done not just six days a week but seven days a week. Is it lawful for a nurse or a doctor to help people who are sick on the Sabbath day? Of course it is. Is it lawful to save life rather than take it? The irony is that the Pharisees were ready to bring charges against Jesus for violating the Sabbath, for doing good on the Sabbath, for healing on the Sabbath, and they were plotting to kill Him. That was a gross violation of the Sabbath, of the sanctity of the day that God has set apart for our well-being. And finally, we read that the Pharisees **were filled with fury and discussed with one another what they might do to Jesus** (v. 11).

The Bible warns us about grieving the Holy Spirit (Eph. 4:30). In the days before the flood, God looked at the evil in this world and said, "My Spirit shall not abide in man forever" (Gen. 6:3). There's a point when His compassion ends, His mercy stops, and His anger erupts. Therefore, don't harden your hearts when you hear the Word of God. The Holy Ghost uses the Word of God to quicken our consciences, to make us aware of our rebellion against God. Nothing has the power to bring us to health like the Word of God, and so let us not hear a story like this and then be like the Pharisees and say, "Oh, those bad Pharisees." When we do that, we're just like them. But my prayer as a Christian is "O God, don't be angry with me. Don't let me give You cause to be furious with me. Don't let me grieve You because my heart is hardened." When we hear a story like this, we want to say: "Lord, You are the Lord of the Sabbath. What do You want from me? Give me ears to hear and a heart that is open to embrace everything that You say."

28

THE TWELVE APOSTLES, PART 1

Luke 6:12–16

In these days he went out to the mountain to pray, and all night he continued in prayer to God. And when day came, he called his disciples and chose from them twelve, whom he named apostles: Simon, whom he named Peter, and Andrew his brother, and James and John, and Philip, and Bartholomew, and Matthew, and Thomas, and James the son of Alphaeus, and Simon who was called the Zealot, and Judas the son of James, and Judas Iscariot, who became a traitor.

This short passage has great historical significance, because on this occasion Jesus appointed twelve of His disciples and gave them the office of Apostle. History notes that this small handful of men later turned the world upside down. It is amazing what God did, and is continuing to do, with this group of people as a result of their ongoing influence.

In these days he went out to the mountain to pray, and all night he continued in prayer to God (v. 12). That Jesus separated Himself from His disciples and from the multitudes for seasons of prayer is not unusual. But Luke adds the detail that **all night He continued in prayer to God**. That's a long time to spend in prayer, and I think even Jesus reserved that kind of marathon of prayer for extraordinary occasions. We know of the intensity of His prayer in the garden of Gethsemane before He was betrayed and tried and killed. But here, we see Jesus wrestling all night in prayer before the Father, as He was about to select His Apostles who would carry on His ministry after Jesus left this planet.

From the beginning we are told that one of the twelve who were selected **became a traitor** (v. 16). Jesus knew from the beginning about Judas' plans and desires. Yet, in the course of this time of prayer, Jesus certainly wrestled with, among other things, the decision to select the one whom He knew would betray Him.

The Office of Apostle

When day came, he called his disciples and chose from them twelve, whom he named apostles (v. 13). People sometimes talk about the twelve disciples and the twelve Apostles as if a disciple was the same thing as an Apostle. That's not the case. Jesus had many more disciples than twelve. On one occasion, He sent seventy-two of them out on a preaching mission (10:1–12), and from this larger band of seventy-two disciples, He selected twelve to be Apostles. The term *disciple* means a learner or a student. In this period in Jewish history, disciples were not merely students; they were also followers of certain leaders, such as a rabbi or John the Baptist.

An apostle was different, and the role of an apostle was one of great significance. The role of a student was considered a somewhat lowly position, one similar to that of a servant. But an apostle was one who was bathed in authority. In the ancient world, an *apostolos* was "one who was sent." Someone who filled that role functioned as an emissary or ambassador or a representative of someone in a high position. For example, kings might send out apostles to represent them, and they carried with them the authority of the one who sent them. So, when Jesus separated twelve men and gave them Apostolic authority, He was assigning to them His own authority so that what they said and what they taught carried with it the full weight of Jesus' authority.

The first Apostle in the New Testament, and the greatest Apostle in the New Testament, indeed the supreme Apostle in the New Testament, was Jesus Himself. Jesus said, "For I have not spoken on my own authority, but the Father who sent me has himself given me a commandment—what to say and what to speak" (John 12:49). The Father had given Him all authority on heaven and earth (Matt. 28:18). So when Jesus spoke, He spoke with the authority of the One who sent Him, and the One who sent Him was God. In a similar manner, Jesus then selected His Apostles and said to them, "The one who hears you hears me, and the one who rejects you rejects me, and the one who rejects me rejects him who sent me" (Luke 10:16).

This is important to remember at a time when people try to draw lines of distinction between Jesus and the authors of the Scriptures. The truth is, if we want to have Christ, we must receive the teachings of His prophets and Apostles, because they carry the authority of the One who commissioned them. Scripture tells us that the foundation of the church is not Jesus; it's the prophets and the Apostles (Eph. 2:20). In the building metaphor, it is the prophets and the Apostles who are described as the foundation, and Jesus is the chief cornerstone. The Bible says there's no other foundation that can be laid, but that which is laid in Christ Jesus (1 Cor. 3:11), but the whole foundation is built upon the prophets and the Apostles. When we reject the prophets and Apostles, we reject the very foundation of the church. As the psalmist says, "If the foundations are destroyed, what can the righteous do?" (Ps. 11:3). The foundations of the church are built in large measure on these people who are mentioned here in this text.

Simon Peter

Simon, whom he named Peter (v. 14). In every list of the Apostles given in the New Testament, Simon Peter is the first one mentioned (Matt. 10:1–4; Mark 3:13–19). That's a fascinating point because he was not the first disciple. His younger brother Andrew preceded him in discipleship, and it was his younger brother who introduced Peter to Jesus (John 1:35–42).

Peter is first on every list, and it's probably not because he was the first bishop of Rome (as the Roman Catholic Church claims) but because he clearly had a position of leadership among the Apostles. He became the spokesman for them. He's known as a man who was impetuous and in some ways unreliable. His performance throughout the earthly ministry of Jesus would have earned him the nickname "the sand" rather than "the rock" (see Matt. 16:18). However, after the death and resurrection of our Lord, Peter was indeed the rock of the early church.

During the ministry of Jesus, we see this wavering spirit of Peter. He's bold enough to walk out onto the water following Jesus, but also he is the one, when he doubts, who starts to sink (Matt. 14:22–33). He distinguishes himself at Caesarea Philippi, when Jesus asked His disciples, "Who do people say that the Son of Man is?" (Matt. 16:13). Some of the answers were John the Baptist, Elijah, Jeremiah, and one of the prophets. Jesus says, "But who do you say that I am?" (v. 15). It was Simon who gave the great confession, "You are the Christ, the Son of the living God" (v. 16). And with that confession of faith, Jesus turned to Simon and said: "Blessed are you, Simon Bar-Jonah! For flesh and blood has not revealed this to you, but my Father who is in heaven. And I tell you, you are Peter, and on this rock I will build my church, and the gates of hell shall not prevail against it" (vv. 17–18).

Soon after Jesus called Simon "the rock," He gave him another name because Jesus announced to His disciples that they were going to go back to Jerusalem, and there Jesus would be handed over to the Gentiles and be judged and be killed. Peter said: "Far be it from you, Lord! This shall never happen to you" (v. 22). Imagine that: "Far be it from You, *Lord.* No, *Lord.* You cannot do that, *Lord.*" Jesus listened to His close friend and disciple, and when He looked at Peter, He saw something else, and He said, "Get behind me, Satan!" (v. 23).

The same Simon Peter who gave the magnificent confession of faith also denied Jesus. During Jesus' trial, Peter was confronted not by the authorities, not by the soldiers, but by a maid who asked if Peter was one of the followers of Jesus. Peter cursed with a loud voice, denying three times that he even knew Jesus. The same Simon Peter later met with the risen Christ on the shore of the Sea of Galilee and was asked three times by Jesus, "Simon, son of John, do you love me?" As he had denied Jesus three times earlier, now Peter affirmed his love for Christ three times, "You know that I love you." Jesus said to him, "Feed my sheep" (John 21:15–17).

Peter's ministry later was a great blessing to the church as persecution broke out in Jerusalem against the Christians. Peter was imprisoned (Acts 12). The rest of the Apostles met in secret and prayed diligently for the release of Peter. Their prayer time was interrupted by a knock at the door. A servant girl recognized Peter's voice and came and told the others. They dismissed her, saying, "It is his angel!" (v. 15). As they were praying that God would rescue Peter from his imprisonment, Peter arrived, but they didn't believe it. They thought it was his ghost at the door.

Peter's ministry continued into the AD 60s. He was arrested by the Romans under the tyranny of Nero, who also saw to it that the Apostle Paul would be executed that same year. Simon Peter was thrown into the Mamertine Prison in Rome, where he was tortured before he was taken out of that prison to the Circus Maximus and executed by crucifixion. Because he said he was not worthy to be executed in the same manner as Jesus was, he was crucified upside down.

Andrew, James, and John

Andrew his brother (v. 14) was the first disciple who was called. He had originally been a follower of John the Baptist, and he heard John the Baptist point to Jesus as the One whom he was announcing as the coming Messiah (John 1:35–42). Andrew transferred his allegiance from John the Baptist to Jesus, obviously with John's blessing. Andrew brought his older brother Simon to Jesus, and so the two brothers became disciples and both were elevated to the level of Apostles.

In AD 70, Andrew also suffered martyrdom. His crucifixion was on a cross that was in the shape of an X. Tradition tells us that when he saw the cross that had been prepared for his execution, he broke out in joy. He said, "For my whole life has been for the cross." He was delighted that he could join his Savior in death through crucifixion. He was tied to that cross, and he lived on that cross for three days before he died.

The other two disciples mentioned here are **James and John** (v. 14). They, along with Peter, are normally considered to be the inner circle of the Twelve. These three were present at the transfiguration of Jesus (Matt. 17:1–7). Just as Andrew and Peter were brothers, so James and John were brothers. They were known as the sons of Zebedee and were also known by the nickname Boanerges, "Sons of Thunder" (Mark 3:17), because they wanted Jesus to bring down fire from heaven. These were firebrand disciples. They were not meek and mild. They were ready to turn the world upside down. They were the ones who had their mother intercede with Jesus, asking that when He came into His kingdom her two sons could be placed at His right and left hands (Matt. 20:20–28).

James the son of Zebedee is sometimes called James the Greater to distinguish him from **James the son of Alphaeus** (v. 15), who was called James the Less. James the Greater had the distinction of being the first Apostolic martyr in Christian history. He was not the first Christian martyr. The first martyr, of course, was Stephen, but the first of the Twelve, the first of the Apostles, to be martyred was James in the year AD 44 during a time of persecution by Herod Antipas (Acts 12:1–2).

His brother John had the distinction of being the only one of the Twelve not to suffer a violent death. Ten out of the twelve were martyred for the faith. One out of the twelve took his own life in remorse, and that of course was Judas. Tradition tells us that all the rest of the Apostles suffered and died for their faith. It was said of John that he suffered and lived for the faith.

That John escaped martyrdom does not mean that he escaped suffering. He was subjected to suffering throughout his whole life, which was a long life. He was the last of the Apostles to die.

John wrote five books of the New Testament: the Gospel of John; 1, 2, and 3 John, and the book of Revelation. He was the only Apostle to author a Gospel. Peter wrote 1 and 2 Peter, and it is thought that John Mark, author of the Gospel of Mark, was Peter's disciple and set down Peter's teaching in his Gospel, but Peter was not the author. John was known as the disciple whom Jesus loved, and he was also known for being the disciple or the Apostle of love. His admonishment to the Christian community was always "Beloved, let us love one another" (1 John 4:7).

Under the emperor Domitian, John was exiled to the island of Patmos in the Aegean Sea, where he received the heavenly vision that he recorded, as Jesus instructed him to, in the book of Revelation. In that book, we have a marvelous vision of the triumph of Christ over all His enemies and the triumph of His people, who will participate in that victory.

John suffered many times. The church father Tertullian records that Domitian ordered John to be plunged into a pot of boiling oil but that John miraculously survived unscathed. Tradition tells us that on another occasion, he was supposed to be executed by poison. He drank the poison and it didn't affect him. He didn't die until the Lord was ready to take him.

Philip and Bartholomew

The New Testament doesn't give us a lot of information about **Philip** (v. 14), but he is introduced very early in the Gospel of John when we're told that he came to Nathanael and said to him, "We have found him of whom Moses in the Law and also the prophets wrote, Jesus of Nazareth, the son of Joseph" (1:45). Philip, in bearing witness to Jesus, made his confession of faith that Jesus was the One who had been prophesied through the Old Testament Law and the Prophets, indeed, the One who was the Messiah.

Later on, we see Philip on the occasion of the feeding of the five thousand, and he is the one who calculated the expense that would be involved in buying provisions to feed that vast multitude (John 6:7). Because of that incident, some people have unfairly dismissed Philip as just another calculating person, because he should have realized that Jesus had the power and the ability to feed all of those five thousand people without having to buy food. But this was a passing comment, and we cannot infer that it was characteristic of Philip and his whole life.

Philip the Apostle is not to be confused with Philip the deacon and evangelist, who is found throughout the book of Acts and who meets the Ethiopian eunuch in Acts 8 and explains Isaiah 53 to him.

Philip is also noteworthy for having said to Jesus, "Lord, show us the Father, and it is enough for us" (John 14:8). Philip was saying: "We've seen all these wonderful things that You've done. We've witnessed the turning of the water into wine, the walking on the water, the calming of the sea, the raising of Lazarus, and all the rest of these wonderful miracles, but there's one thing that we want. Give us the big one, Jesus. Show us the Father, and then we'll be completely satisfied."

If there was ever a time when Jesus seems to be exasperated with one of His Apostles or disciples, it was on this occasion, because He said to Philip, "Have

I been with you so long, and you still do not know me, Philip? Whoever has seen me has seen the Father. How can you say, 'Show us the Father'?" (John 14:9). What a powerful statement that Jesus makes regarding the significance of His incarnation, "Whoever has seen me has seen the Father."

Many of the Apostles became missionaries to other lands after Pentecost. Tradition tells us that the missionary outreach of Philip went all the way to ancient Gaul, modern-day France. He is recorded as the first to bring the gospel of Jesus Christ to France, and then he spent much time in Turkey. He engaged in confrontation with pagan priests there, and as a result he was martyred in AD 80. He was doubly martyred, if that's possible. First he was stoned almost to the point of death, and then they finished by crucifying him.

Bartholomew (v. 14) is mentioned in the Synoptic Gospels and Acts but not in the Gospel of John. So it is generally believed that he was the Apostle known as Nathanael, whom Philip brought to meet Jesus. Philip said, "We have found him of whom Moses in the Law and also the prophets wrote, Jesus of Nazareth, the son of Joseph," and Nathanael famously responded, "Can anything good come out of Nazareth?" (John 1:45–46).

Jesus saw Nathanael coming toward Him and said of him, "Behold, an Israelite indeed, in whom there is no deceit!" (v. 47). The Gospels do not tell us a lot about Nathanael, but Jesus' description of his character is profound. He was a guileless person, one without deception, without dishonesty, without manipulation. Nathanael heard this pronouncement and asked, "How do you know me?" Jesus answered him, "Before Philip called you, when you were under the fig tree, I saw you" (v. 48). It wasn't just Peter who made a great confession of faith among the Apostles. We read here of Nathanael's confession of who Jesus is: "Rabbi, you are the Son of God! You are the King of Israel!" (v. 49).

The Scriptures don't speak much more of this guileless Israelite, but tradition tells us that he also became a missionary and went to Armenia, where he and Jude/Thaddaeus started the first Christian church there. His ministry there got him into conflict with the local priests of pagan religion, and he was martyred by being flayed alive and then beheaded. Interestingly, Armenia in the fourth century became the first state to adopt Christianity as its official religion.

29

THE TWELVE APOSTLES, PART 2

Luke 6:12–16

In these days he went out to the mountain to pray, and all night he continued in prayer to God. And when day came, he called his disciples and chose from them twelve, whom he named apostles: Simon, whom he named Peter, and Andrew his brother, and James and John, and Philip, and Bartholomew, and Matthew, and Thomas, and James the son of Alphaeus, and Simon who was called the Zealot, and Judas the son of James, and Judas Iscariot, who became a traitor.

We met **Matthew** (v. 15) already in the Gospel of Luke. He was also known as Levi, the tax collector whom Jesus called from his tax-collecting business, and who then threw a party for Jesus and his tax-collector friends that created such hostility from the Pharisees that they sought ways to do away with Jesus (5:27–32).

Matthew wrote the Gospel that bears his name. Of the four Gospels, his is the one with the most references to the Old Testament. It was clearly written for a Jewish audience. He too became a missionary and, according to tradition, took the gospel to Ethiopia and established a church there. But in AD 60, he also got into problems with the local pagan priests, and as a result he was beheaded as a martyr to the faith.

Thomas

Thomas (v. 15) is held in infamy as the skeptic of the resurrection. He's called Doubting Thomas and he's also called Didymus, "the Twin." But if we look at the other references to Thomas in the New Testament, we see that it's unfair to simply dismiss him as a skeptic. When things escalated during the last days of Jesus' life and Jesus told His disciples that He was going to be arrested and suffer and die, most of the disciples wanted no part of that. But it was Thomas who said, "Let us also go, that we may die with him" (John 11:16). He was willing to accompany Jesus to the point of death.

When, in his zeal, he saw his Savior executed, taken down from the cross and buried, and the other Apostles told him that Jesus had been raised from the dead, Thomas did not believe it. Perhaps it was to protect his own faith, as he was so hurt by the loss of Jesus, so devastated by His execution, that he wouldn't allow himself to believe anymore. His faith had crumbled, and there was no more room for hope in this man. Thomas told the other disciples, "Unless I see in his hands the mark of the nails, and place my finger into the mark of the nails, and place my hand into his side, I will never believe" (20:25).

Eight days later, Jesus' disciples were inside again and Thomas was with them and Jesus appeared in their midst. He said to Thomas: "Put your finger here, and see my hands; and put out your hand, and place it in my side. Do not disbelieve, but believe" (v. 27). That was the offer Jesus made to Thomas. The Scriptures don't tell us if Thomas actually touched the risen Christ. The presence of Jesus with His outspread hands may have been enough to convince him. Thomas then gave one of the highest professions of faith of any of Jesus' disciples of Jesus when he said, "My Lord and my God!" (v. 28). It is notable also that Jesus did not reject this worship from Thomas, as do others in Scripture who are not worthy of worship, such as angels and Apostles.

Thomas then later became a missionary to India, and in the year AD 72 he suffered martyrdom by being killed with a spear. But his confession rings down through the ages to this day.

James Son of Alphaeus, Simon the Zealot, and Judas Son of James

The last four Apostles whom we've not mentioned include **James the son of Alphaeus** (v. 15), also known as James the Less; **Simon who was called the Zealot**; **Judas the son of James** (v. 16); and finally **Judas Iscariot**. Regarding the first three men, there is little information given to us in the New Testament.

Regarding the last one mentioned, much has been written and much has been spoken of since his betrayal of our Lord.

Before we turn our attention to him, let's look briefly at these first three. We've mentioned James the son of Alphaeus, who is also known as James the Less. Some people think "the Less" means that he was younger than the other James, the brother of John. Others think it means that he was shorter than the other James. We hear almost nothing about him in the New Testament. What is perhaps most significant in the New Testament record of James has to do with his mother. His mother was one of the Marys who was at the foot of the cross on the day of crucifixion and also one of the Marys who got up before dawn and went to the tomb of Jesus to anoint His body with spices. And, of course, it was James' mother along with Mary Magdalene and the other Mary to whom the angels announced the resurrection.

Tradition tells us that James was also a missionary. He went to Syria, but in AD 62 he was recalled to Jerusalem and tried by the Jewish leaders as a heretic. He was taken to the pinnacle of the temple and told to publicly renounce Jesus. Instead, he reaffirmed his conviction that Jesus is the Messiah and the Son of God, whereupon he was thrown to the ground. But that did not kill him; it merely broke his leg. To finish the job, the executioners hit him in the head with a large stone and killed him.

Simon the Zealot is interesting because he is noted as a member of a group of first-century Jews known as Zealots. The Zealots were not so named because they were zealous about spiritual matters; the object of their zeal was political. They were passionately committed to overthrowing the Roman government and driving the Romans from the land. The Zealots were involved with an incident in AD 73–74 where Roman forces besieged the fortress of Masada. As the Romans breached the fortress, they found that the Zealots had committed mass suicide rather than being captured. Some have described the Zealots as ancient terrorists, so it's one of the strange acts of providence that Jesus selected for His inner core of Apostles a man who was a tax collector raising tribute to support the Roman cause and at the same time a Zealot to work side by side with the former tax collector.

Tradition tells us that Simon also was a missionary. He is often considered part of a missionary team with Jude/Thaddaeus. They traveled across the ancient Near East before they were both martyred in Syria in AD 65.

Judas the son of James is also known as Jude and also as Thaddaeus (Matt. 10:3). Once again, next to nothing is known about him. He is almost certainly not the author of the epistle of Jude, who is traditionally held to be the Lord's brother. The Armenian church credits him, along with Bartholomew, with founding the church there.

Judas Iscariot

That brings us to a name that is identified with treachery and betrayal: Judas Iscariot, of whom much is written in the New Testament. I want to consider his role in the plan of God for redemption. Here, we see that he was selected by Jesus to be an Apostle.

First, we want to look at his name. There's a difference of opinion among biblical scholars as to its meaning. Some argue that it simply refers to a section of Judea named Kerioth, so Judas Iscariot was from that place. If that is the case, then Judas was the only one of the Twelve who was not a Galilean. Others argue that the etymology of *Iscariot* goes back to the Semitic word for "dagger," *sicari*, which was the symbol of certain assassins. Judas has been called at times Judas the Assassin or Judas the Dagger-Man. Though he didn't use a dagger on Jesus, Judas did nevertheless stab him in the back, as it were. He betrayed Jesus for thirty pieces of silver and led the soldiers to Jesus in the garden, where He was arrested. Judas indicated in the darkness to the soldiers which one was Jesus by kissing Him (Luke 22:47–53; see Matt. 26:15).

In his speech at Pentecost, Peter said:

> "Men of Israel, hear these words: Jesus of Nazareth, a man attested to you by God with mighty works and wonders and signs that God did through him in your midst, as you yourselves know—this Jesus, delivered up according to the definite plan and foreknowledge of God, you crucified and killed by the hands of lawless men. God raised him up, loosing the pangs of death, because it was not possible for him to be held by it." (Acts 2:22–24)

Here the Scriptures tell us that Jesus was delivered by the determined purpose and foreknowledge of God, that Jesus' betrayal was not an accident of history. It was not a mistake or an accident. No, this act of treachery was ordained by almighty God from the foundation of the world, and that causes us no small amount of consternation. How could God ordain that someone would betray the innocent Jesus and then be held accountable for such treachery? Could not Judas on the day of judgment say: "What else could I do? I was merely fulfilling Your purpose. I was simply doing Your will. It was You who ordained that Satan would enter into me, and then Satan made me do this diabolical act." How do we deal with that?

Remember that this is certainly not the first time in biblical history where we see wickedness perpetrated by people where they are working out the counsel of almighty God. Consider, for example, the greatest Old Testament act of redemption, the exodus. God heard the cries of His people and determined to redeem them from their bondage, and the instrument that He used was the most powerful man on the face of the earth: Pharaoh, king of the Egyptians.

When God sent Moses to Pharaoh to demand that he let the Israelites go, He told Moses, "I will harden Pharaoh's heart" (Ex. 7:3) Sure enough, "Pharaoh's heart was hardened, and he would not listen to them" (v. 13), and he obstinately refused to let the people of God go. The series of plagues came and were visited upon the people of Egypt and on Pharaoh, and after each plague, Pharaoh began to relent. "But the LORD hardened Pharaoh's heart, and he did not let the people of Israel go" (10:20), and so Pharaoh remained obstinate in his resistance to the mandate of God. Finally, God said, "I will harden Pharaoh's heart, and he will pursue them, and I will get glory over Pharaoh and all his host, and the Egyptians shall know that I am the LORD" (Ex. 14:4). God hardened Pharaoh's heart so that the people might know and clearly understand that it was God in His grace who delivered them and not Moses or the will of the people or the benevolence of Pharaoh, but that salvation was of the Lord.

The question is twofold: Why did God harden Pharaoh's heart? And how did God harden Pharaoh's heart? Scripture is quite clear as to why He hardened Pharaoh's heart: that it would be manifest that it was the Lord God Almighty in His mercy and grace who was redeeming His people. That was one of the purposes. The other purpose is that God's hardening of Pharaoh's heart was an act of divine judgment. It wasn't as though Pharaoh was an innocent, righteous bystander who had only good intentions toward the poor oppressed Hebrew people. No, Pharaoh was altogether wicked.

One of the things that God does again and again in church history is exercise judgment in a poetic manner. He gives people over to their own wicked desires. One of the things by which God exercises mercy and ministry to us is by restraint. He keeps us from living out the fullness of our sinful inclinations. The thing that the most wicked people in history—people such as Hitler, Stalin, and Nero—all had in common was the virtual absence of earthly restraint on their lives. They had that absolute power that corrupts absolutely. There was nothing to hold them in check, except the sovereign restraint of God.

All God had to do for such men to be even worse was to remove His restraints. He could let Hitler do what he wanted to do, remove His hands from Stalin and give Stalin true reign in his wickedness to do what he wanted to do, and take away the restraint from Nero so Nero could live out the kind of life he was inclined to live. That's what it means to be abandoned by God, to be given over to Satan by God.

Martin Luther said that when God hardened Pharaoh's heart, He didn't create fresh evil in his heart. There was plenty of evil already there. The way God hardens the heart is by removing the restraints and giving a person over to his own wickedness. Pharaoh's heart was already recalcitrant. It was already a heart of stone before God had any of the plagues afflict him.

Judas was a devil from the beginning. Judas was an unregenerate, corrupt, treacherous, lying, thieving crook before he met Jesus. God worked through his corruption to bring about the greatest work of salvation in all of human history. What Judas meant for evil, God used for good (Gen. 50:20).

30

THE BEATITUDES

Luke 6:17–23

And he came down with them and stood on a level place, with a great crowd of his disciples and a great multitude of people from all Judea and Jerusalem and the seacoast of Tyre and Sidon, who came to hear him and to be healed of their diseases. And those who were troubled with unclean spirits were cured. And all the crowd sought to touch him, for power came out from him and healed them all.

And he lifted up his eyes on his disciples, and said:

"Blessed are you who are poor, for yours is the kingdom of God.

"Blessed are you who are hungry now, for you shall be satisfied.

"Blessed are you who weep now, for you shall laugh.

"Blessed are you when people hate you and when they exclude you and revile you and spurn your name as evil, on account of the Son of Man! Rejoice in that day, and leap for joy, for behold, your reward is great in heaven; for so their fathers did to the prophets."

In the Old Testament, God would give His word to His prophets, and they would preface their announcements by saying, "Thus says the Lord." These pronouncements came in two distinct forms. There were "oracles of weal," which were good pronouncements, and "oracles of woe," which were prophetic pronouncements from God that expressed His wrath and judgment. For example, in the book of Amos, the prophet pronounced judgment by saying,

"Woe to those who are at ease in Zion, and to those who feel secure on the mountain of Samaria" (Amos 6:1). In the New Testament, Jesus condemned the Pharisees for their hypocrisy, saying: "Woe to you, scribes and Pharisees, hypocrites! For you travel across sea and land to make a single proselyte, and when he becomes a proselyte, you make him twice as much a child of hell as yourselves" (Matt. 23:15). It was a dreadful thing to hear a pronouncement from God that included oracles of doom, but it was a wonderful thing for God to pronounce you blessed.

Blessings and Woes

This passage begins the Sermon on the Plain, Luke's version of the Sermon on the Mount (see Matt. 5–7). In Luke 6:20–26, Jesus proclaims four beatitudes, or blessings, and four woes.

Oracles of weal were usually prefaced by the word *blessed*. Psalm 1 begins: "Blessed is the man who walks not in the counsel of the wicked, nor stands in the way of sinners, nor sits in the seat of scoffers; but his delight is in the law of the LORD, and on his law he meditates day and night. He is like a tree planted by streams of water that yields its fruit in its season, and its leaf does not wither. In all that he does, he prospers" (vv. 1–3).

Being "blessed" in this sense does not simply mean "happy"; that's a horrible distortion of the biblical concept of blessedness. In our culture, the word *happy* has been just about as trivialized as any word can be. When we're talking about beatitudes pronounced by almighty God, we're not talking about mere sentimentality. The idea of blessedness contains the idea of happiness, but it is so much deeper.

Numbers 6 contains a passage called the Aaronic blessing. It contains three lines: "The LORD bless you and keep you; the LORD make his face to shine upon you and be gracious to you; the LORD lift up his countenance upon you and give you peace" (vv. 24–26). These three lines exhibit a literary form called parallelism. The second and third lines are ways of restating the first line, so that blessing and keeping are the same as being gracious and likewise the same as giving peace. And ultimately, these lines tell us that blessedness is to be brought into an intimate relationship with almighty God, so that He would literally make His face radiate and make the refulgence of His glory shine on you. When the Bible pronounces blessing, it doesn't mean, "Be happy"; it means, "May you understand in the depths of your soul, in the deepest chamber of your heart, the sweetness of the presence of God as you live before His face every moment."

Blessed are the Poor

"Blessed are you who are poor, for yours is the kingdom of God" (v. 20). Verses 20–23 are Luke's version of the Beatitudes, which are also found in Matthew 5:2–12. This particular beatitude differs slightly from what we find in Matthew. Some scholars say that Luke has abridged Jesus' sermon, while others say that He preached this sermon on more than one occasion and did so with slight differences. We should not be troubled by any variations between Luke's telling and Matthew's. In Matthew's version, Jesus says, "Blessed are the poor in spirit, for theirs is the kingdom of heaven" (Matt. 5:3). Luke's version lacks the qualification "in spirit." Being poor in spirit means being humble, and it is not exactly the same as simply being poor. In saying, **"Blessed are you who are poor,"** Jesus may be referring again to the poverty in their spirit or the humiliation that they suffer, but I believe He pronounces His blessing on these disciples because of their economic status, because they are poor with respect to the riches of this world.

The Bible has a lot to say about the poor, and what it says does not always agree with what people say about the poor. Often, we hear very simplistic descriptions of poor people, that they are lazy or not willing to work. But the Old Testament distinguishes among four distinct groups of people who are poor, and it evaluates these groups differently. For three out of four of the groups, the announcement of God is mercy and love and kindness. For the fourth group, the announcement is condemnation.

The first group includes those who are poor as the result of catastrophe—the farmer whose crops have been wiped out by famine, a person whose possessions have been destroyed by a tornado or an earthquake, or a laborer with a dreadful disease that has left him incapacitated and incapable of engaging in productive labor. God is greatly concerned that these people be cared for, and significant and distinct provisions were given to the people of Israel in the law to make sure that these people were taken care of.

The second group includes those who are poor as a result of oppression—those who have been enslaved or have had their property taken from them by the powerful. We have a tendency to think that the powerful that are in view here are for the most part the businessmen, the wealthy, who are squeezing the life out of the poor laborers, but that was not the chief consideration. The principal people in view as oppressors were governments. Kings like Ahab, who confiscated Naboth's vineyard (1 Kings 21), and other kings who enslaved their people like Pharaoh, who get fabulously wealthy by squeezing all the wealth they can squeeze out of their subjects.

So, the principal violators of the poor in the Old Testament were those invested with governmental power, and that's as true today as it was then. We fail to recognize so often the ways in which government destines people for poverty. For instance, state governments collect billions of dollars every year in lottery tickets. And the vast majority of people who buy lottery tickets are the people who can least afford it, but the government knows that poor people will buy these tickets, knowing that they're hoping for the big payoff. It's sad to see people who have such little disposable income throw it away on a virtually hopeless dream of getting rich. That's how we keep people poor. God is concerned for people who are oppressed by the state, and His judgment falls on kings and governments that enslave their own people and keep them tied to welfare.

The third group includes those who are poor for righteousness' sake. Notice that Jesus says, **"Blessed are you poor,"** speaking to His disciples. He is talking directly to people who have voluntarily given up their quest for wealth in order to serve Christ. I've never met a missionary in my life who was motivated to go into mission work in order to become rich. There are people who willingly set aside the hopes of financial gain in order to be servants. Peter and John left their nets. Matthew left his tax-collecting table. They gave up everything to follow Jesus, and He called them blessed.

The fourth group is mentioned several times in the Bible. They are those who are poor as a result of slothfulness. They simply will not work. They despise the creation mandate to be fruitful and to labor. Paul speaks candidly on this point: "If anyone is not willing to work, let him not eat" (2 Thess. 3:10). That sounds harsh, but Paul was also aware of the other three categories. He says there is no dole for someone who is trying to live at the expense of his neighbor's labor. Today in the United States of America, we have people voting to have the government take from one group and give it to them without their working. That is sinful. You as a Christian must never ask the government to take from somebody else and give his possessions to you. That's evil. That's legal theft.

But woe unto us when we assume that anybody who's poor is poor because he's lazy, because that's just not true. There are people who are poor who are not lazy, and there are people who are poor because they're lazy, and we have to be able to distinguish between them if we're to be concerned with biblical ethics and biblical righteousness.

31

BLESSINGS AND CURSES

Luke 6:21–26

"Blessed are you who are hungry now, for you shall be satisfied.

"Blessed are you who weep now, for you shall laugh.

"Blessed are you when people hate you and when they exclude you and revile you and spurn your name as evil, on account of the Son of Man! Rejoice in that day, and leap for joy, for behold, your reward is great in heaven; for so their fathers did to the prophets.

"But woe to you who are rich, for you have received your consolation.

"Woe to you who are full now, for you shall be hungry.

"Woe to you who laugh now, for you shall mourn and weep.

"Woe to you, when all people speak well of you, for so their fathers did to the false prophets."

"Blessed are you who are hungry now, for you shall be satisfied" (v. 21). In Matthew's version, it's "Blessed are those who hunger and thirst for righteousness, for they shall be satisfied" (Matt. 5:6). Sometimes the New Testament writers use a technique called ellipsis, which means something is stated in brief but it leaves the implications unstated. That may be simply what Luke is doing here when he fails to spell out the kind of hunger and thirst that Jesus is speaking about.

We are people who have great ambitions and drive and goals, and we train diligently so we can be successful or so we can achieve a higher station in life. But who among us has the consummate goal of our lives to be righteous?

Jesus' priorities were different. He said, "But seek first the kingdom of God and his righteousness, and all these things will be added to you" (Matt. 6:33). The word translated "first" is the word *prōtos*, not first chronologically but first in importance. This is a challenge for us. We often seek with great passion everything but the kingdom of God, everything but righteousness. We need to have a passion for godliness.

Jesus said, "My food is to do the will of him who sent me" (John 4:34). He, of all men who ever lived, hungered and thirsted for righteousness, and He achieved it. We in the Western world have a hard time relating to the concepts of real hunger and thirst because few among us have ever experienced the depths of physical hunger. Few among us have ever been at the edge of starvation where a piece of bread would be the greatest joy that we can experience. But that's what Jesus was talking about. In the ancient Near East, they had real hunger, the kind of hunger that is experienced in Third World nations even today, and Jesus blesses such people.

The Values of the Kingdom

Jesus drew stark contrasts in this sermon—between hunger and satisfaction, grief and joy, poverty and wealth, being despised by human beings and being honored by them. There is another contrast that lies behind these, and it is the contrast between the present world and when the kingdom is fulfilled. We live in a topsy-turvy world, a world where the values of the kingdom of God have been turned upside down. We want everything that we can possibly have now. But Jesus is saying that this present world, this vale of tears, this place of want and poverty, is not the final chapter of world history. Jesus came to proclaim His kingdom that He was going to establish, and when that kingdom is consummated, there will be no more poverty. There will be no more hunger. There will be no more sin, no more grief, no more tears. But in the meantime: **"Blessed are you who are hungry now, for you shall be satisfied. Blessed are you who weep now, for you shall laugh"** (v. 21). The mourning and pain of this world are not the final chapter of the human experience.

"Blessed are you when people hate you" (v. 22). How's that for a life goal? Notice, He didn't stop there and say that anybody who is reviled and anybody who is cast out and anybody who is hated is going to be great in the kingdom of God. Many people are reviled because their behavior is repulsive or their character is despicable. No, He said, **"Blessed are you when people hate you and when**

they exclude you and revile you and spurn your name as evil, on account of the Son of Man!" If you're excluded, if you're hated or reviled because you are a Christian, then you come under the benediction of Christ and are called blessed.

"Rejoice in that day, and leap for joy, for behold, your reward is great in heaven; for so their fathers did to the prophets" (v. 23). He didn't just say, "Smile and be content." He said: "Rejoice! How great is it for you to be in that situation, for your reward is great in heaven." Some people say that heaven is going to be exactly the same for everybody who's there and that everybody's reward will be the same. But the New Testament tells us that there will be a graduation of rewards in heaven. Jesus said to work for those rewards. He promised great reward for those who are abased for His sake, **"for so their fathers did to the prophets."**

Oracles of Woe

Finally, in stark contrast to these benedictions, Jesus now moves to the flip side, to the oracles of woe, the pronouncement of divine judgment and the curse of almighty God. Some people have a hard time with this because they have a view of God as a cosmic bellhop who's there to do our bidding, who's incapable of wrath, incapable of judgment. Don't believe it. Our God is a consuming fire, and it's a fearful thing to fall into His hands. To experience the curse of God is the worst calamity that could ever befall a human being, and the only person who ever experienced it in its absolute fullness was Jesus on the cross.

But now comes the warning. **"But woe to you who are rich, for you have received your consolation"** (v. 24). Just as there are different kinds of poor people in the Bible, so it is with the rich. The Bible says scary things about the rich, but there is no absolute condemnation of being rich. The Bible does not say there is something inherently evil about being wealthy. Abraham was one of the wealthiest men in the world; Job was one of the wealthiest men in the world; Joseph of Arimathea was blessed of God with wealth. Yet, wealth carries a peculiar danger, and it is this: when somebody is really wealthy, it is easy for him to focus on the power of his wealth and on his independence, relatively speaking, and to think he can live without God. But there comes a day when we come into situations where all the money in the world is not enough to get us out, and that day that the Lord promises is coming is the day of judgment.

There's a myth, another myth associated with wealth, one that you hear all the time and in every political campaign. The idea is the only way a person can become wealthy is at the expense of somebody else. The rich get richer and the poor get poorer, and if a person is wealthy, that's proof—that's all the evidence you need to know—that they are corrupt, that they're selfish, that they're greedy.

This is not the case. Henry Ford became one of the wealthiest men of his era not by tromping on the backs of people but by making automobile transportation affordable to almost every family in the United States through mass production. His wealth brought a boon not simply to himself but to the whole nation.

Jesus was not saying that if you're wealthy, you're doomed. But He was saying how hard it is for a rich man to get into the kingdom of God. "It is easier for a camel to go through the eye of a needle than for a rich person to enter the kingdom of God" (18:25), because the rich man tends to put his trust in his riches rather than in the riches of Christ.

"Woe to you who are full now, for you shall be hungry" (v. 25). Again, He was not condemning having a good meal. What is in view is a philosophy called hedonism, which defines good in terms of pleasure and the avoidance of pain. The problem is that hedonism is subject to a paradox. If your foremost goal is to seek pleasure and you fail to achieve it, you will be frustrated. And if you achieve your goal, you will be bored. So if your life is defined strictly in terms of the pursuit of pleasure, you're doomed either to frustration or to boredom.

"Woe to you who laugh now, for you shall mourn and weep" (v. 25). Jesus was saying: "If you're full now, because that's all you're concerned about is your belly, the day is coming when you will starve. You can laugh now, but the hour is coming where you will mourn and you will weep." Woe to those who see life as a game, who are cynics, who make fun of the things of God. When you do that, you open yourself to the curse of God, and you have a date with the house of mourning.

"Woe to you, when all people speak well of you, for so their fathers did to the false prophets" (v. 26). Woe to you when everybody speaks well of you. Watch out for that person of whom everyone speaks well. The only way to have a reputation where everybody speaks well of you is to wear two faces and to be a man pleaser, to make sure that you please everybody around you. If you are a man pleaser, you cannot please God (Gal. 1:10). So if you're going to be a disciple of Christ, all men will not speak well of you, and in order to be a Christian, you must do as your Lord did: make yourself of no reputation.

False prophets were the most popular men in Israel. Jeremiah came and said that the judgment of God was coming. The false prophets said, "No, it isn't. Peace, peace!" and there was no peace. Likewise, the church that proclaims "God loves you unconditionally" will be full. It is easy to live in a place where God does not require anything—no repentance, no faith. But that is not biblical. The truth is that He loves His people in the Beloved. He loves His Son unconditionally, but everybody else has to put their trust in that Son to receive the ultimate blessing of God.

32

LOVE YOUR ENEMIES

Luke 6:27–36

"But I say to you who hear, Love your enemies, do good to those who hate you, bless those who curse you, pray for those who abuse you. To one who strikes you on the cheek, offer the other also, and from one who takes away your cloak do not withhold your tunic either. Give to everyone who begs from you, and from one who takes away your goods do not demand them back. And as you wish that others would do to you, do so to them.

"If you love those who love you, what benefit is that to you? For even sinners love those who love them. And if you do good to those who do good to you, what benefit is that to you? For even sinners do the same. And if you lend to those from whom you expect to receive, what credit is that to you? Even sinners lend to sinners, to get back the same amount. But love your enemies, and do good, and lend, expecting nothing in return, and your reward will be great, and you will be sons of the Most High, for he is kind to the ungrateful and the evil. Be merciful, even as your Father is merciful."

"**Love your enemies**" (v. 27). This is one of the most radical teachings that ever came to us from the lips of Jesus. Certainly, those who heard this mandate on this occasion were shocked by it, and certainly the scribes and the Pharisees were utterly hostile to it, but if we look at it from a different perspective, we will see that even in this teaching there was nothing new. When He gave His explanation—for example, of the Ten Commandments—His ideas seemed then to be shocking, but He told the people that the law that says "You shall not murder" (Deut. 5:17) carries with it the implication that you should not even be angry at a person without just cause. He taught not only that we should not commit the actual act of adultery but that the law against such things is violated when we even have lustful thoughts in our minds (Matt. 5:21–30). Jesus didn't add new content to the Ten Commandments; rather, He explained the full intent of the law of God as it was originally given.

He was doing the same thing here. For the great commandment given by God to His people in the Old Testament was this: "You shall love the Lord your God with all your heart and with all your soul and with all your strength and with all your mind, and your neighbor as yourself" (Luke 10:27). The Pharisees had a narrow interpretation of what was included in that great commandment, and they restricted their understanding of one's neighbor to fellow Jews. The mandate to love one's neighbor did not apply to Gentiles or foreigners who were outside the camp. Jesus is simply spelling out the full import of the Great Commandment.

I'll go even a step further and say that Jesus' exposition of the Great Commandment indicates that the Great Commandment was only an exposition of the original commandment that God gave to every creature when He stamped His image on every human being. That image carried with it the mandate to live in such a way as to mirror the character of God, so these mandates from Jesus are informed by how God relates to us. We, who are by nature the enemies of God, constantly receive from Him His beneficence and His benevolent love. Even though we are His enemies, He has loved us, and He has loved us when we were altogether unlovely; and when we were not thankful to Him, He was merciful to us; and when we sinned against Him, He never returned evil for evil. God's pattern of relating to His people is the same pattern that Jesus taught us to display as imitators of Him who is God incarnate.

Love Your Enemies

"But I say to you who hear, Love your enemies" (v. 27). What did He mean? He didn't mean that you have to have feelings of affection toward those who are your enemies. Here, as almost everywhere in the Scriptures, love is more a verb than a noun. We could translate it this way: "Be loving toward your enemies."

Jesus went on to spell out what that means. It has to do with how we behave toward those who are our enemies. Not everybody out there is our friend, so we as Christian people need to learn how to deal with those we can identify as our enemies. **"Do good to those who hate you"** (v. 27). That's what it means to love your enemy; you do good to those who hate you, you bless those who curse you. Now, what's our flesh going to do when somebody curses us? We want to curse them right back. If somebody wants to harm us, we don't want to do good to them.

"Bless those who curse you, pray for those who abuse you" (v. 28). If you want to put this into action, try this experiment for thirty days. If there's somebody you don't like, or someone you don't get along with, be it a coworker, your boss, or whoever, even if it's your biggest enemy, try praying for them. Try praying for them every single day for thirty days. Some amazing things may happen in your relationship with them or in their life, but you can be sure that things will happen in your own heart because you will be heeding Jesus' call to pray for those who curse you.

"To one who strikes you on the cheek, offer the other also, and from one who takes away your cloak do not withhold your tunic either" (v. 29). The action in view here was getting struck on the right cheek, and the only way to strike someone on the right cheek is to use the back of the hand. This was the classical way that Jewish people would insult somebody. So what Jesus was saying here is if somebody insults you by giving you the back of the hand, turn the other cheek. Let him insult you over and over, but do not return insult for insult. And if he wants your coat, give him your shirt as well. If somebody comes and asks you for help, help him.

"Give to everyone who begs from you, and from one who takes away your goods do not demand them back" (v. 30). The Bible does not deny the legitimacy of loaning money for interest. What the Bible denies is usury, the kind of interest that is so heavy and burdensome that it exploits the person in need. If you want to see what usury is, look at the interest rates on your credit cards. They are so ungodly, these rates of interest, that they are usurious and in direct violation of the law of God. But Jesus went beyond that: **"And as you wish that others would do to you, do so to them"** (v. 31). If somebody needs it, give it to him, even if it means you're not getting anything back. In other words, don't use the help of your brother for your own profit.

"If you love those who love you, what benefit is that to you? For even sinners love those who love them. And if you do good to those who do good to you, what benefit is that to you? For even sinners do the same. And if you lend to those from whom you expect to receive, what credit is that to you? Even sinners lend to sinners, to get back the same amount. But love your enemies, and do good, and lend, expecting nothing in return, and your reward will be great, and you will be sons of the Most High, for he is kind to the ungrateful and the evil. Be merciful, even as your Father is merciful" (vv. 32–36). If there is a core meaning to these exhortations, it's this: mercy, not vengeance. God is an avenging God. God promises to make unjust things just. God says, "Vengeance is mine, I will repay" (Rom. 12:19). But He reserves vengeance for Himself; we are not to show vengeance but are to imitate Him in His mercy.

Now again, when it comes to public matters, there's still a legitimate place for the role of the state and for the role of church courts and so on. But Jesus had Christian personal ethics in mind here. We as Christians should be known as people of mercy because we've been recipient of mercy, and as God has been kind to us, so we ought to be kind to our neighbors.

33

JUDGE NOT . . .

Luke 6:37–42

"Judge not, and you will not be judged; condemn not, and you will not be condemned; forgive, and you will be forgiven; give, and it will be given to you. Good measure, pressed down, shaken together, running over, will be put into your lap. For with the measure you use it will be measured back to you."

He also told them a parable: "Can a blind man lead a blind man? Will they not both fall into a pit? A disciple is not above his teacher, but everyone when he is fully trained will be like his teacher. Why do you see the speck that is in your brother's eye, but do not notice the log that is in your own eye? How can you say to your brother, 'Brother, let me take out the speck that is in your eye,' when you yourself do not see the log that is in your own eye? You hypocrite, first take the log out of your own eye, and then you will see clearly to take out the speck that is in your brother's eye."

"Judge not, and you will not be judged" (v. 37). This verse is probably the only verse that every pagan in America knows is in the Bible. They may not know what John 3:16 says, even if they see the reference in bold letters at sporting events. But they know this one, because anytime the church makes a comment about any practice that the church deems to be a sinful practice, the pagan is quick to quote the Scriptures by saying: "Oh, don't you judge! You're not supposed to judge us."

While this statement is so well known, it is the subject of great misunderstanding.

So what was Jesus saying when He uttered these words? First, let's look at what He was not saying. Our Lord was not saying that we are to do away with any discernment of the difference between good and evil. It requires a discerning mind to know the right thing to do.

God's Word calls us, from beginning to end, to be mature and knowledgeable in our discernment, that we might recognize evil when it appears, that we might flee from it, and that we might know what is the good and righteous thing to do. The judgment of discernment, the ethical evaluation, is not what was being prohibited here by our Lord Jesus. Rather, He was speaking of a different kind of judgment: the judgment of condemnation.

Jesus' prohibition takes the form of *casuistic law* rather than *apodictic law*. Apodictic law takes the form of an unconditional statement that applies universally, while casuistic law is a moral axiom that in general is a good thing to observe, but it is not a moral absolute. We find many examples of casuistic law in Proverbs; the aphorisms in that book tell us how things generally are or provide general principles that are good to observe. When it comes to judging others, Jesus could not possibly have meant to issue a universal prohibition. Why? Because there are times when we are to sit in judgment of our brothers and sisters. For example, in church discipline, a person is brought before the authorities in the church and tried and a judgment is issued, just as a person is brought to trial in a criminal case and judged by the jury or the judge and has a sentence passed on him if he is guilty.

The Judgment of Charity

Jesus was not doing away with civil courts or church courts when He said, **"Judge not, and you will not be judged."** Instead, our Lord was addressing a personality trait we find sometimes that involves being judgmental in one's spirit and hypercritical of other people. This has to do with how we pass judgment on other people. We make a distinction between different kinds of judgment: either harsh and severe judgment or what is often called the judgment of charity.

The judgment of charity is what we call the "best case" analysis. It involves giving the benefit of the doubt. We're not always sure whether a person is as guilty of a particular sin as it appears. Even in our law courts, we are very careful to weigh evidence and to make sure that, before anybody is convicted of a crime and is subjected to penalties, a particular standard of proof has been met. In civil cases, the standard of proof is "the preponderance of evidence," meaning that there is a better than 50 percent chance that the plaintiff's claim is true. But in the criminal courts, the standard is "beyond a reasonable doubt." Now, reasonable doubt is not the same thing as being beyond a shadow of a doubt.

If that were the standard, nobody would ever be convicted of a crime. Beyond a reasonable doubt means there is no plausible reason to believe otherwise. In both civil and criminal courts, the burden of proving the case is on the one who is making the charge, not on the defendant. That is true for a reason, lest in our hostility and our desire for vengeance we be guilty of judging beyond a sober and serious measure.

So our Lord told us here to be very, very careful that we are ready at any moment to give our neighbor the benefit of the doubt if there is doubt, to give the charitable judgment whenever possible. Sadly, the person to whom we most frequently give the charitable judgment is ourselves. We usually reserve best-case analysis for our own activity. We can spin our indiscretions and our sins in such a way as to make them appear virtuous, which is exactly one of the problems we face as fallen human beings.

What Jesus was saying here is not isolated from what He said just a few sentences earlier when He set forth the Golden Rule and told us to love our enemies. When He asked us to be quick with the judgment of charity and to flee a censorious spirit, He was filling out the principle of doing for others what we would have others do for us. If we want other people to give us the benefit of the doubt, then we must stand ready to give them the benefit of the doubt.

At the same time, the judgment of charity cannot be the judgment of naivete. Some people have such an exalted view of the basic goodness of human beings that they can't believe for a moment that anybody ever intends to do evil. This is clearly unbiblical, for the Bible tells us that "the heart is deceitful above all things, and desperately sick" (Jer. 17:9) and that we do evil, that the machinations of our sins can be so wicked and destructive that they bring harm to multitudes of people. We don't look at the world through rose-colored glasses and assume the good intent of everybody's behavior.

"Judge not, and you will not be judged; condemn not, and you will not be condemned; forgive, and you will be forgiven" (v. 37). What if you offend somebody and they apologize and ask you for forgiveness, and you say: "Oh no! Not now, not ever"? When we refuse to forgive those who repent of their sins, we expose ourselves to God's eternal justice rather than His mercy. I would hate to stand before God and ask Him to forgive me of my lifetime of sin and have Him look at me and say, "Don't you remember that day when somebody sinned against you and they repented and apologized and asked for your forgiveness, and you refused to give it, and now you want Me to forgive you?"

A Generous People

"Give, and it will be given to you. Good measure, pressed down, shaken together, running over, will be put into your lap. For with the measure you use it will be measured back to you" (v. 38). Isn't that wonderful? It's a description that comes from the ancient marketplace. In the Old Testament laws for the operation of Israel, God prohibited false weights and measures, because false weights and measures are an injustice. God holds people, nations, and businesses accountable for just weights and measures. In the ancient world, you would go to the marketplace and buy a bushel of grain or a bushel of corn, and there were ways to stack those ears of corn in the bushel. Now you can fill a bushel up with a lot of empty air in there, or you can shake that bushel and pack that corn or shake that grain and pack the grain until the bushel was filled to its utter capacity. **"Pressed down, shaken together, running over."** If you give like that, that's what you'll get back.

Jesus was talking about the practical applications of the Christian faith. He was saying, "My people are to be generous people." The Bible says, "God loves a cheerful giver" (2 Cor. 9:7). He doesn't love a stingy giver. In fact, stinginess is something that should never be part of our lives. Now, let me ask you this: How many times have people in your life called you generous? How many times have they called you stingy? Jesus said: "I want you to be generous. I want you to give in great measure, and the more you give, the more you'll get, because our God is a generous God and not a stingy God."

A Call to Walk Carefully

He also told them a parable: "Can a blind man lead a blind man? Will they not both fall into a pit?" (v. 39). Jesus was not talking simply about physical blindness here. He was talking about spiritual blindness. We need to be led by those with keen sight into the truth of God if we want to stay out of the ditch.

"A disciple is not above his teacher, but everyone when he is fully trained will be like his teacher" (v. 40). Who is our teacher? Jesus is the Master. Jesus is our Rabbi. We're His disciples. We're His students. We're not above our Master. But He wants us to be like our Master. He wants us to learn from our Master. He wants us to pursue and to seek the very mind of Jesus.

"Why do you see the speck that is in your brother's eye, but do not notice the log that is in your own eye?" (v. 41). A speck of dust in contrast to a wooden plank. We could draw a cartoon about this. We would see two people walking down the street, one man with a totally indiscernible speck of dust in his eye that would take a microscope to detect it, and he's nearing a man with a wooden plank sticking out of his eye. And the man with the wooden plank comes up to the brother with the speck and says: "Brother, you have a speck in your eye. You need to take it out." The other guy says, "How can you even see in my eye with that plank sticking out of your own eye?" Jesus said this is how foolish we are. We're so quick to see the imperfections in everybody else, but we're blind to our own myopia. We're blind to the log or the beam or the plank that's in our own eye.

"How can you say to your brother, 'Brother, let me take out the speck that is in your eye,' when you yourself do not see the log that is in your own eye? You hypocrite, first take the log out of your own eye, and then you will see clearly to take out the speck that is in your brother's eye" (v. 42). Jesus was not teaching us anything here more than to do unto others as we would have others do unto us. He was not teaching us any more than the Apostles taught us when they said that there is a love that covers a multitude of sins (1 Peter 4:8). Keep your handkerchief in your own pocket, and let your brother take the speck out of his own eye. This is the teaching of Jesus for His people.

34

GOOD AND BAD FRUIT

Luke 6:43–45

"For no good tree bears bad fruit, nor again does a bad tree bear good fruit, for each tree is known by its own fruit. For figs are not gathered from thornbushes, nor are grapes picked from a bramble bush. The good person out of the good treasure of his heart produces good, and the evil person out of his evil treasure produces evil, for out of the abundance of the heart his mouth speaks."

In the canons of the discipline of logic are many types of fallacies, both formal and informal, and one of the most common informal fallacies is called the either-or fallacy, or the fallacy of the false dilemma. That fallacy is committed when we try to reduce the possible options to only two, when in fact there could be a third option. However, there are situations where there really are only two alternatives. For instance, you're either alive or you're dead; there are no other options.

Jesus in this passage reduces the options to two when He talks about good trees and bad trees. Throughout the Scriptures, and particularly in the New Testament, we hear such distinctions between two things. For example, in the church, we find sheep and goats, which is to say we find people who are truly saved and people who are not (Matt. 25:31–46). There are only two options—you're either born of the Holy Spirit or you're still in the flesh. There is no middle ground. Of course, it's of eternal importance for everyone in the church to come to a clear understanding as to what their status is.

Good Fruit

Jesus set before us the following options about these matters: **"For no good tree bears bad fruit, nor again does a bad tree bear good fruit"** (v. 43). That is to say, if the tree is rotten to the core, that which will come from that tree will be rotten as well. So also, a bad tree does not produce good fruit. Jesus was saying that every good tree produces good fruit, and every bad tree produces only bad fruit. **"For each tree is known by its own fruit"** (v. 44).

The issue of fruit was one of the points of debate during the Protestant Reformation of the sixteenth century, and it was related to the issue of justification. Martin Luther made the declaration that the just shall live by faith and that to be justified in the presence of God occurs by faith and by faith alone, not by faith mixed with good works. In the Roman Catholic system, justification begins at baptism as a sacerdotal act administered by the priest whereby the grace of justification is infused into the soul, and when that soul assents to and cooperates with it, the person is then in a state of justification before God. That state of justification lasts until a person commits a mortal sin, which kills that justifying grace, so that the person loses his justification, though he still may retain his faith.

What is the remedy? According to Rome, the remedy was through another sacrament, the sacrament of penance, which Rome calls the "second plank" of justification for those who have made shipwreck of their souls. If someone commits a mortal sin, he goes to confession and receives absolution from the priest, but it doesn't stop there. In order for that person's justification to be restored, he must do works of satisfaction. Those works may be seemingly small and insignificant, such as saying so many "Our Fathers" or so many "Hail Marys," but they produce what Rome calls *congruous merit*, merit that is sufficiently meritorious that makes it fitting or congruous for God to restore that person to a state of justification.

That state remains until and unless that person commits another mortal sin, whereupon he has to go through the process again. If a person dies without mortal sin on his soul but still has venial sins remaining, he still does not enter the gates of heaven but must first go to purgatory, where those impurities are cleansed away. When he is fully and finally cleansed, which may be after one day or after a million years, then his soul is finally able to enter heaven.

Luther reacted strenuously against this system. He said the gospel promises that at the very moment you put your trust in Jesus Christ, all that He is and that He has becomes yours. Paul wrote, "Since we have been justified by faith, we have peace with God through our Lord Jesus Christ" (Rom. 5:1), just as Abraham was counted righteous the moment he believed God (Rom. 4). The good news for us is that even though we are sinners, we can still be justified in the sight of God by putting our faith in Him. At the moment we put our faith in Him, we receive a covering, the imputed righteousness of Jesus Christ. Just as the atoning blood covered the mercy seat in the Old Testament, so the righteousness of Jesus is transferred to our account the moment we put our faith in Him.

Any works we bring to the table count for nothing. The only righteousness that will count for us in the sight of God, Luther said, is a righteousness that is *extra nos*—outside of us. It is an alien righteousness. It is somebody else's righteousness; it is the righteousness of our Savior. The minute we put our trust in Him, He covers our filthy rags with His righteousness, and God pronounces us just in His sight. We come with nothing in our hands. No good deeds, no list of achievements. The only thing that will get us into the presence of God is the righteousness of Christ.

So, then, the questions in the sixteenth century, and the questions that persist today are, What about works? Doesn't Jesus call us to do good works? Isn't our Lord profoundly concerned about the fruit that we produce? If we're regenerate people, if we're justified people, will we not manifest that by the fruit that we bear?

In the 1980s, a major controversy broke out in the evangelical world called the Lordship Salvation controversy. There were those in one camp who said that you can be saved if you put your trust in Jesus as Savior. If you embrace Jesus as Savior and don't receive Him as your Lord, you can still be saved. That is, since justification is by faith and by faith alone, you can have a faith that is alone. You can have a faith that never brings forth fruit, a faith that never produces good works, and still be justified. Part of that was a result of the very wide dissemination of a distorted view of salvation that was associated with the concept of the carnal Christian. The idea is that we can receive Jesus as Savior and be saved and yet remain altogether carnal, showing no fruit whatsoever.

That's not the biblical doctrine. Luther said justification is by faith alone, but not by a faith that is alone. That is, the only kind of faith that saves you is a legitimate faith, a living faith, not a mere dead profession of faith. If you have faith, even though the works that you produce out of that faith don't count toward your justification, nevertheless they are necessary manifestations of that true faith. That is, if you don't have works, it means you don't have faith, and if you don't have faith, you don't have justification. All you have is a profession of faith, and all that qualifies you to be is a goat in the church, a bad tree that brings forth only bad fruit.

Out of the Heart the Mouth Speaks

"For figs are not gathered from thornbushes" (v. 44). If you want to go gather figs, you go to a fig tree. You don't go to a thornbush. And you know, not all fig trees are good fig trees. There is the account where Jesus cursed a fig tree, and the Bible tells us that when He did it, it wasn't even the season for figs (Mark 11:12–14). So if there's ever an event in the Bible where it seems that we see an arbitrary judgment of God in Christ, it was when Jesus cursed the fig tree.

The Holy Land has many, many varieties of figs. The vast majority of those fig trees bear fruit in a particular season. There is such a thing as fig season, but not all fig trees bear figs then. A few varieties of fig trees bear their figs outside of fig season. And when they do, they're regarded as a delicacy. On this occasion, Jesus saw a fig tree from a distance and it was in leaf. And the sure sign in Palestine of the presence of figs is the presence of leaves. So our Lord said, "Here's one of these fig trees with this unusual variety of figs." He walked over, and there were leaves and no figs. The tree was a hypocrite. The tree gave the outward signs of fruit, but it had no fruit. Jesus used that as a prophetic object lesson to describe not fig trees but people who give the appearance of fruit but have no fruit.

"Nor are grapes picked from a bramble bush" (v. 44). Again, if you want to plan a vineyard and raise a choice crop of grapes, you don't start with bramble bushes. You need vines that will produce grapes.

"The good person out of the good treasure of his heart produces good, and the evil person out of his evil treasure produces evil, for out of the abundance of the heart his mouth speaks" (v. 45). It's interesting that the Greek word here for "treasure" is the word *thēsauros*, from which we get the English word *thesaurus*. A thesaurus is a collection of the treasury that is ours in human language, and Jesus uses this same term for the storehouse of the heart. And that thesaurus is either a storehouse of goodness or a storehouse of corruption. And the Old Testament tells us, "As he thinketh in his heart, so is he" (Prov. 23:7, KJV). Jesus is telling us what a man treasures in his heart determines what he is.

35

BUILD ON THE ROCK

Luke 6:46–49

"Why do you call me 'Lord, Lord,' and not do what I tell you? Everyone who comes to me and hears my words and does them, I will show you what he is like: he is like a man building a house, who dug deep and laid the foundation on the rock. And when a flood arose, the stream broke against that house and could not shake it, because it had been well built. But the one who hears and does not do them is like a man who built a house on the ground without a foundation. When the stream broke against it, immediately it fell, and the ruin of that house was great."

In the conclusion to Luke's Sermon on the Plain, Jesus asked, **"Why do you call me 'Lord, Lord,' and not do what I tell you?"** (v. 46). We are still focusing on this problem of making a profession of faith in Christ that is not a true one. To appreciate the full impact of these words, let's look at the fuller version of this passage in Matthew's Sermon on the Mount: "Not everyone who says to me, 'Lord, Lord,' will enter the kingdom of heaven, but the one who does the will of my Father who is in heaven. On that day many will say to me, 'Lord, Lord, did we not prophesy in your name, and cast out demons in your name, and do many mighty works in your name?' And then will I declare to them, 'I never knew you; depart from me, you workers of lawlessness'" (Matt. 7:21–23).

The repetition of a name in the Bible usually signifies intimacy, as with "Abraham, Abraham" (Gen. 22:11); "Moses, Moses" (Ex. 3:4); "Martha, Martha"

(Luke 10:41); and "Saul, Saul" (Acts 9:4). So these people who Jesus said would call Him "Lord, Lord" were not going to be simply claiming a passing acquaintance with Jesus; they were going to be saying: "I have a deep, personal affection for You. I know You, Jesus, intimately. I've taken You as my Savior." Jesus will say to those on that occasion: "Excuse me, I don't believe I know you. You say you went to church, you were a pastor, you were a missionary, you were a member of the session or the deacons, you were a tither. But I don't know you. Please leave. Depart from Me, you workers of lawlessness."

This is one of the scariest passages in the New Testament. Jesus was talking about church members here. He was talking about people who've made a public profession of faith in Him. Jesus said it's going to happen that these people will honor Him with their lips, while their hearts are far from Him (Matt. 15:8). Jesus later said to His disciples, "If you love me, you will keep my commandments" (John 14:15). The test for the fruit is obedience. Anyone can say that they love Jesus, but the proof is in obedience.

So Luke put it in question form: **"Why do you call me 'Lord, Lord,' and not do what I tell you?"** (v. 46). When you say "Lord," you're saying: "You're my authority. I submit to Your kingship. I acknowledge that You are sovereign over me and that whatever You command me, I am under obligation to do." So Jesus says, "Well, why do you say that I'm your Lord when you don't do what I tell you to do?"

The Difference between Hearing and Obeying

He followed up that question with this brief parable about the builders. He says, **"Everyone who comes to me and hears my words and does them, I will show you what he is like"** (v. 47). In the Greek language, there is a distinction between the verb "to hear," *akouō*, and the verb "to obey," *hypakouō*, which we might say is "hyper-hearing." The difference between hearing and obeying is the difference between hearing and really hearing. The one who really hears Jesus will obey Him. And that person **"is like a man building a house, who dug deep and laid the foundation on the rock. And when a flood arose, the stream broke against that house and could not shake it, because it had been well built"** (v. 48).

The land of Israel is substantially desert, and throughout the region are innumerable wadis. A wadi is a dry gulch, an empty creek bed that is only filled with water under extraordinary circumstances of rainfall. Israel has two rainy seasons, the former rains and the latter rains. For most of the year, there is little to no rainfall. But when the rains come, and when it rains hard, all the rain drains into the wadis and gathers there. The streams become like mini tsunamis, where the water comes rushing down the wadi. The power of that water coming down the wadi is something you don't want to get caught in.

The one who hears the words of Jesus and obeys is like a man who builds a house and takes care, as he builds this elegant structure, to dig deeply. He goes down to the level of rock, and then when he hits the rock, he builds his foundation. And then on top of that solid foundation, the house is built. If you build a house like that, it can withstand all the torrential rushing water when it comes and vehemently beats against the house.

"But the one who hears and does not do them is like a man who built a house on the ground without a foundation. When the stream broke against it, immediately it fell, and the ruin of that house was great" (v. 49). You see the contrast. The second house may be palatial, but it's built on sand. It has no firm foundation, and it looks beautiful for a season until the floodwaters come. When the stream beats vehemently against that house, it does not merely creak and groan; it collapses. It has no strength to withstand negative forces against it, and it crumbles. And Jesus said, **"The ruin of that house was great."**

The Church's Foundation

We frequently hear the idea that Jesus is the foundation of the church. "The church's one foundation," we sing, "is Jesus Christ our Lord." That's not exactly the way that the Scriptures describe the church building. Rather, we're told that "no one can lay a foundation other than that which is laid, which is Jesus Christ" (1 Cor. 3:11). The general image of Jesus is not that He's the foundation but that the foundation is laid in Him and that He is the chief cornerstone: "The stone that the builders rejected has become the cornerstone" (Luke 20:17).

What, then, is the foundation of the church? According to the Scriptures, the church is "built on the foundation of the apostles and prophets, Christ Jesus himself being the cornerstone" (Eph. 2:20). In the book of Acts, we get a glimpse of life in the primitive Christian church after Pentecost in Jerusalem: "And they devoted themselves to the apostles' teaching and the fellowship, to the breaking of bread and the prayers" (Acts 2:42). The people of God gathered together on Sunday, and they steadfastly continued in the Apostles' doctrine. That means that at the heart of the gathering of the early church on the Lord's Day was a devout attending to the preaching of the Word of God. The study of Apostolic doctrine is the study of the Word of God, because where you find the Apostolic doctrine is in sacred Scripture.

Now, if the Apostles and the prophets are the foundation of the church, we find that foundation in sacred Scripture. At the end of the New Testament, in the book of Revelation, we read of the new Jerusalem that comes down from heaven (Rev. 21). She had a great and high wall with twelve gates and twelve angels at the gates and names written on them. And then in verse 14, we are told that the city had twelve foundations, and on them were the names of the twelve Apostles of the Lamb. In the city of God, the foundation is built on the Apostles.

That's why the early church came together to devote themselves to the study of the doctrines of the Apostles. If we're going to live as faithful Christians, we have to be rooted and grounded in the Apostolic Word. To be grounded in the Word of God is to dig the foundation of your life down to bedrock, where you take that Word, you embrace that Word, and you are able to stand against anything the world, the flesh, and the devil throw at you. But if you don't have that foundation, that foundation in the Apostolic Word, then you're building your house on sand. And when the storm comes, what you'll experience is ruin.

We all must ask ourselves what we're building our lives on. We might say that we are of course building our lives on Christ. And we might have the fruit of our obedience to demonstrate the truth of our profession. You see how this follows after what Jesus was saying in the previous passage. We are known by our fruits, not by our verbal professions. Again, what we do will not get us into the kingdom of God—only trust in Christ can get us there. But the test of whether our trust is real, the test of whether our faith is sincere, the test of whether our justification is authentic, is our fruit, our obedience.

We live in a country where still more than four out of five people say they believe in God. Yet, practically speaking, we live as if there is no God. If you found out today that there is no God, how would your life change? Are you one of those people who hypothetically affirms the existence of God and the lordship of Jesus Christ, but for all practical purposes you live as if there were no God? That's how a lawless person lives. There's no fear of God in such a person. He doesn't care what comes out of his mouth. He doesn't care if he keeps his promises, because his house is built on sand. But if you build your house on the Word of God and you build your house on Jesus Christ, the everlasting Rock, even a tsunami cannot ruin your life.

36

THE CENTURION'S SERVANT

Luke 7:1–10

After he had finished all his sayings in the hearing of the people, he entered Capernaum. Now a centurion had a servant who was sick and at the point of death, who was highly valued by him. When the centurion heard about Jesus, he sent to him elders of the Jews, asking him to come and heal his servant. And when they came to Jesus, they pleaded with him earnestly, saying, "He is worthy to have you do this for him, for he loves our nation, and he is the one who built us our synagogue." And Jesus went with them. When he was not far from the house, the centurion sent friends, saying to him, "Lord, do not trouble yourself, for I am not worthy to have you come under my roof. Therefore I did not presume to come to you. But say the word, and let my servant be healed. For I too am a man set under authority, with soldiers under me: and I say to one, 'Go,' and he goes; and to another, 'Come,' and he comes; and to my servant, 'Do this,' and he does it." When Jesus heard these things, he marveled at him, and turning to the crowd that followed him, said, "I tell you, not even in Israel have I found such faith." And when those who had been sent returned to the house, they found the servant well.

**ow a centurion had a servant who was sick and at the point of death, who was highly valued by him** (v. 2). I like this fellow, this centurion who sent elders of the Jews to Christ, pleading that Jesus

would come and heal his servant who was sick to the point of death. He was a man of some status in the nation of Rome, being a commander of a hundred or more troops. And he was loved by the Jews, as we read here, because he had been very generous. He was obviously a man of wealth and had spent his money to build a synagogue for the Jewish people there in Capernaum. The Jews came to Jesus and asked Him to help this man because **"he is worthy"** (v. 4).

When the centurion heard about Jesus, he sent to him elders of the Jews, asking him to come and heal his servant (v. 3). Please note the remarkable concern and care that this powerful and wealthy man had for a slave, for a servant who had no social standing in the community. Yet this man was so exercised about the well-being of his slave that he sent the message to Jesus pleading for Jesus to come and heal his servant.

Back in the days when I ministered in western Pennsylvania, I was involved in an organization called "The Value of the Person" that ministered in the arena of labor and management relationships. One of the things we were concerned about was how employees were treated by management. A problem that the management of any organization faces, inevitably, is the necessity from time to time to terminate employees, and that's never a happy occasion. Sometimes, employees must be terminated because of immorality or illegal activities. Sometimes, they need to be terminated simply because they are not able to meet the responsibilities they have in a competent manner. Many times, terminations come because of economic downturns that require that the organization trim its staff, and so people are laid off not for any fault of their own.

But there is one type of termination that is often missed and yet is very important, one that I learned about by working closely with people in the arena of labor and management. In every organization, inevitably there will be managers who are kind, considerate, and upright to their bosses but are cruel and uncaring to their subordinates. I urged people in management in various organizations to make sure that if they have managers in those positions who are tyrannizing their subordinates, they must be removed. When the wolf comes into the sheepfold, it is the duty of the shepherd to protect the sheep.

This centurion was not such an employer. This man cared deeply about those who were under his command, all the way down to the slave who was working for him in his house. And to demonstrate and manifest that concern, he sent a message to Jesus asking for Jesus' help. **And Jesus went with them. When he was not far from the house, the centurion sent friends, saying to him, "Lord, do not trouble yourself, for I am not worthy to have you come under my roof"** (v. 6). This is the second thing I love about this centurion. Everybody else was telling Jesus, **"He is worthy to have you do this for him,**

for he loves our nation, and he is the one who built us our synagogue" (vv. 4–5). "You've got to go and help this man," they were saying. "You've got to heal his servant because here's a man who deserves Your help. He is eminently worthy. He's been kind to us as Jews. In fact, he's even built for us a synagogue, and we don't expect that from Roman centurions. So, Jesus, however busy or tired You may be, please make an exception and come and help this man."

But the centurion sends a completely different message. As much as he wants Jesus' help, he says to Him through the messengers: "You don't have to come to my house. I'm not worthy that You would come under my roof. Maybe these excited Jewish friends of mine have exaggerated my worth, but I'm not asking You to come because I deserve it or because I'm worthy." This man understood grace. He understood it in a way that very few people in Israel understood it—and in a manner that very few people understand it even in the church today.

The One with Authority

"Therefore I did not presume to come to you. But say the word, and let my servant be healed" (v. 7). We read at the end of the story that the servant was healed, and obviously all Jesus had to do to heal him was to say the word. There are two things I want to consider about that. How is it possible for Jesus to heal somebody simply by word? We're talking about the One who is God incarnate, the One who had the authority over heaven and earth, and the centurion recognized that. He said, **"For I too am a man set under authority, with soldiers under me: and I say to one, 'Go,' and he goes; and to another, 'Come,' and he comes; and to my servant, 'Do this,' and he does it"** (v. 8). In other words, "I understand, Christ, that You have authority. You have authority over life. You have authority over death. You don't have to be here. Just say the word."

There is a stark difference between this attitude and the attitude of Mary and Martha when their brother Lazarus died (John 11). Jesus came four days too late to keep Lazarus from dying, and they were distressed. They said, "Lord, if you had been here, my brother would not have died" (v. 21). They didn't understand. Jesus didn't have to be there to save Lazarus. He could have done it from a distance. And when He did come, how did He raise Lazarus from the dead? He stood before the tomb, and He opened His mouth and uttered a command, saying, "Lazarus, come out" (v. 43). And the one who had been dead for four days began to breathe, his heart began to beat, brain waves were rushing through his head, and he emerged from his tomb alive and well by the power of the word of Christ.

When I was in college, I started out as a history major and then changed to a

Bible major. In my sophomore year, I was required to take a social science, and I elected to take a course in philosophy, which I soon regretted immensely. The professor was dry as dust. He lectured the first day on David Hume. I didn't know what he was talking about, and from there he went on to Immanuel Kant and all these philosophers. I was bored, so I sat in the back row of the classroom. And then shortly into the term, the professor gave a lecture on Augustine and on Augustine's concept of the creation of the universe, and I started to listen. I put down my notebook. I heard him tell how Augustine said that the Lord God Almighty created the whole universe *ex nihilo*, out of nothing. He didn't just shape and form some preexistent matter. Out of nothing, He created the entire universe. "How did He do it?" the professor asked. Through what he called the "divine fiat." *Fiat* is the imperative form of the verb "to be." He said God called the universe into being by the power of His voice, giving a divine imperative, saying, "Let there be light," and the lights came on.

I couldn't believe it. It was like I had a second conversion, a conversion to God the Father, to His transcendent majesty and power. I left the classroom that day, went downstairs to the registrar's office, and changed my major to philosophy, because my eyes were opened to the power of God, who could create the whole world by the sound of His voice. That's all it took for Jesus, who was God incarnate, to heal this centurion's servant. He didn't have to be there. He just had to say the word, and by His word, the man was healed.

The Mystery of the Incarnation

When we look at Christ and the mystery of the incarnation, we see the perfect union of the divine and the human. In the mystery of the incarnation, we understand that when God took upon Himself a human nature, the divine nature didn't stop being divine, and the human nature was truly human. There was not a composite being that was a deified humanity or a humanized deity. Two distinct natures, divine and human. Notice that when Jewish elders went to Jesus, they said, "Please, come here." Throughout the New Testament, we see Jesus moving from place to place. We read at the beginning of the text that **after he had finished all his sayings in the hearing of the people, he entered Capernaum** (v. 1).

The Bible here is discussing what Jesus did according to His human nature, because according to His divine nature, He was already in Capernaum. When Jesus went to Capernaum, He made the journey according to His human nature. He had to travel the distance between those two points. But when Jesus, according to His humanity, was on His way to Capernaum, He was already there according to His divine nature. In the incarnation, the divine nature retained its attributes, one of which was omnipresence or ubiquity. When we understand the incarnation, when the divine nature united with the human nature, the divine nature was not contained within the human nature. This is expressed in a grand theological principle: *Finitum non capax infinitum*—"the finite cannot contain the infinite."

Even in the incarnation, Jesus' divine nature still retained its attribute of omnipresence, while His human nature remained confined to one location. This is why we can say that according to His human nature, Jesus is no longer present with us. As He told His disciples, He was going away, and He would come again. According to His human nature, He's in heaven at the right hand of God. Yet according to His divine nature, Christ is never absent from us. And wherever the divine nature is, Jesus the person is. However, because of the close and inseparable union between the natures of Christ, when we commune with the divine nature, we commune with the whole Christ. Jesus' human nature is in heaven, the human nature is still united to the divine nature, and when Christ is present here with us, He is really and truly present in His personhood. His person is really and truly everywhere, and this One who healed the centurion's servant by His word heals us through the power of His word.

37

THE WIDOW'S SON

Luke 7:11–17

Soon afterward he went to a town called Nain, and his disciples and a great crowd went with him. As he drew near to the gate of the town, behold, a man who had died was being carried out, the only son of his mother, and she was a widow, and a considerable crowd from the town was with her. And when the Lord saw her, he had compassion on her and said to her, "Do not weep." Then he came up and touched the bier, and the bearers stood still. And he said, "Young man, I say to you, arise." And the dead man sat up and began to speak, and Jesus gave him to his mother. Fear seized them all, and they glorified God, saying, "A great prophet has arisen among us!" and "God has visited his people!" And this report about him spread through the whole of Judea and all the surrounding country.

Each of the writers of Gospels in the New Testament had to be selective. They had to choose from a large list of episodes from the life of Jesus. John told us that if all the things that Jesus did had been reported in the Apostolic works, there would not be a book big enough to contain them all (John 21:25). Sometimes we wonder, "Why did Luke (or Mark or Matthew or John) select this episode or that episode?" When we come to this text, we don't have to think very long about why this episode is included in Sacred Writ. If this were the only passage that survived from the life of Jesus, there is enough in it to reveal to us His sweetness, His excellency, His person, His power, and His saviorhood. We can live the rest of our lives trusting just this much information about the Lord Jesus Christ.

Luke begins by telling us when it happens. He said that it happened **soon afterward** (v. 11). Soon after what? Soon after he healed the centurion's servant (Luke 7:1–10). But here, what we have is not somebody who is sick unto death but rather somebody who had already died and the burial process was under way.

There was always a burial procession because, by law, Jewish people had to be buried outside the city. They didn't have hearses or police escorts. There was a procession, where the person who had died was carried not in a coffin as we have today but in an open bier. That was a couch-like structure that was heavier and bigger and more substantial than a stretcher or a litter. The corpse was placed on this bier, and people carried it to the burial plot. This was usually done within twenty-four hours after death occurred.

The Lord Jesus came upon this funeral procession, and presumably without any invitation, He interjected Himself into this solemn ceremony. We're told that Jesus had just left Capernaum, and He was followed by **his disciples and a great crowd** (v. 11).

As he drew near to the gate of the town, behold, a man who had died was being carried out, the only son of his mother, and she was a widow, and a considerable crowd from the town was with her (v. 12). What do we know about the people involved? We know that the woman whose son had died was a widow. She had already buried her husband. That was significant to a woman in ancient Israel. The Bible places great priority on the need for the Christian community to give care to widows and orphans because, in many cases, the only support that a widow could expect to gain in the ancient world was from her children, her sons. This woman had only one son, and now he had died. She was in an extremely precarious position.

Jesus Has Compassion

And when the Lord saw her, he had compassion on her and said to her, "Do not weep" (v. 13). This is the first time in Luke's Gospel that he calls Jesus *kyrios*, "Lord." This title translates the Old Testament title *Adonai*, meaning "my sovereign One," "the One who rules over all things with all authority and all power." The title that was reserved for God is now given to the Son of God, who is God incarnate.

The first thing Luke tells us is that **the Lord saw her**. He saw her in her grief, in the depths of her sorrow, in the midst of her mourning. This woman did not escape the notice of the Son of God. I find that extremely comforting for anyone who goes to the house of mourning, that the Lord Jesus Christ sees us when we weep, when we suffer, and when we die just as He saw this pitiable woman from the city of Nain. Luke tells us that when He saw her, **he had compassion on her**. Is there anyone whose compassion we need more than the compassion of the Son of God, who was like us in every respect except sin, who understands our feelings? As He saw that woman, He saw her heartbreak. Surely, she was on the brink of despair. He could see her tears flowing down her cheeks, and He was not unfeeling. He felt it in His own soul.

You can't read the next portion without understanding that when He saw her, immediately **he had compassion on her**, and then He spoke. Remember the first words He said to this lady: **"Do not weep."** She perhaps thought: "Who is this man who tells me not to weep? Of course I'm weeping. My heart is broken." Don't you wish you could've been there and heard the tone of voice that Jesus used when He said to her, **"Do not weep"**? I think there was a hint in the very sound of His voice that He was not rebuking her for a public spectacle of grief, nor was He asking her to be stoic in her grief. There must have been something tender, comforting, something that gave a hint of power over grief and over mourning when Jesus said to her, **"Do not weep."**

Jesus Raises the Boy to Life

Then he came up and touched the bier, and the bearers stood still. And he said, "Young man, I say to you, arise" (v. 14). Touching the open bier meant risking becoming impure, because it was forbidden for Jews in the ancient world to touch the dead. But Jesus had authority over death, and He touched this open coffin. **The bearers stood still.** They stood there as amazed and stunned as the woman was. When Jesus spoke again, it wasn't to the pallbearers and it wasn't to the mother. This time, the Lord spoke to the young man who was dead. And He said, **"Young man, I say to you, arise."**

Three times in the New Testament, we see our Lord raising people from the dead: Jairus' daughter (Luke 8), Lazarus (John 11), and here the widow of Nain's son. When Jesus raised people from the dead, all that He needed was the same power He displayed the day before in healing the centurion's servant. It took from Him only a word from His mouth: "Young man, I'm talking to you. I know you're dead. Get up! Arise!" **And the dead man sat up and began to speak, and Jesus gave him to his mother** (v. 15).

This is the One who said, "I am the resurrection and the life. Whoever believes in me, though he die, yet shall he live, and everyone who lives and believes in me shall never die" (John 11:25–26). On the last day, in the twinkle of an eye, He is going to say to all who were dead in Christ, "Arise!" and we will join Him in the power and the glory of His resurrection, and children will be presented to parents, husbands to wives, parents to children in the great resurrection.

Fear seized them all, and they glorified God, saying, "A great prophet has arisen among us!" and "God has visited his people!" (v. 16). This was the normal response of the crowds when Jesus performed a miracle. They were terrified and yet they glorified God. Why? Because they knew they had just witnessed something that only God could do. So they glorified God and they said, **"A great prophet has arisen among us!"** Oh, indeed, it was a great prophet and more than a great prophet.

They go on to say, **"God has visited his people!"** In Luke 1, we saw the concept of the visitation of God. The idea behind the divine visitation is wrapped up in the Greek verb *episkopeō* and its noun form, *episkopos*, from which we get the words *episcopal* and *episcopalian*. The episcopalian form of church government is based on rule by bishops, and it is so named because a bishop is an *episkopos*, or "overseer."

The incarnation was like the Old Testament act of redemption where God heard the cries of His people when they were in bondage in Egypt, and He issued the command, "Let my people go" (Ex. 5:1). Now the Lord God omnipotent visits His people in the person of His Son. The Apostle Peter calls Jesus "the Shepherd and Overseer [i.e., Bishop] of your souls" (1 Peter 2:25). It's one thing to have a pastor, but when the Bishop comes—and it's not just the bishop of the local diocese; it's the Bishop from heaven—that is a momentous event. This is the great Shepherd of the sheep, the Good Shepherd who calls us His sheep and who cares for us as a good shepherd cares for his lambs and who watches over us as the Bishop of heaven. The people understood that the spectacle that had unfolded during this funeral procession was a divine visitation, an intrusion from the transcendental realm, a visit of God Himself into the midst of His people.

Do you see why I say if these were the only verses we had in the whole New Testament, they would be enough to cause us to dance all the rest of our days, even into our graves? Because the Bishop who saw the widow of Nain also sees us and is moved by compassion. But He doesn't just feel sorry for us; He acts for us, bringing life out of death, joy out of sorrow.

38

JOHN THE BAPTIST

Luke 7:18–35

The disciples of John reported all these things to him. And John, calling two of his disciples to him, sent them to the Lord, saying, "Are you the one who is to come, or shall we look for another?" And when the men had come to him, they said, "John the Baptist has sent us to you, saying, 'Are you the one who is to come, or shall we look for another?' " In that hour he healed many people of diseases and plagues and evil spirits, and on many who were blind he bestowed sight. And he answered them, "Go and tell John what you have seen and heard: the blind receive their sight, the lame walk, lepers are cleansed, and the deaf hear, the dead are raised up, the poor have good news preached to them. And blessed is the one who is not offended by me."

When John's messengers had gone, Jesus began to speak to the crowds concerning John: "What did you go out into the wilderness to see? A reed shaken by the wind? What then did you go out to see? A man dressed in soft clothing? Behold, those who are dressed in splendid clothing and live in luxury are in kings' courts. What then did you go out to see? A prophet? Yes, I tell you, and more than a prophet. This is he of whom it is written,

" 'Behold, I send my messenger before your face,
who will prepare your way before you.'

I tell you, among those born of women none is greater than John. Yet the one who is least in the kingdom of God is greater than he." (When all the people heard this, and the tax collectors too, they declared God just, having been baptized with the baptism of John, but the Pharisees and the lawyers rejected the purpose of God for themselves, not having been baptized by him.)

"To what then shall I compare the people of this generation, and what are they like? They are like children sitting in the marketplace and calling to one another,

" 'We played the flute for you, and you did not dance;
we sang a dirge, and you did not weep.'

For John the Baptist has come eating no bread and drinking no wine, and you say, 'He has a demon.' The Son of Man has come eating and drinking, and you say, 'Look at him! A glutton and a drunkard, a friend of tax collectors and sinners!' Yet wisdom is justified by all her children."

As a result of His astonishing act of raising someone from the dead, the reputation of Jesus swelled throughout the land. One of the places where that report had been carried was a dungeon five miles from the Dead Sea, where John the Baptist had been incarcerated for daring to publicly critique the morality of the king. John was languishing in prison at the same time the popularity of Jesus was on the rise among the populace. Obviously, John was confused. He was hearing all the great things that Jesus had done, and while Jesus was doing these great things, John was in prison, and he was wondering about this.

There are commentators who assume that the reason John the Baptist sent messengers to Jesus with the question **"Are you the one who is to come, or shall we look for another?"** (v. 19) was not that John's confidence regarding Jesus was shaken. They believe John was a prophet, and he was having his disciples ask Jesus this question for their sakes, to confirm their faith, for John was going to transfer the allegiance of his disciples to Jesus. I think that's a stretch. We have to go with what the text itself says. It's John who asked the question, and the reply that Jesus gives is not simply for the benefit of John's disciples, for Jesus said, **"Go and tell John . . ."** (v. 22). So Jesus was obviously receiving this question as though it came from John, and He gave the response to John.

Why should it be a strange thing for John to have doubts? He had gone on public record proclaiming Jesus as the One who was to come, the Lamb of God who would take away their sins, the One who would be greater than John the Baptist (Luke 3; see John 1:19–34; 3:22–30). He was the one who baptized Jesus in the River Jordan. John had made his public proclamation of the person of Jesus, and whatever his personal expectations were of Jesus, they were as yet not fulfilled.

Is it impossible for a prophet of God to go through a dark night of the soul, a time of doubt? Consider the prophets of the Old Testament such as Jeremiah, who was ready to give up his office when he had had enough of the derision heaped upon him by the people: "The word of the LORD has become for me a reproach and derision all day long. If I say, 'I will not mention him, or speak any more in his name,' there is in my heart as it were a burning fire shut up in my bones, and I am weary with holding it in, and I cannot" (Jer. 20:8–9). Or Elijah, who cried out, "I, even I only, am left, and they seek my life, to take it away" (1 Kings 19:10). Or consider Jonah, who boarded a ship to escape the responsibilities of the word of prophecy that God had given him. We could go on citing examples of the real humanity of the prophets of God in the Old Testament who, just like everybody else, had moments of doubt and confusion in times of distress and in times of trouble.

John had to be wondering as he languished in this horrible dungeon: "Where is Jesus? Did I make a mistake? Did I proclaim the wrong one to be the Lamb of God?" Finally, he sent two of his disciples to Jesus to ask Him, **"Are you the one who is to come, or shall we look for another?"**

The One Way to God

Before we look at Jesus' response to this, a word of application. Do you know how many millions of people today are not convinced that Jesus was the One? The whole Jewish nation is still waiting for the Messiah, having rejected Jesus and being convinced that He was not the One who was to come. Every Muslim on this planet believes that Jesus was not the One who was to come, and there are others who are looking for a hero who can fulfill the role of the rescuer, the deliverer, the savior. They are not satisfied with Jesus.

Then there are millions of people who believe that Jesus was one of the ones who was to come but is by no means the only one. They will acknowledge that Jesus is one way to God but will shrink in horror at the suggestion that He's the only way to God. I can't think of any profession more repugnant to a secular culture than the profession that there's only one way to God and that one way is Jesus.

The Word of God says, "There is one mediator between God and men" (1 Tim. 2:5). There's only One who has given an atonement. If we think that God is stingy and lacking in grace by restricting it to one way, we need to ask ourselves: "Why is there any way? What have we done that would merit God's being moved to provide any way of salvation?" But in His glorious grace, He has given to us the *monogenēs*, the only begotten of the Father.

If you're not willing to stand for that, it may very well be that you're an unregenerate person. It is here where your loyalty to Christ comes to the test. Are you going to please men and bow to political correctness in a pluralistic and relativistic culture? Or are you convinced that Jesus Christ is God's only Son, the only One to provide an atonement for our sins, the One whom God raised for our justification, the One whom God has appointed as Judge of the whole world? Jesus will judge—not Muhammad, not Confucius, not the Buddha. Muhammad is dead. Confucius is dead. The Buddha is dead. Only Jesus has been raised and elevated to the right hand of God the Father, where He sits right now as the King of kings and the Lord of lords.

Jesus Answers John

And he answered them, "Go and tell John what you have seen and heard: the blind receive their sight, the lame walk, lepers are cleansed, and the deaf hear, the dead are raised up, the poor have good news preached to them. And blessed is the one who is not offended by me" (vv. 22–23). Jesus is not angry at John the Baptist's question. He's patient, and he points out some of the miracles He had performed. The thing that would have created such a marvel in the land was to see people who've been blind from their birth having their eyes opened so they could see, the lame leaping for joy, the deaf hearing, the dead raised.

Why does Jesus include that **"the poor have good news preached to them"**? This was part of the agenda set in the book of Isaiah for the Lord's Anointed, the Messiah: "The Spirit of the Lord God is upon me, because the Lord has anointed me to bring good news to the poor" (Isa. 61:1). Jesus points to Isaiah 61 as providing the answer to John's question. Nobody else was fulfilling the prophetic description of the Messiah.

Jesus added, **"And blessed is the one who is not offended by me"** (v. 23). That's a very important beatitude. Why is it that professing Christians are so reluctant to say Jesus is the only way? We know how the world thinks about that. We know they can't stand to hear that, that it is utterly offensive to them. So what do we do? We want to flee from the offense, and we want to say to them: "Well, Christianity is right for me, but whatever you believe is fine for you. You pray to your god and I'll pray to mine." Jesus pronounces a benediction on the believer who is not offended by Him.

The Greatest Old Testament Prophet

When the messengers leave, Jesus gives a commentary about John. It is basically a hymn of praise for John the Baptist. Jesus said to the multitudes concerning John, to those people who went to the Jordan River and thronged along the riverbanks that they might be baptized by John: **"What did you go out into the wilderness to see? A reed shaken by the wind? What then did you go out to see? A man dressed in soft clothing?"** (vv. 24–25). The chief caricature of the pastor today is that of a wimp, where there is no manliness, no strength, only weakness and hypocrisy. This is not the image of John the Baptist. He lived in the wilderness and survived on locusts and wild honey. He was the toughest man in Israel at the time.

"What then did you go out to see? A prophet? Yes, I tell you, and more than a prophet" (v. 26). Of course they went out to see a prophet. That was the attraction after four hundred years of silence from God. Since Malachi, no prophet had arisen in Israel, and then from the traditional meeting place between God and His people, a new prophet came proclaiming the kingdom of God and calling people to repent and be baptized.

"This is he of whom it is written, 'Behold, I send my messenger before your face, who will prepare your way before you'" (v. 27). The Old Testament prophets not only prophesied about the coming Messiah, but they also prophesied about the prophet who would be the herald of the Messiah. So John himself is not just a prophet; he's the subject of prophecy and the object of prophecy. He was himself prophesied by the Old Testament prophets. Jesus, citing Malachi 3:1, said he's a prophet; but he's more than a prophet. He's *the* prophet, the herald of the Messiah, the one who would usher in the messianic era.

Then Jesus gives this astonishing comment: **"I tell you, among those born of women none is greater than John"** (v. 28). Who was the greatest prophet in the Old Testament? Was it Jeremiah or Isaiah or Ezekiel or Daniel or Amos or Moses? No, the greatest prophet of the Old Testament was John the Baptist. You may think, "John the Baptist was in the New Testament, not the Old Testament," but though we read about him in the New Testament, it was still the period of the Old Testament. The New Testament hadn't yet started. In terms of redemptive history, John the Baptist belonged to the old covenant. And Jesus said there was none greater than he.

After giving such wonderful praise to John the Baptist, Jesus goes on to say, **"Yet the one who is least in the kingdom of God is greater than he"** (v. 28). To put this in perspective, let's assume for the sake of illustration that we are least in the kingdom of God. Yet we can take some comfort in knowing that despite our "leastness" in the kingdom of God, we're still greater than John the Baptist. This seems strange at first glance, because we know that John the Baptist in some respects is far greater than we are in terms of his importance to the scope of redemptive history. If we are thinking of greatness in terms of status, do we think in heaven, when God gives out the rewards for faithfulness and obedience, that our reward will be greater than that of John the Baptist? Of course not. I'm sure that my reward in heaven won't look anything like the reward that will be given to John the Baptist for his martyrdom and his fidelity and his convictions and confession of Christ Jesus.

What then does it mean to say that the least in the kingdom of heaven is greater than John the Baptist? We have to consider the meaning of greatness in this context. There's a clue to this in the book of Genesis when Noah gave his patriarchal blessing to his three sons. He said, "Blessed be Shem, enlarged be Japheth, and cursed be Canaan the son of Ham" (see Gen. 9:24–27). So one was blessed, one was cursed, and the middle son, Japheth, was enlarged, in the sense made greater. The context of that language from the Old Testament had to do not only with the size of the tribes that would come out of Japheth but also with the degree of blessedness that Japheth and his sons and daughters would experience. The greatest level of blessedness was given to Shem and to his sons and daughters. But then the second-greatest level of blessedness would go to the descendants of Japheth. The quantitative terms of large and small, of great and small, are defined in terms of blessedness.

What I believe Jesus is saying in this problematic statement about John the Baptist is that even though there is none born of women greater than John the Baptist, nevertheless he who is least in the kingdom of God is in a greater state of blessedness than even John the Baptist enjoyed. John the Baptist was the last of the Old Testament prophets, and he was the prophet selected to be the herald of the coming Messiah, to introduce Jesus as the One who would be crowned the King, as the One who would bring in the new covenant. But John was still on the outside looking in. Anyone who is born after the cross, after the resurrection, and particularly after the ascension of Christ, is living in a better situation in terms of redemptive-historical salvation than all the saints in the Old Testament.

The Apostle Peter refers to "the things that have now been announced to you through those who preached the good news to you by the Holy Spirit sent from heaven, things into which angels long to look" (1 Peter 1:12). The covenant that we are in, we are told, is a better covenant. The situation that we are in is a better situation, and it all has to do with the kingdom of God.

There are those in the Christian church who have been profoundly influenced by theology that teaches that the kingdom of God is something that is totally in the future. But the New Testament makes it clear that while the kingdom of God will be consummated in the future, it has truly been inaugurated already in the past. Jesus' coming was to begin the kingdom of God. John the Baptist preached, "Repent, for the kingdom of heaven is at hand" (Matt. 3:2), and Jesus said, "If it is by the finger of God that I cast out demons, then the kingdom of

God has come upon you" (Luke 11:20). In a very real sense, the kingdom is here. So our situation historically, in terms of redemptive history, is far greater than anything John experienced even though he was an eyewitness of Jesus and actually baptized Him.

(When all the people heard this, and the tax collectors too, they declared God just, having been baptized with the baptism of John, but the Pharisees and the lawyers rejected the purpose of God for themselves, not having been baptized by him) (vv. 29–30). John the Baptist came as a prophet, and he called the people to repent because the kingdom of God was at hand. But it was the religious establishment that refused.

Wisdom Justified by Her Children

"To what then shall I compare the people of this generation, and what are they like? They are like children sitting in the marketplace and calling to one another, 'We played the flute for you, and you did not dance; we sang a dirge, and you did not weep'" (vv. 31–32). What does this mean? This was what children did when the marketplace was empty and they had some space to play. They would create games. Kids are great at inventing games. But sometimes they don't agree, and they fuss among themselves as to what they should play. Jesus said, in effect, this is how the people were. They were like kids who play the flute, saying, "We're going to have a happy time of dancing." And some of the others say: "We're not dancing. We don't want to play the flute game." "OK, let's play funeral." So they played the funeral dirge, but others refused to join in, saying: "No! No! We're not going to play funeral. We're not going to mourn." This is the way children behave. That's what this generation of adults was like. They were childish.

"For John the Baptist has come eating no bread and drinking no wine, and you say, 'He has a demon.' The Son of Man has come eating and drinking, and you say, 'Look at him! A glutton and a drunkard, a friend of tax collectors and sinners!'" (vv. 33–34). John the Baptist came in his asceticism, and they rejected him. Jesus came at a time of feasting, not a time of mourning, and He ate with the people. He was accused of being a drunkard, a glutton, and a friend of tax collectors and sinners. They rejected John the Baptist because he was too austere. They rejected Jesus because He was too happy and pleasant.

"Yet wisdom is justified by all her children" (v. 35). This is a very important statement. Jesus made a figurative use and application of the word that is translated "justify" or "justification" in the New Testament. This plays a critical role in the whole history of the Reformation. The Reformation was fought over the battle of justification. How are we justified in the sense of reconciled to God?

God is just; we're unjust. He is holy; we're not. Paul labors the point that the only way we can be justified is not by our deeds or our works, because they're always tarnished. And he says, "By works of the law no human being will be justified in his sight" (Rom. 3:20). So we have to be justified by faith and by faith alone, which means the only way we can be justified before God is by putting our trust and our faith in Christ and in His works, in His righteousness.

Then along comes James, who writes in his epistle: "What good is it, my brothers, if someone says he has faith but does not have works? Can that faith save him?" (2:14). James answers that question by saying that dead faith never justifies anybody. At the end of that chapter, he goes on to say, "Was not Abraham our father justified by works when he offered up his son Isaac on the altar?" (v. 21). So we have Paul saying we're justified by faith, and James saying we're justified by works. How do we resolve this?

They're clearly not talking about the same kind of justification. When Paul talks about justification in Romans, he is talking about how we are made justified in the sight of God. James asks, "Was not Abraham our father justified by works when he offered up his son Isaac on the altar?" (James 2:21). Justified before whom? Did God have to wait to see whether Abraham was going to give Isaac on the altar before He knew whether Abraham's faith was genuine? Of course not. According to Paul, Abraham was justified in Genesis 15, but according to James, it was not until Genesis 22. James is saying that someone's claim to have faith is justified—that is, it is shown to be a true claim—before other people when he manifests or shows or demonstrates the reality of that faith by his works. James uses the term "justified" in the sense of manifesting or demonstrating something in exactly the same way Jesus uses it here in this text when He says, **"Wisdom is justified by all her children"** (v. 35).

Jesus is not saying that wisdom is brought into a reconciled relationship with a just and holy God by having children. He's saying that wisdom is shown to be wisdom by its fruits, by the results that are manifested. We don't know whether a decision we make is a wise course of action. We will only know for sure when we see the results. The wisdom of John the Baptist and the wisdom of Jesus Christ was made plain and manifest by the power of God, showing the whole world that these men were the men of God.

39

THE FORGIVEN WOMAN

Luke 7:36–50

One of the Pharisees asked him to eat with him, and he went into the Pharisee's house and reclined at table. And behold, a woman of the city, who was a sinner, when she learned that he was reclining at table in the Pharisee's house, brought an alabaster flask of ointment, and standing behind him at his feet, weeping, she began to wet his feet with her tears and wiped them with the hair of her head and kissed his feet and anointed them with the ointment. Now when the Pharisee who had invited him saw this, he said to himself, "If this man were a prophet, he would have known who and what sort of woman this is who is touching him, for she is a sinner." And Jesus answering said to him, "Simon, I have something to say to you." And he answered, "Say it, Teacher."

"A certain moneylender had two debtors. One owed five hundred denarii, and the other fifty. When they could not pay, he cancelled the debt of both. Now which of them will love him more?" Simon answered, "The one, I suppose, for whom he cancelled the larger debt." And he said to him, "You have judged rightly." Then turning toward the woman he said to Simon, "Do you see this woman? I entered your house; you gave me no water for my feet, but she has wet my feet with her tears and wiped them with her hair. You gave me no kiss, but from the time I came in she has not ceased to kiss my feet. You did not anoint my head with oil, but she has anointed my feet with ointment. Therefore I tell you, her sins, which are many, are forgiven—for she loved much. But he who is forgiven little, loves little." And he said to her, "Your sins are forgiven." Then those who were at table with him began to say among themselves, "Who is this, who even forgives sins?" And he said to the woman, "Your faith has saved you; go in peace."

Earlier we heard Jesus speak of the hypocrisy of those who criticized John the Baptist for one thing and Jesus for just the opposite. It seemed that no matter what a prophet of God did, the Pharisees were inclined to reject him and to condemn him. That episode is followed by an invitation that comes from one of the Pharisees whose name was **Simon** (v. 40). We're not sure who this Simon was, except that he was **one of the Pharisees** (v. 36). Since the Pharisees were so hostile toward Jesus, why would one of them invite Jesus to his house for dinner?

The Bible doesn't tell us, but it may be because he wanted to probe Jesus to test His reputation of being a prophet. He may have wanted to discover something about Him, or perhaps he wanted to trap Jesus into condemning Himself. In any case, Simon the Pharisee asked Jesus to a banquet, and our Lord acquiesced.

One of the Pharisees asked him to eat with him, and he went into the Pharisee's house and reclined at table (v. 36). **Reclined at table** meant He reclined on a couch because that's the way they ate in the banquets of that day—on couches where people leaned on their left elbow and kept their right hand free to eat the food that was presented to them.

A Sinful Woman

And behold, a woman of the city, who was a sinner, when she learned that he was reclining at table in the Pharisee's house, brought an alabaster flask of ointment (v. 37). The text doesn't say she's a prostitute. History and tradition assume that she was one because she was given the designation of **sinner**. Though there are many other sins besides that one, at the same time, that was the euphemism for *prostitute* that was frequently used in antiquity. Whatever her sin was, it was considered egregious, and it was one for which she was notorious. She was not a rank-and-file, run-of-the-mill, commonplace sinner. She was a serious sinner, possibly a professional sinner.

We know she wasn't invited to the banquet because a Pharisee would not invite a notorious, sinful woman to his house. The Pharisees embraced the idea of salvation by segregation—that is, by keeping themselves at a safe distance from sinners—because to come into any kind of contact with them would be to pollute themselves and their own holiness. This was one of the common complaints they made about Jesus: that He was a wine bibber, that He was a glutton, and that He associated with tax collectors and other kinds of sinners. We can only suspect then that when this woman heard about the party, what interested her was not the banquet itself but that Jesus was going to be there.

We don't know how she got in the house. We can assume she was well dressed. She was carrying an **alabaster flask of ointment**. Perhaps the gatekeeper saw this attractive woman coming, bearing a gift, and assumed she was invited. The Bible doesn't tell us how she got in the house, but it does say that she got in somehow.

The Woman Honors Jesus

Standing behind him at his feet, weeping, she began to wet his feet with her tears and wiped them with the hair of her head and kissed his feet and anointed them with the ointment (v. 38). This woman came in and cried so many tears that they fell down and wet the feet of Jesus enough that she dried His feet with her hair. Perhaps she was embarrassed, but she saw that her tears were soaking the feet of Jesus. Her intent when she came was not to dishonor Him, so she leaned over and, taking the strands of her hair, tenderly wiped away her tears from our Lord's feet. Can you imagine the shock that rippled through the house?

But she wasn't finished. When she dried His feet, she **kissed his feet**. She didn't come in and kiss Him on the cheek or on the forehead. She humbled herself to kiss His feet. And then she **anointed them with the ointment**.

When the Pharisee who had invited Jesus saw this, he spoke to himself. He didn't speak to Jesus. He didn't speak to the woman. He didn't speak to his friends. This was a soliloquy in his mind. He spoke silently to his own conscience, saying, **"If this man were a prophet, he would have known who and what sort of woman this is who is touching him, for she is a sinner"** (v. 39). Jesus knew what he was saying to himself and said to him, **"Simon, I have something to say to you"** (v. 40).

What Jesus had to say to this Pharisee was a parable, none more simple in the teachings of Jesus. He said: **"A certain moneylender had two debtors. One owed five hundred denarii, and the other fifty"** (v. 41). A denarius was the unit of pay for a day's wages. So the debtor who owed fifty denarii owed fifty days' worth of wages. The other man owed five hundred denarii, which would be obviously about two years' worth of his income. That's a lot of indebtedness for a common person in Israel to be carrying. Jesus went on to say, **"When they could not pay, he cancelled the debt of both"** (v. 42). He freely forgave the debt. There weren't any strings attached to this mercy. He simply canceled the debt, no repayment. There was nothing they could do to merit it. The man who was owed the money said that they didn't have to pay.

Then Jesus asked Simon the Pharisee, **"Now which of them will love him more?"** (v. 42). I love the answer that Simon the Pharisee gives: **"The one, I suppose, for whom he cancelled the larger debt"** (v. 43). Isn't it obvious that the one who had been forgiven ten times more than the other was ten times more thankful, ten times more loving? But as hard as it was to admit, Simon at least allowed it as a supposition that one of them would love more than the other. So Jesus said to him, **"You have judged rightly"** (v. 43). This was one of the few times this Pharisee made a judgment that was right.

Forgiven Much

Then turning toward the woman he said to Simon, "Do you see this woman? I entered your house; you gave me no water for my feet, but she has wet my feet with her tears and wiped them with her hair" (v. 44). Customarily, there was not only a basin for foot washing but also a towel to dry them. Simon didn't give any water for Jesus to wash His feet, which was a common courtesy. No water, no towel. This woman supplied the water and the towel. **"You gave me no kiss, but from the time I came in she has not ceased to kiss my feet"** (v. 45). When Jesus came in, Simon didn't kiss Him, even though it was the custom in the ancient Near East to kiss friends, even men, on the cheek. But the woman went so far as to kiss His feet. **"You did not anoint my head with oil, but she has anointed my feet with ointment. Therefore I tell you, her sins, which are many, are forgiven—for she loved much. But he who is forgiven little, loves little"** (vv. 46–47).

All who came to Simon the Pharisee's house that evening came for a party. But this woman came to go to church. She came because Jesus was there, and she came to worship Him, to adore Him, to praise Him, to thank Him, to honor Him, to glorify Him, and to serve Him. When we gather for worship, are our tears flowing out of our shame and out of our gratitude? Do we come to give extravagant praise and thanksgiving to Jesus? This was not a token offering of praise and thanksgiving. This was an extravagant act of worship coming from a woman who had experienced extravagant grace for the forgiveness of her sins.

Finally, Jesus turned His attention to her. **And he said to her, "Your sins are forgiven"** (v. 48). There are two kinds of people in the world: people whose sins have been forgiven and those whose sins have not been forgiven. There are two kinds of people in this world: those who repent of their sins and those who remain steadfast in their impenitence. There are two kinds of people in this world: those who heap lavish praise and adoration on Jesus and those who refuse to submit to Him. It's very simple.

There is nothing greater than hearing the Lord Jesus Christ say, **"Your sins are forgiven."** I know on September 13, 1957, in my heart I heard the Lord Jesus say that to me, and that was the defining moment of my life, because there is no greater gift that the Lord God can give any of us than to cancel our debt, to erase the ledger, and to forgive us for every sin that we've ever committed. The more we understand that, the greater the love we have for Him, because He who is forgiven much loves much.

40

THE PARABLE OF THE SOWER

Luke 8:1–15

Soon afterward he went on through cities and villages, proclaiming and bringing the good news of the kingdom of God. And the twelve were with him, and also some women who had been healed of evil spirits and infirmities: Mary, called Magdalene, from whom seven demons had gone out, and Joanna, the wife of Chuza, Herod's household manager, and Susanna, and many others, who provided for them out of their means.

And when a great crowd was gathering and people from town after town came to him, he said in a parable, "A sower went out to sow his seed. And as he sowed, some fell along the path and was trampled underfoot, and the birds of the air devoured it. And some fell on the rock, and as it grew up, it withered away, because it had no moisture. And some fell among thorns, and the thorns grew up with it and choked it. And some fell into good soil and grew and yielded a hundredfold." As he said these things, he called out, "He who has ears to hear, let him hear."

And when his disciples asked him what this parable meant, he said, "To you it has been given to know the secrets of the kingdom of God, but for others they are in parables, so that 'seeing they may not see, and hearing they may not understand.' Now the parable is this: The seed is the word of God. The ones along the path are those who have heard; then the devil comes and takes away the word from their hearts, so that they may not believe and be saved. And the ones on the rock are those who, when they hear the word, receive it with joy. But these have no root; they believe for a while, and in time of testing fall away. And as for what fell among the thorns, they are those who

> hear, but as they go on their way they are choked by the cares and riches and pleasures of life, and their fruit does not mature. As for that in the good soil, they are those who, hearing the word, hold it fast in an honest and good heart, and bear fruit with patience."

Before Luke records for us Jesus' teaching of the parable of the sower, he gives us a brief historical note by saying, **Soon afterward he went on through cities and villages, proclaiming and bringing the good news of the kingdom of God. And the twelve were with him** (v. 1). Luke then tells us that also with Him were **some women who had been healed of evil spirits and infirmities** (v. 2).

Mary, called Magdalene, was one of them, **from whom seven demons had gone out** (v. 2). This poor woman has suffered from the characterization of having been a harlot. There's not a scintilla of evidence anywhere in Scripture that she was ever a harlot, and she is an outstanding example of fidelity to the Lord Jesus Christ. It was to this woman that Jesus first revealed Himself on resurrection morning.

And Joanna, the wife of Chuza, Herod's household manager, and Susanna, and many others, who provided for them out of their means (v. 3). One commentator says that this was the women's aid society that supported Jesus during His earthly ministry. Luke's Gospel is noted as giving more attention to women than any of the other Gospels. No, the women were not numbered among the Apostles, but they did have a significant role in the entourage of Jesus during His earthly ministry. Here their nobility, their sacrifice, and their fidelity are noted by Luke.

The Four Soils

And when a great crowd was gathering and people from town after town came to him, he said in a parable, "A sower went out to sow his seed" (vv. 4–5). Here is a story taken from the agricultural methodology of Jesus' day. At this time, seed was not sown in the fields in the way it normally is in our country. Rather, when it came time for planting, the sower would have a large bag slung over his shoulder, and it was filled with the seed that he was going to plant. Unlike farmers today, he would not plow the field first and then sow the seed, but rather, he would go through the field sowing the seed, and the little wind currents would carry the seed where it would—sometimes into the middle of the field, sometimes into the path alongside or in the middle, or on those sections of the field under which there were hidden outcroppings of limestone. Wherever the currents carried the seed, there the seed landed. When he was done sowing the seed, then he would take his plow, and he would plow the seed into the earth and wait for the rain to come to have the seed be germinated.

"And as he sowed, some fell along the path and was trampled underfoot, and the birds of the air devoured it. And some fell on the rock, and as it grew up, it withered away, because it had no moisture. And some fell among thorns, and the thorns grew up with it and choked it" (vv. 5–7). In every season, each time seed was sown by a farmer, certain things took place. Some of the seed that was cast about would fall along the path that was beaten down, that was hardpan, and it had no possibility of penetrating into the earth. And the seed that was cast in that manner never germinated and never bore fruit but was plucked by the birds of the air and seemed to be wasted. Some of the seed that fell upon the rock had nowhere to go under the ground, and when the plow came through, it couldn't break up the rock, and so the seed rested just barely below the surface on the stone but had no possibility of taking root. Some of the seed fell along the sides of the field, where other things were already growing, thorns and brambles, and the seed would fall in the middle of that and it could take root. There was earth there, but when it took root and began to grow alongside the thorns and the brambles, the seed was choked out and died without coming to fruition.

"And some fell into good soil and grew and yielded a hundredfold" (v. 8). Then Jesus explained that in the parable, there was seed that fell on good earth. Not earth that was hardpan, not earth that was stone, or that was covered with thorns and brambles, but fine soil with the nutrients needed for germination and growth right there. And this seed took root and it grew and produced a hundredfold, a wonderful crop. **As he said these things, he called out, "He who has ears to hear, let him hear"** (v. 8). This was a call to understand what Jesus was saying.

At that point, the disciples weren't sure whether they understood the point of the parable. So they asked Jesus, "What does this parable mean?" Jesus answered the question and explained the meaning of the parable. But before He did, He said something that is often disturbing to people as they read this text of sacred Scripture. He said, **"To you it has been given to know the secrets of the kingdom of God, but for others they are in parables, so that 'seeing they may not see, and hearing they may not understand'"** (v. 10). Jesus' answer is a quote from Isaiah 6:9.

We normally assume that the point of a parable is to clarify some difficult aspect of Jesus' teaching. But actually, the parables had a dual purpose. For those who had ears to hear, the parables were given to reveal the hidden things of the kingdom of God. But at the same time that the parables were given to some people to explain, elucidate, and clarify the teaching of Jesus, Jesus spoke in parables to others to hide from them the truth of the gospel. Why would He do that? Parables were given not only to reveal but also to conceal. To those whom God had given ears to hear, it was revelation. But for those whose hearts were hardened, who did not have ears to hear, whose necks were stiff and who didn't want to hear the Word of God, who had a basic antipathy and hostility to the things of God, the parables were a form of divine judgment. It's as though God were saying to these people, "You don't want to hear Me? Then I won't let you hear Me."

God's justice is poetic. He gives people over to their sins. If their hearts are hardened by their own sin, He says: "Let that hardened heart be even more hardened. Let that stiff neck be even more stiff. If that's what you want, that's what you'll get." This is a perfectly just judgment of God with respect to people who do not want to have God in their thinking.

Jesus said this parable was given to reveal things about the kingdom to the disciples, so He now explains it for them. **"Now the parable is this: The seed is the word of God"** (v. 11). That's the first thing we have to understand about this story. It's about seed being cast into the wind and onto the earth and into thorns and brambles. It is not simply an exercise in agriculture. It is about the preaching of the Word of God. The seed represents God's Holy Word.

"The ones along the path are those who have heard; then the devil comes and takes away the word from their hearts, so that they may not believe and be saved" (v. 12). The Holy Word is preached, and those by the wayside hear, but the devil comes like the birds of the air and takes that Word from their hearts, lest they should believe and be saved. There are people reading this now, I'm sure, who are reading this parable just as Jesus gave it, and it is falling on ears that can understand it intellectually, but it doesn't pierce the soul. It doesn't penetrate the heart. Such a heart is still in the possession of the enemy, and he wants to do everything in his power to keep that Word from entering into the soul. Though the Word is heard outwardly, it isn't heard inwardly.

"And the ones on the rock are those who, when they hear the word, receive it with joy. But these have no root; they believe for a while, and in time of testing fall away" (v. 13). Some look at this parable and think that what it teaches is that people can be saved and lose their salvation. They can be in a state of grace and be justified, but it doesn't last. That flies in the face of everything else the Bible teaches us about the perseverance of the saints. The Bible tells us that those whom the Lord redeems, He preserves. He gives to them the seal and the guarantee of the Holy Spirit. And we are told, "He who began a good work in you will bring it to completion at the day of Jesus Christ" (Phil. 1:6). And John writes: "They went out from us, but they were not of us; for if they had been of us, they would have continued with us. But they went out, that it might become plain that they all are not of us" (1 John 2:19).

Salvation Is of the Lord

John goes to great lengths to teach us that God the Father has given the Son a people. And those whom the Father gives to the Son come to the Son, and nothing can snatch them out of His hand (John 10:1–18, 28–29). I don't believe for a second that a true believer ever loses his salvation. He may have periods of backsliding or he may be engaged in a serious and radical fall from grace, but never a full and final fall. We say it this way: "If you have it, you never lose it. If you lose it, you never had it." That's the paradox in this situation.

In our fallen condition, while we're spiritually dead, we can still perceive something of the benefits of the gospel. The gospel is good news. As creatures made in the image of God, though our consciences have been seared by sin, we still, even in our natural condition, have an ability to feel guilt. For some people, that's all they feel. They're guilty, and they know they're guilty. The euphemisms and rationalizations that we as human beings do to assuage our guilt don't work. When somebody preaches the gospel of grace and forgiveness of their sins, they jump at it. There's an emotional response. But as the parable indicates, it is superficial. It is a response only on the surface, a momentary emotional response, not one that comes from the depths of the soul.

It's like seed that falls on that tiny little bit of earth under which there's stone, and it takes root for a short time, and it springs up, but the roots don't go deep enough to sustain life. As soon as the sun comes up, it is scorched, and it withers and dies, bringing no fruit whatsoever. That describes false conversions, which is one of the deadliest dangers that we deal with in the church. We're justified not by a profession of faith but only by a possession of genuine faith. Anybody can say they believe. Anybody can have their hearts tingling for a moment, but real conversion turns the life upside down.

The question is not, When and where were you converted? That's not the point. The question is, Are you converted? Not that you answered an altar call, not that you raised your hand, not that you prayed the sinner's prayer, not that you signed a card. Are you converted? Does the Holy Spirit dwell in your heart? Has your life been changed by the regenerating grace of God the Holy Spirit? The only test for that is whether you bear fruit.

"And as for what fell among the thorns, they are those who hear, but as they go on their way they are choked by the cares and riches and pleasures of life, and their fruit does not mature" (v. 14). Like the seed that fell on the stone, these at least take root. Maybe their profession lasts a little longer than those who fell upon the stones. But these that fell upon the thorns never leave the thorns and are choked by the thorns. Were these converted people who fell away? I don't think so. Their conversion experience was spurious. It was not the real thing. That's why it's so important that we hear this parable lest we go through life blithely and blindly assuming that we are in a state of grace when we're far from the kingdom of God. That's why we need to search our hearts to make our calling and our election sure, lest we be deceived.

"As for that in the good soil, they are those who, hearing the word, hold it fast in an honest and good heart, and bear fruit with patience" (v. 15). It is not that only good people respond to the gospel. That's not the point that Jesus is making. No, the good soil is the soil that has been changed by God the Holy Spirit. It is the good soil, where the seed takes root because God the Holy Spirit has prepared it, tilled it, and made it fertile, which is something we cannot do for ourselves. But those whose hearts have been changed by the Holy Spirit, when they hear the Word, they love the Word. They embrace the Word and obey it. They bring forth the fruit of conversion, the fruit of real salvation in abundance, a hundredfold.

I think that's the point of this very interesting but difficult parable. It's the reason why many commentators don't even call it "the parable of the sower." They call it "the parable of the soil," because it's the soil that determines whether the fruit comes forth and whether the seed germinates—the soil that has been prepared by the Holy Ghost. He who has ears to hear, let him hear.

41

THE PARABLE OF THE LAMP

Luke 8:16–21

"No one after lighting a lamp covers it with a jar or puts it under a bed, but puts it on a stand, so that those who enter may see the light. For nothing is hidden that will not be made manifest, nor is anything secret that will not be known and come to light. Take care then how you hear, for to the one who has, more will be given, and from the one who has not, even what he thinks that he has will be taken away."

Then his mother and his brothers came to him, but they could not reach him because of the crowd. And he was told, "Your mother and your brothers are standing outside, desiring to see you." But he answered them, "My mother and my brothers are those who hear the word of God and do it."

To further amplify the point that our Lord was making in the parable of the sower, He gives this smaller parable of the lamp. Jesus says, **"No one after lighting a lamp covers it with a jar or puts it under a bed, but puts it on a stand, so that those who enter may see the light"** (v. 16). Lamps in ancient Israel were simple pieces of pottery, like a saucer that has the front of it pinched together. In that saucer was oil, and in the front of the lamp where it's pinched together, a wick was inserted that basically floated on the oil. And the wick was then ignited.

I don't know how much light is created by such a lamp as this, but I doubt it would intimidate Thomas Edison. It's not the kind of thing that we use to bring light into the darkness of our homes at night. It had very little power of illumination. As little as it is, Jesus said: "Do you think that anyone, once they've put the flame to the wick in such a lamp, will take the lamp and put something over it or put it under the bed? If a person wants to have any usefulness from such a lamp, he would put it on a stand where it is elevated, where the maximum amount of light would be given to the darkness of the room."

The point that Jesus was making is simple. He was saying that the light that comes from the Word of God is truth, truth that must never be hidden. We're not to take the Word of God, as we understand it and it takes root in our hearts, and put it under a cover or hide it under the bed. Rather, we are to put it in a place of prominence where it can be made manifest and where it can be seen clearly by all who are present.

The Day of Judgment

"For nothing is hidden that will not be made manifest, nor is anything secret that will not be known and come to light" (v. 17). Here, Jesus is referring to the day of judgment, which will be the day of great epiphany. It will be the day when all of truth will be made clear and be revealed. This has two sides to it, a positive side and a negative side. The positive side is this: our Lord is saying that on that day, the Word of God will be manifested clearly and finally as the truth. On the day of judgment, every mouth will be stopped and no one will be able to gainsay the truth claims of Christ. That Christ is the Son of God, that Christ is our Savior, will be so clear and so plain that everybody who repudiates that claim, everybody who rejects that truth, will be put to utter shame.

So, in the first instance, the good news is that in that grand epiphany, the truth will be demonstrated to be the truth once and for all, and every lie and every falsehood will be destroyed. But the downside of it is that the secrets of men's hearts, the things that we do in darkness, the things that we seek to hide from the world, will all come into open view. That's a scary thought, isn't it? It's been said that there are skeletons in everybody's closet and that there are things about ourselves that we would not want the whole world to know.

Think for a moment of those things in your life that you would most like to keep secret forever and know that it is impossible for them to remain hidden. Not only the truth about the gospel will be made clearly known, but also the truth about me and the truth about you. Nothing that is hidden will remain hidden. Everything that is concealed now will be revealed then. This is not good news to sinful people because, as the Word of God tells us, we are by nature not the children of light but the children of darkness. John tells us, "And this is the judgment: the light has come into the world, and people loved the darkness rather than the light because their works were evil" (John 3:19). That's why we choose the darkness rather than the light.

This problem is not something new; it began in the garden of Eden. After the very first act of transgression, there was the first cover-up. The initial response of Adam and Eve to their sin was an experience of shame and awareness of their nakedness. Adam's first action was to hide. He hid from God, whereas previously they were delighted when God walked in the coolness of the garden, and they rushed to enjoy His fellowship. But after sin entered their lives, they didn't want God to see them, so they hid. They sought out the darkness. They wanted a place where they could be concealed, hidden from the view of God.

We might think that there's nothing sillier than to hide a lamp after we've lit it. But there is something sillier, and that is thinking that we can find a place in this universe where we can hide from almighty God. No such place exists. We could go into the darkest hole in the universe and still not escape the gaze of God. The psalmist said, "Search me, O God, and know my heart! Try me and know my thoughts! And see if there be any grievous way in me, and lead me in the way everlasting!" (Ps. 139:23–24). And he said, "Even before a word is on my tongue, behold, O Lord, you know it altogether. . . . Where shall I go from your Spirit? Or where shall I flee from your presence? If I ascend to heaven, you are there! If I make my bed in Sheol, you are there!" (vv. 4, 7–8).

Fast-forward to the New Testament, where Jesus said, "I tell you, on the day of judgment people will give account for every careless word they speak" (Matt. 12:36). Think about that. Every casual, cavalier, off-the-cuff remark that we've ever made, we're going to have to own up to. Not to mention the carefully devised lies and angry statements that we have made. All those will come into the judgment because our Lord said, **"Nothing is hidden that will not be made manifest, nor is anything secret that will not be known and come to light"** (v. 17). These are sobering words. Jesus was saying to us and to His disciples: "Live in the light. Let the truth be in the light. Don't hide the Word of God. Don't hide yourself from the Word of God."

We are called to be people of the light, people who have received the truth of God, who have been commissioned to proclaim the truth of God, to let it be known. Does everybody who knows you know that you're a Christian? I hope if they do, it's not because you're obnoxious about it. I hope that they know it because it is evident to them. Anybody who knows you should know and appreciate that you're a follower of Christ. If they don't know, maybe it's because the light you have received has gone under the couch or under the bushel. The truth of God is the light of the world, and we are called to be people of that light.

As Jesus finished teaching, somebody interrupted Him and said, **"Your mother and your brothers are standing outside, desiring to see you"** (v. 20). Jesus took the opportunity to teach an important lesson when He said, **"My mother and my brothers are those who hear the word of God and do it"** (v. 21). This is a brilliant statement of one of the most important doctrines set forth in the New Testament, the doctrine of adoption. This doctrine means that through the grace of God, everyone who puts their faith in Christ is adopted into the family of God. Jesus calls us His brothers and His sisters, and we are adopted then by the heavenly Father.

42

THE CALMING OF THE STORM

Luke 8:22–25

One day he got into a boat with his disciples, and he said to them, "Let us go across to the other side of the lake." So they set out, and as they sailed he fell asleep. And a windstorm came down on the lake, and they were filling with water and were in danger. And they went and woke him, saying, "Master, Master, we are perishing!" And he awoke and rebuked the wind and the raging waves, and they ceased, and there was a calm. He said to them, "Where is your faith?" And they were afraid, and they marveled, saying to one another, "Who then is this, that he commands even winds and water, and they obey him?"

In the eighteenth century, a watershed event occurred in Western civilization. It began in Germany, where it was called the *Aufklärung*, and then it spread rapidly to England and then to France, culminating in what we call in Western history the Enlightenment.

The Enlightenment was not a uniform, monolithic movement where all the thinkers and philosophers agreed on every point. There were many intellectuals who were ardent atheists, but there were also many intellectuals of that period who remained steadfast in their affirmation of belief in God. The most militant of the atheists were numbered among the *Encyclopédistes*, including the two most notorious of that group, Denis Diderot and Baron d'Holbach. D'Holbach was known as "the personal enemy of God." These atheists believed that the new discoveries of modern science had made the God hypothesis an unnecessary, outdated opinion that science now repudiated.

They came to this conclusion by saying the God hypothesis was no longer necessary because now we know that the origin of life, and indeed the origin of the whole universe, came to pass through the power of spontaneous generation. They got this idea initially from observing mud puddles that were far removed from streams, rivers, oceans, and lakes. They looked at mud puddles and found that in a few days after their formation, they could see movement in the mud puddles of tiny tadpoles that they thought obviously had come into existence spontaneously. They didn't consider other possibilities. But they were confident in their assertion of this new view of spontaneous generation, meaning that life and the whole universe came out of nothing spontaneously.

When we look at that today, we see that that's not only bad theology and bad philosophy but also bad science. It violates the most fundamental principle of science and philosophy: *ex nihilo nihil fit*—"out of nothing, nothing comes." If there was ever a time that there was nothing, the only thing that can possibly be here right now is nothing, because you can't get something out of nothing. The doctrine of spontaneous generation was not science; it was magic. It was like bringing the rabbit out of the hat, without a rabbit, without a hat, without a wand, and even without a magician. Nevertheless, it had a tremendous impact on the thinking of Western intellectuals.

The Persistence of Religion

The atheists of the nineteenth century were convinced that their work had already been accomplished by those in the eighteenth century, whom they believed refuted the idea of the existence of God. The problem that the atheists of the nineteenth century faced—men such as Karl Marx, Ludwig Feuerbach, Friedrich Nietzsche, and especially Sigmund Freud—was, since now we know that there is no God, why is it that in our anthropological investigations, no matter how far we go, we find religion? They pondered, if there's no God, why is it that human beings are not only *Homo sapiens* but also seem to be *Homo religiosus*, that is, incurably religious? They felt the burden of accounting for this universal appearance of religion in light of what they believed was the accomplished proven fact that there is no God.

In a word, if there's no God, why is there so much religion? Virtually all the major atheists of the nineteenth century agreed that religion arose historically out of the psychological needs of human beings, as an antidote to human fears and uncertainty. Marx spoke of religion as "the opiate of the masses," the drug that dulls our senses to the terrors and unpleasantries that surround us in this world.

Nobody was more inventive and more comprehensive in his attempt to account for religion than was Sigmund Freud in his work *The Future of Illusion*. Freud argued this way: The biggest problem we face as human beings is the threat of death, and that threat comes to us from many angles. With the widespread presence of wars and murders, one of the things that we learn to fear is other human beings, but we have come to gain a certain assurance of how to deal with hostile people by adopting various and sundry methods. If somebody's angry with me and threatening me, I can beg him for mercy so he might refrain from bringing me harm. Or I can give him laudatory expressions, saying: "Why would you want to harm me? I'm your number one fan in the world. So please don't hurt me." Or we can try to bribe or negotiate: "I'll give you ten thousand dollars if you spare me." We've learned all those techniques to deal with people who are hostile to us. They don't always work, but sometimes they do.

But in addition to the threat of violent human beings, we also have the threat of disease, of natural catastrophes like earthquakes, floods, and fires. The question is this: How do you negotiate with cancer? What good is it to plead with a fire? How do you bribe a flood? All these inanimate forces that threaten to destroy us are immune to all the devices we use to ameliorate hostile people. According to Freud, we tend to personalize these impersonal forces as animistic religion does. They suppose that the flood or the storm or animals like the crocodile are inhabited by living spirits. So the animist tries to appease these hostile spirits by giving worship to them, making idols of them; and even though these idols don't have real ears or real mouths, the animist still speaks to them, prays to them, and honors them with worship.

The next step is the sacralization of these forces, or considering them sacred and divine. Out of all this comes the beginnings of religion, and the religion gets more and more abstract and more and more sophisticated. That theory found many converts in the nineteenth century. One of the things that I find so interesting about this episode in the life of Jesus is that it seems to contradict Freud's theory.

The Fear of the Holy

One day he got into a boat with his disciples, and he said to them, "Let us go across to the other side of the lake" (v. 22). When Jesus and His disciples started in the boat, the lake was placid and tranquil. This was the Sea of Galilee, a body of water that is subject to unexpected storms, violent winds coming off the Mediterranean Sea and through the mountains on the edge of Israel that form a wind tunnel. When this happens, it instantly can turn the lake into a maelstrom, a horrendous, life-threatening situation. That's what happened in this case.

So they set out, and as they sailed he fell asleep. And a windstorm came down on the lake, and they were filling with water and were in danger (vv. 22–23). Jesus and His disciples were out on the water when a violent storm came. The boat was filling with water, and the winds were howling; the waves became so high that the boat was in danger of capsizing. The Bible tells us they were afraid. Of course they were afraid. They were afraid for their lives. These forces of nature were about to destroy them. In the meantime, Jesus was sound asleep in the back of the boat.

And they went and woke him, saying, "Master, Master, we are perishing!" (v. 24). I wonder what they expected Jesus to do in this situation, but this I do know, that they certainly did not expect Him to do what He did.

And he awoke and rebuked the wind and the raging waves, and they ceased, and there was a calm (v. 24). He talked to the wind and to the water and gave a command. The imperative that comes from the lips of Jesus is this: "Peace! Be still!" (Mark 4:39). Instantly, the wind ceased. There wasn't the slightest zephyr in the air. Instantly, the sea became as smooth as glass. He then rebuked His disciples, saying, **"Where is your faith?"** (v. 25).

The question I have is, What was the disciples' reaction? What would you expect it to be? You would think they would rejoice and thank Jesus for saving them. That's the response that you would expect, isn't it?

But that's not the response the disciples had. The Scriptures tell us that after the threat of nature was removed by Jesus, instead of eliminating their fear, their fear was intensified. **And they were afraid, and they marveled, saying to one another, "Who then is this, that he commands even winds and water, and they obey him?"** (v. 25). Suddenly, they were in the presence of something that was more terrifying than the violence of this storm. They looked at Jesus in a way they hadn't before. And they said among themselves: "What manner of man is this? Who is this man?" We don't have a category for Him. He is *sui generis*, in a class by Himself. No human being has ever spoken to the wind and made it behave or calmed a troubled sea with the mere force of his voice.

They realized that they were in the presence of something more terrifying than the violent forces of nature. This is what Freud didn't expect or understand. The disciples were in the presence of the holy. They were in the presence of One who had no category, because He was transcendent. He was other. He was different. He was higher. He was holy. And there is nothing on this planet more frightening than to be in the presence of the holy.

John Calvin wrote that people are completely fearless in certain circumstances, but the Scriptures uniformly relate that people who previously were self-secure and safe are reduced to trembling when God appears to them in His holiness. This is what the disciples experienced. They were in the presence of the holy on that boat, on the Sea of Galilee. What's the significance of this?

The supreme Old Testament act of redemption was the exodus. The Jewish people had been enslaved under the tyranny of Pharaoh, and they were miserable. They cried and groaned, until finally we read in the Scriptures that "God heard their groaning, and God remembered his covenant with Abraham, with Isaac, and with Jacob" (Ex. 2:24). God then appeared in the Midianite wilderness to Moses, saying, "Do not come near; take your sandals off your feet, for the place on which you are standing is holy ground" (3:5). And God gave the command to Moses to go to the court of Pharaoh, the most powerful leader on earth. Moses, a Midianite shepherd, went with a message from God that said simply, "Let my people go" (5:1).

Why did God command that Pharaoh let these slaves go? Was it simply because He was acting to rescue them from the misery of their experience in slavery? Certainly, that was an important element of it, but it's not the whole story. Moses was commanded to say, "Let my people go"—and here is the purpose—"that they may hold a feast to me in the wilderness" (5:1). Now, the dramatic story of rescue in the Old Testament had, as its ultimate goal, that these people who were rescued might come and worship God.

If we fast-forward to the New Testament, we see the elaborate work of redemption that Christ, the new Moses, accomplished for us in saving His people. We know what He saved them from—He saved them from the wrath of God. But what did He save them for? The answer to that question is worship. One of my greatest concerns for the church is that worship in so many churches has become casual. Casual worship is a contradiction in terms. No person ever comes into the immediate presence of a holy God in a cavalier manner. You don't come into the presence of God dressed like you were going to the beach. Sometimes, we reveal how casually we take worship. When we come to worship, this is holy ground. We come not with a servile fear but with a godly fear, a sense of reverence before Him. A sense of fear and trembling that was experienced by the disciples in that boat on the Sea of Galilee. Yes, they were frightened, and they should have been, because they were in the presence of the Holy One of Israel, before whom even the demons from hell scream in terror.

We come to church for a variety of reasons. But the ultimate reason that we are to come, if we are mature in our faith, is to worship Him, to bow down before Him, to sing our praises to Him, to offer the sacrifice of praise to our God, and to adore Him with the fear of the Lord that is the beginning of wisdom.

43

LEGION

Luke 8:26–39

Then they sailed to the country of the Gerasenes, which is opposite Galilee. When Jesus had stepped out on land, there met him a man from the city who had demons. For a long time he had worn no clothes, and he had not lived in a house but among the tombs. When he saw Jesus, he cried out and fell down before him and said with a loud voice, "What have you to do with me, Jesus, Son of the Most High God? I beg you, do not torment me." For he had commanded the unclean spirit to come out of the man. (For many a time it had seized him. He was kept under guard and bound with chains and shackles, but he would break the bonds and be driven by the demon into the desert.) Jesus then asked him, "What is your name?" And he said, "Legion," for many demons had entered him. And they begged him not to command them to depart into the abyss. Now a large herd of pigs was feeding there on the hillside, and they begged him to let them enter these. So he gave them permission. Then the demons came out of the man and entered the pigs, and the herd rushed down the steep bank into the lake and drowned.

When the herdsmen saw what had happened, they fled and told it in the city and in the country. Then people went out to see what had happened, and they came to Jesus and found the man from whom the demons had gone, sitting at the feet of Jesus, clothed and in his right mind, and they were afraid. And those who had seen it told them how the demon-possessed man had been healed. Then all the people of the surrounding country of the Gerasenes asked him to depart from them, for they were seized with great fear. So he got into the boat and returned. The man from whom the demons had gone begged that he might be with him, but Jesus sent him away, saying, "Return to your home, and declare how much God has done for you." And he went away, proclaiming throughout the whole city how much Jesus had done for him.

What happened immediately after the calming of the storm we don't know, because Luke doesn't take up the narrative until the boat in which Jesus and the disciples are sailing reaches shore. What follows immediately is only more trauma and more terror, because as the boat comes in to land on the shore, it is greeted by the wild man whom Luke describes here in the text.

Then they sailed to the country of the Gerasenes, which is opposite Galilee. When Jesus had stepped out on land, there met him a man from the city who had demons (vv. 26–27). The New Testament looks at this matter of invisible, wicked spirits and takes it seriously. Many people today don't believe Satan exists. One possible reason for this is that he has been caricatured as a grotesque character in a red suit and a long tail, with a pitchfork and horns. But that description is not from Scripture. In fact, that is the very opposite of the way the devil is described. He's described as being disguised as an angel of light who goes about seeking to devour as he will (2 Cor. 11:14; 1 Peter 5:8). He appears, as we say in theology, *sub specie boni*, "under the auspices of the good."

From where did that popular image come? It came from the Middle Ages, when the church was acutely conscious of the reality of Satan, and they wanted to ward off his influence. They said that the point of vulnerability of Satan was his pride. In order to attack his pride, they invented wild caricatures of him, making him look ludicrous, and later generations said, "I don't believe in that devil." Nobody did when that image was first projected. That was done to insult Satan.

We have the record here of a man whom we're told is demon possessed, but he differs from other demon-possessed individuals. To what degree? Anyone who is demon possessed is in a serious state. It's a horrible thing to have to experience or to contemplate, but if demon possession can admit to degrees, this man was severely demon possessed. If for no other reason, it was for the number of demons that had entered into him. Clearly, the New Testament sees the possibility of demon possession as involving more than one demon on any occasion. In this case, we're told that this man is possessed by a multitude of them.

For a long time he had worn no clothes, and he had not lived in a house but among the tombs (v. 27). The area that is described here is on the edge of the Sea of Galilee, where it rises up as a steep cliff. At the top of the cliff was built a cemetery that has multiple graves and tombs, most of which were filled, but some of which were still vacant. This poor soul was living not in the streets of the city in a cardboard box but in the wilderness. He had been banished from his hometown and lived naked in a tomb.

Son of the Most High God

When he saw Jesus, he cried out and fell down before him and said with a loud voice, "What have you to do with me, Jesus, Son of the Most High God?" (v. 28). The voice that came out of this man was not his own voice. It was the demonic voice that addressed the question. There is irony here. The last time we saw a question in this text, it was raised by the disciples when Jesus calmed the storm: "What manner of man is this? Who is this man?" Well, the answer to that question is provided by the demons. The demons didn't have to say, "What manner of man is this?" They knew exactly what manner of man He was, and they recognized what the disciples didn't recognize: that they were in the presence of God incarnate. They used the title **"Son of the Most High God."**

The phrase "Most High God" is not a description of God that is normally used in the New Testament. Yet in the realm of anthropology, scholars from around the world have discovered religion among the most remote people and among animistic tribes that have evil spirits that they have to appease, spirits that indwell the trees, the crocodile, or the rhinoceros. Their religion does not focus on a monotheistic deity, but anthropologists, when they probe the people about their religion, have discovered that they have a vague memory of a god who's on the other side of the mountain, the god who is not a part of their daily lives. They refer to him as the "Most High God," which verifies what the Apostle Paul tells us about God's revealing Himself plainly and clearly to all people everywhere (Rom. 1:18–23). False religion cannot extinguish the revelation that God gives of Himself. So in every tribe and every tongue and every nation, there is an awareness, repressed as it may be, not only of a God, not only of the God, but of the Most High God.

There's a Latin term in technical theology to describe God. He's called the *ens perfectissimum*, "the most perfect being." The term is somewhat redundant, in that it talks about the superlative degree of perfection. If something is perfect, it can't be most perfect, because most perfect gains nothing over the perfect. If you're perfect, you've reached the ultimate limit of what can be. But as a matter of intentional hyperbole, theologians speak of the most perfect being, because they can't find an adequate way to extol the perfection that resides in God. The demons understand that, and they recognize Jesus, and they cry out, **"I beg you, do not torment me." For he had commanded the unclean spirit to come out of the man** (vv. 28–29).

(For many a time it had seized him. He was kept under guard and bound with chains and shackles, but he would break the bonds and be driven by the demon into the desert) (v. 29). More background is supplied by Luke. This man was demon possessed when he was in the town, and he behaved in this wild manner while there, so much so that he was a threat to the well-being of the citizens, so they bound him as tightly as they could. But no matter how tightly they bound him, he broke his bonds and freed himself, so the people drove him into the wilderness.

The Appointed Time

Jesus then asked him, "What is your name?" And he said, "Legion," for many demons had entered him. And they begged him not to command them to depart into the abyss (vv. 30–31). The spokesman for the demons identified himself by the name **Legion**. A legion in Roman categories consisted of soldiers numbering six thousand. If you take this literally, the demonic being is saying, "Our name is Legion because there are six thousand of us in this man." However, it is probably an instance of hyperbole that nevertheless indicates that the man was possessed by a multitude of demonic spirits.

The abyss they feared was a bottomless pit and clearly is symbolic of hell itself. If we compare this with the other Synoptic Gospels, another element is added to it where they begged Jesus not to command them to go into the abyss "before the time" (Matt. 8:29). These demons knew what their future held. They knew their destiny. They knew that God in His sovereignty had appointed a day when the demons would be shut up forever in the abyss, but that time had not yet come. The atonement had not yet been made, the kingdom of God had not reached its consummation as it would at the end of the age, and the demons knew that the day in which they would be sent into the abyss was way off in the future. At least, that was the theology they had been taught by the prince of demons, Satan himself.

Jesus knew that *kairos*, that time that God had appointed, was not yet. On the surface, it seems as though Jesus was now negotiating with these demons, because they were reminding Him that it was too early to be sent there. We see then that Jesus didn't send them into the pit. Some commentators look at that and say, "Here, Jesus is surrendering to the pleas of these evil beings," but He wasn't. Jesus acknowledged, by His actions, that it wasn't the time to send them into the pit, but it was time for them to come out of the man.

Now a large herd of pigs was feeding there on the hillside, and they begged him to let them enter these. So he gave them permission. Then the demons came out of the man and entered the pigs, and the herd rushed down the

steep bank into the lake and drowned (vv. 32–33). This causes a hue and cry among people who say: "Jesus wasn't such a good guy after all. He was unfair, unjust, and cruel to these animals." But Jesus understood the difference between human beings and the beasts of the field. Jesus created the world, and He knew that the animals were created for man, not man for the animals. Jesus knew nothing of a world where fish eggs were protected and unborn human beings were destroyed. That was as foreign to His way of thinking as anything could be.

Pigs were considered unclean animals by the Jews. A lot of Gentiles lived in the Decapolis (the region where this episode took place), and this was probably a Gentile herd of swine. But the point is, if it took invading the pigs with demons to rescue one human being from Satan, Jesus would sacrifice the whole herd of pigs. Jesus told us that God notices the landing of every bird in the air, every sparrow that lands is noticed by God, and are you not worth more than a bird (Matt. 10:26–33)? Are you not worth more than a pig? Of course you are, in the scheme of creation.

When the herdsmen saw what had happened, they fled and told it in the city and in the country (v. 34). They went running back home and said: "You can't believe what happened out there. This fellow came along, and He's cured that wild man, and He sent the demons into our pigs. Then the pigs went down the hill and into the water and drowned."

The People Fear

Then people went out to see what had happened, and they came to Jesus and found the man from whom the demons had gone, sitting at the feet of Jesus, clothed and in his right mind, and they were afraid (v. 35). Not only had Jesus calmed the sea, but He had also healed a human being who was tormented by demons and who now was of sound mind. What was the response of the townspeople? It was the same response the disciples had in the boat on the Sea of Galilee: **they were afraid**. The reason the demon-possessed man was sent to the tombs in the first place was because the people were afraid of him. Now, when they found him calm, clothed, and in his right mind, they were scared. What does this tell you?

And those who had seen it told them how the demon-possessed man had been healed. Then all the people of the surrounding country of the Gerasenes asked him to depart from them, for they were seized with great fear. So he got into the boat and returned (vv. 36–37). As we have noted, nothing terrifies a human being more than being in the presence of the holy, and these townspeople realized that they were in the presence of One who was holy and they were not. They wanted Him to go away from them. Some wonder why Jesus was killed. He wasn't killed because He was bad; He was killed because He was holy, and He had to be done away with.

The man from whom the demons had gone begged that he might be with him, but Jesus sent him away, saying, "Return to your home, and declare how much God has done for you." And he went away, proclaiming throughout the whole city how much Jesus had done for him (vv. 38–39). I don't know that I was ever possessed by demons but I was certainly in bondage to sin, as every unbeliever is, and I served Satan rather than God as every unbeliever does. But once God rescues us, He gives us the duty to proclaim His great works to the whole world.

44

JAIRUS' DAUGHTER

Luke 8:40–56

Now when Jesus returned, the crowd welcomed him, for they were all waiting for him. And there came a man named Jairus, who was a ruler of the synagogue. And falling at Jesus' feet, he implored him to come to his house, for he had an only daughter, about twelve years of age, and she was dying.

As Jesus went, the people pressed around him. And there was a woman who had had a discharge of blood for twelve years, and though she had spent all her living on physicians, she could not be healed by anyone. She came up behind him and touched the fringe of his garment, and immediately her discharge of blood ceased. And Jesus said, "Who was it that touched me?" When all denied it, Peter said, "Master, the crowds surround you and are pressing in on you!" But Jesus said, "Someone touched me, for I perceive that power has gone out from me." And when the woman saw that she was not hidden, she came trembling, and falling down before him declared in the presence of all the people why she had touched him, and how she had been immediately healed. And he said to her, "Daughter, your faith has made you well; go in peace."

While he was still speaking, someone from the ruler's house came and said, "Your daughter is dead; do not trouble the Teacher any more." But Jesus on hearing this answered him, "Do not fear; only believe, and she will be well." And when he came to the house, he allowed no one to enter with him, except Peter and John and James, and the father and mother of the child. And all were weeping and mourning for her, but he said, "Do not weep, for she is not dead but sleeping." And they laughed at him, knowing that she was dead. But taking her by the hand he called, saying, "Child, arise." And her spirit returned, and she got up at once. And he directed that something should be given her to eat. And her parents were amazed, but he charged them to tell no one what had happened.

In the last passage, after Jesus cast out Legion, the people were filled with fear, and they begged Jesus to leave. They said, "Please go." In this passage, we have a ruler of the synagogue entreating Jesus, "Please come."

Now when Jesus returned, the crowd welcomed him, for they were all waiting for him. And there came a man named Jairus, who was a ruler of the synagogue. And falling at Jesus' feet, he implored him to come to his house (vv. 40–41). The synagogue in those days was ruled by elders, and those who had that position were held in high esteem in the community. This, then, was a man of some status, and when he came to Jesus, he humbled himself completely and fell at the feet of Jesus. He was a desperate man. Luke tells us the reason for his desperation: **he had an only daughter, about twelve years of age, and she was dying** (v. 42). Clearly this ruler would have summoned the best physicians in Capernaum to treat his daughter, but whatever treatments she received were not successful. His only hope at this point was Jesus.

As Jesus went, the people pressed around him (v. 42). The crowd that had welcomed Him on the shore witnessed Jairus' begging Jesus to come and save his daughter. The whispering went among the crowd, and they all fell in step with Jesus. Some had probably been eyewitnesses of other miracles that Jesus had performed. The multitudes thronged around Him. And then Jesus was interrupted on His way to Jairus' house.

The Hemorrhaging Woman

And there was a woman who had had a discharge of blood for twelve years, and though she had spent all her living on physicians, she could not be healed by anyone (v. 43). This woman is given no name, only a condition. Here's a woman who, presumably the same year that Jairus' daughter was born, came down with a chronic case of hemorrhaging, wherein she lost her health first of all, and Luke tells us that she **had spent all her living on physicians** but **she could not be healed by anyone**. She had lost her health, and she had lost her wealth. Furthermore, since she had this hemorrhaging, she would have been ceremonially unclean and therefore would have lost her status and her reputation in the Jewish community. Everything that was important to her—her health, her money, her status in the community—was gone, for twelve years. She was as desperate in her condition as Jairus was in his, having a daughter who was dying.

She came up behind him and touched the fringe of his garment, and immediately her discharge of blood ceased (v. 44). As Jairus had come and fallen down before Jesus, now this woman may have reasoned in her heart, "If I can just touch His garment. I don't need to have Him lay His hands on me or say anything to me or touch me. I'm unclean, and it would be presumptuous of me to ask Him to touch me. But if I can touch the fringe of His garment, I'm sure that will be all that is necessary." Here was a woman who had no reason to trust that any man could ever heal her. Yet when she saw Jesus, she seemed to know that if she could touch the hem of His garment, she would be healed. She came from behind Him and touched the border of His garment, and instantly the flow of blood stopped, the hemorrhaging finished.

And Jesus said, "Who was it that touched me?" When all denied it, Peter said, "Master, the crowds surround you and are pressing in on you!" But Jesus said, "Someone touched me, for I perceive that power has gone out from me" (vv. 45–46). Now this poor woman was cowering in terror. The last thing she wanted to do was to come forward and say, "I did it." But in the meantime, Jesus wanted to know who touched Him, and everybody denied it. Peter, always impetuous and prone to correcting Jesus, said, **"Master, the crowds surround you and are pressing in on you!"** Do you hear the tone in Peter's voice? "How are we to know who touched You? All these people are bumping and pushing against You, and You're asking us who touched You." Jesus ignored the outburst from Peter and simply said, **"Someone touched me, for I perceive that power has gone out from me."**

This statement can tell us something about Jesus. When Jesus used His power to redeem people from whatever condition they were in, it was costly for Him. When He calmed the storm, when He healed the man of a legion of demons, He was drained of the power. Now as He was on His way to deal with the dying daughter of Jairus, He felt the power go out of Him again. He understood that the departure of strength from His body occurred when His redeeming power was being used in a saving way.

And when the woman saw that she was not hidden, she came trembling, and falling down before him declared in the presence of all the people why she had touched him, and how she had been immediately healed (v. 47). This is the second person who has fallen down before Jesus in this narrative—first Jairus and now this woman. She declared to Him in the presence of all the people that she touched Him, and in the presence of all the people she said why she touched Him.

And he said to her, "Daughter, your faith has made you well; go in peace" (v. 48). I wonder how old she was. She'd had this condition for twelve years. She wasn't a child. She may have been as old as Jesus, and yet Jesus called her **"Daughter."** Don't miss the significance of that. We are not by nature sons and daughters of God. God is not the Father of us all. In biblical terms, God is the unique or sole Father of His only begotten Son and all the rest of His children are adopted. There's no other way to get into the family of God except through adoption. And the only way you can be adopted into the family of God is through God's only Son. This trembling woman, telling the story, wondered what Jesus was going to do. The first thing He did was welcome her into God's family by calling her **"Daughter."** He was going to heal Jairus' daughter, and on their way He stopped to heal what is now His own daughter. **"Your faith has made you well; go in peace."** It wasn't her faith that had the power to heal her, as some mistakenly believe. But it was because of her faith in Christ, as a consequence of her faith, that she was healed.

Jairus' Daughter Raised

While he was still speaking, someone from the ruler's house came and said, "Your daughter is dead; do not trouble the Teacher any more" (v. 49). In John 11, when Jesus got to the home of Mary and Martha and Lazarus, four days after Lazarus had died, the women said, "Lord, if you had been here, my brother would not have died" (vv. 21, 32). Do you know how many millions of people have assumed in their lifetime that it was too late for them to meet Jesus or to have Jesus do anything for them? If you are still alive, then it's not too late.

But Jesus on hearing this answered him, "Do not fear; only believe, and she will be well." And when he came to the house, he allowed no one to enter with him, except Peter and John and James, and the father and mother of the child. And all were weeping and mourning for her, but he said, "Do not weep, for she is not dead but sleeping" (vv. 50–52). This is a common way of Jewish speaking that speaks euphemistically. Jesus was saying she wasn't dead in the sense of dead once and for all, gone forever, but she just needed to be woken up.

And they laughed at him, knowing that she was dead (v. 53). What's the antecedent of *they* here? Who was it that ridiculed Jesus when He said this? Peter, James, and John? The mother and the father? No. The ones who ridiculed Him were the crowd that was pressing around outside wailing and playing the music. Who were they? They were the professional mourners who gathered as soon as the death occurred. These professional mourners were paid to play the flute and to wail and to cry at funerals. When a person who had a death in the family was somebody of means, as soon as the news of death came, the mourners would flock to the home where the death had occurred. These mourners ridiculed Him, because they knew the girl was dead.

But taking her by the hand he called, saying, "Child, arise" (v. 54). There it is again—the divine effectual call. The means by which the world came into being was by divine imperative. Lazarus came out of that tomb because Jesus called him out of the tomb. If you are in Christ, it's because God the Holy Spirit called you out of darkness into light. He just didn't invite you; that call was not simply the outer call of preaching. It was the inner call of God the Holy Ghost, the omnipotent God who brought you alive from spiritual death, what we call in theology "the effectual call of God." This is a foretaste of the last judgment, when all who are in Christ will hear the same effectual call, and the dead in Christ will rise at the sound of His voice.

And her spirit returned, and she got up at once. And he directed that something should be given her to eat. And her parents were amazed, but he charged them to tell no one what had happened (vv. 55–56). Luke understood that she was not comatose, because when you're comatose your soul doesn't leave the body. She wasn't sleeping, because when you're sleeping your soul doesn't leave the body. This little girl was dead, because her soul had gone. Jesus called it back and reunited her soul with her body, and she arose immediately. Jesus then continued to show compassion even as the girl's parents were paralyzed in amazement, as He looked after her needs by directing that she be given some food.

45

THE SENDING OF THE TWELVE

Luke 9:1–6

And he called the twelve together and gave them power and authority over all demons and to cure diseases, and he sent them out to proclaim the kingdom of God and to heal. And he said to them, "Take nothing for your journey, no staff, nor bag, nor bread, nor money; and do not have two tunics. And whatever house you enter, stay there, and from there depart. And wherever they do not receive you, when you leave that town shake off the dust from your feet as a testimony against them." And they departed and went through the villages, preaching the gospel and healing everywhere.

This passage is brief, but in the history of redemption, it is one that is extremely important because it marks a transition point in the earthly ministry of Jesus that will have radical ramifications for the whole future of Christianity.

And he called the twelve together and gave them power and authority over all demons and to cure diseases (v. 1). Jesus called His twelve disciples, and He summoned them for a particular reason. In this text, we see a critically important transition in the lives of the twelve disciples. Now, the disciples are becoming Apostles.

Sometimes we have the tendency to think that the terms *disciple* and *apostle* are synonyms, but that's not the case. A disciple (Greek *mathētēs*) is a learner, a student. An apostle is something quite different. An apostle (Greek *apostolos*, meaning "one who is sent") is one who is commissioned and called by a superior—such as a king, a general in the army, or, in this case, the Lord of glory—and is sent out, carrying the authority of the one who sent him. It is much like an ambassador may have been authorized, in the ancient world, to speak with the authority of the king who sent him. Similarly, Jesus selected, from His disciples, twelve men whom He would send with His authority. As He would say elsewhere, "The one who hears you hears me, and the one who rejects you rejects me, and the one who rejects me rejects him who sent me" (Luke 10:16).

He called them to Himself for this purpose: to give **them power and authority over all demons and to cure diseases** (v. 1). They had no power or authority in themselves. But the authority and power by which they were to exercise their ministry of healing and of preaching was by the power and authority of Christ. In the book of Acts, after Peter and John healed the man by the Beautiful Gate (see 3:2), they were dragged before the Sanhedrin, and the leaders of Israel said, "By what power or by what name did you do this?" (Acts 4:7). They responded, "By the name of Jesus Christ of Nazareth, whom you crucified, whom God raised from the dead" (v. 10). Further, the authority by which the New Testament was written was the authority of Christ. If you reject the New Testament Apostolic witness, you reject the One who commissioned the Apostles to write what they did.

And he sent them out to proclaim the kingdom of God and to heal (v. 2). The kingdom of God was the central theme of Jesus' own preaching. Just as John the Baptist had come on the scene earlier and said, "Repent, for the kingdom of heaven is at hand" (Matt. 3:2), Jesus came with the same message. This was a new time in history. This was the time of the breakthrough of God's kingdom. Why? Because God's anointed King was here. Jesus, who had been preaching the kingdom of God throughout His earthly ministry, now sent His disciples as Apostles to preach His message through the villages and towns in Galilee. He sent them to preach the kingdom of God and to heal the sick.

And he said to them, "Take nothing for your journey, no staff, nor bag, nor bread, nor money; and do not have two tunics" (v. 3). In other words, the mandate that Jesus is giving is this: "You're to go out there and travel light. You're to be on the move every moment, and you don't need to take anything to even meet your own basic needs."

He goes on to say that they're basically to depend upon the Jewish principle of hospitality that was part of the law of Moses—that, if a stranger is in your gates, you are to give shelter, food, and hospitality to him. Jesus was sending

His representatives to the Jewish people, and He said, **"And whatever house you enter, stay there, and from there depart"** (v. 4). Jesus was saying, in effect: "When you're finished with your ministry in that particular village, you leave that house. But I don't want you going into one house and, if you don't like the menu, going to another house and seeking better quarters or better food. You go to one place. You stay there until your mission is done, and it's the people's responsibility to support you while you're involved in this mission."

The Limits of God's Patience

"And wherever they do not receive you, when you leave that town shake off the dust from your feet as a testimony against them" (v. 5). Even if you've seldom read Scripture, you have probably heard of the idiomatic expression "shake the dust off your feet." This was not just an idiom that Jesus invented; it was an idea with which His disciples were already familiar. Remember when God called Moses out of the Midianite wilderness and He spoke to Moses out of the burning bush? He said, "Moses, Moses! . . . Do not come near; take your sandals off your feet, for the place on which you are standing is holy ground" (Ex. 3:4–5). To this day, we refer to the land of Israel as the Holy Land. It was the land promised by God to Abraham and to his descendants. The Holy Land, when it began to be inhabited by the Hebrew people in the Old Testament, was considered sacred. Everything outside the borders of Israel was pagan, and pagans were considered unclean. When a Jew went on a journey that would take him across the borders of Israel into a pagan land, he would be standing on ground that was not holy ground but contaminated ground. It was contaminated by the sin of the residents in these pagan regions. When the Jew came back to Israel, his custom was that before he crossed into the Holy Land again, he would stop and literally shake the dust off his feet, lest he bring pagan contamination to the Holy Land.

What is radical about Jesus' directive here is that He was sending His people not into Gentile, pagan countries but to Jewish villages and towns, preaching the gospel of the kingdom of God. He said to His Apostles, **"And wherever they do not receive you, when you leave that town shake off the dust from your feet as a testimony against them."** The gesture is testimony to the Jews' unbelief.

We see a scary concept here that is found throughout Scripture, and it's this: God's patience will not last forever. Some people postpone their repentance and say: "I will be committed to God tomorrow. I will change my ways tomorrow. I will give my life to Christ tomorrow. But not today." The young Augustine's prayer before his conversion was "Grant me chastity and continence, but not yet." He was taking advantage of God's patience and long-suffering. But the Bible warns us that God's patience does not endure forever. There is a limit to it, and there may come a time in a person's life when it is too late. We sometimes say it's never too late, but after you die, it's too late. The Bible tells us, "It is appointed for man to die once, and after that comes judgment" (Heb. 9:27). If you want to postpone your repentance, make sure that you don't postpone it till after you die, because then it's too late. But here's the scary thing: in some instances, it may be too late before you die.

Go back to the Old Testament, to the book of Genesis, to a familiar story there: the story of the flood that wiped out the whole world except for the family of Noah. When God saw that the earth was completely corrupt, He said, "My Spirit shall not abide in man forever" (Gen. 6:3). At that time, the end of God's patience had come. He destroyed the whole creation except for the family of Noah. If we go to the book of Revelation, the angel announces, "Let the evildoer still do evil, and the filthy still be filthy, and the righteous still do right, and the holy still be holy" (22:11). Now, what does that mean? We see in Genesis and in Revelation, and all through the Old Testament prophets, that there comes a time when God gives impenitent sinners over to their sin. Let us not tempt the Lord in His grace and in His patience. You cannot hear the gospel and be neutral to it. If you receive it, you enter heaven forever. If you reject it, you've hardened your heart, and you are heaping up wrath against the day of wrath.

46

HAUNTED BY GUILT

Luke 9:7–9

> Now Herod the tetrarch heard about all that was happening, and he was perplexed, because it was said by some that John had been raised from the dead, by some that Elijah had appeared, and by others that one of the prophets of old had risen. Herod said, "John I beheaded, but who is this about whom I hear such things?" And he sought to see him.

In this brief interlude, Luke describes a man who is haunted by guilt. Well it was that he should be, for his guilt was connected to an atrocity that was committed under his rule. We may recall that particular atrocity. We'll look at Mark's account of what had gone before this event:

> King Herod heard of it, for Jesus' name had become known. Some said, "John the Baptist has been raised from the dead. That is why these miraculous powers are at work in him." But others said, "He is Elijah." And others said, "He is a prophet, like one of the prophets of old." But when Herod heard of it, he said, "John, whom I beheaded, has been raised." For it was Herod who had sent and seized John and bound him in prison for the sake of Herodias, his brother Philip's wife, because he had married her. For John had been saying to Herod, "It is not lawful for you to have your brother's wife." And Herodias had a grudge against him and wanted to put him to death. But she could not, for Herod feared John,

> knowing that he was a righteous and holy man, and he kept him safe. When he heard him, he was greatly perplexed, and yet he heard him gladly.
>
> But an opportunity came when Herod on his birthday gave a banquet for his nobles and military commanders and the leading men of Galilee. For when Herodias's daughter came in and danced, she pleased Herod and his guests. And the king said to the girl, "Ask me for whatever you wish, and I will give it to you." And he vowed to her, "Whatever you ask me, I will give you, up to half of my kingdom." And she went out and said to her mother, "For what should I ask?" And she said, "The head of John the Baptist." And she came in immediately with haste to the king and asked, saying, "I want you to give me at once the head of John the Baptist on a platter." And the king was exceedingly sorry, but because of his oaths and his guests he did not want to break his word to her. And immediately the king sent an executioner with orders to bring John's head. He went and beheaded him in the prison and brought his head on a platter and gave it to the girl, and the girl gave it to her mother. When his disciples heard of it, they came and took his body and laid it in a tomb. (Mark 6:14–29)

This is one of the most grisly stories that we read anywhere in the New Testament. Just a brief word of background about it: Herod, one of the sons of Herod the Great, was given a portion of his father's kingdom—thus, he was called a *tetrarch*—and that portion included Galilee. Herod had been married to a neighboring king's daughter. The marriage was arranged chiefly to secure a political alliance with the neighboring country, with which Israel had had intermittent bouts of conflict. After the marriage was arranged, Herod's eye turned away from his wife and toward the wife of his brother. Her name was Herodias. So he dismissed his wife and—illegally, immorally, and against the law of God—took his brother's wife, Herodias, for his own wife. When that happened, John the Baptist publicly denounced Herod for this immoral action.

Herod, as we're told, was fearful of John the Baptist. He respected John the Baptist and recognized that John the Baptist was a righteous man, indeed, a holy man. Herodias, his wife, couldn't stand the public humiliation that followed from John the Baptist's denunciation of her illicit marriage to Herod. She endeavored to have her husband arrest John the Baptist and keep him in custody, where he couldn't do them any more harm. If you read the pages of the Old Testament, you can't help but see the parallel between this episode and the way Jezebel constantly pestered her husband, Ahab, to go after the prophet Elijah because he had spoken against their wicked practices.

Weak as he was, Herod surrendered and acquiesced to the wishes of his wife and placed John under arrest. The occasion came for the celebration of Herod's birthday. He invited the nobles and the people of great status to the celebration. As part of it, the daughter of Herodias, Salome—who presumably was the daughter from Herodias' previous marriage—performed a dance in front of Herod and his guests. Herod was so moved by this dance that in his exuberance, he offered up to half of his kingdom as a reward for whatever the young girl requested. She consulted with her mother. This was Herodias' great opportunity. She told her daughter to ask for the head of John of Baptist served on a platter. Herod, who had made an unlawful vow, thought that he was duty-bound to fulfill this vow. What he should have done was said, "My vow was unlawful, and I must be released from it." He didn't want to embarrass himself in front of his guests and fail to keep his word, so he ordered the executioner to go to the dungeon, kill John the Baptist, and present his head on a platter. In the midst of Herod's birthday celebration, instead of a cake, they brought the severed head of a prophet of God and paraded it before the guests.

Now, Herod is hearing stories about this miracle worker in Galilee. He listened to the reports and the analysis that others gave. Some said that **John had been raised from the dead** (v. 7). Others said that the prophet **Elijah had appeared** (v. 8). And still others, that **one of the prophets of old had risen** (v. 8). When we look at parallel texts, we see that Herod was most convinced of the first option: that this miracle worker must have been John the Baptist come back. **Herod said, "John I beheaded, but who is this about whom I hear such things?" And he sought to see him** (v. 9). Herod wanted to deal with this man. Do you feel the moral anguish that's going on here in the soul of Herod? He knew that he'd had John the Baptist beheaded for no just reason. There was nothing he could do to get rid of the weight of this.

The Crushing Weight of Guilt

Guilt is one of the most powerful, demoralizing, paralyzing, disintegrating, and destructive forces in all the world. I remember the very first time I administered the Lord's Supper. It wasn't to a congregation assembled but was in a hospital, to a woman who was dying. Before I gave her the sacrament, she told me that she had something to confess. She told me that years before she'd had an abortion, and that she was convinced that the cancer from which she was dying was a consequence of that and was God's judgment on her. After she'd had her first child, a daughter, she became pregnant a second time. But her husband was adamant that he didn't want another child and insisted that she have an abortion, so she had her unborn baby killed. As she was facing death in a matter of days, she was haunted by that guilt. I said: "Before you participate in the sacrament, you need to understand the gospel. Yes, abortion is an egregious sin and weighty sin, but it is not the unforgivable sin. We have a Savior who can forgive you of that sin and remove that guilt from you before you die." She confessed that sin to God, and she was forgiven by Christ. She received the sacrament, and she died in faith. I'll never forget that—the impact that unresolved guilt can have on people.

When we're burdened by our guilt, the first thing we try to do is deny it. We'll say, "Well, what I did really wasn't a sin," or "I can find so many of my friends who have done the same thing," or "This is acceptable in our culture." We give reasons why this behavior is OK. We deal with the guilt by denial. Or we try to rationalize our guilt. I'm not talking just about abortion. I'm talking about all those couples today who have eschewed marriage and live together without being married, in a blatant assault against the sanctity of an institution that God established and ordained. They carry on as if there were no God or as if they were exempt from the commandments of God. There's also the widespread practice of adultery. In the New Testament, Paul says, "But sexual immorality and all impurity or covetousness must not even be named among you, as is proper among saints" (Eph. 5:3). And yet the church is filled with unrepentant fornicators. We try to use the "everybody's doing it" excuse to relieve ourselves of guilt. The other problem with guilt is the more we repeat our sins or deny our sins or rationalize our sins, the more hardened our hearts become, and as Jeremiah said, we "have the forehead of a whore" (Jer. 3:3). We've lost the capacity to blush. That's what impenitence does to us. We try all these ways to escape from the reality of guilt.

Guilt is objective. Guilt has nothing to do with our feelings. It is an objective state of affairs whereby we incur guilt when we break the law of God. It doesn't matter how we feel. Even if we don't feel guilty about it, we are still guilty. Guilt feelings are our subjective response. It's a good thing that Herod had guilt feelings, because nothing is more wicked than to be a sociopath who incurs guilt and doesn't feel any guilt about it.

On the other side of the coin is forgiveness, and feelings of forgiveness. Forgiveness is an objective state; feeling is a subjective state. A young woman came to me, beside herself because of her guilt. She confessed her sin and said, "I've prayed to God ten times to forgive me for this sin, and I still don't feel forgiven. What can I do?" She wanted a deep, profound, theological answer. I said, "I want you to get on your knees and confess your sin to God." She said: "What? That's what I'm trying to tell you. I've done that already ten times, and it didn't work." I replied: "I'm not telling you to ask God to forgive you again for what you've asked Him for ten times. Now I want you to ask God to forgive you for your arrogance." Her response was: "What arrogance? How could I be more humble? I've been groveling at the feet of God and telling Him how sinful I am." I continued: "Did not God say that if you confess your sins, He is faithful and just to forgive your sin? So you have confessed your sin, but for you, the truth is that you're not forgiven because you don't feel forgiven. Therefore God isn't faithful, God isn't just, God doesn't do what He says He's going to do. Your unbelief is now worse than your original sin. That's what you need to confess."

I don't care if we feel forgiven. I do care if we *are* forgiven. Feeling forgiven is a bonus. It's a wonderful benefit, but the reality that we're looking for as sinners is the reality of God's forgiveness, because if God forgives us, we are forgiven.

47

THE FEEDING OF THE FIVE THOUSAND

Luke 9:10–17

On their return the apostles told him all that they had done. And he took them and withdrew apart to a town called Bethsaida. When the crowds learned it, they followed him, and he welcomed them and spoke to them of the kingdom of God and cured those who had need of healing. Now the day began to wear away, and the twelve came and said to him, "Send the crowd away to go into the surrounding villages and countryside to find lodging and get provisions, for we are here in a desolate place." But he said to them, "You give them something to eat." They said, "We have no more than five loaves and two fish—unless we are to go and buy food for all these people." For there were about five thousand men. And he said to his disciples, "Have them sit down in groups of about fifty each." And they did so, and had them all sit down. And taking the five loaves and the two fish, he looked up to heaven and said a blessing over them. Then he broke the loaves and gave them to the disciples to set before the crowd. And they all ate and were satisfied. And what was left over was picked up, twelve baskets of broken pieces.

If you've attended church much at all, you've heard this story and probably know it from beginning to end. You know that Jesus **withdrew apart to a town called Bethsaida** (v. 10). There, He **spoke to them of the kingdom of God and cured those who had need of healing** (v. 11). And, as it was coming toward evening, the disciples had a sense of concern and compassion for this multitude that numbered **five thousand men** (v. 14). That doesn't count the women and children. The disciples said, **"Send the crowd away to go into the surrounding villages and countryside to find lodging and get provisions, for we are here in a desolate place"** (v. 12). It's interesting to me that, once again, we have the disciples coming to Jesus and giving Him advice as though He needed it. How like the disciples we are in our prayers when we try to give counsel to God Almighty and to be His instructors. Jesus didn't debate with them. He said, **"You give them something to eat"** (v. 13). The disciples wondered how they were to do that when they had only **five loaves and two fish** (v. 13). Jesus instructed the disciples, **"Have them sit down in groups of about fifty each"** (v. 14).

He took the five loaves and the two fish and, by the power of God, multiplied and multiplied and multiplied them so that every person who was gathered there not only was fed, but was fed to the point of satisfaction. **And they all ate and were satisfied** (v. 17). The Gospel writer Mark says they were "filled" (Mark 6:42, NKJV). It was not like passing around a little piece of bread during communion. These people were filled to a sufficient level by the bread and the fish that Jesus provided for them, **and what was left over was picked up, twelve baskets of broken pieces** (v. 17). He didn't just give them what they needed. He gave them way beyond their needs. When God blesses His people, He blesses them abundantly.

The Reality of Miracles

The New Testament writers saw a singular significance to this particular miracle. It's the only one—apart from the resurrection—contained in all four Gospels. On the other side of that coin, this particular miracle has been singled out by critics and skeptics as an example of mythological teachings of the New Testament. This miracle has been targeted by those who, since the Enlightenment, have embraced the philosophy called naturalism. Naturalism teaches that we have nature around us, and nature is all there is. There's no supernatural, so anything that we find in the Scriptures that suggests a supernatural event must be rejected out of hand, because we can't believe in the supernatural.

When the naturalists invaded the church in the nineteenth century, we saw a movement spawned in Europe that was called nineteenth-century liberalism. It wasn't just liberalism in general, but it had a specific agenda, a specific philosophy, a specific theology. Nineteenth-century liberalism was based on the assumption that the Bible is to be criticized by biblical scholars and demonstrated to be false in many places. Nineteenth-century liberals took out of the New Testament record anything that smacked of supernaturalism—the virgin birth, the atonement of Christ, the resurrection of Christ, the transfiguration of Christ, the ascension of Christ. All the miracles of Jesus were thrown out wholesale. Early in the twentieth century, a Swiss Neoorthodox theologian named Emil Brunner wrote a book called *Der Mittler* (*The Mediator*), in which he explored the mediatorial work of Jesus. When he looked at the theories of nineteenth-century liberalism, he said, "This is unbelief." The unbelief that characterized nineteenth-century liberalism became a pervasive influence in what are called the mainline churches here in the United States, which, for the most part, have become monuments of unbelief.

How did the nineteenth-century liberals deal with the feeding of the five thousand? The ironic thing is, though they rejected supernaturalism—and they were committed naturalists—they still wanted to find some viable place for religion and for ethics. Though they rejected the supernatural claims of Jesus, they lauded Him for His ethical insights and honored Him as a great moral teacher. They also said there's still room for religion that gets us in touch with our inner feelings and our spirituality. Does that sound familiar? People who are rank pagans, who deride any biblical theology, still talk about being "spiritual," whatever that means. How did they treat this New Testament narrative?

One theory was that it was a wholesale, fraudulent myth—the kind of myths that are made up in the imaginations of people who have some high esteem for a local hero or some other great person. They say, "In the New Testament record, Jesus, whoever He really was in history, was a man about whom many myths were created to extol His significance, but we can't take this record seriously as history." This spawned a movement in nineteenth-century thought called the quest for the historical Jesus. The assumption behind the quest for the historical Jesus was that you can't find the historical Jesus in the New Testament. We have to reach beyond it, underneath it, inside it in order to understand who He was. We have to demythologize it and come up with something that is rational and natural. So the first explanation was that it was just myth.

Another theory came forth that was even more critical. It said the feeding of the five thousand was not only a myth but it was an intentional fraud perpetrated by Jesus Himself. Jesus knew He was going to depart from the city to a place outside where food wasn't available, and He planned a scheme to make it look as though He had supernatural power. Before the crowd assembled, Jesus had His disciples buy a great supply of bread and fish and conceal it in a secret cave where He would be giving His message. Then, as He had instructed His disciples, He stood in front of the hidden entrance to the cave and when it was time to eat, the disciples formed a kind of "bucket brigade," passing the food through the cave to Jesus' back. Like a magician who pulls silk scarves forever out of his sleeve, Jesus pulled out bread and fishes to perform this seeming miracle. The staging of such a thing would be almost more miraculous than the miracle itself.

The third theory was that Jesus didn't perform a physical miracle of multiplying loaves and fishes, but what our Lord did was perform an ethical miracle. Some people—like the little boy mentioned in John 6:9—thought ahead and were prepared, bringing their lunches for the occasion, but many people, in their excitement to see Jesus and to hear Him, were derelict. They forgot to pack a lunch and didn't make adequate preparations, and like the foolish virgins of the parable (Matt. 25:1–13), they came unprepared. Of course, the people who didn't have any food were looking at those who were eating, and they were hungry. Jesus persuaded those who had food to share voluntarily with those who did not. This was one of the first biblical accounts of the redistribution of wealth under the impetus of the teaching of Jesus. Jesus was so persuasive that the people shared their lunch. Of course, that does radical violence to the New Testament text and completely depletes it of the significance found in the biblical text.

The Emptiness of Naturalism

If you're a naturalist, nothing makes any difference. There's no one home up there, and if there's no one home, all you have is nature, and you don't live your life out in an environment that is hostile to you. Mother nature is not hostile; she's indifferent, which is even worse. The stones, the rocks, the cells, the stars, the animals are indifferent to you and to your circumstances, because from the perspective of nature, you're nothing more than a grown-up germ. You're a cosmic accident. Your origin comes from nothingness and is meaninglessness, and you are sitting on one cog of a huge wheel of a vast cosmic machine that is running down inexorably to the abyss of meaninglessness. There are two poles to your life: one that begins in meaninglessness and the other that ends in meaninglessness. The naive humanist tries to borrow some capital from Christianity when he says, "We have to protect human dignity and to tolerate everybody." Why make such a statement? If you start with meaninglessness and you end with meaninglessness, what you have at every point in between is meaninglessness.

The only philosophy I respect at all apart from Christianity is total nihilism, where nothing matters. But you see, if naturalism is all there is, who cares whether black people or white people sit at the back of the bus. Neither the black nor the white has any dignity whatsoever. Who cares if we kill fifteen million unborn children? They're so much domestic garbage to begin with if you're a naturalist. If you're a naturalist, there's no such thing as right; there's no such thing as wrong. All you have are personal preferences. If the stronger person has his personal preference over the weaker person, then he'll use his club on the weaker guy's preferences. That's the way it is in naturalism.

Assume that on that day in Galilee, Jesus of Nazareth fed thousands of people to their satisfaction with five loaves and a few fish. What that means is the radical breakthrough of the supernatural into the natural. What that means is that Jesus of Nazareth is not just a clever ethical teacher. It means that He is who He said He was—the incarnate Son of God. It means not only that God is but that He cares. He dwells among us, and He deals with our sin, with our disappointment, and with our pain. What that means is that every human being is made in the image of God, and that who sits at the back of the bus matters, and it matters forever. It means that your life matters, not just for now but forever.

Nineteenth-century liberalism spilled over into the twentieth century, and we were plunged into the existential theology of the *hic et nunc*, the here and now. This is all there is. You only go around once, so eat, drink, and be merry, for tomorrow we die. And nobody cares. Or at least nobody ought to care, because the word *ought* is a meaningless word.

We don't seem to see what's at stake here. I remember when I was in seminary, dealing with professors who believed this kind of higher critical theory and who couldn't wait to attack the integrity of the Scriptures. I talked to one of these professors and said: "I understand that you don't believe the Bible is the Word of God, but I don't understand why you seem to delight in teaching that. I would think that if you came to the conclusion that the Bible is not the inspired Word of God, that it's a conclusion that you would reach with tears. Because without this, we're without Christ. And without Christ, we're without hope. And we are, as the Apostle Paul declared, 'most to be pitied [1 Cor. 15:19].'"

What difference does it make? All the difference in the world. Jesus is the Bread of Life who was there to feed those thousands of people who were hungry, and He is the same Bread of Life who feeds us when we come to Him today. What interest should we have in adoring, worshiping, praising, or working for a myth? The nineteenth-century liberals were wrong—desperately, fatally, eternally wrong. Thank God.

48

PETER'S CONFESSION AND OURS

Luke 9:18–27

Now it happened that as he was praying alone, the disciples were with him. And he asked them, "Who do the crowds say that I am?" And they answered, "John the Baptist. But others say, Elijah, and others, that one of the prophets of old has risen." Then he said to them, "But who do you say that I am?" And Peter answered, "The Christ of God."

And he strictly charged and commanded them to tell this to no one, saying, "The Son of Man must suffer many things and be rejected by the elders and chief priests and scribes, and be killed, and on the third day be raised."

And he said to all, "If anyone would come after me, let him deny himself and take up his cross daily and follow me. For whoever would save his life will lose it, but whoever loses his life for my sake will save it. For what does it profit a man if he gains the whole world and loses or forfeits himself? For whoever is ashamed of me and of my words, of him will the Son of Man be ashamed when he comes in his glory and the glory of the Father and of the holy angels. But I tell you truly, there are some standing here who will not taste death until they see the kingdom of God."

In this text, there's an echo of the question that had haunted King Herod, where he was troubled by the reports coming to him of a man who was going about the countryside healing people and performing amazing miracles. Was it some prophet? Was it Elijah coming? Or the worst of his nightmares would have been that it was the reappearance of John the Baptist, whom he had executed. Now that same issue is brought up by Jesus to His disciples when they came to Him while He was alone praying.

He asked them, "Who do the crowds say that I am?" (v. 18). The disciples would have been aware of what was being discussed among people in the nearby villages. **And they answered, "John the Baptist. But others say, Elijah, and others, that one of the prophets of old has risen"** (v. 19). Jesus received this information without any substantial comment. It's as if He were to respond that it was interesting information, but His concern was not so much what people out there were saying about Him but rather what the disciples thought. **Then he said to them, "But who do you say that I am?"** (v. 20).

The Identity of Jesus

I'm tempted to assume that every sentient adult in the United States has at least enough information about Jesus (if from no other source than those messages that come through the extended Christmas season each year) to have formed some opinion as to the identity of Jesus. I wonder: "What is that identity that they've assumed? What do they think about Jesus? Do they think He is a mythological character? Do they echo the liberalism of a century ago, that Jesus was a prophet or a great ethical teacher?"

I haven't canvassed everybody in America, but I encountered a friend recently whom I have known for many years. He's a man who wouldn't enter a church building other than to pay his last respects to a friend who had died. He's a profane man, and his vocabulary is regularly laced with blasphemies. Though I know he has a high regard for me, and I trust that he loves me, nevertheless, his favorite pastime in my presence is to mock me for my religious convictions. He raises his hands and says, "Praise the Lord, R.C.!" This is the way he likes to tease me, so I thought he would be a good candidate to ask his opinion of Jesus. I said to him, candidly, "I have a sermon this Sunday, and I would like your help with it." He seemed surprised that I was seeking information for my sermon from him. I said: "I'm speaking on a passage from the Bible where people were asked their opinion of Jesus, and I'm curious as to what your opinion is. Who do you think Jesus was?"

He didn't respond in his normal, silly manner, but rather, he became somewhat sobered by the question. And he said, "I'm going to have to think about it." So I said, "Fair enough." About four hours later, I saw him and asked, "Have you thought about the question I asked you?" He responded: "Actually, I've thought about little else in the last few hours, and I have come to a conclusion as to what I think about Jesus. I think that He's the Son of God and that God sent Him into the world."

That was the last answer I expected from him, and it gave me pause. I thought, "How is it possible that somebody could come to the conclusion that Jesus is the Son of God and behave as this man does?" As I contemplated my own question, I thought of two personages who have manifested that possibility clearly by their behavior. The first one is Satan himself. He knew, during Jesus' entire earthly ministry, that Jesus is the incarnate Son of God, and, as much as he understood that intellectually, he hated it passionately. He knew who Jesus was, but he was not interested in following Him, only in destroying Him. In the biblical record, the first personages who recognized the deity of Christ behind the hidden veil of His humanity were the demons from hell, so for them, it wasn't a problem of a lack of knowledge of His identity. It was a lack of affection for the One who was the Son of God. But that's Satan, and we put him in a separate category than human beings.

Then I thought of another person who was convinced that Jesus is the Son of God and, despite that knowledge, was altogether unconverted and unregenerate. The day before I was regenerated by the Holy Spirit, if you would have asked me: "What is your opinion of Jesus? Who do you think He was?" I would have been unhesitant in my response: "Clearly, He is the Son of God." I believed that in my head, but there wasn't an ounce of affection in my heart for the One whom I believed to be the veritable Son of God.

Thinking that through even more, I began to wonder, "How many people out there have that same contradictory understanding of Jesus intellectually, while their hearts are so far removed from Him?" I began to think of the precious people whom I love so dearly who make up my congregation and thought again of the great Augustine of Hippo's definition of the church as a *corpus permixtum*, a mixed body. Augustine was simply reflecting on the teaching of Jesus Himself, who said that in the assembly, there will always be tares among the wheat (Matt. 13:24–30). There will be the unconverted among the converted. And who knows who they are? I don't have the ability to read anyone's heart any more than anyone has the power to read my heart. I don't know who is soundly and truly converted and who remains unconverted and on their way to everlasting torment.

We should be able to know the state of our own hearts. Even if I'm unsure about my state, I know that the Scriptures tell me that I am to make my calling sure (2 Peter 1:10)—that the assurance of salvation is a real possibility, and not only a possibility, but an obligation for every Christian.

In Matthew's account, it was Peter who answered the question, "Who do you say that I am?" "Simon Peter replied, 'You are the Christ, the Son of the living God.' And Jesus answered him, 'Blessed are you, Simon Bar-Jonah! For flesh and blood has not revealed this to you, but my Father who is in heaven. And I tell you, you are Peter, and on this rock I will build my church, and the gates of hell shall not prevail against it'" (Matt. 16:15–18). If you understand that Jesus is the Son of God—not simply in an intellectual manner—then Christ will say to you, "Blessed are you." For there is no greater blessing than to know the Son of God.

The Suffering of Christ

And he strictly charged and commanded them to tell this to no one (v. 21). It was not yet the hour to make the truth of that affirmation public. But He went on to say this: **"The Son of Man must suffer many things and be rejected by the elders and chief priests and scribes, and be killed, and on the third day be raised"** (v. 22). In Matthew's account, Peter, the rock, who made the great confession, immediately made a dreadful confession when he presumed to tell Jesus what Jesus was not allowed to do and what He was to do.

What Jesus said to the disciples was this: **"The Son of Man must"**—must, it's necessary, there is no other possibility. He was going by divine, sovereign constraint. It absolutely had to happen. It was His mission. **"The Son of Man must suffer many things and be rejected by the elders and chief priests and scribes, and be killed, and on the third day be raised."** This was not a solitary venture. He told them these things not because He wanted their compassion or comfort or sympathy. He told them this so that they would understand what it meant to follow Him. Jesus continued, **"If anyone would come after me, let him deny himself and take up his cross daily and follow me"** (v. 23). Perhaps it's that part that people who deny that Jesus is the Son of God don't want to hear. They don't want to embrace the consequences that Jesus sets forth. When it comes right down to it, you either deny Christ and follow yourself, or you deny yourself and follow Christ, because you can't follow Christ and yourself.

"Let him deny himself and take up his cross daily and follow me." The first time I read that in the New Testament, I was puzzled by it. Jesus was asking people to pick up their crosses and follow Him every day when He hadn't been crucified yet. Where did the cross come into this? It was too early for the cross; it hadn't happened yet. We know what the imagery suggests. The Romans required, in crucifixion, that on the way to his execution, the condemned person had to carry the heavy wooden crossbeam that would then be affixed to the vertical beam forming the cross on which the person would be placed for crucifixion. We know the account of our Lord's crucifixion, that He had been severely beaten, so they compelled Simon of Cyrene to carry the crossbeam for Him (23:26).

There is evidence that the Jews under Roman rule were familiar with this Roman form of execution, and they had developed an idiom called "bearing one's cross," which meant to the Jew, "enduring the worst that the world can throw at you." It is not out of place for Jesus to use this metaphor. To "take up the cross daily" is to take up our Lord's cross daily, to identify with His humiliation. Even our baptism, which signifies many things, signifies our being buried and raised together with Christ (Rom. 6:4). As the Apostle Peter tells us, unless we're willing to involve ourselves with the humiliation of Jesus, we won't experience involvement with His exaltation (1 Peter 5:6). To be a follower of Christ is not to be a follower of self or to be one who flees from the humiliation and the suffering that are involved with being a Christian.

The Grand Paradox

Jesus then told the grand paradox: **"For whoever would save his life will lose it, but whoever loses his life for my sake will save it"** (v. 24). In one sense it appears that to be a Christian is to have a throwaway life. But to throw away one's life for Christ is to find life forever. **"For what does it profit a man if he gains the whole world and loses or forfeits himself?"** (v. 25). What profit, what gain is it? Jesus suggested that we look at the bottom line at the debits and the credits, the assets and the liabilities. He was speaking in economic language, in terms of profit. Jesus asked in Matthew 16:26, "What shall a man give in return for his soul?" Many of us have read dramatic stories and literary tales about people selling their souls to the devil as if that were something extraordinary. The vast majority of human beings do it every day, trading their souls for what the world offers. What profit is it to a man if he gains the whole world if it costs him his soul?

"For whoever is ashamed of me and of my words, of him will the Son of Man be ashamed when he comes in his glory and the glory of the Father and of the holy angels" (v. 26). This is a sober warning from Jesus. If we confess Him before men, He will confess us before His Father. If I say to my friends: "I love Jesus. I believe Jesus is the Son of God, and I'm prepared to follow Him at whatever cost it is," and if I mean that and do it, then Jesus will say to the Father: "I love R.C. He's mine." But if I am ashamed of Jesus, if I try to harbor a secret faith, and I don't want anybody to know lest they think I'm strange or weird or foolish, then He will say to the Father: "R.C. Sproul? Yes, I know who he is, and Father, I'm ashamed of him." Can you imagine anything worse?

"But I tell you truly, there are some standing here who will not taste death until they see the kingdom of God" (v. 27). Luke mentions these words almost in passing. There is no consensus as to what moment or event

Jesus was referring to in this somewhat cryptic statement. There are many who suggest that, since Luke placed it right before the transfiguration, that Jesus was referring to their witnessing that transfiguration only a few days after He made this pronouncement. Others have suggested that Jesus was referring to the resurrection; others, to His ascension; or still others, to the day of Pentecost, or to the fall of Jerusalem in AD 70, which is the view I favor. The language that our Lord uses here involves what we call a particular negative proposition, signaled by the use of the word *some.* In the canons of logic and the laws of immediate inference, when a particular negative is expressed, it assumes that the opposite and equal particular is affirmed. In simple language, what that means is when Jesus said, **"There are some standing here who will not taste death until they see the kingdom of God,"** the inference was that some of them *would* taste death before that happened. That makes it highly unlikely that this prophecy would come to pass just a few days later.

49

THE TRANSFIGURATION

Luke 9:28–36

Now about eight days after these sayings he took with him Peter and John and James and went up on the mountain to pray. And as he was praying, the appearance of his face was altered, and his clothing became dazzling white. And behold, two men were talking with him, Moses and Elijah, who appeared in glory and spoke of his departure, which he was about to accomplish at Jerusalem. Now Peter and those who were with him were heavy with sleep, but when they became fully awake they saw his glory and the two men who stood with him. And as the men were parting from him, Peter said to Jesus, "Master, it is good that we are here. Let us make three tents, one for you and one for Moses and one for Elijah"—not knowing what he said. As he was saying these things, a cloud came and overshadowed them, and they were afraid as they entered the cloud. And a voice came out of the cloud, saying, "This is my Son, my Chosen One; listen to him!" And when the voice had spoken, Jesus was found alone. And they kept silent and told no one in those days anything of what they had seen.

I think it's the case with the vast majority of preachers that when they rise to exposit the biblical text, they suffer from a sense of personal inadequacy. That's certainly true for me. This text, however, brings us face-to-face with one of the most profound moments that has ever taken place. To try to plumb the depths of this is not only a herculean task but an impossible one.

Now about eight days after these sayings he took with him Peter and

John and James and went up on the mountain to pray (v. 28). I sometimes like to speculate about what it would have been like to have been alive during the days of Jesus' ministry on earth. How wonderful it would have been to be an eyewitness to the things He did during those years—to have seen the transformation of water to wine at the wedding feast of Cana; to see the resurrection from the dead of the widow of Nain's son, or Jairus' daughter, or Lazarus; or to have been an eyewitness of the resurrection or of the ascension.

It's hard to think of wanting to have seen anything more beautiful than the resurrected Christ, but short of that, the one event in all of human history I would want to be an eyewitness of was this one, the transfiguration. In this moment, God removed the veil, and the concealed deity of Christ burst through the cloak of His humanity, displaying itself in nothing less than the pure radiance and refulgence of divine glory. Only five human beings were privileged to be eyewitnesses of that event: three contemporaries, and two who had been brought there from the past days of history—namely, Moses and Elijah. But we're told here that it was only the inner circle of disciples—**Peter and John and James**—who were invited to go with Jesus as He went up on the mountain to pray.

The event took place not during Jesus' conversation with the disciples but while Jesus **was praying** (v. 29). Peter, John, and James were merely onlookers. **The appearance of his face was altered, and his clothing became dazzling white** (v. 29). Suddenly, what the Greek calls a *metamorphosis* took place before their very eyes—a radical transformation of the visage of Jesus. We read that, as He prayed, **the appearance of his face was altered**—metamorphosed, changed. Jesus' face began to shine. In Matthew's account, the shining of His face is noted as having been so intense that it was as the brightness of the sun (Matt. 17:2).

The Glory of God

There is, of course, an episode in biblical history where another person's face began to shine like this. We find it in Exodus 34:29–35. Thousands of years before the transfiguration of Jesus, Moses ascended Mount Sinai to meet with God. After he beheld a portion of God's glory, his face became radiant. It was shining so brightly that when he appeared to Joshua and to Aaron and to the others, they became terrified. They asked him to veil his face because the intensity and the brilliance of that shining glory frightened them.

In that episode, the refulgent glory that was coming from the face of Moses was simply a reflection. It wasn't the glory of Moses. The glory that was being reflected there was a heavenly glory, a divine glory. This is the glory—the *kabod* or weightiness—that belongs uniquely and singularly to God Himself, His eternal glory, which is made manifest throughout history in different times through the appearance of the shekinah, that cloud of radiance and brightness that blinds those who look at it. It is that heavenly glory that God says He will share with no creature: "My glory I give to no other" (Isa. 42:8). He doesn't share His glory with Moses. He displays it. It is so bright that the face of Moses can't absorb it; it can only reflect it.

The difference between that and the transfiguration of Christ is that in Christ's transfiguration, the radiance on the face of Jesus was not a reflection. It was the divine glory coming from the second person of the Trinity, who shares the fullness of the divine glory. We sing, "Glory be to the Father, and to the Son, and to the Holy Ghost; as it was in the beginning, is now, and ever shall be." Here, the eternal glory of the Son of God that was hidden by the frame of His humanity burst out.

His clothing became dazzling white (v. 29). Mark says his clothes "became radiant, intensely white, as no one on earth could bleach them" (Mark 9:3). This was a white that was pure, without any defect, without any blemish.

Peter, James, and John saw this take place. They saw the glory of God, the divine nature right before their eyes. This experience left an impression on these three men that they would never forget. John began his Gospel: "In the beginning was the Word, and the Word was with God, and the Word was God" (John 1:1). He went through the rest of the prologue, and at the end of the prologue, he said, "And the Word became flesh and dwelt among us, and we have seen his glory, glory as of the only Son from the Father, full of grace and truth" (v. 14). John couldn't write that Gospel without first saying, "We saw His glory."

Likewise, Peter wrote: "For we did not follow cleverly devised myths when we made known to you the power and coming of our Lord Jesus Christ, but we were eyewitnesses of his majesty. For when he received honor and glory from God the Father, and the voice was borne to him by the Majestic Glory, 'This is my beloved Son, with whom I am well pleased,' we ourselves heard this very voice borne from heaven, for we were with him on the holy mountain" (2 Peter 1:16–18). During the ministry of Jesus, and even after His death, resurrection, and ascension, Peter had his well-known lapses. But the one thing he never forgot is what he saw on that holy mountain when Christ was transfigured before him.

Moses and Elijah

And behold, two men were talking with him, Moses and Elijah, who appeared in glory and spoke of his departure, which he was about to accomplish at Jerusalem (vv. 30–31). Moses represented the law and Elijah stood at the head of the long line of prophets. We can say here that on the Mount of Transfiguration, the divine nature broke through in the presence not only of the disciples but also of the law and of the prophets, of Moses and Elijah, who had called the people's attention to the One who would come. This episode came soon after Peter's Caesarea Philippi confession, when he said, "You are the Christ, the Son of the living God" (Matt. 16:16). The Messiah would not only be an anointed human being, but He also would be the divine Son as well. One of the ironies of this text is that Moses, the mediator of the old covenant, was not allowed to enter the promised land. He could look at it, but God denied him entry into it.

Now hundreds and hundreds of years later, Moses was in the promised land with Elijah. They took a brief leave from heaven, where they beheld the glory of the Father day and night, and came to the earth to behold the glory of the Son. Moses and Elijah appeared on the Mount of Transfiguration in the glory they brought with them and spoke of Jesus' **departure, which he was about to accomplish at Jerusalem**. Jesus had told the disciples after the Caesarea Philippi confession that He had to go to Jerusalem to suffer and to die (Luke 9:22). As He was about to make that journey, the Father sent Moses and Elijah to Him perhaps in answer to His prayer. The Scriptures don't say what Jesus was praying about, but given the intensity of His prayer in Gethsemane, He was perhaps praying about the cup that the Father had placed before Him. The Father sent Moses and Elijah to comfort Him and to encourage Him concerning His coming death.

Now Peter and those who were with him were heavy with sleep, but when they became fully awake they saw his glory and the two men who stood with him. And as the men were parting from him, Peter said to Jesus, "Master, it is good that we are here. Let us make three tents, one for you and one for Moses and one for Elijah"—not knowing what he said (vv. 32–33). Peter didn't want to leave. It was a mountaintop experience. He had no interest in going to Jerusalem or in continuing to preach. Peter wanted to bask in the glory he had just experienced. How like all of us Peter was, wanting to stay there on the mountain. With his attempt to encourage, he tried once more to dissuade Jesus from His destiny.

The Father Speaks

As he was saying these things, a cloud came and overshadowed them, and they were afraid as they entered the cloud (v. 34). Was it the shekinah or an ordinary cloud? Luke doesn't tell us. **And a voice came out of the cloud, saying, "This is my Son, my Chosen One; listen to him!"** (v. 35). Only three times in the New Testament are we told that God speaks audibly from the heavens. The first time was at the baptism of Jesus, when the dove descended, the heavens opened, and the Father spoke, saying, "This is my beloved Son, with whom I am well pleased" (Matt. 3:17). This is the second time, and the third is in John 12:28. In this pronouncement on the Mount of Transfiguration, God repeats what He said at Jesus' baptism but changes the message slightly. He gives the same affirmation of Jesus' sonship: **"This is my Son."** But He also calls Jesus **"my Chosen One"** and adds the command to **"listen to him!"** This is an interesting command, for the disciples had tasted the glory of God and had had a glimpse of the majesty of Jesus Christ. Why would they not want to hear everything that He had to say? How could they not have heeded and wanted to hear every word that came from the mouth of the One who had just been transfigured in front of them?

And when the voice had spoken, Jesus was found alone. And they kept silent and told no one in those days anything of what they had seen (v. 36). Later, of course, they talked about what they had seen and heard and told everybody. But for now, it wasn't time for talking. It was time for hearing, which they did.

Every one of us who is in Christ Jesus will one day see this same glory. It's inherent in Jesus. The author of Hebrews says that Jesus is "the radiance of the glory of God" (1:3). When we enter into glory, and our eyes are overwhelmed by the brilliance of the light, and we try to find the source of that light, we'll see Jesus—not for a moment, but forever—in the blinding glory of God. We missed the transfiguration the first time, but we won't miss it the next time.

50

THE GREATEST

Luke 9:37–48

On the next day, when they had come down from the mountain, a great crowd met him. And behold, a man from the crowd cried out, "Teacher, I beg you to look at my son, for he is my only child. And behold, a spirit seizes him, and he suddenly cries out. It convulses him so that he foams at the mouth, and shatters him, and will hardly leave him. And I begged your disciples to cast it out, but they could not." Jesus answered, "O faithless and twisted generation, how long am I to be with you and bear with you? Bring your son here." While he was coming, the demon threw him to the ground and convulsed him. But Jesus rebuked the unclean spirit and healed the boy, and gave him back to his father. And all were astonished at the majesty of God.

But while they were all marveling at everything he was doing, Jesus said to his disciples, "Let these words sink into your ears: The Son of Man is about to be delivered into the hands of men." But they did not understand this saying, and it was concealed from them, so that they might not perceive it. And they were afraid to ask him about this saying.

An argument arose among them as to which of them was the greatest. But Jesus, knowing the reasoning of their hearts, took a child and put him by his side and said to them, "Whoever receives this child in my name receives me, and whoever receives me receives him who sent me. For he who is least among you all is the one who is great."

The transfiguration of Jesus Christ was one of the most glorious moments in history. Yet, the next day, when Jesus came down the mountain to meet the rest of the disciples, He walked into a maelstrom of controversy and trouble.

Luke 9 begins, "And he called the twelve together and gave them power and authority over all demons and to cure diseases" (v. 1). That was the moment when the disciples became Apostles, because Jesus transferred to them authority and power—the authority and power to preach, to heal, and to cast out demons. Now, when Jesus came down from the Mount of Transfiguration, He found nine of His disciples, who had received that commission and been granted that power and authority, failing to exercise what had been given to them.

The New Testament tells us that every person who is in Christ has been visited by the Spirit of God and empowered for ministry. Paul tells us that we don't all have the same gift. Our gifts differ, but we all are gifted to participate in the ministry of the kingdom of God. He says: "Having gifts that differ according to the grace given to us, let us use them: if prophecy, in proportion to our faith; if service, in our serving; the one who teaches, in his teaching; the one who exhorts, in his exhortation; the one who contributes, in generosity; the one who leads, with zeal; the one who does acts of mercy, with cheerfulness" (Rom. 12:6–8). Every believer has been empowered to serve in some capacity. The disciples were gifted to heal and to cast out demons, and they failed to exercise their gifts in a meaningful way in this case.

The Gaze of God

On the next day, when they had come down from the mountain, a great crowd met him. And behold, a man from the crowd cried out, "Teacher, I beg you to look at my son, for he is my only child" (vv. 37–38). The French existentialist philosopher Jean-Paul Sartre, one of the most famous atheists of the twentieth century, gave a critique of the existence of God, saying that if God exists at all, and if He is omniscient, that means that we all live our lives beneath His gaze. To be subject to the gaze of God is to be reduced to an object, like a monkey in the zoo, and we lose our very humanity. Sartre couldn't stand the thought of God's being a cosmic voyeur who was looking down at us through the keyhole of heaven and monitoring our every move. He thought that was the ultimate loss of freedom and dignity. There is in the heart of the atheist a profound desire for God not to look at him but to overlook him and ignore him.

This is our most base response to the existence of God. As we saw in the garden of Eden, the first impulse of Adam and Eve, after their initial transgression of the law of God, was to run and hide. They didn't want God to see them, because they were ashamed. The tragedy is that Sartre had not yet experienced the benevolent gaze of God, the healing gaze of God, the compassionate look of God. David, when he had known forgiveness, said to God: "O Lord, you have searched me and known me! . . . Even before a word is on my tongue, behold, O Lord, you know it altogether. . . . Where shall I go from your Spirit? Or where shall I flee from your presence? If I ascend to heaven, you are there! If I make my bed in Sheol, you are there!" (Ps. 139:1, 4, 7–8).

David said, "Please look at me!" And that's what this man was saying: "Jesus, look at my son! Don't pass by and fail to notice him in his pain and in his misery." He was asking Jesus to look at his son, not with the look of judgment or scorn, but with the gaze of mercy and of healing. **"I beg you to look at my son, for he is my only child."**

"And behold, a spirit seizes him, and he suddenly cries out. It convulses him so that he foams at the mouth, and shatters him, and will hardly leave him" (v. 39). This sounds like a definition or a description of epilepsy, but remember that Luke was a physician and knew the difference between normal epilepsy and a demonically induced epileptic convulsion. Jesus understood that this was no mere disease but rather was an invasion from hell into this little boy's life. The man says, **"And I begged your disciples to cast it out, but they could not"** (v. 40). The disciples failed. They had the authority. They had the power, but it didn't work. If we ever find a time in sacred Scripture where our Lord displays annoyance or frustration, here it is. **Jesus answered, "O faithless and twisted generation, how long am I to be with you and bear with you?"** (v. 41).

There's a dispute among scholars as to whom Jesus was addressing. Was He addressing everyone in the crowd, including the scribes who were there, the disciples, and everyone else? Or was He particularly addressing the disciples? I think the latter more than the former. I think His annoyance was particularly with His own disciples, whom He had commissioned and to whom He had given power and authority. In this attempt at healing the young boy, they acted without faith, and they participated in the perversity of that generation. The word translated **"twisted"** is sometimes translated "perverse." In our culture, we often associate that word with some kind of sexual deviation. But when the Bible speaks of perversion, it means something that goes beyond sexual behavior. Jesus linked together faithlessness and perversion. What perversion means here in the text is "that which is crooked" or "that which is distorted." Jesus was addressing not only His disciples but also the generation at that time.

The culture into which Jesus came was twisted. It was distorted. The values that they held dear were things that were noxious to the Lord God, and what was precious in the sight of God was despised in their culture. Theirs was a twisted culture because it was a faithless culture.

When human beings fail to trust God, they twist their lives into all kinds of crazy shapes. Consider our own age. The sanctity of life has been twisted; the sanctity of marriage has been distorted. We are twisted; we're distorted and therefore faithless.

The Demon Cast Out

"Bring your son here" (v. 41). Jesus didn't come down the mountain just to complain about the perversity of this generation. Of course He was going to accede to the man's request to see his son. **While he was coming, the demon threw him to the ground and convulsed him** (v. 42). This was this boy's last convulsion. This was this demon's last victory over this young boy because **Jesus rebuked the unclean spirit and healed the boy, and gave him back to his father** (v. 42). That demonic spirit had snatched the boy from his father, but once Jesus healed him and rebuked the enemy, He gave the boy back to his father. That's what Jesus does.

And all were astonished at the majesty of God (v. 43). The Greek word translated "astonished" (*ekplēssomai*) is one we hear again and again in the New Testament in response to the miraculous works of Jesus. Regularly and characteristically, when people beheld His works, they were utterly amazed. But notice the locus of their amazement here. They **were astonished at the majesty of God**. Isn't it interesting that, twenty-four hours earlier, Peter, James, and John had been terrified at the majesty of God as it exploded in front of them on the Mount of Transfiguration? Now, at the bottom of the mountain, the crowd, which hadn't seen a transformed Christ or seen the radiance of His face, was amazed at His power over hell. They caught a glimpse of the majesty of God. Isn't it interesting that they realized, at least for the moment, that they weren't simply in the presence of an extraordinary man? They had just witnessed a work of God, and it displayed His majesty, His glory, His splendor, His grandeur in the healing of the boy.

But while they were all marveling at everything he was doing, Jesus said to his disciples, "Let these words sink into your ears: The Son of Man is about to be delivered into the hands of men" (vv. 43–44). This wasn't the first time He told them that, but their response this time wasn't any different than it was in the other times. **But they did not understand this saying** (v. 45). Why? For one thing, the Jews in their expectation of the Messiah only looked at the royal pomp of the coming Son of David, and they didn't tie it together with the Suffering Servant of God found in the book of Isaiah. That understanding of the messianic office did not become clear until after the cross. **It was concealed from them, so that they might not perceive it. And they were afraid to ask him about this saying** (v. 45). God hid it from them for His own purposes.

The Least and the Greatest

An argument arose among them as to which of them was the greatest (v. 46). The disciples were arguing about which one of them would be the greatest in the kingdom of God. What's wrong with wanting to be great? Nothing—and everything. It's been said by one theologian that most sins really are nothing more and nothing less than a distortion or a twisting of some virtue. When God created human beings and made them in His own image, He gave to them, as part of their humanity, an aspiration for significance. Is there anybody who wants their life to be insignificant, to be meaningless, to be useless, to be an exercise in vanity? We want our lives to count, but sometimes we want it to count for the wrong reasons. We become competitive; we become vicious toward rivals who would find a higher station than we achieve, who would receive the promotion we want or win the championship we covet. We begin to be envious and jealous of them and then to despise them. How many of the Ten Commandments address our twisted desires for greatness? To want to be great in faith, to want to be great in service, is a noble thing, but to want to be the greatest in the kingdom of God at the expense of other people is perversity.

But Jesus, knowing the reasoning of their hearts, took a child and put him by his side and said to them, "Whoever receives this child in my name receives me, and whoever receives me receives him who sent me. For he who is least among you all is the one who is great" (vv. 47–48). Christ tells us to become as little children. Sometimes we use that as an excuse for infantile Christianity. He calls us to be childlike, but never childish. We're called to be "babes" in evil. But in our understanding, we're called to be adults and mature, knowledgeable of the things that God reveals to us in sacred Scripture. In what sense are we to be like children? In the sense of trusting our heavenly Father. Anybody can believe *in* God, but to *believe* God is what is involved in the Christian life—to trust Him. When He says, "Do this and live," we know that that's how we are to behave. When He tells us the things that He loves, we trust that they're good, and when He tells us the things that He abhors, we trust that they are abhorrent. Little children don't get into deep theological disputes with their parents; there is that *fides implicita,* an implicit trust or faith that they give to their parents. That's what Jesus is saying: "Trust Me! You can't believe in Me and then not trust Me." Because that's what faith is. It's trust. And so He says, **"He who is least among you all"**—by which He means he who is most trusting—**"is the one who is great."**

51

DISCIPLESHIP

Luke 9:49–62

John answered, "Master, we saw someone casting out demons in your name, and we tried to stop him, because he does not follow with us." But Jesus said to him, "Do not stop him, for the one who is not against you is for you."

When the days drew near for him to be taken up, he set his face to go to Jerusalem. And he sent messengers ahead of him, who went and entered a village of the Samaritans, to make preparations for him. But the people did not receive him, because his face was set toward Jerusalem. And when his disciples James and John saw it, they said, "Lord, do you want us to tell fire to come down from heaven and consume them?" But he turned and rebuked them. And they went on to another village.

As they were going along the road, someone said to him, "I will follow you wherever you go." And Jesus said to him, "Foxes have holes, and birds of the air have nests, but the Son of Man has nowhere to lay his head." To another he said, "Follow me." But he said, "Lord, let me first go and bury my father." And Jesus said to him, "Leave the dead to bury their own dead. But as for you, go and proclaim the kingdom of God." Yet another said, "I will follow you, Lord, but let me first say farewell to those at my home." Jesus said to him, "No one who puts his hand to the plow and looks back is fit for the kingdom of God."

Luke tells us that immediately after the debate as to who would be the greatest in the kingdom of God, John replied, **"Master, we saw someone casting out demons in your name, and we tried to stop him, because he does not follow with us"** (v. 49). Some say that John was just offering this comment as a diversion to deflect the words of rebuke that Jesus had just given to them. Others say that it was an earnest concern that John had seen somebody actually casting out demons using the name of Jesus, but he wasn't one of the Twelve and presumably not one of the seventy-two in the broader company of Jesus' disciples (10:1–12). John was concerned about this and wanted Jesus to stop the man from carrying out this ministry that he was doing in the name of Jesus. Instead, Jesus saw a spirit that was contrary to authentic discipleship to Christ. He saw a narrow exclusiveness, a parochial attitude that said, "If he's not part of our group in its purest form, then he has nothing whatsoever to do with us." Does that sound familiar? Do we not commit this same offense again and again? "He may claim to be a Christian, but he's not really Reformed, so we can't trust him," or "He's not an Episcopalian or a Lutheran as we are, so we can't trust him."

The Spirit of Exclusion

I don't know of anybody who's a greater fan of Martin Luther than I am, but one of the low points of the Reformation took place when the attempt was made to create a unified front between the Reformers of Switzerland and the followers of Luther in Germany. At Marburg, Germany, representatives of both sides—including Huldrych Zwingli from Switzerland—met for a colloquy or dialogue to try to hammer out a position of unity so that they could stand together for the Reformation. They couldn't agree on some points regarding how Christ is present in the Lord's Supper. Both sides believed that He is present, but the mode of that presence was a matter of dispute. Luther insisted on the physical, corporeal presence of Christ in the sacrament, and at one point he pounded the table repeating, "*Hoc est corpus meum!*"—"This is My body." He insisted that the only way we can take these words of Jesus is in the fullest corporeal sense.

Zwingli and the others said, "But Jesus said, 'I am the vine'; 'I am the door.' Can't the word *is* be used in a way that it represents something without this insistence on literalism?" They couldn't get together. That was sad enough, but the saddest thing was when Luther turned to Zwingli and said, "You are an *andern Geist*," a different spirit. He questioned Zwingli's Christianity altogether. Luther was like John at this point: "If you don't agree with us at every point, then you're really not of Christ." Jesus will have none of that.

Jesus said to him, "Do not stop him, for the one who is not against you is for you" (v. 50). We should learn not only from that tragedy at Marburg but also from this encounter here in the Scriptures.

But that spirit of exclusion got worse. **When the days drew near for him to be taken up, he set his face to go to Jerusalem. And he sent messengers ahead of him, who went and entered a village of the Samaritans, to make preparations for him. But the people did not receive him, because his face was set toward Jerusalem** (vv. 51–53). Where was He received? He was thrown out of Galilee. They wouldn't accept Him in Judea. The Samaritans rejected Him. The Gerasenes expelled Him. Everywhere He went, He was unwelcome. When James and John saw this rejection by the Samaritans, they said, **"Lord, do you want us to tell fire to come down from heaven and consume them?"** (v. 54). Elijah did just that in his confrontation with the priests of Baal in 1 Kings 18. The disciples, because they were offended, wanted to give the Samaritans a taste of the wrath of God. Have you ever wanted God to pour down fire from heaven on someone who offended you? Is this not our nature, even as Christians, to flee from God's wrath for ourselves but also to push our neighbor into the direct path of it? Again, Jesus will not have it. **But he turned and rebuked them** (v. 55).

The Cost of Discipleship

And they went on to another village. As they were going along the road, someone said to him, "I will follow you wherever you go" (vv. 56–57). Do you hear what this man is saying? "Lord, Lord, my Sovereign One, the One who has absolute authority over me—whatever You say for me to do, I'll do it. Wherever You tell me to go, I'll go." I'll never forget the time when, right after my conversion, I was welcomed into a small group of college men who met weekly for prayer, Bible reading, and hymn singing. One of my favorite hymns was "Where He Leads Me I Will Follow." As a young Christian, singing those words thrilled my soul, but in the back of my mind I wondered: "Do I really mean this? Will I follow Him wherever that path takes me?" I wanted so much to be sincere.

And Jesus said to him, "Foxes have holes, and birds of the air have nests, but the Son of Man has nowhere to lay his head" (v. 58). The fox who raids the vineyards, when he wants rest and to seek refuge, he returns to his den, and he sleeps in that place until he's refreshed and strengthened once more to go out. How marvelous it is to watch birds coast on the currents of the air without any labor, or at other times fly into the breeze, flapping their wings and working so hard to make progress against the wind. When they get tired, they fly back to their nests, and there they receive rest and refreshment until the morrow and take flight again. The Son of Man didn't have a nest. He didn't have a den. He didn't have a house. He had nowhere to lay His head. "If you want to follow Me, don't count on plush accommodations at the next stop, because I don't have any. Are you sure you want a life like this?" Jesus was saying to this man that there's not a lot of glamour in following Him.

To another he said, "Follow me." But he said, "Lord, let me first go and bury my father" (v. 59). This man asked to postpone his following Jesus, be it ever so briefly, because of a family emergency. The family emergency was that his father had died and he wanted to go bury him before he could follow Him. Now, in Jewish categories, if there ever was a legitimate excuse for avoiding service, it was to make certain that one of your loved ones received a proper burial. Among the rabbis, the need to give a burial for one's father especially—and burials took place very shortly after death—was reason to be excused from religious services and any other service requirement. This was seen as one of the highest priorities that a Jewish person could have, to make sure that his loved one received a proper burial. Surely, Jesus did not despise that tradition. For Jesus to call somebody not to go home and bury their father would require a calling so high, so holy, so important, that it would make the burial of one's own father pale in significance. **And Jesus said to him, "Leave the dead to bury their own dead. But as for you, go and proclaim the kingdom of God"** (v. 60).

Yet another said, "I will follow you, Lord, but let me first say farewell to those at my home" (v. 61). This man said he would follow, but not today—maybe tomorrow. Do you relate to this? "Someday, I will devote myself unequivocally to following Jesus, but first, I have other matters to attend to. I have other things to take care of. Following Jesus with all of my heart and soul is something I would like to do, but at the moment, it is not my top priority." If you don't want to follow Jesus as a top priority in your life, He doesn't want you as a disciple. Elsewhere, our Lord said, "But seek first the kingdom of God and his righteousness, and all these things will be added to you" (Matt. 6:33). Jonathan Edwards said this: "The seeking of the kingdom of God is the chief business of the Christian life." It's not a secondary endeavor. It's not a postscript to your devotion. The overwhelming majority of people who claim to be Christians follow Him with no more than half their hearts. Their devotion is an add-on, but it is not what defines their lives. To be a disciple of Jesus Christ is to have the following of Jesus Christ be that which defines who you are as a person.

Jesus said to him, "No one who puts his hand to the plow and looks back is fit for the kingdom of God" (v. 62). Here Jesus drew an illustration from the agrarian culture of the day. Jesus was saying that it would be absurd for a man to go out to plow his field and, as he started to plow the rows that he would soon plant, to look back over his shoulder to see how straight the furrows were. If you're trying to plow straight ahead while your eyes are straight behind you, can you imagine where that plow is going to go? So Jesus said, "Once you start, don't turn your eyes away from your goal." Remember what the passage told us about where Jesus' focus was? **He set his face to go to Jerusalem** (v. 51). He didn't say, "Let's go to Jerusalem! No, wait a minute! Let's go back to the Mount of Transfiguration." His vocation was to go to Jerusalem, and as He set out to fulfill His mission, there was no turning back.

This raises the question of the perseverance of the saints. Is it possible for a person to begin in grace and lose his salvation? There were those who joined the disciples group of Jesus who then turned away. John said: "They went out from us, but they were not of us; for if they had been of us, they would have continued with us. But they went out, that it might become plain that they all are not of us" (1 John 2:19). Once you sign up, you're in for the duration. Once you set your hand to the plow, if you look back—like Lot's wife looked at Sodom—you're liable to turn into a pillar of salt. But those who have been born of the Spirit of God, whose lives have been changed and who are now walking with Jesus Christ—they may stumble, they may lose resolve from time to time, but their faces are set in one direction: to finish the course of following Him.

52

THE MISSION OF THE SEVENTY-TWO

Luke 10:1–20

After this the Lord appointed seventy-two others and sent them on ahead of him, two by two, into every town and place where he himself was about to go. And he said to them, "The harvest is plentiful, but the laborers are few. Therefore pray earnestly to the Lord of the harvest to send out laborers into his harvest. Go your way; behold, I am sending you out as lambs in the midst of wolves. Carry no moneybag, no knapsack, no sandals, and greet no one on the road. Whatever house you enter, first say, 'Peace be to this house!' And if a son of peace is there, your peace will rest upon him. But if not, it will return to you. And remain in the same house, eating and drinking what they provide, for the laborer deserves his wages. Do not go from house to house. Whenever you enter a town and they receive you, eat what is set before you. Heal the sick in it and say to them, 'The kingdom of God has come near to you.' But whenever you enter a town and they do not receive you, go into its streets and say, 'Even the dust of your town that clings to our feet we wipe off against you. Nevertheless know this, that the kingdom of God has come near.' I tell you, it will be more bearable on that day for Sodom than for that town.

"Woe to you, Chorazin! Woe to you, Bethsaida! For if the mighty works done in you had been done in Tyre and Sidon, they would have repented long ago, sitting in sackcloth and ashes. But it will be more bearable in the judgment for Tyre and Sidon than for you. And you, Capernaum, will you be exalted to heaven? You shall be brought down to Hades.

"The one who hears you hears me, and the one who rejects you rejects me, and the one who rejects me rejects him who sent me."

The seventy-two returned with joy, saying, "Lord, even the demons are subject to us in your name!" And he said to them, "I saw Satan fall like lightning from heaven. Behold, I have given you authority to tread on serpents and scorpions, and over all the power of the enemy, and nothing shall hurt you. Nevertheless, do not rejoice in this, that the spirits are subject to you, but rejoice that your names are written in heaven."

Do you believe in God? Do you believe in Jesus as the Son of God? Do you believe in hell? If you say yes to the first one, you have to say yes to the second one because the true God is the One who has confirmed in power and in glory the unique sonship of Jesus. If you believe in the first, you will believe in the second, and if you believe in the second, you must believe in the third.

Our Lord Jesus taught more about hell than He did about heaven, and yet this is one of the more unpopular subjects in sacred Scripture. Even those of us who say we believe in hell do so barely, for if we were truly persuaded of hell's existence as a place of eternal judgment of God, it would change our passion to reach out with the gospel to those for whom we have any feeling or concern.

Throughout the New Testament, we see Jesus teaching that there will be a judgment day. That is inescapable. Though we would seek to deny it, and the world around us ridicules it, nevertheless, the idea that a human being can go through his life with impunity, without being held accountable, is utterly foreign to the teaching of God. Each one of us will be present at that day of judgment.

After this the Lord appointed seventy-two others and sent them on ahead of him, two by two, into every town and place where he himself was about to go (v. 1). Luke 10 begins so much as chapter 9 did. Chapter 9 began with Jesus sending out the Twelve. Now, He's sending out seventy-two. This larger group of disciples under Jesus' authority was commissioned by Him to go out two by two **into every town and place where he himself was about to go**.

The Lord of the Harvest

And he said to them, "The harvest is plentiful, but the laborers are few. Therefore pray earnestly to the Lord of the harvest to send out laborers into his harvest" (v. 2). He said that the harvest was ripe. It was ready for the sickle. It was abundant. Of course, He was speaking metaphorically. He wasn't sending these men out to do agricultural work. He was sending them out to do the task of evangelism. He was sending them into a fallen world, but into an area of that fallen world in which God was growing His people. He said there was a multitude of people out there ready to enter the kingdom of God, but the laborers were few. So He sent these disciples, but He instructed them to pray that the **"Lord of the harvest"** would send out workers into the harvest.

Whose harvest is it? It's not the harvest of the disciples. It's the harvest of God. Who is the Lord of the harvest? The Lord of the harvest is not the preacher or the evangelist. The Lord of the harvest is God. It's His harvest. He prepared it. It's ready to be harvested, and He's sending out people to bring it. Jesus made it clear here and throughout the New Testament that we don't bring the fruit. We plant the seed, we water the seed, but only God can bring the increase (1 Cor. 3:7). God is the only One able to give people ears to hear and hearts ready to respond to the message. No amount of eloquence, learning, or erudition is good enough or strong enough to bring any human being from spiritual death into the kingdom of God.

Why then does He tell us to pray for laborers if our labor isn't enough to redeem anybody? God doesn't need us. God could speak from the sky. He could write in the sky with His own finger as He wrote the Ten Commandments. He doesn't need me and He doesn't need you. What are we supposed to pray? That He will send out laborers, because the labor and the harvest is one of the most beautiful and fulfilling opportunities and privileges that God gives to His people. He can do it without us, but He chooses to do it with us, to give us the privilege of bringing in the harvest as His servants.

The Kingdom Has Come Near

"Go your way; behold, I am sending you out as lambs in the midst of wolves. Carry no moneybag, no knapsack, no sandals, and greet no one on the road. Whatever house you enter, first say, 'Peace be to this house!' And if a son of peace is there, your peace will rest upon him. But if not, it will return to you. And remain in the same house, eating and drinking what they provide, for the laborer deserves his wages. Do not go from house to house. Whenever you enter a town and they receive you, eat what is set before you. Heal the sick in it and say to them, 'The kingdom of God has come near to you'" (vv. 3–9). What is Jesus saying here? The announcement of the gospel of the kingdom of God, to the Old Testament Jews, was a hope they had of something in the distant future. Now this hope had broken into time and space, and the moment of supreme crisis had arrived. "The kingdom of God is right here, right next to them, among them," Jesus said.

Then Jesus said something dramatic: **"But whenever you enter a town and they do not receive you, go into its streets and say, 'Even the dust of your**

town that clings to our feet we wipe off against you. Nevertheless know this, that the kingdom of God has come near.' I tell you, it will be more bearable on that day for Sodom than for that town" (vv. 10–12). He told the seventy-two to say that the kingdom of God has come near to you, but He said, if that message is rejected, it will be more tolerable in the day of judgment for Sodom than for those who don't accept the message.

That truth hasn't changed. If you hear the gospel when it is near you and you don't heed it, it will be more tolerable for the citizens of Sodom and Gomorrah on the day of judgment than it will be for you. If you walk away unconverted on the day of God's judgment, you will wish that you had been a citizen of Sodom and Gomorrah, because God's judgment will be less severe on them than it will be on you.

There are many people who believe that God's judgment for all sin is the same, that all sins are equally grievous to God. No. Jesus again and again talks about lesser and greater sins, lesser and greater judgment. The Apostle Paul warns: "Because of your hard and impenitent heart you are storing up wrath for yourself on the day of wrath when God's righteous judgment will be revealed" (Rom. 2:5). Every time we sin, we make a new deposit into that treasury of wrath. People might think that if they have committed one sin, they might as well keep going. For instance, if someone has lusted, he ought to go on and commit adultery. After all, James said, "For whoever keeps the whole law but fails in one point has become guilty of all of it" (James 2:10). But that does not mean we should keep on sinning. James means that the slightest discretion is a violation of the whole law. James doesn't say that every sin is equally offensive to God. Jesus teaches clearly that there will be degrees of judgment in the day of judgment. A sinner in hell would give everything he had, do everything that he could, to make the number of his sins in his lifetime one less.

"Woe to you, Chorazin! Woe to you, Bethsaida! For if the mighty works done in you had been done in Tyre and Sidon, they would have repented long ago, sitting in sackcloth and ashes. But it will be more bearable in the judgment for Tyre and Sidon than for you. And you, Capernaum, will you be exalted to heaven? You shall be brought down to Hades" (vv. 13–15). Jesus went on to pronounce an oracle of doom against the contemporary cities who had heard the gospel. The greater judgment comes with the greater light. The more light you have been given of the things of God, the more information you have been given about the kingdom of God, the more liable you are for your response to that message.

"The one who hears you hears me, and the one who rejects you rejects me, and the one who rejects me rejects him who sent me" (v. 16). If you reject the Apostolic testimony, you reject the Christ who authorized it, and if you reject the Christ who authorized the Apostolic testimony, you reject the One who sent Christ—the Father.

The Disciples Return

The seventy-two returned with joy, saying, "Lord, even the demons are subject to us in your name!" (v. 17). The seventy-two were excited. The mission was a success. They were amazed that even the demons were subject to them in His name. Jesus responded, **"I saw Satan fall like lightning from heaven"** (v. 18). But He didn't stop there. He said, **"Behold, I have given you authority to tread on serpents and scorpions, and over all the power of the enemy, and nothing shall hurt you"** (v. 19).

Have you ever thought about the little things in the circumstances of your life and asked, "What if?" Our lives are the sum of millions of small decisions. Behind all the circumstances of history is the Lord of history, and it's only by His divine providence and His sovereign authority that we exist at all. Our very lives are a gift from almighty God, and our lives did not come about as a result of fortuitous circumstances or by chance, but by the eternal decree of almighty God.

You are alive by the providence of God. Do you ever count all your blessings instead of counting sheep? What are you happy about? Your family, your health, your job, your achievements? What are the things in your life for which you are most grateful? If you were to write them down and rate them, what would they be? Jesus gives us the answer as to what they should be.

Written in Heaven

"Nevertheless, do not rejoice in this, that the spirits are subject to you, but rejoice that your names are written in heaven" (v. 20). Do not rejoice in your power, or in your success, or in your authority, but **"rejoice that your names are written in heaven."** The greatest joy any Christian can have is to understand that of all the people in this fallen world, by the sheer grace of almighty God, our names are written in heaven. To have your name written in heaven means that is where your citizenship is. And if your name is written in heaven, then God wrote it there. The only One who writes your name in the Lamb's Book of Life is God, and He writes it in from all eternity.

God does not look down the corridor of time and say: "Who is going to hear My message and respond? Those who will say yes, I'll write in My book, and those who will say no to the gospel, I'll keep their name out of the registry." This is a common interpretation of the biblical teaching of divine sovereign election where God's election is thought to be conditional—it depends on your foreseen works. The Bible clearly refutes that error, and yet it persists.

God does know everything that has happened and everything that will happen in this world. He does know everything that you and I have ever done. Not only that, He knows what you and I are going to do tomorrow. When we talk about the possibility of what may happen tomorrow or what we could conceivably do tomorrow, we call those things contingencies. A master chess player, when he reads the board in front of him, considers the contingencies. He's considering the possible moves that his opponent will make in the course of the game. He then sets up his strategy accordingly, but he doesn't know for sure what his opponent is going to do on the chessboard. He just knows the possibilities.

When we speak of God's omniscience and God's knowing the future, it's not simply that God knows all the possibilities and that God knows all the contingencies. He does know all the contingencies. He does know everything theoretically that you and I could do, and so we say in theology that God knows all contingencies, but He knows nothing contingently. That means that the reason God knows what's going to happen is not because He knows what *might* happen. It's not that He has a crystal ball. The reason He knows the future is because He ordains it sovereignly and eternally. He wrote names in heaven in eternity past. If you're a Christian, it is not because of anything you have done or ever will do but surely by the grace of God alone.

The ultimate question I have in theology when I consider my redemption is this: Why me? Lord, why did You open my eyes? Why did You change my heart? Why did You open my ears? Why did You give me a delight for those things that formerly I despised? It's the pearl of great price. It's the greatest gift ever. Jesus says, "Here's the ground of your ultimate joy: that your names are written in heaven."

53

THE RETURN OF THE SEVENTY-TWO

Luke 10:21–24

In that same hour he rejoiced in the Holy Spirit and said, "I thank you, Father, Lord of heaven and earth, that you have hidden these things from the wise and understanding and revealed them to little children; yes, Father, for such was your gracious will. All things have been handed over to me by my Father, and no one knows who the Son is except the Father, or who the Father is except the Son and anyone to whom the Son chooses to reveal him."

Then turning to the disciples he said privately, "Blessed are the eyes that see what you see! For I tell you that many prophets and kings desired to see what you see, and did not see it, and to hear what you hear, and did not hear it."

The only legitimate reason anyone ever says yes to Christ and receives Him and all His benefits is because of God's grace and by His grace alone. That idea is central to the Reformed faith that we embrace. Having that in front of us, look now at this text that includes within it what I call the strangest prayer ever recorded in the New Testament by Jesus.

In that same hour he rejoiced in the Holy Spirit (v. 21). Before we look at His prayer, we understand that this prayer is given in an attitude of profound joy that Jesus, the incarnation of the second person of the Trinity, is now inclined by the third person of the Trinity, the Holy Spirit, to a profound sense of joy as He addresses the Father, the first person of the Trinity. This is a Trinitarian text all the way through it.

The Election of God

There is no time gap between Jesus' saying to His disciples "Rejoice that your names are written in heaven" (v. 20) and His moving apart from them under the influence of the Holy Spirit in a spirit of joy to express His gratitude to His Father: **"I thank you, Father, Lord of heaven and earth, that you have hidden these things from the wise and understanding and revealed them to little children; yes, Father, for such was your gracious will"** (v. 21). Many people respond with hostility to the idea of God's eternal sovereign election. Every time I encounter such a response, I feel obliged to be patient, because nobody fought that doctrine more fiercely than I did for the first five years of my Christian experience.

In seminary, I took a course in the theology of Jonathan Edwards. That was my first mistake. I took it under the tutelage of the United States' leading authority on Jonathan Edwards. That was my second mistake. My third mistake was to write a little note that I put on my desk that said: "You are responsible to believe, to teach, and to preach what the Bible says is the Word of God. What the Bible says is true, not what you want it to say." You combine those three mistakes, and it was three strikes and I was out. By the time Edwards was through with me, he took Paul's epistles, and particularly Romans, and particularly Romans 9, and thoroughly convinced me of election and predestination. "OK," I said, "that's what the Bible teaches. I have to accept it, but I don't have to like it."

Then a short time after that, I began to see the sweetness of the tender mercy of God and why the Apostle Paul himself would interrupt his own writings and break into praise and say things such as, "Oh, the depth of the riches and wisdom and knowledge of God!" (Rom. 11:33). I've realized that the only way I am in the kingdom of God is not because of some work that I have performed or some response that I have given but because of the grace of God. It took me a while to enjoy the doctrine, but that was not a problem for Jesus. Jesus didn't need the help of Jonathan Edwards. Jesus didn't have to read Romans 9, because it wasn't even written yet, but Jesus, the incarnate Son of God, knew from eternity past that the Father had willed to save for Himself and for His Son a group of people out of a mass of fallen humanity, by His grace. He also understood that that predestination was double.

There are theologians who believe in what is known as single predestination. That means that from all eternity, God has designed and willed in His perfect counsel to save some, and by His eternal decree, it is absolutely certain that those whom He has foreordained and elected to this salvation will come to faith. However, as for the rest of humanity, He leaves them to their own devices. He offers them the gospel. If they want to come, they can come. It's just that they're not predestined to come, but if they want to come, they can. There's no negative side to single predestination. There's no flip side of reprobation, where from all of eternity God has decreed that some people will never come to faith. In double predestination, the decrees on both sides are absolute. God has decreed some to salvation, while He has chosen to pass over the others and not extend His salvation to them. He has decreed to save some. He has decreed not to save others.

Some say that God is a gentleman. He will not impose His will on people. He'll offer Himself to anybody who wants Him, but unless they come on their own free will, He will leave them to their own devices, because God can't violate the free will of the sinner. The problem with this view is that it leads to the conclusion that no one will be saved, because if God leaves everybody in the state that they are without intruding Himself into their sinful nature, they have no hope of salvation. Remember, we are by nature children of the darkness, dead in our sin and trespasses, and Jesus told Nicodemus plainly that unless God the Holy Spirit regenerates us, we will not and we cannot come to Christ (John 3:5–8; Eph. 2:1–3). In ourselves, we cannot, because we will not, come to Christ, and we're not able to do what we don't want to do. That's what free will means.

We have to deal with both sides of the issue, and this is what Jesus does in a spirit of joy in His prayer. **"I thank you, Father, Lord of heaven and earth"** (v. 21). He identifies God as the Sovereign One of all creation, the One who governs all things in creation. Everything in the universe is under His authority, under His power. **". . . that you have hidden these things from the wise and understanding"** (v. 21). What? Jesus is grateful that His Father has concealed the kingdom from some people?

We might think of this concealment as passive. No one will see the kingdom of God unless it's revealed to them, as we saw with Peter's confession at Caesarea Philippi. God could reveal the fact that Jesus is the Christ to everybody if He so desired, but He chose to reveal it to Peter and to the others whom He purposed to save. Concealment is the absence of revealing. If the Holy Spirit doesn't reveal it to someone, then, in fact, it's been concealed from him because his natural preference is to live in the darkness. God's general revelation has been given to all people since they took their first breath, and yet, in their fallen humanity, they reject God's revelation in nature.

But even this is not strong enough. Look at Isaiah 6, after Isaiah sees the Lord high and lifted up in the heavenly temple and he hears the call of the Lord, saying, "Whom shall I send, and who will go for us?" Then Isaiah said, "Here I am! Send me" (v. 8). So God said to Isaiah: "Go, and say to this people: 'Keep on hearing, but do not understand; keep on seeing, but do not perceive.' Make the heart of this people dull, and their ears heavy, and blind their eyes; lest they see with their eyes, and hear with their ears, and understand with their hearts, and turn and be healed" (vv. 9–10). In effect, God told Isaiah that his ministry first of all was designed to harden the hearts of these people.

Why would God do such a thing? You've heard the phrase *poetic justice*, where the punishment is suited to the crime. We read in the Scriptures again and again the warning that God, at some point, will give people over to their sin and that His judgment is poetic in this sense. "You want to be an adulterer? Then be one. I'll give you over to adultery. You want to be a thief? Then be one. I'll give you over to being a thief. If you don't want to see Me with your eyes, I'll make you blind. If you don't want to hear Me, I'll make you deaf." The concealing that is done is a judgment on people who don't want the things of God. The mystery, since all of us in our natural state don't want to hear it, is why He doesn't conceal it from us all.

Notice that Jesus thanked the Father for concealing it from **"the wise and understanding"** (v. 21). Paul said of the Corinthian believers, "For consider your calling, brothers: not many of you were wise according to worldly standards" (1 Cor. 1:26). The wiser you are, the more brilliant you are in your unconverted state, the more hostile you are to the things of God. It's a thing incredible to me that some of the most brilliant minds are the ones who are most antagonistic to the things of God. One of the almost absolute universal presuppositions of modern science is naturalism, which rules out in advance any scientific inquiry into or exploration of the supernatural.

Instead, God has revealed Himself **"to little children"** (v. 21). Pray that your friends who have not yet come to faith are not those from whom God will perpetually conceal Himself. As long as they're alive, we hope that the lights will come on and they will perceive the sweetness of God's grace that shows them the loveliness of Christ.

The Will of God

"Yes, Father, for such was your gracious will" (v. 21). In Romans 9, Paul talks about Jacob and Esau: "When Rebekah had conceived children by one man, our forefather Isaac, though they were not yet born and had done nothing either good or bad—in order that God's purpose of election might continue, not because of works but because of him who calls—she was told, 'The older will serve the younger.' As it is written, 'Jacob I loved, but Esau I hated'" (vv. 10–13). It was God who made the choice, not Jacob or Esau.

Then Paul asks a rhetorical question, anticipating his readers' negative response: "What shall we say then? Is there injustice on God's part?" (v. 14). How does he answer that question? Paul says, "By no means!" and he then reminds the people of what God said to Moses: "I will have mercy on whom I have mercy, and I will have compassion on whom I have compassion" (v. 15; see Ex. 33:19). Here's an important truth to understand. When God, in looking at the whole of fallen humanity, has mercy on some, what do the rest get? They get justice. Nobody gets injustice. Nobody deserves to be saved. Nobody deserves even to have an opportunity to be saved. You either get mercy or you get justice, but you never get injustice.

"All things have been handed over to me by my Father, and no one knows who the Son is except the Father, or who the Father is except the Son and anyone to whom the Son chooses to reveal him" (v. 22). In our natural state, we don't know who God is. In our natural state, we know *that* He is, but we don't know *who* He is. We don't know who Christ is. The only One who really knows who the Son is, is the Father. The only One who knows who the Father is, is the Son and the one to whom the Son wills to reveal Him. Pray that the Son would reveal Himself to those whom you love.

Then turning to the disciples he said privately, "Blessed are the eyes that see what you see! For I tell you that many prophets and kings desired to see what you see, and did not see it, and to hear what you hear, and did not hear it" (vv. 23–24). Think of Abraham. He left the land of his father, not knowing where he was going. He sought a city that was not the work of man's hands but whose builder and maker was God. He went to the promised land, and the only thing he ever saw was his grave (Heb. 11:8–10). He and all the other Old Testament saints died in faith, looking past the horizon to that moment in time when the Messiah would appear. Jesus said to His disciples: "That time is now. You see it. You hear it, and all who come after you, because of these things, will hear it and see it."

54

THE PARABLE OF THE GOOD SAMARITAN

Luke 10:25–37

And behold, a lawyer stood up to put him to the test, saying, "Teacher, what shall I do to inherit eternal life?" He said to him, "What is written in the Law? How do you read it?" And he answered, "You shall love the Lord your God with all your heart and with all your soul and with all your strength and with all your mind, and your neighbor as yourself." And he said to him, "You have answered correctly; do this, and you will live."

But he, desiring to justify himself, said to Jesus, "And who is my neighbor?" Jesus replied, "A man was going down from Jerusalem to Jericho, and he fell among robbers, who stripped him and beat him and departed, leaving him half dead. Now by chance a priest was going down that road, and when he saw him he passed by on the other side. So likewise a Levite, when he came to the place and saw him, passed by on the other side. But a Samaritan, as he journeyed, came to where he was, and when he saw him, he had compassion. He went to him and bound up his wounds, pouring on oil and wine. Then he set him on his own animal and brought him to an inn and took care of him. And the next day he took out two denarii and gave them to the innkeeper, saying, 'Take care of him, and whatever more you spend, I will repay you when I come back.' Which of these three, do you think, proved to be a neighbor to the man who fell among the robbers?" He said, "The one who showed him mercy." And Jesus said to him, "You go, and do likewise."

This passage is often called the parable of the good Samaritan. It might say that in bold letters in your Bible. These subheadings are not part of the actual biblical text but they are helps for us, rendered for us by the editors of the Scriptures.

This is certainly a legitimate heading for this passage. Another good name for it might be "The Contest between the Lawyer and the Teacher," because we have two people engaged in a conversation, and not only in conversation but in a thinly veiled debate. It is a debate between the *nomikos* or the lawyer, the one who is an expert in the law, and the *didaskolos* or teacher, Jesus.

Jesus, going about the countryside like an itinerant rabbi, had received from the masses the title of *teacher*. There is no record in the New Testament of Jesus' studying under the great rabbis or theologians of His era or having earned a degree that would have given Him this kind of academic credibility. But we're told again and again that He spoke as One having authority, because His mentor was not Gamaliel in Jerusalem but God the Father in heaven who revealed many things to the Son incarnate. Jesus was acclaimed by the masses as being a teacher par excellence.

And behold, a lawyer stood up to put him to the test (v. 25). This was a professional, one who was recognized as an expert in the Jewish law. When we think of lawyers today, we think of those who practice civil or criminal law. A lawyer in Israel was an expert on the law of Moses. This law included not only the laws that governed the religious community but also the laws that governed the state. Old Testament Israel was a theocracy, meaning there was no separation between church and state. The civil laws were governed by the same rules that governed the cultus, or the religious life of the people.

This man was the expert, the professional, and we're told that he stood up and tested Jesus. We could read it another way, that he came to challenge Jesus. He came to expose Jesus' naivete, to reveal to the adoring public that Jesus was simply an amateur and that he, the lawyer, was of course the professional. He tested Jesus by asking Him a fundamental question about those things related to the law of God, saying, **"Teacher, what shall I do to inherit eternal life?"** (v. 25). This was not a genuine inquiry. A man seeking salvation would come to Jesus and humbly say, "Lord, tell me how I can get into heaven." But the lawyer is probing Jesus' understanding of theology.

He said to him, "What is written in the Law? How do you read it?" (v. 26). Jesus, as He often did, answered a question with a question. His response could have been taken as an insult. "You're a lawyer, and you're asking Me what you must do to inherit eternal life? What's written in the law? You know what's written in the law. What's your understanding and your reading of it?"

And he answered, "You shall love the Lord your God with all your heart and with all your soul and with all your strength and with all your mind, and your neighbor as yourself" (v. 27). The lawyer answered by going to the most basic of the laws of Israel, found principally in the Shema, and Jesus affirmed his answer. **And he said to him, "You have answered correctly; do this, and you will live"** (v. 28).

The Place of the Law

Jesus knew that the man had not kept the Great Commandment since he got out of his bed that morning. He had never kept it fully for a single minute from the day he was born, and in that regard the lawyer was no different from us, because none of us has kept the Great Commandment fully from the day we were born. Jesus had just put the basic law right in front of this man's face.

In Reformed theology, when it comes to the meaning of the law of God and its significance, we follow John Calvin's idea of the threefold use of the law. There are three basic functions that the law performs for us. One of the most important functions of the law is as a mirror by which we see ourselves against the measuring rod of the law of God. It's a terrible thing to look at. Our tendency is to not judge ourselves by the law of God but to judge ourselves in comparison to the behavior of our friends and neighbors. When we do that, we come out thinking of ourselves very highly.

But not so in comparison to the law of God. Once we lift our gaze to heaven and consider what kind of being God is and look into the mirror of His law, then not only do we discover who God is, but we discover who we are. As the Apostle Paul tells us, the function of the law is as a schoolmaster to drive us to Christ because the law reveals our sin (Gal. 3:23–29).

We are unable to understand the mercy of God until we understand the law of God and how the law of God reveals to us our sin and our hopeless inability to justify ourselves. The law drives us to Christ, who alone can justify sinners who are unjust. The lawyer who challenged Jesus made the worst mistake he could possibly make. He thought he could justify himself. Probably most people think the same, that they can say to God, "I led a good life." Compared to what? Compared to the law of God? Not a chance.

God doesn't need to remind us of each of the Ten Commandments or of the holiness code of Exodus. He can simply say in the day of judgment: "Did you love Me with all your heart? Did you love Me with all your soul? Did you apply your mind every day to seeking the deepest possible understanding of My Word? You can't justify yourself." If anybody should have known better, it was this man who was a student of the law. He was a lawyer.

But he, desiring to justify himself, said to Jesus, "And who is my neighbor?" (v. 29). The lawyer who tried to put Jesus to the test thought he could justify himself. He expected to trip Jesus up with his question. He wanted to know how expansive the neighborhood was and how many people he was commanded to love as he loved himself. Jewish tradition said that it was only the Jewish community that was in view here. Those who were unclean, the Gentiles and the Samaritans, who were outside that community, were not to be included in the mandate to love one's neighbor.

Jesus could have answered it very plainly by saying: "Everyone in the world is your neighbor. Each human being with whom you have contact, you are to love as much as you love yourself." That could have been the end of the discussion. Instead, Jesus said, "Let Me tell you a story."

A Dangerous Journey

Jesus replied, "A man was going down from Jerusalem to Jericho" (v. 30). It's just a few miles from Jerusalem to Jericho. New Testament Jericho is a different city from Old Testament Jericho, whose walls came tumbling down under the onslaught of Joshua and his troops. On the way from Jerusalem to New Testament Jericho, you travel through the barren wilderness under the heat of the sun. Jericho was an oasis, and as you crossed the wilderness, you'd see in the distance green trees and water running in streams and canals.

"He fell among robbers, who stripped him and beat him and departed, leaving him half dead" (v. 30). The problem was that the road between the two cities was isolated, and it was a perfect place for ambush. Predators and robbers hid in the hills along the way, and when they saw somebody coming unprotected, they attacked, as happened in this case. They attacked the man, stripped him of his clothing, beat him, and left him on the side of the road half dead.

"Now by chance a priest was going down that road, and when he saw him he passed by on the other side" (v. 31). Here we find a priest who saw the man lying on the side of the road apparently near death, and he passed by on the other side. Jesus doesn't tell us why he did this. New Testament scholars love to speculate on this point. They think the man thought he was dead, so if the priest were to walk over and touch him, then he would contaminate himself. Others guess that he thought the robbers might still be nearby, and he didn't want to meet the same fate that this poor fellow had met. Others say he just was too busy.

"So likewise a Levite, when he came to the place and saw him, passed by on the other side" (v. 32). What was the difference between a priest and a Levite? All priests were Levites, but not all Levites were priests. There were other duties in the cultus that were assigned to Levites besides the priesthood. They would take care of the buildings and of the liturgies and that sort of thing without rising to the level of the priesthood. Both the priest and the Levite were professional ministers. And both of them left the dying man on the side of the road.

The Compassion of God

"But a Samaritan, as he journeyed, came to where he was, and when he saw him, he had compassion" (v. 33). Now Jesus gets to the crux of the matter. We call this man the Good Samaritan, but to the Jew and to this lawyer, there was no such thing. The Jews had no dealings with Samaritans (John 4:9). But Jesus said it was the Samaritan who saw the man on the road and **"had compassion."** We tend to cheapen this concept in our culture today. We say, "I feel your pain," and walk on the other side of the street. Of course, true compassion goes far beyond mere feelings. If a person has real compassion, he doesn't just feel it; he shows it. In Psalm 103:13, we read, "As a father shows compassion to his children, so the Lord shows compassion to those who fear him." What father would leave his son half dead in a ditch because he had an appointment somewhere else?

God's compassion for His children took Jesus to the cross. God didn't just feel bad for us. Jesus didn't just take care of us. He demonstrated that compassion by doing everything to heal us and to redeem us. This Samaritan, as he journeyed, came to where the man was and when he saw him he had compassion. He had compassion, so then what? The Samaritan went to him. Do you see the different directions? The man is in the ditch, and the priest goes one way; the Levite goes the same way; but the Samaritan goes a different way, directly to the man.

"He went to him and bound up his wounds, pouring on oil and wine. Then he set him on his own animal and brought him to an inn and took care of him. And the next day he took out two denarii and gave them to the innkeeper, saying, 'Take care of him, and whatever more you spend, I will repay you when I come back'" (vv. 34–35). We have a hymn called "Jesus Paid It All." The Samaritan here reminds me of Jesus. Luther had an expression when he was asked what it means to love your neighbor. He said that it means you have to be Christ to your neighbor. Now Luther was not so crass as to imagine that you could ever save your neighbor, that you could ever offer an atonement for your neighbor. He meant that you do for your neighbor what Jesus would do in His compassion, so that your neighbor will see Jesus working through you.

"Which of these three, do you think, proved to be a neighbor to the man who fell among the robbers?" (v. 36). No human being was ever asked an easier question by Jesus. The lawyer got it right. **He said, "The one who showed him mercy." And Jesus said to him, "You go, and do likewise"** (v. 37).

The Essence of Christianity

In the nineteenth century in Germany, it seemed as though all the theologians were writing on the vision, the being, or the essence of things. A famous church historian of the time, Adolf von Harnack, wrote a little book on the essence of Christianity called *What Is Christianity?* He tried to reduce the whole of the Christian faith to two primary theses: the universal fatherhood of God and the universal brotherhood of man. God is the Father of all men, and we are all brothers of one another. As brilliant as Harnack was, he was incorrect on both counts.

God is the Creator of all people, but He is not the Father of all people. Ultimately, He's the Father of One, His *monogenēs*, His only begotten Son. By extension, all those who are united to His Son by faith are adopted into the family of God. No one is ever born a Christian; by nature, we are children of the devil. The only way we can be children of God is to be adopted, and the only way we can be adopted is through the Son. That's how we enter the family of God.

What about the universal brotherhood of men? This also is not taught in Scripture. The image in Scripture again depicts only those who are in Christ as included in the brotherhood and in the sisterhood. You are my brother if you have the same Father that I do. If your Father is God and my Father is God, we are brothers. The Bible doesn't teach the universal brotherhood. It does teach the universal neighborhood of God. All men are not my brothers, but all men are my neighbors.

All men and women are my neighbors, which means, as we see in the Great Commandment, that I have to love everyone. In biblical terms, love is more a verb than a noun. I don't have to like everybody, but I need to love them. To love everyone means to be loving to them, to do what love demands for everyone you come across, whether you like him or not, whether he's a Jew or he's a Samaritan. In pointing to these truths, Jesus taught this lawyer the ABCs of the law of God.

55

MARTHA AND MARY

Luke 10:38–42

Now as they went on their way, Jesus entered a village. And a woman named Martha welcomed him into her house. And she had a sister called Mary, who sat at the Lord's feet and listened to his teaching. But Martha was distracted with much serving. And she went up to him and said, "Lord, do you not care that my sister has left me to serve alone? Tell her then to help me." But the Lord answered her, "Martha, Martha, you are anxious and troubled about many things, but one thing is necessary. Mary has chosen the good portion, which will not be taken away from her."

Now as they went on their way, Jesus entered a village (v. 38). There's some ambiguity in the text here. First, Luke tells us that *they* went, presumably meaning that Jesus and His disciples were on a journey, and that Jesus then entered a certain village. It's not likely that when they got to the village, the disciples went one way and Jesus went the other way alone. Probably, when He entered the village, His disciples entered as well. That will become significant.

And a woman named Martha welcomed him into her house (v. 38). Luke doesn't name the village where this took place, but he names a woman, Martha, and her sister, Mary. We can safely assume that this is the same Mary and Martha who had a brother, Lazarus, whom Jesus raised from the dead (John 11). They were close friends of Jesus and gave Him housing when He came to or near Jerusalem. The unnamed village that is unnamed here was most likely the village of Bethany on the eastern slope of the Mount of Olives outside Jerusalem (see John 11:1).

And she had a sister called Mary, who sat at the Lord's feet and listened to his teaching. But Martha was distracted with much serving (vv. 39–40). One sister is in the kitchen; the other one is in the gathering room. The sister who's in the kitchen is engaged in service. Presumably, she's preparing dinner either for Jesus and her siblings or for Jesus and the Twelve. Maybe it's not even the preparation of the meal that's in view here. It could be that they had already eaten and Martha retired to the kitchen to clean the dishes and get everything taken care of while Mary remained behind to chat with Jesus.

And she went up to him and said, "Lord, do you not care that my sister has left me to serve alone?" (v. 40). You can feel and sense the frustration of Martha. With every dish she cleaned, she was thinking: "Where's my sister, Mary? She's out there having a wonderful chitchat with Jesus, and she leaves me with all this work." Martha was upset, so she went to see Jesus, and she reproached Him. Isn't it interesting how people call Him Lord and then seek to correct Him? Next came the direct corrective: **"Tell her then to help me"** (v. 40).

Notice how Jesus replied. His response to her rebuke was tender. **But the Lord answered her, "Martha, Martha . . ."** (v. 41). There are about fifteen times in the Bible when a person is addressed by the repetition of his name. "Moses, Moses." "Abraham, Abraham." "Absalom, Absalom." "Saul, Saul." "My God, my God." It was a Jewish idiom of personal affection. Don't miss Jesus' tone in His response to Martha. She had just rebuked Him and told Him what to do. He said to her, **"Martha, Martha."** Can you hear the tenderness coming from His lips?

"You are anxious and troubled about many things, but one thing is necessary. Mary has chosen the good portion, which will not be taken away from her" (vv. 41–42). Jesus was not saying: "Mary did the good thing. You did the bad thing."

In John 17, Jesus prayed His High Priestly Prayer, in which He prayed for all of those whom the Father gave Him, as well as for His disciples, and He prayed for you and me and all those who would come to faith because of the testimony of the Apostles. Listen to one of the things He prayed for:

> I am praying for them. I am not praying for the world but for those whom you have given me, for they are yours. All mine are yours, and yours are mine, and I am glorified in them. And I am no longer in the world, but they are in the world, and I am coming to you. Holy Father, keep them in your name, which you have

> given me, that they may be one, even as we are one. While I was with them, I kept them in your name, which you have given me. I have guarded them, and not one of them has been lost except the son of destruction, that the Scripture might be fulfilled. But now I am coming to you, and these things I speak in the world, that they may have my joy fulfilled in themselves. I have given them your word, and the world has hated them because they are not of the world, just as I am not of the world. I do not ask that you take them out of the world, but that you keep them from the evil one. They are not of the world, just as I am not of the world. (vv. 9–16)

"Sanctify them," Jesus said to the Father. "These are the ones You gave Me, and You've saved them. You've justified them, but now, Father, please sanctify them. Change them. Make them holy. Make them conform to My image."

Jesus was praying for our sanctification. What did He ask the Father to do? How did He ask for us to be sanctified? "Sanctify them in the truth; your word is truth" (v. 17). That's why we study—not so that we can make an A in a theology exam or boast of great knowledge and be puffed up intellectually, but so that we may be made holy by the truth of God. That was what was happening to Mary. Martha was serving. Mary was being sanctified.

56

A SIMPLE WAY TO PRAY

Luke 11:1–4

Now Jesus was praying in a certain place, and when he finished, one of his disciples said to him, "Lord, teach us to pray, as John taught his disciples." And he said to them, "When you pray, say:

> "Father, hallowed be your name.
> Your kingdom come.
> Give us each day our daily bread,
> and forgive us our sins,
> for we ourselves forgive everyone who is indebted to us.
> And lead us not into temptation."

His name was Peter. He had a barbershop in a small town. One afternoon when he was trimming the hair of one of his regular customers, he looked as the front door opened, and he saw a notorious outlaw entering his shop, a man who was wanted by the authorities dead or alive. A princely sum had been offered as a reward for this man's capture.

The outlaw asked the barber for a haircut and a shave. Peter lathered the man's face and neck. He stropped his razor and moved the blade to the man's face and to his neck. As Peter had the sharp edge of the blade pressed against the throat of the outlaw, Peter knew that all he had to do was exert some extra force and he could kill the man and claim the reward.

But the last thing in Peter's mind was killing the outlaw. Though the man was wanted by the authorities, he was Peter's hero, and not only his hero but his mentor in spiritual things. The man in the barber chair was Martin Luther.

While Peter was shaving the great Reformer, he took the opportunity to ask him a spiritual question. He knew of Luther's reputation, not only for being a brilliant theologian and courageous Reformer but for being a titan of prayer, someone who gave himself to prayer every day for two to three hours.

He said, "Dr. Luther, can you please teach me how to pray?" The disciples asked the same question of Jesus when they noticed the obvious connection between Jesus' life and His prayer. Luther said to Master Peter, the barber of Wittenberg, "Certainly, I will teach you something of this matter." After his shave and haircut, Luther went to his study and wrote a small booklet not for the world but simply for his barber. He titled it *A Simple Way to Pray*.

That little book is still available. We can all read it and be instructed by it. But to profit from it, as Luther indicated to his barber, one must first take the time to memorize portions of three key things: the Ten Commandments, the Apostles' Creed, and the Lord's Prayer. The reason for this, Luther pointed out, is that these three portions can guide us in our seasons of prayer. We will turn our attention to the Lord's Prayer as it is found in this passage.

The Lord's Prayer

Now Jesus was praying in a certain place, and when he finished, one of his disciples said to him, "Lord, teach us to pray, as John taught his disciples." And he said to them, "When you pray, say . . ." (vv. 1–2). When Jesus gave this model prayer, He didn't say to His disciples, "When you pray, pray this." It's not that He was giving us a mandate to recite this prayer over and over again. There's nothing wrong with that, of course. He was saying: "When you pray, pray like this. This is the model I'm giving you. This is the example to show you how you should pray."

"Father, hallowed be your name" (v. 2). When Luther taught Peter to pray, he encouraged him to focus on the majesty of God, to get on his knees and say: "O God, You are from everlasting to everlasting. You are immortal, invisible, the only wise God. You are infinite, eternal, immutable, omniscient, and omnipresent. You are all of these magnificent things, O God. You transcend us by Your majesty to such a degree that we are absolutely overwhelmed that we can come into Your presence and say, Abba Father. Your being fills every corner of this universe, and there is nowhere that we can flee from Your presence. You are here and there and everywhere at every moment. Yet Your natural habitat, O God, is not this world, for You dwell in heaven. We are of the earth, earthly, but You are of heaven, heavenly."

"Father" is merely the address. It contains no great petition. The first petition of the Lord's Prayer that Jesus gave to His disciples, the number one priority that Jesus gave for us to pray, is **"hallowed be your name."** We pray that God's name would be regarded as sacred, holy, that it would be treated not only with respect but with reverence and adoration by every creature in heaven and on earth.

My spirit sinks when I hear people use the name of God in a flippant manner and never give it a thought. I want to say to them, "Don't you know that God will not hold you guiltless for using His name in this cavalier way?" (see Ex. 20:7). It's part of our culture. We are a nation that has no fear of God and no respect for Him. I understand that Christians are capable of any sin. I know that Christians without thinking can use the name of God in a disrespectful way. But I don't know how a person who has any love and reverence for God can be so irreverent with a use of His name.

If you're examining your own life and your own soul, and it's something that you do regularly, this may be your first clue and best clue about the state of your salvation. You may be dreadfully lost and not aware of it. Jesus said, "It is not what goes into the mouth that defiles a person, but what comes out of the mouth; this defiles a person" (Matt. 15:11). I realize that in our culture, it doesn't seem all that important, but Jesus made it the number one priority for our prayer.

"Your kingdom come" (v. 2). At the center of Jesus' preaching was the proclamation of the kingdom of God. When we look at Jesus' model prayer, we see at the center of its concern is the kingdom of God. When we follow Jesus' example in prayer, the chief concerns we bring before God are not the simple matters that plague us on a daily basis but the success and the extension of the kingdom of God.

Jesus taught His disciples to pray for the manifestation of God's reign on earth. He taught them to pray for a love and a hunger and a thirst for His kingdom. God has given us a King in Jesus, but the world is blind to His kingdom. We ought to pray that God's kingdom, which is so hidden from the eyes of fallen humanity, would be made known, so that His kingdom would come here as it already is manifest in heaven.

"Give us each day our daily bread" (v. 3). God knows our needs. He knows we can't survive without the necessities of life. We need food and shelter and so many other things every day. We need those things that sustain us. Every one of those things comes from God's gracious hand. Jesus taught us to pray that God would continue to sustain us and that He would take away our anxiety, that we might not be anxious about what we should eat or what we should drink or what we should wear (Matt. 6:25–34).

May we be grateful for the necessary gifts that God bestows so liberally on us. He has done so even though we have rebelled against Him. We have committed cosmic treason. We have defied His law. We have asserted our wills over His. The only way we can possibly stand in His presence is if He forgives us and provides for us a righteousness that is not our own.

He has done that in Christ. He has made us just, not by our own achievements, not by our own merit, not by our own righteousness, but by the righteousness of Jesus. He has covered our sinfulness with Christ's righteousness and has made our sins, which once were scarlet, white as snow. Though they were crimson, He has made them like wool (Isa. 1:18).

"And forgive us our sins, for we ourselves forgive everyone who is indebted to us" (v. 4). Our sins are ultimately against God, as David understood (Ps. 51:4). As we become aware of our sins, may we bring them to the Father and ask that He would blot out our transgressions, purge us with hyssop, and make us clean, that the bones that He has broken would rejoice, because as far as the east is from the west, He has removed our transgressions from us (Pss. 51:7–12; 103:12).

We have been free in receiving God's grace and mercy, but we are often loath to extend it to others. We do not forgive the debts against us as we have asked Him to forgive our debts against Him. Let us pray that the Lord would give us a forgiving heart, one that understands the great debt of which we have been forgiven in Christ.

"And lead us not into temptation" (v. 4). We know that God is so holy that He is incapable of ever enticing us to sin (James 1:13–14). Rather, He calls us to flee from sin, to come out of the darkness and into the light. Let us pray that He would never allow us to be naked and exposed to the wiles of the devil, that he would not allow us to be subjected to a test of our fidelity like what Job endured. May God put a hedge around us and protect us, not just from the world, the flesh, and the devil but from ourselves and from our own evil inclinations. May God deliver us from Satan, from the enemy, the one who goes about us roaring, lying, and seeking to devour whom he will, the one who disguises himself as an angel of light that he may deceive us and accuse us and bring us into despair and to ruin.

We often boast of our own strengths as if we are the source of them. What glory do we have? Our feet are clay; our frames are dust. We come to the Lord with nothing in our hands. All glory, laud, and honor belong to Him and to the Lamb, who is worthy to receive glory and power and honor and dominion now and forevermore (Rev. 4:11).

What Luther did for his barber, Jesus did for us. He taught us how to pray. He taught us to pray as He prayed. He taught us how to pray for the things He prayed for. That's what godly prayer is about.

A good way to learn to pray as Jesus prayed is to immerse yourself in the Psalms of the Old Testament. That is Spirit-inspired prayer. Fill your soul with the Psalms, along with the Ten Commandments, the Apostles' Creed, and the Lord's Prayer. The church will only be as strong as its prayers.

57

ASKING AND KNOCKING

Luke 11:5–13

And he said to them, "Which of you who has a friend will go to him at midnight and say to him, 'Friend, lend me three loaves, for a friend of mine has arrived on a journey, and I have nothing to set before him'; and he will answer from within, 'Do not bother me; the door is now shut, and my children are with me in bed. I cannot get up and give you anything'? I tell you, though he will not get up and give him anything because he is his friend, yet because of his impudence he will rise and give him whatever he needs. And I tell you, ask, and it will be given to you; seek, and you will find; knock, and it will be opened to you. For everyone who asks receives, and the one who seeks finds, and to the one who knocks it will be opened. What father among you, if his son asks for a fish, will instead of a fish give him a serpent; or if he asks for an egg, will give him a scorpion? If you then, who are evil, know how to give good gifts to your children, how much more will the heavenly Father give the Holy Spirit to those who ask him!"

And he said to them, "Which of you who has a friend will go to him at midnight and say to him, 'Friend, lend me three loaves, for a friend of mine has arrived on a journey, and I have nothing to set before him' . . ." (vv. 5–6). It's not by accident that this parable in Luke's Gospel is situated immediately after Jesus' teaching on the Lord's Prayer because this parable illustrates some of the important elements of prayer. The story that Jesus tells is about a man and two of his friends.

An important principle that God enjoined on His people under the old covenant was the principle of hospitality. The old covenant community was to take care of sojourners and strangers, not just friends. In this case, Jesus tells of a man who received an unexpected visit from one of his friends. Because it was unexpected, he wasn't prepared. He didn't have food needed to provide it for his visitor. But he had another friend, perhaps his next-door neighbor, to ask for help, as we might when we run out of flour or sugar. This is part of the reciprocity that we enjoy in any kind of human community.

". . . and he will answer from within, 'Do not bother me; the door is now shut, and my children are with me in bed. I cannot get up and give you anything'?" (v. 7). Jesus asked if we can imagine a friend next door refusing a request for help from his friend. What kind of neighbor would do something like that?

"I tell you, though he will not get up and give him anything because he is his friend, yet because of his impudence he will rise and give him whatever he needs" (v. 8). Even if your friend were reluctant to get up and answer your request, if for no other reason apart from your friendship, he will be annoyed enough by your persistence to put an end to it and get up and give you whatever you need.

Ask, Seek, Knock

"And I tell you, ask, and it will be given to you; seek, and you will find; knock, and it will be opened to you. For everyone who asks receives, and the one who seeks finds, and to the one who knocks it will be opened" (vv. 9–10). Jesus told this story to illustrate an important principle about praying. Remember that the focus of the Lord's Prayer is the kingdom of God. It is not about our particular needs where we use prayer simply as a lever to induce God to give us things that we desire. But Jesus was not saying that it's wrong to ask God for things that we need or things that we would like Him to do. He encourages us right here by saying, **"Ask."** James wrote, "You do not have, because you do not ask" (James 4:2). We're encouraged by Christ and by the Apostles to bring our requests before God.

At the same time, the Bible tells us that the Father knows what we need before we ask Him (Matt. 6:8). The purpose of our prayers is not to go through a grocery list of things that we need in order to inform God of our situation. He already knows it. If He already knows and He's inclined to give these things, why bother to ask? Again, the purpose of asking is not for God's benefit. It's for our benefit.

Jesus was encouraging us to open our hearts to our Father and to tell Him our concerns. He knows them, of course, but He wants to hear from us. Jesus knows that it's good for us that we have the opportunity to come to Him and pour out our hearts to Him. Jesus said, **"Ask, and it will be given to you; seek, and you will find"** (v. 9).

This is one of the most misunderstood passages in the entire New Testament. This misunderstanding has brought in its wake a revolution in worship in our day. Worship is now designed in many churches not as a time of offering praise to God but as an arena for evangelism where we bring people who are outside of the faith into church. So, the Sunday morning service is tailored to accommodate unbelievers. This dynamic is called being "seeker sensitive"—sensitive to those unbelievers who are seeking after God but as of yet have not found Him. The hope is that in the worship service, those unbelievers who are seeking God will come to faith and find Him.

The only problem with this strategy is that it is completely and utterly doomed to failure. If we tailor worship for unbelieving seekers, we are tailoring our worship for no one, because there's no such thing as an unbeliever who is seeking after God. The New Testament makes that abundantly clear. In Romans 3:9–12, the Apostle Paul quoted from Psalms 14:1–3 and 53:1–3. He wrote: "We have already charged that all, both Jews and Greeks, are under sin, as it is written: 'None is righteous, no, not one; no one understands; no one seeks for God. All have turned aside; together they have become worthless; no one does good, not even one.'" The natural disposition of fallen human beings is not to seek after God. There's not a one of them who seeks after God. The natural activity of the unbeliever is to flee from God. Think of Paul on the road to Damascus. He was not seeking Christ. He was seeking Christians that he might destroy them.

This question was once raised to Thomas Aquinas: Why is it we seem to find people who are searching after God and yet the Bible says no one seeks after God? How can that be? Thomas in his wisdom explained that people search for happiness, for meaning in their lives, for healing from their afflictions. They search for relief from the paralysis of their guilt. These people are searching for those things that only God can give them, and we conclude that since they're searching for the gifts of God, they must be searching for God. The problem is that in our unregenerate state we want the gifts of God without God. We delude ourselves if we think that unbelievers seek after God.

Jesus said, "But seek first the kingdom of God and his righteousness, and all these things will be added to you" (Matt. 6:33). But we don't begin to seek God until we are converted. Once a person is converted, that's not the end of the search; it's the beginning of the search. Jonathan Edwards said seeking after

God is the central pursuit of the Christian life. The day we meet Christ is the day we start a lifelong pursuit to know Him more deeply and more fully. We must understand that seeking is something that is the business of the believer. Jesus says to those who are believers that if you seek, you will find. Again, Jesus is giving this in the context of prayer for believing people. Search for Him with all your heart and you will find Him more deeply every day.

"Knock, and it will be opened to you" (v. 9). In His letter to the lukewarm church of Laodicea in the book of Revelation, Jesus said: "Those whom I love, I reprove and discipline, so be zealous and repent. Behold, I stand at the door and knock. If anyone hears my voice and opens the door, I will come in to him and eat with him, and he with me" (Rev. 3:19–20). How many times have you heard this text used in the context of evangelism, where the gospel is preached and the preacher says, "Jesus is knocking at the door of your heart, and if you will open the door and ask Jesus into your heart, He will come in and abide with you forever"?

The context in which this verse is given is not an evangelistic context. Jesus is not knocking on the hearts of unbelievers; He's knocking at the door of the church. That may seem strange, because we like to think that our church is open for anybody to come in. Certainly, our doors are always open for Jesus to come in. The Lord Jesus Christ shouldn't have to knock to come into His church. However, there are tens of thousands of churches in this world from whose entranceway Christ is forbidden. The last person invited into those churches is Christ Himself.

There is a theological concern for this application of the text that was addressed initially to the church and not to the unbeliever. When we say to the unbeliever, "Jesus is knocking on the door of your heart, and if you open your heart, He will come in," we forget that Jesus doesn't knock on the door of people's hearts. You don't become converted because Jesus asks you to let Him into your life. You, in your unregenerate state, are unable to stir yourself from your spiritual death and open the door to your heart so that He can come in. That's not how it works.

When Jesus enters the heart of the unbeliever, He doesn't knock. He comes in and opens the door for you. It's Christ who lets Himself in to our hearts to abide with us forever through His grace. If Jesus knocked on the heart of the unregenerate and asked them to open and let Him in, Jesus would be knocking forever. No one would open the door. Dead people don't open doors. We are by nature spiritually dead. But Jesus does knock on the door of His people's hearts. He comes to us in the weakness of our faith, in the feebleness of our devotion, and invites us to go into a deeper personal relationship with Him.

"What father among you, if his son asks for a fish, will instead of a fish give him a serpent; or if he asks for an egg, will give him a scorpion? If you then, who are evil, know how to give good gifts to your children, how much more will the heavenly Father give the Holy Spirit to those who ask him!" (vv. 11–13). As the end of the parable suggests, what Jesus will give us is what we need. It will nourish and strengthen us this day and forevermore. The final point of the parable is that our heavenly Father delights to give the glorious gift of the Holy Spirit to those who ask Him in faith.

58

A HOUSE DIVIDED

Luke 11:14–26

Now he was casting out a demon that was mute. When the demon had gone out, the mute man spoke, and the people marveled. But some of them said, "He casts out demons by Beelzebul, the prince of demons," while others, to test him, kept seeking from him a sign from heaven. But he, knowing their thoughts, said to them, "Every kingdom divided against itself is laid waste, and a divided household falls. And if Satan also is divided against himself, how will his kingdom stand? For you say that I cast out demons by Beelzebul. And if I cast out demons by Beelzebul, by whom do your sons cast them out? Therefore they will be your judges. But if it is by the finger of God that I cast out demons, then the kingdom of God has come upon you. When a strong man, fully armed, guards his own palace, his goods are safe; but when one stronger than he attacks him and overcomes him, he takes away his armor in which he trusted and divides his spoil. Whoever is not with me is against me, and whoever does not gather with me scatters.

"When the unclean spirit has gone out of a person, it passes through waterless places seeking rest, and finding none it says, 'I will return to my house from which I came.' And when it comes, it finds the house swept and put in order. Then it goes and brings seven other spirits more evil than itself, and they enter and dwell there. And the last state of that person is worse than the first."

The first time we meet the devil in the Bible is in the garden of Eden, where he is introduced in chapter 3 of Genesis with the somewhat cryptic and ominous foreboding words "Now the serpent was more crafty than any other beast of the field that the LORD God had made" (Gen. 3:1). Jesus tells us this serpent was the father of lies (John 8:44), and he used the power of the lie to seduce our primordial parents and to bring the whole creation into ruin.

It's the same serpent that assaulted our Lord in the wilderness and did everything in his power to seduce Jesus and to prevent Him from fulfilling the mission the Father had given to Him. But fortunately for us and for the world, the second Adam stood firm and overcame the enemy (Matt. 4:1–11). Even with that victory of Jesus, Satan's assault against Him did not cease but followed Him every step of His earthly ministry, as we see in this passage.

Now he was casting out a demon that was mute. When the demon had gone out, the mute man spoke, and the people marveled (v. 14). Jesus cast out a demon from a man who was mute, which allowed the man to speak. Everyone who knew this man knew that he didn't have the ability to speak. When Jesus performed this miracle the people were absolutely astonished, but not everyone celebrated this victory over the demonic world. The enemies of Jesus, chiefly the scribes and Pharisees, took this occasion to bring perhaps the greatest insult against Jesus that they ever did. It was in this moment that they came very close to committing the unpardonable sin.

But some of them said, "He casts out demons by Beelzebul, the prince of demons" (v. 15). They said that Jesus cast out demons by the power of Satan. It's one thing to be hostile to Jesus, but it's something else to say He was in league with the devil.

While others, to test him, kept seeking from him a sign from heaven (v. 16). Others who were there wanted to test Him further, but He knew what they were thinking. So He responded to the charge that He was performing these works by the power of Satan.

Casting Out Demons by Beelzebul

But he, knowing their thoughts, said to them, "Every kingdom divided against itself is laid waste, and a divided household falls. And if Satan also is divided against himself, how will his kingdom stand? For you say that I cast out demons by Beelzebul. And if I cast out demons by Beelzebul, by whom do your sons cast them out?" (vv. 17–19). Jesus said that's a foolish supposition to think that Satan would use his power in Jesus to destroy his own kingdom. Jesus had just delivered a man who was under the control of a junior-grade demon who reported to Beelzebul—one of his minions, one of his lieutenants. Would Satan destroy his own army if he wanted his kingdom to stand?

This is how Jesus gave His initial response to the charge that He was doing His miracles through the power of Satan. There are a few things we need to get clear. In the first place, these leaders, many of whom were scholars, did not deny that Jesus was doing miracles. They didn't accuse Him of duplicity by performing sleight of hand or cleverly devised tricks. They fully acknowledged that Jesus was doing miracles. But the issue was this: By whose power was Jesus able to perform these astonishing signs and wonders?

In John 3, Nicodemus came to Jesus at night with a differing view from that of his fellow Pharisees. He said to Jesus in a complimentary and flattering way, "Rabbi, we know that you are a teacher come from God, for no one can do these signs that you do unless God is with him" (v. 2). At that point, here was one Pharisee whose thinking was sound. Nicodemus acknowledged that the miracles of Christ were authentic, and he took the next step and said Jesus could not do them apart from the power of God. Notice what Nicodemus didn't say. He didn't say, "Jesus, we know that You're a teacher sent from God or from Satan, or You wouldn't be able to do the things that You're doing." Nicodemus had eliminated the second alternative, the idea that Jesus had been sent from Satan.

Nicodemus understood that only God can empower a miracle, that Satan does not have the ability to perform miracles. Satan is not God. Satan is a creature. He's stronger than we are, more crafty than we can be, but he doesn't have the attributes of God. I doubt if you and I will ever meet Satan in our lives because as a creature, he can only be at one place at one time. He's spending his time assaulting the big boys and the big girls. He sends his junior-grade demons to torment us. We'll never have to deal with him as Jesus did and Luther did because he's not divine. He doesn't have the attribute of omnipresence; nor is he omnipotent.

False Signs and Wonders

Doesn't the Bible warn us against the miracles of Satan? The Apostle Paul warned in 2 Thessalonians 2:

> Now concerning the coming of our Lord Jesus Christ and our being gathered together to him, we ask you, brothers, not to be quickly shaken in mind or alarmed, either by a spirit or a spoken word, or a letter seeming to be from us, to the effect that the day of the Lord has come. Let no one deceive you in any

> way. For that day will not come, unless the rebellion comes first, and the man of lawlessness is revealed, the son of destruction, who opposes and exalts himself against every so-called god or object of worship, so that he takes his seat in the temple of God, proclaiming himself to be God. . . . The coming of the lawless one is by the activity of Satan with all power and false signs and wonders, and with all wicked deception for those who are perishing, because they refused to love the truth and so be saved. (vv. 1–4, 9–10)

This passage refers to "the man of lawlessness," who is often equated with the Antichrist. The term *anti* in Greek does not simply mean "against"; it also means "in place of." The Antichrist will be not only an opponent of Christ but also one who wants to usurp the position of Christ, to take His place and establish himself as the great authority.

Paul wrote that this one, the man of lawlessness, who comes in the power of Satan, will come with the power of lying signs and wonders. These signs will be wonderful and powerful enough to deceive, if possible, the elect (Matt. 24:24). What does it mean to say that Satan has the power to perform "false signs and wonders" (2 Thess. 2:10)? Does Paul mean that Satan will come doing bona fide miracles in support of a falsehood or a lie? Or does he mean that those signs and wonders are not true signs and wonders but only appear to be so?

I think it's the latter. Paul means that Satan can perform signs that are so prodigious as to deceive—if it were possible—even the elect of God. Nevertheless, as clever and as impressive as these signs may be, they are phony. They are not real miracles.

When God called Moses in the Midianite wilderness, He said to him, "Come, I will send you to Pharaoh that you may bring my people, the children of Israel, out of Egypt" (Ex. 3:10). Moses was impressed by the presence of God, of course, but he worried that the Israelites would not believe that God had sent him. He said, "But behold, they will not believe me or listen to my voice, for they will say, 'The Lord did not appear to you'" (4:1). How did God answer Moses' question? He told him to throw his staff on the ground. It turned into a snake. Then He said to pick it up by the tail. Moses did so, and it turned back into a staff. Then He told Moses to put his hand in his cloak and then to pull it out. His hand was leprous. He told Moses to put his hand back in his cloak and to pull it out again, and it was clean. The Lord was saying that the way the Israelites and Pharaoh would know that He had sent Moses was through signs. God empowered Moses to do miracles. All of history was changed because God empowered Moses to perform true miracles, not false signs and wonders.

When Moses went to the palace and told Pharaoh the message from God, Pharaoh summoned his wise men and magicians. Aaron threw down his staff, and it turned into a snake. But then the magicians of Egypt threw down their staffs, and they also become snakes. A standoff, right? But then Aaron's staff swallowed up their staffs (7:8–13). The magicians were practiced in sleight of hand. Perhaps they had empty staffs that already had snakes in them. But there was a limit to their magic; they eventually confessed when they could not replicate Moses' miracles, "This is the finger of God" (8:19).

Theologians who have defended the idea that Satan can perform genuine miracles make a fine distinction. In classic theology, part of the definition of a miracle is a work that is accomplished *contra naturam*, against nature—violating the normal laws of nature like having an axe head float (2 Kings 6:5–7), a virgin bringing forth a child (Isa. 7:14; Matt. 1:18–25), or turning water into wine (John 2:1–11). Those are not natural occurrences. Something working *contra naturam* must be involved in order for them to happen.

Can Satan perform miracles against nature? He is a supernatural being, an angelic being, and he has more powers than we do. But he's not the Lord of nature or the author of nature, so he cannot work *contra naturam*. Furthermore, he certainly cannot work *contra peccatum*, or against evil, which is Jesus' point here. Satan cannot but work for the cause of evil. He only works *pro peccatum*, for evil. Jesus, on the other hand, had the power to work *contra naturam* and always worked *contra peccatum*.

Why am I concerned about it? The author of Hebrews wrote: "Therefore we must pay much closer attention to what we have heard, lest we drift away from it. For since the message declared by angels proved to be reliable, and every transgression or disobedience received a just retribution, how shall we escape if we neglect such a great salvation?" (Heb. 2:1–3). The salvation that comes to us in Jesus Christ is not a mean salvation. It's not an insignificant salvation. It's not one way of salvation. It is a great salvation. This is the greatest work of benevolence that the providence of God has ever wrought in history.

That's the way of the world. God provides a great salvation. We neglect it; we dismiss it; we overlook it. It's a rhetorical question that is raised here by the author of Hebrews: "How shall we escape if we neglect such a great salvation?" Let's make it personal. How could I escape the judgment of God if I neglected that great salvation? How could you possibly escape if you neglect that salvation?

The Purpose of Miracles

The author of Hebrews continued, "It was declared at first by the Lord, and it was attested to us by those who heard" (v. 3). This great salvation was announced by Jesus to the disciples, who confirmed or authenticated it. How was the word of this great salvation confirmed? God confirmed it by bearing witness with signs and wonders and various miracles.

The truth of sacred Scripture, the truth of the gospel, the truth of Christ was authenticated by miracles. That was God's way of confirming that the message that was delivered was His truth. Do you see what's at stake? If Satan can really perform true miracles, then the miracles of Christ, the miracles of the Apostles, the miracles of Moses confirm nothing. Satan is clever. He can disguise himself as an angel of light. He goes about as a roaring lion seeking those whom he can devour, but he's not God. There is a limit beyond which he cannot go. That's why we give a tight definition of a miracle. It's not helpful when people get loose about the definition of a miracle and say, "Every time a baby is born, that's a miracle." No, when a baby is born, that's a wonderful thing, but it's not a miracle.

A miracle is the last thing that you would expect to happen. It is extraordinary; there's nothing ordinary about it. A miracle by definition is so extraordinary, so unusual, that it demands our attention. God answers prayers every day—inward things that we don't see. But nobody is raising people from the dead. Nobody is making axe heads float. Nobody performs these kinds of works that only God can do.

When miracles—true miracles—come to pass, they bring with them divine certification. That was the point of the miracles, principally and chiefly: to prove once and for all that Jesus is the Christ, the Son of the living God.

"When the unclean spirit has gone out of a person, it passes through waterless places seeking rest, and finding none it says, 'I will return to my house from which I came.' And when it comes, it finds the house swept and put in order. Then it goes and brings seven other spirits more evil than itself, and they enter and dwell there. And the last state of that person is worse than the first" (vv. 24–26). You can have a demon cast out, and it may roam about the dry places, but if it's not replaced by the Holy Ghost, it will come back with all its friends, and your end will be worse than your beginning. We can respect the power of Satan, but let's not give him the power and authority that only God possesses.

59

SEEKING A SIGN

Luke 11:27–36

As he said these things, a woman in the crowd raised her voice and said to him, "Blessed is the womb that bore you, and the breasts at which you nursed!" But he said, "Blessed rather are those who hear the word of God and keep it!"

When the crowds were increasing, he began to say, "This generation is an evil generation. It seeks for a sign, but no sign will be given to it except the sign of Jonah. For as Jonah became a sign to the people of Nineveh, so will the Son of Man be to this generation. The queen of the South will rise up at the judgment with the men of this generation and condemn them, for she came from the ends of the earth to hear the wisdom of Solomon, and behold, something greater than Solomon is here. The men of Nineveh will rise up at the judgment with this generation and condemn it, for they repented at the preaching of Jonah, and behold, something greater than Jonah is here.

"No one after lighting a lamp puts it in a cellar or under a basket, but on a stand, so that those who enter may see the light. Your eye is the lamp of your body. When your eye is healthy, your whole body is full of light, but when it is bad, your body is full of darkness. Therefore be careful lest the light in you be darkness. If then your whole body is full of light, having no part dark, it will be wholly bright, as when a lamp with its rays gives you light."

As he said these things, a woman in the crowd raised her voice and said to him, "Blessed is the womb that bore you, and the breasts at which you nursed!" (v. 27). This woman, though not a prophetess, pronounced an oracle of weal. She pronounced a divine blessing, not simply on Jesus but on His mother, the one who gave birth to Him and who nursed Him.

This passage forms part of the Rosary that the Roman Catholic Church recites: "Hail Mary, full of grace, the Lord is with thee; blessed art thou among women and blessed is the fruit of thy womb, Jesus. Holy Mary, Mother of God, pray for us sinners, now and at the hour of our death." In the Rosary, Mary is called *theotokos*, the Mother of God, and is called "blessed" because she gave birth to Jesus. Surely, no woman in the history of the world received a higher honor or a greater measure of blessedness than this peasant girl, who was given the honor of bearing in her womb the baby who would save the world.

But he said, "Blessed rather are those who hear the word of God and keep it!" (v. 28). Jesus' response was astonishing. Jesus said that as blessed as Mary was to be His mother, we who believe in Him are even more blessed. We have received an even greater blessing than she did by being recipients of the Word of God. We hear the Word of God written as it is enunciated here in sacred Scripture. But there's a condition attached to that blessedness. It comes not simply in hearing it but in obeying it.

In the Greek language, there's a strange twist of wording. The Greek word meaning "to hear" is *akouō*; the Greek word meaning "to obey" is *hypakouō*. The second word means that if someone obeys what he hears, he experiences "hyper-hearing." That is hearing that is not simply surface-level and that goes in one ear and out the other; it is hearing in an emphatic way that results in doing what the word commands. If you hear the Word of God and obey it, our Lord pronounces a blessing on you that is greater than the blessing that the Father gave to His own mother.

When the crowds were increasing, he began to say, "This generation is an evil generation" (v. 29). Jesus tacitly pronounced an oracle of woe on the generation of His contemporaries. The Scriptures tell us that all generations are evil because all generations are made up of corrupt human beings. But Jesus singled out that generation as particularly evil and wicked. I think the reason for that is it was the most blessed generation that ever walked the face of the earth. This was the generation that experienced the visitation of God incarnate. This was the generation that was on the earth when divine light shone on the planet in an unprecedented manner. This generation, because of that light, that extraordinary light, had a much more somber obligation to respond. To reject the Messiah in the midst of this kind of extraordinary light accentuated the evil of that generation.

The Sign of Jonah

"It seeks for a sign, but no sign will be given to it except the sign of Jonah" (v. 29). Jesus went on to define why He found that generation so particularly evil. It sought a sign; it wanted proof that Jesus was who He said He was. It wanted to see miracles. Notably, the Apostle John doesn't speak about miracles in his Gospel; he speaks about signs. One of the principal words in his Gospel is the Greek word *sēmeion*, which is translated "sign."

A *sign* is something that has *significance*. Significance differs subtly from the word *symbol*; a symbol participates in that which it points to. But a sign points to something outside of itself, something beyond itself. When you drive toward the city of Orlando and you see a sign that says "Orlando 5 miles," you're not in Orlando. You're headed to Orlando. You're going in the direction of Orlando because you're following the sign that directs you there. But once you pass the city line, you're no longer outside looking to something in the future, but you're in it.

That evil generation sought some kind of special sign that would prove to them that He was the Messiah, that He was God incarnate. Notice, He said this to a group of people who had just seen Him cast out a demon and who accused Him of doing so by the power of Beelzebul. Jesus responded by saying, "But if it is by the finger of God that I cast out demons, then the kingdom of God has come upon you" (v. 20). In other words, this was the sign. Jesus had just given them a sign, and it went right past them. They wanted a bigger sign, a better sign. Jesus said, **"No sign will be given to it except the sign of Jonah"** (v. 29). How did Jonah get into this discussion? How is Jonah a sign? Jesus explained that elsewhere. He said in Matthew's Gospel, "For just as Jonah was three days and three nights in the belly of the great fish, so will the Son of Man be three days and three nights in the heart of the earth" (Matt. 12:40). He pointed here to the ultimate sign, the supreme sign, the most significant thing that God did in Christ: His resurrection.

Paul said to the Athenians on Mars Hill, "The times of ignorance God overlooked, but now he commands all people everywhere to repent, because he has fixed a day on which he will judge the world in righteousness by a man whom he has appointed; and of this he has given assurance to all by raising him from the dead" (Acts 17:30–31). Those of you who are still looking for signs, those of you who are still waiting to be convinced, who are looking for more evidence from God than He's already given, your hope is futile. You are on a fool's errand because God has already provided you with the ultimate sign.

God commands all men everywhere to repent because of the resurrection, the ultimate sign. So Jesus said: **"No sign will be given to it except the sign of Jonah. For as Jonah became a sign to the people of Nineveh, so will the Son of Man be to this generation"** (vv. 29–30).

Something Greater

"The queen of the South will rise up at the judgment with the men of this generation and condemn them, for she came from the ends of the earth to hear the wisdom of Solomon, and behold, something greater than Solomon is here" (v. 31). The queen of Sheba made that journey for the sake of learning wisdom. The reputation of Solomon and his wisdom had gone to the far corners of the earth, and the queen of Sheba was so impressed that she just had to meet him, whatever it took. Jesus said, **"Something greater than Solomon is here."** So the queen of Sheba and her entourage **"will rise up at the judgment with the men of this generation and condemn them"** for ignoring the invincible sign of Christ Himself.

"The men of Nineveh will rise up at the judgment with this generation and condemn it, for they repented at the preaching of Jonah, and behold, something greater than Jonah is here" (v. 32). Jonah was a great man, despite all his flaws and imperfections. He was a prophet of God. He pronounced the word of God, and the pagan people of Nineveh repented en masse. It was Nineveh's great awakening. And Jesus said, **"Something greater than Jonah is here."** The implication is that if you won't hear Jesus, whom will you hear?

Letting Light Shine

"No one after lighting a lamp puts it in a cellar or under a basket, but on a stand, so that those who enter may see the light" (v. 33). What's the point of hiding a lamp? It obviously makes more sense to put it on a lampstand so everyone who comes in can see the light.

Then Jesus made an analogy: **"Your eye is the lamp of your body. When your eye is healthy, your whole body is full of light, but when it is bad, your body is full of darkness"** (v. 34). The way we perceive light is through the organ of the eye. If your eyes are not functioning and if you're blind because your eyes no longer work, then your life is a life of darkness.

"Therefore be careful lest the light in you be darkness. If then your whole body is full of light, having no part dark, it will be wholly bright, as when a lamp with its rays gives you light" (vv. 35–36). Jesus was accusing that generation of being blind, and their blindness extended through their whole lives. If you don't have the light of Christ in your heart and in your soul, no matter how well your eyes function organically, you're living in utter darkness. Your destiny will be an eternity of darkness. That image of darkness is used biblically to describe our fallen condition, where by nature as children of darkness we prefer the darkness rather than the light.

If we stand in the light, we are stripped naked, as it were, exposed of all our sin. The light of the gospel does that. That's why we flee from it. It exposes us until we rejoice in it and we are covered by the gracious righteousness of Christ. The gospel is the light of the world because Christ is the light of the world. Without Him, your whole life is darkness. With Him, it's nothing but light.

60

WOE TO THE HYPOCRITES

Luke 11:37–54

While Jesus was speaking, a Pharisee asked him to dine with him, so he went in and reclined at table. The Pharisee was astonished to see that he did not first wash before dinner. And the Lord said to him, "Now you Pharisees cleanse the outside of the cup and of the dish, but inside you are full of greed and wickedness. You fools! Did not he who made the outside make the inside also? But give as alms those things that are within, and behold, everything is clean for you.

"But woe to you Pharisees! For you tithe mint and rue and every herb, and neglect justice and the love of God. These you ought to have done, without neglecting the others. Woe to you Pharisees! For you love the best seat in the synagogues and greetings in the marketplaces. Woe to you! For you are like unmarked graves, and people walk over them without knowing it."

One of the lawyers answered him, "Teacher, in saying these things you insult us also." And he said, "Woe to you lawyers also! For you load people with burdens hard to bear, and you yourselves do not touch the burdens with one of your fingers. Woe to you! For you build the tombs of the prophets whom your fathers killed. So you are witnesses and you consent to the deeds of your fathers, for they killed them, and you build their tombs. Therefore also the Wisdom of God said, 'I will send them prophets and apostles, some of whom they will kill and persecute,' so that the blood of all the prophets, shed from the foundation of the world, may be charged against this generation, from the blood of Abel to the blood of Zechariah, who perished between the altar and the sanctuary. Yes, I tell you, it will be required of this generation. Woe to you lawyers! For you have taken away the key of knowledge. You did not enter yourselves, and you hindered those who were entering."

As he went away from there, the scribes and the Pharisees began to press him hard and to provoke him to speak about many things, lying in wait for him, to catch him in something he might say.

The church is full of hypocrites. At least that's the judgment that I hear over and over again from those who are critics of the Christian faith and of the church. It's one of the most common objections to the truth claims of Christianity. The problem is that it's wrong. There are certainly some, of course, but to say that the church has a plenitude or a fullness of hypocrites in her midst is simply slander.

Why is this charge made so frequently? It's probably because people don't understand what hypocrisy actually is. People on the outside of the church notice that we come to church on a regular basis, and then during the week, they observe us. They watch our activities. They listen to our words. They see that we sin. And then they say, "You say you're a Christian, but you sin; therefore, you must be a hypocrite." Well, if we claim as Christians to be without sin and then we sin, we would indeed be guilty of the sin of hypocrisy.

If these people's complaint were that the church is filled with sinners, then that would be correct. In fact, the Christian church is the only organization that I know of that requires a person to be a sinner to join it. Hypocrisy is a sin, but it is one sin among many. It is the sin of saying that we don't do a certain thing but then we do it.

D. James Kennedy used to respond to the charge that the church is full of hypocrites by saying: "There's always room for one more. Why don't you come and join us?" Then he would say, "If you find a perfect church, please don't join it, because you would surely ruin it."

Hypocrisy involves engaging in pretense. In the church, it involves the pretense of being more righteous than we actually are, more holy than we actually are. Though Jesus was clear in His judgment about all kinds of sins, He was particularly expressive about the sin of hypocrisy, as we see in this text.

While Jesus was speaking, a Pharisee asked him to dine with him (v. 37). There's already a hint of hypocrisy here because it is clear as we follow the text that this invitation from the Pharisee was not genuine. He wasn't inviting Jesus over to eat because He was an honored guest. He didn't invite Him into his house for dinner because he wanted to offer Him a gracious meal or to extend a particular kindness to Him. No, the invitation to dinner was to set a trap for Jesus, to catch Him doing or saying something that could be occasion for them to rise up in judgment against Him.

Clean Hands

So he went in and reclined at table. The Pharisee was astonished to see that he did not first wash before dinner (vv. 37–38). Rabbinic law required that before eating, one must go through a cleansing rite, not as a matter of hygiene but merely as a matter of liturgy according to tradition. It was not a requirement that God made in His law; it was the requirement that the Pharisees added to the law of God. Jesus didn't do it. Why not? He knew what He was doing. He didn't point it out, but He was saying no to these regulations that had been invented by the Pharisees. They had nothing to do with the kingdom of God. David asked, "Who shall ascend the hill of the LORD?" (Ps. 24:3), and the answer was, "He who has clean hands and a pure heart" (v. 4). The man who came to dinner that day had the cleanest hands in human history and a heart completely absent of any impurity whatsoever. Jesus had no need to wash His hands.

And the Lord said to him, "Now you Pharisees cleanse the outside of the cup and of the dish, but inside you are full of greed and wickedness" (v. 39). The Pharisee was offended. Jesus understood what he was thinking, so He began to rebuke him: "You're so zealous to put on this facade of purity and of cleanliness that you make sure there are no blemishes outside. You're like a person who after dinner cleans the outside of the cup or the outside of the plate and doesn't bother that part of the plate where all the dirt has accumulated. Your hands may be clean, but your hearts are filthy. Your minds are filthy. Your thoughts are greedy and corrupt. Oh, foolish ones."

Don't miss the importance of that. Jesus warns in the Sermon on the Mount against using the term "fool" in an unjust way (Matt. 5:22). To call somebody a fool in biblical terms was not to make a statement about his intelligence. The Old Testament says that "the fool says in his heart, 'There is no God'" (Ps. 14:1). Foolishness was the opposite of wisdom to the Jew, and the fear of God is the beginning of wisdom. If you're a fool, that means there's no fear of God in you. You may fear people. You may fear your boss. But you don't have any reverence for, awe of, respect for, or fear of God. That's what Jesus was saying: **"You fools! Did not he who made the outside make the inside also? But give as alms those things that are within, and behold, everything is clean for you"** (vv. 40–41).

Tithing Mint and Neglecting Justice

Then He raised the ante. The antithesis of the blessing of God was the curse of God. The way the curse was pronounced by the prophet was by the oracle of doom, which was signaled by the word "woe." At the end of the book of Revelation, we read about the day of God's ultimate judgment: "Then I looked, and I heard an eagle crying with a loud voice as it flew directly overhead, 'Woe, woe, woe to those who dwell on the earth' " (Rev. 8:13). Here, Jesus used the oracle of the prophet against the Pharisees. He said to them, **"But woe to you Pharisees! For you tithe mint and rue and every herb, and neglect justice and the love of God. These you ought to have done, without neglecting the others"** (v. 42).

In Matthew's parallel version, Jesus said: "You tithe mint and dill and cumin, and have neglected the weightier matters of the law: justice and mercy and faithfulness. These you ought to have done, without neglecting the others" (Matt. 23:23). The Pharisees were scrupulous. They gave 10 percent of all their produce. They didn't cheat God out of a nickel. If they found an extra piece of mint along the road, they took one-tenth of it and gave it to God. But they neglected the weightier things, things that are much more important than tithing, such as the love of God and working for truth and righteousness. They obeyed the little things but wouldn't obey the big things. What does that say to the rest of us who won't even obey the little things? It's not that we shouldn't be tithing. No, He said these things "you ought to have done." But we must not neglect the weightier things in the name of scrupulous obedience.

Woe to the Scribes and Pharisees

"Woe to you Pharisees! For you love the best seat in the synagogues and greetings in the marketplaces" (v. 43). Synagogues were the places where the people came to learn, like an adult Sunday school. They gathered to hear exposition of sacred Scripture. Seats for the dignitaries were placed in the front of the synagogues. Jesus said the Pharisees loved to sit up there in an exalted position where everybody could see them and to have people greet them in public, saying, "Good morning, Rabbi." They loved having positions of respect in the religious community.

"Woe to you! For you are like unmarked graves, and people walk over them without knowing it" (v. 44). When the pilgrims came to Jerusalem for the feast, it was required of the people who had graveyards to make sure the graves were visible because to step on a grave defiled a person, making the person unclean. The graves were beautifully marked with whitewash. In Matthew's version, Jesus said: "Woe to you, scribes and Pharisees, hypocrites! For you are like whitewashed tombs, which outwardly appear beautiful, but within are full of dead people's bones and all uncleanness" (Matt. 23:27). That's what a hypocrite is like. What you see is not what you get. What you see disguises and hides what's underneath.

One of the lawyers answered him, "Teacher, in saying these things you insult us also" (v. 45). This lawyer had heard all he could stand from the lips of Jesus. He complained that Jesus, in denouncing the Pharisees, slandered him and his fellow lawyers also. Jesus replied: **"Woe to you lawyers also! For you load people with burdens hard to bear, and you yourselves do not touch the burdens with one of your fingers"** (v. 46). They were adding burdens to the law of God that God never placed there. The burden of Christ is light, but the clergy and the theologians and the lawyers were experts in biblical law. They were theologians. They were adding requirements and rules and regulations to people where God had left them free. Their hypocrisy was such that they wouldn't even obey those things that they had invented to keep the people in bondage.

"Woe to you! For you build the tombs of the prophets whom your fathers killed. So you are witnesses and you consent to the deeds of your fathers, for they killed them, and you build their tombs" (vv. 47–48). In Jerusalem, just outside the city wall, some tombs and statues honoring Old Testament prophets still remain. Jesus pointed out the hypocrisy of building monuments to the prophets whom their fathers had killed. Yet that wicked generation, which claimed to honor the prophets, would have killed the prophets too.

"Therefore also the Wisdom of God said, 'I will send them prophets and apostles, some of whom they will kill and persecute'" (v. 49). Jesus earlier addressed this group as an evil and adulterous generation. Of all the generations of human beings that have ever lived, this was the one generation that had the unbelievable privilege of being eyewitness to the incarnate Son of God. John begins his Gospel by saying, "He came to his own, and his own people did not receive him" (John 1:11). Every generation of human beings has been rebellious, but none had seen such a visible manifestation of the glory of God on earth as that generation saw when Jesus was working through His earthly ministry.

"So that the blood of all the prophets, shed from the foundation of the world, may be charged against this generation, from the blood of Abel to the blood of Zechariah, who perished between the altar and the sanctuary. Yes, I tell you, it will be required of this generation" (vv. 50–51). In our natural, unconverted state, the basic disposition of our hearts is to hate God. People really get upset about that. They insist that they can't hate God if they don't believe He exists. But no, we all know that God exists, but in our natural state, we just don't want anything to do with Him. Sin is clearly universal. Even pagans would acknowledge that no one's perfect, but they never take the next step and ask, Why not? The truth is that we are born that way. We are born in sin and in rebellion against God. And of all generations, this one, as we have seen, was the worst.

"Woe to you lawyers! For you have taken away the key of knowledge. You did not enter yourselves, and you hindered those who were entering" (v. 52). As a freshman in college, I read an essay from early American literature that was titled "On the Danger of an Unconverted Ministry" by Gilbert Tennent. Do you realize that it was the clergy who killed Jesus? Do you realize that throughout history, those who have been most opposed to the gospel have been the clergy?

I couldn't read the hearts of my professors in seminary, but my feeling was that the vast majority of them were unconverted men. I remember a professor once rebuked a student by saying, "You've come to the seminary with too many preconceived ideas." The preconceived idea that was being rebuked was the idea of Christ. Another seminary professor castigated a student publicly for preaching on the atoning death of Christ. Why would such men go into the teaching ministry? Many people go into the ministry so they can undermine the faith of Christ, so they can attack Christianity. We tend to think that if somebody's a minister, then they're dedicated to the things of Christ. But that's not always the case. Jesus condemned the ministers of His day, saying that they had taken away the key to knowledge and were putting up obstacles in the path of people who were coming to the kingdom of God.

The Plot to Kill Jesus

As he went away from there, the scribes and the Pharisees began to press him hard and to provoke him to speak about many things, lying in wait for him, to catch him in something he might say (vv. 53–54). Try to picture that in your minds—gnashing of teeth, fury, rage at the Son of God. They couldn't have hated Him any more than they did. We are just like this in our natural state. If God the Holy Spirit doesn't invade our souls and change the dispositions in our hearts, we would go to our graves sharing the same hostility against God and His Christ, for we are by nature at enmity with God.

That's why the Bible speaks of reconciliation. That's why the Bible speaks of the gospel as the gospel of peace. That's why we celebrate Christmas, because the Prince of Peace came to take away our anger, to take away our hostility, to overcome that estrangement, and to reconcile us to the Father.

61

FEARING GOD

Luke 12:1–7

In the meantime, when so many thousands of the people had gathered together that they were trampling one another, he began to say to his disciples first, "Beware of the leaven of the Pharisees, which is hypocrisy. Nothing is covered up that will not be revealed, or hidden that will not be known. Therefore whatever you have said in the dark shall be heard in the light, and what you have whispered in private rooms shall be proclaimed on the housetops.

"I tell you, my friends, do not fear those who kill the body, and after that have nothing more that they can do. But I will warn you whom to fear: fear him who, after he has killed, has authority to cast into hell. Yes, I tell you, fear him! Are not five sparrows sold for two pennies? And not one of them is forgotten before God. Why, even the hairs of your head are all numbered. Fear not; you are of more value than many sparrows."

The chapter divisions and verses in the Bible were not in the original manuscripts. I sometimes wonder if it was an itinerant preacher riding around on horseback who put in these chapter divisions, because they don't always make sense. Certainly, the beginning of chapter 12 could fit nicely as part of the conclusion of chapter 11. The beginning of chapter 12 flows naturally out of Jesus' confrontation with the Pharisees in the previous chapter in which He gave them the oracle of woe and pronounced judgment on them principally because of their hypocrisy.

In the meantime, when so many thousands of the people had gathered together that they were trampling one another . . . (v. 1). Everywhere Jesus went, there were huge, thronging crowds that followed after Him, people who wanted to see every miracle that He performed or hear every word that came from His lips. Perhaps people knew that Jesus was eating at the home of the Pharisee, and as word spread, the crowds came out in greater numbers to await His appearance. The multitude was so great that people began to trample one another to get to Him. That's how excited they were to come and see Jesus.

. . . he began to say to his disciples first, "Beware of the leaven of the Pharisees, which is hypocrisy" (v. 1). The first thing He had to say was a warning to His disciples, and presumably not merely the Twelve but the larger number of disciples that He had. This was not the only time that our Lord used the metaphor of leaven for something that can have a destructive power. He was speaking of a little thing that has the ability to spread to the point that it is pervasive. He said hypocrisy is like this; if you allow it in your life, even just a little bit of it—a small amount of Pharisaism, of playacting, pretending, or deceitfulness—you will not be able to contain it. It will spread like a cancer. It will fill your soul and destroy your character.

"Nothing is covered up that will not be revealed, or hidden that will not be known" (v. 2). Jesus says be careful not to live a deceitful life. Any attempt to hide ourselves from the world and maintain a facade of righteousness that is not authentic at some point will certainly be exposed. Think of the first sin ever committed by human beings. As soon as Adam and Eve transgressed the law of God, their immediate experience was an awareness of their nakedness. It was an awareness of shame, and their natural response to their shame was to hide—to flee from the presence of God and hope that He would not be able to see what they had done.

All of us have things about ourselves, about our lives, that we are ashamed of and don't want anybody else to know about. So we pretend that those things are not part of our character. Jesus says to be careful. In the first place, this leaven can destroy you. In the second place, all attempts to conceal our sin will ultimately be futile because everything that is currently covered will be revealed and there is nothing that is hidden that will not be made known.

Making Known What Is Hidden

"Therefore whatever you have said in the dark shall be heard in the light, and what you have whispered in private rooms shall be proclaimed on the housetops" (v. 3). On another occasion when Jesus spoke of the consequences of hiding, He did it in the context of the last judgment. He said, "I tell you, on the day of judgment people will give account for every careless word they speak" (Matt. 12:36). Everything we say in private that we don't want people to know that we said, all the things we've done in privacy that we don't want people to see, will be proclaimed on the housetops. Everything that we've ever said and everything that we've ever done will be made manifest on the day of judgment.

Many Christians have the misguided idea that Christians don't have to worry about this disclosure on judgment day. They assume that it's only the pagan or the corrupt person or the Pharisee who has to fear. After all, we have passed from the judgment to life, and we know that one of the benefits of our justification is that there is now no condemnation for those who are in Christ Jesus. Therefore, if you're a Christian, you don't have to worry about being condemned by God on the last day. On the last day, your judge and your defense attorney will be Jesus Christ. However, even though our entrance to heaven is not based in any way on our good works, and though our good works contribute nothing to our salvation, every one of us will be evaluated on that day according to our works. The truth about our obedience, our sanctification, and our profession of faith will be made manifest.

In the final judgment, the character of every man will be clearly revealed, in the sight of God and in the sight of the man himself, so that all our self-deceptions will be banished. For the first time, we will see ourselves as we really are. One of the things that I've often said about God's grace in the process of our sanctification is that He doesn't reveal all our sin to us all at once. If He did, we wouldn't be able to stand it. But so gracious is our God that He slowly and tenderly convicts us of our sin by the influence of the Holy Spirit as He brings us into conformity to Himself.

One of the ways in which the last judgment is characteristically described in sacred Scripture is with respect to the silence of those who receive the judgment of God. Every tongue will be stopped when God reveals our sin, and we will immediately know the truth of that judgment and the futility of trying to argue about it. Indeed, those who fall under God's judgment will condemn themselves. Further, the judgment will be clear to all those who see.

That may be an oppressive thought to some, but in reality, it's one of the most liberating thoughts that the New Testament gives for several reasons. You often hear the complaint that there's no justice in this world. There are many times in this world where justice is frustrated and not established—but not at the last judgment. In that judgment, perfect justice will prevail, and there will be no injustice whatsoever.

Also, it's liberating to know that there's nothing we can hide from God, either here or in the future. While the pagan trembles at the rustling of a leaf and seeks to hide from the all-seeing eye of God, the believer should delight in knowing that God knows us altogether, and even though He knows us altogether, He redeems us altogether.

The One to Fear

"I tell you, my friends, do not fear those who kill the body, and after that have nothing more that they can do. But I will warn you whom to fear: fear him who, after he has killed, has authority to cast into hell. Yes, I tell you, fear him!" (vv. 4–5). The Old Testament Wisdom Literature says, "The fear of the Lord is the beginning of wisdom" (Prov. 9:10). That fear that the Bible speaks of is not a servile fear that a prisoner has for his torturer. It is more a filial fear, a fear of offending one's father, and it has more to do with living before God in a sense of awe and reverence. That's true as far as it goes, but the word here is not translated "reverence." And it's not translated "awe." As important as those elements are, still the operative word here is "fear." Even Christians need to understand a godly fear, what it means to fear God in a righteous way. Even though we are to come before Him boldly and we can call Him our Father, He's not our chum. He's not our pal. He is the Lord God omnipotent, and when He appears, we will be on our faces before Him, trembling before His majesty.

David said of the ungodly, "There is no fear of God before his eyes" (Ps. 36:1). It's amazing to me how fearless the average person is of God. How is it possible that a creature made in the image of God, who lives impenitently in rebellion against God, has no fear of God as he continues to sin? In more than fifty years of ministry, only two people have told me that they came to faith in Christ because they were overwhelmed by a fear of hell. People go through life not believing in hell. And those who think hell exists are not afraid that they're going to go there. They figure, if there is a God, heaven wouldn't be right if they weren't there. Not only that, many ministers are telling people that God loves them unconditionally. Why should anyone be afraid of a God who loves them unconditionally?

The kingdom of God is ruled by a just and holy Creator for whom we should have fear. This is what Jesus was instructing here. We are afraid of strong people, of criminals who might attack and maim us or even kill us and destroy our bodies. He said not to be afraid of them. The worst that can happen at the hands of such a thug is that they can kill the body. But once we're dead, they can't harm us anymore. Jesus said rather that we are to **"fear him who, after he has killed, has authority to cast into hell"** (v. 5). That's the One for whom we are to have fear.

The Care of God

"Are not five sparrows sold for two pennies? And not one of them is forgotten before God. Why, even the hairs of your head are all numbered" (vv. 6–7). If we stop right there, that would be enough to intensify our fear, wouldn't it? But He's simply saying that God knows every single thing about us. Nothing escapes His notice.

The concept of omniscience is one we cannot comprehend. How is it possible for God to know everything there is to know about everything there is to be known? Every thought, every word, every hair on our head. You would think that this was an opportunity for Jesus to compound His charge for us to fear God. Then He adds these startling words: **"Why, even the hairs of your head are all numbered. Fear not; you are of more value than many sparrows"** (v. 7). Fear God, but in that fear of God, don't think that under the gaze of God you are reduced to insignificance. Even though God knows everything about you as a believer, He places a value upon you as His child that is incalculable. On the one hand, we should fear Him. On the other hand, we should not fear because He has redeemed us in His sight.

Do not fear, for you matter to your Father.

62

THE UNFORGIVABLE SIN

Luke 12:8–12

"And I tell you, everyone who acknowledges me before men, the Son of Man also will acknowledge before the angels of God, but the one who denies me before men will be denied before the angels of God. And everyone who speaks a word against the Son of Man will be forgiven, but the one who blasphemes against the Holy Spirit will not be forgiven. And when they bring you before the synagogues and the rulers and the authorities, do not be anxious about how you should defend yourself or what you should say, for the Holy Spirit will teach you in that very hour what you ought to say."

Throughout these passages, there have been several different issues set forth by Jesus, but there is one common theme that runs through them: the relationship between the mouth and the heart. We heard Jesus give His severe rebuke to the Pharisees for their hypocrisy because they said one thing and did another. Then we heard His warning about the words that we speak in private and in secret that will be public knowledge on the day of judgment. Continuing in this vein, our Lord again spoke about the relationship of the mouth and the heart.

He said, **"Everyone who acknowledges me before men, the Son of Man also will acknowledge before the angels of God, but the one who denies me**

before men will be denied before the angels of God" (vv. 8–9). Later on, in his epistle to the Romans, the Apostle Paul made an observation: "'The word is near you, in your mouth and in your heart' (that is, the word of faith that we proclaim); because, if you confess with your mouth that Jesus is Lord and believe in your heart that God raised him from the dead, you will be saved" (Rom. 10:8–9). Two things are required of believers. First, in their hearts they must have a true faith in Christ for their salvation, and second, that faith in the heart is not to remain hidden there but is to be made manifest through a verbal profession of faith to the watching world.

A Mixed Body

"And I tell you, everyone who acknowledges me before men, the Son of Man also will acknowledge before the angels of God" (v. 8). Jesus was looking forward, as He did in the previous passage, to the day of judgment, when all secrets will be made known and the truth of our status in righteousness will be revealed. Everyone who has made a profession of faith that is not genuine will be shown to be a hypocrite.

Our Lord, on another occasion, said His visible church will always contain tares, or weeds, along with the wheat (Matt. 13:24–30). Augustine said that the church is a *corpus permixtum*, a mixed body containing both believers and unbelievers. We're not saved by being members of the church. We're saved by Christ and by a true faith in Him, and that faith is not to be held in secret. The blessing that Jesus promises to His people is this: "If you confess Me before men, if you let it be known to your family, to your friends, to your neighbors that you are a follower of Jesus, then on that day I will stand up and confess you before the holy angels." What a moment that will be when we appear at the judgment seat and Jesus stands up and says: "He's one of Mine. She's My disciple. I confess her, I confess him before the Father and before all the angels in heaven." What a glorious moment that will be for the believer.

"But the one who denies me before men will be denied before the angels of God" (v. 9). In stark contrast to the blessing experienced by believers is the terror of that moment for those who have denied Him publicly. Are you ashamed of being a Christian? Are you embarrassed that people know you are a Christian? If you are, then Christ will be embarrassed by you, and He will say on that day, "I don't know who that is," and before the angels of heaven He will deny you because you've denied Him in this world. It's a fearful thing if there's a disconnect between our hearts and our lips. If we say it, we have to believe it, and if we believe it, we have to say it.

Blasphemy against the Holy Spirit

That may be scary, but the truly frightening part comes next. Jesus said, **"And everyone who speaks a word against the Son of Man will be forgiven, but the one who blasphemes against the Holy Spirit will not be forgiven"** (v. 10). If anything chills the blood, it is the idea that we could possibly commit a sin that could not be forgiven, either in this world or in the world to come, and if there is such a sin that is absolutely and eternally unforgivable, then it would certainly behoove us to know what that sin is.

There has historically been disagreement over the identity of that particular sin. Some have suggested it is murder; others have suggested it's adultery because it's a sin against the temple of the Holy Ghost (1 Cor. 6:15–20). But those sins, as egregious as they may be, can certainly be forgiven. We see examples of that in sacred Scripture itself. The woman caught in adultery was forgiven by Jesus (John 7:53–8:11). David, in his murder of Uriah, was forgiven by God (2 Sam. 12:13). So the unforgivable sin is clearly not murder or adultery. Jesus identifies it as the sin of blasphemy, and blasphemy has to do with the use of words—in this case, words that are directed specifically against the Holy Ghost.

The law against blasphemy is one of the Ten Commandments, and we live in a culture where the name of God is dragged through the mud in every moment. People commonly say, "Oh my God," not realizing that when they do that, they are committing a sin that is worthy of death. The only way for us to use God's name in a frivolous way is by having a frivolous view of God. It's no wonder that the first petition of the Lord's Prayer was that the name of God would be hallowed, not blasphemed. Using the name of God in vain is a serious sin, but it too is forgivable.

How is it that a person can blaspheme against the Father or against the Son and be forgiven, but if he blasphemes against the third person of the Trinity, there's no hope of forgiveness here or in the world to come? Do we not all agree that the Father, the Son, and the Holy Spirit are equal in dignity, in value, in eternality, and in all the divine attributes? So why should one person of the Trinity be singled out as the One against whom a sin could never be forgiven? The answer is related to the Spirit's work in revealing the character and the person of Jesus Christ.

This warning was given after the Pharisees observed the miraculous works of Jesus and accused Him of casting out demons by the power of Satan in Luke 11:14–23. They accused Jesus of numerous things, and they slandered Him constantly, but on that occasion, they came so close to the unforgivable sin that Jesus saw fit to issue a warning regarding the unforgivable sin of blaspheming against the third person of the Trinity, the Holy Spirit, who reveals the true identity of Christ.

The Pharisees had not yet stepped across the line, but they were close. They should have known who Jesus was. They claimed to search Scripture, but they didn't come to the right conclusion. I believe this is one of the reasons that Jesus prayed on the cross, "Father, forgive them, for they know not what they do" (23:34).

But what happens if the Holy Spirit reveals to you that Jesus is the Christ? What if He makes it manifest to you and shows you the truth—not just a preacher telling it to you, not just a theologian explaining it for you, but God the Holy Spirit illumining your mind and your heart and revealing to you indubitably that Jesus is the Son of God? What if you then call Christ a devil? You have just committed the unpardonable sin.

Can a Christian commit the unpardonable sin? Yes and no. In ourselves, we are capable of any sin, including this one. But God in His preserving grace restrains us and will not allow us to commit this sin.

"And when they bring you before the synagogues and the rulers and the authorities, do not be anxious about how you should defend yourself or what you should say, for the Holy Spirit will teach you in that very hour what you ought to say" (vv. 11–12). When you go to a funeral, what do you say to the loved ones left behind? Here's my advice: don't worry about it. There's no speech that you have to memorize. Just be there. Put your arms around them. Weep with them, and the Holy Spirit will make the communication happen.

63

THE PARABLE OF THE RICH FOOL

Luke 12:13–21

Someone in the crowd said to him, "Teacher, tell my brother to divide the inheritance with me." But he said to him, "Man, who made me a judge or arbitrator over you?" And he said to them, "Take care, and be on your guard against all covetousness, for one's life does not consist in the abundance of his possessions." And he told them a parable, saying, "The land of a rich man produced plentifully, and he thought to himself, 'What shall I do, for I have nowhere to store my crops?' And he said, 'I will do this: I will tear down my barns and build larger ones, and there I will store all my grain and my goods. And I will say to my soul, "Soul, you have ample goods laid up for many years; relax, eat, drink, be merry."' But God said to him, 'Fool! This night your soul is required of you, and the things you have prepared, whose will they be?' So is the one who lays up treasure for himself and is not rich toward God."

Luke recorded in his Gospel how Jesus, while speaking to a crowd, would often be interrupted by somebody in the crowd who would change the subject. In this passage a young man who seemed uninterested in hearing what Jesus was saying had a personal concern that was heavy on his heart, and he was hoping that Jesus would help him solve his dilemma.

Someone in the crowd said to him, "Teacher, tell my brother to divide the inheritance with me" (v. 13). This young man was concerned about the legacy that had been left by his father that was to be shared by his two sons, the elder and the younger. Apparently, the younger one was not satisfied with the division of the estate, and now he was taking advantage of the Old Testament law that called for disputes among heirs about an inheritance to be resolved with the help of a rabbi (Num. 27:1–11; Deut. 21:15–17).

But he said to him, "Man, who made me a judge or arbitrator over you?" (v. 14). Jesus was recognized as a rabbi because of the profundity of His teaching, but there's little reason to believe that He had gone through the formal steps of officially becoming a rabbi or that He was in an official capacity to render a verdict in this dispute.

And he said to them, "Take care, and be on your guard against all covetousness, for one's life does not consist in the abundance of his possessions" (v. 15). Jesus, of course, was much more concerned about proclaiming the kingdom of God rather than settling disputes among siblings over the degree of their inheritance. So He said to the people as well as to the man, **"Take care, and be on your guard."** We've heard Him say something similar recently: "Beware of the leaven of the Pharisees, which is hypocrisy" (v. 1). His concern here was different; rather than warning against hypocrisy and the Pharisees, He warned against covetousness.

The Danger of Covetousness

The tenth commandment is "You shall not covet" (Ex. 20:17). Have you ever wondered why God in His infinite wisdom included a law against coveting in His top ten commandments for us? Perhaps God knows something about what leads to stealing, about what leads to jealousy, about what leads to murder and to war. Covetousness is the cause of a person's wanting for himself what God in His beneficence has graciously bestowed on someone else. The sin of covetousness reveals something about the darkest part of our fallen humanity. In his letter to the Romans, Paul wrote:

> For the wrath of God is revealed from heaven against all ungodliness and unrighteousness of men, who by their unrighteousness suppress the truth. For what can be known about God is plain to them, because God has shown it to them. For his invisible attributes, namely, his eternal power and divine nature, have been clearly perceived, ever since the creation of the world, in the things that have been made. So they are without excuse. For although they knew God, they did

> not honor him as God or give thanks to him, but they became futile in their thinking, and their foolish hearts were darkened. (1:18–21)

God brings the whole human race to His tribunal and convicts the whole human race of two fundamental things, the two most basic sins of all of us. The first is the refusal to honor God as God, and the second is the refusal to be grateful.

No one can honor God and have a heart full of gratitude to Him and at the same time be covetous. Covetousness is the antithesis of contentment with the goodness of God. Covetousness always wants more. But Jesus warned, **"One's life does not consist in the abundance of his possessions"** (v. 15).

The Danger of Greed

And he told them a parable, saying, "The land of a rich man produced plentifully, and he thought to himself, 'What shall I do, for I have nowhere to store my crops?' And he said, 'I will do this: I will tear down my barns and build larger ones, and there I will store all my grain and my goods. And I will say to my soul, "Soul, you have ample goods laid up for many years; relax, eat, drink, be merry"' " (vv. 16–19). There are three things to note about this rich man. The first was that he was greedy. No matter how great the crop was, no matter how much he had in storage, he wanted more.

Billionaires have been interviewed and asked, "What drives you? Don't you have enough money yet?" "How much do you want?" They reply, "Just a little bit more." Unlike the Apostle Paul, who was able to be content in whatever state he was in (Phil. 4:11), most of us are never content with what we have. We want more. No wonder greed is historically considered one of the seven deadly sins.

The second thing we learn about this man is that he was selfish. There's not a hint that he wanted to share anything out of his abundance with other people. For him, charity was not an option. All he could think about was how he could keep everything that he had earned.

A Christian is a generous person. How can a Christian not be generous? For every Christian has his being only by the generosity of almighty God. What do we have that we haven't received from God?

Jesus warned people about that greed. But worse than being greedy and worse than being selfish, this man was incredibly foolish. Listen to what he said: **"I will say to my soul, 'Soul, you have ample goods laid up for many years; relax, eat, drink, be merry'"** (v. 19). That last phrase has a long history; it goes back not only centuries but millennia. Even before the Epicureans who debated with the Apostle Paul on Mars Hill in Athens, there was a group called the Cyrenaics who invented what we might call crass hedonism.

Hedonism says that the good is found in the avoidance of pain and the attainment of pleasure. The Cyrenaics' creed was this: Get as much pleasure as you possibly can get. Drink to excess, get drunk, get intoxicated. Eat to the point of gluttony. Enjoy sex until you're satiated by it because that is the good life. That's found in eating and drinking and being merry. Let's have a party. Let's be happy. Let's eat and drink.

The Epicurean philosophers came along and said: "No, that kind of crass hedonism always ends in either boredom or frustration. If you get too much pleasure, you're bored; not enough, and you're frustrated." The Epicureans wanted to refine this. They wanted just enough to drink, just enough of the finest cuisine, just enough sex. They believed this would keep the level of pleasure at the optimum.

The phrase "eat, drink, be merry" is found elsewhere in Scripture. The Apostle Paul used a similar phrase when writing to the Corinthians, some of whom were denying the resurrection of Christ. He said: "If the dead are not raised, 'Let us eat and drink, for tomorrow we die'" (1 Cor. 15:32).

The creed of the American culture is not the Apostles' Creed; it's the hedonist creed. "Eat, drink, be merry" is the creed of the fool. The most useless thing you can do with your life is to spend it seeking pleasure and avoiding pain when blessedness is yours for the asking.

"But God said to him, 'Fool! This night your soul is required of you, and the things you have prepared, whose will they be?' " (v. 20). The reason the man in Jesus' parable said "eat, drink, be merry" is that he had many goods laid up. He thought he had security for his old age. But Jesus responded that a contrary report came from God.

"So is the one who lays up treasure for himself and is not rich toward God" (v. 21). Jesus applied the parable in this manner by saying that the person who lays up treasures for himself, no matter how great that treasure is, but who is not rich toward God is a pauper. He's poverty stricken. Jesus said elsewhere, "For what will it profit a man if he gains the whole world and forfeits his soul? Or what shall a man give in return for his soul?" (Matt. 16:26).

He who lays up treasure for himself and is not rich toward God is like the rich fool—greedy, selfish, and foolish. May we never be called greedy, selfish, or foolish by God. Take heed, Jesus says, lest you succumb to covetousness.

64

THE END OF ANXIETY

Luke 12:22–34

And he said to his disciples, "Therefore I tell you, do not be anxious about your life, what you will eat, nor about your body, what you will put on. For life is more than food, and the body more than clothing. Consider the ravens: they neither sow nor reap, they have neither storehouse nor barn, and yet God feeds them. Of how much more value are you than the birds! And which of you by being anxious can add a single hour to his span of life? If then you are not able to do as small a thing as that, why are you anxious about the rest? Consider the lilies, how they grow: they neither toil nor spin, yet I tell you, even Solomon in all his glory was not arrayed like one of these. But if God so clothes the grass, which is alive in the field today, and tomorrow is thrown into the oven, how much more will he clothe you, O you of little faith! And do not seek what you are to eat and what you are to drink, nor be worried. For all the nations of the world seek after these things, and your Father knows that you need them. Instead, seek his kingdom, and these things will be added to you.

"Fear not, little flock, for it is your Father's good pleasure to give you the kingdom. Sell your possessions, and give to the needy. Provide yourselves with moneybags that do not grow old, with a treasure in the heavens that does not fail, where no thief approaches and no moth destroys. For where your treasure is, there will your heart be also."

What are you afraid of? What do you worry about on a daily basis? Think about those two questions over the course of your day and your week. Each night before you go to bed, ask yourself: "What am I afraid of? What do I worry about?"

In this passage Jesus addresses the problem of anxiety, the feeling of uneasiness of mind or fearful concern. He often issued commands not to be afraid, as He does in this passage. **"Fear not"** (v. 32), He said. He knew us in our human condition. He knew that all of us in our fallenness go through life on the edge of anxiety.

All kinds of anxieties abound, and we must distinguish in the first place between specific anxiety and nonspecific anxiety. Specific anxiety involves those fears that we have common to our life—fears of illness, fears of job loss, and that sort of thing. A study was done a few years ago concerning married men in America that concluded that the number one thing that married men in America worry about is money, specifically with respect to their ability to care for and provide for their families. Before marriage, men feel responsible to take care of themselves, but once they enter into the marriage contract, they feel the weight and the burden of providing not only for themselves but for their wives and their children.

The survey also revealed a startling fact: when men gather, they talk about politics, women, sports, business, and all the rest, but the one thing they never talk about is their insecurities about their ability to provide for their families.

These are specific anxieties. There is also nonspecific anxiety, which is more generalized; it is not focused on any one thing in particular. A philosophy that emerged in the nineteenth century called existentialism had a lot to say about nonspecific anxiety.

Existentialism reached its acme in the West after World War II with the atheistic form of existential philosophy made popular by men such as Jean-Paul Sartre and Albert Camus. But one of the most important voices of that movement was Martin Heidegger, who said that one of the root problems that every human being encounters is the sensation of dread. But this dread is undefined, amorphous, vague; it is something that just constantly eats away at us, and yet we can't define it or explain it. We may go see the counselor and say, "I'm anxious; I'm fearful." He may say to us, "What are you afraid of?" The answer may be, "I don't know; I'm just scared."

Heidegger painted a grim picture of this. He said that every human being experiences what he called a sense of having been hurled chaotically into life with no sense of purpose or destiny, and that sense of having been cast in a meaningless way into life eats away at the soul day in and day out.

Individuals attend school, and their teachers or professors tell them that the universe and human life came into being through macroevolution and that they are cosmic accidents, that they are grown-up germs sitting on a wheel of a vast cosmic machine that is destined for annihilation. They're told they come from nothingness and their future is nothingness, and that eats away at their own sense of significance. That's this vague anxiety.

Do Not Be Anxious

And he said to his disciples, "Therefore I tell you, do not be anxious about your life, what you will eat, nor about your body, what you will put on" (v. 22). Jesus addressed in this discourse specific fears and anxieties that we encounter. I doubt if there's any commandment of God I've broken more frequently than this one not to be anxious. That, of course, is a judgment on my confidence and faith in God.

Jesus tells us that He is with us (Matt. 28:20). If we knew with full assurance every second of our lives that Jesus is right next to us, why would we be afraid of anything? How could we be afraid of anything if we knew that the Lord was standing right beside us? David said, "Even though I walk through the valley of the shadow of death, I will fear no evil" (Ps. 23:4). What's the reason he gives? Because he was not afraid of death? No. Because he was happy in the shadows? No. "For you are with me; your rod and your staff, they comfort me."

That's why living the Christian life means focusing on the Word of God to such an extent that we become more and more conscious of the presence of Christ with us. "Behold," He said, "I am with you always. I am with you on the battlefield. I am with you in the hospital. I am with you in the ambulance. I am with you at the cemetery. I am with you when the bank notice comes of foreclosure. Behold, I'm with you always, even to the ends of the earth."

". . . what you will eat, nor about your body, what you will put on. For life is more than food, and the body more than clothing" (vv. 22–23). I have a hard time preaching on this text personally. This was my father's favorite biblical text, and I watched him die over a period of three years with four strokes, the fourth of which killed him. For most of that time, he was confined to a chair with a magnifying glass that he used to read his Bible. He had much to be anxious about. He wasn't earning any money. He wasn't able to care for his family. He didn't know whether his children were going to be able to go to college. He didn't know if he was going to survive another week.

He said to me with gnarled speech and a sagging jaw, "Be anxious for nothing, what you should eat, what you should drink, what you should put on." I was just amazed because he wasn't anxious, and I, as a high school student, was. My father clung to this text to the very end of his life.

"Consider the ravens: they neither sow nor reap, they have neither storehouse nor barn, and yet God feeds them. Of how much more value are you than the birds!" (v. 24). Have you ever seen a raven go into a field with a plow or use its beak to furrow the fields and then come the next day with a mouthful of seed, dropping it here and there into the furrows? Have you then seen it cover up the seed with its wings and then fly up to the nearest tree to wait for the rain to come and for the seed to germinate? Have you then seen it come afterward and reap the harvest and take the fruit of that harvest to a barn and fill it up for future contingencies? Of course not. Ravens don't sow or reap or store grain. But God feeds them. And we, Jesus said, are of much more value than birds.

"And which of you by being anxious can add a single hour to his span of life? If then you are not able to do as small a thing as that, why are you anxious about the rest?" (vv. 25–26). Worry all you want; you won't add an hour to your life or an inch to your height. Those things are beyond our control. If you're not able to do these things that are the least, why would you be anxious for the rest?

"Consider the lilies, how they grow: they neither toil nor spin, yet I tell you, even Solomon in all his glory was not arrayed like one of these" (v. 27). Did you ever see a lily go to a factory and punch in its time card? Have you gone into a garden and seen the lilies working at a loom with the shuttle flying in and out between the yarn in order to produce a beautiful garment with which to be clothed? Of course not.

"But if God so clothes the grass, which is alive in the field today, and tomorrow is thrown into the oven, how much more will he clothe you, O you of little faith! And do not seek what you are to eat and what you are to drink, nor be worried" (vv. 28–29). Jesus was not saying as the rich fool had said: "Eat, drink, be merry" (v. 19). This is not some giant welfare program that God is offering through the lips of His Son. Of course we're supposed to work and to be productive, but the productivity to which we're called is not to go about our lives with paralyzing fear and anxiety.

Seek First the Kingdom

"For all the nations of the world seek after these things, and your Father knows that you need them. Instead, seek his kingdom, and these things will be added to you" (vv. 30–31). At this point, Jesus was summarizing some of the things that He taught elsewhere. He was talking about priorities. In the Sermon on the Mount, He said, "But seek first the kingdom of God" (Matt. 6:33). Everything else is secondary. I've heard people say cynically, "Money isn't everything; it's the only thing." I've heard them say, "Money isn't everything, but it's way ahead of whatever is in second place." What's in first place in the value system of God is seeking His kingdom.

Unbelievers don't seek after God. They don't seek His kingdom. The seeking of the kingdom of God is the activity of the converted person. When you were converted, it wasn't because you were seeking after God but because God found you and turned your life inside out. From that moment of conversion—and for the rest of your life—you should be busily engaged in seeking more and more of the things of God. That's what discipleship and sanctification are.

"Fear not, little flock, for it is your Father's good pleasure to give you the kingdom" (v. 32). How tenderly Jesus spoke here. Do you know who the **"little flock"** is? It's you and me. We are His lambs, His little flock. He was not rebuking us but rather comforting us. He said: "Don't be afraid, little flock, for it is your Father's good pleasure to give you the kingdom. That's My legacy for you. That's your inheritance."

"Sell your possessions, and give to the needy. Provide yourselves with moneybags that do not grow old, with a treasure in the heavens that does not fail" (v. 33). This is not a universal mandate for everybody to divest themselves of all worldly goods. That was not Jesus' point here. He was saying to give freely, without anxiety, in light of God's gracious provision of all our needs, and to see to it that we are storing up treasure in heaven as we seek after His kingdom.

". . . where no thief approaches and no moth destroys. For where your treasure is, there will your heart be also" (vv. 33–34). It is natural for us to put our hearts where we have most heavily invested in this world. If your number one investment is the kingdom of God, that's where your heart will be. If your number one investment is accumulation of riches, that's where your heart will be. Put your heart and your treasure with the kingdom of God. When you do that, you'll have nothing to fear.

65

THE FAITHFUL SERVANT

Luke 12:35–48

"Stay dressed for action and keep your lamps burning, and be like men who are waiting for their master to come home from the wedding feast, so that they may open the door to him at once when he comes and knocks. Blessed are those servants whom the master finds awake when he comes. Truly, I say to you, he will dress himself for service and have them recline at table, and he will come and serve them. If he comes in the second watch, or in the third, and finds them awake, blessed are those servants! But know this, that if the master of the house had known at what hour the thief was coming, he would not have left his house to be broken into. You also must be ready, for the Son of Man is coming at an hour you do not expect."

Peter said, "Lord, are you telling this parable for us or for all?" And the Lord said, "Who then is the faithful and wise manager, whom his master will set over his household, to give them their portion of food at the proper time? Blessed is that servant whom his master will find so doing when he comes. Truly, I say to you, he will set him over all his possessions. But if that servant says to himself, 'My master is delayed in coming,' and begins to beat the male and female servants, and to eat and drink and get drunk, the master of that servant will come on a day when he does not expect him and at an hour he does not know, and will cut him in pieces and put him with the unfaithful. And that servant who knew his master's will but did not get ready or act according to his will, will receive a severe beating. But the one who did not know, and did what deserved a beating, will receive a light beating. Everyone to whom much was given, of him much will be required, and from him to whom they entrusted much, they will demand the more."

According to His human nature, Jesus is no longer present with us, but according to His divine nature, He is never absent from us. He has ascended bodily to heaven, where He sits at the right hand of the Father, but He promised at the time of His departure that He would return. In the text above we hear our Lord telling us that we are to be ready, in a spirit of vigilance, waiting in a mode of preparedness for His return.

"Stay dressed for action and keep your lamps burning" (v. 35). Jesus began with an admonition. People of antiquity were normally clothed in long flowing robes that went to their ankles. But when they were called to action as soldiers in the military or were to be involved in some kind of an emergency, in order to be prepared for quickness of motion, they would hike up their robes and put on a large belt, into which they would tuck the ends of the robes. This way, their knees would no longer be hindered by the fabric of the garment and they would be able to move at a moment's notice with alacrity.

"And be like men who are waiting for their master to come home from the wedding feast, so that they may open the door to him at once when he comes and knocks" (v. 36). This is a call to be ready. On those who are ready, He pronounced another beatitude: **"Blessed are those servants whom the master finds awake when he comes. Truly, I say to you, he will dress himself for service and have them recline at table, and he will come and serve them"** (v. 37).

Jesus said something so astonishing here that He had to preface His announcement with the word **"truly."** That word means that there is not a shadow of a doubt about it. It is astonishing that the master would gird himself for service and have the servants recline at table, and that the master would come and serve them. The master, when he comes, will come not to be served but to serve (Mark 10:45).

"If he comes in the second watch, or in the third, and finds them awake, blessed are those servants!" (v. 38). The Jews divided the night into three watches, the Romans into four. The master would probably not return during the first watch, but if he came in the second watch or in the third watch, in the wee hours of the morning after everyone else in the village had gone to bed, he would want to find his servants ready and their lamps still burning. Stay ready, Jesus said, no matter how late it may be. Even though you may grow weary and maybe even cynical, saying, "He still isn't here; He's probably not coming at all, so we might as well go to bed," resist those impulses. Jesus said the servant whom the Lord finds waiting when He comes is blessed.

"But know this, that if the master of the house had known at what hour the thief was coming, he would not have left his house to be broken into" (v.

39). If the master knew that somebody was going to break into his house and steal from him, he would not have left the house but would have watched it.

Be Ready

"You also must be ready, for the Son of Man is coming at an hour you do not expect" (v. 40). I believe the event of which Jesus is speaking here is His consummate return at the end of the age when He comes back for His church. No one knows the day or the hour of His return, so we must be ready.

Peter said, "Lord, are you telling this parable for us or for all?" (v. 41). Peter's question is in response to Jesus' parable, and it prompts Him to tell a second parable. Peter wanted to know if the call to be ready was simply for those Apostles whom Jesus was leaving behind to care for the church or if this teaching was meant for all people by extension. The answer Jesus gave make it clear that these warnings were not uttered merely for the first-century disciples or Apostles but for Christians of all times until our Lord returns.

And the Lord said, "Who then is the faithful and wise manager, whom his master will set over his household, to give them their portion of food at the proper time?" (v. 42). He was asking not about what, where, or why but about who. Who is the faithful steward? Who is the wise steward whom his master will make ruler over his household to give them their portion of food in due season?

"Blessed is that servant whom his master will find so doing when he comes. Truly, I say to you, he will set him over all his possessions" (vv. 43–44). This is another benediction. The manager or steward in biblical terms was not the owner of the house. He didn't own the property. He was hired to manage the possessions of the master. The biblical concept is clear: we are called to be stewards of the earth and stewards of everything that God has entrusted to us. This is our Father's world, not ours. My house is not my house; it's His house. My life isn't my life; it's His. Everything I have I hold as a steward for the Lord, and He will require from my hands faithful and wise stewardship of all that He gives to me.

"But if that servant says to himself, 'My master is delayed in coming,' and begins to beat the male and female servants, and to eat and drink and get drunk, the master of that servant will come on a day when he does not expect him and at an hour he does not know, and will cut him in pieces and put him with the unfaithful" (vv. 45–46). This is one more example of stewards who mirror the behavior of the rich fool who said in his heart, "Eat, drink, be merry" (v. 19). The master of that servant will come on a day and in an hour when the servant is not looking for him just as he did to the rich fool.

Jesus said he will cut the servant in pieces. Can it get any more graphic than that? The master comes home and finds the steward beating the rest of the employees, exploiting them, making a mockery of his stewardship. If possible, it gets worse, a whole lot worse, because the judgment on this unfaithful steward is not merely being cut in pieces. Jesus had warned earlier in the chapter: "I will warn you whom to fear: fear him who, after he has killed, has authority to cast into hell. Yes, I tell you, fear him!" (v. 5). What is worse than being cut in half is that he, the unfaithful steward, will be **"put . . . with the unfaithful."**

This is what makes the text so scary. He was not talking about people who are on the outside of the church. He was not talking about rank pagans who have nothing to do with the kingdom of God. He was talking about people who are inside the church and have been appointed stewards of the kingdom of God, who have made professions of faith, who perhaps come to church each Sunday, and He may have been referring to ministers, who have an extra high responsibility of stewardship.

"And that servant who knew his master's will but did not get ready or act according to his will, will receive a severe beating. But the one who did not know, and did what deserved a beating, will receive a light beating" (vv. 47–48). Jesus talked about the proportionate punishment that comes in hell. I often hear from people who think all sins are equally heinous in the sight of God and that hell has just one level of punishment.

Jesus talked about those who hear the Word and fail to keep it. They will receive a severe beating. There are those who are outside the church and don't hear the Word and don't have the advantage of listening to expository preaching every Sunday morning. Though they've still sinned, they will receive a lighter beating. The judgment for those who are in the house of God and who hear but do not respond will be much greater than for those who have never heard.

"Everyone to whom much was given, of him much will be required, and from him to whom they entrusted much, they will demand the more" (v. 48). Jesus concluded this parable by saying that much will be required of those on whom much has been bestowed. To answer the question "What does the Lord require of you?" we must answer another question: "What has the Lord bestowed on you?"

66

THE DIVIDING CHRIST

Luke 12:49–59

"I came to cast fire on the earth, and would that it were already kindled! I have a baptism to be baptized with, and how great is my distress until it is accomplished! Do you think that I have come to give peace on earth? No, I tell you, but rather division. For from now on in one house there will be five divided, three against two and two against three. They will be divided, father against son and son against father, mother against daughter and daughter against mother, mother-in-law against her daughter-in-law and daughter-in-law against mother-in-law."

He also said to the crowds, "When you see a cloud rising in the west, you say at once, 'A shower is coming.' And so it happens. And when you see the south wind blowing, you say, 'There will be scorching heat,' and it happens. You hypocrites! You know how to interpret the appearance of earth and sky, but why do you not know how to interpret the present time?

"And why do you not judge for yourselves what is right? As you go with your accuser before the magistrate, make an effort to settle with him on the way, lest he drag you to the judge, and the judge hand you over to the officer, and the officer put you in prison. I tell you, you will never get out until you have paid the very last penny."

The text begins with a statement that Jesus made concerning the reason for His incarnation, and His explanation is not just difficult but also shocking. On other occasions, Jesus gave other reasons for His coming to this world: "I came that they may have life and have it abundantly" (John 10:10); "For even the Son of Man came not to be served but to serve, and to give his life as a ransom for many" (Mark 10:45); "For this purpose I was born and for this purpose I have come into the world—to bear witness to the truth. Everyone who is of the truth listens to my voice" (John 18:37). But on this occasion, He gave another reason for His coming, one that indeed is surprising for us to hear.

The Coming Judgment

"I came to cast fire on the earth" (v. 49). If somebody asked you, "Why did Jesus come into this world?" I doubt you would have answered that He came to cast fire on the earth. But that's what He said here. He's not only announced that He was going to send fire on the earth, but He communicated His own feelings about that task, saying, **"Would that it were already kindled!"** Jesus was now baring His soul, saying something about His deepest longings. What are we to make of that?

Scholars have historically interpreted this text in different ways. Perhaps the most common way is to say that Jesus was saying, "I wish that the Father would send the fire of judgment on the earth that He has been holding back, and I wish He would do it quickly." Yet, if Jesus were to express a joy of anticipation of a fierce divine judgment on this earth, we would tend to shrink in horror at such a thought. I doubt if there are many things more despicable to our thinking in twenty-first-century America than the idea that God would consume the earth with wrath and judgment. I think back to the attacks of 9/11. The day after, on September 12, two prominent preachers announced that they believed that what happened the day before was an expression of the judgment of God. The public outcry was so great against them that they apologized for their remarks.

When I saw the attack and the people's response I thought, "Isn't it interesting that Americans believe it is possible for God to bless our country, but they don't think that He can judge a nation and bring it to ruin?" If we ask God to bless our country, we have to admit that He might not and that our desire is in vain.

There is perhaps no more difficult doctrine than the doctrine of hell. Almost everything that we know about hell in the New Testament comes to us from the mouth of Jesus, not from the Apostles. The Apostles didn't deny or overlook it, but the vast majority of texts in Scripture about hell come from Jesus. I'm guessing that God knew we wouldn't accept that doctrine from anybody less than Jesus. Even from His lips people find it odious.

In seminary, a student once asked, "If I go to heaven and find that my mother's not there but that she's in hell, how can I possibly be happy in heaven?" The professor looked at the student and said, "Young man, don't you know that when you get to heaven you'll be so purified from sin, so sanctified by the Holy Spirit, that you'll be much more concerned about the glory of God than you will be about the well-being of your mother?" There was an audible gasp from the students in the class.

I couldn't believe what the professor had said, but I thought a lot about it afterward. I realized that I'm a sinner and all my friends and family are sinners. Everybody that I love is a sinner. I have so much more in common with sinners than I have with God in His perfection and His holiness. My concerns always favor the side of those like me. The professor was saying that at some point, we will be so in love with the glory of God that when we see the vindication of His righteousness and His holiness and the punishment of wickedness, we'll be able to rejoice in it. Jesus was without sin. His meat and His drink were to do the will of the Father. He was a man of sorrows and of profound compassion. There has never been a more compassionate human being in the history of the world than was Jesus. This Jesus looked at Jerusalem and, knowing what fate would befall it in the near future, wept over the city; He said: "O Jerusalem, Jerusalem, the city that kills the prophets and stones those who are sent to it! How often would I have gathered your children together as a hen gathers her brood under her wings, and you were not willing!" (13:34). Yet it was that same man of compassion who said, **"Would that it were already kindled!"** That's one possible interpretation.

A second possible interpretation is that Jesus knew the judgment of God was coming and He just simply wanted to get it over with. That line of thinking is linked to the next statement of Jesus: **"I have a baptism to be baptized with, and how great is my distress until it is accomplished!"** (v. 50). It is interesting that Jesus had just told His disciples not to be anxious (vv. 22–34), yet here He revealed a profound state of distress, a profound concern for Himself and for what was waiting for Him in the near future. But what did He mean?

Jesus was already baptized. He'd been baptized in the Jordan River by John the Baptist. John baptized Him with water. The baptism that Jesus was speaking of here was not a baptism of water; it was a baptism of fire, the fire of divine judgment. So, why did He use the Greek term *baptizō*, "to baptize"? The term provides a vivid picture of the fullness of God's wrath. The fire of the Father's wrath would not merely touch Jesus or harm Him a little bit or singe His hair. No, all of God's wrath that should be poured out on every one of His people for their sin would be poured out on Jesus instead. Jesus was looking toward the cross, the most vicious expression of divine wrath that we find anywhere in Scripture. This would be no mere display of God's displeasure; it would be real judgment. The fullness of hell itself was to come upon Him. At this point, Jesus was saying, "I want to get it over with, to cry from the cross, 'It is finished!'"

"Do you think that I have come to give peace on earth? No, I tell you, but rather division" (v. 51). We call Jesus the Prince of Peace. We think about peace every Christmas Eve—peace on earth and goodwill toward men. Isn't that why He came? Jesus said no; He came rather to divide. It seems to be a bad thing to divide people. We tend to think that He came to reconcile and to bring healing everywhere. But here He said that He came to bring division.

When the New Testament talks about the appearance of Christ, it uses the Greek word *krisis*. We get the English word *crisis* from it, but the translation of the word *krisis* is not "crisis"; it's "judgment" or "division." Jesus was saying that all human history will be divided by Him.

Division over Jesus

"For from now on in one house there will be five divided, three against two and two against three. They will be divided, father against son and son against father, mother against daughter and daughter against mother, mother-in-law against her daughter-in-law and daughter-in-law against mother-in-law" (vv. 52–53). People will be divided over Jesus. The most dividing question in the history of the world is, What do you do with Jesus?

The first week I became a Christian, I came home and said to my mother, assuming a joyous response would be forthcoming, "Mother, I became a Christian this week." She responded: "What? You've always been a Christian." I said, "No, Mom, what I mean is, I've come to know Christ as my Savior." She had no idea what I was talking about at that point. By the grace of God, she came to know, but in the meantime, my sister, my cousins, and my uncles and aunts did everything but disown me because I had committed my life to Christ. That act cost me many friends. I was shocked at the intensity of the hostility and animosity toward Christ.

We do everything we can to mollify the situation, to water down the divisive character of Christ, but Christ made it clear: there is no neutrality. You're either for Him or you're against Him. Whether you're for or against Him is the most critical issue for you eternally. If you're not for Him, you're against Him. If you stay against Him, you will be against Him and He against you forever.

He also said to the crowds, "When you see a cloud rising in the west, you say at once, 'A shower is coming.' And so it happens. And when you see the south wind blowing, you say, 'There will be scorching heat,' and it happens. You hypocrites! You know how to interpret the appearance of earth and sky, but why do you not know how to interpret the present time?"

(vv. 54–56). In the midst of this crisis, He pointed out that the people of that time could predict the weather but they couldn't discern the present time. They didn't know how critical it was for human history that He was there then.

"And why do you not judge for yourselves what is right? As you go with your accuser before the magistrate, make an effort to settle with him on the way, lest he drag you to the judge, and the judge hand you over to the officer, and the officer put you in prison. I tell you, you will never get out until you have paid the very last penny" (vv. 57–59). Jesus was telling us not to wait until the last judgment to come to Him. If you do, it will be too late. The judge of all the earth will hand you over to judgment, and you won't get out until you pay the last cent, which means you won't ever get out, because you are a debtor who is unable to pay your debts. This is a hard saying. Christ divides between those who embrace Him, put their trust in Him, and those who ignore Him or reject Him.

67

THE LOCUS OF ASTONISHMENT

Luke 13:1–5

There were some present at that very time who told him about the Galileans whose blood Pilate had mingled with their sacrifices. And he answered them, "Do you think that these Galileans were worse sinners than all the other Galileans, because they suffered in this way? No, I tell you; but unless you repent, you will all likewise perish. Or those eighteen on whom the tower in Siloam fell and killed them: do you think that they were worse offenders than all the others who lived in Jerusalem? No, I tell you; but unless you repent, you will all likewise perish."

There were some present at that very time who told him about the Galileans whose blood Pilate had mingled with their sacrifices (v. 1). For many in and around Jerusalem, it was a scandal. On a feast, presumably Passover, some pilgrims had journeyed to the city to offer their sacrifices in the temple, and when they went in, they were met by soldiers, sent by Pontius Pilate, who massacred them in cold blood. It was a gory scene. As these pilgrims were bringing their animal sacrifices and offering them, Pilate's soldiers cut up the worshipers' bodies so that when blood spurted out, it mixed with the blood of their sacrifices.

When the word of this slaughter reached the streets, people were confused and frightened. They asked the question that all believers do when tragedies like this take place: Where was God in all of this? These were pious Jews. They weren't rebellious Jews. They were people who made the journey to Jerusalem to offer the sacrifice of praise to their God.

One suggestion that came from those who speculated about this tragedy was that though the people killed seemed outwardly pious, they must have actually been inwardly corrupt or God would not have allowed this to happen. They thought there must be a relationship between the degree of sin that we commit and the degree of suffering that we experience. They had forgotten the book of Job, where Job's friends wrongly came to the conclusion that because of the desperate degree of Job's suffering he must have been the worst of all sinners.

They probably weren't there when Jesus answered a similar question concerning the man born blind (John 9), and they rushed to judgment. But beyond that was the bigger question of how a just and holy God can allow something like this to happen.

Philosopher John Stuart Mill posed one of the most famous arguments against Christian theism. It goes like this: Christians claim that God is good and that He is omnipotent, but these things cannot both be true, not with all the pain, suffering, and tragedy there is in this world. If God is good, He would see all the pain and all the suffering and He would surely eliminate it, unless He were unable to. If He wanted to get rid of pain and suffering but He can't, then He's not omnipotent, and if He is omnipotent and doesn't rid the world of pain and suffering, then He's not good.

Mill overlooked two salient points that were not part of his thinking—namely, the holiness of God and the sinfulness of human beings. If God is holy and we are sinful, there must be pain and sorrow in this world until it is all redeemed. Jesus, however, understood the struggle that these people were having regarding this tragic event, and He gave an answer to their question.

Mercy and Justice

And he answered them, "Do you think that these Galileans were worse sinners than all the other Galileans, because they suffered in this way? No, I tell you; but unless you repent, you will all likewise perish" (vv. 2–3). He said they were vexed with the theological problem as to why His Father allows suffering and pain in the world, but they were asking the wrong question. The question they should have been asking was "Why wasn't I slaughtered along with the others?"

He then took it another step: **"Or those eighteen on whom the tower in Siloam fell and killed them: do you think that they were worse offenders than**

all the others who lived in Jerusalem? No, I tell you; but unless you repent, you will all likewise perish" (vv. 4–5). The Scriptures make clear that all of us from time to time are victims of injustice, and all of us at one time or another have injured others unfairly and unjustly. When we experience injustice at the hands of men, Jesus tells us we ought not faint but ought to pray, for He said, "Will not God give justice to his elect, who cry to him day and night?" (18:7). God promises to make right those injustices that we have either committed or received from others. But not once have we ever received an injustice from the hands of God. We have never been treated unfairly or unjustly by God.

I taught theology for more than fifty years, and I've heard literally thousands of questions from students asking about difficult theological questions. One I hear often is closely related to what is dealt with here: Why did God allow this to happen? People ask, "Why did my baby die?" "Why did my husband die?" I get that kind of question all the time. Do you know the question I almost never hear? "Why did God save me?" That's the biggest mystery in theology.

I could give two different answers to that question. The first one is this: I don't know. And the second one is this: because He would not allow His Son to suffer the travail of the cross and not be satisfied. The only reason I can give for why God would save me or save you or save anybody is to honor His Son. It was certainly not because we deserved it in and of ourselves. We deserve what Jesus talked about here: to be slaughtered in the temple or to be crushed on the sidewalk. That's what we deserve. That's justice. Anything else is mercy.

We tend to be forgetful people. We take God's mercy for granted. The first time we taste the tender mercy of God, our hearts are overwhelmed with gratitude and we start singing, "Amazing grace, how sweet the sound," but the second time we're not quite so amazed or quite so grateful. By the third time, we not only expect it but demand it because now we believe we're entitled to the grace of God, and if we get anything less, we're not only confused but become angry.

Though we may experience profound pain, grief, and sorrow that's so deep it could lead us to the pit of despair, there is no possible just ground for anyone ever to be angry with God. There are a million reasons for God to be angry with us, but there is not one reason justly for us to be angry with Him. But we grow accustomed to His grace and confuse justice and mercy.

If you ever think God owes you mercy, if you think for a second that God is obligated to be gracious to you, then let a bell go off in your brain that reminds you that you have confused justice and grace. Although God's character is to be generous with His mercy, and although He is gracious, remember that grace is always unrequired and voluntary. On the one hand, we can expect it because of His consistency of character, but we can never presume upon it. We should never be surprised by grace because God is so gracious. On the other hand, we should always be surprised by His grace because it is amazing and because we don't deserve it.

That's what our Lord was saying. Unless you repent, you will perish just like the Galileans in the temple and the people on whom the tower fell, so put your trust and your hope in His mercy and let God be God.

68

THE PARABLE OF THE BARREN FIG TREE

Luke 13:6–9

And he told this parable: "A man had a fig tree planted in his vineyard, and he came seeking fruit on it and found none. And he said to the vinedresser, 'Look, for three years now I have come seeking fruit on this fig tree, and I find none. Cut it down. Why should it use up the ground?' And he answered him, 'Sir, let it alone this year also, until I dig around it and put on manure. Then if it should bear fruit next year, well and good; but if not, you can cut it down.' "

George Whitefield was one of the greatest preachers ever anointed by God and was one of three men, along with John Wesley and Jonathan Edwards, whom God used to bring about a time of spiritual revival in eighteenth-century America called the First Great Awakening. If you study that period of church history and the preaching of Whitefield, Wesley, and Edwards, you will see a common theme that ran through their preaching. It was the theme of conversion. If you are not converted to Christ, as these men emphasized, your destiny is the wrath of God forever.

Conversion requires the presence of saving faith and contains within it the need for authentic repentance. That's why in the previous text, Jesus said to those who were befuddled by the tragedies that had come to Jerusalem, "Unless you repent, you will all likewise perish" (vv. 3, 5). Jesus said "unless," which introduced a necessary condition for some consequence to follow. Jesus said, "If you don't do this, if you don't repent, you will perish."

We don't want to perish. We want to be spared. We want to be rescued. We want to be saved from that judgment. Edwards preached frequently on this theme, and he understood that in all probability there were people who came to his church and listened to his sermons every Sunday who remained unconverted. He also was convinced that unless the Holy Spirit changed the inclination of their hearts through the supernatural work of regeneration, they would never repent, and they would never come to saving faith.

Some of those people in Edwards' congregation realized that they were unconverted and knew the only way they would be converted would be through the merciful sovereign act of God and His saving grace. They asked Edwards, "What then can we do?" He developed a doctrine that was called the doctrine of "seeking," where he appealed to their enlightened self-interest. He appealed to them to repent as far as they could in their unregenerate state.

In theology, we distinguish between two kinds of repentance. There is the repentance that we call *attrition*. That's the repentance that is motivated by a fear of punishment. It's a repentance that is driven by a desire to get a ticket out of hell, to be rescued from perishing. It's the repentance of Esau. It's the repentance of your little child when you catch him with his hand in the cookie jar and he says: "I'm so sorry. Please don't spank me." That repentance is driven not by a genuine sorrow for having sinned and disobeyed but by a desire to escape the consequences of punishment.

Edwards understood clearly that attrition, that kind of repentance, will never lead to salvation. True repentance is the repentance that we call contrition, where our hearts are broken because of our sin. We are awakened to the fact that we have grievously offended God, and our sorrow is real. Men and women of faith who experience the repentance of contrition are people who are reconciled forever to almighty God.

Edwards said that even if someone is not inclined to true sorrow, true contrition, he can still take advantage of his enlightened self-interest and seek after God. He may then save you. Edwards was saying that if you're not sure that you're converted or if you're convinced you're not, don't leave the church. Make sure you're here every Sunday.

The Centrality of the Church

We know that God saves people outside the church and sometimes in spite of the church and against the teaching of the church. But the main place where the means of God's saving grace are concentrated is the church. It is in the church where you hear the Word of God, and God uses His Word as His primary means to bring people to faith. "So faith comes from hearing, and hearing through the word of Christ" (Rom. 10:17). God Himself has chosen the foolishness of preaching as the method by which He will save His people. If you're unconverted, don't take Sunday off to play golf. Be in church, and pray that under the preaching of the Word of God, you will be saved.

And he told this parable: "A man had a fig tree planted in his vineyard" (v. 6). Jesus continued to teach about the need for repentance and the evidence of true repentance in this parable about a fig tree in a vineyard. Why would someone plant a fig tree in a vineyard? A vineyard is a place where you grow grapes, not figs.

The vineyard of an ancient Jewish farmer was sometimes called his fruit field because the vineyard was the best place to grow not only grapes but also other types of fruit. It was not unusual for the Jewish farmer to plant fruit trees in the vineyard alongside his grapevines because that section of his land received the best care and contained the best soil.

If a farmer wanted to grow a productive fig tree, the best place to grow it was in the vineyard. Just as Edwards said, if you want to grow a repentant sinner, the best place to grow him is in the visible church, where the means of grace are concentrated. In terms of agriculture, God's means of grace for this fig tree were best found in the middle of the vineyard.

The Fruit of Repentance

"And he came seeking fruit on it and found none" (v. 6). The man came seeking fruit on the fig tree. Figs on fig trees are usually concealed by the foliage and are not evident from a distance. The owner had to come close to inspect the fig tree to see if there was any fruit on it, but he found none.

Throughout His teaching, Jesus was concerned that His people bear fruit—chiefly, the fruit of repentance. And yet, this emphasis is not always recognized. There is a school of thought in theology that teaches a doctrine of the work of the Holy Spirit that is not only seriously defective but fatally so. It teaches that in rebirth, the Holy Spirit can bring a person to salvation and to saving faith without that person's ever being changed. Theologically, this is a manifest impossibility. Any human being who has been regenerated by God the Holy Spirit is, by necessity, a changed person. It's impossible to be born of the Spirit and not be changed.

This is a ghastly distortion of biblical truth, and it's ghastly not simply because it's bad theology but because the consequences are severe. It encourages people who have made a profession of faith but who don't possess the faith they profess into believing that they are saved even when there is no evidence of it.

In Reformed theology, we harp on the doctrine of justification by faith alone. With Martin Luther, we agree that it is the article upon which the church stands or falls. We affirm the idea that the works we do in this world add nothing to our justification. To be justified by faith alone is to be justified by Christ alone.

Yet, Luther was quick to add that we are justified by faith alone but not by a faith that is alone. True faith always manifests itself in the fruits of repentance and good works. The good works don't justify us, but if they're not there, that's evidence that there is no real faith. If there's no real faith, there's no justification. The presence of fruit is absolutely essential to be assured of the reality of your conversion. If you are converted, do you have fruit? Or when the Lord comes and examines you and looks for fruit in your life, will He say, "There is none"?

"And he said to the vinedresser, 'Look, for three years now I have come seeking fruit on this fig tree, and I find none. Cut it down. Why should it use up the ground?' " (v. 7). The tree is not bearing fruit, so it is useless. And not only is it useless, but it's also harmful because it's taking the nutrients from the soil and space in the vineyard.

Now Is the Time

"And he answered him, 'Sir, let it alone this year also, until I dig around it and put on manure. Then if it should bear fruit next year, well and good; but if not, you can cut it down' " (vv. 8–9). Jesus didn't tell us what happened to the fig tree. We don't know if in the fourth year, when it had more exposure to the things that would cause it to bear figs, it blossomed and bore fruit; we don't know if after the fourth year it was still barren and whether it passed the limit of the loving-kindness, tender mercy, and grace of the owner.

Jesus used this parable to amplify what He had taught the people on the occasion of the tragedies that had befallen their city. In this parable, our Lord is not saying, "If you repent someday"; He is saying, "Now is the time." You can't assume three more years of patience, three more years of long-suffering. God commands us to repent of our sins now.

If you have lived this long without ever having truly repented of your sins or fled to Christ for your forgiveness and your healing, today may be your last chance. You may not have next week or even tomorrow. Don't presume on the grace of God. If when you lay your head on your pillow tonight, you remain unconverted, I pray that you would not sleep until you're on your knees before the living God, taking advantage of the blessed redemption that He has given to all who repent and believe in the Lord Jesus Christ.

69

A LITTLE LEAVEN

Luke 13:10–21

Now he was teaching in one of the synagogues on the Sabbath. And behold, there was a woman who had had a disabling spirit for eighteen years. She was bent over and could not fully straighten herself. When Jesus saw her, he called her over and said to her, "Woman, you are freed from your disability." And he laid his hands on her, and immediately she was made straight, and she glorified God. But the ruler of the synagogue, indignant because Jesus had healed on the Sabbath, said to the people, "There are six days in which work ought to be done. Come on those days and be healed, and not on the Sabbath day." Then the Lord answered him, "You hypocrites! Does not each of you on the Sabbath untie his ox or his donkey from the manger and lead it away to water it? And ought not this woman, a daughter of Abraham whom Satan bound for eighteen years, be loosed from this bond on the Sabbath day?" As he said these things, all his adversaries were put to shame, and all the people rejoiced at all the glorious things that were done by him.

He said therefore, "What is the kingdom of God like? And to what shall I compare it? It is like a grain of mustard seed that a man took and sowed in his garden, and it grew and became a tree, and the birds of the air made nests in its branches."

And again he said, "To what shall I compare the kingdom of God? It is like leaven that a woman took and hid in three measures of flour, until it was all leavened."

Now **he was teaching in one of the synagogues on the Sabbath** (v. 10). We are not told the location of this synagogue, but we can assume that this was perhaps Jesus' last opportunity to teach publicly in a Jewish synagogue before His crucifixion. It was customary in those days for a visiting rabbi to be invited to expound the Old Testament text that was designated for that day. Jesus, having been invited, assumed that role of teacher and was explaining an important text of the Old Testament. While He was doing this, He interrupted Himself.

And behold, there was a woman who had had a disabling spirit for eighteen years. She was bent over and could not fully straighten herself (v. 11). A disabled woman appeared in the synagogue. Jesus could not help but notice her because of her obvious deformity. She was a woman who was bent over and couldn't straighten her back. Modern interpreters have suggested that the woman suffered from a condition called spondylosis deformans; it involves a deformed spine in which the bones of the spine are fused together into a single, rigid mass. This forces the person to walk stooped over.

Luke tells us she had been afflicted with this infirmity **for eighteen years**. Not only was the deformity grotesque in appearance, but it was also at times exceedingly painful. Jesus was giving an exposition when He noticed the woman bent over come into the synagogue.

When Jesus saw her, he called her over and said to her, "Woman, you are freed from your disability" (v. 12). We don't know why she was there. Perhaps she had heard that Jesus was there and knew of His reputation, so she made her way painfully and slowly to the place where He was teaching. When Jesus saw her, He stopped His teaching. He called her to come forward. He did two things: He spoke, and He touched her.

And he laid his hands on her, and immediately she was made straight, and she glorified God (v. 13). He laid His hands on her. And then, not gradually or slowly but immediately, for the first time in eighteen years, the woman stood up straight. Her spine was healed, and the affliction was removed from her. And she gave praise to God.

Mercy on the Sabbath

But the ruler of the synagogue, indignant because Jesus had healed on the Sabbath, said to the people, "There are six days in which work ought to be done. Come on those days and be healed, and not on the Sabbath day" (v. 14). It was the responsibility of the ruler of the synagogue to establish the liturgy for the day and even to issue the invitation to the visiting rabbi who would interpret the Old Testament passage. This man was shocked by what he saw, and in his judgment the Sabbath day in the synagogue was not the place to carry on a healing ministry. In his anger, he addressed the crowd, telling them that if they wanted to be healed, they should come on one of the other six days of the week. The rebuke was aimed at the woman, of course, and also implicitly at Jesus.

Then the Lord answered him, "You hypocrites! Does not each of you on the Sabbath untie his ox or his donkey from the manger and lead it away to water it? And ought not this woman, a daughter of Abraham whom Satan bound for eighteen years, be loosed from this bond on the Sabbath day?" As he said these things, all his adversaries were put to shame, and all the people rejoiced at all the glorious things that were done by him" (vv. 15–17). Jesus called him a hypocrite because he would not have considered it a violation of the Sabbath day to give the necessary requirements of life to his livestock but was offended when Jesus did the same for a human being. The man's value system was broken. He placed a higher value on his donkey or his ox than he did on human beings. As Jesus said these things, His adversaries were put to shame.

Does it strike you as strange, in this topsy-turvy world, that beasts of the earth are treated with more dignity than human beings? People protest the treatment of animals, attacking the keeping of animals in zoos, decrying the use of animals as food sources, or agitating for the protection of endangered species. I love animals, and I don't want to hurt them, but where is the outrage over the systematic destruction of living human beings? Recently it was said that the worst crime of the twentieth century was the Holocaust, perpetrated by Adolf Hitler and his henchmen with the extermination of six million Jews. Yet more than sixty million babies in the United States have been slaughtered in the womb since *Roe v. Wade* in 1973, not because a Hitler is orchestrating it but because we're doing it ourselves to our own children. There is a deathly silence in the land about that.

In nineteenth-century England, William Wilberforce protested slavery in Parliament year after year, and year after year he was soundly defeated. Slavery was an established convention. In the end, Wilberforce won his battle against slavery. Abortion on demand has been established as a societal convention in our culture, making it almost impossible to overturn.

The Growing Kingdom

He said therefore, "What is the kingdom of God like? And to what shall I compare it? It is like a grain of mustard seed that a man took and sowed in his garden, and it grew and became a tree, and the birds of the air made

nests in its branches" (vv. 18–19). We know that the mustard seed was one of the tiniest seeds that could be found in the Holy Land. Jesus said: "Look what you can get from this tiny little seed. You put it in the ground, you water it, and you wait. Soon, a little sprout comes up out of the earth, and it begins to grow until it becomes not just a bush but a tree, ten feet, eleven feet, up to fifteen feet tall, with a strong canopy. And it is dense in its vegetation—so dense that birds seek it out as a place to find rest or even build their nests. All of that from this infinitesimally small seed."

And again he said, "To what shall I compare the kingdom of God? It is like leaven that a woman took and hid in three measures of flour, until it was all leavened" (vv. 20–21). Jesus was saying again that this is what the kingdom of God is like. Small beginnings yield great and vast fruit.

Within forty years from the time Jesus spoke that parable, the kingdom of God had penetrated every locale in the Roman Empire. He started with a handful of people, and they leavened the whole lump. The little seed that was planted by Jesus has since grown into a tree that keeps us in its branches today, two thousand years after the life of Jesus.

Small things can grow and will grow. The gates of hell cannot prevail against it because it's the kingdom of God, not the kingdom of men. With God, all things are possible. With Christ, all things are possible. A woman bent in half can be made straight, and a culture twisted and distorted can be turned right side up when the people of God act like the people of God.

70

THE NARROW WAY

Luke 13:22–35

He went on his way through towns and villages, teaching and journeying toward Jerusalem. And someone said to him, "Lord, will those who are saved be few?" And he said to them, "Strive to enter through the narrow door. For many, I tell you, will seek to enter and will not be able. When once the master of the house has risen and shut the door, and you begin to stand outside and to knock at the door, saying, 'Lord, open to us,' then he will answer you, 'I do not know where you come from.' Then you will begin to say, 'We ate and drank in your presence, and you taught in our streets.' But he will say, 'I tell you, I do not know where you come from. Depart from me, all you workers of evil!' In that place there will be weeping and gnashing of teeth, when you see Abraham and Isaac and Jacob and all the prophets in the kingdom of God but you yourselves cast out. And people will come from east and west, and from north and south, and recline at table in the kingdom of God. And behold, some are last who will be first, and some are first who will be last."

At that very hour some Pharisees came and said to him, "Get away from here, for Herod wants to kill you." And he said to them, "Go and tell that fox, 'Behold, I cast out demons and perform cures today and tomorrow, and the third day I finish my course. Nevertheless, I must go on my way today and tomorrow and the day following, for it cannot be that a prophet should perish away from Jerusalem.' O Jerusalem, Jerusalem, the city that kills the prophets and stones those who are sent to it! How often would I have gathered your children together as a hen gathers her brood under her wings, and you were not willing! Behold, your house is forsaken. And I tell you, you will not see me until you say, 'Blessed is he who comes in the name of the Lord!' "

He went on his way through towns and villages, teaching and journeying toward Jerusalem (v. 22). Luke introduced this discourse by telling us that Jesus was continuing His journey to Jerusalem in somewhat of a leisurely pace, going through each village and town along the way and taking the opportunity to preach the kingdom of God and to heal those who were afflicted.

And someone said to him, "Lord, will those who are saved be few?" (v. 23). Have you ever asked that question? Did you ever wonder what proportion of fallen humanity will make it to heaven? Is it the majority of humankind that God saves, or is it but a remnant? What percentage of your friends and neighbors will go to heaven, and what percentage will spend eternity in hell? I believe very few people think about that in any degree because we live in such a pluralistic culture. The assumption is that most, if not all, people who die will go to heaven. Perhaps God is so kind, so tenderhearted, so merciful that His eternal plan is to save the vast majority of mankind. I hope that's the case, but I have little reason to believe it.

It seems to me that Scripture is overwhelming in its teaching to the contrary and that the vast majority of people who have ever lived are either now or will soon be in hell forever. Can you even begin to bear such a thought?

Paul makes it clear in Romans that the entire world—every man, woman, and child—is by nature exposed to the wrath of God because every single person is in a natural state of rebellion and hostility to almighty God (Rom. 1:18–23). Why would a righteous Judge, a holy God, be concerned to save any of us?

We know of one occasion in the Old Testament when God destroyed the world with a flood because "the Lord saw that the wickedness of man was great in the earth, and that every intention of the thoughts of his heart was only evil continually" (Gen. 6:5). Whatever the number of human beings on earth at that time, only a handful were saved—Noah and his family. Why should we think that God would save the majority of us? The most vexing theological question is actually why He would save anybody.

Few Will Enter

And he said to them, "Strive to enter through the narrow door" (vv. 23–24). The word that is translated "strive" is the Greek word from which we get the English word *agony*. That is, He was not saying that we ought to have a casual interest in entering through the narrow door. But if necessary, we should pummel ourselves until we're bleeding. We should exert ourselves with whatever full measure we have to make sure that we get through the narrow door.

"For many, I tell you, will seek to enter and will not be able" (v. 24).

There's a parallel here to what Jesus taught in the Sermon on the Mount. On that occasion, Jesus said: "Enter by the narrow gate. For the gate is wide and the way is easy that leads to destruction, and those who enter by it are many. For the gate is narrow and the way is hard that leads to life, and those who find it are few" (Matt. 7:13–14). Jesus drew a contrast between two things: the size of the gate and the number of those who enter. Two gates—a narrow one and a wide one. Many will enter through the wide gate and go to destruction, while few will enter through the narrow gate and find life.

We live in a culture that tells us daily that the most important virtue is to be broad-minded, and the most politically incorrect thing is to be narrow-minded. People ask: "What? There's only one way to God? Jesus is the only way? How narrow is that?" Society wants us to embrace pluralism and relativism—no one has an exclusive claim to truth; that's way too narrow-minded. I hear people describe themselves as "broad" evangelicals. A broad evangelical is an oxymoron. If you're evangelical and believe the gospel, then you've chosen the narrow path, and you've said this way and none other. One Christ, no more. Jesus is the *monogenēs*, the only begotten of the Father. All the rest are thieves and robbers. But there are thieves and robbers at every gate that is wide. They are beckoning, inviting, seducing, controlling, and saying: "Come through my gate. It's plenty wide for all of us. It doesn't matter what you do or what you believe. This gate's big enough for everybody, so you can all come."

When the Door Is Shut

"When once the master of the house has risen and shut the door, and you begin to stand outside and to knock at the door, saying, 'Lord, open to us,' then he will answer you, 'I do not know where you come from' " (v. 25). It's bad enough that Jesus taught us that the gate is narrow and that there are few who find it, but it gets worse. Here He talked about what happens when the door is shut. The narrow gate allows access into the kingdom of God. It is the door to heaven, but there comes a time when even the narrow gate is shut. Once that door is shut, there's nothing anyone can do to open it.

This is again similar to Jesus' words in the Sermon on the Mount: "Not everyone who says to me, 'Lord, Lord,' will enter the kingdom of heaven, but the one who does the will of my Father who is in heaven. On that day many will say to me, 'Lord, Lord, did we not prophesy in your name, and cast out demons in your name, and do many mighty works in your name?' And then will I declare to them, 'I never knew you; depart from me, you workers of lawlessness'" (Matt. 7:21–23). When Jesus said He didn't know them, He didn't mean that He was unaware of them. He meant that He didn't know them savingly. He repeated that warning here. People will say, **"Lord,"** feigning an intimate knowledge of Christ, and He will answer them, **"I do not know where you come from"** (v. 25). Then they will say, **"We ate and drank in your presence, and you taught in our streets"** (v. 26), and He will respond, **"I tell you, I do not know where you come from. Depart from me, all you workers of evil!"** (v. 27).

"In that place there will be weeping and gnashing of teeth, when you see Abraham and Isaac and Jacob and all the prophets in the kingdom of God but you yourselves cast out" (v. 28). Jesus described the state of those who are barred from entering as **"weeping and gnashing of teeth."** If you die and wake up in hell, what will be your response? There are only two possible responses. People will sob uncontrollably forever, or they will gnash their teeth. What does that mean? When people become enraged at other people, they don't just grit their teeth; they gnash their teeth against them. That's a metaphor that describes unmitigated fury. You wake up in hell, and you shake your fist at heaven. You see Abraham, you see Isaac, you see the prophets, you see your next-door neighbor entering eternal felicity, but you're left out. You're too mad to cry, so you gnash your teeth while saying: "That's not fair, God; why would You put me here? I was a good person."

"And people will come from east and west, and from north and south, and recline at table in the kingdom of God. And behold, some are last who will be first, and some are first who will be last" (vv. 29–30). What if Jesus is right? Then it's time to do everything you can do to get yourself in the presence of the means of grace and to take hold of the saving Christ.

The Plot of Herod

At that very hour some Pharisees came and said to him, "Get away from here, for Herod wants to kill you" (v. 31). Luke interrupted this narrative by saying that after Jesus gave this address, some of the Pharisees came to Him. Every time we see the Pharisees with Jesus, they're trying to trap Him, trick Him, arrest Him, or find a way to get Him executed. This time, they came to warn Him that Herod Antipas, the one who murdered John the Baptist, was seeking to kill Him, saying that He should leave Galilee and go to Judea. Were these Pharisees trustworthy? Probably not. They likely wanted Him out of Galilee and in Judea, where they had jurisdiction.

And he said to them, "Go and tell that fox, 'Behold, I cast out demons and perform cures today and tomorrow, and the third day I finish my course. Nevertheless, I must go on my way today and tomorrow and the day following, for it cannot be that a prophet should perish away from Jerusalem'" (vv. 32–33). It's as if He was saying, "Don't worry, Herod; I'm going. My time is limited, and I'm on My way to Jerusalem because that's where the prophet must go to die."

Jesus Laments over Jerusalem

"O Jerusalem, Jerusalem, the city that kills the prophets and stones those who are sent to it! How often would I have gathered your children together as a hen gathers her brood under her wings, and you were not willing! Behold, your house is forsaken. And I tell you, you will not see me until you say, 'Blessed is he who comes in the name of the Lord!' " (vv. 34–35). Having mentioned Jerusalem, He uttered this famous lament over the city. Jesus believed that the reason these people wouldn't come to Him was because they were not willing to. They exercised their free will to say no to Jesus' invitation.

Why wouldn't they come? The answer is they wouldn't come because they couldn't come. Jesus said, "No one can come to me unless the Father who sent me draws him" (John 6:44). God has to enable you to come to Christ because you can't come to Him without divine intervention. They would not come because they could not. But why is it that they could not? They could not because they would not. This sounds like a vicious circle. They would not because they could not, and they could not because they would not. What do I mean?

The answer has to do with free will. Free will is the ability to choose what you want without coercion, and we have this ability. Not only are you free to choose what you want, not only may you choose what you want, but you must choose what you want because the very essence of free choice is choosing what you want most at a given moment. The problem with the people of Jerusalem was not that they didn't have a free will; it's that they didn't want Jesus. If you don't want Him, not only will you not choose Him, but you can't choose Him, since if you're free, you can't choose what you don't want. So, they could not because they would not. They would not because they could not, because they didn't have the power to act against their own free will.

Some say that God saves as many people as He possibly can. If that's the case, then we should be Universalists, because God has the authority and the power to save every last sinner on this planet. But such people say that God cannot save anybody who doesn't want to be saved. God is a gentleman, and He can't impose His will on an unwilling sinner and intervene and change the disposition of that sinner's heart. But what cosmic law is there that forbids the Creator from re-creating the creature for the creature's eternal salvation? What kind of God is that who cannot act in such a way? God can save all, and He can certainly save most people. But in His perfect righteousness and wisdom, He has decided from all eternity to save but a few. That is His sovereign right, and it is for His glory.

71

THE WAY OF HUMILITY

Luke 14:1–14

One Sabbath, when he went to dine at the house of a ruler of the Pharisees, they were watching him carefully. And behold, there was a man before him who had dropsy. And Jesus responded to the lawyers and Pharisees, saying, "Is it lawful to heal on the Sabbath, or not?" But they remained silent. Then he took him and healed him and sent him away. And he said to them, "Which of you, having a son or an ox that has fallen into a well on a Sabbath day, will not immediately pull him out?" And they could not reply to these things.

Now he told a parable to those who were invited, when he noticed how they chose the places of honor, saying to them, "When you are invited by someone to a wedding feast, do not sit down in a place of honor, lest someone more distinguished than you be invited by him, and he who invited you both will come and say to you, 'Give your place to this person,' and then you will begin with shame to take the lowest place. But when you are invited, go and sit in the lowest place, so that when your host comes he may say to you, 'Friend, move up higher.' Then you will be honored in the presence of all who sit at table with you. For everyone who exalts himself will be humbled, and he who humbles himself will be exalted."

He said also to the man who had invited him, "When you give a dinner or a banquet, do not invite your friends or your brothers or your relatives or rich neighbors, lest they also invite you in return and you be repaid. But when you give a feast, invite the poor, the crippled, the lame, the blind, and you will be blessed, because they cannot repay you. For you will be repaid at the resurrection of the just."

This is the third episode given to us in Luke of encounters Jesus had with the Pharisees with respect to the issue of healing people on the Sabbath day (see 6:6–11; 13:10–17). It seems that there was no end to this dispute, as the Pharisees considered this activity of Jesus one of the most sacrilegious and blasphemous things He did during His earthly ministry. Remember, these are Pharisees. They were so named because in the intertestamental period, they saw the moral decline of their own nation. People were moving away from a desire to obey the law of God. The Pharisees called themselves the "set-apart ones." They were uniquely devoted to keeping every law that came from God in the Old Testament.

Some of them were convinced that if someone kept the law perfectly for one day, that action would induce God to send the long-awaited Messiah. The irony is that the Messiah was standing before them.

These men, who had dedicated themselves to the pursuit of righteousness, had degenerated into a group of hypocrites. They were involved in a charade. Their joy was to parade their righteousness and their holiness not before God but before the eyes of men. What they lusted for was the applause of human beings. It was an exercise in hypocrisy, a pretense, as their righteousness was not genuine. Nothing exposes the counterfeit like the genuine. When Christ came into their midst, they couldn't stand Him. Their overwhelming desire was to get rid of Him, by execution if necessary.

Here it happened again. They invited Him to dinner on the Sabbath. Jesus came, knowing full well that it was a trap. They hadn't invited Him out of kindness or friendliness or out of a desire to honor Him; rather, they invited Him to catch Him in another violation of the Sabbath.

One Sabbath, when he went to dine at the house of a ruler of the Pharisees, they were watching him carefully (v. 1). The Pharisees were watching Him closely. Every eye was on Him. What was He going to say? What was He going to do?

And behold, there was a man before him who had dropsy (v. 2). This man may have suffered from acute edema, possibly manifesting a serious illness involving the heart, the kidneys, or the liver. He might have been a plant; perhaps the Pharisees went out and found someone they could put before Jesus to see if He would heal again on the Sabbath, as He had done on two other occasions.

And Jesus responded to the lawyers and Pharisees, saying, "Is it lawful to heal on the Sabbath, or not?" (v. 3). Jesus asked His host a question. He put His petition before the court, before He acted, and asked them to give a judgment. Is it lawful to heal on the Sabbath day? Well, in fact it was, according to Jewish law, as there were exceptions to the prohibition against work. Those exceptions involved emergency situations when human beings or animals were in severe distress.

There was one sect among the Jews, the Essenes, whose members were even more narrow and scrupulous than most Pharisees. We know from the Dead Sea Scrolls that the Essenes had a prohibition against assisting an animal in giving birth if it was the Sabbath day. And if someone's animal gave birth and the newborn animal fell into a pit, it couldn't be rescued on the Sabbath day. But that narrow view was not the traditional view of the Pharisees, and Jesus knew that.

But they remained silent (v. 4). In response to Jesus' question, the Pharisees said nothing. The room was silent. They didn't know what to say to Jesus. **Then he took him and healed him and sent him away** (v. 4). Then Jesus again directed His attention to the Pharisees.

And he said to them, "Which of you, having a son or an ox that has fallen into a well on a Sabbath day, will not immediately pull him out?" And they could not reply to these things (vv. 5–6). This is the same argument that He used on a previous occasion (13:15–16). Again, they couldn't answer Him. Jesus then punctuated His action by giving a parable.

Places of Honor

Now he told a parable to those who were invited, when he noticed how they chose the places of honor, saying to them, "When you are invited by someone to a wedding feast, do not sit down in a place of honor, lest someone more distinguished than you be invited by him, and he who invited you both will come and say to you, 'Give your place to this person,' and then you will begin with shame to take the lowest place" (vv. 7–9). Can you picture it? A wedding feast was a memorable time with places set for those who came and who were holding high offices. It was similar to this very feast to which the Pharisees had invited Jesus.

At a normal dinner party, the host had three U-shaped couches. People reclined to eat their meal. The tables were established with priorities. Table number 1 was for the most-honored guests. Table number 2 was for the next group. Table number 3 was for the group after that. The person who was in the highest honor sat at the bottom of the U. Then those at his left and at his right were also in this pecking order of honor. There weren't any reserved signs or name signs placed at each table. It was open seating, but everybody was supposed to know their place. When the host, who was at the highest place, reclined, he expected the two places beside him to be occupied by the most highly honored guests.

Jesus watched what was going on. There was a mad scramble among the invited guests to try and be next to the host or get closer to the host. Nobody wanted to sit in seat number 9. That was for the lowly person among the guests. But it was foolish to take the highest seat, because there was a chance that the person would be disgraced when the host came and directed him to move to the back of the room.

"But when you are invited, go and sit in the lowest place, so that when your host comes he may say to you, 'Friend, move up higher.' Then you will be honored in the presence of all who sit at table with you. For everyone who exalts himself will be humbled, and he who humbles himself will be exalted" (vv. 10–11). It is better to humble yourself so you can be exalted.

Before the Face of God

He said also to the man who had invited him, "When you give a dinner or a banquet, do not invite your friends or your brothers or your relatives or rich neighbors, lest they also invite you in return and you be repaid. But when you give a feast, invite the poor, the crippled, the lame, the blind, and you will be blessed, because they cannot repay you. For you will be repaid at the resurrection of the just" (vv. 12–14). Jesus was talking about something basic to our humanity. Ungodly ambition and the quest for recognition and for honor and glory in this world show that your gaze is in the wrong place; it is fixed on this terrestrial plane. You need to lift up your eyes to heaven. The Reformers had an adage that said: "We are to live our lives *coram Deo*, before the face of God. Everything we do should be done before God, under His authority, and to His glory, not bound to this world and to the ambitions that define our earthly estate."

Several years ago, I was involved in one of the most painful theological controversies of my life. The issue at stake was so weighty and severe that I felt constrained to stand in opposition to some of my closest friends and comrades in the faith.

The Bible teaches us, as much as possible, to live at peace with all men. We are not to be quarrelsome or contentious, but there are times when the line has to be drawn, where a person cannot tolerate the intolerable. That's what happened in the sixteenth century. That's what happened at the Diet of Worms when Martin Luther said he was unable to recant his teachings.

I was in agony over this issue, and I went by myself into a church. I opened my Bible to Galatians, where the Apostle Paul wrote these words: "I am astonished that you are so quickly deserting him who called you in the grace of Christ and are turning to a different gospel" (Gal. 1:6). Paul was expressing Apostolic astonishment that some of the Galatians, who embraced that gospel by which they were redeemed, had moved away from it so quickly to what he said was a different gospel. Then he corrected himself, saying, "Not that there is another one" (v. 7). The Apostle understood there is only one gospel. There are not two gospels. He said, "But there are some who trouble you and want to distort the gospel of Christ" (v. 7).

Then he said this: "But even if we or an angel from heaven should preach to you a gospel contrary to the one we preached to you, let him be accursed" (v. 8). Paul said let such a man be cursed by God. If anyone preaches any other gospel to you than what you have received, let him be accursed.

Before I went to the church that day, I had read that passage a hundred times. I knew the Apostle Paul had told us that we're not to negotiate or compromise or exchange the gospel in any way whatsoever and that if any would seek to pervert that gospel, they were under the judgment of God. I knew that. I knew what happened in the sixteenth century at the Council of Trent, where the Protestant doctrine and an understanding of justification by faith alone was subjected to the denunciation of Rome: "If anyone says a man is justified by faith alone, apart from the works of the law, let him be anathema." The Reformed doctrine of justification was cursed by Rome in the sixteenth century.

I knew that the Roman Catholic understanding of the gospel and the Reformed understanding of the gospel were not the same. They can't both be right. One is the gospel; the other one isn't. I knew what the pressure would be to soften that difference and negotiate the article upon which the church stands or falls. I kept coming back to Galatians: If anyone, even an angel from heaven, even your best friend or your co-laborer, preaches a different gospel, you can't negotiate it. No matter what.

All those times I read that passage, I stopped at the end of verse 9 and didn't go on to verse 10. That day in the empty church, I read verse 10: "For am I now seeking the approval of man, or of God? Or am I trying to please man? If I were still trying to please man, I would not be a servant of Christ." Paul was not saying that we should be as displeasing to human beings as we possibly can; nor was Jesus saying that it's always wrong to have a dinner party where you just bring your friends in. Jesus was talking about the sin of being a people pleaser.

There are moments in our lives when every Christian has to face this question: Do I please these people, or do I please God? The Bible is a history of what happens to people who faced that choice and decided to please God rather than man. It's a bloody history. It's not a pleasant thing to lose friends. It's not a pleasant thing to have your reputation tarnished because you wouldn't play ball. With respect to the gospel, it's never, ever, ever a game. It's a commitment where eternity hangs in the balance.

It's better to lose a thousand friends or a thousand relatives than to lose the gospel. If you seek to please men rather than God, it might get you into the most honored seat in the house—until He comes and says: "Please move. Go to the back of the house. Will those who have kept the faith, honored Me, and sought more than anything to please Me rather than seeking the applause of this world come up here and sit at My Father's table?" Whom do you want to please? The world or the Lord of the world?

72

THE PARABLE OF THE GREAT SUPPER

Luke 14:15–24

When one of those who reclined at table with him heard these things, he said to him, "Blessed is everyone who will eat bread in the kingdom of God!" But he said to him, "A man once gave a great banquet and invited many. And at the time for the banquet he sent his servant to say to those who had been invited, 'Come, for everything is now ready.' But they all alike began to make excuses. The first said to him, 'I have bought a field, and I must go out and see it. Please have me excused.' And another said, 'I have bought five yoke of oxen, and I go to examine them. Please have me excused.' And another said, 'I have married a wife, and therefore I cannot come.' So the servant came and reported these things to his master. Then the master of the house became angry and said to his servant, 'Go out quickly to the streets and lanes of the city, and bring in the poor and crippled and blind and lame.' And the servant said, 'Sir, what you commanded has been done, and still there is room.' And the master said to the servant, 'Go out to the highways and hedges and compel people to come in, that my house may be filled. For I tell you, none of those men who were invited shall taste my banquet.' "

In the previous passage, Jesus had been invited to a dinner at the home of a Pharisee, and with the other Pharisees in attendance, a trap was set for Jesus. In the Pharisees' opinion, Jesus violated the Sabbath day by healing a man with dropsy. Jesus took that occasion not only to heal the one so afflicted but also to instruct those who were there concerning humility. He followed that instruction with this parable.

When one of those who reclined at table with him heard these things, he said to him, "Blessed is everyone who will eat bread in the kingdom of God!" (v. 15). We don't know if this was said cynically or skeptically, since those who were in attendance were opposed to Jesus. Or perhaps this person was a secret disciple of Jesus' like Nicodemus. Whether he spoke cynically or genuinely, what he said abounds with truth.

We have here another beatitude or blessing. Who is blessed in this context? The man said, **"Blessed is everyone who will eat bread in the kingdom of God!"** Blessed is the person who comes to the table of God in the heavenly kingdom.

As Mephibosheth, the crippled survivor in the Old Testament, was invited to dine at the king's table in the house of David (2 Sam. 9:10–11), so all who are born of the Spirit, redeemed by Christ, and adopted into His family are invited to the heavenly feast that God has prepared in all eternity, the marriage feast of the Lamb with His bride. All of us who are in Christ, who are in the invisible church, are His bride. We will participate in that bridal feast.

The Banquet Is Ready

But he said to him, "A man once gave a great banquet and invited many. And at the time for the banquet he sent his servant to say to those who had been invited, 'Come, for everything is now ready'" (vv. 16–17). After the man pronounced the benediction, Jesus told a somewhat troubling parable. What lay behind this text was an ancient Jewish custom that when a major feast was prepared by a wealthy person, two invitations were given.

The first invitation went out to the guests whom the host was asking to attend. The people would then respond, and presumably being invited to a feast such as this was a great privilege and honor. So, the invitees would usually accept. When the meal was prepared and the time was at hand, those who had said they were coming would be notified that the time had arrived for the feast to begin. The guests would then come and participate.

In this parable, the servant went and gave the second invitation to those who had accepted the first invitation, but things didn't go as expected: **"But they all alike began to make excuses"** (v. 18). Even though they had said they would come, when the time actually came, each of them refused to come. They offered excuses to the servant who summoned them.

"The first said to him, 'I have bought a field, and I must go out and see

it. Please have me excused.' And another said, 'I have bought five yoke of oxen, and I go to examine them. Please have me excused.' And another said, 'I have married a wife, and therefore I cannot come'" (vv. 18–20). Jesus included members of that group with respect to their excuses. The first one said he had to go look at a piece of land he had purchased. Who buys a piece of land sight unseen? Even if he were foolish enough to do that, the land would still be there the next day. There was no pressing need for that guest to absent himself from the feast because he bought a field.

The second was like the first. The most important animal to the ancient Jew was the ox. The ox was the beast of burden that was responsible for so many activities of labor for the farmer. This man said he had bought five yoke of oxen and had to test them. Did the man not test them before he bought them? Or did he think the oxen would die that day and he wouldn't have an opportunity to check them out the next day? That's not a good excuse.

The third man said he got married. Did he get married that day? Did the man not know the date of the banquet or of his wedding when he accepted the invitation to come to the feast? How feeble are all these excuses.

The Invitation Given to Others

"So the servant came and reported these things to his master. Then the master of the house became angry and said to his servant, 'Go out quickly to the streets and lanes of the city, and bring in the poor and crippled and blind and lame.' And the servant said, 'Sir, what you commanded has been done, and still there is room.' And the master said to the servant, 'Go out to the highways and hedges and compel people to come in, that my house may be filled. For I tell you, none of those men who were invited shall taste my banquet'" (vv. 21–24). Jesus said that the servant reported all of this to his master, and the master of the house was disappointed with this news. The master extended the invitation to the rejected, the despised, those who were outside. Here you can sense Jesus' meaning: "Go over the borders of Israel. Go to the Gentiles. Go to those people who were no people and let them now be known as My people." To you and to me, the invitation is now given.

We have a tendency when we read Scripture to think, How could they be so foolish and wicked as to say they were going to the banquet and fail to show up? But that's who we are. We can see several similarities between us and the invitees of the parable.

First, we also often fail to keep our commitments. Each of us who is a church member, in order to join that church, made a pledge, a vow, a commitment to participate in the life of the church. Everybody who's married has made a vow to maintain honor in their marriage. Every one of us who is employed or who is an employer has entered into agreements with those who labor with us or for us to do certain things.

In a word, we are people who make commitments in every aspect of our lives, and we often don't keep those commitments. So, in that regard we're like the people who said they would come to the feast but in their busyness were nowhere to be found. That's who we are in our fallen condition.

Second, these were people who put second things first. Jesus had said, "But seek first the kingdom of God and his righteousness, and all these things will be added to you" (Matt. 6:33). But their eyes were fixed on the things of this world.

There's nothing wrong with buying a field. There's nothing wrong with buying oxen. There's nothing wrong with getting married. Typically, our whole concentration is fixed on this world. We rarely think of heaven or of eternal matters. It used to be said of Christians that they were so heavenly minded they were no earthly good. Now the problem is the opposite. We're so earthly minded we're no heavenly good. We need to lift our gaze to heaven and think of the things that God has stored up for us for eternity. Every bone in our bodies, every fiber of our being screams that the significance of human life far transcends the daily activities in which we're engaged, but for the most part we're mindless, thoughtless about eternal matters. So, buying a field, testing oxen, or working out a marriage becomes far more important to us than our eternal destinies.

Finally, people who have made a profession of faith don't possess the profession they've made. No one has ever entered heaven by a profession of faith. If you have faith, you're supposed to profess it, but professing it doesn't mean you have it. Every one of these people professed that they were coming to the banquet, but no one came. They said, "I'll come," and then they said, "I cannot come." That has to do with our ultimate state of things.

Maybe you heard an evangelist preach a sermon, and you walked down the aisle and made a commitment of faith. Perhaps you prayed the sinner's prayer or something of that sort, and the next day you forgot it. The people who make that commitment but don't keep it, people whose eyes are fixed on this world and not on heaven, people who profess faith in Him but don't possess the faith they profess, are the ones of whom Jesus said, **"None of those men who were invited shall taste my banquet"** (v. 24).

73

THE COST OF DISCIPLESHIP

Luke 14:25–35

Now great crowds accompanied him, and he turned and said to them, "If anyone comes to me and does not hate his own father and mother and wife and children and brothers and sisters, yes, and even his own life, he cannot be my disciple. Whoever does not bear his own cross and come after me cannot be my disciple. For which of you, desiring to build a tower, does not first sit down and count the cost, whether he has enough to complete it? Otherwise, when he has laid a foundation and is not able to finish, all who see it begin to mock him, saying, 'This man began to build and was not able to finish.' Or what king, going out to encounter another king in war, will not sit down first and deliberate whether he is able with ten thousand to meet him who comes against him with twenty thousand? And if not, while the other is yet a great way off, he sends a delegation and asks for terms of peace. So therefore, any one of you who does not renounce all that he has cannot be my disciple.

"Salt is good, but if salt has lost its taste, how shall its saltiness be restored? It is of no use either for the soil or for the manure pile. It is thrown away. He who has ears to hear, let him hear."

If we have a desire for evangelism, a concern for our loved ones and friends who don't know Christ, sometimes we'll do everything that we can think of to win them to Jesus. We'll plead with them. We'll beg them. We'll cajole them. We'll give them all kinds of marvelous promises of how their lives will be wonderfully changed if they will come to Jesus.

It's a good thing that we desire to see others come to Jesus, but we often forget that when Jesus called people to come to Him, He often went about it in a different way than we do. We want to make the path to Christ as easy as we possibly can. Jesus would caution them. That's what He did in this text.

Now great crowds accompanied him, and he turned and said to them, "If anyone comes to me and does not hate his own father and mother and wife and children and brothers and sisters, yes, and even his own life, he cannot be my disciple" (vv. 25–26). He posted a warning to all who would come to Him, laying out the price of being His disciple. Are you willing to hate your mother, your father, your brother, your sister, your wife, your children? Are you ready to hate yourself? Because if you're not, Jesus said you can't be His disciple.

Have you ever heard an evangelist or preacher include that in his evangelistic message? We're stunned by these words. Jesus told us to love our neighbor, to love our mothers and fathers and our children, but here He said we have to hate our mothers and our fathers and our children and our wives. He couldn't possibly mean this. We stumble over the word **"hate"** here and tend to interpret it the way we use it customarily in our own culture. But if we look carefully at how the Bible uses that term, we see that it frequently—but not always—means to love less.

Genesis 29 tells us the story of Jacob and his marriages to Leah and Rachel. Jacob worked seven years for Rachel, but then he was tricked by her father, Laban, into marrying Leah. He then had to work another seven years for Rachel. The passage tells us that Jacob "loved Rachel more than Leah" (v. 30). In the next verse, it says, "Leah was hated" by Jacob (v. 31). In using the terms interchangeably, Scripture indicates that because Jacob loved Leah less than he loved Rachel, the love that he had for Leah seemed like hate.

Our Lord is not saying that we are to despise or abhor our parents or our children or our spouses, but the devotion we give to Jesus must be even greater than that which we give to the dearest ones of our family and friends. This sometimes leads to conflict with the ones we love the most. So Christ tells us the cost: "What I demand from My disciples is that their first devotion, their first love, must be to Me. You must love Me more than your family. You must love Me more than you love yourself; otherwise you can't be My disciple. Unless you're willing to bear your cross as I must bear Mine, you can't be My disciple."

Counting the Cost

"For which of you, desiring to build a tower, does not first sit down and count the cost, whether he has enough to complete it? Otherwise, when he has laid a foundation and is not able to finish, all who see it begin to mock him, saying, 'This man began to build and was not able to finish'" (vv. 28–30). Jesus illustrated the need to count the cost of being His disciple with a pair of examples. The first has to do with building. If you build a house or an outbuilding, or if you build a tower or a silo, before you build it, you ask how much it is going to cost. Do you have the money to complete the job? If you start building without having what you need to complete the job, you will show yourself to be foolish.

"Or what king, going out to encounter another king in war, will not sit down first and deliberate whether he is able with ten thousand to meet him who comes against him with twenty thousand? And if not, while the other is yet a great way off, he sends a delegation and asks for terms of peace" (vv. 31–32). The second example Jesus used has to do with warfare. Military commanders must be sure they have the troops and equipment necessary to defeat their enemy, or else they will come to ruin.

"So therefore, any one of you who does not renounce all that he has cannot be my disciple" (v. 33). There is something paradoxical about being a Christian. On the one hand, is there anything sweeter or more blessed? Is there anything that can possibly produce more joy than being a Christian and being in Christ, knowing that all the sins you've ever committed have been forgiven, knowing that He has gone into His Father's house to prepare a place for you to live forever?

What a wonderful thing it is to enjoy the Christian life. Sometimes I wonder how people who aren't Christians are able to cope with human existence. The Bible says that without Christ we are without hope (Eph. 2:12). We are hopeless, and we are living in a state of hopelessness. People may protest and say: "I'm having a great time and having all kinds of fun. I'm living the dream." They may be having all kinds of fun, but it is a futile fun and they know it.

On the other hand, living the Christian life means you've given your life away. Life in Christ in this world is a throwaway life because you're not your own anymore. You're no longer autonomous. Now you're under the lordship and the command of the Prince of Glory. You're baptized; you're given the sign not only of all the promises of salvation that come with the sign but also of your death and resurrection in Christ.

In baptism, we participate in the death and the burial of Jesus. As the Apostle Paul tells us again and again in the New Testament, if we're not willing to identify with and participate in the humiliation of Christ, we'll never participate in His exaltation (Rom. 6:4; Col. 2:12). To the Colossians, Paul wrote this: "Now I rejoice in my sufferings for your sake, and in my flesh I am filling up what is lacking in Christ's afflictions for the sake of his body, that is, the church" (Col. 1:24).

Sometimes Paul the Apostle is hard to understand, and this is one of those places. What did he mean that he was "filling up what is lacking in Christ's afflictions"? Was there some deficiency in the sufferings of Jesus that had to be fulfilled by the Apostle Paul? Did the Father say to the Son, "You did a good job as far as it went, but I have to wait for the Apostle Paul to finish the job"? No, Paul was not saying that there was any lack of merit or efficacy in the sufferings of the Lord Jesus on our behalf. Rather, Paul was saying the suffering of Christ in His body did not end with His death but continues in the sufferings of His body, the church.

The testimony of history shows how the afflictions of those who identify with Jesus continue to add to the total summation of the sufferings of His body even to this very day. You know that around the world there are many hot spots of persecution. Christians are being executed daily by hostile forces. Even in America, where we enjoy many freedoms, there is a growing hostility toward all who take the name of Christ. It's possible, and even likely, that in the near future Christians in America will be tempted to say about Christ, "I do not know Him" (see Luke 22:57).

This isn't a scare theology. This is the truth. Jesus said, "If the world hates you, know that it has hated me before it hated you" (John 15:18). So count the cost; it's a heavy price. But when you count the cost of anything, along with it you have to count the value of that which you're getting in return. In return for the cost of your life is the "pearl of great value" (Matt. 13:46). It is priceless to own Him and to have Him own you. It is worth everything, for as He said: "For what will it profit a man if he gains the whole world and forfeits his soul? Or what shall a man give in return for his soul?" (Matt. 16:26). What do you profit if you gain the whole world and lose your own soul?

"Salt is good, but if salt has lost its taste, how shall its saltiness be restored? It is of no use either for the soil or for the manure pile. It is thrown away. He who has ears to hear, let him hear" (vv. 34–35). To be a disciple of Christ is to be salt for Him—not salt that's lost its saltiness. Jesus wants disciples who have counted the cost and who keep their salt no matter what.

74

THE LOST FOUND

Luke 15:1–10

Now the tax collectors and sinners were all drawing near to hear him. And the Pharisees and the scribes grumbled, saying, "This man receives sinners and eats with them."

So he told them this parable: "What man of you, having a hundred sheep, if he has lost one of them, does not leave the ninety-nine in the open country, and go after the one that is lost, until he finds it? And when he has found it, he lays it on his shoulders, rejoicing. And when he comes home, he calls together his friends and his neighbors, saying to them, 'Rejoice with me, for I have found my sheep that was lost.' Just so, I tell you, there will be more joy in heaven over one sinner who repents than over ninety-nine righteous persons who need no repentance.

"Or what woman, having ten silver coins, if she loses one coin, does not light a lamp and sweep the house and seek diligently until she finds it? And when she has found it, she calls together her friends and neighbors, saying, 'Rejoice with me, for I have found the coin that I had lost.' Just so, I tell you, there is joy before the angels of God over one sinner who repents."

Now the tax collectors and sinners were all drawing near to hear him. And the Pharisees and the scribes grumbled, saying, "This man receives sinners and eats with them" (vv. 1–2). Isn't it interesting how Jesus drew sinners to Himself? Yet sinners tend to flee from us. I wonder what they saw in Him that they don't see in us. Sometimes we think that God has appointed us not to be vessels of grace but to be the policemen of the world. But Jesus somehow was approachable by the sinner. They flocked to Him to hear Him.

Some people were a little bit angry about that. The Pharisees and the scribes murmured against Him. Jesus recognized that broken sinners came to Him and were eager to hear His teaching, but the elite of the culture, the so-called righteous Pharisees, were angry that Jesus would stoop to associate Himself with such people. To instruct the scribes and Pharisees, Jesus gave a series of parables.

So he told them this parable: "What man of you, having a hundred sheep, if he has lost one of them, does not leave the ninety-nine in the open country, and go after the one that is lost, until he finds it?" (vv. 3–4). The man doesn't say, "That's a 1 percent loss. I'll write it off on my taxes." Instead, he goes and searches for the sheep. **"And when he has found it, he lays it on his shoulders, rejoicing"** (v. 5). This was a strong indictment against the Pharisees, because Jesus was telling them that they didn't care about the sheep, who are His Father's people. Jesus said elsewhere, "For the Son of Man came to seek and to save the lost" (19:10). Notice that Jesus didn't say, "I came to call people to repentance," and hang up a sign that says, "All of you who want to repent and be saved, sign in please." He is seeking them. He goes out to find them. He goes out of His way to find the ones who are lost.

The image of Jesus as the Good Shepherd who finds and brings back His sheep reminds me of a crisis time in my life. When I was a boy, my father became sick unto death and suffered four strokes starting when I was thirteen, and he died when I was seventeen. After the third stroke, he was paralyzed and confined to his chair. The only two times he got out of his chair were to go to his bed, into which I lifted him, or to go to our table for dinner. He could be propped up in a chair and eat dinner there; his legs were paralyzed.

He was too heavy for me to carry him. I was just a sixteen- or seventeen-year-old boy. The way we did it was that I would go to where he sat on his chair and bend down with my back against him. My father hung his arms, fireman style, around my neck, and I held on to his arms and stood up with him on my back. Then I dragged him to the table. It was a difficult thing, but there was something that happened humanly that's indescribable. He was utterly helpless, and he had to depend on his son to get him to the place where he got his daily bread. That is a humiliating thing for a man to have to do. Through the arms, through the hands, through the physical contact, without any words spoken—imagine the emotion that passed through us.

In a similar way, Jesus goes and finds us helpless sheep and carries us when we cannot go ourselves. There is tenderness involved in the way the Shepherd brings that lost sheep back. He doesn't go with a chain or collar and put it around the sheep's neck and drag it bleating and kicking back home. He puts the sheep around His neck and carries it home. The thing about lost sheep is that they don't know they're lost. The worst part of being lost is to be lost and not know that you're lost.

"And when he comes home, he calls together his friends and his neighbors, saying to them, 'Rejoice with me, for I have found my sheep that was lost.' Just so, I tell you, there will be more joy in heaven over one sinner who repents than over ninety-nine righteous persons who need no repentance" (vv. 6–7). The man's joy is so intense that he calls together his friends and his neighbors to celebrate. This points to a greater truth: that nothing causes more joy in heaven than repentance of one sinner. Each time I see a person come to Christ, I think: "They're setting the tables above. There's a party tonight in heaven. The angels are coming together and they're rejoicing."

"Or what woman, having ten silver coins, if she loses one coin, does not light a lamp and sweep the house and seek diligently until she finds it? And when she has found it, she calls together her friends and neighbors, saying, 'Rejoice with me, for I have found the coin that I had lost.' Just so, I tell you, there is joy before the angels of God over one sinner who repents" (vv. 8–10). These parables emphasize the delight that God has in human repentance.

75

THE LOST SON

Luke 15:11–32

And he said, "There was a man who had two sons. And the younger of them said to his father, 'Father, give me the share of property that is coming to me.' And he divided his property between them. Not many days later, the younger son gathered all he had and took a journey into a far country, and there he squandered his property in reckless living. And when he had spent everything, a severe famine arose in that country, and he began to be in need. So he went and hired himself out to one of the citizens of that country, who sent him into his fields to feed pigs. And he was longing to be fed with the pods that the pigs ate, and no one gave him anything.

"But when he came to himself, he said, 'How many of my father's hired servants have more than enough bread, but I perish here with hunger! I will arise and go to my father, and I will say to him, "Father, I have sinned against heaven and before you. I am no longer worthy to be called your son. Treat me as one of your hired servants." ' And he arose and came to his father. But while he was still a long way off, his father saw him and felt compassion, and ran and embraced him and kissed him. And the son said to him, 'Father, I have sinned against heaven and before you. I am no longer worthy to be called your son.' But the father said to his servants, 'Bring quickly the best robe, and put it on him, and put a ring on his hand, and shoes on his feet. And bring the fattened calf and kill it, and let us eat and celebrate. For this my son was dead, and is alive again; he was lost, and is found.' And they began to celebrate.

"Now his older son was in the field, and as he came and drew near to the house, he heard music and dancing. And he called one of the servants and asked what these things meant. And he said to him, 'Your brother has come, and your father has killed the fattened calf, because he has received him back safe and sound.' But he was angry and refused to go in. His father came out and entreated him, but he answered his father, 'Look, these many years I have served you, and I never disobeyed your command, yet you never gave me a young goat, that I might celebrate with my friends. But when this son of yours came, who has devoured your property with prostitutes, you killed the fattened calf for him!' And he said to him, 'Son, you are always with me, and all that is mine is yours. It was fitting to celebrate and be glad, for this your brother was dead, and is alive; he was lost, and is found.' "

The context of this parable once again is a confrontation that Jesus had with the Pharisees and the scribes. At the beginning of chapter 15, we read that all the tax collectors and sinners drew near to Jesus in order to hear Him, but the Pharisees and the scribes complained about this. They said, "This man receives sinners and eats with them" (v. 2). That's the reason Jesus gave these three parables. He had heard the criticism that He had associated with tax collectors and with sinners, and not only was He associating with them, but He was actually sharing meals with them.

The Pharisees and the scribes were aghast because this violated every principle they held precious. They practiced the kind of spiritual apartheid in which they actually believed that salvation comes through segregation, by keeping oneself at a distance from anyone who is tainted with evil of any kind, and they saw Jesus spending time with the sinners and with the tax collectors. Jesus was with the tax collectors and sinners not because He wanted to be like them but because He was driven by compassion.

Jesus said on another occasion, "Those who are well have no need of a physician, but those who are sick. I have not come to call the righteous but sinners to repentance" (5:31–32). That's where He spent his time. In responding to this vigorous criticism from the scribes and the Pharisees, He told two brief parables before the larger one that we've just read. Jesus then came to the larger story.

And he said, "There was a man who had two sons. And the younger of them said to his father, 'Father, give me the share of property that is coming to me.' And he divided his property between them" (vv. 11–12). In the ancient world, just as happens today, inheritances were passed down to children and grandchildren after the death of the owner of the estate. On rare occasions, a wealthy owner could give a trust fund to his children or give them certain gifts in advance of his death. But it was exceedingly rare. That would mean liquidating his assets in order to distribute them among his heirs. It would usually in such cases involve a potential long-term loss of the real value of the estate.

That didn't bother this son. He said: "Father, I want my inheritance, and I want it now. I don't want to have to wait until you die." This was a case of a young man who did not believe in delayed gratification. He wanted it now so he could spend it now.

We don't want to identify ourselves with this young man who didn't want to defer or delay gratification, but we are like him when we spend money that we don't have, when we live beyond our means, and when we steal from our creditors by delaying our payment to them.

Credit card debt is an epidemic in America. It's crippling to people, but credit card debt comes when we live beyond our means, when we become prodigal and profligate just like this man in the story. That's bad stewardship. It's not how God wants His people to live.

In this case, the young man says, **"Give me the share of property that is coming to me."** An incredible part of this story is that the father agreed to it. The father allowed his son to go with his inheritance.

"Not many days later, the younger son gathered all he had and took a journey into a far country, and there he squandered his property in reckless living" (v. 13). The first thing this young man did after receiving his early inheritance was to gather it together and leave home. He left the confines of his family and the restraints of his parents. He didn't just go to the next town where somebody might know him; he went to a far country where he was anonymous. He went into the darkness where no one could see him so he could do the things he had always wanted to do without restraints.

Every year I see the news accounts of spring break in Florida. The news shows the unbridled debauchery of college students far from school, far from home. Every time I see that I wonder if their parents are watching this on television. Do their parents know what they're financing on spring break? Do they have any idea what their children are doing when they go into a far country?

This young man went to a far country where nobody knew him so he could have the mother of all parties. He was like a sailor on shore leave with a pocket full of money. No restraints. Certainly, finances were not a restraint. There in this far country, **"he squandered his property in reckless living."**

"And when he had spent everything, a severe famine arose in that country, and he began to be in need. So he went and hired himself out to one of the citizens of that country, who sent him into his fields to feed pigs. And he was longing to be fed with the pods that the pigs ate, and no one gave him anything" (vv. 14–16). A *prodigal* is somebody who is involved in radical, lavish waste. He was wasting his money and his time, but far worse, he was wasting his life. He consumed his wealth in riotous living and in harlotry. He became penniless and had to live with the pigs.

We all have known loved ones who have wasted their lives in this kind of lifestyle. They often land in misery, in shame, and in jail, with their hearts still hardened. Is there anything more tragic than a wasted life? It's one thing to waste a paycheck, but to waste a life is the tragedy of all tragedies.

Jesus told this story because He cares about people like this young man. The Pharisees didn't care about a young man wasting his fortune and living with the pigs, but the Lord of glory cared. The point of this parable is the same as the point of the parables of the lost sheep and the lost coin. When those who are lost are found, it's a time for joy and celebration even in heaven.

The Divine Light Dawns

"But when he came to himself . . ." (v. 17). This is the turning point in the life of the Prodigal Son. Each of these three parables has a crisis point. Obviously, the turning point of the parable of the lost sheep is when the shepherd, after seeking diligently, finds the lamb and tenderly picks it up, puts it on his shoulders, and brings it home. The turning point in the parable of the lost coin is when this poor woman, after sweeping her house and looking in every nook and cranny, finally saw that tiny glint of silver and found the coin that meant so much to her.

The crisis moment of this parable is when the Prodigal Son **"came to himself."** It's a strange way of describing his condition. People who get involved in a downward spiral, such as is described in the life of the Prodigal Son, will often go to great lengths of personal disintegration and destruction. They have to hit bottom before there is hope of repentance and transformation of their character. Many people don't hit bottom until they reach the bottom of the grave in which they are buried.

There are those remarkable moments we've seen in people's lives who are on an arc of total destruction who reach bottom and then are redeemed. It's at this moment in the story that the Prodigal Son hit bottom, and when he did, he came to himself. How did he do this? I'm going to suggest that he came to himself not by himself, because any person who reaches this level of degradation—someone who is dead in sin, who is torpid, who is in so deep a slumber that no alarm clock could possibly awaken him—cannot turn around and come to himself by himself.

When somebody is in a coma or is unconscious and he awakens, we say that he "came to." That's the case with this young man. He was in a spiritual coma and he came to. He was resuscitated and roused to wakefulness not by himself but in the only way anyone ever comes to. He was awakened by God, by the power of God the Holy Spirit.

In Matthew 16, Jesus gathered His disciples and said, "Who do people say that the Son of Man is?" They said, "Some say John the Baptist, others say Elijah, and others Jeremiah or one of the prophets." Jesus said, "But who do you say that I am?" This is a question that every one of us has to answer. Peter replied, "You are the Christ, the Son of the living God." When Peter uttered those words to Jesus, Jesus immediately responded with a benediction. He said to His impetuous disciple: "Blessed are you, Simon Bar-Jonah! For flesh and blood has not revealed this to you, but my Father who is in heaven" (vv. 13–17).

Jesus said Peter was blessed because he had been awakened to an understanding of who Jesus is. He confessed the truth not by flesh and blood, not by his education, but by means of a revelation that came directly and immediately to him from God the Father.

Jonathan Edwards' sermon "A Divine and Supernatural Light" catapulted him to fame throughout New England. It contains his exposition of Peter's confession, stressing that the light that came to Peter was not human; it was divine. It was not natural but supernatural. It was a light that only God can give to awaken a soul that is dead. A divine and supernatural light is that which happens when a soul is born of the Spirit and regenerated by God. There's nothing you can do to cause yourself to be regenerated by the Holy Spirit. This is a sovereign act of divine grace that is wrought not by means but by the immediate power of God the Holy Spirit in everyone who believes.

Edwards said: "It is a divine and superlative revelation of the excellency of God and of Jesus Christ. A glory that is greatly distinguished from everything that is earthly and temporal. There is a vast difference between having an opinion that God is holy and gracious and having a sense of the loveliness and the beauty of that holiness and grace." How you view Jesus, if you view Him in a saving way, is not a mere mortal opinion. If you have an understanding not only intellectually but where the heart and the soul are enflamed to see the beauty and the excellency and the glory of that divine grace, it is a gift of God.

If you don't understand what Edwards is saying here, you're still dead. You're still in the pig pen; you haven't been awakened. You haven't been really converted until the soul not only understands who Jesus is but also sees the beauty and the glory and has a sheer delight in the soul that is in love with the Savior.

Through this divine and supernatural light, the young man came to himself and said: **"How many of my father's hired servants have more than enough**

bread, but I perish here with hunger! I will arise and go to my father, and I will say to him, 'Father, I have sinned against heaven and before you. I am no longer worthy to be called your son. Treat me as one of your hired servants'" (vv. 17–19). He had sinned against his father and his brother, but chiefly his sin, as all sin, is against God.

David in the midst of his repentance from the profound sins of adultery and murder spoke out in anguish, saying, "Against you, you only, have I sinned and done what is evil in your sight" (Ps. 51:4). Hyperbole? No, ultimately the One against whom he sinned was God Himself. God will not awaken a person to grace and to salvation without at the same time convicting him of sin.

Martyn Lloyd-Jones said that his mission as a minister was to preach both the law and the gospel because his great longing was to see people awakened and converted to Christ, but he understood that no one is ever converted without first being convicted by God of his sin.

You really don't understand the gospel as good news until you understand it is the good news of God forgiving you for your sin. You don't need a divine and supernatural light to be aware of your sin. We still have consciences even in our fallen condition. As corrupt as we are and as much as we put callouses on our consciences and sear the conscience and try to do away with conscience altogether, the natural conscience of fallen man is still intact enough to let us know that we are sinners. You can know that you're a sinner without being born again, but you can't be born again without knowing that you're a sinner.

It's not a mere opinion but something that grasps the soul. We see it in this young man when he came to himself and said: **"I will arise and go to my father, and I will say to him, 'Father, I have sinned against heaven and before you. I am no longer worthy to be called your son. Treat me as one of your hired servants'"** (vv. 18–19). That's what repentance is. It is turning back to the one you have offended. **"And he arose and came to his father"** (v. 20).

Remember, he had gone to a far country, and you may wonder how the young man was going to get back home. He was out of resources. He didn't have a penny to his name; he couldn't buy a donkey or a camel to ride. The only way he could go was to walk. The longer he walked, the more tired he became and the more tattered and soiled his clothes became. He came looking like a beggar.

A Father's Love

"But while he was still a long way off, his father saw him and felt compassion, and ran and embraced him and kissed him" (v. 20). His father saw him from a distance. Jesus didn't explain in this story how the father could have recognized the young man from so far away. I think it must have been the way he walked, the way he moved. There was no mistaken identity here. The father knew immediately. He lifted up his robe and girded it about his waist, and the father with wobbly knees and old legs took off running. He ran and ran, and when he got there, like the shepherd who found his lost sheep and the woman who found the coin that she had lost, he rejoiced.

This son who had disgraced the father coming home in filthy rags was greeted by his father, who fell upon his neck and kissed him. That's what God does for every sinner who repents. He runs to you and He hugs you and He kisses you in your filth. That's the way God works.

"And the son said to him, 'Father, I have sinned against heaven and before you. I am no longer worthy to be called your son'" (v. 21). The father said something like, "I know all that, son, but I don't care," and he gave a command to the servants: **"But the father said to his servants, 'Bring quickly the best robe, and put it on him, and put a ring on his hand, and shoes on his feet. And bring the fattened calf and kill it, and let us eat and celebrate. For this my son was dead, and is alive again; he was lost, and is found.' And they began to celebrate"** (vv. 22–24).

The Older Brother

"Now his older son was in the field, and as he came and drew near to the house, he heard music and dancing. And he called one of the servants and asked what these things meant. And he said to him, 'Your brother has come, and your father has killed the fattened calf, because he has received him back safe and sound.' But he was angry and refused to go in. His father came out and entreated him, but he answered his father, 'Look, these many years I have served you, and I never disobeyed your command, yet you never gave me a young goat, that I might celebrate with my friends. But when this son of yours came, who has devoured your property with prostitutes, you killed the fattened calf for him!'" (vv. 25–30). The other brother, the other son who didn't claim his inheritance early, who didn't go to a far country, who didn't waste his life in riotous living with harlots, was out working as he did every day and heard the sound of music and merriment, and he asked one of the servants what was going on. Upon hearing what his father had done to celebrate his brother's homecoming, the older brother refused to come in. "Not me," he said. "I'll have nothing to do with it." Obviously, he represents the attitude that Jesus was correcting in the Pharisees. The father entreated the older brother, but the older brother complained, "Your son is unworthy. You never killed even a goat for me."

"And he said to him, 'Son, you are always with me, and all that is mine is yours. It was fitting to celebrate and be glad, for this your brother was dead, and is alive; he was lost, and is found'" (vv. 31–32). The angels in heaven rejoiced.

76

THE PARABLE OF THE UNJUST STEWARD

Luke 16:1–13

He also said to the disciples, "There was a rich man who had a manager, and charges were brought to him that this man was wasting his possessions. And he called him and said to him, 'What is this that I hear about you? Turn in the account of your management, for you can no longer be manager.' And the manager said to himself, 'What shall I do, since my master is taking the management away from me? I am not strong enough to dig, and I am ashamed to beg. I have decided what to do, so that when I am removed from management, people may receive me into their houses.' So, summoning his master's debtors one by one, he said to the first, 'How much do you owe my master?' He said, 'A hundred measures of oil.' He said to him, 'Take your bill, and sit down quickly and write fifty.' Then he said to another, 'And how much do you owe?' He said, 'A hundred measures of wheat.' He said to him, 'Take your bill, and write eighty.' The master commended the dishonest manager for his shrewdness. For the sons of this world are more shrewd in dealing with their own generation than the sons of light. And I tell you, make friends for yourselves by means of unrighteous wealth, so that when it fails they may receive you into the eternal dwellings.

"One who is faithful in a very little is also faithful in much, and one who is dishonest in a very little is also dishonest in much. If then you have not been faithful in the unrighteous wealth, who will entrust to you the true riches? And if you have not been faithful in that which is another's, who will give you that which is your own? No servant can serve two masters, for either he will hate the one and love the other, or he will be devoted to the one and despise the other. You cannot serve God and money."

In Luke's Gospel, the parable of the unjust steward follows the parable of the prodigal son. Having considered how the Prodigal Son wasted his father's inheritance and wasted his life, Jesus turned His attention to a different kind of waste, a waste that involved stewardship.

He also said to the disciples, "There was a rich man who had a manager, and charges were brought to him that this man was wasting his possessions" (v. 1). In the ancient world, those who were people of means had servants of different kinds. The chief of them was the one who was hired as the steward of the house. The steward, or manager, was given the responsibility of managing all the goods of the household and all the property of the master who hired him. The steward didn't own those goods or that property. He was simply responsible to manage them.

"And he called him and said to him, 'What is this that I hear about you? Turn in the account of your management, for you can no longer be manager'" (v. 2). This man was a dishonest and unjust steward who was lining his own pockets and in other ways wasting the property of his master. The day of accounting came, and the master discovered what the unjust steward had done. When the man was called to account by his master, he was fired.

The Manager's Plans

"And the manager said to himself, 'What shall I do, since my master is taking the management away from me? I am not strong enough to dig, and I am ashamed to beg. I have decided what to do, so that when I am removed from management, people may receive me into their houses'" (v. 3). Luke doesn't tell us that Jesus said anything of what the steward responded to the master, only what he said to himself. He ruled out digging or begging, but then he came up with a plan. The unscrupulous steward formulated a way to resolve his problem and to ensure the safety of his future.

"'I have decided what to do, so that when I am removed from management, people may receive me into their houses.' So, summoning his master's debtors one by one, he said to the first, 'How much do you owe my master?' He said, 'A hundred measures of oil.' He said to him, 'Take your bill, and sit down quickly and write fifty.' Then he said to another, 'And how much do you owe?' He said, 'A hundred measures of wheat.' He said to him, 'Take your bill, and write eighty'" (vv. 4–7). He called each of his master's debtors. Presumably the master had many people who were in debt to him, and the handling of those debts was the responsibility of the manager. Jesus didn't say what the man said to each one of the debtors. He gave only two as examples for how the steward handled his problem where he reduced what the debtors owed his master.

One of the strong prohibitions of the law of Israel was the law against usurious interest rates—interest rates that weighed down debtors and reduced them to rags. Such activity was condemned by God. Rather than charging usury with respect to interest, it was commonplace among the producers to add interest into the cost of the goods. The typical practice for the olive oil industry was to add 100 percent to the actual cost of the product because of the risk of spoilage with olives and olive oil. The wheat crops were more stable, so the standard rate was a 20 percent increase.

The manager knew all that, so he went to the debtors. He said to the olive debtor: "Reduce your debt by 50 percent. Cut it in half." How do you think that debtor liked that? He said to the man who owed one hundred measures of wheat: "Knock it down to eighty. Take that extra 20 percent out." The steward was looking out for his future. He made sure that he would continue to have a business by making friends with the people who were in debt to the master.

At this point in the parable, Jesus focused His attention on the importance of stewardship and looking out for the future. A good steward never lived beyond his means. He lived on less than he made because he didn't know what would happen tomorrow. He was a wise investor, a careful manager of his master's property. This steward looked out for his own future by making deals with the debtors.

The Manager's Shrewdness

"The master commended the dishonest manager for his shrewdness" (v. 8). Here comes the shocking part. His master found out about the manager's plan, and he knew that the steward had the authority to adjust the amount debtors owed. The owner wasn't going to go to those debtors and say: "I fired my manager, and that new deal he gave to you is null and void. I'm going to hold you responsible for the full amount that we originally agreed on." The master couldn't do that because the steward had the imprimatur of the master.

"For the sons of this world are more shrewd in dealing with their own generation than the sons of light" (v. 8). Jesus said the master commended the unjust steward not because he was honest but because he was clever, because he was shrewd. He said the sons of this world—the unbelievers, the ungodly, the unrighteous, like the unjust steward—are more shrewd in their generation than the sons of light.

The devil has more ingenious strategies to win the battle than we do because we don't tend to think about the future. We don't come up with strategies to defeat the gates of hell. So Jesus said, in effect, "You people should be more like this crooked steward, not by being crooked, but by being strategic in what you do."

Stewarding Our Resources

"And I tell you, make friends for yourselves by means of unrighteous wealth, so that when it fails they may receive you into the eternal dwellings" (v. 9). First of all, when He spoke of unrighteous wealth, Jesus was not talking about ill-gotten goods received through thievery or bribery or cheating. Rather, He was simply using the term that was common for what we would call worldly goods. Jesus was talking to His disciples, those who wanted to follow Him, about how they were to be stewards of their worldly goods. Then He looked beyond that strategy of this world and talked about heaven.

I've heard many ministers say they never preach on tithing. The reason they give is a shrewd one. They say: "If people are Christians, born of the Spirit, and they belong to the kingdom of God, they don't need to be told over and over to give 10 percent of their annual income to the kingdom of God—not necessarily just to the local church but to the work of Christ and of His kingdom. These people know it and they do it gladly. The people who don't tithe aren't going to tithe no matter how often you preach about it and explain their obligation to God."

What concerns me is the people who don't tithe. I don't understand it. How is it possible for a person to be a Christian and steal from God? I know it's possible for people to tithe and even more than tithe and not be Christians. They're people who make a false profession of faith, come to church every Sunday, and tithe but their hearts are still far from God. They might even give their bodies to be burned and still not have saving faith. I understand it, because Jesus made it clear that tithing is not a weighty matter. He commended the Pharisees for tithing their mint and their cumin. He said, "You tithe mint and dill and cumin, and have neglected the weightier matters of the law: justice and mercy and faithfulness. These you ought to have done, without neglecting the others" (Matt. 23:23). What does that mean? It means tithing is not a weighty matter of the law. It's a lesser matter.

Tithing is something that Christians do virtually automatically, so if you do tithe that's no guarantee that you're saved. I think it's possible to be a true Christian and not tithe. I don't know how it's possible, but I think it is. Because we are all sinners, we're all subject to these ties of the flesh, and for many the hardest thing in the world is to let go of any of our money. But how can a person be forgiven of every sin they've ever committed and be promised eternal life, absolute joy, and felicity by our Savior and then steal from Him?

Doesn't the Bible say that everything I have and everything you have comes from God, who in fact owns it? He doesn't own 10 percent of what you have and what I have. He owns 100 percent of what we have. He just asks for 10 percent of it back. We're stewards, not owners, and then we hold it back. We're unjust, unrighteous stewards.

I wish everybody in church knew of the opportunities to work for the kingdom of God that are prevented because of the lack of funds. Before the Berlin Wall came down and before the Soviet empire disintegrated, I lectured for a week in Vienna, Austria, to between fifty and seventy-five pastors, all of whom were from behind the Iron Curtain and had to get special passes for this event. I spent eight to ten hours a day teaching these pastors. One of the things I found out was that the average pastor in that group owned five books. Do you know how much their ministry could have increased just by providing books and other educational helps and tools for them?

That's what Jesus was saying when He said, **"Make friends."** Think about your future, not just your future here but your future where your stewardship will be brought into account and the Lord will discover whether you've been a good steward of the things He's given you or if you've wasted them. Can you imagine standing before Jesus on the day of judgment and hearing Him say to you: "I know you. I gave you everything you had, and as far as My kingdom was concerned, you wasted it."

"One who is faithful in a very little is also faithful in much, and one who is dishonest in a very little is also dishonest in much. If then you have not been faithful in the unrighteous wealth, who will entrust to you the true riches? And if you have not been faithful in that which is another's, who will give you that which is your own? No servant can serve two masters, for either he will hate the one and love the other, or he will be devoted to the one and despise the other. You cannot serve God and money" (vv. 10–13). Jesus doesn't say you shouldn't serve two masters; He says you can't. It's impossible. You can't serve God and your money. You have to ask yourself whom you're going to serve, whose steward you are. He's speaking categorically, universally, to all of us about what it means to be stewards of the kingdom of God. He who has ears to hear the words of Christ, let him hear.

77

PRESSING INTO THE KINGDOM

Luke 16:14–18

The Pharisees, who were lovers of money, heard all these things, and they ridiculed him. And he said to them, "You are those who justify yourselves before men, but God knows your hearts. For what is exalted among men is an abomination in the sight of God.

"The Law and the Prophets were until John; since then the good news of the kingdom of God is preached, and everyone forces his way into it. But it is easier for heaven and earth to pass away than for one dot of the Law to become void.

"Everyone who divorces his wife and marries another commits adultery, and he who marries a woman divorced from her husband commits adultery."

The Pharisees, who were lovers of money, heard all these things, and they ridiculed him (v. 14). After the somewhat lengthy parable of the unjust steward, which was given specifically for the benefit of the disciples, we see that those who were standing outside the group of disciples, listening in to that parable, were the Pharisees.

The Pharisees **were lovers of money**. One of the most misquoted verses in all of sacred Scripture is "Money is the root of all evil." But that's not what the Bible says. It says, "The love of money is a root of all kinds of evils" (1 Tim. 6:10). If the love of money is a root, that root had sprung up in full measure to a forest of trees in the hearts and souls of the Pharisees, and being lovers of money, they were seriously offended by Jesus' teaching on stewardship. Their response to the message that our Lord gave in the parable of the unjust steward was not to flee to Him in repentance but rather to stand back and deride and sneer at Him.

Can you imagine sneering at Jesus? It would seem that behavior could sink no lower than to hold the Son of God in contempt. Yet this is the almost universal reaction of the world to Jesus. All those who are outside the kingdom of God, though they may make empty compliments of Jesus, calling Him a great teacher or a prophet, nevertheless indicate by their response to His Word that in the deepest chambers of their hearts they hold Him in contempt.

And he said to them, "You are those who justify yourselves before men, but God knows your hearts. For what is exalted among men is an abomination in the sight of God" (v. 15). We live in a topsy-turvy world where princes walk in rags and beggars ride on horses. We live in a culture that exalts people of unspeakable immorality. People are praised in our culture when they are an abomination to God. And yet, we're told daily that God loves everybody unconditionally. We don't have room in our thinking or in our theology for the idea that something may be an abomination in God's eyes. We might say that certain behavior patterns are an abomination to Him. God absolutely hates sin. People say that God loves the sinner but He hates the sin. The Bible nowhere says that or even hints at it.

In the Psalms and in the Prophets, it is clear that God abhors the evildoer and that the evildoer is an abomination in His sight. He doesn't send sin to hell at the judgment day. He sends people there because they're an abomination to Him. And there was probably never a more abominable group of people that walked the earth than the Pharisees, who prided themselves on their righteousness and their goodness. These were the people who thought that if they lived a good life, that was enough for them to be justified and to enter the kingdom of God.

How many people do you know who are relying on living a good life to get themselves into heaven? Who is practicing self-justification? Who is resting on his good deeds and his performance to pass the bar of God's justice? There is no more foolish endeavor, no greater fool's errand than to seek to enter the kingdom of God by your own good works. That's not only what the Pharisees did, but that's what they taught everyone else.

The Advent of the New Covenant

"The Law and the Prophets were until John" (v. 16). In speaking of the Law and the Prophets, Jesus did not say that they ended with Malachi, the last prophet, or with Chronicles, the last book of the Jewish Old Testament.

He was talking about the whole progress of the Old Testament, which He said goes right up to and includes John the Baptist. John the Baptist, though he is written about in the New Testament, belonged to the period of redemptive history that we call the Old Testament or the old covenant. The Law and the Prophets ruled up to and included John.

With the advent of John the Baptist's ministry, a crisis point in history took place because John was the forerunner of the Messiah. John proclaimed the crisis of human history when he said, "Repent, for the kingdom of heaven is at hand" (Matt. 3:2). Then he pointed to Jesus and said, "Behold, the Lamb of God, who takes away the sin of the world!" (John 1:29). Jesus began His public ministry, and His message was the same: "Repent, for the kingdom of heaven is at hand" (Matt. 4:17). The Pharisees heard that, and first they yawned, then they sneered, and then they murdered. The last thing they wanted was the kingdom of God.

Passion for the Kingdom

"Since then the good news of the kingdom of God is preached, and everyone forces his way into it" (v. 16). Matthew records Jesus as saying, "From the days of John the Baptist until now the kingdom of heaven has suffered violence, and the violent take it by force" (Matt. 11:12). They were battering down the doors—anything to get into the kingdom of God. And as they were saved, that striving, that pressing, that forcing didn't stop. It accelerated. Paul understood that when he said to his readers, "Work out your own salvation with fear and trembling" (Phil. 2:12). The kingdom of God has never been a casual affair. Jesus rebuked the church at Laodicea because it was lukewarm. He said: "Would that you were either cold or hot! So, because you are lukewarm, and neither hot nor cold, I will spit you out of my mouth" (Rev. 3:15–16).

There are people whom we call nominal Christians who are Christians in name only but have no passion for the things of God. They may understand theology, and they have their intellect tickled by discussions of doctrine, but their hearts are far from the kingdom. They're not pressing into the kingdom of God. The psalmist wrote: "How lovely is your dwelling place, O Lord of hosts! My soul longs, yes, faints for the courts of the Lord; my heart and flesh sing for joy to the living God" (Ps. 84:1–2). Does that sound like what you would say? When you think about coming to church on Sunday morning, do you think, "I can't wait to walk in there"? How lovely is the court of the Lord. My soul longs, it aches, it swoons, it faints to be in the sanctuary of God because my heart and my flesh cry out for the living God.

There are times in church history when the Spirit of God visited the people of God in extraordinary ways. During the sixteenth-century Protestant Reformation, zeal for the things of God swept across the land as the gospel was recovered. During the First Great Awakening in the eighteenth century, with the preaching of George Whitefield, Jonathan Edwards, and John Wesley, God visited His people and woke them up out of their dogmatic slumber, moving people to great passion for the things of God. But the greatest awakening in human history was in the Apostolic Age in the first century, when the King of the kingdom was present in the flesh, and they heard His voice and they listened to His words and they rushed into His kingdom, pressing and striving with all their might to be there.

The kingdom of God is a real place, and if you understand it, then like the psalmist you will long for it and your heart will faint. You will cry out for the living God. I believe that Christianity is rational; you can't get to the heart except through the mind. God wants us heart, mind, and soul. In fact, the more we understand the truth of the things of God, the more our souls are enflamed.

The Uses of the Law

"But it is easier for heaven and earth to pass away than for one dot of the Law to become void" (v. 17). We have all kinds of intellectual and theological debates about the nature and origin of Scripture. Is it just a book written in antiquity by some people who were religious? Or was it indeed superintended and inspired by God? Even people who agree that it was inspired argue over the extent of that inspiration. Some say the Bible as a whole is inspired—there's an organic inspiration about it and basic truths are contained in the Bible with a mixture of errors that come from the pens of human beings. We, however, say it's not just plenary inspiration, meaning the teachings of the Bible as a whole, but it is verbal inspiration, which means that each and every word of Scripture is inspired by God and carries His authority.

I'd like to suggest to you that Jesus didn't believe in plenary inspiration or even in verbal inspiration. Jesus' view of Scripture was jot and tittle inspiration. Not just every word, not just every letter, but every vowel point, every comma, every period was inspired by the Holy Spirit so that not one word of Scripture can possibly fail. I don't want to have a lower view of Scripture than Jesus or a higher view of Scripture than Jesus taught. I want to hold to the position that He taught.

A grievous error has infected the church today. It is called antinomianism, meaning that it is against the law of God. Antinomianism is at the core of the theology of dispensationalism, which is pervasive in evangelicalism. Dispensationalism declares that the laws of the Old Testament have no function in the life of New Testament Christians. The jots and tittles of the law are done with, according to dispensationalism. The law of God is a thing of the past for dispensationalists.

Many churches use the Ten Commandments and the exposition of them to remind people that the law of God is not gone. We speak of three basic uses of the law, the first being that of a mirror. The law of God reveals the character of God and thereby shows us ourselves. We look into that mirror of the law of God and judge ourselves not by the community standards of where we live and of our culture but by the law of God. The psalmist asked, "If you, O LORD, should mark iniquities, O Lord, who could stand?" (Ps. 130:3). We know that when we look in that mirror, we're not going to stand. The law of God reveals to us our utter hopelessness and helplessness of saving ourselves. It acts like a schoolmaster that drives us to Christ.

The second use of the law is as a curb. This is its civil use. Even when it does not change hearts, the law imposes penalties on lawbreakers and thereby acts as a restraint on wickedness in the world.

The third use is as a guide. For the Christian, the law has the extreme value and benefit of revealing to us what is pleasing to God and what isn't. This is crucial for us as Christians, for if we are pressing into the kingdom of God, we need to know what God loves and what He hates.

The Pharisees were supposed to be the experts in the law, yet they were legalists and antinomians at the same time. They were legalists in that they added to the law of God principles and traditions that were not the law of God. They kept people in chains where God had left them free. That's what legalism does. They were also legalists in thinking that they could save themselves through their own righteousness, through their own good works. That is another form of legalism. Finally, they were legalists in trying to find ways to get around the radical demands of God's law. In this, they actually became antinomian, against the law.

Marriage and Divorce

"Everyone who divorces his wife and marries another commits adultery, and he who marries a woman divorced from her husband commits adultery" (v. 18). Nowhere was the Pharisees' error regarding the law more clear than their teachings on marriage and divorce. In the Old Testament law regarding divorce, God said the only ground for divorce is sexual immorality (Deut. 24:1). As Jesus said when the Pharisees tried to trap him in Matthew's Gospel: "Because of your hardness of heart Moses allowed you to divorce your wives, but from the beginning it was not so. And I say to you: whoever divorces his wife, except for sexual immorality, and marries another, commits adultery" (Matt. 19:8–9). Paul later added that divorce is allowed in the case of desertion (1 Cor. 7:15). The Pharisees, however, said that if a wife burned her husband's dinner, that was grounds for divorce. If the husband decided his wife wasn't attractive anymore, that was grounds for divorce. So the Pharisees undermined the sacred institution of marriage.

Where did marriage come from? It came from God. In marriage ceremonies, we say that it was instituted by God and is regulated by God's commandments. We're not free to do whatever we want to do with marriage. Historically, the family unit has been the stabilizing force in every society. We have seen the effects of frivolous views of marriage, as the divorce rate has climbed toward 50 percent, in the breakdown of our society. Unfortunately, our society's solution to the disintegration of the home and of the family and of marriage is to grant no-fault divorce or to do away with marriage altogether. It's more than a trend; it's an epidemic, particularly with our young people who cohabitate without marriage. Too many churches today take the position of not being "judgmental," of not exercising church discipline. A church that will not exercise discipline for gross sin is not a church. Discipline is one of the necessary conditions for a true church.

Now the government defines marriage between a man and a man and a woman and a woman as legitimate and brings repercussions on anyone who refuses to honor them as such. It won't be long until there will be sanctions against preachers who refuse to perform such weddings, and that objection will come not only from the state but also from churches that have already embraced the legitimacy of homosexual marriage. Same-sex marriage is an abomination in the sight of God, and it presupposes that the law of God has failed and that we can live without it.

78

THE RICH MAN AND LAZARUS

Luke 16:19–31

"There was a rich man who was clothed in purple and fine linen and who feasted sumptuously every day. And at his gate was laid a poor man named Lazarus, covered with sores, who desired to be fed with what fell from the rich man's table. Moreover, even the dogs came and licked his sores. The poor man died and was carried by the angels to Abraham's side. The rich man also died and was buried, and in Hades, being in torment, he lifted up his eyes and saw Abraham far off and Lazarus at his side. And he called out, 'Father Abraham, have mercy on me, and send Lazarus to dip the end of his finger in water and cool my tongue, for I am in anguish in this flame.' But Abraham said, 'Child, remember that you in your lifetime received your good things, and Lazarus in like manner bad things; but now he is comforted here, and you are in anguish. And besides all this, between us and you a great chasm has been fixed, in order that those who would pass from here to you may not be able, and none may cross from there to us.' And he said, 'Then I beg you, father, to send him to my father's house—for I have five brothers—so that he may warn them, lest they also come into this place of torment.' But Abraham said, 'They have Moses and the Prophets; let them hear them.' And he said, 'No, father Abraham, but if someone goes to them from the dead, they will repent.' He said to him, 'If they do not hear Moses and the Prophets, neither will they be convinced if someone should rise from the dead.' "

Most people, both inside and outside the church, believe in the reality of heaven. Yet at the same time, most people, both inside and outside the church, deny the reality of hell. For those who claim the name of Christ, especially, this is a strange phenomenon, inasmuch as we have the same source for affirming both heaven and hell—the Lord Jesus Christ. And yet, when Jesus speaks of heaven, many Christians say, "Yes, Lord," but when He speaks of hell, they say, "No way, Lord."

In His earthly teachings as they are recorded for us in the New Testament, Jesus spoke more about hell than He did about heaven. Clearly, it was a matter of great importance and concern for Him. Also, we hear so much more about hell from Jesus than we do from the Old Testament prophets or from the New Testament Apostles.

We are reluctant to believe the truth about hell when we hear it from the prophets or the Apostles, and we believe it only scarcely more when we hear it from Jesus Himself. Yet there is no greater authority on these questions than Jesus of Nazareth. If Jesus was wrong about this, there is no intelligent reason to believe Him about anything. If you're a Christian, denying the reality of hell is simply not an option.

Why do we struggle so much with the idea of hell? There are many reasons, some of which are found in our care, concern, and compassion for our fellow human beings who may end up there. I can't get happy in this life thinking of anyone going into such a miserable place, but of course I'm not yet finished with my sanctification, and I still have a tendency to have more compassion for my fellow human sinners than I have for the glory of God.

There are two significant reasons for our hesitation regarding—and, at times, our revulsion to—the doctrine of hell. The first is that we don't understand who God is. We have little to no understanding of the depth and the breadth and the height of His perfection and of His holiness. The second is that we don't understand the sinfulness of sin.

We are quick to say to err is human and to forgive is divine; we are equally swift to affirm that no one's perfect. The awfulness of sin hasn't really captured our understanding. What repentance we have before God is shallow at best, as we sugarcoat the offenses we have committed, not only against our neighbors but especially and ultimately against God Himself.

The Rich Man

"There was a rich man who was clothed in purple and fine linen and who feasted sumptuously every day" (v. 19). This parable concerns two men, and Jesus began by introducing the first, a rich man, who is traditionally known as

Dives. Dives was a rich man, but this is not a judgment against wealth. Joseph of Arimathea had great wealth. Abraham and Job were two of the wealthiest people in the world. So, there is no inherent evil about this man being wealthy. Dives, however, was the quintessential ostentatious rich man. He dressed like a king, wearing purple, a dye that was almost priceless in antiquity and was reserved almost exclusively for royalty.

"And at his gate was laid a poor man named Lazarus, covered with sores, who desired to be fed with what fell from the rich man's table. Moreover, even the dogs came and licked his sores" (vv. 20–21). Jesus then introduced by way of stark contrast another person in this drama, a beggar named Lazarus. He didn't have a penny to his name, and not only was he impoverished but he was also suffering from endless sores that covered his body, and he was also on the edge of starvation. A compassionate person brought Lazarus near the gate of the wealthy man in the hope that somehow, being in close proximity to such plenteous wealth, the crumbs from the garbage would fall in the direction of Lazarus and keep him alive.

Jesus' mention of dogs would have inspired revulsion. Dogs at that time were not household pets; they were feral creatures, wild and despised. The image Jesus gave of Lazarus' situation was that an unclean, despicable animal came to the poor man not to give comfort to him but to enjoy licking the sores of the beggar.

The Rich Man Asks for Mercy

"The poor man died and was carried by the angels to Abraham's side. The rich man also died and was buried, and in Hades, being in torment, he lifted up his eyes and saw Abraham far off and Lazarus at his side. And he called out, 'Father Abraham, have mercy on me, and send Lazarus to dip the end of his finger in water and cool my tongue, for I am in anguish in this flame'" (vv. 22–24). The rich man was conscious in hell, and he looked and saw Lazarus at Abraham's side. Dives cried out: "Father Abraham, have mercy on me. Send Lazarus to me and let him dip his finger in water and touch my tongue; just give me some relief from hell. Please, have mercy." He asked for mercy. You have to wonder if he even understood the meaning of the word while he was on earth, but at this point he did, and he wanted some. He cried for it.

Two words that you don't ever want to hear from God are *too late*. God is a God of mercy, a God whose mercy is beyond all human comprehension. But I sometimes object inwardly when people in their zeal thank God for His mercy and speak of His "infinite" mercy. If people mean by "His mercy is infinite" that it has no boundaries, that is incorrect. There is a boundary to the mercy of God and that boundary is the end of your life. "It is appointed for man to die once, and after that comes judgment" (Heb. 9:27). If we cry for mercy and cry for Jesus after we're dead, it's too late.

"But Abraham said, 'Child, remember that you in your lifetime received your good things, and Lazarus in like manner bad things; but now he is comforted here, and you are in anguish. And besides all this, between us and you a great chasm has been fixed, in order that those who would pass from here to you may not be able, and none may cross from there to us'" (Luke 16:25–26). Abraham said Dives had received comfort during his life, but now Lazarus was receiving comfort while Dives was suffering. Further, our Lord was telling us in this parable that there is an unbridgeable chasm between heaven and hell. There is no power on Earth or power in hell that will allow you, once you are in hell, to escape and reach heaven.

There is no bridge between heaven and hell. That chasm represents the fixed and permanent position of hell. If you are there, you're there forever. If you have any understanding of the reality of hell, you will crawl on broken glass to the cross to the only One who can bring you safely home for eternity.

If Someone Should Rise from the Dead

"And he said, 'Then I beg you, father, to send him to my father's house—for I have five brothers—so that he may warn them, lest they also come into this place of torment'" (vv. 27–28). Dives, hearing the dreadful words that no one can pass between hell and heaven, begs. Isn't it interesting that at the beginning of this parable Lazarus is the beggar, and now it is Dives who is doing the begging? He asks Abraham to send Lazarus to warn his family about the fate that awaits the unrepentant.

"But Abraham said, 'They have Moses and the Prophets; let them hear them.' And he said, 'No, father Abraham, but if someone goes to them from the dead, they will repent.' He said to him, 'If they do not hear Moses and the Prophets, neither will they be convinced if someone should rise from the dead'" (vv. 29–31). Truer words were never spoken than Abraham's, because One has risen from the dead—the very One who was telling this parable—and people still don't believe it.

If there is a hell, and there is, it makes all the difference in the world for you, for everyone you know, for everyone you love. God grant that we would heed this parable of Jesus and let it pierce our souls and our hearts with a concern for the future of every person we meet. May it weigh heavily on our hearts, because when they die, it's too late.

79

UNPROFITABLE SERVANTS

Luke 17:1–10

And he said to his disciples, "Temptations to sin are sure to come, but woe to the one through whom they come! It would be better for him if a millstone were hung around his neck and he were cast into the sea than that he should cause one of these little ones to sin. Pay attention to yourselves! If your brother sins, rebuke him, and if he repents, forgive him, and if he sins against you seven times in the day, and turns to you seven times, saying, 'I repent,' you must forgive him."

The apostles said to the Lord, "Increase our faith!" And the Lord said, "If you had faith like a grain of mustard seed, you could say to this mulberry tree, 'Be uprooted and planted in the sea,' and it would obey you.

"Will any one of you who has a servant plowing or keeping sheep say to him when he has come in from the field, 'Come at once and recline at table'? Will he not rather say to him, 'Prepare supper for me, and dress properly, and serve me while I eat and drink, and afterward you will eat and drink'? Does he thank the servant because he did what was commanded? So you also, when you have done all that you were commanded, say, 'We are unworthy servants; we have only done what was our duty.' "

And he said to his disciples, "Temptations to sin are sure to come" (v. 1). Our Lord acknowledged that until the kingdom of God is fully consummated, we will still struggle with sin. We will still struggle with offenses that we commit against God. We still have temptations with which we must wrestle.

"But woe to the one through whom they come! It would be better for him if a millstone were hung around his neck and he were cast into the sea than that he should cause one of these little ones to sin" (vv. 1–2). Jesus then pronounced to His disciples an oracle of doom. This is a tremendously important point that Jesus made in this oracle of judgment. It is one thing, He said, for you to sin, but the judgment of God will be even greater on those who tempt others to sin.

In Romans 1:28–32, after Paul gave a list of egregious offenses against God, he concluded, "Though they know God's righteous decree that those who practice such things deserve to die, they not only do them but give approval to those who practice them" (v. 32). There are numerous churches whose pastors tell their people that premarital sex is part of normal puberty and growth, extramarital sex is acceptable to God, same-sex marriage has His approval, and God is not offended by abortion on demand. Many mainline churches have adopted these positions as part of their official sanctions. Woe to those people who encourage others to commit these egregious sins against God. It would be better for that person if they had a millstone hung around their neck.

Jesus' mention of a **millstone** was a reference to the agrarian society of the time. On the threshing floor where grain was ground, there were two large circular stones, one on top of the other. The top stone had a hole in the center into which they poured grain. Oxen were attached to the top stone, and they moved around in a circle, which would cause the top stone to grind the grain against the bottom stone. A human was not able to do this task, except for Samson, who was forced to do it after he was captured by the Philistines (Judg. 16:21). The weight of that stone was so great that if it were put around your neck and you were thrown into the depth of the sea, you would surely drown.

The Call to Forgive

"Pay attention to yourselves! If your brother sins, rebuke him, and if he repents, forgive him, and if he sins against you seven times in the day, and turns to you seven times, saying, 'I repent,' you must forgive him" (vv. 3–4). There's a widespread misconception among Christians that if somebody sins against us, we're duty bound to give them unilateral forgiveness regardless of whether they repent. Jesus, of course, did that when He prayed for the forgiveness of His executioners while He hung on the cross (23:34). But the Bible doesn't teach that we are required before God to give automatic unilateral forgiveness to anyone who sins against us. That's why the New Testament lays out a process for church discipline (Matt. 18:15–20; 1 Cor. 5; 2 Cor. 2:5–11). Jesus said that if we are sinned against, we are to rebuke that person, and if he repents, then forgiveness is not an option; we must forgive.

Jesus went on to say that if that person commits the same sin fifteen minutes later and comes and repents, you have to forgive him again. And if he does it a third time, a fourth time, a fifth time, a sixth time, a seventh time, and then he repents, you can't say to him: "No, that's number seven. Too late; you're done." It doesn't matter how many times we've been sinned against; if the party who offends repents, then we forgive. We have to stand ready to forgive people at any time at a moment's notice.

The apostles said to the Lord, "Increase our faith!" And the Lord said, "If you had faith like a grain of mustard seed, you could say to this mulberry tree, 'Be uprooted and planted in the sea,' and it would obey you" (vv. 5–6). After the admonition to forgive, Jesus gave something of a strange and unexpected story in response to the disciples' request for Him to increase their faith. I don't know too many of us who can actually order a mulberry tree to cast itself into the sea, but Jesus' point was that it doesn't take a lot of faith to forgive somebody who sins against you. Now comes the story that is unexpected.

We Have Only Done Our Duty

"Will any one of you who has a servant plowing or keeping sheep say to him when he has come in from the field, 'Come at once and recline at table'? Will he not rather say to him, 'Prepare supper for me, and dress properly, and serve me while I eat and drink, and afterward you will eat and drink'? Does he thank the servant because he did what was commanded?" (vv. 7–9). Jesus asked His disciples what they would do in this situation. He told them of a master who owned a farm and had a hardworking servant. If you were the master, He asked, would you tell the servant to sit down and enjoy a meal that you prepared for him before you ate? We don't learn of the disciples' response to Jesus' question, but Jesus' point was not the servanthood of the master. He was addressing the situation where a man, the servant, did what he was commanded to do. He did all that he was responsible for, and when he came in at the end of the day, he still had further duties to perform. It was now time for him to prepare his master's dinner. The master was not going to say to the servant: "Sit down. Put your legs up. I'm going to cook you some food and treat you to a lavish dinner." He was not going to say to him, "Thank you so very much for doing what you've been commanded to do."

"So you also, when you have done all that you were commanded, say, 'We are unworthy servants; we have only done what was our duty'" (v. 10).

Here's the point of the parable. Jesus directed His address at this point to His disciples, and therefore also to us. We also, when we have done all the things that we are commanded to do, are to understand that **"we are unworthy servants; we have only done what was our duty."** We have added nothing to the assets side of the ledger. If we have lived a life of perfect righteousness, if we have obeyed every commandment that God has ever given (which we haven't), Jesus said that all we have done is what we were supposed to do. Didn't our Creator make us in His own image? Didn't He call us to mirror and reflect His character? Didn't He say to us, "Be holy, for I am holy"?

If I live a life of perfect holiness, I've done nothing of merit. I've added nothing to the weights and measures of the kingdom of God because I've simply done what was my duty to do. We have many people in the church who still hold on to the idea that what they've accomplished in this life is what will get them into the kingdom of God. Muslims have a view that if your good deeds outweigh your bad deeds, you'll go to heaven, but if your bad deeds outweigh your good deeds, you'll go to hell. Christianity says that if your whole life has nothing but good deeds and you have no bad deeds, without the righteousness of Christ, you'll still go to hell forever because there's nothing you could possibly do to earn your way into the kingdom of God. You can't go to the judgment seat of Christ and say: "I went to church every Sunday for thirty years. I was an elder. I was a minister. I was a deacon. I tithed my money. I fed the poor. I ministered to the sick." God will say: "That's what you were supposed to do. Why should I reward you for doing your duty?"

One of my favorite hymns is "Rock of Ages, Cleft for Me" by Augustus Toplady. There is a line in that hymn that expresses the idea in this parable: "Nothing in my hand I bring, simply to the cross I cling." *Nothing* in my hand. The hand is empty. It brings nothing to the table except my shame, my guilt, and my need. When we come to the cross, we bring nothing in our hand; "Foul, I to the fountain fly; wash me, Savior, or I die." All that has been done to get me into the kingdom of God is done by Christ. He and He alone is the profitable servant. We reap the benefits of His profit. He takes the profit that He has achieved, and He pours it into our hands so that when we stand before God, we have everything. We have perfect righteousness in our hands, but it's His. It's not ours.

I don't add a cent to the profit that is won for me by Christ. What do we have to boast of before God? "Let the one who boasts, boast in the Lord," we are told (2 Cor. 10:17). We have only the righteousness of Jesus, so we bring nothing of our own except our need.

80

CLEANSING OF THE LEPERS

Luke 17:11–19

On the way to Jerusalem he was passing along between Samaria and Galilee. And as he entered a village, he was met by ten lepers, who stood at a distance and lifted up their voices, saying, "Jesus, Master, have mercy on us." When he saw them he said to them, "Go and show yourselves to the priests." And as they went they were cleansed. Then one of them, when he saw that he was healed, turned back, praising God with a loud voice; and he fell on his face at Jesus' feet, giving him thanks. Now he was a Samaritan. Then Jesus answered, "Were not ten cleansed? Where are the nine? Was no one found to return and give praise to God except this foreigner?" And he said to him, "Rise and go your way; your faith has made you well."

On the way to Jerusalem he was passing along between Samaria and Galilee (v. 11). Luke begins this passage by telling us of an event that took place when Jesus was on His way to Jerusalem. In His travels, He passed through Samaria and Galilee. That in itself was unusual.

Scripture tells us that there was a hostile relationship between Jews and Samaritans and that the Jews had no dealings with Samaritans. The hostility was so deeply rooted that when Jews wanted to go between Judea and Galilee, instead of going the shortest route through Samaria, they crossed the Jordan and went up the desert road. They would go out of their way to avoid going through Samaria. Jesus went against that convention and decided to go directly through Samaria.

And as he entered a village, he was met by ten lepers, who stood at a distance . . . (v. 12). Once a person was diagnosed with leprosy in ancient Israel, he suffered the worst of all possible quarantines—not a quarantine that would last a week or two weeks but one that would last for the rest of the person's life. Unless a person was cured of leprosy by some marvelous means, he was sentenced to a solitary life removed from the community, removed from family, removed from the religious institutions. He was a social pariah, and the only fellowship he could have with other human beings was with other lepers. There were reasons why lepers gathered in groups such as this group of ten, because that was the only companionship they could enjoy.

Here in this area on the border between Galilee and Samaria was a commercial highway that brought people from different nations, not just Jews and Samaritans but international people. These ten lepers included Jews and Samaritans, but probably people from other countries were among them also.

. . . and lifted up their voices, saying, "Jesus, Master, have mercy on us" (v. 13). How did the lepers know who Jesus was? They didn't have cell phones, they didn't have radios or television, and they didn't have daily interaction with healthy people. How did they even get the news of Jesus?

The things that Jesus did in Galilee, in Judea, and even in Samaria were things the world had never seen before. A blaze of miracles followed Jesus, and that kind of ministry spread in terms of its news like wildfire throughout the territory. Maybe somebody called out to the lepers, shouting: "There's a man named Jesus! He raises people from the dead! He makes the blind see, the deaf hear, and the lame walk and leap with joy! Watch for Him! Maybe someday He'll come this way! Here's what He looks like! There's always a group following Him! We call Him Master."

I don't know how they'd heard of Him, but how could they not have heard, given who He was and what He was doing? The day they dreamed of, the day they prayed for, took place when, in a distance, there He was. "It's Jesus." You can hear them talking to each other. You can feel their excitement. "Here He comes! He's here! Look, over there! That's Jesus! He raises people from the dead. Maybe He can heal us." So they didn't whisper; they screamed: **"Jesus, Master, have mercy on us."**

The response of Jesus here was unusual. On the other occasions when we see people who are afflicted and suffering come to Him, He reached out and touched them and healed them. He laid His hands on them and said, "Be clean!" and instantly they were healed. But that's not how He did it this time.

When he saw them he said to them, "Go and show yourselves to the priests" (v. 14). According to the book of Leviticus, the priest was authorized to make the diagnosis of leprosy in the first place, and if a person was recovering or if it was a false diagnosis, only the priest's declaration could free him from the quarantine. Jesus didn't say, "Be clean; you're healed." He said to go to the priests. What did that mean? Going to the priest would not be an idle mission. If they showed themselves to the priests, they would be declared clean.

And as they went they were cleansed (v. 14). The lepers weren't cleansed yet when Jesus told them to go to the priests, but they obeyed and started on their way to see the priests in obedience to His command. As they went, they were cleansed, not when they just first saw Jesus, but after they started on their journey to see the priest. Their fingers became whole, their toes were healed, and the horrible sores on their bodies vanished. They were likely beyond themselves with joy and excitement as their bodies were being cleansed with every step they took on their way to the priests.

The Samaritan Turns Back

Then one of them, when he saw that he was healed, turned back, praising God with a loud voice; and he fell on his face at Jesus' feet, giving him thanks. Now he was a Samaritan (vv. 15–16). Imagine ten lepers in a group, watching one another suddenly being made whole. They couldn't wait to get to the priests because they knew that the priests would pronounce them clean. At that point, they would be able to go home again. They could see their wives and embrace their children again. They could worship publicly again. So they hurried along. But one said: "Wait a minute. It was Jesus who made us clean. We must first go back and thank Him and honor Him. I want to let Him know I'm grateful."

The essence of worship is to offer to God the sacrifice of our praise. In Romans 1:18–25, Paul wrote of the fact that God reveals Himself from heaven to every human being and that His wrath is revealed against all unrighteousness and ungodliness of men. The reason men are ungodly and unrighteous is that they suppress the truth of God that He reveals, leaving them without an excuse. Paul went on to say that knowing God, they did not honor Him as God, and neither were they grateful. The two primary sins—the root of every other sin for which every human being in his natural, unconverted state is guilty—are the refusal to honor God as God and ingratitude toward God.

If I were to ask you what is your most base sin, your worst action of evil, would you come up with something like failure to be grateful to God? Probably not, but according to Scripture, that is our fundamental problem. We think

God owes us everything that we receive and much more. If a Christian is truly grateful, he shows it in worship and in service to God. That's the part of this passage that is so precious: the response of the man who was healed. With a loud voice, he glorified God and fell down on his face at the feet of Jesus, giving Him thanks. He was a Samaritan, a leper, and a social outcast, but he fell at the feet of Jesus to thank Him.

Each of us at some time in our lives has suffered from spiritual leprosy. We are by nature lepers, and the God of all mercy and grace, through His beloved Son, has made us clean if we are in Christ Jesus. We all ought to shout our thanksgiving to Him and fall at His feet in honor, adoration, and worship. We've been made clean, and we come to give praise and thanks.

Then Jesus answered, "Were not ten cleansed? Where are the nine? Was no one found to return and give praise to God except this foreigner?" (vv. 17–18). The other nine, of course, were on their way to the priests, as Jesus had told them to do. And yet, Jesus noted that they had not seen fit to come and offer thanks for their cleansing.

And he said to him, "Rise and go your way; your faith has made you well" (v. 19). He was speaking to the man who was still on the ground in a posture of gratitude. This poor leper was clean because the Lord Jesus Christ had cleansed him.

It's your story, it's my story, and it's God's story. How do you show your thanks to Christ? How do you give glory and honor to your Redeemer?

81

THE KINGDOM COME

Luke 17:20–37

Being asked by the Pharisees when the kingdom of God would come, he answered them, "The kingdom of God is not coming in ways that can be observed, nor will they say, 'Look, here it is!' or 'There!' for behold, the kingdom of God is in the midst of you."

And he said to the disciples, "The days are coming when you will desire to see one of the days of the Son of Man, and you will not see it. And they will say to you, 'Look, there!' or 'Look, here!' Do not go out or follow them. For as the lightning flashes and lights up the sky from one side to the other, so will the Son of Man be in his day. But first he must suffer many things and be rejected by this generation. Just as it was in the days of Noah, so will it be in the days of the Son of Man. They were eating and drinking and marrying and being given in marriage, until the day when Noah entered the ark, and the flood came and destroyed them all. Likewise, just as it was in the days of Lot—they were eating and drinking, buying and selling, planting and building, but on the day when Lot went out from Sodom, fire and sulfur rained from heaven and destroyed them all—so will it be on the day when the Son of Man is revealed. On that day, let the one who is on the housetop, with his goods in the house, not come down to take them away, and likewise let the one who is in the field not turn back. Remember Lot's wife. Whoever seeks to preserve his life will lose it, but whoever loses his life will keep it. I tell you, in that night there will be two in one bed. One will be taken and the other left. There will be two women grinding together. One will be taken and the other left." And they said to him, "Where, Lord?" He said to them, "Where the corpse is, there the vultures will gather."

When I come to this text, I'm uncertain at different points what Jesus is referring to. It's not that I haven't studied the text. It's not that I haven't followed the insights of commentators through the ages. I have done that. My homework has been rigorous, but I am still not sure about everything that Jesus says here in this passage. I'm afraid I have no other choice but to be less than dogmatic in my interpretation of the text. Believe me, being less than dogmatic is not my nature at all.

Being asked by the Pharisees when the kingdom of God would come . . . (v. 20). When will the kingdom of God come? Throughout Luke's Gospel, the basic core message in Jesus' preaching was the coming of the kingdom of God. John the Baptist came on the scene first with the announcement, "Repent, for the kingdom of heaven is at hand" (Matt. 3:2). When Jesus began His public ministry, that same announcement was central to His proclamation (4:17). The kingdom of God was at hand.

Jesus' parables are full of references to that kingdom. The kingdom of God is like this; the kingdom of God is like that (see Matt. 13). The Pharisees, who had been trying to trap Him at many different points, finally came to Him and said, "Jesus, You've been talking about the kingdom since you started Your public ministry, so when are we going to see this kingdom?"

The Pharisees were cognizant of the expectation of sacred Scripture. The people at that time were looking for and hoping for a Messiah who would come and drive the dreaded Romans out of their land and free them from that occupation. They expected a political Messiah, a warrior-king who would set the people free. So far, they hadn't seen anything remotely like that, so they were skeptical.

The Kingdom of God Is within You

. . . he answered them, "The kingdom of God is not coming in ways that can be observed, nor will they say, 'Look, here it is!' or 'There!' for behold, the kingdom of God is in the midst of you" (vv. 20–21). Various translations render Jesus' reply differently. Some say "the kingdom of God is within you" (KJV, NKJV), some say "the kingdom of God is among you" (HCSB, NLT), and some say "the kingdom of God is in your midst" (NIV, CSB, NASB). The translation I favor is "the kingdom of God is within you." Commentators say that this phrase means that people were looking for an outward kingdom, but Jesus was saying it's not external. It's not out there; it's in here. It's in people's hearts. It's in the spiritual changes that come to pass when people are submissive to the reign of God and where hearts are in alliance with the purposes of God. That's where the kingdom is.

During the Reformation in the sixteenth century, one of the side issues after the split was the question, What is a legitimate church? Where is the church? Is it in Rome? Is it in Germany? Is it in Switzerland or in Scotland? The Roman Catholics responded to that question by saying, "Where the bishop is, there's the church." The Protestant reply was this: "No, where the Spirit is, there is the church. When the Holy Spirit regenerates people internally, there's the church. It's invisible, but there it is."

The favored interpretation of this text is that Jesus was saying that the kingdom is not something external; it's internal. It's something that exists in the hearts of men. I have some sympathy for that particular interpretation of this passage, but here's one of these places where I am not at all sure. Part of the reason is that if the only place Jesus lives is in my heart, His accommodation is far too small. I know He lives because of the Word of God and because of His resurrection in history. Jesus is alive outside my heart.

I pray that His Spirit is inside my heart, but I serve a risen Master who's alive out there; He's not just in here. Jesus said to Pilate during His interrogation, "My kingdom is not of this world" (John 18:36). It's a supernatural reality, but nevertheless its scope is more than within the hearts of people.

I think Jesus was saying to the Pharisees: "You blind beggars. The kingdom of God is in your midst and you can't see it." I think Jesus said that because where the King is, there is the kingdom. The King of the kingdom was in their midst and had been in their midst for a period of time.

Jesus' Departure

And he said to the disciples, "The days are coming when you will desire to see one of the days of the Son of Man, and you will not see it. And they will say to you, 'Look, there!' or 'Look, here!' Do not go out or follow them. For as the lightning flashes and lights up the sky from one side to the other, so will the Son of Man be in his day. But first he must suffer many things and be rejected by this generation" (vv. 22–25). Jesus at this point was talking to His disciples about something that was near in terms of time. "You're enjoying every day you spend with Me, but the days will come," He said to His disciples, "when you won't have Me in your midst, and you will long to be able to see another day of the Son of Man." Jesus was telling His disciples that He was leaving. This was one of the most difficult things the disciples had to deal with.

He said to them on other occasions, "A little while, and you will see me no longer; and again a little while, and you will see me" (John 16:16). When Jesus said that to the disciples, they were stricken with grief. "Lord, where are You going where we can't come?" He said: "Are you ready to drink the cup I have to drink? Are you ready to be baptized with the baptism that I have been baptized with? No, you're not prepared for that yet, but when I go away, I will not leave you comfortless, but I will send to you another Advocate, even the Holy Spirit" (see John 13:36; 14:16).

We have a number of discourses in which Jesus told His disciples that He would soon be removed from their midst. I think that's what He was talking about here when He said, **"The days are coming when you will desire to see one of the days of the Son of Man, and you will not see it"** (v. 22). After Jesus ascended into heaven, there were multiple false messiahs who appeared in Israel claiming to be the Christ. Public opinion was swayed. Some would say: "He's over here. No, he's over there." Jesus said, "When you see that or when you hear that, don't pay any attention to it."

The Day of the Son of Man

I think He was talking to them about something that was relatively near at hand. He said, **"For as the lightning flashes and lights up the sky from one side to the other, so will the Son of Man be in his day. But first he must suffer many things and be rejected by this generation"** (vv. 24–25). He was speaking of a coming that would be so sudden, so quick, so unexpected that people would not be prepared for it.

When the lightning strikes during a storm and goes clear across the sky, how long does it take? Do you sit down and observe the lightning moving across the sky, taking five minutes to go from one side to the other? No, it's instantaneous. Most commentators say Jesus was talking about His second coming here, His coming at the end of history when He will consummate His kingdom. Perhaps He was, but I don't think so. I think He was describing a different coming, not His final saving coming at the end of the age but His coming in judgment on Israel, which would take place in that generation. In Matthew's Gospel, Jesus said about that judgment, "This generation," which in Jewish terms usually referred to a forty-year period, "will not pass away until all these things take place" (Matt. 24:34).

I'm among those who believe that Jesus was predicting the crashing judgment on Israel that took place with the destruction of the temple and of the city of Jerusalem by the Romans in the year AD 70. It was a historical moment that is all but ignored by the contemporary church, but in terms of redemptive history, it is replete with significance and meaning for Christ and for the church. Regardless of which coming He was describing here—the judgment of AD 70 or His final coming at the end of time—He had things to say about it that would be relevant to both.

"Just as it was in the days of Noah, so will it be in the days of the Son of Man. They were eating and drinking and marrying and being given in marriage, until the day when Noah entered the ark, and the flood came and destroyed them all" (vv. 26–27). What was so significant about the days of Noah? Do you think that Noah built the ark in a week? Scholars have considered all the material that would have been required to build that ark and how much labor would have been involved in putting it together, and they have said it would have taken a significant number of years for Noah to complete that project.

People watched Noah building a boat in the desert and asked him, "Why?" Noah replied, "Because it's going to rain so much that the whole earth will be covered with a flood." They scoffed at Noah and said to themselves, "Let's eat, drink, and be merry and forget about this fool out there building the boat."

They did these things until the day that Noah entered the ark and the flood came and destroyed them all. Every person—man, woman, and child—except for the family of Noah was destroyed by the wrath of God in the flood. Jesus said, "That's the way it's going to be, just that suddenly, when people are going about their normal daily affairs."

"Likewise, just as it was in the days of Lot—they were eating and drinking, buying and selling, planting and building, but on the day when Lot went out from Sodom, fire and sulfur rained from heaven and destroyed them all—so will it be on the day when the Son of Man is revealed" (vv. 28–30). It will be like in the days of Lot. They ate, drank, bought, and sold. They planted. They built. They harvested. They read the stock market. They invested. They did all these things, and suddenly it rained as it had rained in the days of Noah, but this time, the rain wasn't water. It was fire and brimstone.

Sodom and Gomorrah were swallowed up by the wrath of God when they least expected it, but Lot was warned to flee from that wrath. He took his wife and they left Sodom and made their way into the wilderness.

"On that day, let the one who is on the housetop, with his goods in the house, not come down to take them away, and likewise let the one who is in the field not turn back. Remember Lot's wife" (vv. 31–32). Jesus gave further instructions regarding this time, saying that people should not stop to gather their belongings or delay in any way but should flee and not look back. He continued: **"Whoever seeks to preserve his life will lose it, but whoever loses his life will keep it. I tell you, in that night there will be two in one bed. One will be taken and the other left. There will be two women grinding together. One will be taken and the other left"** (vv. 33–35).

And they said to him, "Where, Lord?" He said to them, "Where the corpse is, there the vultures will gather" (v. 37). Jesus' teaching prompted a different question. Instead of asking, "When will the kingdom come?" they now asked, "Where? Where will this take place?" He said to them, **"Where the corpse is, there the vultures will gather."** This gruesome picture is of slain bodies spread across the landscape while the buzzards fly overhead awaiting their feast of human carrion.

This verse can also be translated "Where the body is, there the eagles will gather." We might interpret this as "The bodies of Jewish people, who will be the victims of this dreadful catastrophe, will be marked by the presence of a multitude of eagles." Replicas of eagles were embroidered on the standards and flags of the Roman army. When Rome attacked Judea in AD 66 under orders from Nero, he commanded his general, Vespasian, to capture Jerusalem. When the Roman armies came, they were like a juggernaut as they passed over the borders and destroyed everything in their path.

In the town of Jotapata, every inhabitant was killed except one who went into hiding and was discovered and taken captive by the Romans. His name was Josephus, one of the most important historians of antiquity. Vespasian was recalled to Rome to become emperor. He turned over the reins of conquest to his son Titus to finish the job.

Titus marched to Jerusalem with his troops in AD 69 and besieged the city for months while they camped on the Mount of Olives. Historians tell us that the Mount of Olives was so called because it was covered with gorgeous olive trees that were three or four hundred years old. The Roman soldiers chopped down every tree and used them for firewood. By the time the siege was over, there wasn't a single tree standing on the Mount of Olives.

When finally the attack came, the Romans beat down the walls with their battering rams and used their other sophisticated methods of war. They entered Jerusalem and burned the temple to the ground. They killed 1.1 million Jews and took another hundred thousand captive. It was the end of the temple and the end of Jerusalem for a season.

The Jews who survived fled to other nations and were scattered around the world. But the Christians didn't die in Jerusalem. Jesus had told them to flee to the mountains. "Don't get your suitcases or stay grinding at the mill," He said. "If you stay too long, it will be too late. You need to get up and not go to Jerusalem."

In the ancient world, when an invading army came into people's land, the standard procedure was for the people to flee to protected walled cities, which were mighty fortresses for defense. But Jesus defied the traditional method of escape from an invasion.

Those who went to Jerusalem were killed. Josephus, the historian, recorded that during that fateful hour, several people testified to seeing disturbances in the sky. They said they saw chariots in the air, in the sky, in the clouds, and they heard a voice coming from the sky, saying, "We are departing hence."

If that is true, God was saying to His people in effect: "We are leaving. You didn't want Me. You rejected My Son. You caused Him to suffer and die. You're on your own." Jesus was saying, "When God says He's going to bring judgment, it may tarry. It may tarry for so long that you go along with your daily life, never giving it a second thought until it's too late."

Whether this passage refers to the destruction of Jerusalem or the final judgment, there will be a final judgment for each one of us. When it comes, we won't be expecting it. I have many dear friends who are not believers for whom I pray that the Lord would let them live long enough to come to faith. I pray that when that moment comes, my friends will be not eating and drinking, sowing and reaping, planting and building but be ready, vigilant, diligent. The church in every age, in every generation, is called to be vigilant, watching, waiting, and ready when He comes.

82

THE UNJUST JUDGE

Luke 18:1–8

And he told them a parable to the effect that they ought always to pray and not lose heart. He said, "In a certain city there was a judge who neither feared God nor respected man. And there was a widow in that city who kept coming to him and saying, 'Give me justice against my adversary.' For a while he refused, but afterward he said to himself, 'Though I neither fear God nor respect man, yet because this widow keeps bothering me, I will give her justice, so that she will not beat me down by her continual coming.' " And the Lord said, "Hear what the unrighteous judge says. And will not God give justice to his elect, who cry to him day and night? Will he delay long over them? I tell you, he will give justice to them speedily. Nevertheless, when the Son of Man comes, will he find faith on earth?"

A**nd he told them a parable to the effect that they ought always to pray and not lose heart** (v. 1). There's something odd about the way in which Jesus began this parable. He gave the point of it before He told the story.

In the previous discourse, Jesus talked about His coming and about the catastrophic events that would attend it and about those times of great pain and torment. I don't think it's by accident that this parable followed that discourse because Jesus told His people that though He might tarry for a while and His people would suffer persecution, in the midst of that persecution they ought not lose heart, but they ought to be constantly and persistently in prayer.

The kind of prayer Jesus was advocating is not the juvenile type of desultory prayers that a child might make. Rather, Christ called us to deep levels of prayer, the kind of prayer that is mentioned in James when he said, "The prayer of a righteous person has great power as it is working" (James 5:16). We are called to pray with fervency, with consistency, and with persistence.

That's what our Lord called us to here. The circumstances may be crushing to our spirit and seem apparently hopeless for any good ending; nevertheless, we ought to keep praying, keep praying, and keep praying.

A Corrupt Judge and a Widow in Need

He said, "In a certain city there was a judge who neither feared God nor respected man" (v. 2). To amplify this mandate, Jesus told the parable of two people, a judge and a widow. He began by introducing the judge. This man was appointed to the judicial bench. His call and his responsibility were to administer justice. He had clearly taken an oath to do so, but we're told by Jesus that God was not a part of his agenda. He had no fear of God, no care for God, no consideration for the things of God. He was a totally secular and profane man, without a spiritual bone in his body. Not only was he lacking with regard for God, but he also didn't care about people. Yet, in the providence of God, his vocation was to care about people and to ensure that justice was administered to them.

He didn't care about God or people. The only thing left for him to care about was himself. The decisions he made must have been on the basis of political expediency. There's some irony here, because though this judge is probably a fictional character that Jesus used for the purpose of this teaching, at the end of His own life, Jesus stood before such a judge who had no regard for God or man but only ruled and made decisions on the basis of expediency. Pilate declared to the crowd, "I have found in him no guilt deserving death" (23:22), then a few moments later he ordered Jesus to be crucified (v. 24) because that's what the people wanted.

There's nothing unique about this man. There have been judges throughout history, the world over, who haven't cared about justice. We live in a country today that is supposed to be under God. Yet the government and its minions for the most part have made a declaration of independence from God. God is not in their thinking, and there's a growing hostility toward the things of God.

Every judge in the history of the world will answer at some point to the Judge of all the earth, who never in all eternity rendered a judgment based on expediency. In the kingdom of God, there are no lobby groups. There are no vested interests trying to influence the decision of the court.

This judge embodied all that was wrong with corrupt judges. He had no regard for God, for man, and certainly no regard for the widow, who is the other person in this story. This widow was basically helpless. She had no one to plead her case. She didn't have the means to bring pressure to bear on the court.

"And there was a widow in that city who kept coming to him and saying, 'Give me justice against my adversary.' For a while he refused, but afterward he said to himself, 'Though I neither fear God nor respect man, yet because this widow keeps bothering me, I will give her justice, so that she will not beat me down by her continual coming'" (vv. 3–5). This importunate woman persisted in her appeals to the judge. She came to him, saying, "Get justice for me, please," and the judge said, "Go away." He didn't give her justice after her numerous pleadings, until one day he said to himself: "Even though I don't care about God, and though I have no regard for man, yet because this widow troubles me, I will avenge her, lest by her continual coming to me, she will weary me. She's tiring me out. I don't want to listen to this woman ever again. Every day I come to the courthouse, and she is there begging me to hear her case, pleading with me to give her justice. I'm tired of listening to her. Maybe if I hear her case and give her vengeance, she'll leave me alone."

The Judge of All the Earth

And the Lord said, "Hear what the unrighteous judge says. And will not God give justice to his elect, who cry to him day and night? Will he delay long over them? I tell you, he will give justice to them speedily" (vv. 6–8). The unrighteous judge said he would hear her case simply because she was wearing him out, not because he had any sense of righteousness or any sense of justice. Will not God, Jesus asked, vindicate His own elect who cry out to Him? This isn't a parallel. It's not a simple contrast between a bad judge and a good judge. The relationship between God as Judge and the unjust judge is one of those relationships that occur frequently in Jesus' "How much more?" parables. Jesus was telling us: "If on occasion a crooked, corrupt judge will, if he's pushed far enough, give justice, what about a perfectly just Judge? Was not Abraham right when he said, 'Shall not the Judge of all the earth do what is just?'" (Gen. 18:25).

Abraham's question was rhetorical. What's the answer? The Judge of all the earth isn't able to do anything except what is just. He's never done an unjust thing, and He never will. Everybody has suffered injustices at the hands of other people—but never ever from God.

If you treat me unjustly, I can get on my knees and I can say: "God, this person has treated me unjustly, but what do You want me to learn from it? Even though You have ordained or allowed me to suffer this injustice at the hands of other people, it is certainly a just action on Your part." I've received a lot of mercy and a lot of grace from God, but I've never received an injustice from Him. No one has, because our Lord God omnipotent is a just Judge.

The point is simple. If the unjust judge will once in a while render a just verdict out of expediency, what can you expect from a just judge? Jesus again spoke rhetorically, **"Will not God give justice to his elect, who cry to him day and night?"** (v. 7).

The greatest preacher who ever preached from a pulpit in the United States was Jonathan Edwards. He faithfully served a congregation in Northampton, Massachusetts, for decades. Then one day, that congregation turned on him, led by a man who was spreading false charges in the community about Edwards, accusing him of diabolical things.

Edwards' parishioners came to him and said, "Dr. Edwards, please address these issues." He said, "No, I prefer to remain silent." "Why?" they asked. "Don't you want to be vindicated?" He said that he did want to be vindicated. "That's why I'm keeping silent. If I vindicate myself, I'll get some level of vindication, but if I pray to almighty God and wait for Him to vindicate me, that vindication will be greater than anything any human can bring to pass."

Everybody knows the passage "Vengeance is mine, I will repay, says the Lord" (Rom. 12:19). We hear in the first part, "Vengeance is mine," that He is denying the right of individuals to avenge themselves. That is correct; we're not allowed to avenge ourselves. However, we assume He is saying, "Vengeance is bad." That's not correct. He is saying that seeking vengeance is His prerogative, not ours. Pray to your heavenly Father day and night, for He has promised unequivocally to vindicate us who belong to Him. We become impatient, but He will avenge us.

"Nevertheless, when the Son of Man comes, will he find faith on earth?" (v. 8). Jesus ended this parable with a curious question. We know that Jesus is the God-man. He has a divine nature and a human nature, and though we must never separate those two natures, we can distinguish them. When Jesus became sleepy or when He bled, He did so according to His human nature. Jesus' question seems to suggest there was something He didn't know. Certainly, according to His divine nature, Jesus knew the answer to this question, but according to His human nature, Jesus was expressing a question. "When I come, will I find faith on the earth? Or will it all have disappeared?" If He came today, would He find faith in your house? Would He find faith in your heart?

83

THE PHARISEE AND THE TAX COLLECTOR

Luke 18:9–14

He also told this parable to some who trusted in themselves that they were righteous, and treated others with contempt: "Two men went up into the temple to pray, one a Pharisee and the other a tax collector. The Pharisee, standing by himself, prayed thus: 'God, I thank you that I am not like other men, extortioners, unjust, adulterers, or even like this tax collector. I fast twice a week; I give tithes of all that I get.' But the tax collector, standing far off, would not even lift up his eyes to heaven, but beat his breast, saying, 'God, be merciful to me, a sinner!' I tell you, this man went down to his house justified, rather than the other. For everyone who exalts himself will be humbled, but the one who humbles himself will be exalted."

I cannot imagine any text more important than this one because it focuses on the issue of our eternal destiny. Some will hear and heed and spend eternity in heaven with Christ, and those who reject the message that our Lord gave in this parable will be among the doomed. Since our eternal destinies are on the line, I can't think of anything more important than for us to understand what Jesus said in this parable.

He also told this parable to some who trusted in themselves that they were righteous, and treated others with contempt (v. 9). In 1969, I worked in a church in Ohio as minister of theology and teaching. I also was the minister of evangelism, and I trained people in the Evangelism Explosion program for outreach. We took two hundred people into the community each Tuesday night, visited people in their homes, and presented the gospel to them. We used well-known diagnostic questions to begin the gospel conversation. The first one was this: "Have you come to a place where you know for sure that when you die you will go to heaven?" The large majority of people were not sure they were going to heaven.

The second question was this: "Suppose you were to die tonight and stand before God, and God asked, 'Why should I let you into My heaven?' What would you say?" We tabulated the answers of hundreds and hundreds of people, and 90 percent of them gave some kind of "works-righteousness" answer: "I tried to live a good life." "I went to church every Sunday." "I tithed my income." "I did this good work and performed that good work." Ninety percent of the people answered that they were trusting in their own righteousness.

Probably the worst answer ever given to that question was from my own five-year-old son. I said to him, "Son, if you were to die tonight and stand before God, and God asked, 'Why should I let you into My heaven?' what would you say?" My son answered, "Because I'm dead." My own son believed in justification by death, that all you have to do to go to heaven is die. In reality, that is the popular view of many. People are sinners until they die, and suddenly, they become saints when you attend their funerals and hear the stories that are told.

A Stark Contrast

"Two men went up into the temple to pray, one a Pharisee and the other a tax collector" (v. 10). Jesus introduced two men. They have the same mission initially—they both go to the temple to pray. There, for the most part, the similarities end, as the two men described here are revealed to be a stark contrast.

One is a Pharisee. The other is a tax collector. How different were they? The Pharisees were a group of people who separated themselves from the ordinary people, the people of the earth, and singularly devoted themselves to righteousness, to obeying the law, and they were meticulously scrupulous in their daily devotion to spiritual duties. The law required that the people fast twice a year. The Pharisees fasted twice a week. Zealous for obedience to God, they were regarded in the community as the spiritual leaders of the whole nation, yet it was this group of people who were most hostile to Jesus. These were the men who conspired to kill Him because they were counterfeit, and nothing exposes the counterfeit more quickly than the authentic. They pretended to be righteous. Jesus really was righteous, but they grew proud of their righteousness and boasted of it and displayed it publicly for all to see and to applaud.

The other man in the temple was a tax collector. When the Romans imposed taxes on people they conquered, they hired people from the conquered nation, from the Jews in this case, to go to their countrymen and collect the oppressive taxes. Tax collectors got rich on the commissions they made from serving Rome against their own people. They were the quislings of the day. When the people saw the tax collector, their hearts would swell with fury and hatred against him.

"The Pharisee, standing by himself, prayed thus: 'God, I thank you that I am not like other men, extortioners, unjust, adulterers, or even like this tax collector. I fast twice a week; I give tithes of all that I get'" (vv. 11–12). The Pharisee probably stood near the temple. He raised his head and his hands in prayer, and he thanked God that he was a righteous man. I wonder how much honesty was in that prayer of gratitude.

"But the tax collector, standing far off, would not even lift up his eyes to heaven, but beat his breast, saying, 'God, be merciful to me, a sinner!'" (v. 13). In contrast to the Pharisee, who said he'd never stolen, yet who stole the glory of God and who was not an atheist but was an idolater, stood the tax collector. He was probably by the door of the temple. He, in fear and trembling, wouldn't even lift his face up to heaven. His gaze was on the floor. He brought absolutely nothing to God but his sin. He had nothing to offer to God except his guilt.

"Be merciful. Have mercy. It's only by Your grace alone, not Your grace and my contribution." This man understood the doctrines of *sola fide* and *sola gratia*: justification by faith alone and justification by grace alone. There are tens of thousands of Christians in America today who will affirm justification by faith alone but not justification by grace alone. You really don't believe in justification by faith alone if you think you're adding something beyond your faith, beyond the righteousness of Christ, for you to be justified.

How to Be Justified

The ultimate difficulty that any human being will ever encounter is this: How can an unjust person stand in the presence of a just God at the last judgment? The only way we can stand is to be justified, to be declared just.

When we say that justification is by faith alone, that phrase is shorthand for justification by Christ alone. Faith is the sole instrument by which we grasp hold of Christ, and His justice is transferred to us. God imputes or counts the righteousness of Jesus to those who put their trust in Him. If you trust in yourself, you stand by yourself without Christ. The only way we can ever stand before a just and holy God is if we are clothed in the righteousness of Christ. We add nothing to it in and of ourselves.

The Bible says, "All our righteous deeds are like a polluted garment" (Isa. 64:6). The only One who ever possessed perfect righteousness was Jesus. Muhammad didn't; Confucius didn't; Buddha didn't. That's why there's only one way to God, because there's only One who has done what is required to get us to God—to justify us.

"I tell you, this man went down to his house justified, rather than the other. For everyone who exalts himself will be humbled, but the one who humbles himself will be exalted" (v. 14). The man who couldn't even look up into heaven or get near the Holy of Holies could only beat his chest and repent of his sin, plead for the mercy of God, and throw himself on the mercy of the court. This man walked out that door and went home justified. The Pharisee went home and continued to tithe and continued to fast, but he remained an unjustified person.

If you were to die tonight and stood before God, and He asked you, "Why should I let you into My heaven?" what would you say? I hope you would say, "Because of Jesus, because He's my only hope." Then He will look at you and say: "Please come in. My Son is already here, and He has prepared a place for you that you may bask in His glory now and forevermore."

84

LET THE CHILDREN COME

Luke 18:15–17

Now they were bringing even infants to him that he might touch them. And when the disciples saw it, they rebuked them. But Jesus called them to him, saying, "Let the children come to me, and do not hinder them, for to such belongs the kingdom of God. Truly, I say to you, whoever does not receive the kingdom of God like a child shall not enter it."

Now they were bringing even infants to him that he might touch them. And when the disciples saw it, they rebuked them (v. 15). Jesus had just told the parable of the Pharisee and the tax collector, which He concluded by saying, "Everyone who exalts himself will be humbled, but the one who humbles himself will be exalted" (v. 14). In the very next portion of the text is this incident of parents bringing their children and trying to get close to Jesus to have Him touch their children's heads and pronounce His blessing on them.

The disciples were annoyed. They were angry, and they were trying to prevent the little ones from coming to Jesus. They rebuked the parents, but Jesus turned around and rebuked them.

This has radical implications for infant baptism, but I won't get into that here. Jesus understood that the parents wanted Him to put His hand on their children's heads and pronounce a blessing upon them. He was not thinking that by placing His hand on a child's head He was bestowing salvation. But He did want these children set apart, consecrated, so they would grow up in the understanding and the nurture and the teaching of the things of God.

But Jesus called them to him, saying, "Let the children come to me, and do not hinder them, for to such belongs the kingdom of God. Truly, I say to you, whoever does not receive the kingdom of God like a child shall not enter it" (vv. 16–17). Jesus had been training the Twelve as His disciples, but they hadn't gotten it yet, as is evidenced by their hindering the children. His kingdom belongs to people such as those children. He didn't say that everyone who's an infant or a child is automatically in the kingdom of God. He said that people who are in the kingdom of God have to be like these little children.

It's interesting that Jesus said you have to be like a little child to get into the kingdom of God, because the New Testament has other things to say about children. On the one hand, it rebukes those who want to stay as children. Paul told the Corinthians, "I fed you with milk, not solid food, for you were not ready for it. And even now you are not yet ready" (1 Cor. 3:2). The author of Hebrews wrote: "For though by this time you ought to be teachers, you need someone to teach you again the basic principles of the oracles of God. You need milk, not solid food, for everyone who lives on milk is unskilled in the word of righteousness, since he is a child" (Heb. 5:12–13). We ought not be satisfied with milk. That's for infants, and as we grow into adulthood we ought to dig deeply into the Word of God, to the meat of Scripture, and be nurtured by the meat of the Word of God.

On the other hand, the New Testament commends maintaining a kind of childlike innocence. The Apostle Paul said, "Be infants in evil, but in your thinking be mature" (1 Cor. 14:20). We are told to be infants in evil, not grown-up, sophisticated, for-adults-only kind of sinners. Our sins should be the minor sins that are associated with babies and little children, not gross and horrendous sins that adults commit.

Childish vs. Childlike

Sometimes people say: "I don't want to get involved in the complexities of theology and that sort of thing. I want to just have a childlike faith." But there's a huge difference between a childlike faith and a childish faith. Paul said: "When I was a child, I spoke like a child, I thought like a child, I reasoned like a child. When I became a man, I gave up childish ways" (1 Cor. 13:11).

So, what was Jesus saying here? How are we to be childlike? The answer has to do with the question of authority and *fides implicita*, or implicit faith.

We talk about the terrible twos, that stage where children start to act out a desire for independence. But as they do so, they don't give us sophisticated arguments against our authority. For the most part, they trust our authority as parents even as they try to assert themselves. They trust that we will take care of them and that we have their best interests at heart.

That's what it means to have a childlike faith. It means to trust God implicitly, to believe that He cares for us and that He keeps His promises even if we don't understand all that He's doing. We ought not trust pastors implicitly. We ought not trust the church implicitly. We ought not trust the government implicitly. But we ought to trust God implicitly.

The Apostle John wrote, "If we confess our sins, he is faithful and just to forgive us our sins and to cleanse us from all unrighteousness" (1 John 1:9). How many times before you believe Him does God have to tell you that if you confess your sins to Him, He will forgive them? It's one thing to believe in God, but Christianity is all about believing God. The prophet Habakkuk said, "The righteous shall live by his faith" (Hab. 2:4). Three times that verse is repeated in the New Testament with respect to our salvation (Rom. 1:17; Gal. 3:11; Heb. 10:38), which means to be justified by faith means to be justified by trusting what God says.

That's the biggest problem we have. We don't believe what He says. We would prefer to sin than to obey Him because we don't believe that if we obey Him we can be happy. Not once in the history of the human race has sin brought happiness. It's brought pleasure but never happiness. When God gives His law, it's not because He's a killjoy; it's because He loves us and He knows what is good for us.

God wants from His children *fides implicita*, an implicit trust. And He is the only being who deserves implicit trust. Why shouldn't we trust Him implicitly? Has He ever lied? Has He ever broken a promise? Has he ever uttered a falsehood? His Word is truth. Trust it. That's what Jesus was saying here.

If you don't give that kind of trust to God, you're never going to enter the kingdom of God. Jesus took this opportunity with the little ones to say to the big ones, "Learn from the little ones, because this is how My kingdom is established."

85

THE RICH YOUNG RULER

Luke 18:18–30

And a ruler asked him, "Good Teacher, what must I do to inherit eternal life?" And Jesus said to him, "Why do you call me good? No one is good except God alone. You know the commandments: 'Do not commit adultery, Do not murder, Do not steal, Do not bear false witness, Honor your father and mother.' " And he said, "All these I have kept from my youth." When Jesus heard this, he said to him, "One thing you still lack. Sell all that you have and distribute to the poor, and you will have treasure in heaven; and come, follow me." But when he heard these things, he became very sad, for he was extremely rich. Jesus, seeing that he had become sad, said, "How difficult it is for those who have wealth to enter the kingdom of God! For it is easier for a camel to go through the eye of a needle than for a rich person to enter the kingdom of God." Those who heard it said, "Then who can be saved?" But he said, "What is impossible with man is possible with God." And Peter said, "See, we have left our homes and followed you." And he said to them, "Truly, I say to you, there is no one who has left house or wife or brothers or parents or children, for the sake of the kingdom of God, who will not receive many times more in this time, and in the age to come eternal life."

Jesus was used to multitudes thronging about Him pushing, shoving, trying to get close to Him, people screaming out of their agony of afflictions, the leper crying, "Lord, help us," or the blind and the deaf crying out to Him in their need. If we look at this story, not only in Luke's Gospel but compared with the accounts given to us by Matthew and Mark, we see that this man, known as the rich young ruler, came to Jesus not in a casual manner but with an intensity about him (see Mark 10:17). He didn't come asking to be healed of a malady. He wasn't sick as much as he was curious.

And a ruler asked him, "Good Teacher, what must I do to inherit eternal life?" (v. 18). What would prompt a man like this to rush to Jesus with this question? The Bible tells us that he was exceedingly rich (v. 23), he was young (Matt. 19:20), and he was a ruler with a significant amount of authority and power. From an earthly perspective, he had what everybody else wanted and sought to attain. He had all the wealth he would ever need. He had his youth, and he had power and authority.

But he wasn't satisfied. In one sense, this young man was wise beyond his years because he realized that he did not control his future absolutely. He knew that he did not have security that would last forever. We don't know how much he knew about Jesus, whether he had heard Jesus preach or seen Him perform miracles. I suspect from the context that he may have heard Jesus preach, because the most popular subject of which our Lord spoke in His teaching was the kingdom of God. That was the man's burning question: "How do I get into the kingdom of God? What do I have to do to gain the greatest inheritance that a human being could possibly have—the kingdom of God?"

Understanding What Is Good

This man was not going to be denied. He ran and fell on his knees before Jesus, pleading with Jesus to answer his question, **"Good Teacher, what must I do to inherit eternal life?"** Jesus offered a strange response: **"Why do you call me good? No one is good except God alone"** (v. 19).

Some critics look at this and say that Jesus was denying that He is God because He said that only God is good and since He rejected the appellation that He was a *good* teacher, He must therefore have been denying His deity. But this is by no means the case. Jesus understood that the rich young ruler did not know he was asking this question of God incarnate. From the young man's perspective, Jesus was merely a sagacious and good human being. Jesus said: "No, don't call Me good. You don't know the depth of what goodness is." He challenged the man for his loose understanding of goodness.

The rich young ruler didn't understand goodness, much as many people in the church don't understand it. We are still used to flattering ourselves as good people. We're back there in the temple like the Pharisees saying, "I thank you, Lord, that I'm not like that wretched tax collector over there," and we, disobeying the teaching of the Apostle Paul, judge ourselves by ourselves and judge ourselves among ourselves, and therefore we're not wise. We think that goodness is a relative term, and relative to the standards of this world, we are pretty good.

But God doesn't judge us by the standards of this world. God judges us by His own standard of holiness. The mandate He gives to His creatures is this: "Be holy, for I am holy" (Lev. 11:45). He doesn't lower the bar to accommodate us. He doesn't grade us on a curve. He grades our goodness according to the eternal standard of His own nature. When we are judged according to that standard, we fall short, far short, of the glory of God (Rom. 3:23).

"You know the commandments: 'Do not commit adultery, Do not murder, Do not steal, Do not bear false witness, Honor your father and mother' " (v. 20). Jesus next tested the man's understanding of what goodness is and how it's considered. He did so by looking to the Ten Commandments. But the man was not impressed. **And he said, "All these I have kept from my youth"** (v. 21). Jesus could have told him that if he understood the depth of the implication of the commandments, he would know that he hadn't kept one of the commandments since he rose from his bed that morning. "Don't you realize," Jesus could have said, "that if you have any thought of lust, you have violated the law against adultery, and if you've hated or been angry with somebody without just cause, you've violated the law against murder?" (Matt. 5:21–30). He didn't do that. He selected a few of the commandments and mentioned them to the young man.

Treasuring God's Kingdom

When Jesus heard this, he said to him, "One thing you still lack. Sell all that you have and distribute to the poor, and you will have treasure in heaven; and come, follow me" (v. 22). Jesus did not rebuke the young man for his naivete but said to him that he lacked one thing. Why did Jesus say that? He did not mean that everybody has to embrace poverty to be His follower. God did not require of Abraham that he divest himself of his possessions. Joseph of Arimathea was welcome in the kingdom of God without giving away his wealth. So why did Jesus say that?

The man had just claimed to have followed all of the Ten Commandments from his youth. So, Jesus started with commandment number one: "You shall have no other gods before me" (Ex. 20:3). He tested the young man about his other "god" that was before Him: the young man's riches. Jesus told him to give it all away.

But when he heard these things, he became very sad, for he was extremely rich (v. 23). The rich young ruler ran to Jesus with joyous anticipation; he walked away from Jesus totally disappointed. This man kept his money and he lost the kingdom—the worst transaction he ever made in his life. His value system was empty and futile. We should be able to give everything we have and do anything we can if it means inheriting the kingdom of God. Jesus said, "For what will it profit a man if he gains the whole world and forfeits his soul?" (Matt. 16:26). This man walked away, unable to give up his riches.

Jesus, seeing that he had become sad, said, "How difficult it is for those who have wealth to enter the kingdom of God! For it is easier for a camel to go through the eye of a needle than for a rich person to enter the kingdom of God" (vv. 24–25). What a strange comparison, and what an interesting metaphor. What did Jesus mean? It is said that in the ancient world there was a particularly narrow gate among the many gates around Jerusalem, and it was called the Eye of the Needle. Sometimes merchants would try to get their camels through this narrow gate into the city. When the camel didn't fit, the merchant would have to take all the merchandise off the camel's back and use the stick to get the camel to kneel down into the dirt and slide its knees forward to get through this gate.

There's probably no truth to that at all. I think that Jesus was simply painting a vivid picture of the largest animal the people were familiar with trying to pass through one of the smallest apertures that they would know. It is unfathomable how a camel could go through the eye of a needle, and yet Jesus said it is even harder for a rich man to get into the kingdom of God. In other words, the more riches you have, the less possibility there is that you'll be redeemed.

Those who heard it said, "Then who can be saved?" (v. 26). This idea was unthinkable to the people, for they tended to consider riches a sign of God's blessing. It seemed that no one could be saved, for even people with meager possessions clung to them tightly and longed to make them increase.

But he said, "What is impossible with man is possible with God" (v. 27). It was not just riches that were the problem, but it was good works and good intentions also. Nothing of what we have is good enough to get us through the eye of a needle. It is impossible to work our way into heaven. But what's impossible with us is possible with God. That's one of the greatest definitions of grace that Jesus gives us—that God's grace does for us what we cannot possibly do for ourselves. God's grace overcomes our sin and gets us safely home.

And Peter said, "See, we have left our homes and followed you." And he said to them, "Truly, I say to you, there is no one who has left house or wife or brothers or parents or children, for the sake of the kingdom of God, who will not receive many times more in this time, and in the age to come eternal life" (vv. 28–30). Jesus promises that those who follow Him will be blessed in ways they cannot imagine, ways that will make our worldly wealth seem paltry by comparison.

86

THE BLIND MAN

Luke 18:31–43

And taking the twelve, he said to them, "See, we are going up to Jerusalem, and everything that is written about the Son of Man by the prophets will be accomplished. For he will be delivered over to the Gentiles and will be mocked and shamefully treated and spit upon. And after flogging him, they will kill him, and on the third day he will rise." But they understood none of these things. This saying was hidden from them, and they did not grasp what was said.

As he drew near to Jericho, a blind man was sitting by the roadside begging. And hearing a crowd going by, he inquired what this meant. They told him, "Jesus of Nazareth is passing by." And he cried out, "Jesus, Son of David, have mercy on me!" And those who were in front rebuked him, telling him to be silent. But he cried out all the more, "Son of David, have mercy on me!" And Jesus stopped and commanded him to be brought to him. And when he came near, he asked him, "What do you want me to do for you?" He said, "Lord, let me recover my sight." And Jesus said to him, "Recover your sight; your faith has made you well." And immediately he recovered his sight and followed him, glorifying God. And all the people, when they saw it, gave praise to God.

And taking the twelve, he said to them, "See, we are going up to Jerusalem, and everything that is written about the Son of Man by the prophets will be accomplished. For he will be delivered over to the Gentiles and will be mocked and shamefully treated and spit

upon. And after flogging him, they will kill him, and on the third day he will rise" (vv. 31–33). This text begins ominously. Jesus and His disciples were making their way south from Galilee and were nearing Jerusalem, and Jesus for the third time told His disciples what would soon take place.

The message that He gave is a grim one, and they didn't understand it. In Caesarea Philippi, after Peter's confession was made and the disciples had enjoyed the glorious time on the Mount of Transfiguration, Jesus told them: "It's time to go to Jerusalem, where I will be handed over to the Gentiles. I will suffer and be killed." It is then that we have Peter's response, "No, we're not going to do this." At that time, Jesus changed Peter's name again when He said, "Get behind me, Satan!" (Matt. 16:23).

But they understood none of these things. This saying was hidden from them, and they did not grasp what was said (v. 34). There's something strange about this text. Jesus told them what was going to happen, and the disciples didn't understand what He said because it **was hidden from them**. If Jesus knew it was going to be hidden from them, why did He tell them? The reason is probably so that they would understand after it had all taken place. In addition, it is for our edification today as we read of these events two thousand years later. Remember, after the resurrection, Jesus in His discussion on the road to Emmaus began with Moses and went through the Prophets and showed how He had fulfilled, in detail, with meticulous fullness, each of the Old Testament predictions (24:27, 44). It was only after the scales were removed from the eyes of the disciples that they remembered these things.

A Blind Man Calls to Jesus

As he drew near to Jericho, a blind man was sitting by the roadside begging (v. 35). Luke next described the events as they came near Jericho. Matthew and Mark wrote of Jesus' coming out of Jericho (Matt. 20:29; Mark 10:46), while Luke said He was coming into Jericho. There is a simple solution to this seeming discrepancy. New Testament Jericho is built adjacent to the ruins of Old Testament Jericho, and sometimes the Jews referred to the Jericho from the Old Testament, and sometimes they referred to the Jericho from the New Testament. In order to get into the New Testament Jericho, they had to go out of Old Testament Jericho.

Matthew's Gospel tells us that there were two blind men (Matt. 20:30). Mark makes specific reference to Bartimaeus, who was likely the leader of the two in Matthew's account (Mark 10:46). Luke mentions only one of the two, probably Bartimaeus, but he does not name him.

If the man was born blind, he had never seen anything but darkness. When people would describe the sunset or the waterfall or other people, he had no meaningful reference to understand what they were saying. If he had been able to see and then lost his sight, he of course would have had the memories of vision and then could relate to descriptions of things. In any case, his present experience was that he had no sight.

And hearing a crowd going by, he inquired what this meant. They told him, "Jesus of Nazareth is passing by" (vv. 36–37). The man sat by the road begging for alms by which he might live. Because he was blind, he could not earn a living by doing anything except begging. As some people passed him, they would have mercy and drop alms in his hand. This day he could hear the tumultuous sound of a huge crowd approaching, and he asked someone what it meant. They told him, "Jesus is coming." Notice that the man didn't need to say, "Who's that?" By this time, news of Jesus had spread across the whole country. People had told the blind man about this Jesus who had given hearing to the deaf and sight to the blind and raised people from the dead.

You can imagine that in his darkness, he would have a dream that "Someday, Jesus of Nazareth will pass this way." The only hope this man had to receive his sight rested in Jesus of Nazareth. He knew there was no cure, but he had heard the stories. And now his hope was realized. **And he cried out, "Jesus, Son of David, have mercy on me!" And those who were in front rebuked him, telling him to be silent. But he cried out all the more, "Son of David, have mercy on me!"** (vv. 38–39).

And Jesus stopped and commanded him to be brought to him. And when he came near, he asked him, "What do you want me to do for you?" (vv. 40–41). Jesus, of course, could tell he was blind. Why would Jesus take the time to ask him what he wanted? Everybody was in a hurry, so why didn't Jesus just stop, touch the man, say, "Let your sight be restored," and then go on His way? That's not what He did. Instead, He asked him, **"What do you want me to do for you?"**

True Healing

He said, "Lord, let me recover my sight" (v. 41). Bartimaeus gave the completely wrong answer—an answer that was expected and understandable, one that you would expect a blind man to say when Jesus asked what he wanted Him to do. Of course, the man, being human, is going to say, **"Let me recover my sight."**

If Jesus said to you, "What can I do for you?" what would you say to Him? "Lord, I lost my job. I need a new job." "Lord, my marriage is in trouble. I need to be healed in my marriage." "Lord, I was just diagnosed with terminal cancer. Will You heal me?" If we understand anything about Jesus, we should say to Him: "Jesus, Son of David, have mercy on me. Cover me with Your righteousness. Without it, I'm going to stand before Your Father dressed in filthy rags or naked and ashamed. Save me. Give me what I need the most: Your righteousness, without which I will never enter Your kingdom." Or you could put it another way: "Give me saving faith. Justify me before the Father. It's not my eyes, Lord. It's not my ears. It's not my leprosy. It's my soul. Heal my soul. Take away the darkness from my soul."

And Jesus said to him, "Recover your sight; your faith has made you well" (v. 42). Commentators are a little bit perplexed by this. Jesus gave him what he asked for, but then He added, **"Your faith has made you well."** This could be translated "Your faith has saved you." He may have been saying simply, "Your trust in Me has gotten you past your blindness." Or it may be that Jesus gave this man much more than his ability to see; He gave him Himself.

I'm inclined toward that second view because of what follows. **And immediately he recovered his sight and followed him, glorifying God. And all the people, when they saw it, gave praise to God** (v. 43). If Jesus has given you what you need the most, then is it not the sensible thing to follow Him and to glorify God?

87

ZACCHAEUS

Luke 19:1–10

He entered Jericho and was passing through. And behold, there was a man named Zacchaeus. He was a chief tax collector and was rich. And he was seeking to see who Jesus was, but on account of the crowd he could not, because he was small in stature. So he ran on ahead and climbed up into a sycamore tree to see him, for he was about to pass that way. And when Jesus came to the place, he looked up and said to him, "Zacchaeus, hurry and come down, for I must stay at your house today." So he hurried and came down and received him joyfully. And when they saw it, they all grumbled, "He has gone in to be the guest of a man who is a sinner." And Zacchaeus stood and said to the Lord, "Behold, Lord, the half of my goods I give to the poor. And if I have defrauded anyone of anything, I restore it fourfold." And Jesus said to him, "Today salvation has come to this house, since he also is a son of Abraham. For the Son of Man came to seek and to save the lost."

He entered Jericho and was passing through. And behold, there was a man named Zacchaeus. He was a chief tax collector and was rich. And he was seeking to see who Jesus was, but on account of the crowd he could not, because he was small in stature. So he ran on ahead and climbed up into a sycamore tree to see him, for he was about to pass that way (vv. 1–4). Zacchaeus is one of the most popular characters in the New Testament, at least among children, if for no other reason than the song they learned in Sunday school: "Zacchaeus was a wee little man, a wee little man was he. He climbed up in the sycamore tree, the Lord he wanted to see."

Why was Zacchaeus up in that tree? There are several different answers that we can give to the question, some of which are simple and superficial, some others of which are more significant. The first answer is that he was in New Testament Jericho, which was a town built on a large oasis. Unlike the desolate wilderness of most of Judea, this village had lush vegetation because of the plenitude of water available. It included among the vegetation sycamore trees. So the first answer to the question Why was he in the tree? is because it was there.

Second, the Scriptures tell us why Zacchaeus was in the tree: because **he was small in stature** (v. 3) and he wanted to see Jesus. Clearly, he had heard about Jesus and wanted to know more about Him. Zacchaeus also was aware that everywhere Jesus went, He was surrounded by huge crowds who wanted to see Jesus' latest miracle or to hear the uncanny teaching that would come from His lips. Out of curiosity and out of necessity, Zacchaeus climbed a tree. If he were mixed up in the large crowds, he wouldn't be able to catch a glimpse of Jesus over the people in front of him.

There's still a third reason Zacchaeus was in the tree: he was a tax collector, and not only a tax collector but a **chief tax collector** (v. 2). Tax collectors were some of the most hated and unpopular people in all of Israel because they worked for the Roman occupiers and extorted heavy taxes from the people. Tax collectors were considered collaborators, traitors to their own people. To be a tax collector was to be despised, and to be a chief tax collector was even worse. To escape the hostility and perhaps danger of the crowd, he escaped to safety in the tree.

There was a more significant reason for Zacchaeus to have been in the tree. It wasn't necessarily so that Zacchaeus could see Jesus; rather, it was so that Jesus could see Zacchaeus. According to His human nature, Jesus had probably never before laid eyes on this little man. However, according to His divine nature, Jesus not only knew Zacchaeus, but He knew him from the foundation of the world.

And when Jesus came to the place, he looked up and said to him, "Zacchaeus, hurry and come down, for I must stay at your house today" (v. 5). We know from the Old Testament that the Jewish people, by the mandate of God, placed a premium on hospitality, and it is not unreasonable that Jesus was looking for a place to stay that night. But notice that Jesus didn't say, "Zacchaeus, please extend to Me an invitation to your house for dinner." It wasn't because He was hungry that He wanted to see Zacchaeus.

There's something deeper here in the text. He used the word **"must."** This suggests a necessity. There was an urgency behind Jesus' words. He was saying,

"It is imperative that I come to your house," and we are told the reason for that imperative at the end of this story: **"For the Son of Man came to seek and to save the lost"** (v. 10), especially those who were from the household of Abraham. Jesus said Zacchaeus was **"a son of Abraham"** (v. 9). As interested and as curious as Zacchaeus may have been about the person and the teaching of Jesus, he was a lost man until Jesus came to his house.

In John's Gospel, Jesus said:

> "I am the bread of life; whoever comes to me shall not hunger, and whoever believes in me shall never thirst. But I said to you that you have seen me and yet do not believe. All that the Father gives me will come to me, and whoever comes to me I will never cast out. For I have come down from heaven, not to do my own will but the will of him who sent me. And this is the will of him who sent me, that I should lose nothing of all that he has given me, but raise it up on the last day." (6:35–39)

This is the doctrine of election. Jesus said something profound—and in many cases repugnant to those who heard it—when He said this.

Jesus entered Jericho, looked in the sycamore tree, and saw one whom the Father had given to Him from the foundation of the world. "Zacchaeus, I know who you are. You are one of My sheep. Get down from that tree. I must come to your house, because we have business together of the greatest urgency."

So he hurried and came down and received him joyfully. And when they saw it, they all grumbled, "He has gone in to be the guest of a man who is a sinner." And Zacchaeus stood and said to the Lord, "Behold, Lord, the half of my goods I give to the poor. And if I have defrauded anyone of anything, I restore it fourfold." And Jesus said to him, "Today salvation has come to this house, since he also is a son of Abraham" (vv. 6–9). Zacchaeus came down and Jesus went to his house. But there were many people whom Jesus visited—Pharisees, tax collectors, and various people with whom He met who were lost—and He left them, still lost. Beautiful in this text are the words **"Today salvation has come to this house"** (v. 9).

Has salvation come to your house? I'm not asking whether Jesus has visited your house; I'm asking whether He has brought salvation to your house. On that day, the election of Zacchaeus was realized in space and time. He met his Savior, and he received salvation from Him.

88

THE PARABLE OF THE MINAS

Luke 19:11–27

As they heard these things, he proceeded to tell a parable, because he was near to Jerusalem, and because they supposed that the kingdom of God was to appear immediately. He said therefore, "A nobleman went into a far country to receive for himself a kingdom and then return. Calling ten of his servants, he gave them ten minas, and said to them, 'Engage in business until I come.' But his citizens hated him and sent a delegation after him, saying, 'We do not want this man to reign over us.' When he returned, having received the kingdom, he ordered these servants to whom he had given the money to be called to him, that he might know what they had gained by doing business. The first came before him, saying, 'Lord, your mina has made ten minas more.' And he said to him, 'Well done, good servant! Because you have been faithful in a very little, you shall have authority over ten cities.' And the second came, saying, 'Lord, your mina has made five minas.' And he said to him, 'And you are to be over five cities.' Then another came, saying, 'Lord, here is your mina, which I kept laid away in a handkerchief; for I was afraid of you, because you are a severe man. You take what you did not deposit, and reap what you did not sow.' He said to him, 'I will condemn you with your own words, you wicked servant! You knew that I was a severe man, taking what I did not deposit and reaping what I did not sow? Why then did you not put my money in the bank, and at my coming I might have collected it with interest?' And he said to those who stood by, 'Take the mina from him, and give it to the one who has the ten minas.' And they said to him, 'Lord, he has ten minas!' 'I tell you that to everyone who has, more will be given, but from the one who has not, even what he has will be taken away. But as for these enemies of mine, who did not want me to reign over them, bring them here and slaughter them before me.' "

It was the year 4 BC when the king died. He was called King Herod the Great, but upon his death, the people under his subjugation were not saying, "The king is dead; long live the king." They hated Herod, and they did not consider him great at all because he was a tyrant. When he died, little relief was experienced by the people. He divided his kingdom into four parts, with each of his four sons reigning over a part. To his son Archelaus he gave the portion that included Judea and the city of Jerusalem.

Archelaus continued the brutal policies of his father. Just a few months after he ascended the throne, when the pilgrims massed into Jerusalem for the annual celebration of the Passover, Archelaus was responsible for the slaughter of three thousand Jews. Because of that great slaughter, not only was the Passover disrupted, but many of the worshipers fled in order to escape with their lives and did not finish the celebration of the Passover.

Commentators almost universally agree that the backdrop for this parable was the incident that had taken place in 4 BC in Jerusalem. Archelaus had built an enormous palace in the town of Jericho as well as an aqueduct. The people remembered with bitterness the brutality that had been committed by Archelaus and the atrocities that had been visited upon them.

As they heard these things, he proceeded to tell a parable, because he was near to Jerusalem, and because they supposed that the kingdom of God was to appear immediately (v. 11). This parable provided the occasion for Jesus to tell His hearers that the kingdom that had been promised, that would come from heaven, was not going to happen immediately; there would be a period of time wherein a delay would take place between that present moment and the final coming of the kingdom.

He said therefore, "A nobleman went into a far country to receive for himself a kingdom and then return" (v. 12). When King Herod died, Archelaus, in order to receive the legacy that his father intended for him, could not be given the title of king unless it was approved by the emperor of Rome, so Archelaus took the journey to Rome in order to receive the appointment and title of king. Because of the slaughter that had taken place under Archelaus, fifty delegates of the Jewish community went to Rome to plead with the emperor that he not give the title to Archelaus, saying that Archelaus was a brutal ruler and they didn't want him to rule over them.

There was a compromise of sorts. Archelaus was given the authority to continue his reign over the people, but he was given only the title of tetrarch and not the title of king. Caesar mollified the Jewish protesters by not giving the title that Archelaus desired, but all the responsibility and the power within the kingdom was given to this wicked man nonetheless. Of course, once the delegation returned to Jerusalem and Archelaus came back, he subjected the delegates to further punishment and brutality.

"Calling ten of his servants, he gave them ten minas, and said to them, 'Engage in business until I come'" (v. 13). Thinking of Archelaus, who went to receive for himself a kingdom and then came back, Jesus told the story of a nobleman who called ten of his servants and gave them each a mina, which was a unit of currency. This parable is similar to but not exactly the same as Matthew's parable of the talents (Matt. 25:14–30). A talent was a monetary unit in antiquity, but the word comes down to us not as a description of money but as a word that is used to describe an ability or a gift. This ruler gave ten of his servants one mina each, and he said to them, "While I am absent from you, I want you to produce gains from the money that I am entrusting to you."

"But his citizens hated him and sent a delegation after him, saying, 'We do not want this man to reign over us'" (v. 14). This is again a reference to Archelaus and the opposition to his rule that rose up when he sought to inherit part of his father's kingdom.

The Principle of Stewardship

"When he returned, having received the kingdom, he ordered these servants to whom he had given the money to be called to him, that he might know what they had gained by doing business" (v. 15). The nobleman returned to see what his servants had done with his money. Here we see that this parable is about the principle of stewardship, which we find throughout the New Testament. Stewardship has to do with how we handle our resources. When it comes to the resources of nations and how they should be handled, there is debate regarding the competing economic systems of socialism and capitalism.

There are varieties of socialism. It isn't a monolithic movement, and I believe that historical attempts to bring socialism to bear have often been motivated by a concern for people who are impoverished and oppressed. However, it has not once been effective anywhere in the world, and each time it has been attempted, it has only increased poverty and oppression.

In the middle of the twentieth century, there was a theological movement that attracted widespread attention called liberation theology. It flourished predominantly in South America, though its impact was felt in Western and Eastern Europe, as well as in the United States. Liberation theology was conceived as a conscious attempt to synthesize historic Christianity and Marxist philosophy. If ever there was a fool's errand, this was it, because historic Christianity is utterly, completely, irreversibly, irrevocably incompatible with the tenets of Marxism. Certain things were compromised in Marxism and other things were compromised in Christianity in order to create this blended view. It gave rise to various liberation movements such as gay liberation and feminist theology.

Through liberation theology, it was expected that people would become free and would experience racial, economic, political, and sexual equality. The idea was to take from one group of people what they own and give it to another group of people who do not have as much. This is called redistribution of wealth. In the classroom, it would be similar to a professor giving everyone a C even though some studied while the others did not do the work. That's equal, but it's not at all just.

There are also varieties of capitalism. Not all systems of capitalism are the same either. There are some systems that thrive on greed and exploitation. But when we look at the Scriptures, the economic principle we find is what is called stewardship capitalism. There is a sense in which the Bible teaches the sanctity of private property, which is protected by two of the Ten Commandments, as the eighth commandment prohibits theft and the tenth commandment prohibits covetousness. Also, throughout the New Testament the biblical ethic is concerned with stewardship, the idea being anything we have, anything we have received, and any benefit or physical possession we have comes from God; we ultimately don't own it. God owns it, and He gives it to us as stewards in His kingdom, and we are expected to make good use of it.

The principle that we find in this parable is the principle of productivity. Remember that the very first commandment that God gave the human race was "Be fruitful and multiply" (Gen. 1:28). In the kingdom of God, the spiritual premise is repeated that what God has given to us by His grace was intended to be multiplied, that Christians have been saved not by their works but unto works—that is, we are saved for the purpose of doing what is good and helpful for all the human race. We are stewards of the kingdom of God.

"The first came before him, saying, 'Lord, your mina has made ten minas more.' And he said to him, 'Well done, good servant! Because you have been faithful in a very little, you shall have authority over ten cities'" (vv. 16–17). The master commended the first servant for not wasting the resources entrusted to him but rather putting his capital to work, which is a principle that is the very heart of capitalism. The idea is you live on less than you make, and whatever is left over, you invest. And while you're sleeping, your capital is working. Your earnings have become productive. The Lord wants us to be profitable servants, servants who tend whatever we receive so that it grows and multiplies for the benefit of the kingdom of God.

"And the second came, saying, 'Lord, your mina has made five minas.' And he said to him, 'And you are to be over five cities'" (vv. 18–19). The second servant likewise put his capital to work and was rewarded accordingly.

"Then another came, saying, 'Lord, here is your mina, which I kept laid away in a handkerchief; for I was afraid of you, because you are a severe man. You take what you did not deposit, and reap what you did not sow.' He said to him, 'I will condemn you with your own words, you wicked servant! You knew that I was a severe man, taking what I did not deposit and reaping what I did not sow? Why then did you not put my money in the bank, and at my coming I might have collected it with interest?' And he said to those who stood by, 'Take the mina from him, and give it to the one who has the ten minas.' And they said to him, 'Lord, he has ten minas!'" (vv. 20–25). That's not equal distribution of wealth. God is not going to reward laziness or slothfulness.

The Call to Work

The Bible is much concerned about the plight of poor people, and there are many people who are poor not because they were lazy but because of catastrophe. God's heart is concerned for the well-being and the care of those who are in poverty because of exploitation and because they've been oppressed. It's false to assume that anybody who's poor is poor because they're slothful. That's just not true. On the other hand, there are many people who are poor because they're lazy. In the kingdom of God there is never a license for laziness. Salvation is never a license for sloth. We are called as Christian people to work, to be productive and to multiply what God has given to us.

We are not saved by our works, but we are saved for works. We are saved by our Savior—who has entrusted us with the precious "pearl of great value" (Matt. 13:46) and the things of the kingdom of God—to preach, to teach, and to minister, not to waste our lives for a second.

"'I tell you that to everyone who has, more will be given, but from the one who has not, even what he has will be taken away. But as for these enemies of mine, who did not want me to reign over them, bring them here and slaughter them before me'" (vv. 26–27). Jesus said that those who didn't want Him to be their King will be destroyed before His very eyes, but those who are saved are invited to participate in the full fruits of His kingdom and to enjoy the benefits of His reign over heaven and earth, as even this day He calls us to enjoy the benefits of His salvation.

89

THE TRIUMPHAL ENTRY

Luke 19:28–40

And when he had said these things, he went on ahead, going up to Jerusalem. When he drew near to Bethphage and Bethany, at the mount that is called Olivet, he sent two of the disciples, saying, "Go into the village in front of you, where on entering you will find a colt tied, on which no one has ever yet sat. Untie it and bring it here. If anyone asks you, 'Why are you untying it?' you shall say this: 'The Lord has need of it.' " So those who were sent went away and found it just as he had told them. And as they were untying the colt, its owners said to them, "Why are you untying the colt?" And they said, "The Lord has need of it." And they brought it to Jesus, and throwing their cloaks on the colt, they set Jesus on it. And as he rode along, they spread their cloaks on the road. As he was drawing near—already on the way down the Mount of Olives—the whole multitude of his disciples began to rejoice and praise God with a loud voice for all the mighty works that they had seen, saying, "Blessed is the King who comes in the name of the Lord! Peace in heaven and glory in the highest!" And some of the Pharisees in the crowd said to him, "Teacher, rebuke your disciples." He answered, "I tell you, if these were silent, the very stones would cry out."

Scholars have examined the manifold prophecies that are found throughout the Scriptures that have their fulfillment in the historical Jesus. Some scholars have counted somewhere between 1,000 and 1,200 prophecies with respect to the coming Messiah that were clearly and definitively fulfilled in the life and ministry of Jesus. In fact, that very truth of the fulfillment of specific prophecies should be enough to stop the mouths of the most obstreperous skeptics. That should be proof enough for the claims of Christ to being the Son of God and the coming Messiah.

And when he had said these things, he went on ahead, going up to Jerusalem. When he drew near to Bethphage and Bethany, at the mount that is called Olivet, he sent two of the disciples, saying, "Go into the village in front of you, where on entering you will find a colt tied, on which no one has ever yet sat. Untie it and bring it here. If anyone asks you, 'Why are you untying it?' you shall say this: 'The Lord has need of it.'" So those who were sent went away and found it just as he had told them. And as they were untying the colt, its owners said to them, "Why are you untying the colt?" And they said, "The Lord has need of it" (vv. 28–34). What is unique about the event recounted in this passage is that Jesus went out of His way to orchestrate the fulfillment of a particular prophecy. He didn't do anything extraordinary to make sure that He was born in Bethlehem as was foretold by the prophecy of Micah (Mic. 5:2; Matt. 2:1–6). That fulfillment had to do with the providence of God and the decree of Caesar Augustus for people to return to their city of their birth in order to be enrolled for purposes of taxation. The baby Jesus, according to His human nature, knew nothing of that imperial decree, and so He did nothing to purposefully fulfill the prophecy of the circumstances of His birth.

Here, as an adult, Jesus took matters into His own hands. He knew the Old Testament prophecy found in Zechariah: "Rejoice greatly, O daughter of Zion! Shout aloud, O daughter of Jerusalem! Behold, your king is coming to you; righteous and having salvation is he, humble and mounted on a donkey, on a colt, the foal of a donkey" (Zech. 9:9). Jesus went out of His way to make certain that all the details of that prophecy were precisely fulfilled as they had been spoken hundreds of years before.

Why all this extensive activity to prepare the staging of a fulfillment of prophecy? We have to understand that in terms of the life of Jesus, there is this major parenthesis that takes place between His birth and His death, and that parenthesis has to do with God's kingdom. Remember that in the parable of the minas, Jesus told of the nobleman who was going on a journey and he gave some money to his servants to be invested wisely in his absence. Luke says that Jesus told that parable because His kingdom was not going to come immediately (19:11). He knew that the multitudes expected the coming of the kingdom immediately, and He gave that parable to explain the idea of a delay between Jesus' going away and His return to finally establish His kingdom.

Soon after teaching this parable, Jesus orchestrated this dramatic event that had everything to do with the concept of a kingdom that is coming.

In Matthew's record of the nativity of Jesus, he tells the incident of the coming of the wise men who saw and followed an extraordinary star. The testimony of the wise men, once they arrived in Jerusalem, was that they were trying to locate the stopping place of the star that had guided them, and they inquired, "Where is he who has been born king of the Jews?" (Matt. 2:2).

When Herod understood what was occurring, he inquired of those who were seeking the birth of this new king where He would be found. He asked his scholars to look up the Scriptures to tell him what the location would be of the coming Messiah, and they came to the book of Micah. The scholars informed Herod, "The Messiah will be born in Bethlehem of Judea."

Herod hypocritically and maliciously gave directions to the wise men on how to find the town of Bethlehem, which was about six miles away from Jerusalem, and he said, "Go and search diligently for the child, and when you have found him, bring me word, that I too may come and worship him" (Matt. 2:8). This Herod, who had already killed three of his sons and one wife, had no intention of coming to give homage to the newborn King. Nothing rankled King Herod more than the thought of somebody else succeeding in kingship over the succession plan that he had devised.

After the wise men left and found the Christ child, they were warned not to go back to Herod, learning that Herod intended to come and assassinate the Christ child, and so they fled. When the wise men failed to appear, Herod issued a decree that every male child under two years of age would be executed in the environs of Bethlehem. This is known as the Slaughter of the Innocents (Matt. 2:16).

Fast-forward from the birth of Jesus to the end of His life, where the issue of kingship was still central. Before Jesus arrived in Jerusalem and after the transfiguration, He said to His disciples, "The Son of Man is about to be delivered into the hands of men" (Matt. 17:22; Luke 9:44). With grim anticipation of what was before them, the disciples with heavy hearts moved toward Jerusalem to see what fate awaited Jesus.

Jesus knew what awaited Him in Jerusalem, what was going to take place in hours from that Sunday morning when He came in triumph into Jerusalem. Jesus arrived not as a King on a war horse but as One who was meek and lowly, riding on a donkey.

And they brought it to Jesus, and throwing their cloaks on the colt, they set Jesus on it. And as he rode along, they spread their cloaks on the road. As he was drawing near—already on the way down the Mount of Olives—the

whole multitude of his disciples began to rejoice and praise God with a loud voice for all the mighty works that they had seen, saying, "Blessed is the King who comes in the name of the Lord! Peace in heaven and glory in the highest!" (vv. 35–38). The people in the crowd knew the Scriptures, and when Jesus appeared riding the donkey, they gathered in a huge multitude rejoicing and praising God for the mighty works they had seen. "The Messiah has come, and He's coming now to take His place as the King of the Jews, as the King of Israel. Hosanna; blessed is He who comes in the name of the Lord." They put their garments in the path in front of Him as He rode on the donkey.

Jesus knew where He was going and what was waiting for Him at the end of the week. He knew of His betrayal—He would be turned over to the Romans, and He would stand before Pontius Pilate.

Jesus didn't think for a moment that there would be a revolution and that He was going to seize power and be crowned King of the Jews. The people didn't understand, but He did, and He had just told them a parable that the kingdom was not going to come immediately. But they didn't understand that either. Though there were smiles abounding on the faces of the crowd and they were cheering in ecstasy, Jesus rode with a heavy heart, knowing what His destiny was in the hours that lay before Him.

And some of the Pharisees in the crowd said to him, "Teacher, rebuke your disciples" (v. 39). To add insult to injury, as the people cheered with gusto, the Pharisees said: "These are Your disciples. You're their master. Tell them to be quiet." But Jesus understood that the whole creation groaned in agony waiting for the redemption that Christ alone would bring—He was not only the King and Savior of the Jews but also the King of the cosmos. Going back to that parable of the one who went into the far country to be called a king—at the end the nobleman said judgment would come on those who hated him and did not want him to reign over them.

He answered, "I tell you, if these were silent, the very stones would cry out" (v. 40). Jesus said to the Pharisees: "You don't understand. If My disciples are silent, even the stones will cry out, 'Blessed is He who comes in the name of the Lord. This is our King, the King of all creation.'"

We know, of course, that stones don't have mouths or lips; they're inanimate objects. But remember, in Genesis, after Cain killed Abel, God came to Cain and said: "What have you done? The voice of your brother's blood is crying to me from the ground" (Gen. 4:10). Metaphor? Hyperbole? Perhaps. Or did that blood have a voice that could be heard by almighty God?

90

JESUS WEEPS OVER JERUSALEM

Luke 19:41–48

And when he drew near and saw the city, he wept over it, saying, "Would that you, even you, had known on this day the things that make for peace! But now they are hidden from your eyes. For the days will come upon you, when your enemies will set up a barricade around you and surround you and hem you in on every side and tear you down to the ground, you and your children within you. And they will not leave one stone upon another in you, because you did not know the time of your visitation."

And he entered the temple and began to drive out those who sold, saying to them, "It is written, 'My house shall be a house of prayer,' but you have made it a den of robbers."

And he was teaching daily in the temple. The chief priests and the scribes and the principal men of the people were seeking to destroy him, but they did not find anything they could do, for all the people were hanging on his words.

And when he drew near and saw the city, he wept over it, saying, "Would that you, even you, had known on this day the things that make for peace!" (vv. 41–42). This passage is connected to the account of Jesus' triumphal entry into Jerusalem. While everybody else was rejoicing, Jesus was in a spirit of lamentation. When He drew near and saw the city, our

Lord wept. While the sounds of "Hosanna" were ringing in His ears, His eyes were filled with tears as He beheld Jerusalem, the City of Peace.

He knew the people in that city knew no peace. Just as on another occasion He had lamented: "O Jerusalem, Jerusalem, the city that kills the prophets and stones those who are sent to it! How often would I have gathered your children together as a hen gathers her brood under her wings, and you were not willing!" (13:34). Here, He mourned afresh when He considered what these people had missed.

Jesus loved this city of Jerusalem. He remembered visiting the city as a young boy of twelve (2:41–51). His parents started home, accidentally leaving their son behind. When they returned to the city to find Him, they were amazed to discover their young son astounding the scholars and the rabbis by His prodigious knowledge of Scripture and the things of God. In one sense, the young boy Jesus began teaching in the temple that day and must have recalled the occasion.

The Coming Destruction

"Would that you, even you, had known on this day the things that make for peace! But now they are hidden from your eyes. For the days will come upon you, when your enemies will set up a barricade around you and surround you and hem you in on every side and tear you down to the ground, you and your children within you" (19:42–44). This was not the first time and would certainly not be the last time that our Lord predicted the unthinkable. He prophesied the utter annihilation and destruction of the city that is set upon the hill, the city of God, Jerusalem, one of the wonders of the ancient world, the city that every Jew believed was impregnable and that no human power could ever destroy. Yet, within the time frame of a single generation, that city was annihilated.

Josephus tells us in his account of the destruction of Jerusalem in AD 70 that 1.1 million Jews were slaughtered. The Romans overran the rebellious nation of Israel and destroyed village after village and city after city until the inhabitants of the land fled for safety to that walled fortress, which they believed was indestructible. The Roman forces were led by Titus, who had instructions from his father the emperor to destroy every single inhabitant of the place—men, women, and children.

"And they will not leave one stone upon another in you, because you did not know the time of your visitation" (v. 44). The Holy City was demolished because they didn't know the time of their visitation. What does that mean? We can get a hint earlier in Luke's Gospel, in the song of Zechariah, the *Benedictus*.

In the last part of the song, we read these words: "And you, child, will be called the prophet of the Most High; for you will go before the Lord to prepare his ways, to give knowledge of salvation to his people in the forgiveness of their sins, because of the tender mercy of our God, whereby the sunrise shall visit us from on high" (1:76–78). It was announced by the angel to Zechariah that his wife would bear a son and they would call his name John. John would be the forerunner to announce the coming Messiah. What he was announcing was the visitation of God.

That word *visitation* is an interesting word and an important concept. It translates the Greek word *episkopē*. A related word, *episkopos*, comes to us in the word *episcopal*. It is often translated "bishop," so episcopal church government means rule by bishops. What is an *episkopos* or a bishop? The word *episkopos* has the root *skopos*, from which we get the words *telescope* and *microscope*. It has to do with looking or observing. When the prefix *epi* is added, it intensifies the root. That means a super or intense looking.

The Latin translation of this word comes to us as the word *supervisor*, somebody who's observing or deeply looking at things. An *episkopos* in the ancient world was usually a military officer, a general. From time to time, the general would go to the various military encampments and review the troops. He was coming to inspect them to see if they were prepared for battle. That was the *episkopos*, the general, the supervisor, the bishop. If the troops were found to be battle ready, they would receive the praise of the *episkopos*. But if they weren't prepared, if they weren't battle ready, the judgment and wrath of the *episkopos* would fall upon them.

Throughout the Old Testament, the prophets said that there was a day coming that they called the day of the Lord—the day when God would personally visit His people. Initially, the hope for the future visitation of the Lord was a thing that produced great joy and anticipation among the people. As the Old Testament progressed, the connotation of that day began to be murky, dark, and foreboding. The prophet Amos said: "Woe to you who desire the day of the Lord! Why would you have the day of the Lord? It is darkness, and not light" (Amos 5:18).

In the Gospel of John we are told that though John the Baptist was not the light, he bore witness to the One who was the true light, the light that shone in the darkness. The Apostle John tells us of Jesus, "He came to his own, and his own people did not receive him" (John 1:11). It was the incarnation, the taking on human flesh, by which God came to visit His people and to pour out His grace and His tender mercy, to seek and to save those who were lost.

When the Savior entered Jerusalem to bring peace and redemption, He found a people who were living in abject darkness who knew nothing of the Prince of Peace who was coming. They missed the light of the visitation of God. For them, it was a day of darkness with no light in it. Jesus looked at this city, and He cried over it, saying: "How often would I have gathered you to Myself as a hen gathered her chicks, but you didn't want Me. You wanted no part of Me. You hid your face from Me. You crucified Me. The way of peace you did not know. You missed the day of the heavenly visit that would redeem you and turned that day of visitation into the utter destruction of the city and of the temple in AD 70."

A Den of Robbers

And he entered the temple and began to drive out those who sold, saying to them, "It is written, 'My house shall be a house of prayer,' but you have made it a den of robbers" (vv. 45–46). After weeping over Jerusalem, Jesus went to the crowning point of the city, the magnificent temple built by Herod with architecture unmatched in that era, and drove out the money-changers.

This wasn't the first time. At the beginning of His ministry, He came to the temple and found the money-changers exploiting the people (John 2:13–17), filling their pockets as a result of the exploitive prices charged to the pilgrims who came from all over the country. Every Jew was required to come offer their sacrifices. They didn't want to bring their lambs, goats, birds, or pigeons on the journey because they knew that there would be an abundance of livestock for sale in Jerusalem. The pilgrims came to the city and purchased animals for the sacrifices they gave on the Day of Atonement. A lucrative business venture had been created, with collusion between the merchants, the money-changers, and the priests and clergy of the day. The pilgrims needed to have animals for their sacrifices, and only money from Tyre was accepted currency to pay tithes. Animals had to be purchased and money had to be changed, and the prices were usurious.

The noise in the outer court of the temple sounded like the commodities market in Chicago. Here was the Lamb of God Himself, come to lay down His life for His people, but He could hardly move in the temple because of the buying and selling that was taking place. He quoted Isaiah 56:7 in the first person: **"'My house shall be a house of prayer,' but you have made it a den of robbers"** (v. 46).

The church building isn't the only place where we can worship God or pray. We can say our prayers by our bed, we can pray in the woods, we can pray while we're driving. But there's something special about coming into the house of

God and praying in that place. It's holy ground. That's why God had a house built for Himself. That's what the temple was for.

The secularization of the church bumped into the day of visitation of God's Son. It wasn't the first time. Jeremiah was told by the Lord to go to the temple and say:

> Do not trust in these deceptive words: "This is the temple of the Lord, the temple of the Lord, the temple of the Lord. . . . Behold, you trust in deceptive words to no avail. . . . Go now to my place that was in Shiloh, where I made my name dwell at first, and see what I did to it because of the evil of my people Israel. And now, because you have done all these things, declares the Lord, and when I spoke to you persistently you did not listen, and when I called you, you did not answer, therefore I will do to the house that is called by my name, and in which you trust, and to the place that I gave to you and to your fathers, as I did to Shiloh." (Jer. 7:4, 8, 12–14).

Shiloh had been the central sanctuary for Israel. In Jeremiah's time, it was in ruins, covered with weeds. Jeremiah said, "That's what Jerusalem is going to look like someday." No wonder Jesus wept when He saw the Holy City. It was no longer holy. He saw the temple had become a monument of profanity.

And he was teaching daily in the temple. The chief priests and the scribes and the principal men of the people were seeking to destroy him, but they did not find anything they could do, for all the people were hanging on his words (vv. 47–48). Oh, that God would allow people to hang on the words of Jesus. It's only then that we will have an understanding of the peace that passes understanding. It's only when we hang on Jesus' words that we will come to understand that He's the bishop of our souls and that God has visited us—not to condemn us but to redeem us.

91

JESUS' AUTHORITY AND THE PARABLE OF THE TENANTS

Luke 20:1–18

One day, as Jesus was teaching the people in the temple and preaching the gospel, the chief priests and the scribes with the elders came up and said to him, "Tell us by what authority you do these things, or who it is that gave you this authority." He answered them, "I also will ask you a question. Now tell me, was the baptism of John from heaven or from man?" And they discussed it with one another, saying, "If we say, 'From heaven,' he will say, 'Why did you not believe him?' But if we say, 'From man,' all the people will stone us to death, for they are convinced that John was a prophet." So they answered that they did not know where it came from. And Jesus said to them, "Neither will I tell you by what authority I do these things."

And he began to tell the people this parable: "A man planted a vineyard and let it out to tenants and went into another country for a long while. When the time came, he sent a servant to the tenants, so that they would give him some of the fruit of the vineyard. But the tenants beat him and sent him away empty-handed. And he sent another servant. But they also beat and treated him shamefully, and sent him away empty-handed. And he sent yet a third. This one also they wounded and cast out. Then the owner of the vineyard said, 'What shall I do? I will send my beloved son; perhaps they will respect him.' But when the tenants saw him, they said to themselves, 'This is the heir. Let us

> kill him, so that the inheritance may be ours.' And they threw him out of the vineyard and killed him. What then will the owner of the vineyard do to them? He will come and destroy those tenants and give the vineyard to others." When they heard this, they said, "Surely not!" But he looked directly at them and said, "What then is this that is written: 'The stone that the builders rejected has become the cornerstone'? Everyone who falls on that stone will be broken to pieces, and when it falls on anyone, it will crush him."

One day, as Jesus was teaching the people in the temple and preaching the gospel, the chief priests and the scribes with the elders came up and said to him, "Tell us by what authority you do these things, or who it is that gave you this authority" (vv. 1–2). Some of the Jewish leaders came to Jesus to pose a question to Him. They asked not because they were sincerely looking for an answer but because they were trying to frame a question in such a way as to trap Him and get Him in trouble with the authorities.

They came to Him asking what seemed to be a simple question concerning the source of His authority: "Jesus, what are You doing? You ride into town on a donkey as if You were the Messiah. You appear in the temple, and now You teach these things as if this is Your Father's house. What kind of authority do You have that You speak in such a manner and do the things that You do?"

He answered them, "I also will ask you a question. Now tell me, was the baptism of John from heaven or from man?" (vv. 3–4). Jesus answered their question with another question, concerning the source of John the Baptist's ministry. When He asked that question, they didn't answer at once. Instead, they fell back together as a group **and they discussed it with one another, saying, "If we say, 'From heaven,' he will say, 'Why did you not believe him?' But if we say, 'From man,' all the people will stone us to death, for they are convinced that John was a prophet"** (vv. 5–6). They decided that discretion was the better part of valor. **So they answered that they did not know where it came from. And Jesus said to them, "Neither will I tell you by what authority I do these things"** (vv. 7–8).

The Parable of the Tenants

Actually, He did tell them the answer, but He told them indirectly. **And he began to tell the people this parable: "A man planted a vineyard and let it out to tenants and went into another country for a long while"** (v. 9). It was not uncommon in those days for there to be absentee landlords who, at times, would go away into a far country and leave the production or care of the vineyard to sharecroppers. They were able to participate in profits from the vineyard. It was customary for the owner to receive 25 to 50 percent of the proceeds from the vineyard.

"When the time came, he sent a servant to the tenants, so that they would give him some of the fruit of the vineyard. But the tenants beat him and sent him away empty-handed" (v. 10). As the story proceeds, Jesus said that the owner knew it was time for the tenant farmers to pay their share of the profits to the owner. He sent a servant to them and reminded them: "The due date is now here. It's time for you to pay your share of the crops." Instead of greeting the servant willingly, the tenants beat him and sent him away without the owner's profits.

"And he sent another servant. But they also beat and treated him shamefully, and sent him away empty-handed" (v. 11). The landlord sent another servant but they treated him the same way they had treated the first servant. **"And he sent yet a third. This one also they wounded and cast out"** (v. 12). A third time the owner sent a servant to the tenant farmers asking to be paid what he was owed. This time, they wounded the servant and cast him out.

"Then the owner of the vineyard said, 'What shall I do? I will send my beloved son; perhaps they will respect him.' But when the tenants saw him, they said to themselves, 'This is the heir. Let us kill him, so that the inheritance may be ours'" (vv. 13–14). The owner sent his son, and the tenants killed him so that they could have the inheritance. That's what they did in the story. **"And they threw him out of the vineyard and killed him. What then will the owner of the vineyard do to them? He will come and destroy those tenants and give the vineyard to others." When they heard this, they said, "Surely not!"** (vv. 15–16).

No pious Jew could fail to understand what the point of this story was. Anyone who ever read the book of Isaiah knew that the prophet, speaking for God, metaphorically and symbolically spoke about His people Israel: "Let me sing for my beloved my love song concerning his vineyard: My beloved had a vineyard on a very fertile hill" (5:1). Then, Isaiah went on to say how this vineyard failed to bear fruit, moving God to visit His judgment on His own people: "And now I will tell you what I will do to my vineyard. I will remove its hedge, and it shall be devoured; I will break down its wall, and it shall be trampled down" (v. 5). Jesus extended the metaphor by saying, "I won't let this vineyard become desolate; the owner will give the vineyard to someone else."

Jesus was describing that which was owned and planted by God, how it was abused by the disobedient tenants, and how God sent His messengers, the prophets. One by one they beat them, wounded them, and scourged them, and would not obey, until finally God sent His Son, His only begotten Son, who was not simply beaten and scourged but killed.

The Stone That the Builders Rejected

But he looked directly at them and said, "What then is this that is written: 'The stone that the builders rejected has become the cornerstone'?" (v. 17). With His final summary of the point of the parable, Jesus **looked directly at them**. His piercing gaze reduced them to utter shame. Then, He said this in fulfillment of the Old Testament prophecy: **"The stone that the builders rejected has become the cornerstone"** (see Ps. 118:22).

Italy contains magnificent artwork produced by sculptors of the Renaissance period, and the list of the great sculptors of that era is long—Donatello, Bernini, and so on. The period reached its apex in Michelangelo, the greatest sculptor of the Renaissance.

Michelangelo created a group of unfinished sculptures called *Prisoners*, which consist of figures that look as though like they are coming alive and emerging from the stone but they aren't yet free. Michelangelo saw in his mind the figure he wanted to create out of the stone. He said: "I don't just create them. They're already in the stone, and my job as the sculptor is to take my hammer and chisel and to set those captives free from the stone."

Before Michelangelo began his work, he would visit the area of Carrara, where they had white marble that was unequaled in the world. At the quarry, he meticulously inspected each stone. He searched for the smallest flaw, anything that would mar the stone, any blemish that he could discern with the naked eye. If it didn't perfectly meet his specifications, he would pass it by.

Like Michelangelo, the stonemasons of Israel took great pride in their work and looked for the source material that they would use to build a synagogue or even the temple as Herod did or great majestic homes that dotted the landscape. They also went to the stone quarry and examined each stone for flaws.

The Word of God says that a particular stone that the builders rejected would become the chief cornerstone of the building that God will build. There are many metaphors that describe the church in the New Testament. It is called the body and the bride of Christ. But one of the most vivid images is of a building made of living stones, which are the people of God; the foundation of the building is the prophets and the Apostles, with the chief cornerstone being Christ (Eph. 2:20; 1 Peter 2:5).

Jesus told the Pharisees and the Sadducees, the scribes and the elders, that this cornerstone would be a stumbling block. People will look at it and not find any beauty in it. They will trip over it. They will fall on their faces and fall into ruin. Then, He said, **"Everyone who falls on that stone will be broken to pieces, and when it falls on anyone, it will crush him"** (v. 18). We gather each Lord's Day to meet with the Chief Cornerstone of the church, the One who is a stumbling block to many people.

If you trip over Him, you will fall into pieces, and the Father will take that Chief Cornerstone of His church whom you reject and He will crush you. The Word of God says that on the final day, the day of judgment, every knee will bow to Jesus Christ (Rom. 14:11). Many of those people who will bow to Jesus Christ will do so because they acknowledge Him not only as their Savior but as their King. In a spirit of obeisance and adoration and reverence, they will willingly and joyfully get on their knees in front of Him. Those who despise Him will bow because God will break their knees with a rod of iron. One way or another, everyone will be on their knees.

92

RENDER UNTO CAESAR

Luke 20:19–26

The scribes and the chief priests sought to lay hands on him at that very hour, for they perceived that he had told this parable against them, but they feared the people. So they watched him and sent spies, who pretended to be sincere, that they might catch him in something he said, so as to deliver him up to the authority and jurisdiction of the governor. So they asked him, "Teacher, we know that you speak and teach rightly, and show no partiality, but truly teach the way of God. Is it lawful for us to give tribute to Caesar, or not?" But he perceived their craftiness, and said to them, "Show me a denarius. Whose likeness and inscription does it have?" They said, "Caesar's." He said to them, "Then render to Caesar the things that are Caesar's, and to God the things that are God's." And they were not able in the presence of the people to catch him in what he said, but marveling at his answer they became silent.

The scribes and the chief priests sought to lay hands on him at that very hour, for they perceived that he had told this parable against them, but they feared the people. So they watched him and sent spies, who pretended to be sincere, that they might catch him in something he said, so as to deliver him up to the authority and jurisdiction of the governor (vv. 19–20). After Jesus cleansed the temple and antagonized His enemies after His triumphal entry into the city, His enemies continued to seek ways to undermine His authority and to trap Him so they could gain the intervention of the pagan civil authorities to secure His arrest and execution. As they did on multiple occasions in Luke's Gospel, they came to Jesus with questions. Of course, they always wore a mask of sincerity, coming to Him by way of flattery and by way of false accolades, acknowledging that He was a great teacher and taught only those things that are true and honoring to God. But Jesus wasn't fooled by their flattery. The occasion arose for another attempt to pit Jesus against the ruling government over the issue of the payment of taxes.

So they asked him, "Teacher, we know that you speak and teach rightly, and show no partiality, but truly teach the way of God. Is it lawful for us to give tribute to Caesar, or not?" (vv. 21–22). The word "tribute" here means "taxes." Was it lawful to pay taxes to the hated Roman government? We are told that Jesus **perceived their craftiness** (v. 23). In Genesis, Satan is described as being "more crafty" than all the other creatures God had made (3:1). This same kind of craftiness is employed by the rulers of the Sanhedrin in order to trap Jesus.

But he perceived their craftiness, and said to them, "Show me a denarius. Whose likeness and inscription does it have?" They said, "Caesar's" (vv. 23–24). The denarius was a smaller unit of monetary value that was the standard payment for a day's wages. When the Romans minted coins, they often celebrated in their currency the current ruling Caesar. The denarius had imprinted the image of Caesar, and so He said, "Whose image is on the coin?" Somebody produced the denarius, and the Pharisees said, "Caesar's." On one side of the denarius was a portrait of Caesar, Tiberius Caesar, and the words "Tiberius Caesar, Son of the Divine Augustus."

On the other side of the coin the words read "Pontifex Maximus"—not simply the high priest but the highest priest. The Jewish people had a religion with a priesthood, and they had the great high priest, but according to Caesar and his government, Tiberius Caesar was not only a high priest but the highest priest, claiming to be the son of the divine Augustus. Jesus paid particular attention to the words found on the coin.

Obedience to Authorities

He said to them, "Then render to Caesar the things that are Caesar's, and to God the things that are God's" (v. 25). Clearly, Jesus was teaching the people that they ought to practice civil obedience. In the New Testament, we read the Apostolic mandate to pay taxes to whom taxes are due. We know that governments were created by God, and their officials are ministers of God and supposedly ministers of justice and goodness as well (Rom. 13:1–7). It is the duty of every citizen to pay his taxes. **"Render to Caesar the things that are Caesar's,"** and among the things that are of Caesar are taxes. It was his right to levy taxes. Everyone knew at the time Jesus gave this answer that the taxes imposed by the Roman government were unjust. They were oppressive and unfair. Nevertheless, our Lord commanded that they be paid.

This raises a principle that Christians have to deal with when it comes to obedience to authorities. The principle is very simple, but applying it can be excruciatingly difficult. The principle is that we must always, in every circumstance, obey the civil magistrates unless they command us to do what God forbids or they forbid us from doing what God commands. The Apostles confronted that when they were forbidden to preach the gospel of Christ. Peter and John, joining together with the rest of the Apostles, answered, "Whether it is right in the sight of God to listen to you rather than to God, you must judge, for we cannot but speak of what we have seen and heard" (Acts 4:19–20).

In contrast, we read earlier in Luke's Gospel that a decree went out from Caesar Augustus that "all the world should be registered" (2:1). It was for the purpose of taxation. Everybody had to return to their home city to register in order to be taxed. That is why Mary and Joseph had to make the arduous journey when she was nine months pregnant in order to return to Bethlehem that her baby would be born there. You could imagine the frustration that Joseph felt at this edict. But he did it because being oppressed is never an excuse for disobedience. Joseph understood the principle, and he understood its application and made sure that he and his wife would make this journey to be enrolled for Caesar's taxes.

We now need to apply the principle to rendering to Caesar the things that are Caesar's. We understand that taxes are Caesar's, so we pay our taxes. But then Jesus added that we are also to render **"to God the things that are God's"** (v. 25). To whom are we obligated to bring praise and honor and worship? Certainly not to Caesar. Caesar may have claimed to be the son of God, the divine emperor Augustus, but that claim was a false claim, and no believer in Israel could possibly give worship, adoration, and praise of that sort to Caesar. Worship didn't belong to Caesar. It belonged only to God.

That's why the first great crisis in the early church was when they were commanded to swear a loyalty oath to the emperor and to his divinity, saying, *Kaiser kyrios*—"Caesar is lord." The reason Christians were human illuminators in the gardens of Nero and why they were fed to the lions or slain by the gladiators by imperial edict is because they would not say, *Kaiser kyrios*. Rather, their confession was this: *Iēsous kyrios*—"Jesus is Lord." "Caesar, we'll pay our taxes, we'll drive our chariots within the speed limit, we'll do all these things that you command us to do, but don't ask us to give worship to you. That doesn't belong to you. That belongs to our King, Jesus."

And they were not able in the presence of the people to catch him in what he said, but marveling at his answer they became silent (v. 26). God has never given us a right to steal. We render to God the things that are God's, and obedience to His law always supersedes the will of the majority or the will of a minority. We are to render to Caesar what Caesar is owed and render to God His majesty, His glory, His honor, and obedience to Him. Having heard His answer, not even the Pharisees could argue with Him.

93

THE RESURRECTION AND DAVID'S SON

Luke 20:27–47

There came to him some Sadducees, those who deny that there is a resurrection, and they asked him a question, saying, "Teacher, Moses wrote for us that if a man's brother dies, having a wife but no children, the man must take the widow and raise up offspring for his brother. Now there were seven brothers. The first took a wife, and died without children. And the second and the third took her, and likewise all seven left no children and died. Afterward the woman also died. In the resurrection, therefore, whose wife will the woman be? For the seven had her as wife."

And Jesus said to them, "The sons of this age marry and are given in marriage, but those who are considered worthy to attain to that age and to the resurrection from the dead neither marry nor are given in marriage, for they cannot die anymore, because they are equal to angels and are sons of God, being sons of the resurrection. But that the dead are raised, even Moses showed, in the passage about the bush, where he calls the Lord the God of Abraham and the God of Isaac and the God of Jacob. Now he is not God of the dead, but of the living, for all live to him." Then some of the scribes answered, "Teacher, you have spoken well." For they no longer dared to ask him any question.

But he said to them, "How can they say that the Christ is David's son? For David himself says in the Book of Psalms, 'The Lord said to my Lord, "Sit at my right hand, until I make your enemies your footstool." ' David thus calls him Lord, so how is he his son?"

And in the hearing of all the people he said to his disciples, "Beware of the scribes, who like to walk around in long robes, and love greetings in the marketplaces and the best seats in the synagogues and the places of honor at feasts, who devour widows' houses and for a pretense make long prayers. They will receive the greater condemnation."

This time, those who came to Jesus with a question were members of the group known as the Sadducees, but their motive was the same: to try to trap Him in some kind of heresy that would make Him unpopular either with the government or with the populace. The Sadducees traced their tradition to Zadok, who was high priest during the time of David. They were of the priestly class, and they differed significantly from the Pharisees because, in the first place, they held the Torah at a higher level than the rest of the Scriptures, and second, they rejected the traditions of the Talmud and other portions of rabbinic studies. They did not believe there were grounds for believing in a future life, so they denied the resurrection of the dead.

It was at this point that they pressed Jesus for an answer going back to a citation from Moses with respect to the levirate law (Deut. 25:5–10). That law directed that in the case of a marriage when a man dies, leaving the wife childless, it was the responsibility of his brother to take her as his wife, that she might have the opportunity to bear children. The question that the Sadducees posed to Jesus took this scenario even further.

There came to him some Sadducees, those who deny that there is a resurrection, and they asked him a question, saying, "Teacher, Moses wrote for us that if a man's brother dies, having a wife but no children, the man must take the widow and raise up offspring for his brother. Now there were seven brothers. The first took a wife, and died without children. And the second and the third took her, and likewise all seven left no children and died. Afterward the woman also died. In the resurrection, therefore, whose wife will the woman be? For the seven had her as wife" (vv. 27–33). What Jesus said in response is helpful to a certain degree, but on the other hand, it perhaps raises even more questions for us than we would have if He hadn't answered this.

When it comes to heaven, people have all kinds of questions. Will we know each other in the afterlife? If we do know each other, how is recognition possible? In the resurrection, how old will we be? What about infants? Will we know them in the resurrection? Will they have been grown to adulthood? These are difficult and heartfelt questions. But we really don't know the answers to them. Where God has ceased His divine revelation, we must cease from inquiry.

We don't have all the answers to what life in the resurrected state will be. The

Apostle John wrote: "See what kind of love the Father has given to us, that we should be called children of God; and so we are. The reason why the world does not know us is that it did not know him. Beloved, we are God's children now, and what we will be has not yet appeared; but we know that when he appears we shall be like him, because we shall see him as he is" (1 John 3:1–2). In Paul's teaching on the resurrection, he said that which is sown perishable will be raised unperishable. That which is sown in corruption will be raised in incorruption, sown in mortality will be raised in immortality (1 Cor. 15:42–49). We don't get a comprehensive picture of how that will be.

Another question is, Will people in heaven be able to look down on those who are still on earth and know what's going on in their lives? If so, will they be subjected to pain and anguish by what they watch taking place before their heavenly gaze? In the parable of the rich man and Lazarus, the suggestion is that people can look from heaven and see what is happening on earth (Luke 16:19–31). But these are little glimpses that we get about our heavenly state. For the most part, we have to wait and see. We're now in that state where we look into the glass darkly. We know in part that when we make the transition, our knowledge will be much greater.

If there's anything we can say about the resurrected state, it's that it's going to be almost infinitely better than that which we enjoy in this state. Paul wrote, "For to me to live is Christ, and to die is gain" (Phil. 1:21). In one sense, we have to leave it at that point, simply saying what we know for sure. When we enter heaven, we will lose nothing of substance or of value. What we will experience is only gain. Whatever is or isn't in heaven, one thing we know now: in heaven there will be no sin. Everything that profanes human relationships will be gone. No sin. No deceit. No death. No sickness. No sorrow. How that occurs in the resurrection, we don't know. We must trust God at His word that whatever we experience in heaven will be wonderful and will be nothing but gain.

Equal to Angels

And Jesus said to them, "The sons of this age marry and are given in marriage, but those who are considered worthy to attain to that age and to the resurrection from the dead neither marry nor are given in marriage, for they cannot die anymore, because they are equal to angels and are sons of God, being sons of the resurrection" (vv. 34–36). At first glance, that suggests that we are not in a state of marriage in heaven. Whatever state we'll be in will be better than anything we can imagine now.

He said we will be **"equal to angels"** (v. 36). We will not be angels. Don't get the idea that when we die, we grow wings and live an angelic existence. Some think Jesus means that angels are sexless, and so will we be. We don't know that angels are genderless. I assume that since we have been created male and female, we will remain male and female in heaven. Maleness and femaleness will move to a completely different level in glory, a level that is greater and more wonderful than what we now experience.

"But that the dead are raised, even Moses showed, in the passage about the bush, where he calls the Lord the God of Abraham and the God of Isaac and the God of Jacob. Now he is not God of the dead, but of the living, for all live to him" (vv. 37–38). Jesus was saying that there will be no need to fill the earth and multiply by propagation because death will be no more and we won't have to have children in heaven in order to populate it. All the population of heaven will be there by God's grace for eternity.

In this exchange, Jesus silenced the Sadducees. Even the scribes who had failed already to try to trap Him complimented Him. **Then some of the scribes answered, "Teacher, you have spoken well." For they no longer dared to ask him any question** (vv. 39–40). But then, Jesus turned the table on the Sadducees by asking them a question.

David's Son

But he said to them, "How can they say that the Christ is David's son? For David himself says in the Book of Psalms, 'The Lord said to my Lord, "Sit at my right hand, until I make your enemies your footstool."' David thus calls him Lord, so how is he his son?" (vv. 41–44). This is a provocative question that Jesus put to His opponents. The Bible says that the Messiah who was to come would be the Son of David. Yet, David spoke of the Messiah as David's Lord. How could David have a son who was also his Lord? How do you put those two propositions together in any meaningful way? That's the question Jesus asked of His interrogators, and He supplied the answer for us by citing Psalm 110.

Psalm 110 has a jarring apparent contradiction in it. It contains a conversation between God and someone else. It says, "The Lord says to my Lord: 'Sit at my right hand, until I make your enemies your footstool' " (v. 1). In this quote, in the Hebrew, the name of God is combined with the chief title of God. Earlier in the Psalms, David wrote, "O Lord, our Lord, how majestic is your name in all the earth!" (Ps. 8:1). In that psalm, the name of God, Yahweh, is combined with the chief title of God, Adonai. Though we have in the English text the repetition of the word "Lord," there are two different words in the Hebrew text, which reads, "O Yahweh, our Adonai." Throughout the Old Testament, that supreme title, Adonai or Sovereign One, is reserved for God. That's why it's startling that in this text, Psalm 110, there is a conversation between Yahweh and someone else who is given the title Adonai.

Psalm 110:1 reads, "The Lord [Yahweh] says to my Lord [Adonai]: 'Sit at my right hand.'" Somebody else is given the title of Adonai besides God the Father. "Yahweh says to my Adonai, my sovereign." In the kenotic hymn of Philippians 2:5–10, Paul wrote:

> Have this mind among yourselves, which is yours in Christ Jesus, who, though he was in the form of God, did not count equality with God a thing to be grasped, but emptied himself, by taking the form of a servant, being born in the likeness of men. And being found in human form, he humbled himself by becoming obedient to the point of death, even death on a cross. Therefore God has highly exalted him and bestowed on him the name that is above every name, so that at the name of Jesus every knee should bow, in heaven and on earth and under the earth.

What is that name that is above every name? It's not Jesus. It is Adonai. At the name of Jesus, every knee will bow and every tongue confess that He is Adonai. He is Lord, to the glory of God the Father.

In His exaltation, Jesus ascended to heaven and sat at the right hand of God, where He is appointed by the Father to rule over all the earth, to be the King of kings and the Lord of lords, to be Adonai—David's Lord, Caesar's Lord, your Lord, my Lord. Because He has been given the name that transcends all titles, every time we even hear the name of Jesus, the appropriate response is to be on our knees in obeisance before the One whom God has placed at His right hand and has exalted with such majesty. We confess that Christ is Adonai, David's Son and David's Lord.

And in the hearing of all the people he said to his disciples, "Beware of the scribes, who like to walk around in long robes, and love greetings in the marketplaces and the best seats in the synagogues and the places of honor at feasts, who devour widows' houses and for a pretense make long prayers. They will receive the greater condemnation" (vv. 45–47). Jesus once again uttered words of condemnation, this time aimed at the scribes. Earlier, He had severely rebuked the Pharisees and the scribes for being hypocrites (11:45–52). Here He singled out attorneys who were theologians. They were masters of the Old Testament law. He said: "They love to parade around in glory and enjoy the adulation of the people in the marketplace and the synagogues and be elevated in places of honor. But theirs is a culture of deceit, and to them will come the greater condemnation." They had placed their own honor above the honor of God and of His Son, Jesus the Adonai.

94

THE DESTRUCTION OF JERUSALEM

Luke 21:1–24

Jesus looked up and saw the rich putting their gifts into the offering box, and he saw a poor widow put in two small copper coins. And he said, "Truly, I tell you, this poor widow has put in more than all of them. For they all contributed out of their abundance, but she out of her poverty put in all she had to live on."

And while some were speaking of the temple, how it was adorned with noble stones and offerings, he said, "As for these things that you see, the days will come when there will not be left here one stone upon another that will not be thrown down." And they asked him, "Teacher, when will these things be, and what will be the sign when these things are about to take place?" And he said, "See that you are not led astray. For many will come in my name, saying, 'I am he!' and, 'The time is at hand!' Do not go after them. And when you hear of wars and tumults, do not be terrified, for these things must first take place, but the end will not be at once."

Then he said to them, "Nation will rise against nation, and kingdom against kingdom. There will be great earthquakes, and in various places famines and pestilences. And there will be terrors and great signs from heaven. But before all this they will lay their hands on you and persecute you, delivering you up to the synagogues and prisons, and you will be brought before kings and governors for my name's sake. This will be your opportunity to bear witness. Settle it therefore in your minds not to meditate beforehand how to answer, for I will give you a mouth and wisdom, which none of your adversaries will be able to withstand or contradict. You will be delivered up even by parents and brothers and relatives and friends, and some of you they will put to death. You will be hated by all for my name's sake. But not a hair of your head will perish. By your endurance you will gain your lives.

"But when you see Jerusalem surrounded by armies, then know that its desolation has come near. Then let those who are in Judea flee to the mountains, and let those who are inside the city depart, and let not those who are out in the country enter it, for these are days of vengeance, to fulfill all that is written. Alas for women who are pregnant and for those who are nursing infants in those days! For there will be great distress upon the earth and wrath against this people. They will fall by the edge of the sword and be led captive among all nations, and Jerusalem will be trampled underfoot by the Gentiles, until the times of the Gentiles are fulfilled."

Jesus looked up and saw the rich putting their gifts into the offering box, and he saw a poor widow put in two small copper coins. And he said, "Truly, I tell you, this poor widow has put in more than all of them. For they all contributed out of their abundance, but she out of her poverty put in all she had to live on" (vv. 1–4). Chapter 20 closes with Jesus' condemnation of the scribes, but chapter 21 opens with His commendation of a poor widow. He was observing people in the temple, and He saw those of wealth and affluence going to the offering box and, out of the abundance of their great wealth, putting in their donations.

Then He noticed a widow. She had two copper coins, and Mark's Gospel tells us that together they "make a penny" (Mark 12:42). That's all she had in the world, and Jesus saw her put it in the offering box. For this, she received the blessed commendation of Christ.

We sing, "Take my life and let it be consecrated, Lord, to thee." We make claims of devotion, but I know that whatever devotion I have given in my life to Jesus, whatever sacrifice I have made on any occasion for the sake of His kingdom, pales into utter insignificance in light of the action of this poverty-stricken widow whose offering was seen by Jesus and blessed by Him.

And while some were speaking of the temple, how it was adorned with noble stones and offerings, he said, "As for these things that you see, the days will come when there will not be left here one stone upon another that will not be thrown down" (vv. 5–6). Jesus next uttered one of Scripture's most astonishing prophecies. Jesus looked at the temple as the disciples were admiring the stones and the adornment of the building, and He said to His disciples that the day would come when **"there will not be left here one stone**

upon another that will not be thrown down" (v. 6). Do you realize how radical that prediction was?

The first temple was built by Solomon, and it was a magnificent building. It remained for about four hundred years until it was destroyed by the Babylonians. It was then partially rebuilt under the leadership of Zerubbabel. About twenty years before this scene recorded by Luke, King Herod began work on reconstructing the temple and expanding its platform, and he made it a glorious building.

The vastness, the sheer size, of this temple was extraordinarily noteworthy. Herod, the master architect, chose stones that were huge. They were quarried and brought to Jerusalem. To build the interior of the temple, single white marble stones were used. They were sixty-seven feet long, seven feet high, and nine feet wide. He adorned the building with jewels and gold. The outer portion of the temple was covered with layers and sheets of gold, so brilliant that when the sun came up at dawn, people couldn't look directly at the walls of the temple because the refulgence of its glory was so bright that they had to look away.

The temple was one of the wonders of the ancient world. The city of Jerusalem and its temple were considered impregnable. This was the temple of the Lord, Mount Zion. In the eyes of the Jewish people, it was totally indestructible. But Jesus said of the temple: "It's going away. Not one stone is going to be left on another." It would end in absolute desolation and destruction when God responded to the unbelief of His people and visited them with what Luke calls **"days of vengeance"** (v. 22). Their city and their temple would be destroyed.

When Jesus said that, no one could believe it. Yet, if there's anything that proves the truth of the Bible and the truth of Jesus' claims, it's this singular prophecy that was fulfilled in its details in AD 70, when the Romans annihilated both Jerusalem and the temple. But this text ironically is the text most used to support skepticism and unbelief in the church, because in connection with the prophecy of the destruction of the temple, Jesus said that He would come on clouds of glory at the end of the age, that there would be wars and rumors of wars, as well as famines, pestilence, and plagues. Jesus then said, "Truly, I say to you, this generation will not pass away until all these things take place" (Matt. 24:34).

The skeptics leap at that text. Bertrand Russell, in his book *Why I Am Not a Christian*, said that he was not a Christian because Jesus made a prophecy and it didn't happen in the time frame that He said it would. It seemed that every day I was in seminary, some professor would call attention to the Olivet Discourse (Matt. 24–25; Mark 13; Luke 21) and say that Jesus was a false prophet because His predictions didn't come true. And yet, many of His predictions came true so vividly, so compellingly, that it would seem to prove to the most obstreperous skeptic that Jesus was a true prophet. But the time frame issue hangs out there as a cause for much debate. There is a response to the problem of the time frame.

Consider Luke 21:21–24: **"Then let those who are in Judea flee to the mountains, and let those who are inside the city depart, and let not those who are out in the country enter it, for these are days of vengeance, to fulfill all that is written. Alas for women who are pregnant and for those who are nursing infants in those days! For there will be great distress upon the earth and wrath against this people. They will fall by the edge of the sword and be led captive among all nations, and Jerusalem will be trampled underfoot by the Gentiles, until the times of the Gentiles are fulfilled."** The critical word in verse 24 is "until." In the Greek, the word means "up to a particular point, and then it stops." Jesus was saying: "The city will be destroyed. The temple will be destroyed. The Jewish people will be sent into dispersion throughout all the world until a point in time when that vengeance will end." The only other time that I know of that the Bible speaks of **"the times of the Gentiles"** is in Romans 11:25, when Paul talks about the return of the Jewish people to salvation at some point.

I'm Irish by descent. My great-grandfather came to this country during the potato famine in Ireland in the middle of the nineteenth century. My grandfather marched every year in the Orangemen's parade in Pittsburgh. My mother tucked me into bed every night singing Irish lullabies. My son wears a kilt, and our grandchildren have Irish names, but we don't gather around the table and say, "Next year in Dublin" or "Pray for the peace of Dublin." For all intents and purposes, we've become assimilated into this country. We're Americans, not really Irishmen.

The Jews were sent out of their homeland, dispersed throughout the whole world, in AD 70. The Jews didn't regain their homeland for two thousand years. It wasn't until 1948 that the Jewish nation was reestablished.

95

THIS GENERATION WILL NOT PASS AWAY

Luke 21:25–38

"And there will be signs in sun and moon and stars, and on the earth distress of nations in perplexity because of the roaring of the sea and the waves, people fainting with fear and with foreboding of what is coming on the world. For the powers of the heavens will be shaken. And then they will see the Son of Man coming in a cloud with power and great glory. Now when these things begin to take place, straighten up and raise your heads, because your redemption is drawing near."

And he told them a parable: "Look at the fig tree, and all the trees. As soon as they come out in leaf, you see for yourselves and know that the summer is already near. So also, when you see these things taking place, you know that the kingdom of God is near. Truly, I say to you, this generation will not pass away until all has taken place. Heaven and earth will pass away, but my words will not pass away.

"But watch yourselves lest your hearts be weighed down with dissipation and drunkenness and cares of this life, and that day come upon you suddenly like a trap. For it will come upon all who dwell on the face of the whole earth. But stay awake at all times, praying that you may have strength to escape all these things that are going to take place, and to stand before the Son of Man."

And every day he was teaching in the temple, but at night he went out and lodged on the mount called Olivet. And early in the morning all the people came to him in the temple to hear him.

In the first half of chapter 21, we were introduced to what is perhaps the most astonishing prophecy or prediction ever made. No one expected that this prediction could possibly be fulfilled: the destruction of Mount Zion, the destruction of the temple with no stone left on another, the Jews dispersed and sent into exile, and the Holy City taken by the Gentiles until the days of the Gentiles would be fulfilled.

When Jesus gave this prediction, His disciples came to Him asking questions. Their burning question was not "How will these things take place?" or "Where or why will these things take place?" Their question was "When will these things take place?" In answer to that question, Jesus said it is necessary that certain things will take place first. False messiahs will come, there will be wars and rumors of wars, pestilence and plagues, but even after that it will not yet be the time (vv. 7–19). Then He said, "But when you see Jerusalem surrounded by armies, then know that its desolation has come near" (v. 20).

In the second half of this chapter, Jesus introduced the other element that is so controversial about this text: **"And there will be signs in sun and moon and stars, and on the earth distress of nations in perplexity because of the roaring of the sea and the waves, people fainting with fear and with foreboding of what is coming on the world. For the powers of the heavens will be shaken"** (vv. 25–26). In Old Testament prophecies, when the prophets under the inspiration of God the Holy Spirit predicted catastrophic events of divine judgment on the world, they used language that was heavily laden with images and symbols. They spoke of astronomical perturbations and signs in the heavens. This prophecy is no different in that respect, because Jesus said that there would be such calamitous manifestations of divine judgment at the time of this prediction's fulfillment that the whole world, as it were, would be frozen in terror. The whole atmosphere would be shaken by the powers of God's judgment. **"And then they will see the Son of Man coming in a cloud with power and great glory"** (v. 27).

A Difficult Text

The temple destroyed, the city destroyed, the Jews dispersed, and the Son of Man will come in power and great glory. He went on to say, **"Truly, I say to you, this generation will not pass away until all has taken place"** (v. 32). If this one sentence were eliminated from the text of Luke, there would be no controversy or skepticism. It is this sentence that has raised the hackles of all the skeptics and has poured their attention into a denial of the deity of Christ, the accuracy of Christ, the sinlessness of Christ, and the trustworthiness of sacred Scripture.

Before I try to respond to this, understand that the plot thickens. The problem gets more intense. I believe that the vast majority of Christians rarely feel the weight of the problem of this text. I have seen many attempts to get around it with exegetical gymnastics or torturous attempts to simplify the problem. The plot thickens because there are two other texts that we find in Matthew's Gospel that are also problematic: 16:28 and 24:34. Matthew 16:28 says this: "Truly, I say to you, there are some standing here who will not taste death until they see the Son of Man coming in his kingdom." And 24:34 says this: "Truly, I say to you, this generation will not pass away until all these things take place."

What we have here is a particular negative proposition—something will not take place with respect to some people. "Some" defines the particular rather than the universal. Jesus was not talking about everybody or all people, but He said "some" of His hearers would not taste death until they saw the Son of Man coming in His kingdom.

If you were a first-century disciple and you heard Jesus say, "Some of you will not taste death," what does that communicate? "You're not all going to die before what I'm talking about takes place." He meant that there were people there listening to His words who would see the event He was talking about come to pass. They would live to see it.

Some people say, "Maybe what He was talking about here was not His future ultimate coming but rather the coming of His kingdom that would be manifest in the transfiguration or the resurrection, which was at most a few days or a few weeks away." If somebody says, "Something is going to happen in the next few weeks, and some of you won't die before that happens," that would indicate that perhaps some of those people will die before the event takes place. This wasn't an announcement that was made close to the time of the destruction of Jerusalem.

I hardly think Jesus was going to say, "Some of you are going to live to see the transfiguration or the ascension or the resurrection." It has to be something that at least is farther away than a few days or a few weeks in the future. In Matthew 10:23, He made a similar statement when He said, "When they persecute you in one town, flee to the next, for truly, I say to you, you will not have gone through all the towns of Israel before the Son of Man comes." There are many people who say, "This just did happen." Before the disciples' missionary activities went beyond the borders of Israel, they saw the kingdom of God coming in power. They saw it in the transfiguration, in the ascension, and on the day of Pentecost.

The Lord Is Patient toward You

Jesus was responding to a question about time. When would all these things come to pass? Hence the skepticism; hence the development of the theory of parousia delay. The early church expected Jesus to return shortly. When He didn't, they had to construct a new theology. One of the most controversial texts in all the New Testament between Arminians and Calvinists is that text where Peter says, "The Lord is not slow to fulfill his promise as some count slowness, but is patient toward you, not wishing that any should perish, but that all should reach repentance" (2 Peter 3:9).

What's the context of that? Peter was addressing the problem of the delay of the return of Jesus. He said one day to the Lord is like a thousand years (v. 8), and the reason for the delay of the fulfillment of salvation is that God is not willing that any should perish before all those who are foreordained for redemption have been redeemed. He was not saying God is not willing that any person at all should perish. The antecedent of the word "any" is "you." God is not willing that any of *you* should perish. A careful look at the text indicates that "you" refers to those to whom Peter's letter was written, and it was written to the elect (1:10). Not one person who is numbered among the elect will perish, because Jesus won't come back until all of His elect have been redeemed.

In order to evade the difficulty of this text, some people say Jesus is dividing these things. Some of the things were going to take place between the time He spoke and AD 70, such as the destruction of the city, the destruction of the temple, and the dispersion of the Jews. But His personal return had to be separated from these things. However, the text doesn't allow that. When Jesus described this situation, He said "all these things" (Matt. 24:34), including His coming in power, will occur, so that doesn't solve the difficulty.

The Meaning of a Generation

The most common attempt to ease the apparent problem is the realization that the Greek word for "generation" can mean more than one thing, and it does. We know that Jesus often described that generation of contemporary Jewish people who were alive during His earthly ministry as a wicked and perverse generation (Luke 9:41; 11:29). So the term "generation" can refer to a type of people—people who have fallen into terrible sin and evil, a particular level of heinous perversity.

In one sense, Jesus was describing that contemporary generation as the worst generation in the history of Israel because its sin was so magnified. If any generation should have recognized its Messiah, it was that one. The Bible says, "He came to his own, and his own people did not receive him" (John 1:11). Jesus was describing here the days of vengeance that were going to come upon that generation of evildoers that rejected the Messiah.

Some will say that since there's a difference in the meaning of the term "generation," what Jesus was saying was that that generation would not pass away until all these things came to pass. What they mean is that there will always be wicked people, all the way up until the time of Jesus' coming. I certainly agree that until Jesus comes in His final glory, there will always be sinners here. There's no reason to suspect that that is going to change before His final triumphant coming in glory.

However, the primary meaning of the term "generation" is a particular age group. We distinguish among the millennials and Generation X and baby boomers. In Jewish terms, a generation is understood to mean approximately forty years. I'm suggesting that any disciple listening to what Jesus said when they asked the question "When will these things happen?" would understand Jesus to mean that it would be sometime in the next forty years. That's why the skeptics rally around this text, because they say forty years came and forty years went. During that time, the temple was destroyed and the city was destroyed, but Jesus didn't come back.

If Jesus was wrong in His prediction, then He was a false prophet deserving of being stoned. I don't think there's the slightest chance that Jesus was wrong when He made this prediction. If He wasn't wrong, then I assume that every single thing He was talking about here took place within the space of forty years. The temple was destroyed. Jerusalem was destroyed. The Jews were dispersed. And Jesus came back manifesting His kingdom in power.

Does that mean that I don't believe that He is still coming? No, I believe He's still coming. I don't think that He was referring to His ultimate, consummate fulfillment of the kingdom of God, but He came in judgment in AD 70. Josephus, when he gave his record of the destruction of Jerusalem, talked about the multitude of eyewitnesses who saw signs in the sky. When they looked up, they saw chariots of fire in the sky and heard a voice saying, "We are departing hence." They heard the words of the leaving of divine glory, as the people of Israel had heard centuries before when the chariot of God was leaving, giving Jerusalem over to destruction (Ezek. 10). Jesus came at the end of the Jewish age in judgment.

At the same time, we see a pattern in the Scriptures, particularly in the Old Testament, such as the prophecies of the appearance of Cyrus and ultimately the Messiah. There is an early fulfillment that is later fulfilled in its utter fullness and ultimacy. I still think Jesus is coming back. He is coming back to bring the last judgment when the times of the Gentiles are fulfilled, as Luke mentions here. Before the times of the Gentiles, He came in AD 70 to judge His people, and there's no reason to believe that He is not going to come fully and finally at the end of the age of the Gentiles or the age of the world. He is still coming. He is not finished. He did not fail to appear in AD 70 when He said He was going to come.

He came. He saw. He conquered. And a new age was started. The people of God are now being brought from the Gentile nations from around the world into His body, His church.

96

BETRAYED

Luke 22:1–6

Now the Feast of Unleavened Bread drew near, which is called the Passover. And the chief priests and the scribes were seeking how to put him to death, for they feared the people.

Then Satan entered into Judas called Iscariot, who was of the number of the twelve. He went away and conferred with the chief priests and officers how he might betray him to them. And they were glad, and agreed to give him money. So he consented and sought an opportunity to betray him to them in the absence of a crowd.

Betrayal is a brutal and ugly word. There are numbers of ways in which we sin against God and against each other, but when the word *betrayal* comes up, there's something sickening about it, and we respond in our gut to it. The Revolutionary War traitor Benedict Arnold, who is buried now as a hero in Westminster Abbey, is synonymous with treachery. Yet, the most pernicious betrayal in history was that committed by a friend and disciple of Jesus, Judas Iscariot, who sold his Savior for a handful of money.

Now the Feast of Unleavened Bread drew near, which is called the Passover. And the chief priests and the scribes were seeking how to put him to death, for they feared the people. Then Satan entered into Judas called Iscariot, who was of the number of the twelve. He went away and conferred with the chief priests and officers how he might betray him to them (vv. 1–4). Why did Judas do it? What so motivated him that he would commit this treacherous act? We can look at this from different perspectives. On the one hand, we can look at it from the *proximate cause*, the near-at-hand explanation, as distinguished from the *remote cause*, the more distant view of the matter.

We look first of all from this proximate perspective, and we can see two reasons to explain this dreadful deed. The immediate explanation we get is that Judas did it for the money: **And they were glad, and agreed to give him money** (v. 5). Before he met with Jesus and the disciples for the celebration of the Passover, Judas had already met with the chief priests and the scribes and the Pharisees in secret. He knew the Jewish leaders wanted to capture Jesus quietly and privately when there were not throngs of people around Him. **So he consented and sought an opportunity to betray him to them in the absence of a crowd** (v. 6). The plan was to have Jesus taken at night. A group of soldiers was to be sent under the cover of darkness, and Judas would let the soldiers know who Jesus was by greeting Jesus with a kiss.

The authorities offered Judas thirty pieces of silver to betray Jesus (Matt. 26:15). In the grand scheme of economy, the sum that was paid to Judas for the betrayal was paltry, and after the deed was done and Judas was overcome with remorse, he knew that it was nothing. He went to the scribes and Pharisees and hurled those coins to the ground, and in despair he went out and committed suicide (Matt. 27:3–10). That's one way to explain this act of treachery.

A second explanation is also given in the text. The Bible tells us that before Judas committed this act, **Satan entered into** him (v. 3). Judas was not simply harassed by Satan; he was literally possessed by the prince of evil. Satan entered into the inner core of Judas' being and fired up the avarice and intensified Judas' greed.

Now, we can step back from that and ask, How can Judas be held responsible for his behavior? After all, Satan came into him and possessed his soul. Wouldn't that exonerate him at the judgment seat of God? No, it wouldn't. Satan found a willing companion in Judas. Satan didn't coerce Judas to perform that act; they were partners in crime. Judas acquiesced willingly out of the darkness of his own heart. He didn't need to have Satan possess him; he was happy for that occasion.

The Doctrine of Concurrence

There's a third possible explanation for why he did it, this one not from the proximate view but from the remote view. From the overarching, supernatural view, God Almighty eternally predestined Judas to carry out this act.

If anything would seem to excuse Judas, it would be God's sovereign activity in this entire drama. The Scriptures make it abundantly clear that the action of Judas was not an accident; it was planned from eternity, from the beginning (Acts 2:23). It was decreed by almighty God, and whatsoever God ordains must necessarily come to pass. But, as the Westminster Confession of Faith rightly teaches, "God, from all eternity, did, by the most wise and holy counsel of his own will, freely, and unchangeably ordain whatsoever comes to pass: yet so, as thereby neither is God the author of sin, nor is violence offered to the will of the creatures; nor is the liberty or contingency of second causes taken away, but rather established" (3.1).

We see in the doctrine of God's providence and in concurrence a combining of choices between the human and the divine to bring certain actions and consequences to pass. We see this in the story of Joseph, who said to his brothers who had betrayed him, "As for you, you meant evil against me, but God meant it for good, to bring it about that many people should be kept alive, as they are today" (Gen. 50:20). Likewise, in Judas' case, a heinous evil action was committed. But from a different perspective, the most glorious deed that ever was performed on our behalf was the betrayal of Jesus Christ, because through that work, orchestrated by God's sovereignty, our salvation came to pass.

Judas was willing; he had his own intentions. His purpose was to strike at Jesus. God's purpose was to redeem us through this very same act. We see the same in the Old Testament drama of the exodus, in the contest between the powerful sovereign Pharaoh of Egypt and the even more sovereign being who inhabits the heavens—God. It was really no contest; there was no question of how the drama would end. Test after test, plague after plague, Pharaoh was distressed and then was inclined to say, "Let the people leave." We read, "Pharaoh's heart was hardened" (Ex. 8:19). He changed his mind. Who hardened Pharaoh's heart? God hardened it (9:12).

God did not create fresh evil in the heart of Pharaoh so he would become more obstinate and rebellious against God's salvific plans. All God had to do to harden Pharaoh's heart was to remove His restraint and let Pharaoh act according to his own character. That helps a little bit in understanding the drama of Judas. He was not a victim of fate or a whimsical providence by which God created fresh evil in his heart and forced him against his will to betray the Son of Man. Betrayal was already in the heart of this man.

Jesus Prays for His Own

Jesus said to Judas at the Last Supper, "What you are going to do, do quickly" (John 13:27). This appointment, which had been made from eternity, was fulfilled by one whose heart was already desperately wicked. In His High Priestly Prayer, Jesus said: "I am not praying for the world but for those whom you have given me, for they are yours. All mine are yours, and yours are mine, and

I am glorified in them. And I am no longer in the world, but they are in the world, and I am coming to you. Holy Father, keep them in your name" (John 17:9–11). This was the passionate prayer of Jesus for His disciples, that they would be preserved.

"I have guarded them," Jesus said, "and not one of them has been lost except the son of destruction, that the Scripture might be fulfilled" (v. 12). Judas was never saved; he was never converted. It wasn't that Judas lost his faith. No, he was the son of destruction from the beginning, as the Scriptures tell us.

Going back to the proximate cause, an event that had occurred just a short time before may help us understand how Judas could have committed this act of betrayal. When Jesus was with His disciples in Caesarea Philippi, He asked, "Who do people say that the Son of Man is?" They said, "Some say John the Baptist, others say Elijah, and others Jeremiah or one of the prophets." Jesus said, "But who do you say that I am?" and Simon gave the great confession, "You are the Christ, the Son of the living God." Jesus responded, "You are Peter, and on this rock I will build my church, and the gates of hell shall not prevail against it" (Matt. 16:13–18).

Moments later, Jesus told His disciples that they were going to Jerusalem, where He would be betrayed into the hands of His enemies and He would suffer and die. Peter spoke again: "Far be it from you, Lord! This shall never happen to you." Instead of calling him the rock, Jesus looked at Peter and said, "Get behind me, Satan!" (vv. 21–23). Jesus called him the devil. Jesus was hearing the voice of Satan at that moment, just as He had heard it in the wilderness when Satan tried to entice Jesus to take a detour, a way to escape from the suffering and the death that was required for the atonement (Luke 4:1–13).

Soon afterward, Jesus and the disciples set out for Jerusalem. What were they feeling as they walked? Each step between Galilee and Judea, their hearts were pounding in fear, their minds confused. I'm speculating, but what I think motivated Judas more than anything else to betray Jesus was unmitigated anger. He was furious, saying to himself: "I didn't think I was following somebody who was going to be executed as a criminal. I've wasted years of my life with Jesus. He isn't going to drive out the Romans as I thought He would." Failure, pain, disappointment, and frustration gave rise to anger, and Judas' anger reached a crescendo with every step he took toward Jerusalem.

When they got to Jerusalem, preparations were made for the Lord's Supper. At the table Jesus said, "One of you is going to betray Me." One by one the disciples went around the room, asking, "Is it I?" "Am I the one? Lord, is it I who will betray you?" They were as caught up in this web of confusion and frustration as Judas was. When Judas asked, "Is it I?" Jesus said, "What you are going to do, do quickly" (John 13:27).

Every one of us has been betrayed by friends, and every one of us has betrayed our friends. Jesus wasn't Judas' Savior, but He was Judas' friend. Even in the darkness of the night of betrayal, when Judas approached Him, Jesus called Judas "friend." Then Judas, with his agreed-upon sign, gave to Jesus the kiss of death. Those who came for Jesus carried clubs, and they came with swords and lanterns, and they arrested Him in order to take Him to His trial. Judas watched them go.

You and I know that there are a thousand ways that we have betrayed Jesus by not keeping His commandments. By not willingly participating in His suffering, affliction, and humiliation. By seeking escape from the scandal that is the stone of stumbling to the world in Jesus. Never once has He betrayed you or me.

97

THE LORD'S SUPPER

Luke 22:7–23

Then came the day of Unleavened Bread, on which the Passover lamb had to be sacrificed. So Jesus sent Peter and John, saying, "Go and prepare the Passover for us, that we may eat it." They said to him, "Where will you have us prepare it?" He said to them, "Behold, when you have entered the city, a man carrying a jar of water will meet you. Follow him into the house that he enters and tell the master of the house, 'The Teacher says to you, Where is the guest room, where I may eat the Passover with my disciples?' And he will show you a large upper room furnished; prepare it there." And they went and found it just as he had told them, and they prepared the Passover.

And when the hour came, he reclined at table, and the apostles with him. And he said to them, "I have earnestly desired to eat this Passover with you before I suffer. For I tell you I will not eat it until it is fulfilled in the kingdom of God." And he took a cup, and when he had given thanks he said, "Take this, and divide it among yourselves. For I tell you that from now on I will not drink of the fruit of the vine until the kingdom of God comes." And he took bread, and when he had given thanks, he broke it and gave it to them, saying, "This is my body, which is given for you. Do this in remembrance of me." And likewise the cup after they had eaten, saying, "This cup that is poured out for you is the new covenant in my blood. But behold, the hand of him who betrays me is with me on the table. For the Son of Man goes as it has been determined, but woe to that man by whom he is betrayed!" And they began to question one another, which of them it could be who was going to do this.

Then came the day of Unleavened Bread, on which the Passover lamb had to be sacrificed. So Jesus sent Peter and John, saying, "Go and prepare the Passover for us, that we may eat it." They said to him, "Where will you have us prepare it?" He said to them, "Behold, when you have entered the city, a man carrying a jar of water will meet you. Follow him into the house that he enters and tell the master of the house, 'The Teacher says to you, Where is the guest room, where I may eat the Passover with my disciples?' And he will show you a large upper room furnished; prepare it there." And they went and found it just as he had told them, and they prepared the Passover (vv. 7–13). Jesus knew that in a few hours it would be His task and His mission to be the Passover Lamb. He knew the task had been given to Him by the Father and that He would be sacrificed as an atoning death for His people. His soul was deeply troubled. Yet, with the specter of shame, humiliation, and death before Him, He had a deep desire to celebrate the Passover one more time.

The Passover

And when the hour came, he reclined at table, and the apostles with him. And he said to them, "I have earnestly desired to eat this Passover with you before I suffer. For I tell you I will not eat it until it is fulfilled in the kingdom of God" (vv. 14–16). How many times had Jesus celebrated the Passover? He had done so from the time He was a little boy. Every year His parents would go to Jerusalem and take Him along so that they might celebrate the Passover. This wasn't a tradition that Jesus started. It had been started centuries before at the original Passover.

Let's take a look back in the book of Exodus, where in chapter 11 we read these words:

> The Lord said to Moses, "Yet one plague more I will bring upon Pharaoh and upon Egypt. Afterward he will let you go from here. When he lets you go, he will drive you away completely. Speak now in the hearing of the people, that they ask, every man of his neighbor and every woman of her neighbor, for silver and gold jewelry." And the Lord gave the people favor in the sight of the Egyptians. Moreover, the man Moses was very great in the land of Egypt, in the sight of Pharaoh's servants and in the sight of the people.
>
> So Moses said, "Thus says the Lord: 'About midnight I will go out in the midst of Egypt, and every firstborn in the land of Egypt shall die, from the firstborn of Pharaoh who sits on his throne, even to the firstborn of the slave girl who is behind the handmill, and all the firstborn of the cattle.'" (vv. 1–5)

The final plague was the worst of them all. God sent the angel of death, the avenger, to kill the firstborn child in every house in Egypt, even including the firstborn of their cattle.

But the beautiful part of the story is the Passover. God gave instructions to Moses for the people that began with taking a lamb without blemish. Then He said:

> Then they shall take some of the blood and put it on the two doorposts and the lintel of the houses in which they eat it. They shall eat the flesh that night, roasted on the fire; with unleavened bread and bitter herbs they shall eat it. Do not eat any of it raw or boiled in water, but roasted, its head with its legs and its inner parts. And you shall let none of it remain until the morning; anything that remains until the morning you shall burn. In this manner you shall eat it: with your belt fastened, your sandals on your feet, and your staff in your hand. And you shall eat it in haste. It is the LORD's Passover. For I will pass through the land of Egypt that night, and I will strike all the firstborn in the land of Egypt, both man and beast; and on all the gods of Egypt I will execute judgments: I am the LORD. The blood shall be a sign for you, on the houses where you are. And when I see the blood, I will pass over you, and no plague will befall you to destroy you, when I strike the land of Egypt. (Ex. 12:7–13)

Through Moses, God directed them to prepare a special meal that included bitter herbs to remind them of the time of pain and suffering they spent in Egypt. They were to be girded with belts around their waists, so that their legs would be free to run, as they would depart in haste because it was Passover night. They couldn't take time for their bread to be leavened, so they were to take unleavened bread. It was time to get up and leave Egypt.

Then God said to Moses: "Don't ever forget this night. The night when I passed over My people who were marked by the blood of the lamb." He instituted a Passover feast to be celebrated every year. Even now, hundreds and hundreds of years later, it is still celebrated. It is not a human tradition. It is a divine tradition instituted and established by God Himself.

Each year, as the Passover is celebrated, the son says to the father: "Why are we doing this? Why are we eating this meal?" The father answers, "Because of what happened the night of the Passover when the children of God were set free and left their homes as they were instructed."

The people of Israel believed that their redemption was at hand until they came to Migdol by the sea. They saw this impassable sea in front of them while the chariots of Pharaoh were bearing down on them from behind. Moses raised his hands, and God made a great wind blow so hard that it split the water apart and dried out a passageway so the children of Israel could walk across on dry land. As soon as they got to the other side and the chariots of Egypt pursued them to destroy them, the sea came back together, and the Egyptians were drowned in that deluge (Ex. 14).

Jesus said: "I'm not going to forget the Passover. One last time, I want to celebrate this Passover with you." As they began to go through the liturgy, Jesus changed the tradition. He still had the wine and the bitter herbs, but He altered the words.

The Passover Lamb

And he took a cup, and when he had given thanks he said, "Take this, and divide it among yourselves. For I tell you that from now on I will not drink of the fruit of the vine until the kingdom of God comes." And he took bread, and when he had given thanks, he broke it and gave it to them, saying, "This is my body, which is given for you. Do this in remembrance of me." And likewise the cup after they had eaten, saying, "This cup that is poured out for you is the new covenant in my blood" (vv. 17–20). The church of Jesus Christ was born that night. It was then that Christ instituted the new covenant. He changed the words. Giving the bread to the disciples, Jesus said, "Take, eat; this is my body," and taking the cup: "Drink of it, all of you, for this is my blood of the covenant, which is poured out for many for the forgiveness of sins" (Matt. 26:26–28). **"Do this in remembrance of me"** (v. 19).

That's why the New Testament says Christ our Passover is sacrificed for us. He and He alone supremely qualifies as the paschal Lamb, the Lamb without blemish who marks each of His people with an indelible mark on their souls so that the angel of death and of judgment will pass over us.

In the Old Testament, there are several feasts and festivals that were ordained and instituted by God. Certainly, the Passover was one of the most important, probably the second most important. The most important was called Yom Kippur, the Day of Atonement (Lev. 16).

Just as the people of Israel were called to repeat and rehearse the Passover on an annual basis, they also were to come together every year for the Day of Atonement. In this celebration, the priest placed his hands on a goat, symbolically transferring the sin of the people to the back of the goat. The goat was sent out into the wilderness, outside the camp of Israel, where it symbolically experienced the curse of God. Another goat was sacrificed as a sin offering. Its blood was taken by the high priest into the Holy of Holies and sprinkled on the ark of the covenant. The blood was also sprinkled on the main altar as an act of reconciliation for atonement.

However, even though God instituted a Day of Atonement that was to be repeated every year, it was never in reality a day of atonement. We know that because Hebrews 10:4 tells us that the blood of bulls and goats cannot take away sin. The Day of Atonement was a symbol of the reality that had not yet occurred. The Day of Atonement was a ceremony looking not at what happened with the sacrifice of animals but what would actually happen in the future with the perfect sacrifice and satisfaction of the wrath of God once and for all in the death of Jesus Christ.

Ironically, during the time of Jesus, the separation between the Passover and the Day of Atonement was not several months but just a few hours. The new covenant was instituted in the celebration of the Passover, but those Old Testament covenants had to be finalized and ratified by a blood rite. On the cross, our Lord ratified the new covenant that He instituted just hours earlier in the upper room as His life and blood were poured out for the atonement of sins.

There are different views of the Lord's Supper, and one of the most serious controversies in the Reformation of the sixteenth century was over the Mass. It was over one particular part of the Mass. In the theology of Rome, the Mass is understood to be a repetition of the sacrifice of Jesus. It is an unbloody sacrifice, to be sure, but Rome declares it to be a real and true sacrifice every time the Mass is spoken, and even then, it doesn't effect the forgiveness of sins without purgatory and all the rest of the Roman Catholic sacramental system.

The Mass is not only irreligious; it's blasphemous to suggest that the atonement of Jesus Christ needs to be repeated in any manner. His atonement is finished. It is accomplished. As the author of Hebrews tells us, it was "once for all" (9:12). It was done forever on that Day of Atonement on Calvary. On that day, the Passover was celebrated and the Day of Atonement was accomplished in the blood of the new covenant, the blood of Jesus, which was shed for the remission of your sins.

Do you have the mark of His blood on you? Will the angel of God's vengeance visit you or pass over you? The Passover Lamb has been sacrificed for His elect now and forevermore.

98

PETER'S DENIAL

Luke 22:24–34, 54–62

A dispute also arose among them, as to which of them was to be regarded as the greatest. And he said to them, "The kings of the Gentiles exercise lordship over them, and those in authority over them are called benefactors. But not so with you. Rather, let the greatest among you become as the youngest, and the leader as one who serves. For who is the greater, one who reclines at table or one who serves? Is it not the one who reclines at table? But I am among you as the one who serves.

"You are those who have stayed with me in my trials, and I assign to you, as my Father assigned to me, a kingdom, that you may eat and drink at my table in my kingdom and sit on thrones judging the twelve tribes of Israel.

"Simon, Simon, behold, Satan demanded to have you, that he might sift you like wheat, but I have prayed for you that your faith may not fail. And when you have turned again, strengthen your brothers." Peter said to him, "Lord, I am ready to go with you both to prison and to death." Jesus said, "I tell you, Peter, the rooster will not crow this day, until you deny three times that you know me." . . .

Then they seized him and led him away, bringing him into the high priest's house, and Peter was following at a distance. And when they had kindled a fire in the middle of the courtyard and sat down together, Peter sat down among them. Then a servant girl, seeing him as he sat in the light and looking closely at him, said, "This man also was with him." But he denied it, saying, "Woman, I do not know him." And a little later someone else saw him and said, "You also are one of them." But Peter said, "Man, I am not." And after an interval of about an hour still another insisted, saying, "Certainly this

> man also was with him, for he too is a Galilean." But Peter said, "Man, I do not know what you are talking about." And immediately, while he was still speaking, the rooster crowed. And the Lord turned and looked at Peter. And Peter remembered the saying of the Lord, how he had said to him, "Before the rooster crows today, you will deny me three times." And he went out and wept bitterly.

A dispute also arose among them, as to which of them was to be regarded as the greatest (v. 24). The story begins with an account of a dispute that arose at the Last Supper. Some scholars speculate that it must have centered around the seating arrangements because there was a certain pecking order commonplace in that day. Those who were the closest to the leader sat next to him and those who were the farthest removed were considered to be of lesser importance (see 14:7–11). Perhaps there was a rivalry among the disciples as to who would sit closest to Jesus.

Jesus, of course, was distressed to see this behavior, so He said to them, **"The kings of the Gentiles exercise lordship over them, and those in authority over them are called benefactors"** (22:25). That is, the kings claim to use their power and authority for the well-being of the people, though that is not what they do. He didn't want the disciples to behave in that manner.

"But not so with you. Rather, let the greatest among you become as the youngest, and the leader as one who serves. For who is the greater, one who reclines at table or one who serves? Is it not the one who reclines at table? But I am among you as the one who serves" (vv. 26–27). Jesus was saying that He came to exalt those who serve. "If you're going to follow Me and be My disciples, then you must have the heart of a servant." And so He said, **"You are those who have stayed with me in my trials, and I assign to you, as my Father assigned to me, a kingdom, that you may eat and drink at my table in my kingdom and sit on thrones judging the twelve tribes of Israel"** (vv. 28–30).

It's in this context that Jesus spoke to Simon Peter: **"Simon, Simon, behold, Satan demanded to have you, that he might sift you like wheat"** (v. 31). Jesus here made an allusion to the agriculture of the day. There were different ways to separate the wheat from the chaff. In one system, batches of grain were scooped into a sifter, which was shaken rapidly, and the wheat and the chaff were separated by the sifter. This was not a labor-intensive or difficult task to accomplish, so Jesus was saying sifting Peter like wheat would be an easy task for Satan to accomplish.

Notice that when Judas went to betray Jesus, the text says, "Satan entered into" him (v. 3). The day Judas was possessed by Satan, he was not a believer;

he was corrupt from the beginning. However, Peter was a believer, and believers cannot be possessed by demons. They can be harassed and oppressed and tormented and tempted and accused by Satan. In this case, Jesus said: "Peter, you're such an easy mark. Satan has demanded to sift you like wheat." He went on to say: **"But I have prayed for you that your faith may not fail. And when you have turned again, strengthen your brothers"** (v. 32).

How did Peter respond to this prediction of Jesus? He was insulted by the insinuation that his faith would not hold up, and he protested, saying to Jesus, **"Lord, I am ready to go with you both to prison and to death"** (v. 33).

Jesus said, "I tell you, Peter, the rooster will not crow this day, until you deny three times that you know me" (v. 34). We read later in the chapter, **Then they seized him and led him away, bringing him into the high priest's house, and Peter was following at a distance** (v. 54). He wasn't standing right next to Jesus, saying, "If you want Jesus, you're going to have to go through me." Rather, he thought, "I'm going to watch all this unfold, but I'm going to keep my distance so that I can be safe in the midst of this crisis."

And when they had kindled a fire in the middle of the courtyard and sat down together, Peter sat down among them. Then a servant girl, seeing him as he sat in the light and looking closely at him, said, "This man also was with him." But he denied it, saying, "Woman, I do not know him." And a little later someone else saw him and said, "You also are one of them." But Peter said, "Man, I am not." And after an interval of about an hour still another insisted, saying, "Certainly this man also was with him, for he too is a Galilean." But Peter said, "Man, I do not know what you are talking about." And immediately, while he was still speaking, the rooster crowed (vv. 55–60). At that same moment, immediately, while Peter was still speaking, expressing his denial of knowing Jesus, a sound was heard at the break of day—a rooster crowed. At the same moment the rooster crowed, Jesus appeared in the courtyard, and Luke tells us that **the Lord turned and looked at Peter. And Peter remembered the saying of the Lord, how he had said to him, "Before the rooster crows today, you will deny me three times." And he went out and wept bitterly** (vv. 61–62).

He didn't say, "Peter, I told you so." He didn't have to say anything. Jesus just looked at him. Can you imagine a more agonizing feeling than that which fell on Peter, who had just denied his Lord? Peter went out and wept bitterly in his abject shame and humiliation.

99

JESUS AT GETHSEMANE

Luke 22:35–46

And he said to them, "When I sent you out with no moneybag or knapsack or sandals, did you lack anything?" They said, "Nothing." He said to them, "But now let the one who has a moneybag take it, and likewise a knapsack. And let the one who has no sword sell his cloak and buy one. For I tell you that this Scripture must be fulfilled in me: 'And he was numbered with the transgressors.' For what is written about me has its fulfillment." And they said, "Look, Lord, here are two swords." And he said to them, "It is enough."

And he came out and went, as was his custom, to the Mount of Olives, and the disciples followed him. And when he came to the place, he said to them, "Pray that you may not enter into temptation." And he withdrew from them about a stone's throw, and knelt down and prayed, saying, "Father, if you are willing, remove this cup from me. Nevertheless, not my will, but yours, be done." And there appeared to him an angel from heaven, strengthening him. And being in agony he prayed more earnestly; and his sweat became like great drops of blood falling down to the ground. And when he rose from prayer, he came to the disciples and found them sleeping for sorrow, and he said to them, "Why are you sleeping? Rise and pray that you may not enter into temptation."

This was a night of intense drama that began with the preparation for the celebration of the Passover with Jesus and His disciples. He had requested it, saying, "I have earnestly desired to eat this Passover with you before I suffer" (v. 15). This was the night in which the Lord, in celebrating the Passover, instituted the Lord's Supper and a new covenant that was made in His blood for remission of sin. It was a night of betrayal. It was a night of denial. It was a night of teaching. Our Lord, in the upper room, gave the longest discourse ever to be found in the Bible concerning the person and work of the Holy Spirit (John 14–16). It was a time of intercession where we have the most comprehensive record of the intercession of Jesus for His disciples and, by extension, for us in which He prayed not only for His disciples but for all those who would believe as a result of their missionary outreach, including those of us who are believers today (John 17).

This was a night of great labor and great trouble. It was the night of betrayal, of denial, of arrest, of trial, of mockery, and of torture that would ultimately culminate in Jesus' death. Luke recorded the stakes, saying: **And he said to them, "When I sent you out with no moneybag or knapsack or sandals, did you lack anything?" They said, "Nothing." He said to them, "But now let the one who has a moneybag take it, and likewise a knapsack. And let the one who has no sword sell his cloak and buy one. For I tell you that this Scripture must be fulfilled in me: 'And he was numbered with the transgressors.' For what is written about me has its fulfillment." And they said, "Look, Lord, here are two swords." And he said to them, "It is enough"** (vv. 35–38). Jesus referred to His sending out the Twelve, reminding them of how they had lacked nothing (9:1–6). So it would be after His death.

And he came out and went, as was his custom, to the Mount of Olives, and the disciples followed him (v. 39). At this point, Jesus and His disciples left the upper room. He had just concluded the most comprehensive intercessory prayer that He had ever made for His disciples (John 17). Now the focus of His prayer was an intercession for Himself.

And when he came to the place, he said to them, "Pray that you may not enter into temptation" (v. 40). Jesus went out with Peter, James, and John and the other disciples. When He came to that place in Gethsemane He removed Himself about a stone's throw distance away from them and began to pray alone. Through the Gospel that we have here, as well as the other Gospels, we have an opportunity, as it were, to eavesdrop a bit on this memorable prayer Jesus uttered on His own behalf. **And he withdrew from them about a stone's throw, and knelt down and prayed, saying, "Father, if you are willing, remove this cup from me. Nevertheless, not my will, but yours, be done"** (vv. 41–42).

The Wills of Jesus

In the seventh century a view called Monothelitism arose that subsequently was condemned by the church universally as a pernicious heresy. This false doctrine taught that in the incarnate Christ there is only one will operative, not two. The church had clearly defined its understanding of the person of Jesus in Nicaea and then later at Chalcedon, where the church confessed that Christ is *vera homo, vera Deus*—truly man, truly God. He is one person perfectly united with two natures—a human nature and a divine nature. The natures are not to be confused or mixed, separated or divided. Each nature retains its own attributes.

When Monothelitism arose, it asked how many wills there are in the person of Jesus. He has two natures. Does He have two wills or one will? The extended heresy of the Monophysites, who taught that Jesus has but one nature, asserted that there is just one will, one theanthropic will, a mixed or blended will drawing from both the human nature and the divine nature. The church said no. There are two natures, and the divine nature certainly has a divine will. God Himself is a volitional being. The divine nature of Christ has a volitional aspect, a will, and true humanity that is united with that true deity also includes the faculty of volition, of choosing, of a will. There is a divine will, and the church professed that there is also a human will.

Part of the reason some were inclined to imagine that in the mystery of the incarnation there is only one will operative is that from the day of Jesus' conception in the womb of Mary, His divine will and His human will have been in absolute harmony with each other. At no point in the incarnation was there ever tension between the divine will and the human will. The Scriptures tell us that Jesus' meat and drink was to do the will of the Father (John 4:34). That's what He lived to do.

Every word that proceeded from the mouth of the Father was absorbed and incorporated in the human will of Jesus. His constant desire was to please the Father, and so He did, which the Father announced publicly: "This is my beloved Son, with whom I am well pleased" (Matt. 17:5). There came a moment in the midst of great sorrow, in the midst of profound agony, that tension arose between the divine will and the human will. It is clear that there was one thing that, humanly speaking, Jesus did not want to do. He asked the Father's permission for this task to be set aside.

The depths of that mystery is more than I can comprehend. This was not sin in the sense that Jesus rejected the will of the Father, because He remained willing to do whatever it was that the Father willed. Rather, Jesus was not willing in the sense that He was hoping against hope that another way could be found for Him to fulfill His mission in this world. He, in His agony, on His knees, asked: **"Father, if you are willing, remove this cup from me. Nevertheless, not my will, but yours, be done"** (v. 42). All things being equal, Jesus in His humanity didn't want to do this. But He understood the will of His Father and hastened to add: "Nevertheless, not My will but Your will be done. It is still My will, O Father, to do whatever it is that You will, whatever it is You want Me to do. But please, if there's any way, take this cup away from Me."

Why would Jesus ask for the possibility that that cup would be removed? The only answer we have is to understand what was in that cup. Let us look at another passage at the end of the New Testament. In Revelation 14:18–20, we read:

> And another angel came out from the altar, the angel who has authority over the fire, and he called with a loud voice to the one who had the sharp sickle, "Put in your sickle and gather the clusters from the vine of the earth, for its grapes are ripe." So the angel swung his sickle across the earth and gathered the grape harvest of the earth and threw it into the great winepress of the wrath of God. And the winepress was trodden outside the city, and blood flowed from the winepress, as high as a horse's bridle, for 1,600 stadia.

You may be familiar with the words of that passage in a different form from the "Battle Hymn of the Republic": "Mine eyes have seen the glory of the coming of the Lord. He has trampled out the vintage where the grapes of wrath are stored. He has loosed the fateful lightning of his terrible swift sword. His truth goes marching on." How this became a political song in times of war is questionable. Perhaps the only thing that America could imagine as a simile to ultimate destruction was this passage that speaks of the gathering by the sickle of ripe grapes of wrath to be trampled outside until the skins and the substance of the grapes would be separated and poured into a cup that was to be swallowed by a fallen world of sin. The grapes of wrath are what filled the cup placed before Jesus in the garden of Gethsemane.

How can we grasp what was in there? This metaphor means, borrowing from the vineyard, the process of trampling or treading on the grapes to free the fluid so as to fill up the cup with wrath. If God had this cup in front of you, what would you do? Even if I didn't have to take a sip of its contents, to have the proximity of the cup near my mouth would completely devastate me as a human being, and I could not survive.

God didn't just ask Jesus to put the cup against His lips. No. He said: "Drink it, all of it, to its bitter dregs. Not just a sip, but the entire cupful that this wrath may flow into Your stomach, into Your visceral parts beyond those parts to Your very soul, to the last drop of My wrath."

The cup of God's wrath was His curse on Jesus, the price Jesus had to pay for your redemption and for mine. He was completely and utterly forsaken by God. Nothing less would do. No wonder He trembled in agony at the thought of it.

That is the only way God's righteousness and His justice could be satisfied. Someone had to pay the price for sin, and God gave that cup to Jesus. Nevertheless, Jesus said: "Not My will but Your will. Even if Your will is to forsake Me, to curse Me, to condemn Me, not for My sin but for the sin of My people, give the cup to Me and I'll drink it."

The Agony of Jesus

And there appeared to him an angel from heaven, strengthening him. And being in agony he prayed more earnestly; and his sweat became like great drops of blood falling down to the ground (vv. 43–44). Was that simply a metaphorical description saying that the sweat was so intense and so heavy that it was like blood? Some argue in that manner, while others say no, it wasn't just *like* blood; it *was* blood. The intensity of what our Lord experienced in Gethsemane was so great that the capillaries in His forehead burst and blood began to seep from His pores down His face. Just a few hours later, His enemies would take a crown made from thorns and make puncture wounds in His forehead as they put it on Him. That was nothing compared to what He experienced in Gethsemane as He contemplated the cost of our salvation.

The biggest reason we don't understand this text is that we don't really believe in the wrath of God. We have been brainwashed by a secular culture that totally rejects any idea of there being wrath in God. But the Scriptures make clear that God is furious at sin and that His wrath is real.

And when he rose from prayer, he came to the disciples and found them sleeping for sorrow, and he said to them, "Why are you sleeping? Rise and pray that you may not enter into temptation" (vv. 45–46). Three times as Jesus prayed, He came to His disciples (Matt. 26:40–45). Each time He found them asleep and He roused them. "Can't you watch with Me for one hour?"

Jesus didn't say to His disciples, "Please come along and watch *over* Me." He said, "Come and watch *with* Me." The impression we get is that Jesus was completely isolated and alone, as His disciples fell asleep and failed in the request He gave to them to watch with Him. We know that an angel from heaven came and strengthened Him (Luke 22:43). Jesus went from the darkness of the garden, where the soldiers were waiting with their swords and the clubs and where the kiss of death would be placed upon His cheek, and He was delivered into the hands of the Gentiles to be forsaken and cursed by God. This was the price He paid for our redemption.

100

THE ARREST OF JESUS

Luke 22:47–53

While he was still speaking, there came a crowd, and the man called Judas, one of the twelve, was leading them. He drew near to Jesus to kiss him, but Jesus said to him, "Judas, would you betray the Son of Man with a kiss?" And when those who were around him saw what would follow, they said, "Lord, shall we strike with the sword?" And one of them struck the servant of the high priest and cut off his right ear. But Jesus said, "No more of this!" And he touched his ear and healed him. Then Jesus said to the chief priests and officers of the temple and elders, who had come out against him, "Have you come out as against a robber, with swords and clubs? When I was with you day after day in the temple, you did not lay hands on me. But this is your hour, and the power of darkness."

While he was still speaking, there came a crowd, and the man called Judas, one of the twelve, was leading them (v. 47). Judas came with a great multitude of soldiers, and we assume that the soldiers who were present with swords and clubs were a mixture of members of the temple guard belonging to the Sanhedrin and members of the cohorts of the Roman garrisons in Jerusalem. They came to this designated place where the arrest of Jesus would be made, where it would not take place under the light of day but rather in a secluded spot so that His arrest would be covered by the cloak of darkness. Every aspect of this incident that we see here indicates an action that took place among the children of darkness. It was one of the most wicked acts of all of history, and it was appropriate that it took place not in the light of the sun but in the darkness of the night.

He drew near to Jesus to kiss him, but Jesus said to him, "Judas, would you betray the Son of Man with a kiss?" (vv. 47–48). Judas, the betrayer, had given the soldiers a signal, saying, "The one I will kiss is the man. Seize him and lead him away under guard" (Mark 14:44). And as soon as he had come, immediately he went up to Him and said, "Rabbi!" and kissed Him. There is incredible irony in that a gesture of profound honor and affection, which customarily was given by disciples to their rabbi, was the method used by Judas for a most evil and wicked mission. The kiss itself was an act not only of contradiction but of vengeance. Jesus called out Judas' gesture, pointing out the stinging hypocrisy of his choosing to betray Him with a kiss.

And when those who were around him saw what would follow, they said, "Lord, shall we strike with the sword?" And one of them struck the servant of the high priest and cut off his right ear. But Jesus said, "No more of this!" And he touched his ear and healed him (vv. 49–51). Then they laid their hands on Him, and they took Him. One of those who stood by drew his sword and struck the servant of the high priest, cutting off his ear. Luke did not name the one who drew his sword, but John in his Gospel identified him as Peter, the impetuous and impulsive disciple (John 18:10). So Peter drew his sword and struck the servant of the high priest and cut off his ear. Jesus then rebuked him for it and picked up the man's ear and put it back, and this man whose ear had just been cut off had it restored by the very One whom he was arresting for execution.

Then Jesus said to the chief priests and officers of the temple and elders, who had come out against him, "Have you come out as against a robber, with swords and clubs? When I was with you day after day in the temple, you did not lay hands on me. But this is your hour, and the power of darkness" (vv. 52–53). Every day when Jesus was in the temple teaching, the authorities could have arrested Him, and they could have done so easily. They did not need weapons. But they did not do so then, so that the Scriptures could be fulfilled.

101

JESUS BEFORE THE SANHEDRIN

Luke 22:63–71

Now the men who were holding Jesus in custody were mocking him as they beat him. They also blindfolded him and kept asking him, "Prophesy! Who is it that struck you?" And they said many other things against him, blaspheming him.

When day came, the assembly of the elders of the people gathered together, both chief priests and scribes. And they led him away to their council, and they said, "If you are the Christ, tell us." But he said to them, "If I tell you, you will not believe, and if I ask you, you will not answer. But from now on the Son of Man shall be seated at the right hand of the power of God." So they all said, "Are you the Son of God, then?" And he said to them, "You say that I am." Then they said, "What further testimony do we need? We have heard it ourselves from his own lips."

Now the men who were holding Jesus in custody were mocking him as they beat him. They also blindfolded him and kept asking him, "Prophesy! Who is it that struck you?" And they said many other things against him, blaspheming him (vv. 63–65). It is hard to imagine the kind of arrogance that led these soldiers to blaspheme, to mock, and to strike the Christ, the Anointed One of God, the Son of God incarnate. But it testifies to the humility our Savior was willing to undergo for the sake of His people.

In the book of Isaiah, we read, "The Lord God has opened my ear, and I was not rebellious; I turned not backward. I gave my back to those who strike, and my cheeks to those who pull out the beard; I hid not my face from disgrace and spitting" (50:5–6). If somebody tries to spit in your face, you're going to cover yourself up. If they try to strike you, you will defend yourself. Jesus took it, following the prophetic utterance of the prophet Isaiah in describing what would happen centuries in the future with the Servant of the Lord. He was beaten, and He took it when they spit upon Him.

When day came, the assembly of the elders of the people gathered together, both chief priests and scribes. And they led him away to their council (v. 66). At this time, the high priest was Caiaphas, who was the son-in-law of Annas, and Annas was perhaps the most powerful Jew in the land. Caiaphas reigned from AD 18 to 36. What's remarkable about this mention of Jesus' being led away to the high priest and to the **council** or Sanhedrin, which was the ruling body of the Jews, is that where they went was not to the customary meeting place of the Sanhedrin. Normally, the Sanhedrin was assembled at a place called the Chamber of Hewn Stone, but this time, according to Matthew's account, they convened at the home of the high priest (Matt. 26:57). For the only time in recorded Jewish history, a trial was conducted at night, which was illegal, and was conducted at the home of the high priest.

And they said, "If you are the Christ, tell us" (vv. 66–67). The force of the language tells us that they were not on a truth-seeking mission. They were not gathering facts. They weren't interested in facts. They were intentionally trying to find something that would convict Jesus of a capital offense. This was a witch hunt. And not only that, but other Gospel accounts tell us that they were willing to suborn perjury (Matt. 26:59–61; Mark 14:55–59). They were not interested in finding evidence that would be exculpatory; at this time they only wanted dirt that they could gather together.

Now again, this meeting was not held in the normal place for the meeting of the Sanhedrin, which would be much more open to the public. And all these proceedings were taking place under the cover of darkness, covertly, lest the people in Jerusalem be awakened to what was going on and perhaps march in protest against it. And so, they went to the house of Caiaphas and held the hearing at night, which Jewish law forbade. The hearings could only be held in the day, and also the Jewish law prescribed that no trial could be held on either the Sabbath, a feast day, or the eve of a Sabbath or a feast day. That regulation was violated as well, since this was the day before the Sabbath. Also, Jewish law required that if a capital case was being tried and if a criminal was convicted of a capital crime, then the Sanhedrin would be responsible to meet the next day again to confirm the judgment, because the Jewish law put a hedge around any attempts at kangaroo courts, any attempts of rash and sudden judgments in capital cases. And, of course, Old Testament law required that in a capital case there had to be two eyewitnesses to the crime, and those two eyewitnesses had to agree in their testimony (Deut. 17:6). Everything about this hearing flew in the face of Jewish law.

The members of the Sanhedrin had been consecrated and set apart to protect the law of God, just as our Supreme Court is to protect the Bill of Rights and the Constitution. They don't always do it, and neither did the Sanhedrin, because while they were having Jesus on trial, they broke the Ten Commandments by bearing false witness against the Son of God. And not only did they themselves bear false witness against Jesus, but they encouraged one another to do it.

Jesus Responds

But he said to them, "If I tell you, you will not believe, and if I ask you, you will not answer" (vv. 67–68). Jesus did not directly answer their question. This fulfilled the prophecy of Isaiah: "Like a sheep that before its shearers is silent, so he opened not his mouth" (53:7). Maybe that's why Jesus maintained silence at this point, simply to fulfill the Old Testament prophecy, but I think He had something else in mind. He knew what these people were doing, and He knew that whatever He said—no matter how accurate it was, no matter how sincere it was, no matter how truthful it was—His words would be seized upon, they would be twisted, they would be distorted and used against Him. Better to let these false witnesses give their testimony and Jesus stay quiet than for Him to say anything that they could use against Him.

"But from now on the Son of Man shall be seated at the right hand of the power of God" (v. 69). Jesus here used His favorite self-designation: **"the Son of Man." "Seated at the right hand of the power of God"** is likely a reference to Daniel 7 with its description of a heavenly being who comes to the throne of the Ancient of Days. Jesus said: "I have come from heaven, and I'm going back to heaven. The Son of Man will be appointed to judge the living and the dead." In a sense, Jesus was saying: "Yes, I am the Son of Man, and this is not the last time that we will meet in the context of a trial. I'll be back, and I'll be back with all the authority of heaven, and you will be judged by Me." That was the clear implication when He said, **"The Son of Man shall be seated at the right hand of the power of God."**

So they all said, "Are you the Son of God, then?" And he said to them, "You say that I am" (v. 70). The members of the council by this point had lost their patience. They wanted a direct answer regarding Jesus' claims about

Himself. And Jesus affirmed that it had been said of Him rightly: **"You say that I am."**

Then they said, "What further testimony do we need? We have heard it ourselves from his own lips" (v. 71). At this point, the members of the council were convinced that Jesus was guilty of blasphemy and deserving of death. Here's something interesting about this passage. It was not a capital offense in Israel to claim to be the Messiah even if you weren't the Messiah. You could be charged with lying. You could be charged with stirring up trouble. You could be charged with all kinds of things. But it wasn't a capital offense to call yourself the Messiah. So that wasn't enough to bring a death penalty verdict.

Jewish law carefully defined what blasphemy was. To be guilty of blasphemy, you had to directly curse the name of God. Jesus didn't do that. Jesus blessed the name of God. But what they considered blasphemous was His identifying Himself as the Son of God. But even there, the charge was without Jewish legal foundation. But they condemned Him as deserving of death.

In the meantime, as we have seen, Peter was denying his Lord (vv. 54–62). Beloved, if you are ever in the same situation, if that moment of truth comes for you, that moment where you have to stand up and be counted, if you have to identify yourself as one who belongs to Jesus, remember that Jesus said, "And I tell you, everyone who acknowledges me before men, the Son of Man also will acknowledge before the angels of God, but the one who denies me before men will be denied before the angels of God" (12:8–9). I can't imagine anything more embarrassing than to stand in heaven and have Jesus say, "I'm ashamed of this man," to have Jesus look at me and say, "Shame on you." I pray that the grace of God and the strength of the Holy Spirit will keep you and keep me from ever doing that to Jesus.

102

JESUS ON TRIAL

Luke 23:1–25

Then the whole company of them arose and brought him before Pilate. And they began to accuse him, saying, "We found this man misleading our nation and forbidding us to give tribute to Caesar, and saying that he himself is Christ, a king." And Pilate asked him, "Are you the King of the Jews?" And he answered him, "You have said so." Then Pilate said to the chief priests and the crowds, "I find no guilt in this man." But they were urgent, saying, "He stirs up the people, teaching throughout all Judea, from Galilee even to this place."

When Pilate heard this, he asked whether the man was a Galilean. And when he learned that he belonged to Herod's jurisdiction, he sent him over to Herod, who was himself in Jerusalem at that time. When Herod saw Jesus, he was very glad, for he had long desired to see him, because he had heard about him, and he was hoping to see some sign done by him. So he questioned him at some length, but he made no answer. The chief priests and the scribes stood by, vehemently accusing him. And Herod with his soldiers treated him with contempt and mocked him. Then, arraying him in splendid clothing, he sent him back to Pilate. And Herod and Pilate became friends with each other that very day, for before this they had been at enmity with each other.

Pilate then called together the chief priests and the rulers and the people, and said to them, "You brought me this man as one who was misleading the people. And after examining him before you, behold, I did not find this man guilty of any of your charges against him. Neither did Herod, for he sent him back to us. Look, nothing deserving death has been done by him. I will therefore punish and release him."

> But they all cried out together, "Away with this man, and release to us Barabbas"—a man who had been thrown into prison for an insurrection started in the city and for murder. Pilate addressed them once more, desiring to release Jesus, but they kept shouting, "Crucify, crucify him!" A third time he said to them, "Why? What evil has he done? I have found in him no guilt deserving death. I will therefore punish and release him." But they were urgent, demanding with loud cries that he should be crucified. And their voices prevailed. So Pilate decided that their demand should be granted. He released the man who had been thrown into prison for insurrection and murder, for whom they asked, but he delivered Jesus over to their will.

Then the whole company of them arose and brought him before Pilate (v. 1). Pontius Pilate had the title of procurator, or governor, of a section of the Holy Land. He ruled over Samaria and Judea, but his jurisdiction did not extend to Galilee, where most of the ministry of Jesus had taken place. He was appointed by the Roman government for this task in an outpost far from the center of the Roman Empire. As far as political appointments were concerned, this was not a good job. In fact, it was one of the lowest appointments in the Roman Empire. Political leaders hated to be assigned to the Holy Land because the Jews were always involved in turmoil and debate and felt only disgust toward the Romans.

There's a letter that survives from the Hellenistic Jew Philo that describes Pontius Pilate as a man who was inflexible, obstinate, and known for his cruelty. He was known for railroading prisoners through the system in a capricious manner.

From the perspective of the Christian community, however, Pilate occupied a very important role. Often we will recite the Apostles' Creed or the Nicene Creed. In both cases, Pontius Pilate is mentioned by name. Emperor Tiberius isn't mentioned. No Roman senator was mentioned. Neither Annas nor Caiaphas is mentioned in the creeds of the church. But the one who receives that distinction was Pontius Pilate. The creeds declare, "Crucified under Pontius Pilate" or "suffered under Pontius Pilate." Why is that?

In the ancient world it was understood that a person who occupied a seat of government was not a normal layperson but a *persona publica*. He was the public official who stated judgments that were considered to be under the ultimate governing power of the providence of God. So whatever this *persona publica* pronounced in judgment was understood by many to be the will of God.

In the interrogation of Jesus by Pilate, he listened to the charges being raised against Jesus three times (vv. 2–4, 13–16, 18–22) and came to the same conclusion: **"I find no guilt in this man"** (v. 4). The reason Pilate failed to find fault in Jesus is not because he was failing in discernment. The reason is because there wasn't any fault to find.

Repeatedly, the Scriptures teach us of Jesus' sinlessness, which was absolutely crucial for Him to qualify as the Lamb of God without blemish. Even from the deceitful lips of Pontius Pilate, this petty politician, the announcement is made public. **A third time he said to them, "Why? What evil has he done? I have found in him no guilt deserving death. I will therefore punish and release him"** (v. 22).

Already, those who held Jesus had blindfolded Him and then punched, slapped, and brutally mocked Him. Somebody would punch Him, and say, "Prophesy! Who is it that struck you?" and they said other things against Him, blaspheming Him (22:63–65).

The torture, humiliation, and mockery to which Jesus was submitted was something He knew was going to happen. But in the garden of Gethsemane, He wasn't sweating drops of blood because He was worried about the torture and humiliation inflicted by men. What provoked the passion in Gethsemane was the cup filled with the wrath of God. The pain that He would face later, having to drink that cup, immeasurably outweighed the bruises and beatings and torture to which He was subjected by the hands of men.

And they began to accuse him, saying, "We found this man misleading our nation and forbidding us to give tribute to Caesar, and saying that he himself is Christ, a king." And Pilate asked him, "Are you the King of the Jews?" And he answered him, "You have said so." Then Pilate said to the chief priests and the crowds, "I find no guilt in this man" (vv. 2–4). Pilate listened to the charges brought forth by the Sanhedrin—that Jesus called Himself a King. The only absolutely true and authentic leader in the history of the world was Jesus. If there was anything for which Jesus was never once guilty, it was misleading people.

One of the great ironies of our day is that when people who are unbelievers speak about Jesus, they will heap popular praise on Him. "Jesus was a great ethical teacher. I'll even acknowledge that He was a prophet. I just don't believe that He was God incarnate." It's not hard to find somebody quick to criticize Christians, but people are very slow to criticize Jesus Himself.

But they were urgent, saying, "He stirs up the people, teaching throughout all Judea, from Galilee even to this place." When Pilate heard this, he asked whether the man was a Galilean. And when he learned that he belonged to Herod's jurisdiction, he sent him over to Herod, who was himself in Jerusalem at that time (vv. 5–7). When Pilate discovered that Jesus was from

Galilee, he thought he could avoid making a judgment because he didn't have jurisdiction over Galilee. The ruler of Galilee was the tetrarch Herod Agrippa. He was the one who was criticized for his illicit relationship with his wife by John the Baptist (9:7–9; see Matt. 14:1–12). John was imprisoned, and then on a whim, and by the order of the tetrarch Herod Agrippa, John the Baptist was beheaded. Herod Agrippa was haunted for the rest of his life because he knew the guilt that he bore for that atrocity.

Herod Questions Jesus

When Herod saw Jesus, he was very glad, for he had long desired to see him, because he had heard about him, and he was hoping to see some sign done by him. So he questioned him at some length, but he made no answer (vv. 8–9). Herod was, however, fascinated by Jesus. Though he had never met Jesus, Herod had heard about Him. It was as though Herod was saying, "Who is this man? I want to see for myself." Herod hoped that Jesus would perform one of His miracles. So Pilate sent Jesus to Herod Agrippa, who happened to be in Jerusalem because of the feast. Imagine Agrippa's disappointment when Jesus did nothing. No miracles. No tricks. No words. Agrippa questioned Jesus with many words, and every time he asked Him a question, Jesus didn't respond. He opened not His mouth.

The chief priests and the scribes stood by, vehemently accusing him. And Herod with his soldiers treated him with contempt and mocked him. Then, arraying him in splendid clothing, he sent him back to Pilate. And Herod and Pilate became friends with each other that very day, for before this they had been at enmity with each other (vv. 10–12). The Bible doesn't tell us why Herod Agrippa and Pilate were estranged, but probably it had something to do with Pilate's shedding the blood of the Galileans, one of the most cruel atrocities that he perpetrated, but Herod appeared to be grateful to Pilate for the opportunity to see Jesus.

Pilate then called together the chief priests and the rulers and the people, and said to them, "You brought me this man as one who was misleading the people. And after examining him before you, behold, I did not find this man guilty of any of your charges against him. Neither did Herod, for he sent him back to us. Look, nothing deserving death has been done by him. I will therefore punish and release him" (vv. 13–16). There was an impasse with Agrippa, so he sent Jesus back to Pilate again for further judgment. Again Pilate said: "I can't find anything wrong here. There's no capital offense that He has committed."

Once again, as *persona publica*, Pontius Pilate presented Jesus to the group of men who were assembled there and said the immortal words in Latin, "*Ecce homo!*" "Behold the man!" (John 19:5). Was he simply adding to the mockery of Jesus, or was there a higher message delivered by the providence of God? The name of Pontius Pilate appears in the creeds because he essentially said: "Do you want to know what humanity is supposed to look like? What the new Adam looks like? If you want to know the One who is the express image of His person, then *Ecce homo!* Behold the man!"

The Crowd Demands Barabbas

But they all cried out together, "Away with this man, and release to us Barabbas"—a man who had been thrown into prison for an insurrection started in the city and for murder. Pilate addressed them once more, desiring to release Jesus, but they kept shouting, "Crucify, crucify him!" A third time he said to them, "Why? What evil has he done? I have found in him no guilt deserving death. I will therefore punish and release him" (vv. 18–22). Voices from the crowd said: "But wait a minute! Rome has a custom among the Jews. At Passover each year, we ask that you release a prisoner to us." Pilate said: "I'll follow that custom. Would you like me to give you Jesus?" It was election time. Pilate nominated Jesus. The crowd said, "No, give us Barabbas." Oh, the irony that drips from the name Barabbas, "son of the father." When the Son of the Father was standing next to Barabbas, ironically the crowd elected Barabbas to be released by Pilate.

But they were urgent, demanding with loud cries that he should be crucified. And their voices prevailed. So Pilate decided that their demand should be granted. He released the man who had been thrown into prison for insurrection and murder, for whom they asked, but he delivered Jesus over to their will (vv. 23–25). Pilate called for a basin, filled it with water, stood on the porch, and washed his hands in front of the crowd (Matt. 27:24). "My hands are clean. You get what you voted for. You want a murderer? You want Barabbas? You can have him. So what should I do with Jesus?" They screamed, the Scriptures tell us, urgently, "Crucify Him!" It wasn't the common people who were screaming, "Crucify Him!" It was the group of leaders and thugs and false witnesses assembled by the Sanhedrin screaming for the blood of Jesus. So Pilate, living up to his reputation, acquiesced to the will of the people and sent to His death a man whom he had announced three times was innocent.

103

THE CRUCIFIXION, PART 1

Luke 23:26–31

And as they led him away, they seized one Simon of Cyrene, who was coming in from the country, and laid on him the cross, to carry it behind Jesus. And there followed him a great multitude of the people and of women who were mourning and lamenting for him. But turning to them Jesus said, "Daughters of Jerusalem, do not weep for me, but weep for yourselves and for your children. For behold, the days are coming when they will say, 'Blessed are the barren and the wombs that never bore and the breasts that never nursed!' Then they will begin to say to the mountains, 'Fall on us,' and to the hills, 'Cover us.' For if they do these things when the wood is green, what will happen when it is dry?"

And as they led him away, they seized one Simon of Cyrene, who was coming in from the country, and laid on him the cross, to carry it behind Jesus (v. 26). **Simon** is mentioned in other Gospels as well, and from there we get a little more information about this man. We are told, for example, in Mark's Gospel that he was the father of two sons, Rufus and Alexander (Mark 15:21). We don't know for sure about the spiritual condition of this man. He was from **Cyrene**, which was about ten miles from the Mediterranean coast in Libya, and had come to Jerusalem for the feast days. There was a large Jewish settlement in Cyrene at that time, and so as a practicing Jew, this man came for the holy days of that season. As far as we know, he was not yet a believer in Jesus. He is mentioned here merely as a bystander, an observer, a spectator of the events that were about to take place. This was a parade of sorts, but not the kind occasioned by some joyful celebration.

The criminals who had been condemned to execution had been ordered, as was the custom of their executioners, to carry their crosses from the place of judgment, probably along the Via Dolorosa, the way of grief, to a place outside the city walls, because they were not to be executed within the confines of Jerusalem, the holy city of God. We know that Jesus began the process of carrying His cross—whether it was the entire cross or merely the crossbeam is a question of historical debate. Nevertheless, He started on that journey, but He had been severely beaten and scourged with whips and was in an extremely exhausted condition.

By governmental authority, the soldiers who were attending the execution had the right to requisition or compel some bystander to assist in the task of carrying the cross. These authorities looked to Simon of Cyrene.

What Simon of Cyrene did in carrying the cross of Jesus earned him absolutely no merit for himself. This was not a work of the law that would grant him access into the kingdom of God. He could not rest on the virtue of his personal sacrifice, albeit a sacrifice that was not voluntary. He could not look to that as a reason for getting into the kingdom of God. All that aside, this obscure fellow from Libya, who was just a bystander, watching as Jesus struggled with His cross and being conscripted to carry it, was a most blessed human being.

Tradition indicates that Simon watched the spectacle of the crucifixion of Christ and listened to the words that Jesus spoke, and on that day, Simon of Cyrene became a Christian. He could say till the day he died: "I saw it happen. With my own eyes, I witnessed His death. I heard His voice. I heard Him say, 'Father, forgive them, for they know not what they do.' I heard Him cry from the cross, 'My God, my God, why have You forsaken Me?' I heard Him say, 'I'm thirsty.' I watched it all unfold, and I heard it." There were thousands of people there that day who heard and saw the same thing, but only he could say: "I carried the cross of Jesus. I'm blessed to have participated in the affliction and the great passion of Jesus."

Each of those who saw the death of Jesus with their eyes, who heard His words from the cross, had different views of the significance of what they were watching. Caiaphas had an evaluation of it: "This execution is politically necessary. It's good for one man to die for the nation" (see John 11:49–50). The centurion later would say, "Truly this man was the Son of God!" (Mark

15:39). But there was nothing plainly evident in this scene on Golgotha that said to the world that this was an event of cosmic significance. This was the ultimate Yom Kippur, the supreme Day of Atonement, because this man was not simply being executed as a criminal, experiencing in Himself the wrath of men, but He had become a curse for us—His work that day was an atonement for the sins of His people. Not until the Epistles expressed to us the depths and riches through God's revelation of the meaning and the significance of that event would its meaning be evident to an onlooker or a spectator.

The People Mourn

And there followed him a great multitude of the people and of women who were mourning and lamenting for him (v. 27). We don't usually use the term **lamenting** today. We talk about **mourning**. We talk about grief, and we understand that kind of pain. But the term *lament* has almost passed from our vocabulary. The first time I went to the Rijksmuseum in Amsterdam, I saw an incredible collection of paintings from the brush of Rembrandt van Rijn. Out of these great works of art, these masterpieces, my favorite was a portrait of Jeremiah with his head in his hands, and in the background, the city of Jerusalem is in flames from the sacking of the Babylonians in 586 BC. The title of the painting is *Jeremiah Lamenting the Destruction of Jerusalem*.

I point this out for a reason. Rembrandt captured on canvas a man in grotesque agony as he is lamenting for something holy, something precious. Jesus saw the real thing, not just a painting. He saw **women who were mourning and lamenting**, torn asunder with the poignancy of their grief. Jesus spoke to them in one sense, tenderly, and another sense, ominously.

But turning to them Jesus said, "Daughters of Jerusalem, do not weep for me, but weep for yourselves and for your children. For behold, the days are coming when they will say, 'Blessed are the barren and the wombs that never bore and the breasts that never nursed!'" (vv. 28–29). He was warning the women of the coming destruction of the temple and Jerusalem in AD 70 when the wrath of God was to fall upon the Jewish nation. **"Then they will begin to say to the mountains, 'Fall on us,' and to the hills, 'Cover us.' For if they do these things when the wood is green, what will happen when it is dry?"** (vv. 30–31). That's an enigmatic statement. Here is the One who is going into the flames of divine wrath as green wood. Nobody throws green wood into the fire because it won't burn. You dry the wood so that it will ignite easily and quickly and be engulfed in the flames, but the green wood just smolders and smokes. Jesus was saying: "They're going to throw Me into the flames as green wood. What's going to happen to the dry wood?" He said to them: "You haven't begun to lament. You haven't begun to understand grief. When the full judgment of the Father comes on this nation, you'll be screaming for the hills to fall and crush you and cover you, to shield you from that wrath that is to come."

He wasn't on the cross yet, but already He had encountered Simon of Cyrene and the weeping daughters of Jerusalem. Even then, He looked beyond to the curse He was to bear, to the curse of God's wrath that was yet to come.

104

THE CRUCIFIXION, PART 2

Luke 23:32–43

Two others, who were criminals, were led away to be put to death with him. And when they came to the place that is called The Skull, there they crucified him, and the criminals, one on his right and one on his left. And Jesus said, "Father, forgive them, for they know not what they do." And they cast lots to divide his garments. And the people stood by, watching, but the rulers scoffed at him, saying, "He saved others; let him save himself, if he is the Christ of God, his Chosen One!" The soldiers also mocked him, coming up and offering him sour wine and saying, "If you are the King of the Jews, save yourself!" There was also an inscription over him, "This is the King of the Jews."

One of the criminals who were hanged railed at him, saying, "Are you not the Christ? Save yourself and us!" But the other rebuked him, saying, "Do you not fear God, since you are under the same sentence of condemnation? And we indeed justly, for we are receiving the due reward of our deeds; but this man has done nothing wrong." And he said, "Jesus, remember me when you come into your kingdom." And he said to him, "Truly, I say to you, today you will be with me in paradise."

Two others, who were criminals, were led away to be put to death with him. And when they came to the place that is called The Skull, there they crucified him, and the criminals, one on his right and

one on his left. And Jesus said, "Father, forgive them, for they know not what they do" (vv. 32–34). The Gospels record seven sayings that Jesus uttered from the cross, but we don't know exactly in what order they were spoken. Traditionally, however, it is thought that the first statement Jesus uttered from the cross was His plea for forgiveness for those who put them there: **"Father, forgive them."** In this dramatic statement from the cross, Jesus prayed not for Himself, not for His disciples, not for His friends, but for His tormentors, His executioners, those who were committing this most despicable act. Jesus was already functioning as an intercessor, as the Great High Priest, pleading for the Father's forgiveness for these gross sinners. He appended a reason for that request, something of a mitigating circumstance, when He said, **"for they know not what they do."**

In Scripture, there are varying degrees of culpability for the sins we commit. One of those mitigating circumstances is ignorance. Though ignorance does not excuse people entirely for their sinful actions, in the Old Testament sacrificial system, there were particular sacrifices that were offered for those sins that were done in ignorance. In 1870 at the First Vatican Council, Pope Pius IX referred to Protestants as schismatics and heretics. That rhetoric softened between then and the Second Vatican Council in 1962–65, where Protestants were called "separated brethren." Even as harsh as the statements of Pius IX were in 1870, he declared that some Protestants who were guilty of egregious sin nevertheless suffered from what he called invincible ignorance. Invincible ignorance was distinguished from vincible ignorance, as you might presume. Vincible ignorance is ignorance that is easy to overcome, that rarely offers an excuse for any form of wicked behavior. Vincible ignorance is ignorance that could have and should have been overcome. Invincible ignorance, on the other hand, as defined by Pius IX, is ignorance that is very difficult or almost impossible to overcome.

Pius was saying that the Protestant rebels—traitors to the church, schismatics and heretics—nevertheless have their guilt mitigated to some degree because they suffered from invincible ignorance. Since the sixteenth century, Protestants have grown up hearing that Rome is a false church. What would you expect them to believe in those circumstances? They grew up hearing and believing a gross error (from Rome's point of view). As a consequence, they are deeply marred in their tragic sense of ignorance.

When Jesus adds ignorance as a mitigating circumstance, when He pleads for the forgiveness of His executioners, I have to ask, Was it vincible or invincible ignorance? The scribes and the Pharisees and the priests had a vast knowledge of Scripture. They were theologians, students of the Bible, and they enjoyed a certain mastery over sacred Scripture. They read repeatedly all the prophecies recorded in sacred Scripture about the coming Messiah. Yet, when He came, not only did they miss Him, not only did they reject Him, but they murdered Him. Jesus asked for their pardon because of their ignorance. He said, **"They know not what they do."** Later on, the Apostle Paul said of the event of the cross, "None of the rulers of this age understood this, for if they had, they would not have crucified the Lord of glory" (1 Cor. 2:8).

In the Scriptures we have literally scores of titles that are ascribed to Jesus that define His person and His work. One of my favorite titles for Jesus is the one given by the Apostle Paul in that verse, where he calls Jesus "the Lord of glory." Jesus is not just the Lord of the church, not only the Lord of the Jews, not simply the Lord of the Gentiles, not the Lord of all pagans in this world, but the Lord of glory. He doesn't just possess glory; He is its King, its sovereign, its Lord. The Lord of glory Himself became flesh. He left the glory behind Him. He embraced the opposite of glory, which was humiliation, and we killed Him. The Lord of glory was on the cross that day.

Jesus Is Mocked

And they cast lots to divide his garments. And the people stood by, watching, but the rulers scoffed at him, saying, "He saved others; let him save himself, if he is the Christ of God, his Chosen One!" The soldiers also mocked him, coming up and offering him sour wine and saying, "If you are the King of the Jews, save yourself!" There was also an inscription over him, "This is the King of the Jews." One of the criminals who were hanged railed at him, saying, "Are you not the Christ? Save yourself and us!" (vv. 34–39). Even while Jesus was praying for their forgiveness, their hostility toward Him was escalated, and they began to taunt and mock Him. In fact, there were defined here different groups of people making fun of Jesus in His condition. People stood by watching, but the first group, the **rulers**, those in positions of the highest authority in Israel, scoffed at Him, saying, **"He saved others; let him save himself, if he is the Christ of God, his Chosen One!"** The second group, the **soldiers**, also mocked Him, coming up and offering sour wine to Him, saying, **"If you are the King of the Jews, save yourself!"** They could read the inscription put above Him: **"This is the King of the Jews."** There were rulers and soldiers who mocked Jesus, and also **one of the criminals** who was hanging beside Him said, **"Are you not the Christ? Save yourself and us!"** He didn't believe that Jesus could do it.

These men all had the same message: "If You can save others, then save Yourself." People who had witnessed the miracles of Jesus were there. Some realized that He actually did give sight to the blind and hearing to the deaf and saved them from their miserable condition. They said: "But what now, Jesus? You saved everybody else, but You can't save Yourself?"

In the English language, we have two words that sound similar. In fact, the words are differentiated by only one letter. One word is *could*; the other one is *would*. Could or would. We talk about could have, should have, would have, and so on. We know that the sound to the ear is somewhat similar. The difference between these two little words is vast.

What they were saying about Jesus is that He did not save Himself because He *could* not. They were mocking Him by saying He couldn't do it, which means He didn't have the power or the ability to do it.

Jesus Restrains His Power

Among the many people gathered at the place of The Skull to witness the execution of Jesus were tens of thousands who were hidden from human view. The spectators from heaven on high included myriads and myriads of the heavenly hosts. Had Jesus called on one of those angels observing this scene, that is all it would have taken to destroy every Roman and every political leader there. The whole garrison of soldiers would be no match for an angel from heaven, but there was a host of them at the call of Jesus. All Jesus had to do was nod, and the angels would appear.

But let's leave the angels out of it for just a second. Who is the Lord of glory? Who is this who was being crucified? He is the God-man. He is God incarnate, not the impotent God incarnate, but the omnipotent, almighty God incarnate. According to His human nature, while He was hanging on the cross, Jesus was physically helpless and unable to save Himself. That human nature was still perfectly united with the divine nature. According to His divine nature, Jesus only had to say a single word to stop this travesty. As Scripture says, "He utters his voice, the earth melts" (Ps. 46:6). He could have saved Himself in a heartbeat. The reason He didn't save Himself was not because He *could* not but because He *would* not. That makes all the difference in the world. And the reason He would not is the covenant of redemption.

Many people have never heard of the covenant of redemption. They've heard of the covenant of works, the covenant of grace, the new covenant, the old covenant, the covenant with Abraham, the covenant with David, the covenant with Noah, and the covenant with Adam. The supreme covenant, the ultimate covenant, was not made in Shechem or in Jericho, but it was made in heaven before the world began, before creation began. It was a covenant within the Godhead itself, established from eternity, a covenant in which the three members of the Godhead were in perfect agreement. That unity of purpose, from all eternity, was to create a race of human beings who would fall and who would be redeemed. Among the persons in the Trinity, it was the Father who would send the Son. It was the Son who would accomplish that redemption. It was the Holy Spirit who would apply that redemption for the eternal glory of God.

Jesus, according to His human nature, wrestled in the garden of Gethsemane about what lay ahead of Him, but He knew that an agreement had been made, a pact, the covenant of redemption. The Son had made a covenant with the Father and with the Spirit. His mission when He became incarnate was to keep the covenant, the contract, that had been made in eternity and that was worked out in history.

We are by nature covenant breakers. We break covenant with God every hour of our lives. The Father and the Son and the Spirit, when they agree on something, never violate a covenant. When He became incarnate, the Son of God worked out in space and time the agreement that had been conceived in eternity. People talk about election and predestination, but those concepts pale into insignificance when we look at the covenant of redemption made in eternity.

The Repentant Thief

But the other rebuked him, saying, "Do you not fear God, since you are under the same sentence of condemnation? And we indeed justly, for we are receiving the due reward of our deeds; but this man has done nothing wrong" (vv. 40–41). The criminal who had railed at Jesus was rebuked by the criminal who hung on the other side of Jesus. How many hours had passed since Pontius Pilate had said, "I find no fault in Him"? Now, the criminal who was being executed next to Jesus said: "I can't find any fault in Him. He hasn't done anything wrong."

And he said, "Jesus, remember me when you come into your kingdom" (v. 42). That man tenderly said to Jesus: "I know who You are. You are the Lord of glory, and God has prepared a kingdom for You. When You enter it, remember me." Jesus spoke again, telling him, **"Truly, I say to you, today you will be with me in paradise"** (v. 43). He had no idea, probably, how loaded that statement is.

There's a heresy out there called *psychopannychia*, or soul sleep, that says that people, when they die, fall asleep for centuries and centuries, and then at some future date, they wake up and then they go to heaven. People who hold to this view punctuate Jesus' words this way: "I say to you today; you will be with Me in paradise sometime." Jesus was saying, "Today, I'm not just going to remember you; you're going to be with Me in paradise."

105

JESUS DIES

Luke 23:44–49

It was now about the sixth hour, and there was darkness over the whole land until the ninth hour, while the sun's light failed. And the curtain of the temple was torn in two. Then Jesus, calling out with a loud voice, said, "Father, into your hands I commit my spirit!" And having said this he breathed his last. Now when the centurion saw what had taken place, he praised God, saying, "Certainly this man was innocent!" And all the crowds that had assembled for this spectacle, when they saw what had taken place, returned home beating their breasts. And all his acquaintances and the women who had followed him from Galilee stood at a distance watching these things.

It was now about the sixth hour, and there was darkness over the whole land until the ninth hour, while the sun's light failed (vv. 44–45). In antiquity, the Jewish people counted the hours beginning at 6 a.m. Luke tells what took place at the sixth hour, which was noon. It lasted until the ninth hour, or 3:00 p.m. To help us understand this text, let's go back to the first page of sacred Scripture.

The Old Testament Scriptures begin with the words "In the beginning, God created the heavens and the earth" (Gen. 1:1). The text goes on to say of that primordial situation: "The earth was without form and void, and darkness was over the face of the deep. And the Spirit of God was hovering over the face of the waters" (v. 2). You get the picture—formlessness, emptiness, and a total impenetrable darkness. The Spirit of God hovered over the waters, and for the first time in recorded history, God spoke.

He uttered a commandment, a divine imperative, a divine fiat, where He spoke into this darkness, "'Let there be light,' and there was light" (v. 3). There was no hesitation at that moment, no delay between the command and its fulfillment. No sooner had the words escaped the lips of God than the lights came on. Remember that this was before God made the sun, before He made the moon. This was before there was a single star shining in the sky. But the power of the voice of God was enough to vanquish this impenetrable darkness. Probably the source of that light of creation was the same as the one in the book of Revelation, where we're told in the final chapters that in the new heaven and the new earth there will be no temple, there will be no lamp, there will be no artificial lighting, there will be no sun, no moon, no stars, for the glory of God and of the Lamb will be its light (Rev. 21:23; 22:5). At the dawn of creation, the first act of the Creator was to call out of nothing and out of the darkness a glorious and victorious light.

In Luke 23:44–45, we see the polar opposite, the exact antithesis of what took place at the dawn of creation when the cycle was completely reversed. At noonday, when the sun was at its apogee, God said, "Let it be dark," and the darkness came. *Ex nihilo*, out of nothing—not from an astronomical perturbation, not from an extended solar eclipse, but again by divine, supernatural fiat. The world was plunged again into utter darkness.

Three hours of absolute darkness **while the sun's light failed**. This was the first day in the history of this planet after God created the sun to bring warmth and light to the planet that this created orb failed in its duty. Every day since the creation of the world, the sun has been shining. You don't always see it. It can be hidden by the darkness of the clouds or by a solar eclipse, or it can be on the other side of the earth, or you could live at the polar ice caps and experience perpetual winter and six months of darkness.

On the day Christ died, the sun failed, while the Son was victorious over heaven and over hell. Anytime we see the metaphor of darkness in sacred Scripture, it is associated with a judgment of God. On the Day of Atonement, the scapegoat had the sins of the people transferred by the high priest onto its back, and then the goat was dismissed outside the borders of the encampment of the people of God and sent into the wilderness, what was called the outer darkness. In the crucifixion of Christ, when the full measure of the judgment of God against evil fell on His beloved Son, when His beloved Son was sent into the wilderness outside the camp, outside the city, being cursed entirely by the Father, God turned out the lights.

The crowd had been mocking Him and taunting Him, tormenting Him, saying: "If You are the Christ, get down off the cross. You saved others; can You not save Yourself?" When this event took place, every one of the taunts, every one of the mockeries, every one of these torments was stopped instantly as every mouth was silenced as the people were plunged into total darkness. They were there to watch the spectacle, to laugh at Jesus at high noon, to see Him exposed to humiliation, when suddenly they couldn't see their hands in front of their faces. Do you have any idea how terrified this multitude was? It wasn't momentary blotting of the sun. It lasted across the whole land for three solid hours. They trembled. They could hear Him talk, but they couldn't see Him anymore.

The Curtain Is Torn

And the curtain of the temple was torn in two (v. 45). Thirty feet high, forty-five feet wide, the temple curtain was the wall of partition between the Holy Place in the temple and the *Sanctum Sanctorum*, the Holy of Holies, where only the high priest could go once a year on the Day of Atonement, and even then, only after going through elaborate rituals of cleansing. Again we go back to the dawn of creation, when God breathed into the dirt of Adam and Adam became a living soul. Then He created a helpmate suitable for Adam from his rib. He made his wife, Eve (Gen. 2:7, 18–22). The first foreboding tension that we encounter in the book of Genesis is in chapter 3, where we read, "Now the serpent was more crafty than any other beast of the field that the LORD God had made. He said to the woman, 'Did God actually say, "You shall not eat of any tree in the garden"?'" (v. 1).

That's not what God said. The serpent knew that wasn't what He said. Adam and Eve knew it wasn't what He said, but they were tricked and tempted, and they succumbed to the temptation. Suddenly, their eyes were opened, and they were naked and ashamed. This was the first time in human history that man and woman sought out the darkness. They looked for a place to hide, a place where the gaze of God would not penetrate. Because of their nakedness and because of their shame, they hid themselves, and when the Creator came in the cool of the evening, He called to His creatures saying, "Where are you?" (v. 9). "And he said, 'I heard the sound of you in the garden, and I was afraid, because I was naked, and I hid myself.' He said, 'Who told you that you were naked? Have you eaten of the tree of which I commanded you not to eat?'" (vv. 10–11). Of course, they had, and the first act of God's redeeming grace was to cover His shamed creatures with skins that He made from animals to hide their guilt (v. 21).

That was an act of mercy, but what followed was an act of judgment where God expelled and banished Adam and Eve from Paradise (vv. 22–24). He made them leave and to live east of Eden. And not only that, for the first time in human history, God appointed an earthly government. He assigned a sentinel, an angel with a flaming sword, to guard the entrance to Paradise lest Adam and Eve would try to sneak back in. A "no admittance" sign was posted on Paradise, because they were expelled into the darkness.

Throughout Jewish history, the expulsion of Adam and Eve from the immediate presence of God was symbolized through the pages of the Old Testament, through the construction first of the tabernacle, then of the temple, with a wall of partition made out of several layers of cloth. It was not made out of wood or gold that could be smashed by sledgehammers. Anybody who wanted to go and destroy that wall of separation could do so, for if they sent blows against it the plied cloth would simply give.

On this ultimate Day of Atonement, the temple curtain was torn—not by an earthquake, not from the ground up, but by the hand of God from the top down, as if the Lord God omnipotent reached down because of the atoning work of Jesus Christ, took the veil of the temple, and ripped it (Matt. 27:51). He tore down the sign that said "no admittance." All those who are covered by the righteousness of Christ and are justified by His life and death now, as a result of being justified, have peace with God and *access* into His presence (Rom. 5:1–2). The sentinel that stood at the gates of Paradise had his sword extinguished and put back in his scabbard as he was dismissed from service, as for the first time since the fall we could go home without shame and without fear to the presence of God.

The Death of Jesus

Then Jesus, calling out with a loud voice, said, "Father, into your hands I commit my spirit!" And having said this he breathed his last (v. 46). We have recorded for us seven sayings that Jesus spoke from the cross. No one Gospel writer mentions all of them, but this presumably was the last one. With His last breath, He made a commitment to the Father. You would suspect that the words Jesus spoke in the last moment of His life would be hardly audible at all, as He was speaking with His last breath. But Jesus cried out with a loud voice, **"Father, into your hands I commit my spirit!"** Into the hands of the One who had just poured out every drop of wrath on Him. Into the hands of the Father who had put this curse on Him.

In this, Jesus was like Job but infinitely magnified. Job had said, "Though he slay me, I will hope in him" (Job 13:15). Jesus said: "Never mind the torture.

Never mind the wrath. Father, I commit My soul to You." And **he breathed his last**.

Now when the centurion saw what had taken place, he praised God, saying, "Certainly this man was innocent!" (v. 47). This centurion **praised God**. Not Caesar. Not Zeus. He praised the God of heaven and earth and proclaimed Jesus' innocence. Not, "I think He was innocent." Not "I hope He was innocent." Not "Maybe He was innocent." No, he said, **"Certainly,"** echoing the very judgment of Pontius Pilate: "I find no guilt in this man" (v. 4).

And all the crowds that had assembled for this spectacle, when they saw what had taken place, returned home beating their breasts (v. 48). This was an indication of fear and trembling. When it was all over, they went home in self-torment, beating their breasts, after what they had witnessed when the lights came back on and what they heard of the commitment of Jesus. **And all his acquaintances and the women who had followed him from Galilee stood at a distance watching these things** (v. 49).

106

THE BURIAL

Luke 23:50–56

Now there was a man named Joseph, from the Jewish town of Arimathea. He was a member of the council, a good and righteous man, who had not consented to their decision and action; and he was looking for the kingdom of God. This man went to Pilate and asked for the body of Jesus. Then he took it down and wrapped it in a linen shroud and laid him in a tomb cut in stone, where no one had ever yet been laid. It was the day of Preparation, and the Sabbath was beginning. The women who had come with him from Galilee followed and saw the tomb and how his body was laid. Then they returned and prepared spices and ointments.

On the Sabbath they rested according to the commandment.

Isaiah 53 reads almost like an eyewitness account of the crucifixion of Jesus. Beginning at verse 7, it reads, "He was oppressed, and he was afflicted, yet he opened not his mouth; like a lamb that is led to the slaughter, and like a sheep that before its shearers is silent, so he opened not his mouth." One of the most critical portions of this record is reported by the New Testament Gospel writers, as we've seen in Luke's Gospel. There's a pattern in the New Testament with respect to the description of the life of Jesus that swings like a pendulum between humiliation and exaltation. It's not a consistent, monolithic pattern where Jesus is always on one path, such as humiliation, and then switches to another path that is one of exultation. But rather, in the middle of humiliation, there may be brief moments of exaltation that break through.

Just as we would often miss the significance of this text of Isaiah, we sometimes have the tendency to look at the pattern as if the nature of the humiliation of Jesus was His death, and then we see the glorious burst of exultation with His resurrection. We draw the line between humiliation and exaltation at the resurrection. That's not where the Bible draws the line. If we read carefully, in Isaiah 53 we see where that line between humiliation and exaltation is drawn by God: "And they made his grave with the wicked"—referring to His being crucified between two thieves—"and with a rich man in his death, although he had done no violence, and there was no deceit in his mouth" (v. 9). It wasn't in the resurrection that the exaltation began; it was in the burial of Jesus that it all started.

For many years I mistakenly told the story that the bodies of those who were crucified were customarily discarded on the garbage dump outside Jerusalem in the Valley of Hinnom, which was known as Gehenna. Gehenna was described as a garbage dump where the fires never ceased because garbage was thrown into it every day, and every day there was more refuse to be burned. Recently, I learned that a burning garbage dump outside Jerusalem is something that occurred after the time of Jesus. What we know now is that the bodies of those who were crucified were divided into two categories: those who were executed as criminals were returned to their families for burial, and those who were crucified for sedition were not allowed to be given to their families.

Jesus would have been numbered among the seditious; therefore, according to Roman practice in the first century, His body was to be thrown out into the wilderness like so much carrion and left to be devoured by the vultures. Can you imagine the body of Jesus being desecrated by vultures—picking at His skin, His muscles, until He was stripped down to a skeleton? The last words of Jesus before He died were "Father, into your hands I commit my spirit!" (Luke 23:46). The last commitment Jesus made was of His soul. He committed it to the Father. As human beings, we are both body and soul. We know the soul of Jesus was in heaven with the Father. What about His body? There was a double commitment. The Son committed the care of His Spirit or His soul to the Father, and the Father made a commitment regarding the care of His Son's body.

In Psalm 34, we are told with respect to the Messiah that "he keeps all his bones; not one of them is broken" (v. 20). In Psalm 16, which is quoted in Acts, we read, "For you will not abandon my soul to Sheol, or let your holy one see corruption" (Ps. 16:10; see Acts 13:35), so there was the tent of protection draped across the body of Jesus, and God changed the normal course of history in the person of Joseph of Arimathea.

Pilate ordered Jesus' death. He also ordered a sign be attached at the top of the cross, saying "Jesus of Nazareth, the King of the Jews" in three languages. The Jews didn't like that, and they interceded, asking Pilate to change the sign. He said, "What I have written I have written" (John 19:19–22).

Joseph and Nicodemus Bury Jesus

Pilate hated the Jews. He was not about to change his decrees with respect to the disposition of the bodies of those guilty of sedition until the burial of Jesus. **Now there was a man named Joseph, from the Jewish town of Arimathea. He was a member of the council, a good and righteous man, who had not consented to their decision and action; and he was looking for the kingdom of God** (vv. 50–51). Joseph was from the same town that Samuel is traditionally said to have been from; it was about twenty miles north of Jerusalem. Joseph was described as **a member of the council** of the Sanhedrin and **a good and righteous man**. When God the Holy Spirit takes His time to describe a fallen human being as good and righteous, that's an extraordinary thing. Joseph of Arimathea was an extraordinary man. Presumably he was not present at the meeting of the Sanhedrin, for he **had not consented to their decision and action**, and the decision of the Sanhedrin to have Jesus murdered by crucifixion was probably unanimous.

The Bible talks about two members of the Sanhedrin who were secret disciples of Jesus. One was Joseph of Arimathea. The other was Nicodemus. Nicodemus, along with Joseph of Arimathea, cared for the body of Jesus (John 19:39–40).

Joseph of Arimathea **went to Pilate and asked for the body of Jesus** (v. 52). God had made a promise that He would not allow His Holy One to see corruption. Just as the Son had committed His soul to the Father, the Father was committed to the care of the body of the Son, and so He melted the heart of Pilate, and Pilate gave permission for Joseph to have the body.

Then he took it down and wrapped it in a linen shroud and laid him in a tomb cut in stone, where no one had ever yet been laid (v. 53). Tradition tells us that Joseph was aided in that task of mercy by Nicodemus. Imagine the two of them gazing at the dead body of Jesus after the crowd had dispersed, leaving Jesus to hang limply in death on the cross. Can you imagine the emotion, the tenderness, as Joseph pulled the spikes from Jesus' hands? He wrapped Jesus' body **in a linen shroud** carefully, reverently, wrapping the arms, the legs, the torso, the neck, and even the head of Jesus in precious linen, **and laid him in a tomb cut in stone**. Note this detail: **where no one had ever yet been laid**. This was a virgin tomb, never desecrated by death, where no residual portion of decay and corruption could linger. It was a tomb of solid stone. We're told in John 19:38–40 that Joseph and Nicodemus not only wrapped the body of Jesus with the linen but also administered precious spices to His body. It was Nicodemus who produced the spices. This was a royal burial.

It was the day of Preparation, and the Sabbath was beginning. The women who had come with him from Galilee followed and saw the tomb and how his body was laid. Then they returned and prepared spices and ointments. On the Sabbath they rested according to the commandment (vv. 54–56). The women who had followed Jesus went home because it was **the day of Preparation** and they couldn't do anything more until after the Sabbath. **On the Sabbath they rested according to the commandment**, and on the first day of the week they brought spices and ointment to anoint the body of Jesus, not knowing how well His body had already been prepared by Joseph and Nicodemus.

107

THE RESURRECTION

Luke 24:1–12

But on the first day of the week, at early dawn, they went to the tomb, taking the spices they had prepared. And they found the stone rolled away from the tomb, but when they went in they did not find the body of the Lord Jesus. While they were perplexed about this, behold, two men stood by them in dazzling apparel. And as they were frightened and bowed their faces to the ground, the men said to them, "Why do you seek the living among the dead? He is not here, but has risen. Remember how he told you, while he was still in Galilee, that the Son of Man must be delivered into the hands of sinful men and be crucified and on the third day rise." And they remembered his words, and returning from the tomb they told all these things to the eleven and to all the rest. Now it was Mary Magdalene and Joanna and Mary the mother of James and the other women with them who told these things to the apostles, but these words seemed to them an idle tale, and they did not believe them. But Peter rose and ran to the tomb; stooping and looking in, he saw the linen cloths by themselves; and he went home marveling at what had happened.

But on the first day of the week, at early dawn, they went to the tomb, taking the spices they had prepared. And they found the stone rolled away from the tomb, but when they went in they did not find the body of the Lord Jesus (vv. 1–3). It was still dark when the women left for the tomb; dawn was just breaking. A gigantic stone had been placed over the entrance to the tomb (Matt. 27:60), and so their biggest concern was this: "Who will roll away the stone for us from the entrance of the tomb?" (Mark 16:3). These women had no idea how they were going to move that stone, but they came anyway in their devotion and in fear and trembling. When they arrived at the tomb, **they found the stone rolled away**, and **they went in**. The tomb was empty, and they were perplexed. "Who has taken our Lord? Where have they put Him?"

While they were perplexed about this, behold, two men stood by them in dazzling apparel. And as they were frightened and bowed their faces to the ground, the men said to them, "Why do you seek the living among the dead? He is not here, but has risen. Remember how he told you, while he was still in Galilee, that the Son of Man must be delivered into the hands of sinful men and be crucified and on the third day rise" (vv. 4–7). We celebrate the Lord's Day every Sunday morning because that was the day of resurrection, and these two men, obviously angels, said to the women, **"He is not here, but has risen."**

And they remembered his words, and returning from the tomb they told all these things to the eleven and to all the rest (vv. 8–9). The women went to the tomb not knowing how they would move the stone, but it was already moved and two angels were there. They saw their dazzling clothing, but Jesus wasn't there. The graveclothes were there, but He was gone. God would not allow His Holy One to see corruption.

People have read this for centuries, and they reject its truth, saying it is a myth and that no one comes back from death. But the Scriptures say, "God raised him up, loosing the pangs of death, because it was not possible for him to be held by it" (Acts 2:24). Death had no claim on Him whatsoever. Though He died for the sins of people, Jesus remained sinless, and corruption had no title to Him; death had no title to Him. And so He got up, and He walked out of the tomb.

Now it was Mary Magdalene and Joanna and Mary the mother of James and the other women with them who told these things to the apostles, but these words seemed to them an idle tale, and they did not believe them. But Peter rose and ran to the tomb; stooping and looking in, he saw the linen cloths by themselves; and he went home marveling at what had happened (vv. 10–12). Regardless of how many times you have read this or how many Easters you've lived through, is there anything more marvelous to hear than that death could not hold Him because the Father would not allow His Holy One to see corruption?

108

THE ROAD TO EMMAUS

Luke 24:13–35

That very day two of them were going to a village named Emmaus, about seven miles from Jerusalem, and they were talking with each other about all these things that had happened. While they were talking and discussing together, Jesus himself drew near and went with them. But their eyes were kept from recognizing him. And he said to them, "What is this conversation that you are holding with each other as you walk?" And they stood still, looking sad. Then one of them, named Cleopas, answered him, "Are you the only visitor to Jerusalem who does not know the things that have happened there in these days?" And he said to them, "What things?" And they said to him, "Concerning Jesus of Nazareth, a man who was a prophet mighty in deed and word before God and all the people, and how our chief priests and rulers delivered him up to be condemned to death, and crucified him. But we had hoped that he was the one to redeem Israel. Yes, and besides all this, it is now the third day since these things happened. Moreover, some women of our company amazed us. They were at the tomb early in the morning, and when they did not find his body, they came back saying that they had even seen a vision of angels, who said that he was alive. Some of those who were with us went to the tomb and found it just as the women had said, but him they did not see." And he said to them, "O foolish ones, and slow of heart to believe all that the prophets have spoken! Was it not necessary that the Christ should suffer these things and enter into his glory?" And beginning with Moses and all the Prophets, he interpreted to them in all the Scriptures the things concerning himself.

> So they drew near to the village to which they were going. He acted as if he were going farther, but they urged him strongly, saying, "Stay with us, for it is toward evening and the day is now far spent." So he went in to stay with them. When he was at table with them, he took the bread and blessed and broke it and gave it to them. And their eyes were opened, and they recognized him. And he vanished from their sight. They said to each other, "Did not our hearts burn within us while he talked to us on the road, while he opened to us the Scriptures?" And they rose that same hour and returned to Jerusalem. And they found the eleven and those who were with them gathered together, saying, "The Lord has risen indeed, and has appeared to Simon!" Then they told what had happened on the road, and how he was known to them in the breaking of the bread.

That very day two of them were going to a village named Emmaus, about seven miles from Jerusalem, and they were talking with each other about all these things that had happened (vv. 13–14). This journey was a distance of about seven miles, a short enough trip but one that would take about an hour and a half at a normal pace. **While they were talking and discussing together, Jesus himself drew near and went with them. But their eyes were kept from recognizing him** (vv. 15–16).

And he said to them, "What is this conversation that you are holding with each other as you walk?" And they stood still, looking sad (v. 17). This stopped them in their tracks. **Then one of them, named Cleopas, answered him, "Are you the only visitor to Jerusalem who does not know the things that have happened there in these days?"** (v. 18). It was as if they had said to Him, "Where in the world have You been?" Then they recounted the events regarding His death and the reports of His resurrection (vv. 19–24).

In response, Jesus rebuked them. He said: **"O foolish ones, and slow of heart to believe all that the prophets have spoken! Was it not necessary that the Christ should suffer these things and enter into his glory?"** (vv. 25–26). He didn't call them stupid. He didn't say that they were unintelligent or uneducated. He called them **foolish**, and in Jewish categories the term *fool* does not describe somebody of low intelligence. It's not an intellectual assessment. It's a moral one. To be called a fool by God is to come under His judgment, because it is the fool who "says in his heart, 'There is no God'" (Ps. 14:1).

The problem wasn't that they had a poor teacher. Romans 1:18–20 says that God has revealed Himself clearly to every human being. Everybody in this world knows without a doubt that God exists because God Himself has made it clear to them. The English word translated "plain" (v. 19) in the Greek is *phaneros*.

In the Latin, it's *manifestum*. It's not some isolated esoteric, obscure, shadowy knowledge. It's plain. It's manifest.

We don't even need the testimony of creation because God has planted the knowledge of Himself in our very souls and in our consciences. We know who He is, but before the new birth, we are slow to acknowledge Him because, as the Scriptures tell us, we don't want to have God in our thinking. The biggest barrier to what we perceive to be our joy and happiness is the law of God, and we want to do away with it. We want autonomy. We want the freedom to do whatever we want to do, not what He commands us to do, and so the Scriptures tell us we will not have Him in our thinking. The deepest and most pernicious bias of all human inclination is the bias against our blessed Creator Himself.

Christ the Center of Scripture

And beginning with Moses and all the Prophets, he interpreted to them in all the Scriptures the things concerning himself (v. 27). No professor had ever so eloquently, persuasively, and convincingly laid out the whole of the text of sacred Scripture and a summary of all redemptive history such as was heard on the road to Emmaus. Jesus Himself was the instructor: "Let Me tell you what the Scriptures say about Me."

Luke doesn't tell us where Jesus started with Moses, but I imagine it was very early when God pronounced the curse on the serpent and said that the offspring of the woman would bruise the head of that serpent while the offspring of the serpent would bruise the heel of the offspring of the woman (Gen. 3:15). Surely, He mentioned the covenant with Noah (Gen. 9:8–17) and the covenant with Abraham, how Abraham believed God and it was counted to him as righteousness (Gen. 15:6). Where did that righteousness come from? Not from Abraham, but from the One who would come and fulfill all righteousness.

Jesus must also have recounted how God had commanded His disciple Abraham to sacrifice his son—his only son, the one whom he loved, Isaac—and sent him on a journey to Mount Moriah, where he was to offer his son as a living sacrifice (Gen. 22). While they were walking, the boy looked at his father and said, "I see the firewood and the fire, but where's the lamb to sacrifice?" Abraham answered his son, "Jehovah-Jireh, the Lord will provide." When they reached that mountaintop, Isaac was tied up and placed on the altar. Abraham's blade was above his son's chest, and just as he was ready to plunge it into the boy, a voice came from heaven, saying, "Abraham, Abraham! . . . Do not lay your hand on the boy or do anything to him, for now I know that you fear God, seeing you have not withheld your son, your only son, from me" (vv. 11–12). Abraham turned, and there was a ram caught by his horns in the thicket. The substitute was provided. The ram was slain on Mount Moriah, and near that place two thousand years later, God took His Son, His only Son, the Son whom He loved, Jesus, and offered Him on a wooden offering place. But no one cried out, "Stop."

Then on to Jacob, his sons, Joseph, the migration to Egypt, the enslavement of the people, and the appearance of God in the burning bush. God said to Moses: "Moses, Moses, put off your shoes from your feet, for the ground that you're standing on is holy ground. I have heard the cries of My people in Israel, and I want you to go to Pharaoh and say to him, 'Let My people go.'" And Moses went (see Ex. 3).

Pharaoh resisted and fought against Moses through plague after plague after plague after plague, until finally came the night of Passover, when God dispatched the avenger, the angel of death, to destroy the firstborn of all the Egyptians. But God said to the people of Israel, "Take the blood of the lamb, sprinkle it on your doorposts, and when I see that blood, My angel will pass over you" (see Ex. 12). Moses was instructed by God to set a memorial day that would be celebrated every year so the people would never, ever forget the exodus from Egypt.

Jesus took the men walking to Emmaus through the Old Testament to Isaiah, Jeremiah, Daniel, Ezekiel, the Valley of the Dry Bones (Ezek. 37), Micah's small prophecy about a tiny village that would be the exact location where the Messiah would be born (Mic. 5:2), the "sun of righteousness" that would appear (Mal. 4:2), even to the last recorded prophecy in the book of Malachi regarding the coming of Elijah (4:5–6). From Genesis to Malachi, Jesus opened up the Scriptures to these men.

Notice He said that all these things were **"necessary"** (v. 26). It wasn't an accident that Judas betrayed Jesus that night. It wasn't an accident that the bloodthirsty rulers of the Jews conspired to destroy Him. These things were ordained from the foundation of the world. They had to happen. The people of God had two thousand years of prophetic preparation, but how slow they were to believe all those things that were written in the Law and the Prophets.

So they drew near to the village to which they were going. He acted as if he were going farther, but they urged him strongly, saying, "Stay with us, for it is toward evening and the day is now far spent." So he went in to stay with them. When he was at table with them, he took the bread and blessed and broke it and gave it to them. And their eyes were opened, and they recognized him. And he vanished from their sight. They said to each other, "Did not our hearts burn within us while he talked to us on the road, while he opened to us the Scriptures?" (vv. 28–32). Don't miss this. This wasn't simply a matter of intellectual conviction. It wasn't just the setting forth of the *notitia*, the necessary data of the content of our saving faith. There was more here than simply the engagement of the mind. It was visceral. The Spirit of God pierced their souls and their hearts, and they said one to the other, "Did not our hearts burn within us as He spoke to us from His Word?"

109

JESUS APPEARS

Luke 24:36–53

As they were talking about these things, Jesus himself stood among them, and said to them, "Peace to you!" But they were startled and frightened and thought they saw a spirit. And he said to them, "Why are you troubled, and why do doubts arise in your hearts? See my hands and my feet, that it is I myself. Touch me, and see. For a spirit does not have flesh and bones as you see that I have." And when he had said this, he showed them his hands and his feet. And while they still disbelieved for joy and were marveling, he said to them, "Have you anything here to eat?" They gave him a piece of broiled fish, and he took it and ate before them.

Then he said to them, "These are my words that I spoke to you while I was still with you, that everything written about me in the Law of Moses and the Prophets and the Psalms must be fulfilled." Then he opened their minds to understand the Scriptures, and said to them, "Thus it is written, that the Christ should suffer and on the third day rise from the dead, and that repentance for the forgiveness of sins should be proclaimed in his name to all nations, beginning from Jerusalem. You are witnesses of these things. And behold, I am sending the promise of my Father upon you. But stay in the city until you are clothed with power from on high."

And he led them out as far as Bethany, and lifting up his hands he blessed them. While he blessed them, he parted from them and was carried up into heaven. And they worshiped him and returned to Jerusalem with great joy, and were continually in the temple blessing God.

As they were talking about these things, Jesus himself stood among them, and said to them, "Peace to you!" (v. 36). The disciples were talking about the things that had transpired and had been noticed and reported by the men who were on the road to Emmaus when Jesus Himself stood in their midst. On the road to Emmaus, Jesus at first was not recognized by the men making the journey, for "their eyes were kept from recognizing him" (v. 16). His person was concealed from their understanding. He listened to their conversation, to their consternation and confusion about all the things that had transpired and the rumors that were flying through the city. Jesus asked them what things they were talking about, and they said: "Are You the only person in Jerusalem who doesn't know what has happened? This One who we hoped to be the Messiah was crucified, and then we heard these rumors that He was resurrected."

Here Jesus appeared again, and with the usual greeting He said to them, **"Peace to you!" But they were startled and frightened and thought they saw a spirit** (vv. 36–37). They thought they saw a ghost. They still didn't know what to believe despite the reports they had heard. **And he said to them, "Why are you troubled, and why do doubts arise in your hearts? See my hands and my feet, that it is I myself. Touch me, and see. For a spirit does not have flesh and bones as you see that I have." And when he had said this, he showed them his hands and his feet** (vv. 38–40). "Touch Me," He offered to the skeptic Thomas (John 20:24–29).

And while they still disbelieved for joy and were marveling, . . . (v. 41). Notice that they **disbelieved for joy**, not for fear. They were saying, "This is just too good to be true." The doubts that were assailing their hearts were because they couldn't believe the happiness that would be theirs if it were so. Jesus said, "Look, it's so. It is I Myself. Touch Me."

. . . he said to them, "Have you anything here to eat?" They gave him a piece of broiled fish, and he took it and ate before them (vv. 41–43). Only Luke would give us this detail. They gave Him a piece of broiled fish. Luke, under the superintendence of the Holy Ghost, told us how the fish was prepared. He took it, and right before their eyes He ate it.

In the other Gospels, there are further stories of Jesus' appearance before His ascension. There are several occasions when He visited the disciples in Galilee and in Jerusalem before He ascended to heaven. On one occasion, the disciples were gathered together and the door was shut and locked for fear of the Jews, and suddenly Jesus appeared in their midst (John 20:19–23). What are we to make of this description of what He looked like? What we find here in the text of Scripture is both continuity and discontinuity. Continuity in the regard that the body that was laid in the tomb was the same body with which Jesus came out of the tomb.

It wasn't that somebody stole the body and hid the body or that God gave Him some kind of new spectacular body to replace the old one. It was the same body.

There also is obvious discontinuity. Some dramatic changes had taken place. The body with which He was raised was a glorified body, a heavenly body, a body that had been significantly altered from the one that He took into the tomb. Though it was the same, yet it was different. We really don't know how different it was. It was still a human body, and it still had human attributes. God didn't communicate His divine attributes to the human nature of Jesus so that Jesus' body could be in Boston and Philadelphia and Pittsburgh and New York at the same time. No, His body was still limited by space and time, although it had been changed.

The Apostle Paul wrote in 1 Corinthians: "But someone will ask, 'How are the dead raised? With what kind of body do they come?' . . . So is it with the resurrection of the dead. What is sown is perishable; what is raised is imperishable. It is sown in dishonor; it is raised in glory. It is sown in weakness; it is raised in power. It is sown a natural body; it is raised a spiritual body" (15:35, 42–44). Here the Apostle set forth the contrast between our normal earthly bodies that we take to the grave and the heavenly bodies with which we will be clothed in the resurrection, so that we will have the same kind of glorified bodies in heaven as Jesus had that day after the resurrection.

Then he said to them, "These are my words that I spoke to you while I was still with you, that everything written about me in the Law of Moses and the Prophets and the Psalms must be fulfilled." Then he opened their minds to understand the Scriptures, and said to them, "Thus it is written, that the Christ should suffer and on the third day rise from the dead, and that repentance for the forgiveness of sins should be proclaimed in his name to all nations, beginning from Jerusalem. You are witnesses of these things. And behold, I am sending the promise of my Father upon you. But stay in the city until you are clothed with power from on high" (vv. 44–49). Jesus then gave them some final instructions. This was the same message that He gave to the men on the road to Emmaus. It wasn't an accident that these things came to pass. They had to be fulfilled. It was on the orders of the sovereign God, who declared from heaven that what was spoken of the Messiah in the Psalms, what was spoken of the Messiah in Moses, what was spoken of the Messiah in the Prophets had to take place at every level and in every detail. He said, "I told you these things."

The Ascension

And he led them out as far as Bethany, and lifting up his hands he blessed them. While he blessed them, he parted from them and was carried up into

heaven (vv. 50–51). With just a few words, Luke described at the end of his Gospel the ascension of Jesus into heaven.

Let me just augment this brief statement that is made here in Luke's first volume with what he wrote at the beginning of his second volume, the book of Acts, where we read: "And when he had said these things, as they were looking on, he was lifted up, and a cloud took him out of their sight" (1:9). That was not an ordinary cloud. That was the shekinah cloud. That was the glory cloud that was the mode of transportation for the Son of Man as He was lifted up into heaven.

"And while they were gazing into heaven as he went, behold, two men stood by them in white robes, and said, 'Men of Galilee, why do you stand looking into heaven? This Jesus, who was taken up from you into heaven, will come in the same way as you saw him go into heaven'" (vv. 10–11). "What are you doing? Why are you standing still in a stupor gazing into the clouds? If you had a giant telescope you wouldn't be able to see His entrance into heaven, because it isn't simply a matter of geography that divides heaven and earth; it is a dimensional difference." Still, as He was leaving they were watching, and they didn't want to move as long as they could see the slightest glimpse of Him in His glorious departure.

Jesus had predicted earlier that He would ascend into heaven. Do you notice something strange about the way that He made that prediction? He said, "No one has ascended into heaven except he who descended from heaven, the Son of Man" (John 3:13). We read the Old Testament. We know that Enoch was translated (Gen. 5:24). We know that Elijah was taken up (2 Kings 2:11–12). We know that the Old Testament saints were carried to the bosom of Abraham and into paradise (Luke 16:22). Just as Jesus went up, so they went up. There are all kinds of Old Testament saints who ascended into heaven, but here Jesus said nobody ascends into heaven except the One who has descended from heaven.

He's not using the word *ascension* in the commonplace, ordinary vernacular. The verb in and of itself simply means "going up." If pilgrims would go to Mount Zion, to Jerusalem, for a festival, they ascended to Jerusalem. Here, Jesus was using the word in a very narrow, technical sense that is unique. He was saying, "I am the only One who in this way and in this manner ascends to heaven, because no one else ascends except the One who first has descended from heaven." At the beginning of his Gospel, Luke wrote about the descension of Christ—His coming from heaven, His being born in lowliness and humility, laid in the manger and wrapped in swaddling cloths, coming as a baby. That's how it started, with the incarnation. Then, the climax, the culmination of Jesus' earthly stay, is recorded at the end of the book, when the One who had descended now ascended.

What does the ascension mean? There are a couple of references that we have to understand. First, it's significant that Jesus didn't just go up. It's about where He was going and why He was going. Let me give you a parenthesis at this point. When Jesus first told the disciples, "Yet a little while and the world will see me no more" (John 14:19) and "Where I am going, you cannot come" (8:21), they were crushed. When they heard that, they said: "Are You leaving us? You can't leave us. What would we do without You? We would be in abject misery." Even at the time of His death, they scattered like lost sheep, with their spirits destroyed. The worst news they could hear from the lips of Jesus was the announcement that they had heard—that in a little while, in just a short time, He would be taken from them.

Then, as He tried to explain that mystery to His disciples, He said to them, "It is to your advantage that I go away" (16:7). I don't think the church has ever believed that. We still live in a time of longing for the good old days when Jesus was on earth. If we could just have watched Him raise Lazarus from the dead, if we could have seen Him walk on the water, if we could have seen Him turn the water into wine, then we wouldn't have to live by faith or by the testimony of the Word of God. We would have been eyewitnesses to His glory. It doesn't get any better than that.

"Yes, it does get better than that," Jesus was saying. "It gets way better than that, but only if I leave." Why was it better? Because of where He was going. He was going to His coronation. He was going to His investiture, to be seated at the right hand of God in the seat of cosmic authority, the highest political office in the universe. We're worried now every day about the next election, but whoever wins this election cannot unseat the King of kings and the Lord of lords, because the Lord God omnipotent reigns, and Jesus was going to His ascension, to His coronation, that He might be the King of kings, not just the best king that ever was, but the King of all the other kings, the Lord of all the other lords, and all authority is given to Him on heaven and earth.

That's just the beginning. That's not the only reason He went away. He also went away to be installed as our Great High Priest forever "after the order of Melchizedek" (Heb. 6:19–20). The old covenant sacrificial system centered on the Day of Atonement, the forgiving of the sins, on a yearly basis. There is only one person that was allowed to go into the Holy of Holies, and that was the high priest, and only after going through all kinds of ritualistic cleansing. This had to happen every year.

For century after century after century, there were successive Days of Atonement with different people functioning in the office as the high priest. Their appointment to the high priesthood was temporary, but this High Priest was the High Priest appointed to be High Priest forever in heaven. This High Priest doesn't go into the earthly sanctuary and the tabernacle or into the temple, but He went up to the heavenly Holy of Holies, and there He brought His atoning sacrifice and offering for all time for our sins as He ministers as our High Priest (Heb. 9:11–12, 24–28).

And they worshiped him and returned to Jerusalem with great joy, and were continually in the temple blessing God (vv. 52–53). When the disciples finally understood those things, they threw their hats in the air when they realized where He was going. Their tears were dried up forever. They said: "There goes our King to His coronation. There goes our High Priest departing from among us to bring the perfect sacrifice before the Father forever and ever and ever." No wonder they were rejoicing, because finally they understood what most of us still haven't understood—that it was better for Jesus to leave than it was for Him to stay.

In the book of Revelation, we read:

> And between the throne and the four living creatures and among the elders I saw a Lamb standing, as though it had been slain, with seven horns and with seven eyes, which are the seven spirits of God sent out into all the earth. And he went and took the scroll from the right hand of him who was seated on the throne. And when he had taken the scroll, the four living creatures and the twenty-four elders fell down before the Lamb, each holding a harp, and golden bowls full of incense, which are the prayers of the saints. And they sang a new song. (5:6–9)

If you look at the history of redemption in the Bible, every time God did a new and mighty work of redemption for His people, they would celebrate it with a song. "I will sing to the Lord, for he has triumphed gloriously; the horse and his rider he has thrown into the sea," says the Song of Moses (Ex. 15:1). "From heaven the stars fought, from their courses they fought against Sisera," says the Song of Deborah (Judg. 5:20). In the New Testament, the incarnation is celebrated by Mary's song, the *Magnificat*: "My soul magnifies the Lord" (Luke 1:46). Or the song of Simeon, the *Benedictus* (2:29–32). We see the songs of the saints. Now there's a new song on the occasion of the homecoming of Jesus.

In the upper room, Jesus had prayed, "Father, glorify me in your own presence with the glory that I had with you before the world existed" (John 17:5). In the ascension, Jesus came home, and the prayers of the saints uttered a new song: "Worthy are you to take the scroll and to open its seals, for you were slain, and by your blood you ransomed people for God from every tribe and language and people and nation, and you have made them a kingdom and priests to our God, and they shall reign on the earth" (Rev. 5:9–10). John continued:

> Then I looked, and I heard around the throne and the living creatures and the elders the voice of many angels, numbering myriads of myriads and thousands of thousands, saying with a loud voice, "Worthy is the Lamb who was slain, to receive power and wealth and wisdom and might and honor and glory and blessing!" And I heard every creature in heaven and on earth and under the earth and in the sea, and all that is in them, saying, "To him who sits on the throne and to the Lamb be blessing and honor and glory and might forever and ever!" (vv. 11–13)

Handel captured this well in his *Messiah:* "And He shall reign forever and ever and ever and ever and ever and ever."

Luke gives us the perspective from the earth looking up into heaven. John gives us the perspective of the welcoming committee for the homecoming of the Son of Man into the heavenly place where they sang a new song. Now you know the rest of the story.

INDEX OF NAMES

ABOUT THE AUTHOR

Dr. R.C. Sproul was founder of Ligonier Ministries, founding pastor of Saint Andrew's Chapel in Sanford, Fla., first president of Reformation Bible College, and executive editor of *Tabletalk* magazine. His radio program, *Renewing Your Mind*, is still broadcast daily on hundreds of radio stations around the world and can also be heard online. He was author of more than one hundred books, including *The Holiness of God*, *Chosen by God*, and *Everyone's a Theologian*. He was recognized throughout the world for his articulate defense of the inerrancy of Scripture and the need for God's people to stand with conviction upon His Word.